RAGWINGS OVER THE SACRAMENTO RIVER

Early aviation in Sacramento County,
the westside counties,
and the far northern counties
of the Sacramento Valley
1909–1939

(Volume III of the Aviation in Northern California 1910–1939 series)

BY

Allen Herr and Kathe Herr

OTHER TITLES BY ALLEN HERR

Aviation in Northern California 1910–1939 Volume I: San Francisco Bay Area & Volume II: Yuba, Sutter, and Butte Counties

STANSBURY
PUBLISHING
Chico, Ca.

RAGWINGS OVER THE SACRAMENTO RIVER

Early aviation in Sacramento County, the westside counties, and the far northern counties of the Sacramento Valley 1909–1939

Volume III of the Aviation in Northern California 1910–1939 series

Copyright © 2018 by H. Allen Herr and Kathe Herr

ISBN: 978-1-935807-39-1 paperback
ISBN: 978-1-935807-55-1 eBook

Library of Congress Control Number: 2018933973

Second Edition with some new text and cover wording

Stansbury Publishing is an imprint of Heidelberg Graphics

Front cover. Artist's conception of Woodland's Dan Best in his Staggerwing Beechcraft climbing over an irrigation canal and recently harvested rice fields of the western Sacramento Valley, circa 1937.

Back cover. Boeing Air Transport airliner over the state capitol. This Boeing Model 80A was photographed in February 1930.

All rights reserved. No part of this book may be be reproduced or transmitted in any form or by any means, electronic or mechanical, including photocopying, recording, or by any information storage and retrieval system, without permission in writing from the copyright holders or publisher, except for reviews.

DEDICATION

We would like to dedicate this book to the following who have devoted their lives to aviation, worked harder than most, and have loved every minute in the air.

It has been an honor knowing and being inspired by Ben Middleton through our journey in aviation. Ben spent many years flying Ag-cats here in rice country then moved on to corporate helicopter flying in a Hughes 500. One of his last jobs was flying an OV-10 Bronco for the Bureau of Land Management. He flew lead plane for the borate bombers making their drops on forest fires. He was recently given the FAA Wright Brothers Master Pilot Award for 50 years of safe flying. Ben will soon fly the Texas Parasol ultra-light aircraft he just finished building.

Then there is Ed Nelson, aerobatic instructor extraordinaire. He also was an ag-pilot and later flew for FedEx. For over three decades, Ed was the fixed base operator managing the airport at Sidney, Nebraska. He has since moved his flight instruction business and Champion dealership to Kimball, Nebraska. We think Ed is happiest when flying his Pitts S-2B.

Others in our aviation journey that we would like to thank and who are still upright include Norman, Dennis, and Jim Stadel.

We have the warmest of memories and deeply miss those who have left us: Ted Herr, Duane Pangle, Jim Martin, and John Baldwin.

There are two aviation heroes of the "Greatest Generation" with whom Allen had the briefest exposure, but came away feeling justified that all of his heroes are aviators. The first was the late Col. Howard Lee Baugh, husband of Allen's sixth grade long-term substitute teacher, Mrs. Baugh, at Del Paso Heights Elementary School in North Sacramento. She noticed Allen was always drawing pictures of airplanes and carrying around airplane books. Mrs. Baugh asked her husband to take Allen on a tour of McClellan Air Force Base. To this day, he remembers sitting in a B-66 and climbing all through an SA-16 Albatross. With the Baugh children, Allen followed the colonel on a long scary climb to the top of an enormous hangar, through the roof, and into the McClellan control tower. From there he could see every plane parked on the base. Being a big P-51 fan, what stuck in his memory was a line of more than a dozen P-51Ds parked wingtip-to-wingtip (one was down on a wing due to a collapsed landing gear). They would be sold at auction the next year. For an 11-year-old boy, crazy about airplanes, it was a glorious moment. Many years later, Allen learned Colonel Baugh was one of the famed Tuskegee Airmen; credited with 1.5 victories during World War II.

Twenty years later, Allen and Kathe were planning a trip to the 1975 Mojave Air Races and, a few months before the races, Kathe, out of the blue, called R. A. "Bob" Hoover and asked if he would give her husband a ride in his P-51D, *Ol' Yeller*, at the races. He said he would and he did. For Allen it was an amazing experience, but what has stuck with him all these years was the incredible kindness of the great warrior, test pilot, and world-renowned aerobatic ace. Sadly, the aviation community lost Bob Hoover recently.

CONTENTS

LIST OF ILLUSTRATIONS   Page ix

INTRODUCTION   Page xi

ACKNOWLEDGEMENTS   Page xiv

PART I
SACRAMENTO COUNTY EARLY FLIGHT

CHAPTER 1   Page 1
Knabenshue's dirigible flights of 1909 – Roy Crosby flies first – The "Fiesta of the Dawn of Gold" state fair committee hires Hamilton – Ivy Baldwin tries for state fair flying job

CHAPTER 2   Page 19
Charlie Hamilton flies at the state fair – The crash of the Hamiltonian – Kerns and the phony "Bud" Mars – Chappell and Brainard, aeroplane builders – The nation's top exhibition pilots come to Sacramento with Dick Ferris' air circus – Ivan Gates brings the Bay Area's best to fly at the fairgrounds – Bob Fowler and the first power line patrol – Lincoln Beachey at Sacramento

CHAPTER 3   Page 57
Frank Bryant and Sam Purcell fly for the 1917 California State Fair – Liberty Iron Works build JN-4s for war – Mather Field is created – Great War aviators at Sacramento – Jack Irwin

CHAPTER 4   Page 77
Postwar Aviation – Mather Field pathfinder flights – The creation of Del Paso Airport – An airfield at Curtis Oaks – The War Mother's Aero Circus – Sacramento flying in 1921 and 1922 – Sacramento Valley airports in 1922

CHAPTER 5   PAGE 97
Chinese flying school at Courtland – Sierra Aircraft Company and its airfield

– First Annual Sacramento Air Meet – US Air Mail Service plane lands at Sacramento

CHAPTER 6   PAGE 119
A revitalized municipal airport at Del Paso Park – Irwin Airport is abandoned by its creator – Sierra Airport is renamed Eagle Rock Airport

CHAPTER 7   Page 129
Capital Air Lines – The Sacramento Aircraft Show of 1928 – Flying activities at Sacramento airports – Replacing Del Paso Airport – Final years at Eagle Rock Airport

CHAPTER 8   Page 145
New airlines and flying services – Roseville opens an airport – Del Paso hangs on – New municipal airport sites are studied – The Sacramento Aviation Club – NAA Chapter is formed – New management at Del Paso – The first California Air Tour

CHAPTER 9   Page 169
Prominent Sacramento aviators of the 1920s – John Fulton "Jack" Irwin – Henry G. "Andy" Andrews – Ray E. Nicholson – Ingvald Fagerskog – Leo Moore – Walter L. Lockhoof – Jack Beilby – Arthur F. Mickel – Ken Blaney – A. B. Willett

CHAPTER 10   Page 199
A new municipal airport on Freeport Boulevard – Airwar over the Sacramento Valley – A grand airport dedication – New flying businesses on a new airport – Aircraft movements at the new airport – Sacramento flying activities for 1931 through 1933

CHAPTER 11   Page 235
Commercial flying at the new municipal airport – Forrest Earle Bennett – Bob Laurin – Harold G. "Buzz" Slingsby – Summit Flying Service – Kimball Flying Service – Capital Airlines Inc. – Boeing Air Transport – Pacific Air Transport – Century Pacific Lines Ltd. – Consolidated Air Lines – Varney Air Lines

CHAPTER 12   Page 261
Women in aviation – Sacramento's Avis Bielefeld – Sacramento flying activities 1936 and beyond – B-17s at Sacramento Muni in 1937 – Del Paso Airport's final years

PART II.
EARLY AVIATION IN COLUSA AND GLENN COUNTIES

CONTENTS   VII

CHAPTER 13   Page 277
Agricultural flying history – Chasing ducks – Duck patrol in 1920 – Moffett and Hunt in Glenn County – Seeding and dusting crops in the north state – Colonel Livingston Irving – Merced-Wawona Air Lines and Frank Gallison

CHAPTER 14   Page 307
The rice season of 1931 – Early flying attempts at Colusa – Chadwick Thompson flies duck hunters – Colusans choose an airport site – Colusa Airport dedication

CHAPTER 15   Page 325
Albert Lane – A Korean flying school – Postwar barnstormers – Willows Airport established – Willows Airport dedication– Orland's airports – Glenn County flying activities

CHAPTER 16   Page 339
The 1930 Army Air Corps Maneuvers – Floyd Nolta, the Willows Airport manager –Flying activities at Willows – Willows Air Show of 1933 – A larger air show in 1935 – A better air show in 1937 – The best and last air show of the 1930s

PART III.
EARLY FLYING IN TEHAMA, SHASTA, AND YOLO COUNTIES

CHAPTER 17   Page 361
Corning's first airport – Warren Woodson develops an airport – Ben Torrey, airport manager – Pacific Air Transport and West Coast Air Transport choose Corning – Fuel stop for the famous – Corning's first air show – Ben Torrey does it all – Torrey's final days – The Corning Air Show jinx

CHAPTER 18   Page 389
Didier Masson makes first flight in Tehama County – Red Bluff fire patrol base –Gates Flying Circus at the Round-Up – Lindbergh circles Red Bluff – "Aces Up" at the county fair – Red Bluff flying activities – The Gordon and Stryker airplane – Red Bluff loses airport managers

CHAPTER 19   Page 407
Captain Moore and his dirigible over Redding – Frank Bryant and Roy Francis fly first – Air Service fire patrols – Pendleton and Merwin barnstorm Redding – John W. Benton – Flying activities in Shasta County from 1927 – Redding chooses an airport site – Benton Field dedication activities

CHAPTER 20   Page 431
Frank Johnson makes Woodland's first flight – Ivy Baldwin races a train –

Thad Kerns flies an exhibition – Woodland's wartime airport – Charlie Stoffer barnstorms Woodland – The Yolo Fliers Club – O. H. Pratt – Yolo Fliers Club has first air meet – Flier Club Floral Festival Air Meet – William Sanborn killed flying the mail – Best Field – Ernie Moe

ABBREVIATIONS   Page 469

ENDNOTES   Page 471

BIBLIOGRAPHY   Page 487

PHOTOGRAPH CREDITS   Page 490

INDEX   Page 491

ABOUT THE AUTHORS   Page 507

LIST OF ILLUSTRATIONS

Figure Number - Illustration
1 – Frank H. Johnson at Marysville in Feb. 1910
2 – Sacramento and Woodland Airports Map 1910–1939
3 – Roy Knabenshue's dirigible *Toledo III*
4 – Dr. Greene's biplane flown by Roy Crosby
5 – Charlie Hamilton flying his *Hamiltonian*
6 – Hamilton landing at Marysville in March 1912
7 – Chappell and Brainard with their Farman copy
8 – Chappell and Brainard airboat on Sacramento River
9 – Chappell andBrainard airboat attempting river takeoff
10 – Bob Fowler flying the first power line patrol in U. S.
11 – Fred Wiseman sits in his Wiseman-Peters biplane
12 – Globe Iron Works became Liberty Iron Works in Great War
13 – JN-4D Jenny during construction at Liberty Iron Works
14 – JN-4D training planes at Mather Field in 1918
15 – Frank McManus at Mather during the Great War
16 – William Sullivan, a pilot in the Great War
17 – Jack Irwin flying a glider at San Francisco in 1908
18 – Jack Irwin in a Standard Model Curtiss (pusher) in 1912
19 – Jack Irwin props his M-T-2 Meteorplane circa 1926
20 – Adm. Bryd's Fokker *Josephine Ford* at Irwin Airport in 1926
21 – Crissy Field in 2013 – Field has been restored to its 1923 look
22 – Mather Field Open House during 1930 Air Maneuvers
23 – (upper) Del Paso Airport site in 2000
24 – (lower) Del Paso Airport in 1928 aerial view
25 – A participant at War Mothers Air Circus, Curtis Oaks airfield
26 – Walter T. Varney with his Swallow mailplanes
27 – Harry Abbott before service in China
28 – Chinese flying students at Courtland in 1922
29 – A poster for graduation airshow of Courtland's Chinese pilots
30 – Ingvald Fagerskog's airport hangar circa 1929
31 – Pony Express re-enactment with DH-4 airmail plane in 1925
32 – Ingvald Fagerskog in backseat of his JN-4D named *Comet*
33 – (upper) Golden Bear – Harry Abbott and Bert Lane test flew
34 – (lower) A Thomas Morse Scout believed to be Fagerskog's
35 – US Air Mail Service DH-4 with stagecoach
36 – Boeing Model 40A mailplane at Mather Field circa 1928
37 – Barnstormers Thrash and Herzog over Sacramento in 1923
38 – Del Paso Airport Sacramento's first municipal airport 1928
39 – Walter Lockhoof and his Eaglerock on his N. Sacto airport
40 – Blanch Field at Reno, Nev. was airmail stop 1920-1928

41 – Del Paso Airport circa 1927
42 – Del Paso Airport circa 1927
43 – Del Paso pilots meet Bay Area pilot William H. Royle
44 – Ingvald Fagerskog in his new Travel Air 2000
45 – Cessna C-34 forerunner of all Cessna high-wing aircraft
46 – Del Paso Airport during airshow in May 1928
47 – Mather Field at opening of Air Maneuvers April 3, 1930
48 – Opening airshow for new Sacramento Muni Airport 1930
49 – Air Ferries' Loening landing on Sacramento River
50 – Boeing Model 80A transport over Sacramento River
51 – Sac Muni circa 1932 after hangar No. 1 has been moved
52 – Ken Kleaver with Clarence and Al Bielefeld at Shasta
53 – (upper) Curtiss Kingbird eight-place airliner on Sac Muni
54 – (lower) USS *Akron* begins flight up Sacramento Valley
55 – (upper) Kreutzer Tri-motor Air Coach
56 – (lower) Bach Tri-motor Air Yacht
57 – (upper) Ford 4-AT-19 Tri-motor, Cord auto & Bert Lane
58 – (lower) Avis Sutfin Bielefeld
59 – Avis Bielefeld and Ivor Witney with a Fleet Model 2
60 – Women students of Barker and Witney Flying School
61 – Boeing YB-17s at Sacramento Municipal Airport 1937
62 – YB-17s at Sacramento Muni August 1937
63 – Edmund J. Moffett and Ernie Smith at Oakland 1927
64 – Frank Gallison prepares to sow first rice by air
65 – 2002 photo of first Colusa airport site
66 – Clyde "Upside Down" Pangborn leads Orland parade
67 – Bombers pass and review at Mather Field April 1930
68 – Heavy bomber being refueled at Mather April 1930
69 – Night photo during maneuvers reveals Welcome Lindy
70 – Corning airports 1921 and 1926
71 – *Spirit of St. Louis* on Mather Field September 1927
72 – John "Slim" Davis
73 – Redding's Benton Field in 1995
74 – Art Starbuck with Ryan mail plane at Redding 1927-28
75 – Starbuck refuels Ryan at Enterprise Field Redding
76 – Airmail flight Redding, Weaverville & Fall River Mills
77 – (upper) Albert Lane's first plane an OX-5 Standard J-1
78 – (lower) Fokker Super Universal airliner
79 – Membership card for Yolo Fliers Club of 1920
80 – Yolo Fliers Club site in 1995 now Woodland-Watts
81 – JN-4D at opening air meet for Yolo Fliers Club Field
82 – Emory Rodgers in his Pacific Standard
83 – Pacific Standard on Yolo Fliers Club Field
84 – Bristol Tourer - Yolo Fliers Club Field Aug. 22, 1920
85 – Clifford B. Prodger Bristol Tourer pilot
86 – Col. H. H. "Hap" Arnold and L. C. Brand at Yolo
87 – Dan Best with his Stearman C-3 at Best Field
88 – Dan Best and Stearman on Best Field, Woodland 1931
89 – Dan Best flies under the new Knights Landing Bridge
90 – Bristol Tourer at Yolo Fliers Club Field (upper)
91 – Rodgers' Pacific Standard parked at Yolo Fliers Club

INTRODUCTION

The word ragwing is a term used in the aviation community to describe fabric-covered airplanes. We prefer it as the one word that best describes the majority of aircraft discussed in *Ragwings Over The Sacramento River*. This is the final in a trilogy of books that give the reader the fullest possible scope of early airplane flight in Northern California during the years 1910–1939. With the Sacramento River in the title of this last book, it tells where the aerial activities take place—in those counties through which that river runs with the exception of Sutter, Yuba, and Butte counties, which were covered in *Aviation in Northern California 1910–1939 Volume II: Yuba, Sutter, and Butte Counties*.

Even though Sacramento is California's state capital and the most populated city in the valley, it was not the first city in the region to experience an aeroplane flight. Several towns in Sacramento Valley had already enjoyed "first" successful aeroplane flights before Roy Crosby, in the Greene biplane, made the "first" flight for a few hundred Sacramentans in April 1910.

Is it possible the thousands of city residents who came out to watch Roy Knabenshue, exactly one year before, were so impressed by his dirigible flights they felt the aeroplane would be unable to satisfy their interest? After all, Knabenshue had flown around the state capitol twice.

Even though no evidence was found by this author that any local men were successful at aeroplane flight during aviation's Exhibition Years of 1909–1914, the city treated itself to several world-class flying exhibitions by daredevils of the air like Charlie Hamilton, Phil Parmalee, Blanche Stuart Scott, and Charles Willard, who were mostly from the East.

Many Capital City residents flocked to San Francisco in 1915 to watch Lincoln Beachey, Art Smith, Charles Niles, and Silvio Pettirossi, fly their incredible stunts from the North Lawn (today's Marina Green) of the Panama-Pacific International Exposition grounds. Flights which are covered thoroughly in *Aviation in Northern California 1910–1939 Volume I: San*

Francisco Bay Area.

In this work there is much about the development of Mather Field during the Great War, Liberty Iron Works—North Sacramento's greatest contribution to war production, and Mather Field's postwar use for forest fire patrols and an airmail stop.

Also notable in this book is the chapter describing Sacramento's early women pilots and the first women's flying organizations. There is a most informative chapter about the first ag-pilots in central and northern California who herded ducks out of the Glenn, Colusa, and Butte counties rice fields with their Curtiss Jennies. Early in the chapter is a brief description of the army's first experiments of crop dusting in 1921–22.

Certain nomenclature used in this book should be clarified. It took over 15 years following the Wright brother's first flight for the word aeroplane to morph into airplane. Even though the British continue to use it, the word aeroplane in this work is replaced by airplane once America enters the Great War.

There are a few abbreviations used repeatedly throughout the book. They are: ACA/FAI – Aero Club of America/Federation Aeronautiqe Internationale; PPIE – Panama-Pacific International Exposition; DOC – Department of Commerce; ag-flying – agricultural flying; CAA – Civil Aeronautics Authority; and FAA – Federal Aviation Administration.

World War I is usually referred to as the Great War; occasionally it is called the World War, WWI, or just the war. It was the largest conflict to take place during the scope of this book; it began in August 1914. When America entered the Great War on April 6, 1917, army aviators were members of the US Army Signal Corps' Aviation Section. In May 1918, that section was renamed the US Army Air Service, which will be used here regardless of the date of any army aviation activity during the war.

Military aviation is mentioned often in this work, but only as it effected the civilian population or the civilian flying community.

Aircraft identification in most periodicals of the day rarely identified aircraft by their manufacturers' model numbers. For example a Travel Air 2000, which was powered by a Curtiss OX-5 engine, would be identified in most magazines as an "OX-5 Travel Air." The Curtiss JN-4D was referred to as just the "Jenny" or the "OX-5 Jenny." The Curtiss JN-4H was called a "Hisso Jenny" due to its higher horsepower Hispano-Suiza motor. The less precise identification used in those periodicals is also used in this work with apologies to aircraft identification experts.

Introduction   XIII

Referencing the Curtiss pusher biplane, which was responsible more than any other aircraft during the Exhibition Years for bringing aviation to the people of Northern California and possibly the nation, is a little more problematic. The manufacturer later identified it as the Curtiss Model D 1 through D 5. These early planes were handmade at the Curtiss shops with modifications and improvements on nearly every new airframe. It is doubtful any two aircraft were exactly the same. Aviation periodicals of the day referred to the biplane with the catchall term: Standard Model Curtiss. That designation, or occasionally its more colloquial name Curtiss Pusher, is used in this book.

Fig. 1. Col. Frank H. Johnson in his Standard Model Curtiss (Pusher), later known as a Curtiss Model D, as it sits in Knight Park at Marysvillle prior to Johnson making the first successful aeroplane flight in the Sacramento Valley on February 12, 1910.

ACKNOWLEDGEMENTS

Valuable assistance was given to this three-volume project by the diligent employees at the Doe Library's Richmond annex of the University of California at Berkeley. Through them it was possible to obtain the rare aeronautical trade papers and magazines from aviation's early years of 1908 through the early 1920s.

The folks at the circulation desk in the California Room of the State Library at Sacramento were wonderful in supplying the aviation magazines from the mid-1920s and early '30s that were not in our personal collection, and they were ever so patient with Allen's all-day binges, twice weekly, for three years in their newspaper microfilm lab.

There were many who helped in the search for photographs and information for the entire trilogy about early aviation in the Sacramento Valley and the San Francisco Bay Area; thanks must go out to the following people who were such great help in this difficult search. They are: Gordon Werne, an early archivist for the Hiller Aviation Museum; Pat Johnson (2004) and Alex Guilbert (2017) archivists for the Center for Sacramento History; Debbie Seracini, archivist at the San Diego Air & Space Museum; Christina Moretta, photo curator at the San Francisco Public Library; Julie Stark, Curator (now retired)of the Community Memorial Museum of Sutter County; the Mary Aaron Museum in Marysville; Yolo County Archives; Resa Lyn of the Colusa County Library; Ed Beochanz; Gene Russell; Gary Brainard; Donald B. Gray; Linda Liscom; Ed Power; Sutter County Library; Marysville Library; San Mateo County Museum; Butte County Museum; Gridley Museum; and the California Room of the Sacramento City Library.

We want to express many thanks to Larry S. Jackson of Stansbury

Acknowledgements

Publishing for his work on the three books of this series.

—Allen Herr and Kathe Herr
 Yuba City, California
 February 2018

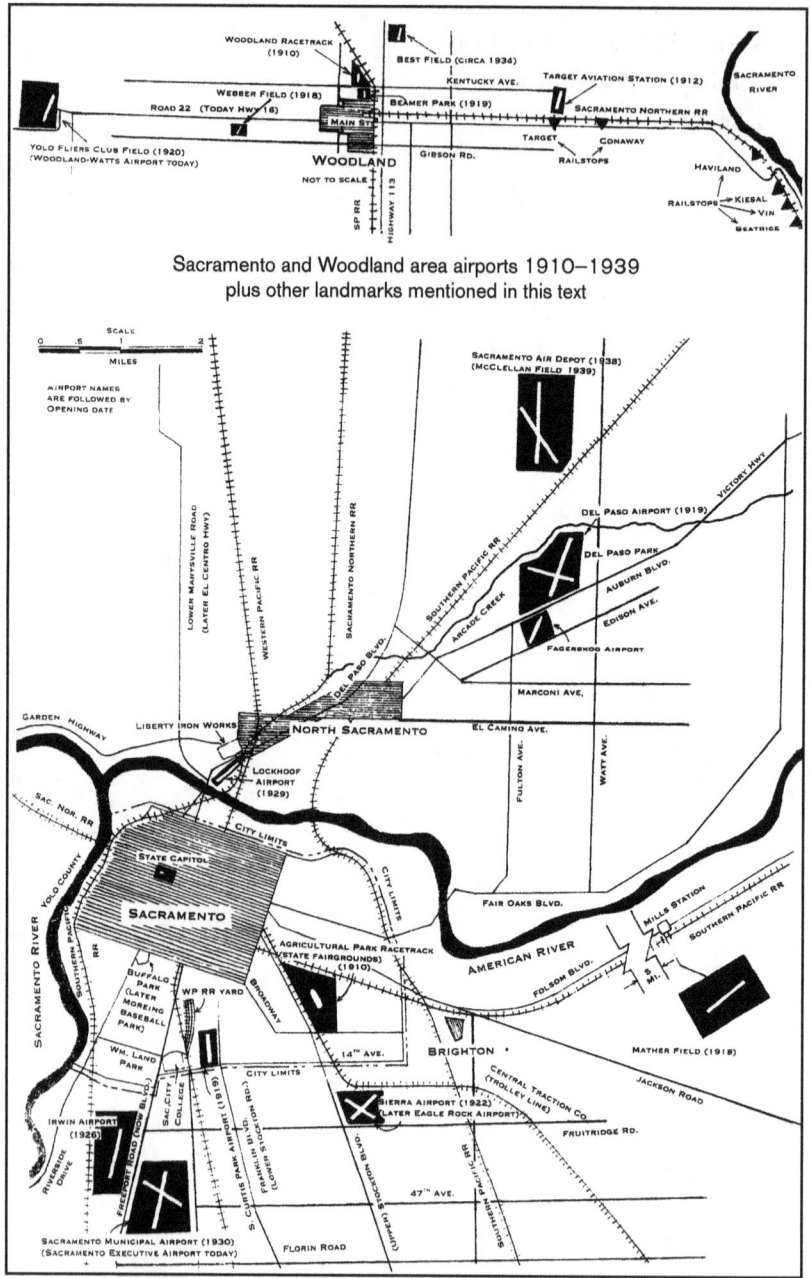

Fig. 2.

Part I. Sacramento County Early Aviation

CHAPTER 1

Knabenshue's dirigible flights of 1909 – Roy Crosby flies first – The "Fiesta of the Dawn of Gold" state fair committee hires Hamilton – Ivy Baldwin tries for state fair flying job

Roy Knabenshue made the most spectacular exhibition flight to yet occur at Sacramento on April 24, 1909. On that day, Knabenshue, who had become one of the most popular aeronauts in America, maneuvered his flying machine twice around the dome of the state capitol in the heart of the city. His machine was not a hot air balloon, and aeroplanes had not yet made a successful flight in California; it was a huge sausage shaped gasbag of transitional aeronautical technology known as a dirigible.[1]

Even though aeroplanes were the future and were making flights in the eastern United States on that April 24 morning ten thousand people assembled to watch Knabenshue fly. They arrived early, but each newcomer who joined the assembled crowd groaned in disappointment when he or she learned the airship wouldn't fly if the developing north wind exceeded 12 mph. He could not safely fly the dirigible, but later in the day he would be ascending in the spherical balloon, *United States*, borrowed from his friend, flying impresario Dick Ferris of Los Angeles.[2]

The people of Sacramento had been looking forward to seeing a dirigible fly at the special citywide festival called Sacramento Day celebrating the 60th anniversary of the city. Knabenshue had established his temporary aviation camp in the old China Slough Basin, an area filled with sand. By the twenty-first, his large tent hangar was up and his dirigible, *Toledo III*, inflated with hydrogen gas. He wouldn't be using the one-man airship like the ones he and Beachey would be flying at Dominguez Hills in nine months.

The *Toledo III* was 112-feet long and powered by a 16hp. motor.[3]

As the day progressed, the north wind blew stronger. Residents of Sacramento Valley know if the north wind blows longer than a day it usually blows for three days. The wind became a threat, and Knabenshue decided to let the gas out of the *Toledo III* before it broke away from its tether. He also took down his tent hangar before it blew down.[4]

The north wind eased up on the twenty-fourth; Knabenshue raised his tent hangar and reinflated the dirigible. He'd promised to make two flights, but the north wind was still exceeding his 12 mph limit. An announcement was made to the thousands assembled that the morning dirigible ascension was cancelled. Some spectators yelled rude remarks at Knabenshue.[5]

At 4:00 PM the wind subsided and Knabenshue announced he would fly. The tent hangar's flaps were thrown open and the large gasbag of the *Toledo III* was slowly walked out by several men gripping the small spruce framework suspended beneath in which Knabenshue and his assistant were standing. Knabenshue made a few adjustments and started the engine. The dirigible was released and ascended on a path to the state capitol. People watched in awe as it maneuvered away from them. Residents along the dirigible's path alerted by the roar of the engine came out of their homes and were stunned at the sight overhead. Some watched from their rooftops.

Knabenshue circled the capitol dome then adjusted his rudder and began a large circular flight back to China Basin where he landed on the spot

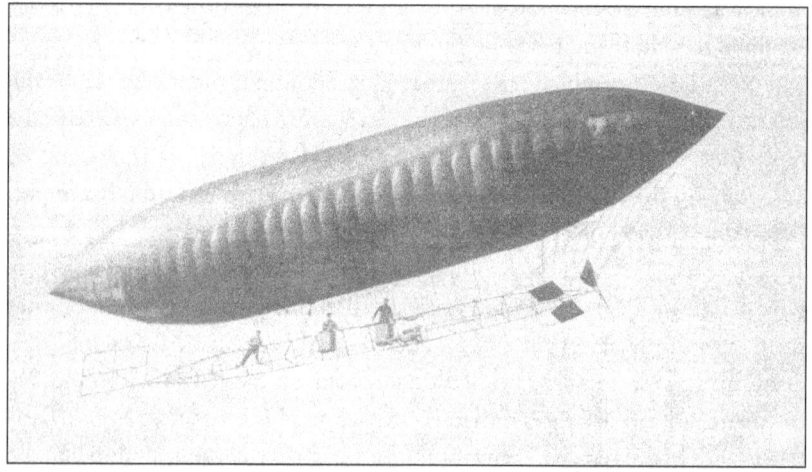

Fig. 3. Roy Knabenshue flying his dirigible, *Toledo III*, in 1908. In April 1909, he would dazzle the people of Sacramento by circling the state capitol twice and returning to his departure point.

of his departure. The crowd was roaring as Knabenshue landed; the flight took 35 minutes.[6] It was the first dirigible flight in the Sacramento Valley.

To cap a successful day of flying, Knabenshue ascended in Dick Ferris' spherical balloon, *United States*. He took five passengers: Bert Adams, Jack Lloyd, John T. Patterson, reporter Harry Gimbal, and Knabenshue's assistant who rode on the ring above the balloon's basket.

The flight of the *United States* was perfect. The balloon ascended from China Basin with its six occupants to 10,000 feet, and slowly drifted southeast overflying the state capitol and then Agricultural Park. After an hour of drifting in flight, Knabenshue began releasing gas to descend. The balloon came down in a farmer's wheat field halfway between the rail stops at Brighton and Florin. Today that is near the intersection of Highway 50 and Power Inn Road in Sacramento.

Several automobiles followed Knabenshue to help recover the balloon and ensure the safety of the passengers at touchdown. The drivers did not wait for permission to enter the field. They barged in tearing down a section of the farmer's fence and damaging his gate. The wheat they were driving over mattered little to them nor did the farmer's protests. They picked up Knabenshue and his passengers then returned to town without fixing the fence.

The following day Knabenshue returned to gather the balloon. The fence had been repaired, and the damaged gate was chained and locked. The farmer denied Knabenshue entry until he was paid $100 for damages. Knabenshue felt that was too much. He called the chamber of commerce officials who hired him. They got the sheriff involved.

The sheriff told everyone he was there to mediate a settlement or to auction off the balloon. This started serious negotiations between the parties. The chamber officials started talking nicely to the farmer, and he lowered his price steadily. After he was bargained down to five dollars, he said he would keep the balloon if he wasn't paid even though he didn't need it. He was paid, Knabenshue loaded his balloon in an automobile and left Sacramento the next day.[7]

The flights by Knabenshue at a track meet and a boat regatta on the Sacramento River made Sacramento Day a great success.

Knabenshue traveled to San Mateo intending to complete the construction of an aeroplane and learn to fly it. He also planned to secure a contract performing dirigible ascensions at the state fair in Sacramento. It is unknown if Knabenshue achieved either of these plans.[8]

In America, A. Leo Stevens had possibly made the first powered balloon flights in 1900 and 1903, however, there are no corroborating witness statements to substantiate those flights.[9]

Hot air or gas filled spherical balloons had been flown in Northern California many times during the last quarter of the nineteenth century, usually by an aeronaut with a nom de theatre preceded by the equally fictitious rank of "captain" or "professor." Two of the most famous aeronauts flying in the north state were exceptions to that rule. They flew under their real names: Park Van Tassall and Thomas S. Baldwin with the rank of captain; after all they were captains of their airships.

Baldwin was a daring showman. Early in his career he not only went up in his hot air balloon, but when it reached a few thousand feet he would jump from it descending by parachute and performing gymnastic acrobatics on a trapeze bar as he came down.[10]

Spherical balloons, whether they used hot air or hydrogen gas for lift, began suffering waning public interest by the beginning of the twentieth century. Once it left the ground, the balloon was at the mercy of the wind; it was not controllable on the horizontal axis. The aeronaut did have some vertical control—he could make the balloon rise and descend—but unless the wind changed direction or he rose to find the wind blowing in the opposite direction, which was rare, he could not return to his departure point. Once launched, he drifted out of sight and the show was over.

The first airship to take flight in America is credited to Dr. August Greth, who flew his dirigible *California Eagle* for 40 minutes rising to an altitude of 2,000 feet above San Francisco Bay before his engine seized forcing him to land in the bay. This was witnessed by hundreds on October 18, 1903, and made front-page news in Bay Area newspapers.

Thomas S. Baldwin, a friend and colleague of Dr. Greth's, built the dirigible, *California Arrow*, and first flew it July 29, 1904, at Idora Park in Oakland. On August 2 he flew the *California Arrow* out and returned to its point of departure; no airship had accomplished such a feat in the United States.[11]

Baldwin's 52-foot dirigible was powered by a 7hp. Curtiss motorcycle engine. The engine's weight plus Baldwin's 200 pounds severely reduced performance. Baldwin planned to compete at the 1904 St. Louis Centennial Fair and hired Roy Knabenshue, a much thinner man, to fly his airship.[12]

With Knabenshue, a veteran balloonist at the helm, the dirigible

California Arrow put all other balloons and airships at the St. Louis fair to shame. Knabenshue did well, but the terms for winning the $100,000 prize were so difficult to achieve he ultimately failed.[13]

Captain Tom Baldwin "launched the airship craze in the United States … [and] together Baldwin and Knabenshue breathed new life into aerial show business with their small, one-man airships."[14] Although the public began to lose interest in free-ballooning its enthusiasm returned when dirigible flight was introduced.

Baldwin sensed the evolution to aeroplane flight. The showman shifted his exhibitions from flying dirigibles to the aeroplane in mid-1910. He built and learned to fly a biplane at Mineola, New York, naming it *Red Devil*.[15] Baldwin flew numerous exhibitions in the *Red Devil*, which was a design copy of the Standard Model Curtiss. He formed one of the early exhibition flying teams then lured exhibition flier J. C. "Bud" Mars away from Glenn Curtiss to join Baldwin's tour of the Orient in 1911.

Roy Knabenshue, who never flew aeroplanes, preferred dirigibles and stayed with the transitional technology until it ran its course. Actually, dirigible technology has continued to this day. After the success as a terror weapon of the rigid Zepplin bombing airships of the Great War and the great passenger airships of the 1930s, non-rigid dirigible designs called blimps were successful at antisubmarine warfare in World War II. They are used for aerial advertising today and for a while were flying sightseeing hops around San Francisco Bay. By 1910 the aeroplane had quickly relieved the slow moving dirigible of exhibition flying.

Knabenshue put dirigible flying aside and managed the aeroplane exhibition team of the Wright brothers in 1910–1911. In 1912 he managed an exhibition team for Glenn Martin. Orville and Wilbur disbanded their exhibition team after star aviators Arch Hoxey and Ralph Johnstone were killed attempting the exceedingly dangerous stunts demanded by the crowds. The short lifespan of an aviator during the Exhibition Years (1909–1914) was an eye-opener for Knabenshue. He stuck with dirigibles to the bitter end.

In January 1910 Knabenshue and Baldwin's other aeronaut, Lincoln Beachey, flew the only two dirigibles to compete at the first Los Angeles International Air Meet in the Dominguez Hills. Later, after wrangling exhibition fliers for the Wrights and Glenn Martin, Knabenshue met Lionel and Louis Armstrong, entrepreneurial brothers from Los Angeles. They would finance construction of Knabenshue's 150-foot dirigible, which carried a passenger car with six double-cockpits powered by a 32hp. engine that pushed the airship along at 25 mph. The 13-place keel car was built in 1913 for Knabenshue in a Sacramento machine shop, possibly that of Chappell and Brainard or A. Meister and Son. The same year, Knabenshue began making passenger-carrying flights at Pasadena. His dream was to start a regularly scheduled airline service with his dirigible, but it was not to be.

During the Great War, Knabenshue was awarded a contract to make 25 captive observation balloons for the US Army Balloon School at Ross Field, Arcadia. He also worked there as advisor to balloon instructors. After the war, he tried to stay in dirigible construction and flying, but was unsuccessful. He took a job with the National Park Service from which he retired in 1949.[16]

Knabenshue's dramatic April 1909 flight at Sacramento had occurred at the height of the dirigible era. No aeroplane flights that can be corroborated had yet been made west of the Mississippi River. The dirigible was still king, but not for long.

IN EIGHT MONTHS, the door was thrown wide open by aeroplanes flying at the Los Angeles Air Meet in the Dominguez Hills. After the meet, citizens of cities and towns throughout California were clamoring for exhibitions of the new technology.

Sacramento residents followed newspaper reports of flying exhibitions taking place daily at America's first air meet in the Dominguez Hills throughout January 1910. They read of Glenn Curtiss making the very first aeroplane flight in the state on January 9th and were particularly interested in the exploits of Roy Knabenshue, who had flown his dirigible exhibition for them only nine months before.

Edgar M. Sheehan, head of California Winery in Sacramento, joined the rush of officials from various California cities to the Dominguez Hills to sign an aviator to fly a first aerial exhibition at their hometowns. Sheehan, a member of the Aerial Navigation Company of Sacramento, thought when he returned from the Dominguez Air Meet it was settled and Sacramento would have an event like Dominguez Hills, even though he did not have a signed contract. After all, he negotiated with Mr. Franciulli, the Herring-Curtiss Company manager of the professional aviators flying for Curtiss, at the Dominguez meet.[17]

Mr. Sheehan was misled or misunderstood the situation. He was late opening negotiations. All available dates were taken for the headlining aviators like Charles Willard, Charlie Hamilton, and even the non-Curtiss flier, Louis Paulhan, from France. Glenn Curtiss wasn't available either; he was going to fly one exhibition for Fresno and Bakersfield following the Dominguez meet and then return home to Hammondsport, New York.

Within a week-and a-half of Sheehan's negotiations, the Sacramento Chamber of Commerce received a letter from Glenn Curtiss inquiring about the availability of land sites to build a factory for the Herring-Curtiss Aeroplane Company. George W. Peltior, vice president of Central California Traction Company, offered Curtiss a site southeast of Sacramento on its rail line for free. He wrote Curtiss the community very much wanted the factory.

Nothing was ever heard from Curtiss regarding the offer. Apparently, Curtiss sent the same letter to nearly every chamber of commerce in the state. Why Curtiss sent out the letter is a puzzle. It is possible he wanted to put some distance between him and the Wright brothers' patent attorneys; much as the early Eastern movie producers had done to escape the Edison Trust. Curtiss also wanted out of his ill-conceived partnership with Augustus Herring, which may have stimulated his desire to move west. Regardless of the reason, Curtiss didn't accept Sacramento's offer.[18]

LAWRENCE E. DARE, an aviation enthusiast from the East and a member of the Aero Club of America, traveled about the country in January 1910 with a collection of large models of the successful aircraft designs of the day. Included was a full-sized working replica of the Farman biplane used by French aviator Louis Pulhan at the recent air meet in the Dominguez Hills. He displayed his collection at various department stores across the nation. Dare's collection included six-foot models of the Wright biplane; the Bleriot, Antoinette, and Santos-Dumont monoplanes; the Chanute glider; and Langley's ill-fated tandem-winged *Aerodrome*, which crashed in the Potomac River in 1903.

Dare's exhibition opened in the Weinstock, Lubin & Co. department store in Sacramento on January 29, 1910. Dare was on hand to explain the models, talk about riding in a Farman biplane, and managing an early air event in the United States. Due to the massive publicity for the air meet in the Dominguez Hills and Louis Paulhan's flights in the Bay Area, just five days before, people flocked to Weinstock's.[19]

An ad hoc committee of 24 influential Sacramentans was formed February 1 to plan a flying exhibition during the California State Fair. The committee's first business was to form an aero club. Committee member Edgar M. Sheehan had explained why an aero club was necessary based on his experience at the Dominguez Air Meet. Sheehan interviewed various aviators there about coming to Sacramento for the state fair. Curtiss, Willard, and Hamilton could perform together at Sacramento for $5,000 ($120,000 in 2016) per day for a six-day run at the fair. Sheehan said an official aero club was needed in Sacramento to allow the Aero Club of America (ACA) and the Federation Aeronautique Internationale (FAI) to recognize any record flights made at the fair. The aviators insisted upon this. They said new records would be set if they flew at the fair.

Sheehan said Jerome Franciulli was in St. Louis at that very moment, meeting with the Aero Club of America. Upon Sheehan's authorization, Franciulli would see to the admittance of the Sacramento Aero Club to the ACA.

The Sacramento Aerial Navigation Syndicate asked Sheehan to represent them to the committee with their request to take part in flying exhibitions at the state fair. The ad hoc committee reorganized itself as the Sacramento Aero Club. J. M. Berry was elected chairman, and H. E. Yardley, secretary. The club then set about organizing a first-class flying meet for the state fair during its "Discovery of Gold Festival," which was soon renamed the "Fiesta of the Golden Dawn."[20]

The Sacramento Aerial Navigation Syndicate offered to give a demonstration before the Sacramento Aero Club on or before June 1 to show good faith they would enter not only two aeroplanes but also a dirigible, a spherical balloon, and a captive balloon. The syndicate assured the club their flying machines were not experiments but proven successful designs.

The aero club members discussed the suitability of Agricultural Park for the air meet. The park was the site of the annual California State Fair and most members believed it was the finest landing site in the area for aeroplanes. It was agreed the meet should be held there, as there was much unobstructed and unlimited level ground in the east and southeast portions of the park. All of the flying events could be started in front of the grandstands at the center of the park.[21]

FEBRUARY 12, 1910, was the last day at Weinstock's for Dare's exhibition, which had been seen by thousands of Sacramento shoppers.[22] Many people traveled north to Marysville that day and the next to watch Col. Frank H. Johnson make the Sacramento Valley's first aeroplane flight in his Standard

Model Curtiss pusher biplane.[23]

The Sacramento Aerial Navigation Syndicate filed its papers of incorporation that same month. Directors of the company were: F. C. Dittmar, James C. Clarke, and Earl Wayne. Little is known of this company; they never made flights for the Sacramento Aero Club.[24]

There was mention by aero club chairman Berry that the Sacramento Aeroplane Company was included in an April newspaper advertisement for the Pankost Boat Supply Company as having purchased an Elbridge Featherweight engine of 40hp. for their aircraft. The Elbridge was a four-cylinder gasoline engine weighing 167 pounds.

The above company was also known as the Sacramento Aerial Company at 1002 J Street, Sacramento. Incorporated in April 1910, the officers were Tracy A. Miller, E. R. Drake, G. H. Seamans, and A. D. Bevan. The company claimed to be building two machines that would be finished by June 1910.[25] Nothing more has been found of this company.

While the Sacramento Aero Club was negotiating with the Curtiss organization for fliers to perform at the fair, other aviators with much less flying experience were vying to be the first to fly at Sacramento.

ROY W. CROSBY, who claimed he was from New York but was really a San Franciscan, planned to make a series of flights at Sacramento beginning March 20. By that date he hadn't arrived. On April 5, he wired Southern Pacific Railroad officials he would be in Sacramento to fly April 16–17. He explained his aeroplane was destroyed in a train crash during shipment to California from New York, and said he had to return to New York for another.[26]

Crosby had opened the 1910 flying season at the Mineola Aviation Field in New York on April 1 with a number of brief flights in Dr. William Greene's newly built biplane. Crosby's longest flight went a distance of 4,000 feet, and he attained a height of 300 feet. He shipped the machine to the West Coast within the next week for exhibition flights there.[27]

Crosby's train crash story was a bad excuse for not showing up on time for his March flights. Based on reports of his activity at Mineola, it was obvious he wasn't ready to fly exhibitions in Sacramento. It appears Crosby's flights on the West Coast were linked to Southern Pacific Railroad's promotions director. Most of the information about Crosby's flights came from Southern Pacific. The railroad announced excursion rates would be in force from all points in the valley during Crosby's stay in Sacramento; the exhibition was advertised by the railroad company throughout the

Fig. 4. On April 15, 1910, Roy Crosby made the first successful aeroplane flight at Sacramento in this Greene biplane named the *Indian Arrow* for the occasion. The design borrows heavily from the French Farman biplane.

Sacramento Valley.[28]

Crosby arrived in Sacramento and had Greene's biplane assembled and ready by April 15. At the fairgrounds in Agricultural Park, during early evening of the fifteenth, Crosby decided to test fly his machine, recently named the *Indian Arrow*. Crosby took off from the racetrack with ease. He flew northward briefly, then came back to the track and landed. He was happy the Greene biplane flew well. As it was being rolled back into its tent hangar, Crosby said, "I have never before made a flight in such perfect weather. If it is this way tomorrow no one will be better pleased than I. The weather will make it possible for records to be broken and my machine can do that with my assistance.

"I do not expect just to skirt the park. What I intend to do is to make some real flights—flights where a man goes more than ten feet off the ground. With my biplane I feel just as safe a thousand feet high as ten feet from the earth."

By flying at Sacramento, Crosby hoped to accomplish two things. The first was to make his initial flights on the Pacific coast and second, he hoped to impress members of the Sacramento Aero Club so they might invite him back in September to fly for prizes at the state fair air meet they were planning.

Regardless of Crosby's plans, what he had accomplished on the evening of April 15 was the first successful powered aeroplane flight at Sacramento, witnessed by park employees and reporters.

Roy Crosby told reporters he would take one or two young ladies up in his plane. Staying at the Hotel Sacramento, he received numerous telephone calls from local young women and 30 perfumed letters were waiting for him at the hotel desk. A few young society ladies came to the hotel in person seeking aeroplane rides, much to the annoyance of Mrs. Crosby who was in town with her aviator husband.

Agricultural Park had additional seating to accommodate 4,000 expected spectators. Round trip tickets from most towns in the valley were marketed on Saturday by the railroad and continued to be on sale Sunday, the last day of flying.[29]

For Crosby's first official flight at Sacramento, Saturday, April 16, only 300 spectators attended but that's not surprising. Most of Southern Pacific's advertising was done in the small farm towns of Northern California. Farming was the north state's biggest employer, and spring was a busy time in farm communities. A five-day workweek was only a dream in 1910. A six-day workweek was standard practice for most jobs, but farmers, ranchers, and their employees worked a seven-day workweek and still do, especially in the spring. Colonel Frank Johnson had flown mid-winter exhibitions in towns near Sacramento, but he had developed a reputation for making low, unexciting flights. Roy Crosby was unknown with no reputation; people weren't sure he would be an exciting risk-taker like Charlie Hamilton.

Crosby's audience included California Governor James N. Gillett and his family. At 1:00 PM they watched Roy walk to his plane parked on the racetrack infield at Agricultural Park. He carefully inspected the *Indian Arrow* then took his seat in the machine. His helper hand propped the engine, and Crosby began his take off roll on the infield. The ground was too rough; Crosby couldn't get enough airspeed to lift off. He tried again with the same results. The crowd gave him a big cheer each time he began a take off run. Roy made attempts to take off for three hours before giving up. It's unclear why this problem didn't bother him the evening before when he made a perfect test flight.

Crosby addressed the crowd in the grandstands. He explained why he was unable to fly, and he asked them to keep their ticket stubs. They would be honored the next day when he would try again. The infield ground would be rolled and improved, or the track railing would be removed so he could take off from the hard-packed, smooth track itself.

As Crosby was walking to the grandstands to make his announcement, someone in the crowd asked him if he was going to fly on Sunday. Roy stopped, took out a cigarette, lit it, and got a dig in at Frank Johnson. He boasted, "My name is not spelt with a J, nor does it sound anything like John. I am going to fly tomorrow and I am going to fly high and long. I am going to show the people of Sacramento what can be done with a biplane when you have smooth ground to start on. I am sorry I couldn't ascend today, but tomorrow well, just watch me!" [30]

On Sunday Governor Gillett and his family were back in the grandstand at the racetrack joining more than 2,000 others to see if Crosby would live up to his boasts.

The center of the infield at the racetrack had been scraped and rolled to remove the roughness and long grass, which impeded Crosby on Saturday. At 4:10 PM Crosby made his first takeoff attempt and failed. For his second try, he made a run towards the grandstands with his mechanic running along side. It appeared Crosby was going to run into the stands full of spectators, so the mechanic grabbed the wingtip and spun the biplane around 180 degrees forcing a ground loop. On the third try at 5:00 PM, Crosby's Greene biplane rose 20 feet into the air then flopped down onto the ground after the engine quit. Two vertical struts between the wings shattered as a result of the drop. By the time his mechanic George Scraggs repaired the vertical struts, it was 7:30; much of the audience had left. Crosby decided to give it one more try before darkness fell.

It was reported, "With a glance at the control plane, Crosby nonchalantly took his seat, the spark began to buzz and with a rush he was off again in the direction of the grandstand. Speeding along the getaway, the biplane rose surely and swiftly for the only flight of the scheduled two days meet." A handful of spectators had remained late enough to see the flight.

Crosby's manager, J. M. Botts, announced after that last flight Crosby would be back and fly for those who couldn't remain, and it would be free. The author could find no record of any further Sacramento flights, or elsewhere for that matter, by Roy Crosby. The Greene biplane was sold to Ivan Gates of San Francisco a short time later.[31]

The Greene biplane design was quite similar to the Farman design flown by Louis Paulhan at the Dominguez Air Meet and at Tanforan Park in January 1910. Wilbur Kimball purchased the first Greene biplane built. He and F. E. Boland made test flights in it, then they made extensive alterations. The rear vertical rudder was removed completely and vertical (rudder like) surfaces were constructed between the wings as on the French Voisin biplane. These verticals worked to maintain lateral control as well as help turn the aircraft left or right. This method worked so well Mr. Boland took his brother up for a short flight. Patents were taken out on this design change.[32]

The vertical surfaces between the wings meant no ailerons on the wing trailing edges or between the wings like those on the Standard Model Curtiss that were used for lateral control. It also meant the Wright's wing warping was not used on the Greene biplane. Dr. William Greene, who designed, built, and flew these biplanes, was able to advertise his aeroplanes did not infringe on the Wrights' or anyone else's patents. How effective and safe Greene's controls actually were is unknown, as is whether his control design could hold up in a court fight with the Wrights.

Back on March 13, Dr. Greene, a member of the New York Aeronautic Society, had installed a Harriman engine in one of his new biplanes with the newly designed vertical surfaces between the wings, and test flying began on the Aeronautic Society's landing grounds at Mineola, New York. This biplane had already been sold to Auchinvole, F. W. Botts, and Roy Crosby of San Francisco to be used for exhibition work. The three men had formed a company and planned to be the western distributor for Greene aeroplanes.

The plane was flight tested by Dr. Greene with its new engine. He flew it from Mineola to the Motor Parkway, a distance of a mile-and a-half. There, Greene announced he would demonstrate the aircraft in accordance with his sales contract. He took off from the parkway and made a circular flight of two miles proving the plane's stability without ailerons or use of wing warping.

After accepting delivery of the plane at the Motor Parkway on April 1, Roy Crosby flew the biplane back to Mineola. Upon arriving over the airfield, he shut the motor down while thirty feet in the air and was surprised he didn't even feel a bump when the plane touched down. Crosby made eleven more flights that day at Mineola. The airplane was not affected by the wind, and Crosby had no problems turning the aircraft. One wonders whether turns made in the Greene biplane were banked turns or uncoordinated skidding flat turns, as an aeroplane might have with four rudders mounted between the wings at the vertical struts. This copied French designers Voisin and Farman, who tried this same wing rudder method. After Crosby was satisfied with the machine, the Greene biplane was taken apart, crated, and shipped to San Francisco where Crosby made further test flights before taking it to Sacramento later in April.

At the time Crosby was trying out his new aeroplane, Greene had four more biplanes in various stages of construction. They were all the same design as Crosby's. By May 1910, there were two Greene aeroplanes flying in the country. It is believed Greene built a total of eight biplanes before he stopped making aircraft.[33]

In April, Col. Frank H. "Millionaire" Johnson Jr. decided he had gained enough experience flying exhibitions with his Curtiss Pusher in the small towns of Northern California and was at last ready to fly an exhibition at the Capital City. He made arrangements to fly three days of exhibitions in Sacramento on May 6–8, 1910, but fate intervened.[34]

The flights at Sacramento never took place because on April 2 Frank Johnson was to fly at the old Neptune Gardens amusement park on the Alameda shoreline. He had made several flights that day and was making one more, which took him quite a distance out over the bay between the grandstands at Neptune Gardens and the Encinal Yacht Club wharf at the south end of Grand Street. He eventually turned back towards his starting point and began to descend. As he reached the shoreline, a wind gust hit the plane pushing the forward elevator boom down into the sandy beach; smashing his elevator and causing Johnson to crash. He was thrown from his seat and hit his head. Stunned and appearing to be seriously injured, he was taken to his tent hangar where he rested and recovered. He was fortunate his injuries turned out to be minor.

On Sunday, the following day, Johnson's Curtiss had been repaired and he made 20 flights—mostly speed runs over a one-mile course laid out on the grounds of the amusement park. He never exceeded 60 feet in altitude and flew mostly at 30 feet. Even though the spectators dangerously crowded his landing site, all his flights that day were successful. During this air meet, Hotchner, Sittman, G. Johnson, Woodside, and Orht flew their gliders and Ivy Baldwin and Park Van Tassell ascended in their balloons.

On Monday, Johnson was making a flight over the bay and his engine quit, forcing him to land in water. Considering his situation, he abandoned the plane and swam ashore. Reportedly, the machine suffered little damage. How that could be after landing in saltwater deep enough the pilot had to swim ashore is incredulous.

These were the first serious accidents Johnson suffered. He had several previous landing accidents, but those were common and damage to plane and pilot was minor. The accidents at Neptune's Gardens could have easily been fatal. It appears Johnson's confidence was quite shaken. There are no further public exhibition flights attributed to Frank H. Johnson, Jr. after his last crash at the amusement park in early April 1910. By mid-June 1910, Johnson had sold his Curtiss to Charles Volmer (Vosner?). He told his critics that Volmer was the only Californian with the nerve to fly the aeroplane.[35]

Meanwhile, the committee for the Fiesta of the Dawn of Gold was still hoping to sign Glenn Curtiss for the weeklong event in September at the state fair. Curtiss initially quoted them a fee of $3,000 a day, which totaled $21,000 ($504,000 in 2016 dollars) for a week of the fiesta. The committee felt that was too much for one exhibition flier. If a better price couldn't be negotiated, they would have to forego an aviation exhibition at the festival.[36]

On June 1 the committee sent Curtiss a counter offer of $14,000 to fly for the week. They were not optimistic; Curtiss had just made the headlines for his historic flight between New York City and Albany for which he received $10,000.[37]

Edgar Sheehan of the festival committee negotiated a deal on July 11 for Curtiss to fly in September for $2,000 per flight. He was to fly twice a day for seven days. This pushed Curtiss' total price even higher to $28,000 for the week.[38]

Ten days later Sheehan received a telegram from Franciulli, Curtiss' manager. Curtiss was unsure he could make the September commitment. However, they could send J. C. "Bud" Mars, one of Curtiss' top exhibition pilots for $10,000 for the week. If Curtiss decided that he could make the dates, then he would replace Mars for $14,000. (These astronomical fees were only paid on the West Coast during the first 18 months of the Exhibition Years, 1909–1914.)

Sheehan replied to Franciulli the festival committee did not want Mars, he was not well-known; the committee was going to negotiate with other aviators.[39]

Finally, it was announced Charles K. Hamilton would fly for the Fiesta of the Dawn of Gold, September 3–10. Hamilton had become the nation's newest hero on June 13, 1910, after he flew from New York to Philadelphia and back in a single day, winning the $10,000 prize. The committee believed Hamilton, whose national exploits put him on the front page of the *Sacramento Bee* twice during June, was the most daring exhibition pilot in America. Hamilton was asking $15,000 for the week, but would take less.[40]

Hamilton's manager, P. A. Young, reported Hamilton would be flying his new, higher powered machine. Named the *Hamiltonian*, his new biplane was a scaled up Standard Model Curtiss with a powerful 110hp. Walter Christie motor, which gave the plane a top speed of 85 mph. Hamilton wanted a guarantee of $2,000 extra if he set any new flying records during the fiesta. The committee agreed to the terms if Hamilton would guarantee not to fly any exhibitions on the West Coast between the end of July and the opening of the state fair in September. Both sides agreed and the deal was set.[41]

Charlie Hamilton's fees, which were reported daily in Sacramento newspapers during the negotiations, caused quite a stir amongst north state wannabe aviators. Few had the wherewithal to do anything about it, but one who did was Ivy Baldwin. Baldwin, a balloonist (aka aeronaut), tried to horn in on the "big money" being negotiated between the festival committee and Charlie Hamilton. Baldwin was under the impression there would be an air meet at the state fair in September with contests and races. The committee, however, had changed its mind about any contests after they found out how much it was going to cost for just one major exhibition star. Baldwin, who for years performed as a balloonist and later flew one of Capt. Thomas S. Baldwin's dirigibles, had recently joined the company of aeronauts who

Fig. 5. Charles K. Hamilton flying his all black 1 ¼ scale Standard Model Curtiss (Pusher) biplane, which he named the *Hamiltonian*. Powered by an experimental engine developing 110-115hp. built by Walter Christie, Hamilton flew several daring exhibitions at the 1910 California State Fair before suffering a bad crash.

Fig. 6. Charlie Hamilton flying from Knight Park at Marysville in March 1912. There he flew from one of America's first generation airports the town's horse racing track. The spectators are obviously unaware of the danger of standing so close to a landing aircraft.

had switched to flying fast heavier-than-air machines instead of the snail's pace gasbags.

Ivy Baldwin's real name was William Ivy. After he began working for the famed Capt. Tom Baldwin, he changed his name to Ivy Baldwin to capitalize on Tom Baldwin's fame. Ivy became a balloonist and gained fame while working for Tom Baldwin. In his later career, he joined the US Army and was put in charge of the army's lone miniscule balloon squadron operating against Spanish forces in Cuba during the Spanish-American War. During the battle for Santiago, Cuba, Sgt. Ivy Baldwin was sent up in a captive balloon to observe the enemy lines. He relayed information vital to the success in capturing San Juan Hill by the US Army's Tenth Cavalry Buffalo Soldiers and the Rough Riders led by Teddy Roosevelt.[42]

Sergeant Ivy's balloon attracted tremendous enemy gunfire during the battle; army reports said the balloon was brought down by gunfire. Ivy survived and a display in the California National Guard Museum in Sacramento states that in July 1898 Ivy was the first American military airman to be shot down in combat![43]

After the war with Spain, Ivy settled in Alameda and worked for Thomas Baldwin flying free balloons and then dirigibles. He eventually ventured out on his own flying dirigibles and, as stated, learned to fly an aeroplane. After some minor exhibition flying with a Curtiss copy in California, Ivy pulled up stakes and moved to Denver, where he spent his remaining years.

During Ivy's plans to take part in the Fiesta of the Dawn of Gold in September 1910, he began flying his Curtiss Pusher in late July from his aviation camp near Webster's Station in Yolo County. This location was a rail stop on the Davis-bound interurban electric train of Sacramento Northern Railway. It was a short distance west, across the Sacramento River, from Sacramento. Ivy had been "grass-cutting" (teaching himself to fly), and honing his skills as an aviator. By August 6 he had made flights of ten minutes to a half-hour in length. He had flown as high as 500 feet and brashly reported his flying was equal to any of the Eastern aviators.

Ivy wanted to meet with the festival committee and convince them to come out to his aviation camp at Swingle in Yolo County and watch him fly. He felt he could demonstrate a daring noteworthy exhibition, and that he was worth a contract for a share of what Charlie Hamilton was going to get for flying the fair.[44]

Ten members of the festival committee, in three automobiles, travelled the rough, dusty roads in Yolo County to watch Ivy Baldwin fly in his

Curtiss copy at Webster Station. The results were quite disappointing. He had engine problems and couldn't make an adequate flight.*

Three days later on the morning of August 11, Ivy Baldwin raced a passenger train with his Curtiss from Webster Station to Sheep Camp, two miles away. The race ended in a tie. Ivy, in his Curtiss, had to deviate from the railroad track and actually fly a distance of three-and-a-half miles. He brought the plane to a stop in front of the Sheep Camp rail stop as the train roared past. The race created a great deal of excitement among passengers enjoying the spectacular race.

Ivy felt racing a fast train would improve his control over the Curtiss, as had his flying low and fast over the tule grass of Yolo County for the past several weeks. G. O. Jamieson, who was with Ivy at Swingle, said of the race, Ivy maintained a speed of more than 50 mph at a height of 60 feet and rose to 200 feet by the end of the race. He said contrary winds caused Ivy to lose ground, or he would have won the race. Consequently, the race was a tie. Ivy said he would race trains every day until the state fair started, but it was too late for Ivy. The committee did not return to watch the race—they had already eliminated him as an aviator for the fair.[45]

The festival committee did authorize time on September 4 to be set aside for amateur aviators to show their skill and win prizes. The prize money was significantly reduced for them. Before any aviator could enter the contests, he had to prove to the committee he could actually fly. No failures or farces would be allowed if they could be prevented.[46]

The festival committee hired Professor L. L. Hill to fly his dirigible on September 3–4, 1910, to open the fair and the Fiesta of the Dawn of Gold. Why they chose Hill to open, rather than Hamilton, may have been due to Knabenshue's successful dirigible exhibitions flown in 1909. Ten thousand people had come to watch Knabenshue. The 2,000 spectators who came to watch Roy Crosby fly in April were the largest audience ever to view an aeroplane flight at Sacramento. It's possible the committee believed more people would come to see Hill's massive dirigible fly, especially after Hill announced he would parachute out of a burning free balloon during the fair. No report has confirmed that jump.[47]

---

*There is strong evidence that Ivy Baldwin made the first successful aeroplane flight in Nevada on June 23, 1910, at Raycraft Ranch near Carson City. It was a trial flight before he flew an exhibition at the Carson City racetrack during the July 3-5, 1910, celebration.

CHAPTER 2

Charlie Hamilton flies at the state fair – The crash of the Hamiltonian – Kerns and the phony "Bud" Mars – Chappell and Brainard, aeroplane builders – The nation's top exhibition pilots come to Sacramento with Dick Ferris' air circus – Ivan Gates brings the Bay Area's best to fly at the fairgrounds – Bob Fowler and the first power line patrol – Lincoln Beachey at Sacramento

Charles Keeney Hamilton, who hailed from New Britain, Connecticut, has been described as, "… a pint-sized, wiry redhead who habitually behaved as if his mainspring [was] wound too tight." He hounded Glenn Curtiss to teach him to fly an aeroplane in October 1909. Before that he was a free balloonist and had learned to fly dirigibles from Roy Knabenshue. In his earlier years he flew (or rode) in the man-carrying box kites of Israel Ludlow. In 1905 or '06, Hamilton rode one of Ludlow's kites to a height of 600 feet being towed by a fast boat on the Hudson River. He was severely injured in a kite test at Daytona Beach, Florida, in 1906.[1]

Hamilton arrived in Sacramento the afternoon of August 31, 1910, with two railcars filled with his two aeroplanes and plenty of spare parts to fly for the state fair. One aeroplane was Charlie's newly built *Hamiltonian*, which was a 1¼ scale Standard Model Curtiss. Instead of the usual 40hp. and 60hp. power plants used in Curtiss aeroplanes, a 110hp. Christie engine powered his *Hamiltonian*. The other aeroplane was a Standard Model Curtiss pusher with a 60hp. engine. It was Charlie's spare machine.

Hamilton's contract stipulated he was to receive $4,000 when he first set foot on the fair grounds and $1,000 a day for the following six days. Also he was to receive an additional $2,000 if he set any new speed, range, or altitude records.

Hamilton had become something of a prima donna. Relations with his teacher, benefactor, and employer, Glenn Curtiss, had reached the point of rupture in July. His contract with Curtiss stated he would pay Curtiss 60 percent of the net income from each flying engagement for using Curtiss' aeroplanes. Less than a year after learning to fly at Curtiss' home field in Hammondsport, New York, and signing an exhibition contract with Curtiss, Charlie decided he didn't want to pay Curtiss such heavy fees. As he saw it, he took all of the risk, so he should get most of the money.

He built the *Hamiltonian* larger than the usual Curtiss machine with the more powerful Christie engine, thus he could claim he was no longer flying a Curtiss built aeroplane. He jumped his contract and struck out on his own no longer taking bookings from Curtiss' manager, Franciulli. Hamilton began booking his own dates; Sacramento was one of the first.

Curtiss sued Hamilton for over $6,500 owed and won a judgment against Charlie for $6,200 plus expenses. Curtiss then went after Hamilton to collect the judgment. It was a problem for Charlie. After he got to his hotel in Sacramento, Hamilton read in a local newspaper his petition for a preliminary injunction to restrain Curtiss from interfering with his contracts to fly exhibitions had been denied. Hamilton had claimed in his petition that Curtiss blocked him from arranging exhibitions in San Francisco and at the Harvard–Boston Air Meet.[2]

When asked by a reporter about the denial of his petition against Curtiss, Hamilton assured him, "There would be no trouble from Curtiss in regard to ... flights in Sacramento ... Sacramento will see me fly. Of that you may rest assured."[3]

Events at the 1910 California State Fair did not go well for aeronaut Hill or his big dirigible. During the opening of the fair's Fiesta of the Dawn of Gold on September 3, Hill was unable to fill his dirigible's gasbag. The 1,800 people who attended the opening event were quite disappointed, as was Miss Ivy Jodoin, Hill's passenger for the ascension. Charlie Hamilton and his manager, P. A. Young, were standing nearby with a few reporters watching Hill's progress or lack thereof. When asked what he thought of Hill's situation, Hamilton bluntly told the reporters, "Hill's dirigible was an unsafe proposition under any circumstances, and that likely as not if it ever did succeed in getting up [it] would probably catch fire." Charlie also said that on Monday, "That black beauty of mine down the field is simply panting to get up into the air and do a few stunts."[4]

The next day, Joseph Carahan ascended in a free balloon at 11:00 AM. When it reached 3,000 feet, he dropped safely from the balloon in a parachute. Professor Hill and his dirigible disappointed everyone again; he was still unable to fill it with gas.

The amateur aviation meet listed in the program was scheduled for the afternoon of September 4. Even though there were prizes of $1,500, not one of the five aeroplanes signed to fly had arrived on the fairgrounds. Two planes from Santa Rosa, undoubtedly those of Fred Wiseman, were damaged there during preliminary flights, as was the single entrant from Los Angeles. Another two entries withdrew at the last minute due to lack of preparation. So far, aviation had made a dismal showing at the California State Fair and its Fiesta of the Dawn of Gold.[5]

The best fliers during aviation's Exhibition Years (1909–1914) achieved what today would be "rock star" fame for their daring and dangerous flying demonstrations. Charlie Hamilton, for certain, was a member of that exclusive group. Twenty-six thousand spectators attended the California State Fair at Sacramento's Agricultural Park on the day of Hamilton's first flight. It was the largest crowd to attend the fair to date. The grandstands were so crowded fair officials opened the south bleachers to relieve the congestion, but the audience kept growing. The Morse patrolmen, the private security hired for crowd control, were unable to control the situation. They were swept away by the throng of people who overran the box seats and reserve section. The California Agricultural Society, who controlled the park, telegraphed at once to the Morse office for more patrolmen. In the meantime, the southernmost of the three grandstands was put on the free list.

The mad scramble on the grounds at such an early hour on September 5 was due to Hamilton's reputation. The weather was perfect and before noon the grandstands were a mass of noisy gesticulating spectators. The racetrack infield finally had to be opened to accommodate the overflow. Four thousand people, all determined to watch Hamilton fly, quickly filled the infield. The few Morse security guards who were supposed to control the crowd were simply ignored and gave up their task as futile.

A little before 9:00, and prior to most of the crowd's arrival, Hamilton made a trial flight to check out his aircraft and engine. A small group of people watched Hamilton's unusual flight. He took off to the south in the *Hamiltonian* and accelerated rapidly. He ascended to 150 feet, made a sudden turn, and returned to land at his starting point. He covered a measured course of two miles in one minute and four seconds. His Christie engine was not running well and needed tuning. He did not want to disappoint the thousands of people who were filling the grandstands to watch him fly at 1:00.

During his one o'clock flight, Hamilton suffered a carburetor problem. He had taken off from the north end of the track's infield using only 150 feet for his take off run. He climbed to 200 feet and started a wide arc at a very fast speed bringing him parallel to the grandstands. As he passed across their view, the crowd jumped to their feet giving Hamilton an ovation he would never have forgotten if he could have heard it over the unmuffled din of his engine.

He sped to the far edge of the park where the roar of his engine could still be heard over the yelling and applause of the spectators. He turned and came back on the same line in front of the grandstands. Directly in front of the stands, his engine began backfiring. Charlie turned in another arc to get back to his starting point. He shut down his engine, and put the biplane down immediately; he had run out of altitude. Charlie had to land the *Hamiltonian* in a field outside the track.

The crowd waited patiently for Hamilton's mechanics to fix the plane and resume the exhibition. But the announcer speaking into a huge megaphone told everyone the flying period was over. Hamilton's engine would take longer to repair. The next flight would occur at 3:00. The announcement was overly optimistic; the 3:00 PM flight was also cancelled. Hamilton was in the air only fifteen minutes on his first day of flying. The crowd wasn't happy but seemed to understand about mechanical problems. They watched a wild west show and other shows at the track then went home.

A reporter wrote that Hamilton "was in the air a scant fifteen minutes, but his skillful maneuvering and utter disregard of personal safety proclaimed him to the crowd as the nerviest sky pilot of modern times."

The *Hamiltonian* was described at the fair as, "… an absolutely new design of the Curtiss type of biplane with a number of Hamilton's own improvements and received its first aerial baptism." The Sacramento flights were his first contracted exhibitions flown in the new machine.[6]

The following day, Hamilton made his first flight shortly before 1:00 for another record crowd. It was a brief two minute flight during which he broke the world record for the quickest take off. In his *Hamiltonian* with its Christie engine, his take off run took only four and four-fifths seconds. Charlie had broken the old record held by Glenn Curtiss of six and four-fifths seconds set at the Dominguez Air Meet in January. Charlie had a much faster headwind when he took off; it was nearly of gale force. Charlie made no more flights for the rest of the day except a quick one to check his engine at 7:00. Once again, he was forced to land in the southern section of the park.

Hamilton's mechanics worked throughout the previous night and most of the day modifying the newly designed Christie engine. (Hamilton was hoping to win the upcoming Gordon Bennett Race in a month at New York's Belmont Park utilizing this powerful new engine. It would not happen because of the cranky engine.) On this day at the fair, his mechanics met with little success. Walter Christie's new motor was giving Hamilton fits. The strong winds all day and the ongoing problem with the engine forced cancellation of further flights for the evening; the *Hamiltonian* was pushed back into its tent.[7]

Charlie made two flights on September 7, about two minutes each. His engine was not firing on all eight cylinders. His mechanics had worked two hours on the carburetor, but couldn't completely fix the problem. Charlie was about ready to fly when a leak was discovered in the gas tank. It was removed and repaired. Another hour was lost, but Charlie finally got up for two short flights. They were just long enough to mollify the audience.[8]

After his pitiful performances on the sixth and seventh, Charlie realized the new, untried Christie engine needed more development; it was letting him down. He needed a backup engine, and he needed it fast. The engine on his backup Curtiss aeroplane was not large enough to adequately power the larger-sized *Hamiltonian*. The problem for Charlie was where to locally obtain an engine larger than the typical 40 and 60hp. engines used on most flying machines of the day? Glenn Curtiss built a more powerful 80hp. engine, but they were rare as hen's teeth. The Curtiss factory was in upstate New York, days away by rail, and Curtiss was not favorably disposed towards Hamilton. The lighter Gnome rotary aircraft engines, capable of 50 to 80 hp, were practically nonexistent in America in 1910; the factory was in France.

The nation's aviation community in September 1910 was small and in Northern California it was miniscule. Telegrams and telephone calls to the few supply houses carrying aviation items in the San Francisco Bay Area revealed to Hamilton the Hall-Scott Motor Company of Oakland had recently built an engine of 75hp. that was currently powering Fred Wiseman and M. Peters' Farman biplane copy at Santa Rosa. The Wiseman-Peters Farman was said to be the first aeroplane built in California and successfully flown in California by a Californian.

Hamilton made Wiseman and Peters an offer they couldn't refuse, and Wiseman had the Hall-Scott removed from the Farman and on its way to Sacramento the following day, Thursday September 8. Wiseman accompanied the motor. He was a professional auto racer and coincidently scheduled to race at the state fair. Wiseman was quite successful in auto racing prior to taking up flying.[9]

Hamilton made three successful flights on the eighth. The crowd again heard backfire explosions of the Christie motor as the *Hamiltonian* flew along the straightaway and around the oval horse racing track at Agricultural Park. At noon Hamilton flew three times around the track, four times during his afternoon flight, and made it five more times around at sunset.

The afternoon flight was a spectacular crowd pleaser. After going around the track twice, he turned out and disappeared behind the horse sheds opposite the grandstands. Many thought Hamilton crashed. Most had sat back down only to jump up en mass as Charlie darted from behind the sheds. He had gone out behind them, stayed very low, reversed his course, and was suddenly coming right at them. As he approached, everyone could see electrical wires directly in front of him. Instead of pulling up abruptly to cross over the wires, Hamilton pushed down and went under to the cheers of thousands. After his fourth trip around the track, he brought his biplane in for a gentle landing next to his hangar tent in the track enclosure.

During his flight at sunset, Hamilton came so close to the occupants at the north end of the grandstands they were sure he was going to crash into them; they jumped from their seats and ran. Of course he pulled up at the last second, and the joke was on them. He then raced against an automobile driven by E. G. Bernthal and A. B. Plughoff, both from San Francisco. It was a 30hp. Overland, which could only reach 40 mph on the rough track. Hamilton lapped the auto after two circuits.

After the race, spectators no longer wondered whether Charlie Hamilton was all he was said to be. They were convinced they had watched the best exhibition pilot in America, which was ironic because the fiesta committee was considering not paying him his $4,000 for the prior two days of "unsatisfactory flights." They had delivered an ultimatum to his manager P. A. Young—Hamilton would have to demonstrate his ability to fly the next day or consider himself through.

Hamilton demonstrated his ability the next day by flying three times around the track and landing. Then he sent his manager to collect his money, or he was packing up his aircraft and leaving. There was a raucous argument amongst the committee members. Many wanted to let him go. Hamilton left the group in disgust telling his manager there was nothing else to be said. Young disagreed and stayed to negotiate until everyone was happy. Two members of the committee went into town and returned with a $4,000 check for Hamilton, who started his plane promptly at 3:00 and made the spectacular second flight of the day, as described above.

When asked about the problem with the committee, Hamilton said there had been, "too many fingers in the pie." He explained his aircraft and engine difficulties were unavoidable and he had lived up to the contract he signed. He said he intended to make long flights in the future and shatter records. He felt the audience's dissatisfaction should disappear. After the day's second flight, ovations from the spectators pretty much confirmed his assumption.[10]

On Friday, the ninth, Hamilton began his flights at 1:00. The flaps of his tent hangar in the racetrack infield were thrown open, and the *Hamiltonian* was pushed to a spot facing the main grandstands where the audience could observe his quick take off. Hamilton opened the throttle, and the big black biplane ran several yards over the ground. The forward elevator planes tilted and the machine leaped into the air. Thousands cheered as the biplane rose to 100 feet. He flew north until he reached the boundary of the park. As he was about to turn, he encountered the same power lines as the day before. He attempted to drop down and fly under them, but he was traveling too fast. Charlie misjudged and pushed down too much. The biplane hit the ground and drove its landing gear up violently. The aircraft was seriously damaged. Hamilton was uninjured, but his mechanics had to get to work on the biplane immediately if he was to make his evening flight. By 7:00 PM the *Hamiltonian* was ready to fly.

The second flight started outside the fairgrounds where Hamilton crashed earlier in the day. The *Hamiltonian* was repaired at the spot it crashed because the landing gear was badly damaged, and the plane couldn't be moved. The grandstands were packed that evening. Many waited more than an hour to watch him race an automobile around the track.

The crowd was on their feet as Hamilton came around for his first lap above the car. The biplane flew very close to the grandstands as it passed by at 100 feet. There was loud cheering as it sped by gently rising to an altitude of 200 feet. By the third lap, the aeroplane was well in front of the car driven by Edgar Sheehan of the Sacramento Aero Club, who was accompanied by newspaper reporters watching the plane. Hamilton began to descend near his tent hangar using a spiral maneuver. At 70 feet the propeller exploded into a cloud of splinters. A split second later Hamilton lost control of the aeroplane, and it plunged straight into the ground.

The front section of the aeroplane was completely destroyed. The pilot, unseen in the darkness, was trapped inside. As with many Curtiss Pusher crashes, Hamilton was injured by the engine behind his seat. In an instant, the shocked crowd rushed from the grandstands towards the crash site. The Morse security guards were once again overwhelmed. There was no holding the people back. The guards tried to reassure those who remained in the stands that nothing serious had taken place.

It was believed Hamilton died in the violent crash. A sense of gloom enveloped the spectators, then great relief when it was announced that even though he had serious injuries Charlie was alive.

Hamilton explained what happened. Coming down the homestretch his rudder jammed. Unbeknownst to him the prop came apart and a piece jammed in the rudder. His mechanics had made a quick fix on the forward elevator control after the first crash, but it didn't hold and came apart when he reefed hard on the steering wheel while trying to move the rudder. With the rudder jammed and no elevator control, the plane nosed over, diving into the ground. The crash was particularly disappointing for Hamilton because the Christie engine was running the best it ever had. He told reporters, "When I hit the ground the machine was going straight down. I almost somersaulted several times and corkscrewed several times and then made a straight shot for the earth. When I hit, the steering wheel jammed me back against the radiator and I was cramped in such a position that I could not get away from the scalding hot water trickling out of the radiator and as a consequence my left leg is pretty badly burned. I feel awfully sore internally and the cuts and bruises about my body and legs also bother me."

When the first men reached the crash site, they found Hamilton conscious. His face was covered with blood, but he managed to bellow, "For God's sake, boys, get me out of this." Fortunately, there was an automobile at the ready; it had just brought a supply of oil for Hamilton's airplane from downtown Sacramento. The injured pilot was gingerly lifted from the tangled wreckage and placed in the car. Physicians were called and Hamilton was taken to his room at Hotel Sacramento.

As he was lifted from the wreckage of the *Hamiltonian*, Charlie, not realizing the seriousness of his injuries, told his two mechanics to work through the night if necessary and get the smaller airplane (a regular-sized Curtiss) ready for flight. "Set her up, boys," said the dazed but determined aviator, "and I'll fly in the morning."

After examining Hamilton at his hotel, a medical team, lead by the outstanding Sacramento surgeon Dr. Junius B. Harris, announced the aviator's wounds were serious but not necessarily fatal. It was thought he might have fractures to his pelvis, and he had a severely lacerated forehead above his right eye with other cuts and bruises about his head and body. These were in addition to the burns he suffered on his left leg from the water in the burst radiator.[11]

The next day Hamilton could sit up in bed for a little while. He ate some eggs and drank some milk. He was in a cheerful mood with Mrs. Hamilton at his side attending him. Fred Wiseman, who had come to Sacramento with his Hall-Scott motor for Hamilton, visited Charlie in his hotel room that day. Hamilton wanted the engine to replace the ill-performing Christie motor. Since Charlie had crashed the *Hamiltonian*, which was severely damaged, there was no rush for him to acquire Wiseman's motor. But Wiseman said he was returning home the next day, so Hamilton bought the 75hp. Hall-Scott.

Hamilton was improving so quickly his manager began making plans for the future. Officials from San Francisco offered to pay Hamilton $5,000 if he would fly nonstop from Sacramento to San Francisco, refuel, and return to Sacramento. Charlie killed the deal after he listened to their proposal and then demanded $10,000 for the flight.

Hamilton got a kick out of reading various newspaper articles describing in detail his death at Sacramento. His laughter soon faded away, and his mood changed to a more somber tone. He asked, "Dead am I? Well they'll have another chance, I guess." [12]

By September 14 Hamilton was able to get down to the hotel's bar with his manager for a drink. His mechanics were putting the *Hamiltonian* back together. Hamilton told a reporter in the bar the heavier parts of the plane were being manufactured in different machine shops around Sacramento in an effort to make the *Hamiltonian* stronger than ever before. He wanted the plane ready to fly so he could break the forty-second mile mark as soon as he was physically able. Edgar Sheehan stopped by to tell Hamilton the fiesta committee was so pleased with his flights they voted to pay him for the day he was unable to fly due to his crash.[13]

Hamilton revealed he had purchased the Hall-Scott engine and was having it installed on the *Hamiltonian* to replace the Christie. The 75hp. engine would drive an eight-foot propeller at 2,000 rpm. He intended to use the new engine for an exhibition flight at Agricultural Park where he planned to break the forty seconds per mile mark.

A large newspaper ad appeared September 22 stating Hamilton, the "Man-Bird," would fly at Agricultural Park at 3:00 PM. He would fly his exhibition in the world's fastest flying machine, the *Hamiltonian*. His exhibition would include the daring and famous "Hamilton glide" and "Hamilton dip" maneuvers. During the flights, Hamilton would attempt to establish a new world's record for speed. Flying would start at 3:00 and cost fifty cents. The ad was premature.[14]

Hamilton wasn't ready to fly on the twenty-second but he decided he could fly on the twenty-fourth and twenty-fifth for free to thank the people of Sacramento for the care and hospitality shown him and his wife during their difficult stay in the city.

On the twenty-fourth, a Saturday, the first day he had flown since his crash, a small but enthusiastic crowd of 500 came to watch him. He made four flights using his newly installed Hall-Scott engine. His last flight of the day, lasting 15 minutes, was his best. After circling the track three times, he ventured outside the park, flying every which way, to the cheers of the audience.

On Sunday, the crowd was twice the size as the day before. Hamilton made three perfect flights of more than 15 minutes each. There was no wind, making for a perfect closing. During take off for his first flight, it appeared Hamilton was going to crash into corrals built in the infield for the Wild West show's cattle, but with a quick tilt of his elevator planes, he jumped off the ground just missing them. At 100 feet he roared over the grandstands and away from the track turning in ever widening circles. He would turn away from the stands only to turn back and head straight for the spectators thrilling them once again. It was obvious to everyone Hamilton was back in his best flying form.

His buzzing the grandstands, the park, and the surrounding area lasted for an hour-and-a-half spread over three flights. At the end of the third flight, an exhausted Hamilton landed on the infield near where he left his cane. He rolled to a stop and got out of his seat, picked up his cane, and started hobbling towards the grandstands looking for his wife.

The San Francisco to Sacramento flight was just hype manufactured by Hamilton's manager, P. A. Young, to keep the press interested. After Charlie

Hamilton's last flight at Agricultural Park, his mechanics began disassembling his plane preparing it for the rail trip to Chicago where he planned to fly the *Hamiltonian* in a 1,000-mile race from Chicago to New York for a combined purse of $30,000.[15]

Hamilton arrived in Chicago, but he was in bad shape physically. He met his old friends, the Curtiss exhibition fliers. Glenn Curtiss had sent all of his fliers to take part in the race. Since Hamilton had defected months earlier, emotions were mixed when they met him. He was still hobbling on his cane and told his old friends of his bad crash at Sacramento, of his burned leg, and his sprained back. To make matters worse, it seems he developed pleurisy on the train trip to Chicago. His friends were all interested in his newly rebuilt *Hamiltonian*. After hanging around Chicago for a while, Hamilton withdrew from the race because of his injuries and illness. He traveled on to New York to await the start of the Belmont Park Air Meet on October 22, 1910.[16]

Some say the Gordon Bennett Cup race was the reason Charlie built the *Hamiltonian*. He wanted to win the Gordon Bennett Cup, the ultimate speed race won by Glenn Curtiss the year before at Reims, France. This time it was taking place at New York's Belmont Park. It was for this race that Hamilton initially purchased the powerful, but untried, Walter Christie engine and built his bigger stronger version of the Standard Model Curtiss to handle the new engine's weight and power.

It all came to naught; the Chicago to New York race was reduced through attrition to only one starter, Eugene Ely, a flier for the Curtiss. He was the only aviator left to start the race, but he too was forced to quit before completing even 50 miles of the 1,000-mile race. No one won the purse.

At Belmont, Claude Grahame-White, an English aviator, won the Gordon Bennett Cup for fastest flight in the world. He sped around the 100 kilometer course in 61 minutes at 62.1 mph. Charlie Hamilton was unable to get his engine running right and dropped out. Had he rehung the Walter Christie motor on the *Hamiltonian*? Some say he did.[17]

FOLLOWING THE FIRST San Francisco International Air Meet at Tanforan Park in San Bruno, January 1911, A. A. Martin, representing an unnamed group of businessmen, signed Eugene Ely and Charles F. Willard for a fee of $7,000 to fly at Sacramento's Agricultural Park racetrack February 4–6. Both were members of the Curtiss Exhibition Team with superb reputations. Willard was Glenn Curtiss' first flying student, and Ely had just become a national hero for landing his Curtiss Pusher on the deck of the US Navy cruiser *Pennsylvania* anchored in San Francisco Bay during the Tanforan Park meet.

A local newspaper assured its readers there would not be a repetition of problems like those suffered by Charles K. Hamilton in his *Hamiltonian* at Agricultural Park the previous September. The article claimed thousands of people traveled from various parts of Sacramento Valley but were disappointed with most of Hamilton's exhibitions because he had problems with an untried motor. Willard and Ely in Curtiss Pushers they had been flying for months, were said to fly maneuvers the people of Sacramento had never seen before. One of the aviators planned to take off from Agricultural Park, fly downtown, and circle the capitol dome.[18]

Ely and Willard arrived in Sacramento and set up their tent hangars in the infield of the racetrack at Agricultural Park the first week of February 1911. They were supposed to fly on February 4, but rain and high winds prevented flying. The next day the rain stopped and Charles Willard was off in his Curtiss climbing to 2,000 feet to give himself more gliding distance should he lose power over the densely populated city on his way to the capitol. The strong wind he encountered at altitude became a problem; turbulence made for a rough flight. Willard said, "At times I would strike a hollow place, the air seeming to drop from under me, and the machine would fall until it reached firmer currents. That was why my course was uneven and extremely dangerous." Willard made it to the capitol and circled the dome. He threw down a message weighted with a quarter coin for Governor Johnson and quickly turned eastward to the fairgrounds racetrack.[19]

Because of rain, high winds, and a soggy landing field, Ely and Willard decided to cut their exhibition short. Their biplanes were "knocked-down" (disassembled), on the fifth, for rail shipment following their limited flights at Agricultural Park. They had to go to Salt Lake City to fulfill another contract.

At Sacramento they were told they would be paid only the $1,000 they received when they arrived; not the $7,000 promised by Martin. They were due $900 from gate receipts for the one day they flew, but city officials refused to pay them if they jumped their contract. Hawley, the city manager, tried to hold the aviators to their contract, but the fliers made it clear bad weather and wet ground made the situation hopeless.[20]

On the one day Willard and Ely flew, it was noticed Willard had an air-cooled seven-cylinder 50hp. Gnome rotary engine mounted on his biplane.

Ely had the usual 60hp. water-cooled Curtiss with cylinders mounted in a V-shape.[21]

Sacramento residents had become cynical and wary of aviation exhibitions scheduled in their city. No professional flying exhibitions had taken place on the advertised dates. This included Knabenshue's dirigible flights back in 1909. There was always a postponement.

STATE FAIR OFFICIALS decided to give aviation another go in 1911 after Hamilton's disastrous crash at the 1910 fair. To save money they hired Fred J. Wiseman who had been the most successful amateur aviator at the air meet in Tanforan Park during January 1911. In February Wiseman had flown the first official airmail from Petaluma to Santa Rosa. Before adopting flying as his profession, Wisman was a champion auto racer and had raced at the state fairs several times. This may have given him an in when the deal was made to hire him to fly an exhibition at the 1911 fair.

Unfortunately, on August 28, while flying at 50 feet during his exhibition at the fair Wiseman's engine quit and his Farman copy rolled half over and crashed into the ground. Wiseman suffered minor injuries and his biplane was reduced to junk.

By November Wiseman was building a plane to cross the Sierra Nevada. Wiseman and his manager Jack McFadden, a salesman for A. Meister and Sons of Sacramento planned a visit to Marysville on November 20th to watch Thad Kerns fly. They were making plans to use Knight Park in Marysville to test Wiseman's aeroplane, which was under construction in the Meisters shop. It was reported that the new plane incorporated details from both Wright and Curtiss machines. It was said to be larger than Robert Fowler's. In the report a photo appeared of Wiseman shaking hands with Thad Kerns; Carl Browne, inventor of the Octoplane, is standing in the background.

The next publicized exhibition in the Capital City was an air meet featuring famous Curtiss exhibition pilot, J. C. "Bud" Mars and Chico's "Bird Boy," as some in the press called Thaddeus Kerns. The exhibition was scheduled for the weekend of December 16–17, 1911, at Buffalo Park in Sacramento.

On the thirteenth, both aeroplanes to be used in the exhibition arrived at the park and were being assembled by mechanics. Thad Kerns arrived from San Francisco that night with newly acquired spare parts he bought from a supplier. It was quick trip by rail for Kerns. He had damaged the landing gear on his Standard Model Curtiss copy during a recent exhibition flight at Woodland. He and his mechanic spent half a day on the fifteenth repairing and assembling his biplane.

Mars, on the other hand, claimed his plane had been damaged during a recent flight in the East. He said he was going to use the biplane designed in Sacramento by Ernest Chappell, a man who later referred to himself as the father of Sacramento aviation, and built by Chappell's partner Ernest Brainard. The Chappell and Brainard biplane was a French Farman copy. However, instead of the typical Farman trailing edge ailerons on the wings, Chappell and Brainard installed Curtiss style ailerons between the wings.

Mars wanted the elevator planes, which were mounted on long booms extending nearly 15 feet in front of the wings, removed. This would make the plane into what soon became known as a "headless biplane." Removal wasn't a quick task on a plane with solid fixed horizontal stabilizers. He said "headless" biplanes were already being built in the East but not in the West.[22]

Mars and an army of mechanics spent nearly two days assembling the Brainard and Chappell biplane. Mars considered the rear elevators too heavy. The afternoon of the fifteenth was spent constructing and installing lighter elevators.

Kerns had his machine assembled in three hours. He claimed his biplane was the easiest and fastest to assemble. He reported expectation of making a lot of money from patents he applied for enabling quick assembly of Curtiss aircraft. Kerns said he built his Curtiss copy in Chico. Kerns, 17, claimed to be the youngest successful aviator in the nation, but at the time so did Farnum Fish, J. C. Kaminski, and Jimmie Ward, all exhibition flyers.[23]

There were aeroplane parts suppliers in San Francisco who made any part of a Standard Model Curtiss a builder needed, including a complete aeroplane. It is doubtful Kerns made every part of his Curtiss himself, but instead did what many aviators in America had to do, he assembled the aeroplane himself out of parts he made and some purchased premade from a supplier. Kerns was well known to the California Aviation Company, a San Francisco parts supplier. The exception to a self-builder, of course, were those few fortunate individuals able to buy Curtiss machines from the factory already assembled. At the time, December 1911, there was a dearth of factory manufactured Curtiss aircraft in the country.

Kerns had made several long flights prior to coming to Sacramento to fly alongside Mars. He had already made a flight of eight miles at Chico,

CHAPTER 2

and made exhibition flights of equal distance at Marysville and Woodland.[24]

Mars and Kerns each told reporters they planned two flights a day in Sacramento. Kerns planned to travel several miles each trip even though he couldn't fly very high with his underpowered engine. Mars said he would set new records at the Capital City.[25]

The first day they were scheduled to fly, the sixteenth, it was revealed the Bud Mars at Sacramento was not aviator J. C. "Bud" Mars of national fame, but a man named J. C. McAuliffe. The real J. C. "Bud" Mars happened to be in San Francisco on business at the time, and he exposed McAuliffe as a phony.

McAuliffe told the press there were two Mars. He said he traveled with the real Bud Mars using the same last name in 1905 when the real Mars was a balloonist. McAuliffe said he did a double parachute jump from a balloon in those days. The real Mars said, many years before he had employed a man named McAuliffe, and the fellow in Sacramento might be that same man—thirteen years ago, he partnered with a man named Beaureguard, and they performed as the Mars brothers.

It became obvious McAuliffe didn't know how to fly, and the meet was a total failure. High winds kept Thad Kerns from flying. He waited a couple of hours until they subsided then made a few runs across the field in an effort to fly, but he never succeeded. He was quite disappointed in the affair and told the press he had no idea McAuliffe was not the real Mars.[26]

Ernest Chappell and Ernest Brainard exposed Mr. McAuliffe. In a letter to the California Aviation Company three weeks later, Brainard wrote, "We have probably been misrepresented by Mr. H. De La Mars. I suppose the said Mr. H. DeLa Mars is the same party who represented himself to us to be Mr. "Budd" [sic] Mars of international aviation fame but who was found out by us and exposed in the newspapers as an imposter. Take a tip from us and [have] nothing to do with him as the truth is not in him [sic]."

Chappell and Brainard, working out of their machine shop, Peerless Iron Works, Second and O streets, quite possibly built the first aeroplane to be constructed in Sacramento. If one wonders why they built a Farman design rather than the ubiquitous Curtiss design, remember that Professor Dare exhibited a full sized replica of the Farman biplane next to his small aircraft models at Weinstock's back in February 1910. Also Roy Crosby made the first successful flight at Sacramento in April 1910 in the Greene biplane, which was a Farman copy. Thus Chappell and Brainard had two major opportunities to study the Farman design up close. They may have discussed the design with Professor Dare and Mr. Crosby. There were suppliers in San Francisco who provided parts for the Farman self-builder.

Twenty years later, Ernest Chappell, by then the superintendent of the city corporation yard and manager of Camp Sacramento, a youth camp, told a reporter after he learned aviators like Charles Hamilton were getting $10,000 to fly at the California State Fair, he wanted a slice of that pie.

Chappell had teamed with two other aviation enthusiasts, the Brainard brothers, and over the next six months they built their version of a Farman in their machine shop. They bought a Gray Eagle air-cooled engine for $900. They built the forward elevators and mounted them on lengths of bamboo. The fuselage was made of laminated spruce. The landing gear wheels came from a small bicycle. The pilot's seat was mounted in front of the wings with the engine and pusher propeller facing to the rear. The gas tank was mounted above the top wing.

The finished aeroplane made its first public appearance at the

Fig. 7. Chappell and Brainard's biplane was a copy of the French Farman design with Curtiss style mid-wing ailerons instead of the Farman's trailing edge ailerons. The Brainard brothers, Omar and Ernest, are standing on the left and right in white uniforms. It is believed that Chappell is sitting in the pilot's seat holding a baby. Jack Irwin is standing to the right of the wing tip in the white hat and pants with a black coat and tie. They are in Buffalo Park, Sacramento, circa 1911.

Sacramento Valley Home Products League parade through downtown Sacramento in 1911. It was not flying but was pushed through the narrow streets by Chappell, Ernest Brainard, and two assistants all wearing white uniforms and hats like early day milk deliverymen.

Chappell told a reporter, years later, of his first attempts to fly the Farman from a field on George Meister's ranch, north of Sacramento. An exclusive group of a dozen people, including Sacramento postmaster Harold J. McCurry, were invited to witness the first flight.

Chappell took off in the Farman and, as the machine began climbing rapidly, Chappell realized all he knew about flying was what he had read in the newspapers. He didn't intend to do any "fancy flying" (stunt flying), but the elevators were very sensitive, and he kept moving them too far overcorrecting each previous move. It appeared to the spectators he was doing the "ocean roll," and they cheered him on. This maneuver was done by exhibition pilots of the day to impress their audiences. Today, Chappell's predicament would be referred to as porpoising due to over-control. Just when Chappell thought he was learning to control the biplane, it pulled up sharply and nosedived into the ground. Chappell said the plane fell about sixty feet suffering heavy damage, but he walked away unscathed. It took three months to repair the aeroplane.

Later Chappell and Brainard attempted to fly the biplane again. This time the machine was mounted on a large flat pontoon with smaller canister shaped floats under each wingtip. The aircraft was headless with a completely new tail section making the entire ship appear as a clone for the first Curtiss hydroplane flown by Glenn Curtiss from the bay at North Island, San Diego, on January 26, 1911.

Chappell and Brainard attempted to fly their hydroplane during a Sacramento Boat Club regatta on the Sacramento River June 1, 1913. Once again, Chappell would be the pilot. After the boat races, his flight was next as a special feature of the grand finale.

The hydroplane ran well picking up speed during its take off run upstream. But with a strong tailwind the hydroplane would not leave the river. Chappell was closing on the Sacramento Northern Railroad's drawbridge at M Street connecting Sacramento to West Sacramento. It was looming larger and larger in his vision, but he couldn't break free from the water. "I thought I was a goner," Chappell recalled. "Just as I neared the bridge we started to rise and as we dove under the span the ship's tail was lapping waves fully three feet high.

"Boy, did I heave a sigh of relief when I saw that bridge behind me! I had no sooner finished thanking my lucky stars, though, than the engine died and we plunged into the water. The plane turned turtle and somehow I managed to get free and was rescued by a boat, once more unscratched."

The plane sank then resurfaced later on the river at Y Street. Brainard and Chappell recovered the engine and left the rest, a tangled mass of debris, in the river. The two men eventually traded the $900 engine for a tree stump puller, which they later sold for $50.[27]

Photographs of the two attempted flights of the Chappell and Brainard biplane reveal the wooden frame wings were constructed then covered with fabric only on the underside of the ribs. According to Joseph Cato, an early flying pioneer and aeroplane builder, this method of covering the wings was used on training aircraft to keep the students on the ground or at least very close to the ground, while they learned the control inputs necessary to fly (also known as the grass-cutting method of flying instruction). If not corrected, this may have been the cause of the Chappell-Brainard aeroplane's difficulty achieving successful flight. Also it is doubtful the pontoon was constructed properly to allow the plane to get up "on the step" prior to breaking free from the water.[28]

The Chappell-Brainard design was originally copied from the basic Farman biplane design of the day and its technique for wing covering was a single covering method in which the wing rib was sewn into a pocket in the wing fabric covering, with the upper curve of the rib left exposed from the pocket—causing the fabric to appear to be only on the underside of the wing ribs. With the upper portion of the ribs exposed there wasn't enough disturbance of the airflow by the ribs to prohibit flight. However, when the entire rib was exposed as described by Cato, the disturbance was enough to keep the airplane on the ground for "grass-cutting" training. Many of the early Curtiss and other aircraft advertised for sale in the aero magazines stipulated that the wings were "double-covered," meaning fabric was applied to both the top and bottom of the wing ribs. There was also a permanent fence a couple inches high that ran perpendicular to the ribs the full length of the top wing. It resembled a modern day spoiler. Being nonretractable, this fence had to cause drastic disruption to the airflow over the wing.

Chappell quit the aviation business a short time later, but Ernest and Omar Brainard, whose main income came from their machine shop, manufactured aviation parts well into the 1930s. They moved their Peerless Iron Works in the 1930s across the river to what is now West Capitol Avenue in

Fig. 8. The Chappell and Brainard airboat. They kept the Farman wings, made the plane "headless" by dropping the front elevator and its long booms, adding a Curtiss rudder and elevators in the tail, and putting the plane on floats. See the small raised fence running parallel about a foot ahead of each wing's trailing edge. Also note that the wing ribs sit on top of the wing fabric; there is no fabric over the top of the ribs. The wings are single covered not double covered in the more traditional manner.

Fig. 9. The airboat making a failed attempt to fly from the Sacramento River circa 1913. The author has found no mention of Chappell and Brainard ever making a successful flight in their biplane(s) and believes this was due to the disruption of the airflow by the fence on the wings and possibly the single wing covering.

West Sacramento and renamed the business Brainard Bros.' Machine Shop & Foundry, which operated well into the 1950s.[29]

The Brainards had a young unpaid apprentice, John Fulton Irwin, working for them during the time they were building biplanes in 1911 and 1912. There will be more about "Jack" Irwin later in this work.

At the time Chappell and Brainard were building their airplane, Carl Browne of Sacramento built an aeroplane of his own design, called the Octoplane, but it never flew.[30]

In January 1912, an advertisement in *Aero* notified aviators that Maxim Rotary Motors Company wanted fliers to bring their aircraft to Maxim's large flying field at Sacramento where the company would install one of their 45hp. motors on any flier's machine, and he could test fly the rotary engine for free. The ad stated the company would like endurance flying done with their motors, but the aviators had to pay their own personal expenses. The company was listed as Maxim Rotary Motors, 1530 M Street, Sacramento, California.[31]

Dick Ferris, the aviation impresario, organized a series of air circuses (air shows) in Northern California after the conclusion of his third Los Angeles International Air Meet at Dominguez Hills during January 1912. Ferris hired several of America's best professional exhibition pilots at the Dominguez meet to form his traveling air circus troupe to fly at the Emeryville racetrack (aka Oakland Motordome) in February. His troupe included Lincoln Beachey, who was rapidly becoming the most sought after of American exhibition pilots. In March, Ferris' troupe moved northeast to Sacramento without Beachey, who had commitments elsewhere. At Sacramento Charlie Hamilton was the ranking exhibition flyer. The troupe later performed at Fresno in April, and in May they flew at Chico.

At Sacramento, Ferris' aviation troupe was made up of Farnum Fish, who at seventeen was the youngest ACA/FAI licensed pilot performing in America, and Miss Blanche Stuart Scott, the first woman to fly solo in America. Charlie Hamilton, Horace Kearney, Phillip O. Parmalee, and Glenn Martin made up the rest of the troupe. They performed at the Agricultural Park racetrack March 2–3, 1912.

The air circus at Sacramento actually began on the last day of February with a long cross-country publicity flight by Horace Kearny in his Standard Model Curtiss. His plan was to fly from San Francisco nonstop to Sacramento. Six miles into the flight, a bad magneto caused his engine to quit and he put down on the mudflats near Noble Station in Alameda County. He touched down perfectly along the tideline but as the plane slowed, his front wheel sank, and he flipped over, partially burying him in mud. He was not hurt, but the forward elevator was crushed. He telegraphed the air circus officials he would be late and traveling by rail. He said his plane would be ready to compete by Saturday, March 2.

Meanwhile several hundred spectators had gathered at the park in Sacramento to watch Kearny land not knowing he had been forced down. Dick Ferris shot fireworks into the air to signal Kearny where to land. After finding out about Kearny's problem, he arranged for Phil Parmalee to go up and put on an impromptu exhibition. The crowd was impressed with Parmalee's flying. Some said it was the best ever to take place in Sacramento. Parmalee and Farnum Fish both flew Wright aeroplanes. Parmalee had been a member of the Wright Exhibition Team, which quietly disbanded in November 1911 after the Wright brothers became appalled at the number of exhibition fliers killed while performing. This air circus would mark the first time a Wright aircraft was seen in the Sacramento Valley.[32]

Everyone watching was excited after Parmalee's flight. Dick Ferris told them, "Wait until you see five or six machines flying at once. That will be some fun."

A reporter commented that prior to Parmalee's flight, aviators, who came to fly at Sacramento were always all "dolled up." They dressed in fur-lined leather coats, long leather gloves, stylish caps, goggles, and leather leggings. Parmalee flew in his street clothes, and his only preparation to fly was turning his Scotch plaid newsboy cap backwards.[33] This cap worn backwards was the badge of an aviator during the Exhibition Years.

The next day the air circus started with a bang after Dick Ferris fired off more fireworks at 2:00. Five aircraft roared off the track at Agricultural Park clawing their way into the air.

Flying actually began earlier in the day. Charlie Hamilton made three test flights in his biplane to be sure his machine was just as he wanted. Horace Kearny and his mechanic were busy assembling his Curtiss; he had just arrived by rail from Alameda. He wanted his plane ready for the next day's handicap race. Parmalee raced against an automobile three times in his Wright and won every time. He and Fish did spiral glides and the "dip of death."

Miss Blanche Scott made two lengthy flights to let everyone know she could fly as well as the men. Dick Ferris wanted Scott to fly a five-mile race against Charlie Hamilton. She refused saying she did not believe in competing with men, and she was not a believer in women's suffrage. She seemed to have no fear and often flew when the wind was raging and turbulence boiling. Glenn Martin, her protector and manager, would not let her go up until he went up and assessed the risk.

Another reason Blanche Scott did not compete in air races and altitude contests in exhibitions was she did not have an Aero Club of America (ACA/FAI) pilot's license. Such a license was necessary for anyone to fly in an ACA/FAI sanctioned air meet for prizes or records. Other aviators at the Sacramento event possessed the necessary licenses and could have had theirs revoked if they competed against Scott. She flew strictly for people's interest in seeing a woman fly, and surely she was being paid for her efforts.

Charlie Hamilton was supposed to make a flight around the capitol, but his mechanics couldn't get the plane adjusted in time. He didn't get into the air until 6:00 PM. The wind was blowing at 20 mph when he took off, but he still made several trips around the race course.

Glenn Martin didn't take off until 6:30. He made several "fancy" maneuvers in his biplane at 800 feet and then spiraled down to 300 feet and landed after several circuits of the racetrack. At this early stage of his exhibition flying career, Glenn Martin was rightfully calling his biplane a Martin-Curtiss. At least then, he was giving Curtiss credit for the only successful design Martin had yet built. A few months later he flew the same design in air meets and listed it solely as a Martin aeroplane. In later years, Martin would claim to have built an aeroplane of his own design, and to have flown it successfully at Santa Ana in August 1909. This claim has never been adequately corroborated.

In the April 6, 1912, issue of *Aero* (later *Aero and Hydro*), one of the first biographies written about Martin stated he had been interested in aviation since 1897. He built several gliders of the Chanute design, but lacked money and "was never able to accomplish anything of note." It claimed he built a machine after the January 1910 Dominguez Air Meet and made short hops and eventually flights of up to twenty minutes. But Martin later said he learned to fly at Curtiss' flying school, North Island, San Diego, which didn't open until 1911. It is obvious that legend creep had not yet infected the 1912 biography in *Aero* written when Martin was still relatively unknown.

In March at Sacramento, Blanche Scott was supposed to fly a Martin-Curtiss plane. She was at her plane ready to fly in her specially made aviatrix's costume, but did not or wasn't allowed to fly because Glenn Martin said the wind was too strong.

In the late afternoon, only Glenn Martin and Farnum Fish competed in the five-mile race. Martin won after engine trouble forced Fish to give up.³⁴ Charlie Hamilton won the handicap race and Parmalee beat Farnum Fish, once again, only this time it was in a contest to see who could make the most perfect figure eight. Parmalee also flew a mail pouch to the Oak Park Post Office in Sacramento from Agricultural Park.

Horace Kearny succeeded in dropping baseballs from 200 feet into the mitts of J. Folk and Patsy O'Rourke, both from a semi-pro Sacramento baseball team. Parmalee, flying the American flag, won the Race of Nations to the cheers of thousands of spectators, and Charlie Hamilton beat a racecar around the track.

Sunday, 5,000 watched Charlie Hamilton take popular actress Miss Culture Odom for her first aeroplane ride. Two minor accidents marred that last day of the meet. Flying events were going as well as the day before until Blanche Scott's exhibition flight demonstrating a maneuver called an "ocean roll," which entails pulling back and pushing forward on the control wheel causing her plane to bob up and down. It was usually performed close to the ground for audience appeal. She misjudged her height and plowed into the ground. There was about four hundred dollars damage, but she was uninjured.

The second accident involved Farnum Fish. After his exhibition flight that included impressive spiral dives, a crowd favorite, his foot slipped off the throttle pedal while landing. His Wright Flyer collided with Parmalee's Wright, which was about to take off. Fish had swooped down from the northwest with the wind behind him, misjudged his distance, and crashed into Parmalee's machine on the racetrack. Both aircraft sustained light damage.

The two-day show was a success. The Sacramento Valley Home Products League sponsored the event, and Sacramento aviation enthusiast and aero club member Edgar M. Sheehan managed it.³⁵

The Ferris troupe of aviators moved on after the show without Charlie Hamilton. Dick Ferris sent him to fly exhibitions at Marysville, Willows, Lodi, and Fresno, to name a few. He wasn't averse to flying his biplane between nearby exhibition sites.

Charlie Hamilton flew the *Hamiltonian* to Marysville March 14, a distance of 42 miles in 33 minutes. He flew exhibitions on the sixteenth and seventeenth and returned to Sacramento on the eighteenth. Professional aviators of the day moved their aircraft between exhibition sites by rail.

On April 23, 1912, Hamiliton flew an exhibition near Lodi at the Sargent Ranch. He made eight flights taking up his wife, followed by Mrs. Sargent, Mrs. Ralls, and Mrs. Hines. Hundreds of automobiles drove to the ranch from Stockton, Sacramento, and Lodi.

A week after the Lodi flights, Hamilton crashed returning to Sacramento. He was said to be limping around Chico waiting for his wrecked airplane to be rebuilt there for the Chico Spring Festival May 3–7. Hamilton flew brilliantly at the festival along with the rest of the Ferris troupe.[36]

The California Aviation Company of San Francisco reported Matthew Mellard of Sacramento ordered a headless Curtiss Pusher copy. The Curtiss copy had a wingspan of 34 feet for the upper wing and 28 feet for the lower. The wing chord was 5 feet, and No. 10 Goodyear rubberized fabric covered the wings. The plane, powered by a 50hp., 4-cylinder Roberts engine, was supposed to be completed by the end of September then tested at Sunset Field in Alameda. It is unknown when this plane was actually built.

Two years later Mellard reported that he had invented a new type of airship, which he claimed had absolute stability. At a hangar he built in North Sacramento adjoining the Oak Grove Picnic Ground, Mellard, who claimed to have been a flying student of Glenn Curtiss', said he had built a heavier-than-air machine with wings curved like parachutes. The craft had a device that automatically adjusted the wings to prevent tipping. Mellard claimed it took no great skill to fly the aircraft and if the engine quit the machine would slowly sink to the ground. There is no evidence that this machine ever flew.[37]

Roy Knabenshue came to Sacramento in May supposedly to organize an air meet for the September 1912 state fair. Since no activities involved aeroplanes during the state fair that year; it must be assumed Knabenshue was organizing balloon or dirigibles flights. At Sacramento crowds historically turned out in larger numbers for lighter-than-air events.[38]

Knabenshue had other business in town several months later in 1913. He took possession of an engine and keel car constructed by W. G. Hansen of Sacramento for a large dirigible he was having built. Knabenshue had the finished envelope filled in Sacramento with gas.[39]

Over a year later another professional flying exhibition took place in the state's capital sponsored by the Sacramento Chamber of Commerce. It was advertised as a "Grand International Aviation Meet … the best aggregation of expert birdmen ever brought together in California," with two-and-a-half hours of "sky vaudeville" promised. Fifty cents paid for parking, admission,

CHAPTER 2   43

and grandstand seats. Shows would start daily at 2:30, April 19–20, 1913, at the state fairgrounds.

The promoter and general manager were, respectively, Bay Area flying impresario Max Friedman of the Motordome Co. of San Francisco and pioneer Cavalry Flat aviator, Ivan R. Gates. They brought the best aviators, all were from the San Francisco Bay Area except young Thaddeus Kerns from Chico.[40] Kerns arrived at the fairgrounds April 16 with his disassembled Curtiss copy and started setting up his required tent hangar before assembling his biplane.[41]

Residents near the fairgrounds looked to the sky just before dusk on the seventeenth after hearing an aeroplane roaring overhead. It made a few dips, curves, and circles before dropping out of sight to land. Roy Francis from San Francisco, piloting the plane, had just finished assembling it in a Western Pacific Railroad Company rail yard, west of the fairgrounds. The crated aircraft had been unloaded earlier in the day from a railcar. Francis couldn't resist putting on a show for the townspeople on his way to the fairgrounds.[42]

By April 18 all the aviators and their planes had arrived. They were: Kerns, Francis, Silas Christofferson, H. W. Blakely, Tom Duck Gunn, and parachutist Leslie Leroy "Sky High" Irvin. All except Kerns and Irvin were professional aviators from the Bay Area.

The meet opened to a respectable crowd of 5,000 the following day. For three hours flying events rolled out like clockwork, keeping aeroplanes in front of the audience every minute of the meet. It was one of the most successful air meets ever held in the north state.

A highlight of the first day occurred when "Sky High" Irving went up with Roy Francis in his Gage twin-tractor biplane. At 2,000 feet Irvin jumped from the plane descending by parachute. Another popular event was an air race between Blakely and Christofferson around a one-mile course. The pilots started from opposite ends of the course and met in front of the grandstands where they turned to race. Blakely with the larger engine prevailed.

Few problems marred the day. One came during the Race of Nations. The Chinese pilot, Tom Duck Gunn, broke two sections off his main plane (wing). His engine had been giving him grief all day, but he felt he had to fly because a great number of his countrymen came to support him. Gunn had yet to make a circuit of the course when he was forced to land with a sick engine. He touched down in a bank (tilted wings) and damaged his plane. He gave up on his engine and wired San Francisco for another. The newer engine came by overnight rail express and Gunn's Chinese mechanics installed the engine and repaired the airframe damage in time for him to fly the next day.

The other problem, on the nineteenth, was Thad Kerns' inability to take off. For power, Kerns' Curtiss now had a Roberts engine, which was not in great condition; it wasn't developing power enough to get him off the ground. It had to be perfectly tuned for maximum horsepower. He spent a lot of time working on his engine and by late afternoon was able to make a 20-minute flight, but Kerns was not a match for the others in competition. However, his flying was acceptable, and he was cheered on by his friends from Butte County who came to support him.

The expert aviators—Christofferson, Blakely, and Francis—gave first class exhibitions the first day of the meet. Blakely was known as a "dare devil" flier and demonstrated a "reckless" flying technique. He stunned the audience with his low-level flying and his fearless dips, dives, and spirals. Roy Francis impressed the crowd with his confident control of the twin-propeller biplane he named *My Girl* for the meet. He carried passengers on two flights during the last day. One was Miss Lulu Holtman, chosen from a group of young Sacramento women requesting rides and second passenger, Mrs. L. Little, of Schurz, Nevada. Mrs. Little wanted to fly with Francis when he and Frank Bryant flew an exhibition at Reno earlier in the year. He told her then that due to the high altitude it would not be safe for him to take up a passenger. He invited her to come down to the Sacramento meet for a ride in his aircraft in thicker air. Silas Christofferson raced an automobile driven by Ed Gardiner around the track. He later competed against Blakely in a figure-eight contest.

Juichi Sakamoto was unable to get his airplane assembled in time to qualify for competition in the two-day meet. He was very disappointed and blamed the railroad company for not delivering his plane to Sacramento on time.

On the last day of the meet, Francis and Blakely came up with an exhibition they called the "Brothers Act." The two aviators came from opposite ends of the track in what appeared to be an impending head-on collision. At the last second, one pilot pulled up and over, while the other pushed down and under avoiding a collision. The crowd loved it.

Other events during the two-day meet included an altitude climb by Francis and Blakely. They climbed for nearly a half hour. Suddenly, Blakely pointed the nose of his plane straight down in a "death dive." Francis disappeared to the west with a mailbag filled with airmail posted at a mailbox on the fairgrounds. He dropped the mailbag at the Oak Park post office, west of the fairgrounds.

On Sunday a larger crowd estimated at 8,000 attended. The same events were carried out with some additions to the final day. Tom Duck Gunn's rebuilt plane was flying with a new engine. He was originally to fly the mail to Oak Park, but the mail sack went through his propeller splintering it to pieces. Thad Kerns made a long distance flight to Yolo County at an altitude of 2,000 feet.

Christofferson raced against a motorcycle driven by Jack Martin and just barely won. The most remarkable aspect of the meet was all of the pilots were Northern California aviators. There wasn't an Eastern or nationally known professional in the lot.[43]

The Bay Area's Hall-Scott Motor Car Company was quite proud three aircraft in the Sacramento meet used its engines. The company began using a photo of H. William Blakely, seated in his Curtiss copy, in their advertising. The other pilots using Hall-Scott engines were Roy Francis and Tom Gunn. Christofferson was using an 80hp. Curtiss engine, and Kerns had a Roberts Six in his Curtiss.[44]

Mrs. Charles K. Hamilton announced in July that she had separated from her husband of five years. Since April 1, she had been working at Nonparel Department Store in Sacramento. She reported she and Charlie were happy until he came into overwhelming fame as an aviator. His drinking had gotten worse as he became more famous.[45]

A. W. Lorain of Sacramento completed his flying tests for an ACA/FAI pilot's license at Curtiss Flying School on North Island, San Diego, as did army Lt. Henry B. Post on August 28, 1913. The two demonstrated excellent handling of their aircraft flying the required figure eights around pylons and landing within 20 feet of the marker flag. They set a record by completing their flying course and getting licensed in only five weeks after they began instruction. They flew a Curtiss with a 30hp., 4-cylinder engine a total of 72 flights for a total flying time of 18 hours (probably "grass-cutting"). Then they flew the Curtiss with a 40hp., 4-cylinder engine, 89 flights for 22 hours. Finally the pair flew the Curtiss with an 8-cylinder 60hp. Curtiss engine, 30 flights for a total of only 4.4 hours. Lorain and Post's totals for the 5-week course came to 191 flights for a total flying time of 44.4 hours. That averages to a little over 22 hours per man to learn to fly and get a license in 1913. Most flights made in the 30 and 40hp. biplanes were logged as "straightaways," meaning the flights ran the length of the course and returned. The flight times included a landing where the aircraft was turned around on the ground then flown straightaway back to the starting point.[46]

It is hard to believe only 2.2 hours, the time spent per man in the 60hp. Curtiss, were spent learning to turn the aircraft. Possibly the 40hp. machine used for straightaways was also used for some turning flights with the 60hp. machine used for 360-degree turns and figure eights.

A. W. Lorain was issued ACA/FAI license No. 263 and Post received No. 264. What happened to Lorain after he left the Curtiss school is unknown. His name doesn't appear in any further aviation periodicals of the day.[47]

ROBERT G. FOWLER, the man who made the second successful transcontinental flight in 1911, signed a contract with the Great Western Power Company in November 1913 to fly power line inspections between Oakland, Brighton (east Sacramento), and Oroville. Fowler was to carry a power company employee as an observer and line repairman. Bob Fowler was trying to develop useful flying jobs that didn't involve dangerous stunt flying exhibitions; power line inspection flying was such a job.[48]

The contract for Great Western Power Co. was to start November 20 at Brighton, but Fowler had damaged his plane on November 16 while flying an exhibition race over San Francisco Bay near the Panama-Pacific Exposition grounds at Harbor View (Fort Mason). Fowler was flying a ten-mile race against Silas Christofferson, Otto Rybitzki, and Adolph Sutro when his engine quit over the bay. He made an excellent landing on his plane's new floats. After he found the source of the engine problem, Fowler asked a nearby canoeist to help him get his engine restarted, which meant hand propping his propeller. The canoeist was able to get the engine started, but his canoe was sucked into the propeller and chopped to pieces. Nobody was hurt, but Fowler's propeller was destroyed.[49]

Having to make repairs and switching the landing gear on his Gage tractor biplane from floats back to wheels, made Fowler nine days late getting to Brighton to fulfill his contract. On November 29 he made his first flights at Brighton. Great Western Power had erected a large tent hangar there in addition to developing a large landing field. The company was anxious to get started with the pioneering flights. Management had gotten the idea from a power company in Germany that had been using airplanes successfully for power line inspection for some time.[50]

Chapter 2

Fowler took off from the newly fashioned airfield next to the patrol station on the Cowell dairy at Brighton. Riding with him in the Gage biplane was patrol lineman Ray S. Kitto. They were off at 8:37 AM following lines to Marysville and on to Oroville. The press made much about this as the first commercial use of an aeroplane. Reporters from *Collier's* and *Leslie's Weekly*, two of the most widely read magazines in America, were in Sacramento for the flight. Technically this was not the first commercial use of an aeroplane. Flying schools had been using aeroplanes commercially to train pilots for quite some time. Pilots were often paid to take up photographers and news reporters. They were paid to fly exhibitions, and they won money flying in races and other contests. Pilots had been flying commercially long before Fowler's power line patrol. Fowler's flights were the first in the nation

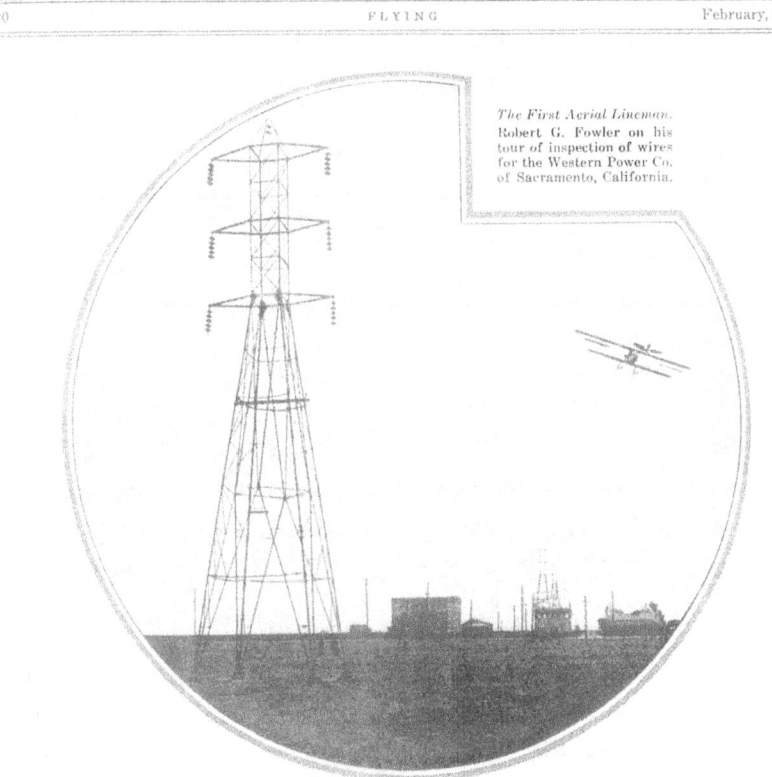

Fig. 10. Robert G. Fowler in his Gage tractor (a puller not a pusher) biplane flying the nation's first power line patrol from Brighton (East Sacramento) to Oroville on November 29, 1913. Seven months earlier in the same plane, Fowler, with photographer Ray Duhem, was the first pilot to fly the entire length of the Panama Canal.

carried out for power line inspection purposes.[51]

On their first flight to Oroville as Fowler's plane neared Palermo, a few miles south of Oroville, Ray Kitto, spotted a shattered insulator on top of one of the steel towers holding heavy transmission lines. Fowler landed in a field a mile-and-a-half outside of Oroville at 10:48. Kitto jumped out and ran to the damaged power line. He tapped into the telephone line that accompanied Great Western's power lines using a portable phone he carried and reached the foreman in the office who answered, "Hello, Hall at Brighton."

"Kitto at Oroville," the patrol lineman replied. "One Thomas disc insulator broken in two at Palermo, on Big Bend line No. 1; line No. 2 O.K."

The problem was located in two hours by plane. It would have taken the ground inspector, who walked the line daily, twelve hours to find the problem. Fowler and Kitto could see the ground inspector at Oroville, Bill Pennington, from three miles away by plane. Fowler usually flew the plane at 800 feet on patrol. Visibility of the lines and insulators was best at that altitude.

After Kitto phoned in his report, he and Fowler went into Oroville for lunch. They returned to the plane and departed at 2:26. D. C. McAuliffe, the line patrolman at Marysville, reported he had them in sight, and by 2:50 they had passed out of view. At Brighton, I. Duren, reported them in sight 28 minutes later, and he lost sight of the plane after Fowler turned west towards Sacramento; they were over the city at 3:20 and Fowler made a circuit around the capitol. He then followed Sixteenth Street out of town and turned for Perkins. He landed just beyond Perkins at Brighton at 3:30.[52]

After his flight to Oroville and back, the Sacramento and San Francisco newspapers declared his endeavor a great success, but due either to a lack of interest or the length of time it was taking to complete a round trip, they dropped the story from their pages. The *Oroville Mercury* stayed on the story reaching a different conclusion.

The newspaper described in more detail Fowler's flight to Oroville. It reported Fowler was originally to land at the old Speedway track at Oroville, but Fowler deemed it unsafe and chose another site believed to be near the junction of the Palermo and Wyandotte roads. The intersection of the roads is very close to the location of Riley Field, Oroville's first airport on Kusel Road. This supports the belief the Riley site may have been used as a landing field as early as 1913. (It would officially be established as an airport for the Army Air Service's forest patrol planes in 1919.) Darby family members, who lived close by, were the first to spot Fowler's plane. A telephone call was placed to Oroville, and an Oldsmobile filled with people came out to greet the plane. Already there waiting, were company linemen Bill Pennington and Leo Wallace. The party from Oroville congratulated Fowler and Kitto on the success of their flight. Nearly everyone then proceeded to sign their names on the fabric wings of Fowler's aeroplane. The wings were covered with hundreds of names including President Woodrow Wilson, who had signed after Fowler flew an aerial circuit over the White House earlier in the year.

Fowler intended to make an immediate return to Sacramento from Oroville, but he was low on fuel. The only gas available at Oroville was low octane, unsafe for his engine. He decided to have better fuel shipped up from Sacramento, which would delay his flight back to Brighton by one day.

Many officials from Great Western Power Company came out to see Fowler. The company was watching this experiment closely. If a success, it could save them a lot of time and money on line inspections. The company had 160 miles of lines. Fowler was under contract to fly an average of two trips per week between Oakland and Oroville. There were eight 90-foot steel towers per mile supporting the transmission lines.[53]

Fowler changed his mind about staying overnight in Oroville. He found adequate gasoline and took off at 2:30 from a field at Villa Verona. The flight back to Brighton was described above.[54]

Brighton was to be headquarters' landing field for Fowler with a turnaround field at Oroville and another at Concord. On leaving Concord, Fowler, as mentioned, would have to cross a range of hills 1,200 feet high to reach Oakland. The turnaround fields were established so there would be no delay for gasoline, oil, water, and repairs if needed.[55]

Fowler and Kitto finally began the second half of the power line inspection, from Brighton to Oakland, on December 4. They departed Brighton at 8:44 AM circling to gain the optimum altitude for line inspection. On reaching an altitude of 800 feet, they struck out in a west-southwest direction. Patrolman I. Duren reported the plane near Hood at 9:00 AM. After passing Hood, they flew into a fog bank, which prevented line inspection, so Fowler landed on the Hollisters' ranch near Hood.

Charlie Hollister was astounded to see an aeroplane landing on his property. Fowler took the rancher on an aerial tour of his ranch after calling Brighton to report he landed. Tom Dillon, Sacramento superintendent for Great Western Power, drove Fowler's mechanic, Mike Silva, down to

Hollister's ranch. Minor repairs were made to the plane. Fowler and Kitto departed the ranch at 1:00 and passed over Isleton and Sherman Island. They overflew Antioch then Clayton and landed at their Concord airfield, refueled and were off at 2:40. They flew over Lafayette, the Contra Costa County line and passed over Oakland a little after 3:00. Four minutes after turning 180 degrees, they exited the county heading north.

Fowler landed back at Concord at 3:25. There they received orders to patrol the main power line from Oakland to Antioch along the Eastern Railroad, one of Great Western's principal feeder lines. They departed Concord a half hour later following the route as ordered. There were no line problems, and Fowler landed back at Brighton at 5:12. The company officials were ecstatic over Fowler's successful flight, and they told him permanent quarters for the crew would be built at Brighton.[56]

Bad weather set in, as it often does that time of the year, and Fowler wasn't able to fly again until December 11. Linemen on the Oroville line were notified Fowler would be flying that morning. He was off about 10:30 with lineman Picket as observer. He circled to gain altitude then headed north to a point 30 miles from Sacramento where the Pacific Gas and Electric lines crossed Great Western's lines. There he was flagged a signal to return to base. He arrived in Brighton and was told to fly the line south of Sacramento to repair lines on islands in the Sacramento River delta. He flew Picket to the Liston District and dropped him off to repair the lines 15 miles south of Sacramento; that was the extent of Fowler's flying for the day.[57]

Fowler made two more trips before the end of December, but all in all, the flying experiment was not a success. Weather in the Sacramento Valley during December can be very ugly. There can be weeks of dark grey fog, which in those early days of aviation made flying impossible.

The results of Fowler's experiments were: He made a total of one full inspection flight of the entire line, which was his first flight, then a half inspection flight followed by two partial inspection flights during the entire month of December. Reportedly, he was supposed to make eight flights per month, so he was paid nothing for a job that, if successful, was supposed to pay $1,500. Poor weather was the reason given for the lack of flying during the span of the contract, and the company decided not to retain Fowler. The *Oroville Mercury* published an article, at the end of December, with the headline FOWLER CANNED FROM PATROL OF G.W. POWER LINE.

On December 23rd Fowler was given three parcels of mail to deliver to the Weinstock & Lubin department store in Sacramento. He flew from Brighton with the mail to a building at 4th & K Streets. From 500 feet he dropped the mail sacks on roof of the building and the company building on L Street. One sack missed and fell in 5th Street. Thousands of people crowded the sidewalks for two blocks to watch Fowler's demonstration of a commercial use for aeroplanes. What they didn't know was the night before Fowler braved a 90 mph gale to fulfill a contract with a West Sacramento company to act as the first flying Santa Claus in history.

After he fulfilled his duties as Santa, Fowler tried to fly back to his hangar at Brighton, but was forced to land on the Swanson Ranch, three miles south of Sacramento. When he returned to his plane the next morning, he discovered it had been blown into the adjacent slough and was badly wrecked. He called for an auto full of spare parts and men to repair the aircraft. The repairs were made and he flew the mail sacks to Weinstock's and returned to his hangar at Brighton. Fowler desperately wanted to find useful commercial jobs for his aeroplane. [58]

It is difficult to understand why Fowler attempted the powerline missions in the month of December with the notorious valley weather. The Bay Area has very different climate than Sacramento Valley and Fowler possibly overlooked the recurring December fog. It's surprising that with the incredible success of Fowler's first inspection flight to Oroville and Oakland, truly remarkable for 1913, that management at Great Western didn't pursue aeroplanes for line inspection during spring and summer when weather in the Sacramento Valley is perfect for flying. Power companies would turn to aircraft for line patrol once again, many years later.

LINCOLN BEACHEY, THE flying phenom, flew an exhibition on October 18, 1914, that left a Sacramento audience awestruck. Once again, the state fairground's racetrack was the site of Beachey's thrilling aerial exhibition. For 50 cents, Sacramentans were able to watch the nation's most famous exhibition flier do aerobatic stunts that no one else in America did. He flew loops in his specially strengthened and modified Curtiss Pusher. He recently became the first pilot in America to do a loop. He was also doing a maneuver, which, unknown to pilots of the day, was even more dangerous than the loop. It was the tail-slide. To do this maneuver, Beachey would pull the nose of his Curtiss straight up vertically, and when the machine ran out of forward speed, it would slide backwards until the nose of the plane would pop over, heading straight down. This maneuver puts tremendous strain on the tail section when it pops over. Aircraft have been known to lose the entire tail assembly off the fuselage during this maneuver. Even today, the Federal Aviation Administration (FAA) requires a placard in some aerobatic aircraft prohibiting the execution of the tail-slide maneuver. This author owned one such aircraft—a Bellanca Decathlon.

Beachey was also flying upside down (inverted) for his audiences. Reportedly, he was also doing a spiral maneuver while inverted. At the time, it was a maneuver that only he did. A very popular stunt Beachey performed at Sacramento did not involve aerobatics. He raced Barney Oldfield, America's most famous auto racer, around the track at the fairgrounds.

The crowd for Beachey's Sunday flying spectacle numbered 6,000 paid ticket holders with the same number outside the fairgrounds who didn't purchase tickets. One local newspaper claimed the crowd was dissatisfied because Beachey only flew four consecutive loops. His fans knew from newspaper reports he had flown ten loops over the White House.[59]

The other Sacramento paper made no mention of crowd dissatisfaction and, in fact, said the crowd, inside the grounds and outside, often cheered loudly at Beachey and Oldfield. The race between the daredevils was the most spectacular ever witnessed at the fairgrounds. Oldfield was driving his 100hp. Fiat Cyclone and was beaten by his friend "Link" by four-fifths of a second in a one-mile race around the track. Beachey flew the entire race just 15 feet above Oldfield's head the entire distance. Occasionally as they raced, Oldfield would have to reach up and push Beachey's wing out of his face so he could see ahead. Beachey did the mile in 51.2 seconds; Oldfield's time was 52 seconds. The audience sat stunned during the race, but when it ended they broke into wild cheers.

Beachey pivoted out to the east at the end of the race climbing to 2,000 feet. He returned over the track and made four consecutive loops with the last one ending just a few hundred feet above the track. His demeanor seemed calm after his loops; he had just completed his 942nd career loop.

Prior to his race against Oldfield, Beachey dropped bombs from 1,500 feet on a makeshift battleship outlined on the track's infield. The ship shot exploding fireworks back at Beachey to simulate the type of Great War tactics believed to be taking place in Europe.

Beachey flew past the grandstands with both hands off the controls, yet still in total control of the biplane. He circled the racetrack three times, and once did a reverse curve (possibly an inverted turn) considered by some impossible to achieve. He climbed to higher altitude, dove 500 feet, turned his aeroplane upside down and flew that way for at least 30 seconds. This was an extremely daring maneuver, and it is doubtful anyone else in America was doing such a stunt.

Barney Oldfield had his one-of-a-kind Walter Christie racer out prior to the big race against Beachey. He shattered all speed records at the fairgrounds' track. His 300hp. Christie racer traveled the one-mile course in 51.4 seconds. Prior to that the course record was 55 seconds.

The day's events went smoothly except when Beachey's engine burned a valve; time was lost while it was repaired. There was no mention in the Sacramento newspapers of Beachey throwing a tantrum and stripping off his clothes in front of the governor before any of his flights at the fairgrounds that day.[60]

Lincoln Beachey would live only five months after his Sacramento exhibition. Some historians consider his fatal crash at the Panama-Pacific International Exposition (PPIE) in San Francisco March 14, 1915, as the true end of aviation's Exhibition Years. Others say the end came with the beginning of the Great War in Europe in August 1914. The war certainly ended exhibitions in Europe, but not so in America. Civilian exhibition flying in America continued until the nation entered the war April 6, 1917.

Flying exhibitions often lost a lot of admission money. It was impossible, once people came to the site, to make them pay to come into an enclosure and watch the exhibition. Most stayed outside the fence to watch the show. Flying exhibitions became an enticement to draw crowds for larger venues such as state and county fairs, or like Beachey's final contract, the PPIE, a world's fair.

The California State Fair had its share of flying exhibitions, but some were less than successful. Robert Defolco attempted a flight in one of John Montgomery's tandem-winged gliders dropped from a balloon on September 6, 1905. Turbulence caused the glider's premature release at 80 feet during the balloon ascent and forced Defolco's shoulder through the delicately constructed glider's main ribs. The glider struck the earth in a lopsided position wrecking the rear wing. The balloon, with the glider gone, sped northward floating in the wind with men giving chase in wagons. Montgomery told the press it was doubtful the glider could be repaired in time for another exhibition. Charlie Hamilton's near fatal exhibition at the 1910 state fair has already been described as has Fred Wiseman's at the 1911 fair. There were flying events at most of the state fairs from the ballooning years through the mid-1920s.

Bay Area exhibition flier Joe Boquel flew for the last prewar state fair in September 1916 in a modified Standard Model Curtiss much like the one used by Lincoln Beachey and his PPIE successor, Art Smith. It would be the last time the old open fuselage aircraft would be flown at the state fair. At future fairs the influence of wartime aircraft construction was made obvious. The exhibition aircraft would have fabric or wood enclosing the plane's fuselage, not just the wing and tail surfaces as on prewar exhibition aeroplanes. The warplanes flying exhibitions during and after the war had more dependable engines that would run longer than 20 minutes without overheating and losing power.

Boquel was a latecomer to exhibition flying, and he was not a man of means. While learning to fly at the Christofferson Aviation School in Redwood City, he worked several jobs, including one as mechanic for the flying school to pay for his lessons. He had a family to support so it took him longer than most to acquire the skills for flying exhibitions. But, he became an expert aerobatic pilot and became well known as a daredevil pilot especially in the western states. He survived several harrowing flights. At San Francisco before his state fair exhibition, he was flying over the city when his engine quit, and he had to glide to the ground powerless. He just missed the Flood Building by 20 feet landing safely in the Civic Center quad.[61]

Joe Boquel was doing many of the same stunts at the state fair as those done by Beachey and Art Smith at the PPIE. He incorporated loops into his routine, just like Beachey and Smith. Boquel took off at 10:00 every night after the fireworks display to fly an aerobatic routine with blazing flares attached to his Curtiss just as Art Smith had done at the PPIE a year earlier. Fairgoers who had seen both pilots do their night flying flare routine, felt Boquel was much more aggressive in his performance. Boquel would bomb a model battleship as Beachey had done on the same grounds eleven months before.[62]

As Boquel did turn after turn with loops thrown in and spiral descents bringing him within 200 feet of the grandstands, everyone on site was holding his or her breath expecting him to hit the grandstand's roof. He straightened out suddenly, flew across the grounds, turned, and landed – rolling to a stop in front of the stands full of cheering people.

Boquel was a native of Normandy, France. He had been in America ten years and had been flying four years. He was 32-years old and claimed he had only had two accidents in his flying career. One occurred just two weeks before in San Francisco when he crashed on landing after a night performance; as he was touching down he was blinded by an automobile's headlights. He said he was badly shaken by the experience.[63]

During the fair, Boquel was introduced to Governor Hiram Johnson following his afternoon aerobatic exhibition on September 4. The crowd had given him a two-minute standing ovation. They demanded a speech from the embarrassed Frenchman; he said a few words and took his seat in the governor's box.[64]

The following day an aviation event concluded quite near the fairgrounds, but the fairgoers never knew anything about it. Sam Purcell, a Bay Area pioneer aviator, decided to crash Boquel's party at the fairgrounds. He planned to fly nonstop from San Jose to Sacramento and land at the fairgrounds, as a way to inform the public of his availability to carry mail, express (freight), and passengers throughout the Great Central Valley. Had he not ran out of gasoline one mile east of the fairgrounds, his plan would have succeeded and the fair crowds would have seen two aeroplanes in the air at the same time. Purcell had flown almost 100 air miles from San Jose when his engine died from fuel starvation. From an altitude of 500 feet, he came down in the Smith Estate Vineyards slightly damaging his machine and injuring himself. He had been in the air for an hour and 45 minutes.[65]

Joe Boquel had a minor problem in the air the next day. After take off his engine began missing right away. No one on the ground knew it, but Boquel flew with one hand while reaching back and working on his carburetor with the other. Able to keep the engine running smoothly, he proceeded to altitude, and carried out his exhibition.[66]

Six hundred soldiers of the California National Guard fought a mock battle on September 7 at the fair. A vast amount of explosives was used, and 16,000 blank cartridges were fired. Governor Johnson and 20,000 spectators viewed the battle from the grandstands. Joe Boquel and Sam Purcell flew their planes throughout the battle acting as scouts and occasionally dropping fake bombs on the troops. The audience loved the spectacle. It was a great day at the fair; earlier two speeding locomotives were crashed head-on into each other. (Ahhh, those were the days.)

Fireworks from Boquel's night exhibitions at the fair often started fires in nearby Elmhurst. Elmhurst residents put the fires out before any damage was done, but one night a blaze Boquel started required three fire companies to extinguish it.[67]

Sam Purcell's self-promotional flight may have paid off. He received a call from the committee putting on the Almond Day celebrations at

Arbuckle in Colusa County on October 6–7, 1916. They negotiated with him to fly at Arbuckle during the events. Purcell asked for $250. He offered to fly from San Jose in his aeroplane and drop almonds and leaflets about Almond Day over towns he passed on his journey. The committee was encouraged with Purcell and sought more subscriptions to pay his fee. Purcell made the flights as contracted.[68]

Unfortunately, Joe Boquel was killed in a crash while flying an exhibition in Southern California just two months after he flew at the state fair. His wife and teenage daughter, who lived in the Potrero Heights district of San Francisco, were awarded a gold medal from the San Diego Exposition committee for his excellent exhibition flying during the exposition. The two women lived in a house that Bocquel (their spelling) built to resemble a biplane. Boquel's wife was a trained nurse and fully supported Joe's love of flying. Even after he began working as a professional exhibition pilot (the purses were smaller by then), she continued to work as a nurse so he could buy an aeroplane.[69]

The Exhibition Years had taken a drastic toll on aviators—particularly those who flew aggressively, on the edge so to speak, having what would later be called "the right stuff." Sadly, their flying machines had not paralleled many exhibition pilots' development and for some their egos clouded a realistic expectation of the capabilities of their questionably constructed machines; a staggering number of pilots did not survive the Exhibition Years. It is interesting to note that of the first 26 aviator deaths in history, none were killed in Curtiss aeroplanes. They were killed flying mostly Wright, Farman, and Bleriot aircraft. Another reason Curtiss' design was so often copied.

Fig. 11. Shown here is the Wiseman-Peters biplane, a Farman copy. In the pilot's seat is Fred J. Wiseman, Northern California's first successful aviator, meaning he was the first self-taught Northern Californian to build and fly his own aeroplane in the north state. He also made the nation's first official airmail flight in this plane on February 17, 1911, from Petaluma to Santa Rosa.

CHAPTER 3

Frank Bryant and Sam Purcell fly for the 1917 California State Fair – Liberty Iron Works build JN-4s for war – Mather Field is created – Great War aviators at Sacramento – Jack Irwin

The California State Fair of 1917 was more subdued than previous years because five months earlier America entered the massive conflict known as the Great War. The emphasis at the annual September event was California's farm and industrial contribution—so necessary to help win the war.

National service was a predominate theme of the 1917 fair. The unqualified loyalty of the California farmer with his ability to produce enormous quantities of foodstuffs was represented by a statue of a man with a hoe. The statue could have been a young teenager or even a middle-aged man, but he was depicted as willing and able to adapt to new wartime requirements.

Each day of the fair four Bay Area aviators flew a fitting demonstration of aircraft use in warfare. Two pilots, Frank Bryant and Sam Purcell, were familiar to Sacramento aviation enthusiasts who had seen their prewar exhibitions. They had given up their prewar open-framed pusher and tractor aeroplanes for the new Curtiss JN-4D Jenny, a tractor type biplane, with a fabric enclosed fuselage; it was designed for use as a military trainer. Bryant and Purcell would demonstrate wartime maneuvers and combat techniques for the state fair audiences. The other pilots who joined them for battle formation demonstrations were Ralph P. Hanson and Dan Davison (or Mayo Boulware) making their debut at Sacramento aviation events.

At 3:00 o'clock daily, the four aviators competed in bomb-dropping contests, spot landing events, and mock air battles. They used bombs filled with bags of oatmeal rather than real explosives. Members of the Pacific Aero Club of San Francisco judged the events; awarding fancy loving cups to the winners.[1]

During a press interview, Frank Bryant, the "grand old man" of aviation in the Bay Area, explained he began training pilots in the Alameda mud flats in 1912 and moved to Redwood City in 1916. He had trained a 100 pilots in the last year-and-a-half, and 18 were now flying for the air services of America or its allies in Europe. He said four of the students were women, the most notable being Helen Hodge and Jeanette Doty. Bryant was very proud that two of his graduates were training military pilots for a flying school at San Diego. The reporter wrote that Frank's son, Harry Bryant was also a pilot and serving somewhere on the war front.[2]

Frank Bryant and Dan Davison competed against each other September 11 in a 10-mile air race at the fair. Their Jennies were described as two "great white birds, sailing aloft through the kindly skies." Bryant won in his Curtiss JN-4D Jenny, powered by a 90hp. Curtiss OX-5 engine, with Dan Davison finishing a half-mile behind him in another JN-4D. Bomb-dropping contests were held the same day with an army tank as the target of oatmeal bombs.[3]

Governor William D. Stephens sat in a box seat the following day watching an aerobatic performance by Dan Davison. Davison flew vertical dives, 90-degree banks, and spiral glides. Afterward, he flew a five-mile race against Sam Purcell.[4]

IN LATE JUNE 1917, the US Congress passed the Aviation Act, which gave the military $640 million to build aircraft and train pilots for war. In late September, a corporation of Sacramento businessmen secured a government contract to build Curtiss JN-4s for the military. The new corporation purchased Globe Iron Works in the city of North Sacramento and renamed it Liberty Iron Works led by James M. Henderson Jr, president, J. A. Jordan, manager, and Harry H. Wetzel, who later became factory superintendent.

Wetzel earned a B.S. in Industrial Engineering at Penn State. While serving in the Army Signal Corps as an aircraft inspector, he met Donald Douglas, the chief civilian aeronautical engineer of the Aviation Section of the Signal Corps, in 1916. In 1921 Wetzel went to work for the Douglas Aircraft Company where he became general manager and eventually vice president.[5]

CHAPTER 3   59

Fig. 12. The Globe Iron Works on Del Paso Boulevard in North Sacramento became Liberty Iron Works in 1917. The iron works would produce training planes for the Army Air Service during the Great War.

Liberty Iron Works claimed they started building Jennies October 6, 1917. That claim was a little premature. The country was in a building frenzy that was causing manufacturing chaos. Getting materials to construct the Jennies was initially a nightmare. J. A. Jordan had claimed himself an expert at building airplanes when the company began operations, but it soon became obvious there was much about aircraft production that Jordan couldn't grasp. Supplies to the factory dropped to a trickle, and planes were not getting built, so E. L. Maddox replaced Jordan.[6]

Liberty Iron Works' production problems forced the government to put the JN-4 contract on hold while a federal grand jury investigated the company. Following the departure of Jordan, the grand jury investigated the conduct at the plant to determine whether it was efficient and could operate at maximum output. They also investigated a report German sympathizers had been hired to work in the factory. The grand jury found Liberty Iron Works was producing as many planes as possible under the circumstances. Shortages of aircraft construction materials hampering production nationwide were well known, and the allegations of German sympathizers working at the factory was never proven.[7]

In early March 1918, James Henderson, Liberty president, and vice president, O. A. Robertson, were in Washington, D. C., getting Liberty Iron's contract reinstated. They also worked to get priority shipment of aircraft quality spruce, steel, and brass to Sacramento so the company could meet some semblance of a production schedule. Henderson returned to Sacramento with good news while Robertson went to Winnipeg, Canada, to try and unravel the problems with getting aircraft quality spruce.

Henderson told a reporter the Aircraft Board in Washington gave approval for Liberty Iron Works to build Jennies in blocks of 100 planes at a time. The factory couldn't choose where its planes would go, but he anticipated many would be sent to the new airfield being built east of Sacramento near Mills Station.[8]

In February 1918 Wetzel left the Air Corps to help with manufacturing training planes at Liberty Iron Works. Liberty Iron Works delivered its first JN-4D in April 1918. If the JN-4 was powered by a Curtiss OX-5 90hp. engine it was designated a JN-4D. JN-4H was the Jenny's designation if a Hispano-Suiza engine, commonly known as a Hisso, was used for power. The Hisso engines used on the JNs supplied either 140hp. or 180hp.

The first JN-4D to fly from the new army airfield at Mills Station

Fig. 13. A Curtiss JN-4D Jenny training plane is manhandled during its construction at the Liberty Iron Works in North Sacramento. During the war, 200 Jennies were constructed at the iron works.

CHAPTER 3

on June 11, 1918, was built by Liberty Iron Works and flown by Lt. J. F. Buffington.[9]

E. L. Maddox resigned as manager of Liberty Iron Works on September 1, 1918, and was replaced by Harry S. Wanzer. Liberty Iron Works built 100 JN-4D aircraft. In October 1918, Liberty delivered its first JN-4D-2 model to the military. By the end of the war, Liberty Iron had completed 100 JN-4D-2 aircraft for a combined total of 200 Jennies built before the company closed its doors forever in 1919 soon after the Great War.[10]

The most important stimulus for the growth of aviation in California's Great Central Valley was the creation of the huge pilot training base near Sacramento. Construction of the airfield began shortly after America entered the World War. It was located 12 miles east of Sacramento at the Mills Station rail stop, thus it was first known as Mills Station Field. The base would become the hub for smaller auxiliary landing fields around the valley to be used for cadet cross-country flights during the war. After the war the base became the main headquarters and departure point for US Army Air Service fire patrols over the forests of Northern California and the state of Oregon. Airfields for refueling and overnight stops for fire patrols were established at valley towns along the western foothills of the Sierra Nevada. In the Great Central Valley, these airfields were located as far south as Fresno and as far north as Redding.

The Curtiss Jenny cost the US government $6,500 each. The Curtiss Aeroplane Co. would later buy JN-4s back from the government following the armistice for less than a third of that price. The company refurbished the aircraft and sold them to ex-army flyers and the general public for $3,500. That price only held for about a year. By 1921, one could buy a Jenny as war surplus, in its crate, direct from the army at Rockwell Field, San Diego, for $200 to $400.[11]

With Liberty Iron Works producing Jennies for the Air Service, the availability of JNs at Sacramento after the war was excellent. Frank W. McManus, the civilian in charge of aircraft maintenance at Mills Station Field during the war, bought JNs built by Liberty Iron Works and started a business selling Jennies to the public. The workmanship of the JNs built by Liberty Iron was considered by many as the best of any JNs built during the war. Some of the other war surplus JNs sold in Northern California were built at factories in San Francisco and Redwood City.

During the war in February 1918, O. A. Robertson, Liberty Iron vice president, had gone to Washington, D. C., working to get Liberty Iron

Works back on track. He reported to Sacramento executives that William Stephens, a government expert in Washington, believed the Mills Station aviation training site would be one of the finest in the country and it had the best chances of becoming a permanent base after the war. Stephens once visited Sacramento to help choose the site.[12]

By March 1918, farmers who owned land on the Mills Station site made satisfactory arrangements enabling the city to buy their land. None attempted to hold out for top dollar. All sold their property at cost or below; some owners suffered great personal losses willingly for the war effort. Such an example was farmer A. W. McDonnell, who sold 184 acres of prime farmland, which had been planted in grain, for a profit of only $62. D. A. Whipple and John Radonich sold their land at nearly cost. Chris Erickson was slow in reaching an agreement for his orchard land through which the railroad spur to the airfield would pass but did sell the government the four acres necessary for the rail line.

A large work gang began building rail line by late March. The Moreing brothers were hired to level the land. The Moreings owned vast grain farmland north of Sacramento and had the necessary land leveling equipment.[13]

Formal approval of the site was made in February 1918, and the army acted rapidly. On March 5, Lt. B. F. Vandenberg arrived in Sacramento to assist in supervising development of Northern California's first US Army airfield. Ten days later, Lt. Samuel P. Burnham arrived leading 1200 workmen in a 12-car Southern Pacific train, and construction of the airfield began.

Captain Albert D. Penney assumed temporary command of the base on April 26. Four days later the 283rd Aero Squadron arrived from San Diego.

The base was known as Mills Station Field until May 2 when it was officially named Mather Field in honor of Second Lieutenant Carl Spencer Mather who was killed on January 30, 1918, while flying from Ellington Field near Houston, Texas.

Major Reuben Fleet became the officer-in-charge of flying at Mather Field on June 10, 1918. The next day the 200th and the 201st Aero Squadrons arrived from St. Paul, Minnesota. Major Delos C. Emmons was given command of the field on June 13 and remained in command until December 17, 1918. Major Walter Wynne succeeded him and Major Dana H. Crissy took over from Wynne on August 4, 1919. (A new airfield created on the Presidio grounds at San Francisco in 1919 was named for Major Crissy after he was killed during the Army Air Service's Transcontinental Reliability and Endurance Race in October 1919.)

CHAPTER 3

At Mather Field on June 16, pilot-training flights began. The first class, reduced to 26 aviation cadets, graduated from primary training three-and-a-half months later.¹⁴

The Sacramento Chamber of Commerce gave a dinner in late June 1918 for Mather's new base commander, Major Emmons, and his staff at the Hotel Sacramento. Emmons used the occasion to announce that 16 planes would fly over Sacramento on the Fourth of July and continue on to overfly Stockton, Woodland, and San Francisco.¹⁵

Development of the Mather Field runway was officially completed June 15, 1918, however, the rest of the base was only partially complete. The land on which the base was located was furnished by the city of Sacramento free for five years with an option to buy, which would happen later.¹⁶

On July 4, Mather's instructor pilots made good on Major Emmons' promise of carrying out a mass flight over Sacramento. Some of the pilots that day made the first flight of Mather aircraft to San Francisco. The official register of Mather flying activities for Independence Day stated, "Formation flight over Sacramento. First flight to Frisco. Marina is not a good landing field. Palace Hotel and Portola Louvre, however, are quite satisfactory [sic]." ¹⁷

Fig. 14. The flight line at Mather Field in 1918. Curtiss JN-4D trainers were the only aircraft based at Mather during the war with the exception of a few de Havilland DH-4 bombers.

The above suggests there were military aircraft using the Marina Green during the war and not a field on the Presidio grounds.

The 1918 California State Fair featured aviation events once again. Instructor pilots from Mather performed flying exhibitions at the September fair; not civilian pilots. (President Wilson had issued an edict banning civilian flying in February and it went into effect on September 1, 1918.) Army JN-4s, flew in formation over the fair and individuals like Lt. Knapp flew aerobatic exhibitions popular with fairgoers. Lieutenant Buffington, the flight commander, did a spectacular inverted flying routine. He was one of the best aerobatic pilots at Mather during the war and was often chosen to fly exhibitions for civilian events around the Sacramento Valley.[18]

While the flying activities at the fair were going on, so was training, and Mather Field suffered its worst flying accident. Two cadets were killed in a midair collision over Walsh Station, east of Mather. The pilots collided head on, possibly while dogfighting. A witness on the ground said one plane tumbled all the way to the ground while the other, under some control, tried to land.

Both pilots were named Wilson, but they were not related. Cadet James E. Wilson from Colorado died in the hospital shortly after the collision. Cadet William G. Wilson, the son of one-time socialist candidate for governor and once Berkeley mayor, J. Stitt Wilson, was killed instantly. One Jenny crashed within a half-mile of the Walsh Station rail stop and the other came down a mile from the station.[19]

Even though the war ended a month-and a-half after the first class of flying cadets graduated, training at Mather Field continued for nearly a year after the war ended. Its enlisted strength during the war numbered 1,100 men. The first class of flying cadets trained under difficult conditions. The flying field wasn't ready; it was only partially leveled. The part leveled was covered with a loose, six-inch layer of dirt that turned into clouds of dust when the propellers of JNs were turning.

Cadets were given dual instruction in the tandem cockpit JN-4D biplanes by instructor pilots, as opposed to the French self-teaching instruction method of "grass cutting" with the cadet alone in an underpowered plane incapable of leaving the ground. At first, cadets at Mather soloed after only two-and-a-half to three hours of dual instruction and graduated from primary training after 30 hours of flying. Later, dual instruction prior to solo was increased to six to eight hours, and total flying time for graduation was increased to 110 hours. This newer regimen decreased accidents and produced superior aviators. The cadets progressed through primary and secondary training, which included dual and solo time to learn aerobatics, formation flying, cross-country flying, and night flying. Photography, gunnery, and artillery coordination were also taught to the cadets. No parachutes were available to flying cadets, nor any US aviators, during the Great War with the exception of aerial observers in the balloon corps.

Raleigh Terry, a flying cadet from Roseville, trained at Mather Field during the war and later described flight training there:

> The ships at that time were equipped with only an altimeter, tachometer and compass in addition to the regular gasoline and oil gauges. For gunnery, a Lewis Gun, drum loaded, was mounted on the center section [above the upper wing] firing over the prop and operated by a trip wire cord in the pilot's seat. Small balloons or six-foot paper parachutes with small sand bags attached were used as targets. A small reservoir near Slough House was used for water targets, although one very irritated farmer is still attempting to identify the aircraft, which killed his prize cow, apparently substituted for a target. Radio at that time was not perfected for training planes and wireless code with blinker lights were used between the ship and ground. Each ship was equipped with a 200-foot antenna, which was reeled out on the side of the fuselage. For mapping and observation the pilot carried a map board and roll strapped to his right leg and jotted down the details of the course as he proceeded. One cadet named Billings found this an unsatisfactory arrangement on one occasion when the map board became unfastened and slipped into the rudder and elevator controls. While forcing his head and shoulders under the control panel to retrieve the map board Cadet Billings found his plane in a bad spin without much altitude.

THE ELEVENTH AND final class, reduced during training to 18 cadets, graduated on January 8, 1919, at Mather. Training had ended for Mather Field. Major Emmons, 110 officers, and 139 cadets were transferred to March Field at Riverside, January 1919. By December 1919, only 17 officers and 32 enlisted men were caring for the airfield. Civilian efforts to keep the base open proved futile. Mather Field was used by the army as headquarters for a small squadron of forest fire patrol aircraft through May 1923. The base was then put on inactive status. In the summer of 1925, the

Fig. 15. Frank W. McManus, the lone civilian in the center of the top row, was head of aircraft maintenance at Mather Field during the war and the government's inspector of aircraft at Liberty Iron Works. He would be instrumental in the creation of Sacramento's first municipal airport at Del Paso Park in 1919.

army returned to Mather with an even smaller detachment of planes to fly fire patrol once again. On July 1, 1925, three DH-4 aircraft and twelve men arrived to carry out fire patrol duties.[20]

Mather Field would be used for various aerial activities during the 1920s and '30s by federal, state, and city government entities. Those activities will be mentioned in the following chronological record of aerial activities in the Great Central Valley.

Thousands of American pilots trained to fly and fight in the World War, but only a small percentage of those who trained in the United States made it across the Atlantic for combat. America entered the war late, and there wasn't time to get pilots trained and transported to Europe. The British and French insisted shipping priority be given to weapons and American infantrymen to replace the thousands of allied troops lost to the Germans in the meat grinder of static trench warfare. Little cargo space was alloted for pilots, their aircraft, and support personnel on supply ships to Europe.

The Allies trained a number of American pilots "over there" who flew combat in France. Among those who did fly combat and were or would be influential in Sacramento aviation include the following men:

William P. Sullivan, one of the founding professors of the pioneering aeronautics program set up at Sacramento City College in the mid-1920s, was an early American volunteer for the war in Europe. He obtained his ACA/FAI hydroplane pilot's license No. 43 upon graduation from Glenn Curtiss's flying school at Hammondsport, New York, in the fall of 1915. He was going to Bermuda with F. G. Eden to open a flying school during the winter months, but his plan fell through. He traveled on to Britain in December 1915. At Northolt, England, he enlisted in the British Royal Flying Corps. He spent three and a-half months in training and was commissioned a lieutenant. Assigned to a base at St. Omer, France, he flew missions against the Germans, many of which were night missions. He returned to America in July 1916.[21] The aeronautics program at Sacramento Junior (now City) College, which is still teaching aviation students in the north state, is one of the few, if not the only, complete aeronautical programs still available at a California junior college.

Fig. 16. Lt. William P. Sullivan, shown here during his wartime service with the British Royal Flying Corps in 1916, would later become one of the early instructors in the aeronautics program at Sacramento Junior (today City) College.

William Van Fleet was born in Sacramento in 1891 to Lizzie (Crocker) Van Fleet and William Cary Van Fleet. Van Fleet was educated in San Francisco and attended the University of California. After college he was in the oil business and helped develop a small submarine, which was purchased by the Japanese, a US ally in the Great War. Van Fleet joined the French Air Service in July 1917. He attended flying schools in France, and from July through August 1918, flew on the Western Front with a French fighter squadron. He was known as a capable and aggressive flier. He transferred to the US Navy in late August and became Naval Aviator No. 1731, stationed at Dunkirk, France. He was awarded the Croix de Guerre with Palm and a US Navy Cross for bravery in combat. He joined the Northern Bombing Group in October and flew with them until the war ended.[22]

Lieutenant L. J. Reese returned home to Sacramento from the war in

March 1919. He and one or two partners started the earliest known postwar flying businesses in the area, which was named the Sacramento Aviation Co. His base of operations was the emerging ad hoc municipal airfield in Del Paso Park adjacent to Auburn Road (later Boulevard), eight miles north-northeast of Sacramento. This airfield became Sacramento's first official municipal airport.

During the war Reese flew with the 96th Daylight Bombing Group. He told reporters upon his return home that his bomb group, which was four squadrons of 12 to 24 bombers in each squadron, was the entire American force of daylight bombers in the American sector of the Western Front. He told of an early mission flown by six bombers from the 96th led by an officer who became lost over Boche lines. Three were shot down, and the rest forced down with their crews taken prisoner. Pilots of the 96th flew the de Havilland DH-4 single-engine biplane bomber. Reese said the DH-4 was satisfactory with an American made Liberty engine, but American pilots were wary of the airplane because of its propensity to catch fire in a fight. The gas tank was positioned right in front of the pilot's cockpit. Slow cruising speed and poor pilot visibility were also aircrew complaints during the war. Later, the fuel tank was moved behind the pilot on a modified version of the DH-4 flown by US Air Mail Service pilots after the war.[23]

By the late 1920s, most civilian pilots in Northern California knew Edison E. "Monty" Mouton. An ex-war flier who, in 1927, became the first federal government aeronautics inspector for the north state. Mouton, born in Sacramento in December 1894, graduated from Sacramento High School and prior to the war worked in hop farming. In May 1917, he joined the US Army Air Service. Sent to France, he trained first as a mechanic and then as a pilot. After the war, he was hired to fly for the US Air Mail Service, a job he held from 1919 to 1927. Mouton flew the first load of transcontinental airmail into Marina Field, San Francisco, on September 11, 1920. In 1927 the Department of Commerce, Aeronautics Branch, hired Mouton who, based at Oakland Municipal Airport, was to oversee the licensing of all pilots, mechanics, and aircraft in the north state, Nevada, and Idaho.[24]

Henry Gay "Andy" Andrews, an Air Service veteran, was a fixture at Del Paso Airport on Auburn Boulevard -- Sacramento's first municipal airport. H. G. Andrews was the best known flying instructor and professional pilot in the Sacramento area for the first two years following the war. On November 2, 1918, Andrews flew the second aircraft in the first squadron of the

CHAPTER 3 69

largest aircraft formation flight ever assembled in the United States—149 airplanes. This formation from Rich Field flew over Waco, Texas, to open the Cotton Palace Exposition, housing the Official War Exhibit of the United States, Great Britain, and France. Also in that first squadron of nine planes with Andrews was Dan E. Davison, a popular San Francisco aviator before and after the war.[25]

With the end of the war, many officers were mustered out of the Air Service at Mather Field. A few of the instructor pilots hung around Sacramento hoping to make connections in what they thought would be flourishing civil aviation work.

JOHN FULTON "JACK" Irwin, returning to Sacramento from wartime duties as a civilian pilot, was a veteran of the city's miniscule prewar aviation industry. He was born in Alameda in June 1892. In 1908 he built a "Chanute" type glider while living in the Noe Valley District of San Francisco. A photo of Irwin's glider in flight, shows a strong resemblance to Wright glider design, however for lateral control Irwin installed Curtiss type mid-wing ailerons. In later years Irwin broke his arm flying the same glider down the

Fig. 17. Jack Irwin flying a glider with the towing assistance of glider club members from the sand dunes of West Ingleside near San Francisco's Ocean Beach circa 1908.

American River Canyon near Auburn. He lost control, spun in, and crashed. It is difficult to understand why he chose such dangerous terrain to fly his glider. Soon after the crash, he moved to Sacramento where he met Ernest and Omar Brainard at their machine shop and foundry at 126 O Street.

Irwin said, "These two men were really very kind to me. I would watch them work and make myself useful as best I could, and it wasn't long before they began teaching me a few of the simple jobs and answering my questions. … They taught me how to make molds from patterns. I made cores of green sand (sand with flour mixed in it). Later I learned to operate lathes and other machines including the use of a drop forge. … I never got any pay; I was just happy to be learning something I felt would be useful."

Irwin helped the Brainards build their Farman biplane copy. As mentioned earlier, Irwin claimed to have built a Curtiss Pusher copy in 1912. An extant photograph shows the Irwin Aero School at the Target rail stop in Yolo County. A Curtiss Pusher copy depicted in the photo is parked next to the Irwin Comet, a tractor biplane, built some time between 1912 and 1916, depending on which of Irwin's stories you believe. He said the photo was taken between 1913 and 1915. Planes are shown sitting in front of a well-built wooden hangar large enough to hold at least two aircraft. The photo is labeled, "The Irwin Aero School," but there is no name on the front of the hangar. Target was a rail stop on the interurban electric rail line that ran from Sacramento to Woodland. It now is located in the Sacramento River overflow area known as the Yolo Bypass, a flood control area for the runoff of winter rain from the Coast Range. Irwin's timeline for aircraft built before 1916 may suffer from "legend creep," as a newspaper article has him leasing property on B. F. Conway's tule ranch in September 1916 to open an aviation school. Target is believed to have been located on that property—as the nearby next rail stop is named Conway.[26]

The Irwin Comet was a cleanly designed early tractor biplane that resembled the early Curtiss JN-1. Like the JN-1, the Comet had a small, square, inadequate looking rudder, but unlike the JN it had a heavy modified Mitchell automobile engine that weighed almost 200 pounds and produced a little under 40 horsepower. Irwin said the engine was used to power two different tractor aeroplane designs of his during his early years. It is unknown which Comet is in the photo with the Curtiss Pusher. Whether the tractor biplanes were successfully flown is also a mystery.

Irwin's early aviation career gets a little confusing when he relates his activities on the Mexican border prior to the Great War. In one article, Irwin

Chapter 3

Fig. 18. Jack Irwin shown here at the controls of a Standard Model Curtiss copy on an airfield at Target, a rail stop on the interurban line between Sacramento and Woodland, in 1912.

states that in 1914 he and 200 other civilian aviators in the United States were requested to bring their aeroplanes, which were early Curtiss, Wright, and Bleriot aircraft, to El Paso, Texas, to help the US Army defend America's border against incursions by the Mexican revolutionary forces of Pancho Villa. Irwin said he and the pilots he met at El Paso became the first government airmen.

It was a curious claim. Irwin said he and the other pilots were never used, but he said one American pilot was hired by Pancho Villa to fly reconnaissance for his army. Irwin said of his Texas adventure, "We didn't have anything to do in El Paso, but we sure drank a lot of liquor."

Irwin told the above story to the *Marin Independent-Journal* in 1961; in 1977 he told a writer for the magazine *Sport Aviation* a different story.[27]

For *Sport Aviation*, he said he was a member of General Pershing's force that went to Mexico in March 1916 to punish Villa for his attack on the town of Columbus, New Mexico, where several US citizens were killed during the attack. Irwin implied he was a member of the First Aero Squadron, which accompanied Pershing's troops with eight Curtiss JN-2 aircraft.

Is it possible Irwin could have been on the border for both events? ¿Quien sabe?

Irwin's stories were consistent about what he did during the Great War. He said an injury kept him from joining the military, but the army hired him as a civilian instructor pilot. He taught flying at Love Field, Dallas, and Scott Field, Illinois, a balloon training base where he flew Jennies.

Later in the war, he was a test pilot of rebuilt Thomas-Morse Scouts at Houston. He remembered a lot of sabotage occurred to the planes he tested. He noticed many mechanical failures. Holes were bored into turnbuckles just inside the last visible thread and then the holes were filled with beeswax to hide the hole. Landing gear fitting repairs were sabotaged by being soldered instead of welded. The gear usually could take the strain of a take off, but would fail on the first or second landing.

Irwin remembered the rotary engines on Tommies had a tendency to catch fire on the landing roll. There was no throttle to slow the engine, just a blip switch on the stick, which cut the ignition completely. The pilot had full power, half power, or no power at all. On final approach to landing, the pilot would kill the engine with the blip switch, but he had to remember to release the switch during the landing roll or the engine would quit. Meanwhile, during the engine-out glide to landing, the unburned gasoline and castor oil mixture was slung all around the inside of the cowling, just waiting to catch fire at the worst possible moment and engulf the plane in flames.

After a few ships were lost this way, Irwin came up with a fix. He had a petcock installed on the fuel line in the cockpit enabling the pilot to turn off the fuel as he entered his landing glide. Just before he flared to land, he would turn the petcock back on. Irwin claimed there were few fires after the modification.

During Irwin's test flying duties, he designed a light aircraft that was his biggest success. The Irwin Meteorplane was a small biplane with a 20hp. engine that Jack was sure would satisfy the passion for flying he believed so many of the thousands of veteran American airmen would have after they returned to civilian life. The Irwin Meteorplane would be available factory assembled or in kit form.

Over the next several years, Irwin sold about 40 factory-built Meteorplanes plus numerous sets of plans for the do-it-yourself builders. Irwin believed about 10 percent of those who bought plans actually built planes. The Meteorplane sold for $1,165 ready to fly from the factory. If one wanted only the parts to build the plane, cost was $400. If the Irwin manufactured 20hp. engine was included, it cost $625 more. Irwin estimated he built 75 to 80 Irwin engines and hundreds of M-T-2 Meteorplane kits.

Chapter 3

Fig. 19. Jack Irwin demonstrates the correct hand propping procedure to start the engine on his M-T-2 Meteorplane circa 1926.

The Meteorplane M-T-2 was only 14 feet long with a wingspan of 20 feet. It was a single-place biplane with the ability to fly for two-and-a-half hours at 80 mph. Its empty weight was 176 pounds. Irwin advertised the Meteorplane in many aviation magazines and *Popular Mechanics*.

In Sacramento after the war, Irwin developed the Meteorplane and sold kits and plans from a location on Yale Street. At the height of Irwin's success with the Meteorplane in 1926, he had purchased land for an airport at the southern end of Twenty-First Street, where Freeport Road (later Boulevard) began at the Sacramento city limits. One history of Sacramento says Irwin Field became Sacramento Municipal Airport in 1930 (today known as Sacramento Executive Airport). Photographs of aircraft taken in 1926 at Irwin Airport reveal the Western Pacific Railroad's track on a high levee running along the western boundary behind the aircraft which confirms Irwin Airport was on the west side of Freeport Boulevard. The 1930 municipal airport was located on the east side of Freeport Boulevard.

This author believes the presence of Irwin Airport in 1926–27 on the west side of Freeport Boulevard allowed Charles T. "Red" Jensen, years later, to skirt federal regulations by grandfathering his crop dusting airfield into

Fig. 20. Irwin Airport led a brief existence in 1926 and early 1927. Jack Irwin constructed a sophisticated floodlight pylon over the airport manager's office and aircraft hangars shown here behind Admiral Richard Byrd's arctic expedition tri-motor Fokker F. VII, named the *Josephine Ford*. Floyd Bennett flew the plane into Sacramento's Irwin Field while on a national tour in 1926. The small biplane under the Fokker's wing is Irwin's Meteorplane.

legally operating within a thousand feet of the municipal airport, because there had been a pre-existing airport on the property Jensen acquired west of Freeport Boulevard. Jensen's private landing strip near the municipal airport was a thorn in the side of the FAA until he died in 1980, the property was sold, and his airport closed.[28]

It is interesting to note in the 1927 *Jane's All the World's Aircraft*, the most authoritative reference book on aircraft then and now, lists Irwin Aircraft Company's location in 1926 at 116-130 O Street, Sacramento. Company officers were President John Fulton Irwin, Vice President Ernest S. Brainard, Secretary S. E. Shelton, and Treasurer Omar L. Brainard.[29]

The Brainard Brothers Foundry and Machine Shop was also located at 126 O Street. It was they who were the actual makers of parts for the Meteorplane under Irwin's supervision and help.* (See end of this chapter)

Jane's also states Irwin built the M-T in 1916. That must have been the designation for Irwin's Comet biplane built at Target before America entered the Great War. Irwin himself said he began thinking and planning for the Meteorplane during the war.

Irwin tried to get a plant going to build the Meteorplane on the airport at Corning, but the deal fell through at the last minute. He believed the deal failed due to the stock market crash of 1929. In later years, Irwin hand-built a few Meteorplanes at the Watsonville Airport while he was airport manager there.

The enforcement in 1927 of new aviation regulations passed by Congress in 1926 made the sale of non-certificated aircraft illegal; this included all types of homebuilt airplanes. It marked the end of the Irwin Meteorplanes and the end of aircraft manufacturing in Sacramento.

During World War II, Jack Irwin worked as a Navy inspector of aircraft construction at Consolidated Aircraft Company in San Diego. He inspected PBY and B-24 aircraft. Jack passed away in 1977. There is an example of his Irwin Meteorplane in the Oakland Museum and another in the California History Museum in Old Sacramento.[30]

Fig. 21. This 2013 photo shows the recent restoration of the US Army's Crissy Field on the Presidio grounds at San Francisco. This airfield was beautifully restored to the way it looked circa 1923, which included the large oval shaped grass landing field. However, not a single restored example of the JN-4 or DH-4 biplanes that flew from the field in those early years can be found there today.

Fig. 22. Mather Field on April 3, 1930. This depicts the air show held by the Army Air Corps to open their month long 1930 Air Maneuvers in the Sacramento Valley. The base was rarely used by the military after the Army forest fire patrols ended in 1921, however, it was the US Air Mail Service stop for Sacramento from 1925 until 1930.

*The Brainard Brothers Foundry and Machine Shop was located at 126 O Street not far from Sacramento's Crocker Art Gallery. On June 5, 1925, at a little after 11 AM Omar Brainard heard gunshots coming from the art gallery. C. M. Jones, a ranch worker from Yolo County, had gone mad and upon entering the gallery began shooting his rifle. He missed the caretaker, M. C. Powers, but shot to death a Canadian tourist, Richard Burnett. Jones then moved back to the front porch of the Crocker and began firing at pedestrians on the surrounding streets. Omar Brainard moved to within 60 feet of Jones and killed him with his shotgun.

A little over fifty years later this author would perform at the Crocker Art Gallery as a member of the Sacramento Symphony with his friend, trombonist Gary Brainard, one of Omar's surviving family members.

CHAPTER 4

Postwar Aviation – Mather Field pathfinder flights – The creation of Del Paso Airport – An airfield at Curtis Oaks – The War Mother's Aero Circus – Sacramento flying in 1921 and 1922 – Sacramento Valley airports in 1922

In December 1918 Army Air Service aviators began a period of aerial exploration and terrain familiarization of the United States. Veteran Air Service pilots remaining in the army after the war knew the topography of France and Italy better than most of America. Aviators took off from Air Service fields across the country to explore and establish best routes between cities and towns. The aircrews of those planes logged the safest terrain to fly over, meteorological conditions, and best sites for emergency landing strips. The latter were important to pilots due to dangerous weather conditions and chronic engine problems that plagued early flight. The public was told these were "pathfinder" missions to help the infant airmail service and future passenger service, but actually the Air Service was finding its way around America.[1]

Aircraft from Mather Field explored California's Great Central Valley, the Sierra Nevada, the Coast Range, and the Pacific Northwest. The first extended pathfinder flight started from Mather December 3–11, 1918. Lieutenant Alander F. Hogland flew to Seattle and back to Mather Field. He flew through rain, fog, sleet, and snow for 1,365 miles in a Jenny! He used 217 gallons of gasoline and averaged 50 mph. His Jenny was powered by a 90hp. OX-5 engine.[2]

On March 22, 1919, three de Havilland DH-4s and one Curtiss JN-4 took off at 9:15 AM from Mather Field for the first crossing of the Sierra

Nevada by airplane. The DH-4s landed at Carson City at 10:45, and the JN-4 landed shortly after noon. Nevada Governor E. D. Boyle entertained the Air Service aviators at the governor's mansion in Carson City. The aircrews of the DHs were Lt. Col. Henry L. Watson, flight leader; Lt. James S. Krull, Mather's officer-in-charge of flying; Lt. Tobin S. Curtis, assistant officer-in-charge of flying; Lt. Francis W. Ruggles, engineering officer; 2nd Lt. Charles W. Schwartz, flying instructor; and Sergeant First Class Leo Conway, aviation mechanic. The pilot of the Curtiss JN-4 was Lt. Frank J. Hackett.

The DH-4s flew at 14,000 feet to make the crossing. They were prepared to go as high as 16,000 if necessary. They carried no oxygen. The JN-4's service ceiling was 12,000 feet, so Lt. F. J. Hackett flew a different lower route than the DH-4s. The Jenny cruised at only 70 mph; the DH-4s cruised at 100 mph. When the aircraft crossed just south of Placerville en route at 9:50 AM, the streets were filled with townspeople staring into the sky.

The next day the DH-4s returned to Mather Field. Governor Boyle flew back with Lt. Tobin Curtis and enjoyed the flight even though heavy mist obscured the Sacramento Valley. The mist was so heavy Lt. Colonel Watson lost his way. He drifted south after reaching Lake Tahoe and flew right past Sacramento without seeing it. He let down into the mist to ascertain his location, and the first town he saw was Lockeford in San Joaquin County, 17 miles north of Stockton. He circled awhile trying to identify the town and finally landed in a nearby plowed field. His DH overturned on landing and was damaged, but he and his passenger got out without a scratch. Watson hired a fellow to watch over the plane, then he and his passenger walked to a rail stop to catch the next train to Sacramento. He informed officers at Mather the plane's damage was not serious; it could be repaired and flown back the next day.

Lieutenant Krull, in one of the other DHs, made the flight from Carson City at 5:00 PM to Mather in only 60 minutes. Over Lake Tahoe, he was leading the flight of three as planned when Lieutenant Curtis crossed over to the left and Watson followed Curtis. Krull stayed on his compass heading and, once past Placerville, knew he was on the most direct route and the shortest time for the return flight. Governor Boyle ate dinner in Sacramento then rode the 10:00 PM train back to Nevada's state capital.

A small accident prevented Lieutenant Hackett from immediately flying his Curtiss JN back from Carson City. He waited for a clear day before returning to Mather.[3]

CHAPTER 4

THE ARMY AIR SERVICE tried everything to demonstrate its importance and its need for sufficient financial appropriations following the war. In addition to the pathfinder flights, it made stronger efforts promoting the benefits that aeronautical technology would soon bring to civilians.

In early 1919, Lt. Jay M. Fetters flew from Mather Field to San Francisco with photographic plates taken that morning in Sacramento of the 363rd Infantry Battalion at the capitol building. He returned the same day with printed copies of the *San Francisco Call*, which published the photos he had brought to the Bay Area that morning!

Lieutenant Krull departed Mather Field to San Francisco at 8:55 AM on May 8 in DH-4 No. 18 and landed at Marina Field at 10:15. He took aboard 250 copies of the *San Francisco Call*, left at 10:55, flew nonstop to Marysville's Knight Park, landing at 12:50. He was greeted by city officials and the local news dealer.[4]

At the time, many California newspapers were claiming to be the first to deliver their papers by air. The *Los Angeles Express* claimed it was first to pull this off when its papers were delivered by plane to San Pedro on March 6, 1919. But the *Fresno Republican* reported they were first when they delivered by air to Madera in 1914. The *Sacramento Bee* preceded them both when Charlie Hamilton delivered copies of the *Bee* to Marysville by airplane on March 15, 1912. But Fred J. Wiseman beat them all by delivering a bundle of the *Santa Rosa Press Democrat* during the first official US airmail flight, between Santa Rosa and Petaluma, on February 17, 1911. Delivering newspapers by air was a typical stunt carried out by exhibition pilots during the Exhibition Years.[5]

Lieutenant Voss, officer-in-charge of flying at Mather Field, relayed to the press that orders had come through from Washington, D.C., requiring him to ready airplanes for daily patrols over national forests of California to provide early detection of forest fires. After a conference with state forester, G. M. Homans, it was agreed patrols would start June 1, 1919.

Voss said two or three aircraft would be in the air at a time, flying an eastern arc from Mather Field north to Oroville, a distance of 150 miles. If the pilot or his observer spotted a fire, they were to fly to the nearest forestry station or settlement and drop a message with pertinent information about the fire.[6]

This was one postwar mission assumed by the Army Air Service that truly was successful and most useful to the state. The Air Service fire patrols were the reason airports were created in towns on the east side and north end of the Sacramento Valley during 1919 through 1922. Jennies and DH-4s on fire patrol were the first airplanes seen by many north valley residents.

Frank W. McManus, who at one time was a chief engineer at Liberty Iron Works on the JN-4D production line and, later, chief civilian aviation engineer for the Army Air Service at Mather, announced to the press he had five JN-4Ds with which he intended to start commercial air service to many small towns surrounding Sacramento. He planned to open his headquarters as soon as he acquired an airfield in Sacramento to use.[7]

Earl Cooper announced he was retiring from auto racing to devote all his time to selling airplanes in Sacramento and San Francisco. He had competed in big auto racing classics for many years. In 1917, he won four of the biggest races on the circuit. His mechanic, Reeves Dutton, would replace him driving the racer. Cooper began making regular trips from Mather Field to ferry Jennies to the Bay Area where he sold them. He said flying the JNs to San Francisco took about an hour and 45 minutes; there was always a headwind. His flights back to Sacramento usually took only 45 minutes.[8]

Cooper started his first business in Sacramento in November 1917. Back then, he sold only automobile tires, later adding Prest-O-Lite auto batteries, and eventually adding the entire Prest-O-Lite line of products. Cooper also acquired the Northern California distributorship for Curtiss Aeroplane Company. In ten months he sold 94 Curtiss aircraft. By June 1920, his company operated a service and repair shop for the JN-4 airplanes he sold.

Aviators L. J. Reese and E. H. Pendleton went before the Sacramento Park Board, which oversaw city parks on July 2, 1919, and each requested ground in Sacramento's Del Paso Park to develop a free landing field for airplanes. The city engineer was ordered by the board to investigate the proposal and report back.[9]

Two days later, Ogle Merwin, an ex-Mather Field aviator, gave Miss Ernestine Virden and later Mrs. J. J. Fitzgerald of the Sacramento Park Board a ride in his JN-4. Merwin circled Sacramento with each of the women. Frank McManus, owner of the Jenny, was hoping to obtain exclusive control of the airfield in Del Paso Park for his headquarters of a regular passenger service to other towns in the state.[10]

The park board met with all interested parties on July 7, and hammered out plans for an "airplane station" at Del Paso Park. After the arguments subsided, the board decided to develop ground for a landing field 1,800 feet long and 600 feet wide. Hangars, a repair shop, and other airport infrastructure were not voted on at the time, but it was decided exclusive use of the airfield would not be granted to any one person or business. The airfield would be open to all fliers who wanted to use it.

E. H. Pendleton, working with Ogle C. Merwin and Frank McManus, was the first to bring the issue before the Sacramento City Commission and then the Sacramento Park Board. He asked that some action be taken during the current meeting. He wanted a five-year lease but offered to develop the landing field even if he were given only a three-year lease.

L. J. Reese, a partner of H. G. Andrews, was incensed at Pendleton's request for immediate action to be taken by the park board. When he remarked that the board was "jamming the thing through," the board's chairman, Dr. W. E. Briggs, rebuked him saying he had no right to presume anything. Tempers cooled and it turned out that all parties were willing to work together on the project.

Reese and Andrews were planning to open an aircraft repair shop, as were Pendleton, Merwin, and McManus. They all said they didn't have the capital to create a regulation flying field, but they could start on a small scale and build from there. They agreed the city should level the field, and the interested parties would lease the ground from the city.

After members of the park board voiced their satisfaction with the airplane rides given them on the previous day, H. G. Andrews spoke. He said an 1,800-foot runway would allow the largest aircraft existing to land at the site since there were no obstructions at either end of the field. Scheduled passenger service would be introduced as soon as the city studied examples of other towns that had developed landing fields.

A week later, John Q. Brown, Sacramento commissioner of Public Works, reported receiving notice in a letter from the Lawson Airline Transportation Company of Milwaukee that in the spring, "Transcontinental air trains will land in Sacramento twice a day … on a regular schedule which will provide for two trains each way daily. … one of its machines (was) ready for a pathfinding trip from New York to San Francisco." In the letter Alfred M. Lawson, company president, asked if the city had a suitable landing field for an airline station to be established. Commissioner Brown said he would tell the company about the Sacramento Park Board's recent action ordering a landing field leveled at Del Paso Park.

In his letter, Lawson described his airplanes as weighing seven tons each and carrying 26 passengers. Half of his planes were planned as sleepers and half for daylight operations with passengers changing planes at bedtime.[11]

Fig. 23. Del Paso Airport, Sacramento's first municipal airport, was located in Del Paso Park where Haggin Oaks Golf Course (shown in this 2000 photo) is today. The airport began operations in 1919 and was in continuous operation until the mid-1930s when it was closed due to golf course construction and the groundbreaking in 1936 for the Air Corps' Sacramento Air Depot (later named McClellan Field) located one mile north.

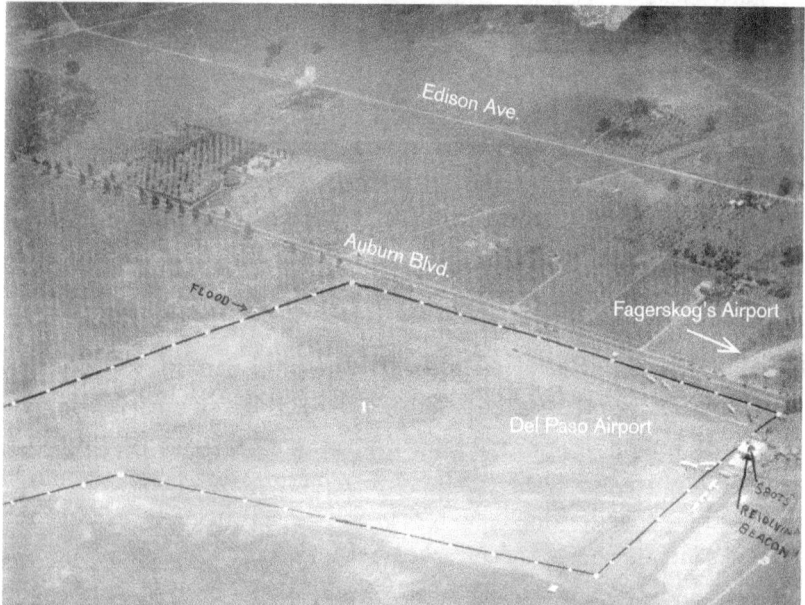

Fig. 24. Del Paso Airport, circa 1928. In the lower right are the large hangar/repair shop and office buildings. The black line with equidistant white dots represents a purposed installation of perimeter lights around the airfield to facilitate night operations. The aircraft in the center of the photo and the elongated perimeter at the lower left indicates the direction of the prevailing winds. Just across Auburn Boulevard from the hangar/repair shop is the northern threshold of Ingvald Fagerskog's runway leading out of the photo to the right. His airport hangar and office are located at the opposite end of the runway near Edison Avenue.

Chapter 4

The park board decided not to lease the aviation field at Del Paso Park, but decided to control the airfield itself. The board appointed E. H. Pendleton to be the city's director of aviation and ordered him to take charge of the field. His position would be without salary, but he would probably be paid a percentage of fees charged at the field. All of the aviators agreed a director (airport manager) was necessary to manage air traffic and settle disputes among the flying businesses on the field. The park board reported several air services had inquired about a landing field at Sacramento, and the board members wanted to hurry development of the airport. They felt aviation technology was developing rapidly, and they wanted the city to be ready. The one sticking point was that work couldn't begin on the landing ground until the crops on the field were harvested.

Ogle Merwin, one of the aviators most interested in the establishment of the new airfield, began flying to other Northern California towns in an effort to encourage those towns to establish airfields so their citizens could enjoy safe air travel. E. H. Pendleton planned to get the airfield at Del Paso Park developed and running as soon as possible. Several airplane businesses and parts distributors planned moving to the new flying field at Del Paso Park.[12]

Commissioner D. W. Carmichael made an effort to obtain airmail service from Sacramento to San Francisco by the end of July 1919, but the postmaster general stated funds were not available for the service.[13]

At a park board meeting, E. H. Pendleton complained about the late harvesting of crops on the airport site. He was told to start working on the field immediately. He promised dust would fly by the end of the week. Pendleton told the park board eleven hangars would be needed on the airfield. Two were necessary for the planned repair shops and nine to house aircraft that had already reserved space on the field. Gasoline and oil service were to be started at once, and water was to be piped in. Instead of a rectangular field 1,800 by 600 feet, a change was made to level an 1,800-foot square field.[14]

A week later grading began on the municipal flying field, soon known to pilots as Del Paso Airport, and indicated on some road maps (there were no air maps at the time) as simply "municipal airport". It was located next to the municipal golf links in Del Paso Park. E. H. Pendleton told a reporter, "There is little possibility that the big planes coming here from the East on commercial runs will be taken down to San Francisco by pilots. The big planes will be exchanged here for smaller ones to enter the perilous atmosphere of the Bay section. That means that Sacramento's field will be the center for Superior California's aviation business." Local aviators were counting on San Francisco's foggy and windy weather conditions to sabotage Lawson Airline's plans to land on a regular schedule at San Francisco's Marina Field.

J. Patterson, a local hatter, flew to Richardson Springs on August 14 with Ogle Merwin. This flight would be the first to land a passenger at a summer resort in the north state. Merwin flew him back to Sacramento two days later. Merwin hoped to start a daily passenger service from Sacramento to Richardson Springs Resort in the Sierra Nevada foothills northeast of Chico.[15]

Frank McManus had his business of refurbishing JNs for the civilian market in operation by September. He completed an aircraft for aviator Fontaine who flew it to Redding with his passenger Miss Genevieve Covell in mid-September. A few days later McManus closed a deal with E. J. Moffett of Colusa for two JN-4s to be used in Moffett's rice field duck patrols around Colusa scaring ducks and geese off the rice. Farmers said the waterfowl were causing unacceptable crop loss.

The Sacramento Aviation Company of L. J. Reese and H. G. Andrews secured the flying concession for the 1919 California State Fair. On August 30, Lt. W. Kauch of the army fire patrol flew a load of figs from Fresno to the fairgrounds' racetrack for display at the fair. September 1, H. G. Andrews was circling the fairgrounds at noon and suddenly his engine quit. He was able to glide to within a few feet of the ground then lost control resulting in his JN nose-diving into the ground. The plane came to rest tail up in the soft earth of a vineyard next to the racetrack on which he hoped to land when he ran out of airspeed. Andrews climbed out without injury, but the landing gear was shattered and the wings, warped badly, would have to be replaced.[16]

Later during the fair, Miss Olive Locke of Arbuckle went aloft with Andrews in another JN-4 belonging to Sacramento Aviation Company. While cruising at 800 feet she threw out clouds of almonds, which rained upon the fairgoers. She was promoting the fifth annual Arbuckle Almond Fair to be held in early October.[17] Andrews and other pilots from the Sacramento Aviation Company flew day and night aerobatic exhibitions at the fair.[18]

A large tent at the fair held displays of the latest inventions in the automobile industry. At the center of the tent sat a Curtiss biplane, which foretold the coming of a new era in motor transportation. The display was Earl

Cooper's, the local distributor for the Curtiss Aeroplane Company. Curtiss was the largest airplane manufacturer in America.

Miss Charlotte Owens, a reporter, interviewed W. H. Jones, Earl Cooper's representative in the tent exhibit. He asked her if she would like to go up in one of Cooper's Curtiss airplanes. Excited at the thought she said yes, but only airplanes belonging to the Sacramento Aviation Company were allowed to fly from the fairgrounds during the fair. Miss Owens had to journey out to Mather Field where Cooper was keeping a spare aircraft during the fair. In a leather flying coat, cap, and goggles, she climbed aboard a new Curtiss. Pilot C. C. Lee, took her to 5,000 feet and flew around Sacramento. Then he closed the throttle and asked her, "How about some stunts?" She nodded and he pulled up into an Immelman maneuver, a half-loop with a half-roll to an upright position. Then he did a Falling Leaf, a slipping maneuver to the left and right resembling a leaf falling from a tree. Aviators used this maneuver more to impress their friends while losing altitude on final approach to landing than for air show work. Lee later demonstrated a spin for Miss Owens. With the earth coming at her in a wild gyration around the nose of the airplane, she had had enough; the flight was over. C. C. Lee claimed 44 Curtiss aircraft had been sold in Sacramento since Earl Cooper Company started in business a few months before.[19]

An airport created for Sacramento Aviation Company in early 1919 was located at the Carrie Cutter Tract in the eastern half of the South Curtis Oaks Housing Division. The runway was between Franklin Boulevard and the eastern boundary of the Western Pacific rail yards off Twenty-first Street, south of Donner Way.

The Cutter family allowed the land to be used as an airfield because of Curtis H. Cutter's great interest in flying. He became one of Sacramento's earliest resident aviators and also one of the city's prominent citizens. He was president of Cutter Lumberyard in Oak Park and later successful in real estate sales.

L. J. Reese founded the Sacramento Aviation Company as its president and general manager with Henry G. Andrews its vice president and chief pilot. The man with the money was prominent Sacramento businessman, Ancil Hoffman, who was company treasurer. Reese had flown bombers in France during the Great War. H. G. "Andy" Andrews had flown over a thousand hours as an army flying instructor at Rich Field, Texas.[20]

The Curtis Oaks airport existed for about a year. It first came to the public's attention when advertisements appeared in regional newspapers promoting Sacramento Aviation Company's barnstorming expeditions through the surrounding counties.

On August 1, 1919, a large ad appeared in the *Marysville Democrat* informing readers Sacramento Aviation Company would bring an aircraft to Knight Park to give local folks 15-minute rides for a dollar a minute. They were promised a conservative ride with no stunting. The weekend before, the company was at Colusa. The ad boasted the company had the best pilots and planes in the Sacramento Valley and would be doing night exhibitions for the upcoming California State Fair. The company's home "aerodrome" was listed as the Cutter Tract in Sacramento. Potential passengers were advised to contact L. J. Reese at the Western Hotel in Marysville. Locals were reminded Reese had taken part in some of the toughest air combat to occur over the Western Front during the Great War. He had spoken about his experiences when he came through Marysville earlier in the year on the Victory Loan train. The Sacramento Aviation Company, with Reese as founder, was said to be, "… prominent in all things, pertaining to the popular flying craze," according to the newspaper.[21]

In July 1919, negotiations were begun with the Cutter family for the donation of some of the Curtis Park lands to the city for a park. It became clear to Reese and his partners the Cutter Tract, part of Curtis Park, was ripe for a housing development. They knew their airport would have to close soon.[22]

On September 17, R. W. Mess, a Sacramento Aviation Company pilot, was departing the Curtis Park airfield in a JN-4 with Milt Cirten, a mechanic, his passenger. A sudden downdraft pulled the Jenny down into high voltage power lines near the airport's boundary. The plane hit the wires, became entangled, and cut some of the Great Western Power Company's lines. The aircraft crashed to the ground and broke in half. Mess was taken to White Hospital and treated for painful injuries to his face and body. Cirten walked away uninjured.

The neighboring Western Pacific rail repair shops had to shut down from loss of electricity until the lines were repaired. The accident worsened the airport's future prospects.[23] The following day, a petition was given to the city commission signed by employees of the Western Pacific rail repair shops. They implored commissioners to close the nearby aviation field that had sprung up. They complained the airfield next door to their shops was a menace to the safety of people living and working nearby. They also mentioned they had been subjected to vile and profane language shouted at them by pilots of the planes landing at the airport.[24] The airport at South

Chapter 4

Curtis Oaks wasn't closed, but Sacramento Aviation Company moved to the new municipal airport developed in Del Paso Park.

In late February 1920, the Walter T. Varney company, whose pilots were based at Redwood City and Marina Field in the Bay Area, got a call from a local company. A Sacramento farmer was desperate to finish plowing his 800 acre farm. He needed a bearing for his tractor that could only be had from the Bearing Supply Co. Varney sent his pilot "Swede" Meyerhoffer with the bearing to Mather Field. There Meyerhoffer discovered the farmer's land was only three miles from Mather. Meyerhoffer took off and flew to the farm, landing next to the broken down tractor. The farmer was stunned; the new bearing came just three hours after he called the bearing company. Swede was flying a Varney Lincoln-Standard powered by a 220hp. Hisso.

BEFORE THE SOUTH CURTIS OAKS airport faded into obscurity, a large aero circus (air show) was held there June 27, 1920, under the auspices of the Sacramento chapter of the American War Mothers Association. Assisting with the air show were the Sacramento Chamber of Commerce, the American Legion, Mather Field officers, and the US Army recruiting office. Spectators were charged 50 cents for admission, and 50 cents to park.[25]

It was probably not a coincidence the "aero circus" just happened to occur at the same time the first homes in South Curtiss Oaks, on Donner Way, became available for inspection by prospective buyers.[26]

The "sky vaudeville," as the press called the War Mothers Aero Circus, was hyped by the press and organizers—"One of the greatest gatherings of famous airmen ever held in the state." Entries in the air show included: Franklin Rose, Bay Area wing walker and stunt pilot who would transfer from a motorcycle to an airplane. Rose was supposed to ride the tail of a bucking airplane rodeo style. Christopher V. Pickup, known to the public for landing an airplane on a downtown Oakland street and an early landing in Yosemite Valley, was to arrive in R. C. Durant's Italian Ansaldo Balilla. The Ansaldo was hyped as a 200 mph (actually 150 mph) airplane said to have fought on the Piave Front in Italy during the Great War. Ex-Lt. Pickup let it be known that due to the Balilla's 90 mph landing speed, he would be flying out of the Yolo Fliers Club Field near Woodland instead of Curtis Oaks' shorter runway. J. T. Cumberpatch, another of Durant's aviators, was to bring the company's 200hp. Hisso powered Standard.

Also scheduled for the air show was the Australian aviator Charles Kingsford-Smith, who would become a world famous ocean flier in 1928, and E. E. "Monte" Mouton, who in three months would fly the first transcontinental airmail into San Francisco. These two pilots would be flying two English Avro 504K biplanes, recently acquired by aviation entrepreneur E. J. Moffett from Bay Area aircraft dealer and pioneer aviator, Bob Fowler.

Colonel H. H. Arnold or Major Henry L. Watson and Major Carl Spatz were to fly in for the air show on the twenty-seventh after inspecting Woodland's new airfield being constructed for the Yolo Fliers Club. Aviators from Mather Field were also scheduled to participate in the War Mother's Aero Circus.[27]

W. L. Morris, a Fresno flying service owner, wired the War Mothers he was sending two aircraft to the event. Four planes from Stockton were planning to fly in for the show. They were to be flown by F. W. Farris, H. E. Buckner, L. C. Gross, and L. A. Bounting. If a parachute arrived in time, Howard R. Smith was to make a parachute jump for the War Mother's event.[28]

Unrelated to the War Mothers air show that week, Cliff Durant's pilot Christopher Pickup, in a Durant Standard, flew Fredrick Sherman, vice president of San Francisco music company Sherman, Clay & Company, from Oakland's Durant Field to Mather Field to meet with his Sacramento branch manager, Irving Heilbron on June 23. After their meeting, Sherman was introduced to a group of Heilbron's employees to whom he delivered a brief pep talk. He mentioned his belief the airplane was the future of transportation; he said he could do a week's work in half a day using an airplane. Pickup flew Sherman to visit his stores in Stockton, Fresno, and San Jose before returning to San Francisco.[29]

On air show day, the twenty-seventh, a stiff wind was blowing at Sacramento, but the War Mothers air show continued. Heavily advertised, over 2,000 people braved the wind and crowded onto the airfield at South Curtis Oaks. Great clouds of dust blew from the runway helped by spinning propellers of the six airplanes at the show. Spectators, tossing their cigarette butts into the dry grass on the airfield, accidently started several fires. Choking dust and smoke delayed the air show's scheduled start by two hours. At 4:00 PM the first planes took off, but not to fly exhibitions. The pilots were giving rides at ten dollars a head. Occasionally they would do a spin or a loop at the request of a passenger, but that was it. The pilot of the *Sun Maid* did some wing walking while he was up. He even hung by his knees from the axle of his landing gear. The plane-to-vehicle transfers never happened nor did the bucking plane demonstration or the parachute jump. Except those

Chapter 4   89

who had ten dollars—a week's wages—to spend on a plane ride, the crowd was angry at the turn of events. The day turned out to be a moneymaker for pilots hopping passengers, but the War Mothers chapter didn't get any of their money. The military's contribution to the disappointing day were static displays showing the internal structure of an aircraft and displays of small tents illustrating daily life of airmen at Mather Field. Two aircraft were sent from Mather; one landed at Curtis Oaks while the other circled the airfield demonstrating the use of wireless radio transmissions to a ground unit on the airfield.

When asked about the lack of exhibition flying, A. E. Wagner, the promoter, said the wind was unfavorable for stunt flying, but this was denied by many of the aviators when asked about the day's circumstances.

Two days after the air show, the War Mothers group disputed the aviators' request for payment. Their lawyers claimed most of the aviators' time was spent giving rides for which the War Mothers received nothing. Attorney Chester Gannon advised the War Mothers not to pay the pilots a cent. However, the War Mothers chapter had already agreed to split ticket receipts with the aviators. Gannon's response was, "It was the boldest piece of bunko that has been put over in a long time and under the guise of patriotism they used the War Mothers. The claim that the wind was unfavorable for stunt flying is unfounded because I have consulted authorities on the subject. It was simply a plan to get the money." The air show was yet another bitter aviation pill Sacramento residents suffered.

It was reported the War Mothers got only $150 and the aviators took in $1,000 at least. Gannon told the press the War Mothers were afraid of being sued and decided to avoid trouble by accepting their meager share.[30] The news reports about the Sacramento War Mothers Aero Circus were the last ones to mention South Curtis Oaks Airport. Housing development in the Cutter Tract forced closure of the airport.

During the 1920 California State Fair, Earl Cooper's pilot/salesman, I. E. Elm of San Francisco, suffered a traumatic accident. Elm was hand propping his Jenny when, allegedly, a boy, playing around the airplane, caught his shirtsleeve on the throttle knob pulling the throttle to full power. Elm, standing in front of the airplane dove to the ground with the spinning prop missing him by inches as the Jenny leaped forward. The "boy" in Elm's story disappears, which leads one to wonder how a boy got his sleeve down inside the cockpit of the Jenny while standing outside of the airplane or even on the lower wing. The boy would have had to be in the cockpit for his shirt to catch on the throttle. It was more than likely the throttle was mistakenly left wide open by the pilot, who didn't chock the Jenny's wheels before propping the plane—a common practice in the early days of aviation, particularly by barnstormers who worked alone. It led to hand propping accidents, often fatal, for pilots and bystanders.

Elm's Jenny jumped forward when it was started, unoccupied with the throttle wide open. It crashed through the inside fence of the racetrack used as the landing field for the fairgrounds. It crossed the track, crashed through the outer railing around the track, and came to a stop against the track's embankment. The wooden propeller was shattered and the wings were damaged, but Elm felt it could be repaired to fly the next day.

The accident happened in front of 50,000 spectators who gathered to celebrate San Francisco Day at the state fair. Elm was about to do stunt flying for the crowd.[31]

THE INTERNAL REVENUE Service ruled in September 1919 that passengers who rode in airplanes for travel or amusement were exempt from paying the war tax. The war tax was a special tax placed on goods and services to help pay for fighting the Great War. Seven months later the IRS reversed itself and assessed a war tax of 8 percent on airplane passengers fares, the same amount paid by train passengers. Freight hauled by airplanes would be taxed 2 percent. Airplanes that only took passengers up for short rides (hops) at several dollars per head would be required to pay the usual vehicle tax of ten dollars per year.[32]

LEO STEVENS, A respected balloon instructor at Fort Omaha, Nebraska, told the press that David Todd, a professor at Amherst College, would try to communicate with Mars from a balloon constructed and piloted by Stevens. The balloon was to be the largest ever built, constructed to rise 50,000 feet. Stevens claimed the balloon would have two compartments, the upper containing hydrogen and the lower for fresh air. Professor Todd was said to have perfected a signaling apparatus for this unusual experiment.[33]

THE NEVADA AVIATION Corporation of Reno claimed to have secured 52 Curtiss JN-4Ds, which were said to be kept at Mather Field in mid-April 1920. The company reportedly had a manufacturing plant at Reno and completed its first Jenny with others under construction.[34]

CHAPTER 4

J. W. Benton, an aviator from the northern Sacramento Valley, flew a 180hp. Hisso JN-4H from San Francisco to Reno in two hours. During landing, he hit a stone wall flipping his plane end for end and totally destroyed it. His two passengers were thrown 20 feet onto a rock pile. They were all treated at the local hospital for bad cuts, bruised hands and feet but were otherwise all right. This was the third airplane accident at Reno's Air Mail Field (named Blanch Field in 1924) in the last week. Benton's was apparently due to the short landing field and a "misarrangement" of landing signals.[35]

Stunt flying for the 1920 California State Fair was performed by Clyde "Upside Down" Pangborn and Jim Hennessy. Pangborn was flying a white JN-4D and Hennessey flew a Curtiss N-9, a slightly larger navy version of the JN-4. As a team they gave free wing walking exhibitions in exchange for the passenger flying concession. Pangborn would walk the wings of the N-9 and afterward both pilots gave airplane rides. They made $2,000 hopping passengers.[36]

Itinerant barnstormers in 1920–1921 found themselves scrambling for fewer dollars at the height of the "little" economic depression following the World War. Groups of aviators, called "flying circuses," were formed. Some were loosely formed teams of two or three Jennies and some were highly organized teams of aviators and stuntmen who were preceded by advance men advertising their flying circus performance date, organizing a landing field, and generally preparing the communities for the arrival of numerous pilots and planes.

The Gates Flying Circus, managed by Ivan R. Gates, was one of the largest and most successful flying circuses to take to the air. In its early days, the Gates group started with two pilots, Clyde Pangborn and Lowell Yerex, and their parachute jumper and wing walker Jinx Jenkins. It grew from there.

Pangborn met Ivan Gates in the spring of 1921 when Gates put together the most successful fly-in/air meet held in Northern California to date. The event was at the Yolo Fliers Club Field, four miles west of Woodland—23 air miles from Sacramento. Several planes and pilots from Mather Field and Sacramento attended the largest aviation event in the area since the end of the war (see Yolo County chapter).[37]

During the summer of 1921, Sacramento was visited a few times by the Friesley Falcon, a twelve-seat, twin-engine, passenger plane built at the Friesley plant near Gridley (see Herr's *Aviation in Northern California 1910–1939*, Volume II, chapters 11–12). The Falcon* (See end of chapter) was the largest plane to visit the area, always landing at Mather Field, which had a longer runway than Del Paso Airport.[38]

H. G. "Andy" Andrews began expanding his sphere of operations from Sacramento's Del Paso Airport. In June 1921, he was photographed with Walter T. Varney and San Francisco "Weather Man" Father Ricard at Redwood City Airport, standing next to the rudder of a JN-4. The rudder had "San Francisco Call" and "staff aeroplane" painted on it. Andrews flew for Varney who owned the plane.

In 1921, Clyde Pangborn once again acquired the flying concession for the California State Fair.[39]

HARRY JOHNSON, A 21-year-old ex-cadet from Mather Field, was killed April 16, 1922, doing wing-walking stunts over Moreing Baseball Stadium during a game at Riverside Boulevard and Broadway in Sacramento. Most of the thousands of fans thought a dummy had been thrown from the plane; a standard trick used by barnstormers. Pilot Fred Kelly told reporters Johnson had performed more difficult stunts in the past. Kelly felt Johnson was stricken with cramps while hanging by his hands from the spreader bar on the JN's landing gear, as Kelly circled over the stadium and surrounding hop fields. Johnson was prone to muscle cramping.

Kelly had looked over the edge of his cockpit at his landing gear and saw Johnson having problems. Johnson was trying to kick his legs in an effort to break the cramps or wrap them around the spreader bar for support. He was unable to do either. Kelly banked the plane in an effort to help Johnson, but this also failed. He pushed the nose of the plane down to get closer to the ground. Johnson couldn't hang on any longer and fell 150 feet. He struck a wire in a hop field and was embedded eight inches deep in soft ground near J. M. Masie's home on Riverside Boulevard. Mr. Masie picked him up and rushed to Sister's Hospital. Doctors said he had died instantly. Kelly was overcome with grief when he saw Johnson let go. It was difficult for him to land the aircraft, and as he walked over and stood beside the body of his friend he broke down.

When his enlistment was up January 1, 1922, Johnson had left the Air Service at Mather Field and from then, until his death, he filled engagements as a stunt flier and sold magazines to make ends meet. He and Kelly shared an apartment on O Street in Sacramento. Mather Field officials said Johnson was known to be a careful flier with 300 hours flying time to his credit. Both men were working for Pioneer Fliers, another flying business managed by the ubiquitous E. J. Moffett. Pioneer Fliers owned the airplane Kelly was flying the day of the accident.

E. J. Moffet was the pioneer organizer of the duck patrol flights in Glenn and Colusa counties in 1919 and 1920. (Later in 1927, he managed Ernie Smith's first attempt to fly to Hawaii.) In 1922, he was reported living in the Maydstone Apartments in Sacramento.[40]

MATHER FIELD STARTED to see civilians landing in January and February of 1922. Sam Eaton, a government airmail pilot stopped at Mather while en route to Reno, as did Cloyd Clevenger on a flight from San Carlos in a Pacific Standard. Maurice "Loop-the-Loop" Murphy and a Mr. Russell flew into Mather from Marina Field during this time.[41]

In May the entire class of 22 flying cadets from Mather Field had completed flight training and would receive commissions in the Army Reserve Corps. Five of the cadets would become notable civilian fliers in the Sacramento Valley: Ive McKinney, Don Templeman, Sid DuBose, Robert Clohecy and Donald M. Cornell.[42] Mather Field reported some civilian flying activity in late spring. W. L. Morris and his mechanic stopped off on a flight from San Francisco to Reno. Robert Tanner in a Jenny with his passenger Mr. M. Delarno stopped at Mather on the way from Gridley to San Francisco.[43]

There were no air maps published in the 1920s. Pilots depended on lists published by periodicals like *Aerial Age Weekly*, which published the following list of the many new landing fields reported to the Office of the Chief of the Army Air Service on January 1, 1922. These were all second generation airports, meaning this was the first land in their communities developed specifically for the use of housing airplanes, repairing them and an area for planes to land and depart. However, the communities below, with the possible exception of Franklin, could not sustain these sites, and no longer exist as airfields. Truckee, Tracy, and Georgetown now have airports at different locations; the rest have no current airports. Some were quite close to Sacramento and others were important to aviators flying to popular destinations like Reno, San Francisco (SF), and Yosemite Valley. Those close to Sacramento were: [1.] **Courtland** – lat. 38°20'N, long.121°30'W, emergency field; 129 mi. from Reno, 58 mi. from San Francisco; nearest RR station at Hood; long distance telephone only; gas and oil available; .5 mi. E and 3 mi. SE of town are large level cultivated fields where a safe landing could probably be made, but take off difficult owing to soft ground and crops; landmark is Grand Island Drawbridge; location is 2 ¼ mi. S of town. [2.] **Franklin** – lat. 38°25'N, long. 121°25' W, emergency field; 122 mi. from Reno, 65 mi. from SF; long distance telephone and telegraph; gas and oil available; tract for landing field adjoining town and ¼ mi. SW of railroad; Landmarks are a church in one corner of field, Western Pacific Depot, and Great Western Power Company's towers. [3.] **Freeport** – lat. 38°27'N, long. 121° 30' W. field 1800 x 2000 feet, located 115 mi. from Reno and 72 mi. from SF on the Southern Pacific RR; long distance telephone only; gas and oil available; landmarks are two steel towers, 185 feet high, one on each side of Sacramento River; location is west of town. [4.] **Natoma** – lat. 38°40'N, long. 121°12' W; 95 mi. from Reno, 92 mi. from SF; long distance telephone only; supplies available; field covered with dredger tailings; landmark is city of Folsom, 1 ½ mi. N; NATOMA painted on both sides of barn. [5.] **Shingle Springs** – lat. 38°40'N, long.120°54'W; field is 1500 x 300 yards, ½ mi. W of town, bounded by highway on the south and railroad on the north; level, hard and smooth; altitude 1000 feet; 7 mi. S and E of the air mail course, on the Placerville branch of the Southern Pacific Railroad.

NEW AIRFIELDS EN ROUTE to prominent locations were: [1.] **Colfax** – lat. 39°07'N, long. 120° 57'W. small emergency field is 600 x 300 feet; soft, wet and level; ½ mi. S of city; altitude 2,422 feet. [2.] **Georgetown** – lat. 38°55'N, long. 120°50'W; field is 70 mi. from Reno and 117 mi. from SF; 18 ½ mi. to Placerville the nearest RR station.; long distance telephone only; field is unplowed land 1800 x 3000 feet, located 1 mi. E of town; slight grade, no obstructions; a large isolated hill on eastern boundary. [3.] **Garden Valley** – lat.38°52'N, long. 120°50'W; field is 70 mi. from Reno and 115 mi. from SF; nearest RR station at Placerville, Southern Pacific about 12 mi. by road; long distance telephone only; no supplies available; not a good landing place, very rocky and hilly. [4.] **Polaris** – lat. 39°23'N, long. 120°10'W; emergency field; 22 mi. from Reno and 165 miles from SF; on the Southern Pacific RR; long distance telephone only; no supplies available; possible landing site 1 mi. north. [5.] **Slatington** – lat. 38°50'N, long. 120°48'W; 73 mi. from Reno and 114 mi. from SF; 6 mi. to RR at Placerville; telephone and telegraph available; supplies available; many suitable landing places. [6.] **Truckee** – lat. 39°20'N, long.120°13W; field good summertime landing, 600 x 2000 feet; near junction of Lake Tahoe and Southern Pacific RRs; deep snows in winter; maintain 15,000 feet crossing Sierras at this point; landing field prepared by the citizens 3 mi. out on the highway; supplies available. [7.] **Suisun** – lat. 38°15'N, long. 122°03'W; field 2000 x 5000 feet; in a strategic position for flying in the Sacramento Valley; level, bounded by fences and a road on the S; supplies available; altitude 100 feet. [8.] **Tracy** – lat. 37°43'N, long. 121°27'W; emergency field; ball ground 1600 x 1100 feet; between RR branch and six big tanks and water tower. [9.] **Yosemite** – lat. 37°45'N, long. 119°37'W; National Park Field.[44]

The landing field at Marysville, **Knight Park**, was taken off the field availability list as of February 1, 1922. It was to be used only as an emergency landing field from that date until July, 1926, when it was closed forever.[45]

Fig. 25. An unknown make or possibly a modified Jenny is believed to be depicted here at the War Mothers Aero Circus (air show) on the South Curtiss Oaks Airfield June 27, 1920, at Sacramento.*

---

*Lewis Wilcoxon was a 20 year-old, played as an outfielder for the Marysville Merchants semi-pro baseball team in 1921. On August 7 Wilcoxon and eight other members of the team assembled at Friesley Field, two miles south of Gridley on Hwy. 99. There they boarded the large twin-engine Friesley Falcon airliner for what was believed to be the first time a baseball team was flown to a game.

Wilcoxon, living in east Sacramento in October 1977, told a *Sacramento Bee* reporter that he "vividly remembered" the team's flight to play the Woodland team that day. The Falcon carried a crew of three, pilots Roy Francis and Bond Spencer plus mechanic Grafton Reed. The plane had only twelve seats so who the other eight team members joining Wilcoxon that day will probably never be known. Wilcoxon remembered that the Falcon couldn't carry the entire team at one time. "So half of us flew to Woodland and came home in cars. The other players drove to Woodland and rode back in the plane. I think we flew at about 1,500 feet, maybe 80 miles per hour. We followed the highway down past Live Oak in Sutter County and then out across the by-pass to Knights Landing (to) Woodland in Yolo County."

The Falcon landed at Yolo Fliers Club Field four miles west of Woodland. They proceeded to the Woodland baseball field where they lost the game 15-5 according to Wilcoxon. He remembered being scared but fascinated by his first flight in an airplane. He said, "The worst part was the takeoff at Gridley. It seemed we were a long time getting into the air." When he looked out the window and saw they were flying he said the "wings seemed to be slapping up and down. I thought we were falling apart. But it got us there. And it got the other half of the team home from Woodland."

As Wilcoxon stated that the entire team did not fly to Woodland in the Falcon it confirms this author's discovery that this entire baseball team did not make the first flight to play a baseball game. However, the August 25, 1919, issue of *Aerial Age Weekly* tells us that during a recent railway strike the Fort Sill, Oklahoma, Post Field Aerial Baseball Club flew to and from a game at Marlow, Oklahoma, in Curtiss planes (probably JN-4s). This occurred two years before the Falcon flew a little more than half of the Marysville Merchants team to Woodland for a game. (See two photos of the Falcon and the Marysville team before takeoff at Gridley and on arrival or departure from Woodland in this author's *Aviation in Northern California 1910-1939 Vol. II.*)

Fig. 26. Walter T. Varney, aviator and aviation entrepreneur, standing in front of his Swallow mailplanes powered by Curtiss K6 motors, which would soon be exchanged for Wright Whirlwind J-4 engines. These planes flew the mail for Varney Air Lines airmail route CAM 5 from Elko, Nev. to Pasco, Wash.

CHAPTER 5

Chinese flying school at Courtland – Sierra Aircraft Company and its airfield – First Annual Sacramento Air Meet – US Air Mail Service plane lands at Sacramento

Chancy Chew of Courtland established a flying school on his farm, 18 miles south of Sacramento, to train Chinese-American aviators for South China Air Service.

Harry Abbott worked as a pilot, parachutist, and wing walker for his father Wayne's flying circus: Abbott's Sky Demons. Abbott was flying an air show at San Jose in early April 1922 when three Chinese brothers from Hawaii approached him: E. I. Young, K. P. Young, and S. Y. Young, who did most of the talking. They asked Abbott to train eight or nine students to fly in two Curtiss Jennies on Chew's farm. They promised him $1,500 a month and requested the instruction be completed by November. Harry discussed the proposition with his wife Dolly and then accepted their offer.

Abbott's Sky Demons, based in the Los Angeles area, were on a barnstorming tour of the San Francisco Bay Area.[1] They were sharing the bill in San Jose with Clyde Pangborn and Lowell Yerex of the Gates Flying Circus. Pangborn was chief of flying operations while Ivan R. Gates handled the business end of the operation. One report states that when Yerex was with the flying circus, he owned the controlling interest, and Gates was simply allowed to act as head of the organization. Before Yerex joined the flying circus, it was often referred to as the Gates-Morris Flying Circus, presumably referring to an earlier partnership between Gates and fellow San Francisco pioneer aviator, William Morris.[2] Of the three Chinese brothers, S. Y.

Young had previously taken instruction from Pangborn.

In Pangborn's biography, the story of the Courtland flying school is given more detail. It states Dan Davison, Bay Area aviator and ex-US Air Mail Service pilot, came to Pangborn and explained he had demolished his airplane while under contract to teach three Chinese to fly. He asked Pangborn to take over the contract, which paid $300 a week. Davison told Pangborn the students had been sent to the United States by Chinese leader Sun Yat-sen and were ensigns in the Chinese navy. Their names were Wong Ping Tung, Nip Kai Hei, and K. Y. (S. Y.) Young. Davison said Young was from Honolulu.

Pangborn assumed the contract and during the next two months soloed all three students and gave them 20 hours of flying time each. When they were finished, Wong asked Pangborn to come to China with them, but Pangborn turned him down. Wong Ping Tung was to become the first commander of a Chinese air service. Later he was air attaché at the Chinese Embassy in Washington, D. C. Nip Kai Hei became a top official in China National Airways, and Young served as a decorated colonel under Tung.

Once this Chinese bonanza was played out, Pangborn was back looking for work in the Bay Area and ran into Ivan Gates at Marina Field in San Francisco. It was then that Pang was invited to join Gates and Yerex in what became the most successful flying circus of the barnstorming era.

Pangborn stayed with the Gates Flying Circus until the very end—spring 1929. In his later years he gained international fame for his record-setting Pacific Ocean flight with Hugh Herndon, and in 1934 he and Roscoe Turner flew a Boeing 247 to third place in the MacRobertson Race from England to Australia.[3]

Earlier in 1922 at the San Jose air meet, according to Harry's son Dan-San Abbott, Harry discussed the job offer to train Chinese pilots at Courtland with S. Y. Young and his brothers. All the while, Joe Dawson, an early Bay Area pilot, was stunt flying at the meet in the Abbott's Standard J-1. The Standard biplane was painted a cream color with "ABBOTT" painted across the upper wing of the biplane and "SKY DEMONS" on either side of the fuselage in brilliant red.

It was typical for barnstormers, especially organized flying circuses, to identify their aircraft in some spectacular manner. Lowell Yerex painted his Hisso JN-4 all red, the color of the Gates Flying Circus aircraft. "YEREX" was painted on the upper and lower wings. The letters were gold with white outlines. Pangborn's JN-4D was still painted white with "PANG" in red

Chapter 5

Fig. 27. Harry Abbott at Courtland, south of Sacramento, on the Sacramento River in the summer of 1922. He was teaching Chinese-Americans to fly so they could serve in Sun Yat-sen's air force in China. Upon their graduation, Abbott would accompany his students to China where Sun Yat-sen made him a colonel in the air force. After Abbott returned to America and due to his size he was termed the "Little Colonel" by his colleagues.

letters on the top wing.[4]

With Chew's school established and the job offer accepted, Harry Abbott and his wife drove from San Francisco to Walnut Grove in a convoy of automobiles containing all of the pilot trainees. Walnut Grove, also on the Sacramento River, was the school's headquarters. It had the only hotel near Chancy Chew's farm, seven miles north at Courtland.

The small farming community of Courtland was populated with mostly Chinese from Ts'ui'hen, a village near Portuguese Macao. Now called Chungshan, it is in the Pearl River Delta of Kwangtung Province in southern China. Dr. Sun Yat-sen, president of the Republic of China, was also from there. The Courtland Chinese were very supportive of Sun Yat-sen's plan to establish a democracy in China. In fact, Chancy Chew acted as a buying agent for Sun Yat-sen's South China Air Service in the United States.

The day after the Abbotts and students checked into the Walnut Grove Hotel for a lengthy stay, they drove out to Chew's farm. The two Jennies they were to use for flight training had arrived by rail and were still in packing crates, which Harry and the students removed from their crates. The students included the aforementioned Young brothers; George Tong from Portland; Fred Wong from Los Angeles; Stephen Lam from San Francisco; and Eugene Chen from Seattle.

While uncrating and assembling the two Jennies, S. Y. Young and some students asked Abbott to come to China with them after their training was completed. Young told Abbott he would guarantee Abbott the rank of captain in the Chinese Air Service, and he would continue being paid $1,500 per month in gold. After Young assured him he wouldn't lose his American citizenship, Abbott accepted the offer.

The two JN-4Ds were repainted yellow with Chinese characters on the underside of the wings spelling CHINESE AIR FORCE in red. Abbott used the time setting up the JNs as instruction in aircraft assembly. The young Chinese-American flying students were highly educated and motivated. After the two planes were assembled, Abbott flight tested them and found everything satisfactory.

Flying at Courtland was done every morning and afternoon weather permitting. Ground instruction consisted of the students learning to tear down, assemble, and maintain the Curtiss OX-5 90hp. engine.

Steven Lam was first to solo and first to gain his ACA/FAI license on May 22, 1922. Each student in turn soloed with both Jennies in constant use every day. As their skills improved, they went on cross-country flights to Suisun City.

In early August, the Abbotts and students went to San Francisco to apply for passports and visas at the Chinese consulate. S. Y. Young came along to search the Bay Area for experts in aircraft construction who might be interested in going to work in China. He signed up Arthur "Pop" Wilde and Guy Colwell. Wilde was one of the best airplane mechanics in the north state, Colwell was also a respected mechanic who had worked for British Bristol Aeroplane Company and more recently for the US Air Mail Service at Marina Field. Dan Davison, the Bay Area pilot who got Pangborn involved with the Courtland flying school, was hired to join the expedition as a flier. Both Davison and Colwell later contracted disease and died in China.[5]

Back at Chew's farm, Abbott continued training his "boys," as he called them, and got them ready to show their skills in an air show for Courtland residents. On September 9, 1922, Abbott and the students put on what they called a "Chinese-American Aerial Circus" on George Johnson's farm. All the students did flying and stunts. Abbott did parachute jumps and wing walking. The show lasted from 1:00 to 7:00. It was a way for the students to say thank you to the farm community whose peaceful mornings and afternoons were often disturbed by the raucous sound of airplane engines. Residents of Courtland, Locke, Walnut Grove, and Isleton turned out in force to watch them exhibit their skills.

Abbott and his students renewed many in Courtland with confidence

Fig. 28. At Courtland in 1922, the Chinese-American flying students service one of their JN-4D training planes.

in flying. There had been an incident two years earlier that shook the community to its core. A Courtland rancher's daughter, Frances E. Lee, a Chinese aviatrix, was killed in Menlo Park. Miss Lee was taking instruction from Bay Area aviator John Fortney. He had been denied permission to fly

Fig. 29. A handmade poster for the graduation air show of Abbott's flying students stated a Chinese-American aerial circus would be held on September 9, 1922 at G. Johnson's farm at Courtland from 1:00 PM to 7:00 PM. Abbott and the students would leave for China the following month.

from the aviation field at Menlo Park, so Fortney moved his plane to a nearby lot and took off with Miss Lee. At 200 feet the wing of his homebuilt monoplane collapsed and Miss Lee jumped out. If she had a parachute, there wasn't enough altitude for it to deploy. Fortney also died in the crash.

With a month-and-a-half of training remaining before Harry Abbott, Dolly, and the students were to sail for China, he concentrated on teaching aerobatics to increase their confidence as pilots. Abbott taught them how to do chandelles, figure eights, spins, loops, and rolls. He worked on formation flying and night flying without lights—training only in moonlight. They practiced bombing with ten-pound sacks of flour. After training ended in October, all students passed their ACA/FAI license tests, and each pilot had acquired 150 flying hours. Mr. Chew purchased surplus army rifles, and the students were trained in the use of small arms. They all did well in ground school. Some did better on engine work, and others did well on airframe work. Local Chinese were confident the students would make excellent leaders of the Chinese Air Force. The Abbotts and the students sailed for China in October 1922 arriving in Shanghai the following month, but that's another story.[6]

SIERRA AIRCRAFT COMPANY began Sacramento operations in mid-1922. Ex-US Army Air Service Reserve Lt. Ive McKinney was the company's Sacramento branch manager and chief pilot. He graduated from Mather Field pilot training in May 1922. McKinney shared instructing duties at Sierra with Robert Clohecy. They had several JN-4Ds in which students got a 30-minute lesson twice a week. The company claimed that after 12 weeks a student would be able to land and take off, do loops, rolls, Immelmann turns, and other aerobatics.[7] Albert Hastings presided over Sierra Aircraft Company's Sacramento, Pasadena, Chico, and Marysville branches.

It is probable the Sacramento branch was the first.

An early report of Sierra Aircraft Company activity came February 1923. Ive McKinney and Harry S. Manwaring sold an aircraft, probably a Jenny, to 71-year-old A. W. Smith of Healdsburg. McKinney and Manwaring also announced plans to take moving pictures of Sacramento and vicinity from an airplane.[8]

McKinney and Robert Clohecy did their best to make the presence of Sierra Aircraft Company known when they set new local altitude records for JN-4D aircraft. Lt. George Love had set the altitude record for JNs in 1920 at Houston, Texas. He reached 9,000 feet. Three years later at Sacramento on March 9, Ive McKinney took off and flew to 11,000 feet. Then Robert Clohecy took off and climbed for two hours to reach 13,500 feet.[9] The records were unofficial, but there was still much hoopla in the press about their achievements.

McKinney flew three passengers to San Diego from Sacramento in March. He also made a flight to San Diego in 4 hours and 50 minutes. When McKinney returned from San Diego on March 16, he told about having to fly at 10,000 feet to avoid a sandstorm, but he said there was sand even at that altitude. Four of the eight cylinders on his engine cut out forcing him to fly at lower altitude. He and his passengers made it over the Tehachapi Mountains and landed at Bakersfield for the night. The next day they continued to Sacramento. While he was in Southern California, McKinney bought a Thomas-Morse Scout and a large quantity of spare parts for the Sierra Aircraft Company.[10]

The Pioneer Aviation Co. of Sacramento offered city Marshal Peck the use of three airplanes and pilots "to ferret out a mysterious rock thrower who has been bombarding Sacramento warehouses with large rocks from some sort of contrivance." (A catapult maybe?)

Jack Shalk, a former acrobat on the Orpheum Theater circuit, was photographed in April, hanging by his teeth from a rope ladder suspended from Ive McKinney's Jenny over the eastern city limits of Sacramento at 3,000 feet. The men were promoting an upcoming air show on May 13, 1923, to raise money for Disabled American Veterans. The air show was to be held at Sierra Aircraft Company's large airfield just south of the orphanage at Stockton Boulevard and Fruitridge Road, one block from the traction company's rail line station.

Army aircraft from Crissy, Mather, and Rockwell fields were participating, as were civilian planes from San Francisco, Oakland, and Sacramento.

JN-4D races of 10 and 25 miles were scheduled. Bob Clohecy would be performing aerobatics, and Ive McKinney would participate in various contests. Sierra Aircraft Company promised to send 14 aircraft from its various branches to the air show. The company planned to send two Thomas-Morse Scouts, one Spad and one Nieuport, representing the fighting planes of the World War. The rest would be Jennys.

The air show went off without any glaring problems on the thirteenth, regardless of superstition surrounding the date. Even when pilot Sydney Du Bose ran over a black cat that had wandered on to the airfield, no one was worried. Nearly 3,000 spectators saw 27 airplanes flown in from Modesto, San Francisco, Stockton, Fresno, and Sacramento.[11]

The day after the meet, police Capt. Robert Dundas decided to enforce one of the state's aviation laws. Lee Flanders flew low over the Sacramento Hall of Justice in preparation to land in the sandy lot north of I Street. Dundas knew state aviation laws forbid aviators to fly below 1,000 feet over a city. He saw Flanders was only a few hundred feet over the police station and apprehended him at another field used by Sierra Aircraft Company on Lower Stockton Road (now Franklin Blvd.).

This was said to be the first arrest in California under the state aircraft laws, which required any pilot overflying a city or town to maintain enough altitude to glide to a safe landing should his airplane's engine fail. Captain Dundas declared that Flanders, from Sonoma, was flying so low the numbers on his plane were visible from the streets below. Flanders denied he was too low. He said if his engine had quit he could have landed in the Sacramento River.

Flanders said he was passing over the city when his right magneto went out and half of the cylinders stopped firing. He admitted to dropping "rather low," but kept his plane over the sand slough near the Southern Pacific rail station, and no one's life was in danger—not even his.

Flanders, flying one of Sierra Aircraft Company's airplanes, was a former airmail pilot and flew in France during the war. Attorneys declared the Flanders case would draw a lot of attention as the first prosecution under the state aviation law of 1921, and it would definitely settle who controlled the air. There were no federal air laws until 1927. Captain Dundas said it was up to him to enforce the motor vehicle laws in Sacramento, and he intended to do so. He said violation of the aviation law was a misdemeanor.

Police Judge O. W. Anderson dismissed the Flanders case on May 18 for insufficient evidence. Flanders had told the judge his engine started running rough forcing him to fly low, then the problem corrected itself allowing him to continue his flight. The newspaper article reporting the dismissal stated the state air law was passed in 1919.[12]

Lt. Corliss C. Moseley landed at Mather Field May 20 on the first leg of a flight from Clover Field, Los Angeles, to West Point, New York. His passengers were Sergeant A. A. Caffery and "Sidlaw Tuffy," a wire-haired fox terrier that insisted on going with Moseley whenever he flew.[13]

Sierra Aircraft Company was in the news again when company pilot Robert L. Clohecy flew octogenarian Gertrude Freeman from Sacramento to the Yolo Fliers Club Field at Woodland. She claimed her husband, Major Freeman, founded the city in 1857 (or 1859). Mrs. Freeman came to California in 1856 riding in an ox cart. She had ridden trains in and out of the state over the years. She went for her first airplane ride on May 23, and she enjoyed it immensely. Ex-state senator Marshall Diggs arranged for her flight.[14]

Albert Hastings, head of Sierra Aircraft Company, filed articles of incorporation in July 1928 with company headquarters listed as Oakland Airport. The business would soon contract as a distributorship for Alexander Eaglerock airplanes in Northern California. The Sierra Aircraft airfield in southeast Sacramento was soon named Eagle Rock Airport.[15]

The Indianapolis 500 on Memorial Day 1923 had special meaning for Sacramentans. America's highest scoring fighter ace from the Great War, Eddie Rickenbacker, was chosen official starter for the race. Rickenbacker visited Sacramento many times—the last was in 1920 when he came to promote General Motors' Sheridan automobiles and the Sacramento post of the American Legion gave a dinner for him at the Traveler's Hotel. Another connection to the Indianapolis race piquing local interest was Harry Hartz taking second place behind Tommy Milton. Hartz was well known in Sacramento. During the war, Hartz was foreman of the fuselage shop at Liberty Iron Works where JN-4s were built for the Army Air Service. Joe Thomas, another racer at Indianapolis that year, also worked at Liberty Iron Works during the war.[16]

In June 1923 an advertisement in the *Sacramento Bee* touted the new Rickenbacker automobile as "a car worthy of its name." It was claimed to be, " The smoothest thing on wheels. If you try it – you'll buy it." The ad included a drawing of the famous "Hat in the Ring" emblem of the 94th Aero Squadron in which Rickenbacker flew during the war. The shield emblem was on the radiator of each Rickenbacker automobile in brilliant enamel.

Fred Bovyer managed Sacramento's Rickenbacker Sales Company.[17]

Walter Varney commissioned Bliss Tire Works in North Sacramento to make a batch of tires to use on the eight JN-4s he bought from the All-In-One plant, formerly the Liberty Iron Works in North Sacramento. Bliss Tire Works cut down 30-inch auto tire tubes to 26 x 4 inches using a special process. A specialist at Bliss had done this during the war at Liberty Iron Works. The tires were for aircraft Varney intended to use for the Checker Air Service he founded in 1925.[18]

Varney made a pathfinder flight from San Francisco to Fresno in late March 1925 flying a Checker Air Service JN and carrying one passenger. Varney made the flight in two hours. Dr. B. M. Rastall, his passenger, told the press, "The day of commercial transportation by airplane is here." He said a modern businessman could make the trip from San Francisco to Sacramento or Stockton in one hour and from Fresno in two hours. He could leave, conduct his business, and be back at San Francisco in time to finish work. Rastall claimed the Bay Area had become one with the Sacramento and San Joaquin valleys, due to availability of Checker Air Service. Varney announced Checker Air Service was sending a nine-plane squadron of aircraft on a promotional formation flight up and down the Great Central Valley and Bay Area routes early next month. It is unknown if this huge formation flight ever took place.[19]

James Crawford "Jimmie" Angel made the Bay Area and Sacramento Valley his center of operations from late 1924 through much of 1927. Eddie Angel, also a pilot, joined his older brother Jimmie in the aviation business, as did their younger brother Parker Angel, who worked as a mechanic and did wing walking for his brothers. Their California operations began at Sacramento in late 1924. (Jimmie Angel's flying career in California is described in detail in the author's book, *Aviation in Northern California 1910–1939 Volume II: Yuba, Sutter, and Butte Counties*.)

Reports of flying activity at Del Paso Park in 1924 are scarce. It is known that pilot Mel Longshore suffered a slight injury when he made a dead stick landing at the city's airport in Del Paso Park on September 21. He was flying a passenger, B. Litz, on a sightseeing ride in a plane based at Del Paso Airport, when he lost power. Golfers on neighboring fairways watched in horror as he attempted an emergency landing with a dead engine, hitting a tall tree with its tail section, and nose-diving into the ground.

On New Years Day 1925, daredevil stunt pilot Sig Smith, was the featured performer at Sacramento's annual New Year's Day athletic program held at McKinley Park. The Sacramento Chamber of Commerce was asked to sponsor Smith's performance but refused when it could not get insurance to cover it. The performance went on anyway; Smith agreed to assume responsibility for doing stunts at his own risk. Smith, flown by Bill Sanders, hung by one hand to the landing gear of the plane. He walked the wings of the plane and again hung from the landing gear as the pilot flew various aerobatic maneuvers.[20]

IN EARLY 1925 following reorganization, the Sacramento Aviation Club planned its inaugural Sacramento Air Meet taking place May 9–10. On the eighth, club president L. D. Packard told the press, "Tomorrow morning everybody in Sacramento will know there's something doing in the air." He promised Sacramento skies would be literally dotted with planes. There would be military and civilian aircraft flying in competitions, races, and stunt flying. Predictions were made of 100 airplanes coming to Mather Field.

Many ex-army aviators were expected for an unofficial reunion with "Mother Tusch" at Sacramento's Senator Hotel. Mrs. C. A. Tusch had turned her Berkeley cottage into a home away from home for young lonely army flying cadets who moved away from home their first time to undergo ground school at the University of California during the war. After the war, her cottage was an aviation shrine attracting numerous aviators passing through the Bay Area who reminisced being there and benefited from the support she gave to help them succeed.

William Sullivan, soon to become one of the founders of the aeronautical program at Sacramento City College, was chosen field director of the meet. Sullivan arranged a special Southern Pacific train to leave the station in Sacramento each morning. It arrived at Mather Field prior to the 1:30 air meet starting time allowing passengers to avoid traffic driving to the airfield.

On Saturday the ninth at 9:30, Mather's gates opened. M. G. Funke of the aviation club received word that the opening event, a cross-country air race starting in Richmond, had eight competing aircraft flying to Mather Field. It was a handicap race since all were different makes with engines of various horsepower. The race would end at Mather around 12:30.

Events for the two days were scheduled as follows: 1:30 competitive formation flying; 2:00 H. G. Andrews and Jimmie Angel would fly aerobatic exhibitions; 2:45 (Saturday only) Fay Lamphiere, queen of the meet, arrives by plane and is welcomed by Captain Lowell Smith, commander of the 1924 Around-The-World-Flight; 2:50 a 25-mile pylon race; 3:25 a dead stick landing competition; 4:15 a battle in the clouds (Army aircraft dog fight); 4:45 US Air Mail Service arrives (leaves mail pouch); 4:50 a squadron of military planes drop smoke and phosphorous bombs.

The following day began with: Navy planes flying demonstrations at 1:50; 2:50 a 50-mile military DH-4 race for the $1,000 Chamber of Commerce trophy; 3:20 a dead stick landing contest for a $200 sterling silver first place trophy and a $75 second place trophy; 4:40 Captain Lowell Smith presented winners' trophies; and at 5:00 an army squadron bombs a mythical city. Major R. F. Rowell, commander of the US Marine Corps squadron attending the meet, dropped two parachute bombs from an altitude of 5,000 feet.

Competition results were: Saturday, R. H. Duke won the opening cross-country race in his plane *The City of Richmond*. Duke, flying a JN-4D, defeated Capt. K. W. Farrow in a JN-4H, Dr. Sterling Bunnell in a Morane monoplane, and five others. No winners were reported for the military aircraft from reserve units and active duty stations at Clover Field, Santa Monica, Crissy field, San Francisco, and Mather Field that competed for best formation flight.

Ingvald Fagerskog, a Sacramento aviator, won the most prizes on the final day. Fagerskog, best known locally for bringing photographs of President Coolidge's inauguration to town for publication in the *Sacramento Bee*, won the Saturday air race for civilian pilots and Sunday's dead-stick contest. Fagerskog was based at Del Paso Airport for several years and bought property across Auburn Boulevard from Del Paso Airport in the fall of 1927 to start his own airport. Since Del Paso's runway was longer, planes from Fagerskog's airport would often taxi across Auburn Boulevard to take off.

Army Lt. C. V. Haynes won the $1,000 trophy for the military DH-4 race. Haynes, from the 91st Observation Squadron at Crissy Field, flew at an average speed of 140 mph. Lt. Willis Taylor, son of Sacramento meteorologist N. R. Taylor, took second place, and Sergeant J. F. Templeman placed third.

Attending celebrities included Round-the-World fliers Lt. Eric Nelson and Capt. Lowell H. Smith. Air meet event officials were: Starters – T. Mealia and Lt. Frank Hackett; Timers – Charles E. Lipps and F. M. French; Judges – Lt. John W. Benton and H. A. Wallace; Inspector – Lt. Walter Miller. Lt. Joe Baily for the army and A. W. Makepeace for the aviation club were in charge of the field and running events.

Chapter 5

Fig. 30. Ingvald Fagerskog's airport circa 1929. There are three Jennies and two Thomas Morse Scout's parked around Fagerskog's large hangar/repair shop. His office building is to right of the hangar. One Jenny had "FLY WITH ME $2.50" on its rudder, but as you can see the price dropped even lower by 1929 and it was removed from the rudder. Fagerskog, an avid air-racing pilot, has the racing number 20 on the tail of the closest Thomas Morse Scout.

The U. S. Air Mail Service plane arrived at 4:10 on the last day of the meet bringing the first airmail to Sacramento by direct air route from the East Coast. Burr H. Winslow, flying a DH-4, landed and gave the mailbags to Sacramento Postmaster Harold McCurry who shook hands with the pilot. Winslow smiled, waved at the cheering crowd of 4,000, then pushed the throttle forward and climbed into the sky heading for Diablo Air Mail Field at Concord. It would be three more weeks, on July 1, 1925, before airmail service officially started.

AN AVIATOR REPORTED as C. Andrews (probably H. G. Andrews) took Oakland music teacher Mrs. Ethel Menz to an altitude of 10,000 feet and dove to 1,200 feet partially restoring the deaf woman's hearing. She planned to go up again hoping for a complete restoration.

There was only one serious injury during the Mather air meet. Parachutist Sgt. Fred Kelly jumped from 1,800 feet with his parachute opening normally, but gusty winds flopped his chute closed causing him to fall faster and strike the ground hard. He was rushed to a hospital. His injuries were first thought to be slight, but soon upgraded to serious. By nightfall he was in critical condition. It is unknown if he survived.

An estimated 20,000 spectators and 90 airplanes attended. It was one of the most spectacular flying events ever held in the Sacramento Valley. Unfortunately, the second annual Sacramento Air Meet never happened.[21]

ANOTHER US AIR Mail Service aircraft landed at Mather Field on July 1, 1925, to officially begin regular airmail service to Sacramento from the East. The de Havilland DH-4 mail plane, No. 372, flown by Clair K. Vance arrived at 3:40 PM from its previous mail stop at Reno. The US Air Mail Service had been flying from Reno to San Francisco since early September 1920, but only stopped at Sacramento for emergencies. Congressman Curry was instrumental getting the airmail to stop at Sacramento and was on hand for the first westbound plane's arrival, as were several Sacramento dignitaries and field radio operator D. H. Cordano. Postmasters from all around the state watched Vance land and taxi. The sunburned pilot shook hands with Congressman Curry, Mayor Elkus, Mr. Engler, and Postmaster McCurry. The radio operator, Cordano, took four mail pouches from the plane, handed them to Congressman Curry, who then gave them to the postmaster. Clair Vance waved, removed his goggles, wiped his forehead, but stayed in his seat. He never shut his engine off; he was on a tight schedule and a few minutes late.

What happened next was bizarre. The crowd around the plane suddenly moved backward as a huge dust cloud enveloped them. A man in buckskins on a wiry horse rode up to the cockpit and shook Vance's hand with some difficulty. His horse was obviously upset by the engine noise and the whirling propeller blowing dust on the animal. But the rider coaxed him close enough for the handshake and used his other hand to give Vance saddlebags representing mail carried by Pony Express riders in 1860. Press photographers took pictures as the rider whirled away from the plane. It just so happened the film director James Cruze was making a movie at Westgate about the Pony Express. He loaned the postal authorities actor Jack Padjan, who was playing the Pony Express rider in his movie, along with the horse, buckskins, and saddlebags.

The opening of airmail service to Sacramento was compared, in the press, to the opening of the Pony Express mail service 65 years prior. In fact, the *Sacramento Union* ran parallel columns describing each event. There were a few old timers still left who witnessed both historical moments.

Vance pushed the throttle forward and was soon back in the air on his way to Concord; the last segment of the transcontinental airmail run.

CHAPTER 5

Fig. 31. To celebrate the beginning of transcontinental airmail service to Sacramento, airmail pilot Clair K. Vance landed his de Havilland DH-4 at Mather Field on July 1, 1925, and accepted the airmail pouch from an actor posing as a Pony Express rider of 1860.

Another feature at the Mather Field airmail inaugural was installation of a radio set for use by the US Air Mail Service and the Army Air Service. The new system was announced during the arrival of La Follette, the postal division superintendent, and D. M. Baker the Sacramento field manager. Radio engineers D. H. Cordano and Hadley Beedle of the Air Mail Service had arrived from Reno and San Francisco fifteen days prior. They started setting up the sixty meter band radio, which would be activated when the necessary tubes arrived from the East. The radio would allow Sacramento to communicate directly with Washington, D. C. Similar sets were being set up at Reno and Concord.

Diablo Air Mail Terminal at Concord was the new alternate western terminus of transcontinental airmail flights. It was created because of the heavy fog that often rolled in over Crissy Field usually in the summer. The eastbound mail would leave from Diablo and the westbound mail was flown directly to Crissy Field unless it was fogged in. Flying from Crissy to Diablo took about 20 minutes. Diablo Field was located about two miles southeast of Concord. It had 2,000 foot east-west and the same north-south runways with a 1,700 foot diagonal runway. It was bounded by West St., Wilson Lane, Denkinger Road, and Clayton Road near Concord.[22]

At Sacramento the regular stop for airmail planes was moved from Mather Field to the municipal airport in Del Paso Park. During hot summer months, the pilots didn't even land. They would dive low over the airport at Del Paso, throw out the mail pouch, and a postal worker walked onto the runway and retrieved it.[23] This method worked well until Burr Winslow tossed the pouch out one day and proceeded to Concord. Winslow received a phone call shortly after he landed there. Where is the mail pouch, a Sacramento postal official wanted to know? Winslow said he tossed it onto the runway. Minutes later a mechanic who checked Winslow's plane handed him the mail pouch. When Winslow tossed it out at Del Paso Airport, apparently the pouch had lodged in the flying wires attached to the horizontal stabilizer on the DH-4's tail and had stuck there, unknown to Winslow.[24]

H. G. "Andy" Andrews taught Sam B. Finnerty to fly and soloed him after eight hours of instruction at Air Service Field in July. Finnerty, a prominent citizen of Linden, flew home in his newly purchased JN-4.[25]

Two de Havilland DH-4s were assigned to Mather Field for forest fire patrol in July 1925. Several pilots were assigned to fly them. However, there would not be patrols flying at regular intervals as in the past. Planes would be flown on an on-call basis when weather conditions or smoke obscured the vision of the mountain top lookout stations or to keep tabs on the direction of an existing fire.[26]

Ingvald Fagerskog, in December 1925, took off from Del Paso with Miss Lydia Alexandra, the original "Good Luck Girl" from the Parisian Follies Bergere, for a flight over downtown Sacramento. Miss Alexandra threw out dancing shoes attached to small parachutes over the center of town near the Senator Theater where she would be performing. Miss Alexandra was starring in *Specialty Ideas*. She caused a sensation swinging out over the heads of audiences and losing her shoes. She had "lost" 5,000 pairs of shoes in five years.

A rocket was fired to signal fans that Fagerskog and Miss Alexandra had taken off. A second rocket was fired when they were over downtown streets, and a final rocket was fired when the shoes were released from the airplane. Stuffed in the toe of each shoe was a coupon for a free subscription to the *Sacramento Union*. Miss Alexandra would lose a pair of shoes at each performance, which also contained a subscription coupon.[27]

Chapter 5   113

Fig. 32. Ingvald Fagerskog is depicted with a woman passenger sitting in the lap of another in the cramped front cockpit of his JN-4D named *Ingvald's Comet*. The Jenny is dark blue or black with stars and a comet painted on the fuselage and wings.

Ingvald Fagerskog took David C. Dome, 91, for his first airplane ride in April 1926. Dome was visiting his son in North Sacramento and saw the Fagerskog airplanes flying from Del Paso Park and decided to go up. He enjoyed the ride immensely.[28]

Charles E. Wilkins had been elected president of the Sacramento Aviation Club in March. Other newly elected officers were Henry G. Andrews – vice president; Charles Lipps – secretary; John Wachorst – treasurer; and as directors – E. G. Funk, H. M. Tucker, C. V. Smith, and William S. Sullivan. Club members who had not learned to fly would be given the opportunity to take lessons at a greatly reduced rate from either H. G. Andrews or Ingvald Fagerskog.[29]

The Sacramento Aviation Club held a meeting in May to urge city manager, H. C. Bottorff to make needed improvements to the municipal airfield in Del Paso Park so the city would not lose out on airmail service, soon to be inaugurated between Los Angeles and Seattle. The projected intermediate stops on the new north-south airmail route were to be at Bakersfield, Fresno, San Francisco, Sacramento, and the Oregon cities of Medford, Eugene, and Portland, and on to the terminus at Seattle. Sacramento might be omitted because of poor landing facilities. Del Paso Airport could only serve small planes. The aviation club brought to Bottorff's attention that as a result of the recent passage of the Air Mail Act, a civilian contractor would fly the new north-south airmail route and the army did not like civilian aircraft using Mather Field. There was the possibility of obtaining an airport improvement grant from the Guggenheim Fund for the Advancement of Aviation if the city of Sacramento matched it.

The aviation club members voted to endorse Colonel Frank P. Lahm for promotion to the rank of brigadier general in the Army Air Service. Their reason for getting involved in army policy was their belief that with high rank he would have a better chance at reviving Mather Field from its dormant state to one of the West's largest airports. Colonel Lahm had always been an eager advocate of such a plan.[30]

The California Development Association contacted the North Sacramento Chamber of Commerce the following month with similar questions. They wanted information on possible landing field sites. The chamber reported a plan to expand the Sacramento municipal field at Del Paso Park. As for new sites, the chamber identified a good flat area of land between Norwood Avenue and the Natomas levee as a possibility. It was convenient to Garden Highway, Western Pacific Railroad, and the interurban Sacramento Northern Railroad.[31]

Sacramento's Del Paso Airport had not caught on with many in the state's flying community. *Western Flying* in its June 1926 issue published a guide of available airports in California, and Sacramento had only one airfield listed—described as "a rectangular landing field, north to south, 2,000 by 1,500 yards, the field is covered with dust two to three inches deep with no vegetation. When muddy it cannot be used. Located five miles from the heart of the city and one mile south of the racetrack and fairgrounds. It was parallel to the Sacramento-Stockton highway. There is a large white circle with a cross in center of the runway. There is a house with windmill on northeast corner and clump of trees just north of the field. Gas, oil and water are available on the field."[32] The above describes the location of Sierra Airport at Fruitridge Avenue and (Upper) Stockton Road. It was the only airport ever located one mile south of the racetrack on the old state fairgrounds (Agricultural Park).

By 1926, Sierra Airport was also called Air Service Field and Antiaircraft Field for reasons unknown. An earlier mention in the March 1926 issue of *Western Flying* listed Air Service Field being located on Upper

Stockton Road, one-half mile from the city limits. The School of Aviation of Sacramento was located on the field. Landings were made diagonally across the field in a southwest or northeast direction, and the prevailing winds came from the southwest. The field was adjacent to a trolley line and had gas, oil, supplies, and a telephone.[33]

The *Western Flying* airport guide did not mention the Sacramento municipal airport, which in 1926 was located in Del Paso Park and had been since 1919.

Information is sketchy, but there definitely was some movement to make Air Service Field the principal airport in the Sacramento area in 1926. It may have had to do with the desire by some city citizens to improve the western section of the 830-acre Del Paso Park to relieve the congested picnic area at the eastern end of the park along Arcade Creek, south of Auburn Boulevard. Superior Court Judge Peter J. Shields, who was the last living member of the committee chosen to negotiate the purchase of the park for the city of Sacramento in 1910, led this improvement movement. The property had been purchased from O. A. Robinson of Minneapolis, Minnesota, who had purchased 44,000 acres of the old Haggin Land Grant.[34] To carry out the improvements sought for Del Paso Airport, it would have to be closed or at least minimized at a critical time when the airmail service needed an improved and expanded site.

At the August 19 meeting of the North Sacramento Exchange Club, the agenda's focal point was the club's decision favoring the Fagerskog family to keep their flying business on the airport in Del Paso Park. During discussions leading up to the club's decision, it was brought up that the Fagerskogs had spent their own money freely developing the Del Paso Park airfield, and they had never had an accident there. The family consistently promoted the Sacramento area in their travels. Most revealing were the statements claiming there was no reason to eject them from Del Paso Park except the suspicion of "politics" and "the development of a rival field south of Sacramento."

The reason given by the city for removing the Fagerskogs was "... that the city could not permit the Fagerskogs to make a profit on their operations." The North Sacramento Exchange Club would not accept this reasoning. They said it was well known that several businesses were making profits in other parts of the park, particularly at the golf course. A resolution was passed favoring the Fagerskogs.

It is doubtful the Fagerskogs came out on top of the situation—Ingvald Fagerskog opened his own airport just a stone's throw across Auburn

Boulevard from Del Paso Airport.

Exchange Club President Lawson then gave at talk about his experiences at Langley Field when he was in the army. He showed a large number of photos of war scenes given to him by General William Mitchell and Captain MacDonald, the official photographer on the field.[35]

The promotion of a rival airport, south of town in 1926, brings up the question of which airport south of town was being promoted. Was it the Sierra Airport/Air Service Field at Fruitridge and Stockton roads or was it Jack Irwin's new airport, which opened in 1926?

E. G. Funke, of the Sacramento Aviation Club, reported that Sacramento had one of the best commercial airports of any town on the West Coast. He was speaking of Irwin Airport on the Victory Highway (Freeport Boulevard). He described the airport as only ten miles south of the city center and had facilities such as hangars, gasoline, beacon lights, wind vane, telephone, and transportation. All aircraft were welcome at Irwin Airport.[36]

Another contemporary description of Irwin Field at Sacramento was published in the December 1926 issue of *Western Flying*. The 150-acre airport was situated on the Victory Highway one mile south of the southern city limits, three to four miles south of the State Capitol. The runway was 2,000 by 300 feet with a landing tee. Hangars were available for rent. There was a tower, lighthouse, ticket office, restrooms, a short order café, and an automobile service station on the grounds. There was a refueling station for aircraft on the field, and the Irwin Aircraft Company was located on the field. The grounds, which were completely level, were 6,000 feet long, 3,300 feet wide at one end, and 1,700 feet wide at the other end.[37] H. G. Andrews, a well-known local pilot in the Sacramento Valley, moved some of his flight operations to the new Irwin Airport at the end of September 1926.

Andrews received a letter from a former flying student on September 28. It was from William P. MacCracken, the newly chosen Assistant Secretary of Commerce for aviation. Andrews had taught him to fly at Waco, Texas, in 1917 during the war. The letter notified Andrews he had been picked as part of a group of prominent aviators to study the early draft of government regulations and rules governing aviation in the United States. He was to view the draft and suggest any further changes.

Charles E. Wilkins, member of the Sacramento Chamber of Commerce, made a resolution to the chamber urging immediate action to develop airports for commercial aviation in the local region. The resolution was adopted.[38]

Floyd Bennett landed at Irwin Airport in December 1926 aboard his trimotor Fokker, named *Josephine Ford*, which he was said to have flown over the North Pole with Admiral Richard Byrd.[39]

Fig. 33. Sitting on Berkeley Airport in June 1929 is the Golden Bear. A scaled down copy of the Ryan Brougham; this aircraft was built by the Neilson Steel Aircraft Company. The Golden Bear was test flown by Harry Abbott and later by Albert Lane.

Fig. 34. This was a Thomas Morse Scout believed to have belonged to Ingvald Fagerskog. The Tommy, as it was called, was the fastest American built war surplus aircraft available to civilians at the end of the Great War. It was a single-seat fighter powered by a rotary engine, thus not too useful to barnstormers during that era. However those who wanted to go fast loved it.

Fig. 35. US Air Mail Service pilots, Burr Winslow and Joe Derham, standing by their DH-4 receive the airmail pouch from Arthur S. Dudley from a stagecoach during a Sacramento mail re-enactment in the 1920s.

CHAPTER 6

A revitalized municipal airport at Del Paso Park – Irwin Airport is abandoned by its creator – Sierra Airport is renamed Eagle Rock Airport

Charles Lindbergh landed his Ryan *Spirit of St. Louis* on Le Bourget Airport at Paris, France, after a 33-hour 30-minute flight across the Atlantic Ocean from New York, which began on May 21, 1927. This single event did more than any other to open the eyes of Americans to the benefits aviation could bring their communities. City officials across the nation began pushing airport construction to the top of the list of community development projects. Lindbergh's flight created an enormous boost in airport development, pilot training, aircraft construction, and aircraft sales. It was known as the "Lindbergh surge."

In June 1927, the Sacramento City Council officially approved the airfield in Del Paso Park to be the city's municipal airport. Until then, even though the airport in the park had been in use since 1919 and was often called the municipal airport, it had never been officially designated as such.[1]

Sacramento postal officials gathered at the municipal airport to greet the first airmail plane landing there on June 20.[2] A few days later, H. G. Andrews and R. E. Nicholson, lessees of the airport from the city, had their business manager W. L. Davie announce they would be starting an air freight and passenger service between Sacramento and the Bay Area. They estimated that by July 15 their service would entail two flights daily.

The same day J. Paulding Edwards announced he would also be starting an air service beginning August 1. His plans, more grandiose, had smaller feeder planes leaving Redding and Bakersfield each morning landing at Sacramento where passengers and freight would transfer to a larger plane departing for San Francisco. Edwards claimed a landing field had been secured across the river at West Sacramento in Yolo County, only 2.7 miles from Sacramento's post office. The field could be reached by automobile in seven minutes. He said his landing field was 6,000 feet wide and 10,000 feet long. He planned to use seven planes; five could each carry a 1,500-pound payload and two could each carry 3,000 pounds of cargo. He had no airfield and his plan was never carried out; it was a pipe dream.

Partners Andrews and Nicholson already had an air service business, but they would learn that any air service to the Bay Area had to be developed gradually on an irregular schedule.[3]

In 1927 the municipal airport in Del Paso Park was a little over 180 acres and not in the tule fog belt where the present day Sacramento International (Metro) Airport is located. Del Paso Airport was 6.7 miles from the city post office, (center of the city). The airport was on Auburn Boulevard, one of the heaviest travelled auto routes into and out of Sacramento. Adjacent to Southern Pacific Railroad's tracks on the west, it was not far from the confluence of the Sacramento and American rivers, making it easy to find by transient aviators.

The city had already built much airport infrastructure over the years including a hangar, fueling station, and administration building. Leveling was done, a deep well drilled and drainage work was begun on the field in the fall of 1927. Runways 3,500 feet by 500 feet had been prepared in addition to taxiways leading from the runways to the hangars. The airport was on the federal lighted airway between Salt Lake City, Reno, and San Francisco. It was already a regularly scheduled airmail stop.

The city pledged to complete development of the airport and had a healthy allowance budgeted for the following year. At least five aircraft were permanently based there by October 1927.[4]

The following month work on the municipal airport was nearly finished. It was named "Lindbergh Field," a name that never caught on with the local flying community. (Many airports across the nation were named or renamed for Lindbergh after his epic flight, but few kept the name. There were too many Lindbergh Fields; it was too confusing. In California, San Diego's Lindbergh Field was the only one to maintain the name.) A magazine reported things about Sacramento's municipal airport a little differently. It stated the runway was "at present" nearly 1,500 feet by 500 feet in the direction of the prevailing winds, and it was "... to be lengthened to about 2000 feet."

The newly organized flying business of Andrews, Nicholson and Morris, formerly Andrews and Nicholson, signed a five-year lease on the airport. It included the administration building, refreshment stand, and fueling station. A 50- by 52-foot hangar was also being constructed for them.

Andrews, Nicholson and Morris acquired the distributorship for Fisk International biplanes. They purchased one for photo work, charter service, and student instruction for their nine flying students. H. G. Andrews, chief pilot, was already doing aerial mapping in addition to instructing. Ray Nicholson also flew for the company. C. E. Morris was a silent financial partner. The partners were said to be building a monoplane of original design with a semi-parasol, thick wing. It was to be powered by a Curtiss OX-5 engine and carried three people. It utilized steel tubing for its internal structure and, depending on the engine used, would cost $1,200 to $1,600. Their plan was to build several prototypes during the fall and winter wet season.

H. G. Andrews had also teamed with H. M. Salisbury of Walnut Grove who designed and was building a small biplane, which they were about to cover with fabric. The biplane was 13 feet long and had a wingspan of 20 feet. A 20hp. Pope motorcycle engine supplied power.

Ingvald Fagerskog built a large hangar directly across Auburn Boulevard from the municipal airport. He kept three Jennies and a Thomas Morse Scout there. He taught several students in the fall, including Milton Tucker who earlier rebuilt a JN-4 and flew it daily.

At Del Paso, Carl Sweeny installed an OX-5 in a light monoplane he had just finished. The plane was believed to be his original design. Ken Blaney, a notable young aviator from Sacramento in the late 1920s, was building a two-place biplane of his own design also powered by an OX-5. Blaney was in process of covering the wings.[5]

Also in the fall of 1927, Irwin Airport, south of Sacramento, was abandoned. Jack Irwin's buildings were dismantled and his plant for building the Meteorplane was moved back into the city. It was a bad time for Irwin. Earlier in August, Irwin had won a large silver loving cup competing in his Meteorplane at an air meet in Visalia.[6] He had high hopes of promoting his small biplane design at the September air races on Felts Field in Spokane, Washington, but he made a hard landing during a test flight there and severely damaged his landing gear, forcing him to pull out of the races. E. B.

Fig. 36. A Boeing Air Transport (BAT) Boeing Model 40A mail plane preparing to depart from Mather Field circa 1927.

Heath in his Heath Parasol won the races in an aircraft slower than Irwin's Meteorplane.

AIRMAIL WAS STILL being flown into Mather Field as late as October 1927. The Boeing Air Transport Company (BAT), since July 1 had been flying its newly acquired transcontinental airmail route from San Francisco to Chicago. BAT officials said that as soon as improvements were completed they would move the airmail service to Del Paso Airport.[7]

Toward that goal Carter Miller of the Department of Commerce (DOC) Aeronautics Branch inspected the municipal airport in December and after his report the city decided to immediately start improvements. Ten thousand dollars was subscribed to pay for the changes, which included a 500-foot cinder runway threshold and powerful lights surrounding the field for night use.[8]

C. C. Allen of Sacramento and Albert Lane of Willows moved their respective Hisso and OX-5 Standards to Stockton where Lane would manage Stockton Airport, which had four hangars along with fuel and repair facilities. Two Jennies were also based there.[9]

Edison E. Mouton assumed his duties as the first DOC Aeronautics

Branch inspector for Northern California in the fall of 1927.[10]

Sacramento's Henry G. Andrews was mentioned on one of the earliest lists, published in 1927, of pilots receiving the first government issued DOC pilot's license. Also listed was Livingston G. Irving, an ex-wartime flier, a Dole Race participant, and pioneer aerial crop duster in the Sacramento Valley.[11]

The 1928 Sacramento telephone book listed three aviation businesses in the Capital City. They were: Andrews, Nicholson & Morris – Municipal Airport; Eagle Rock Airlines – 830 L Street; and Eagle Rock Airport – Stockton Blvd. Eagle Rock Airport also had an advertising box on one page promoting the "Eagle Rock Airport School Of Aviation – Complete flying course under supervision of licensed pilots. Aerial taxi anywhere – Five Miles From Sacramento – Upper Stockton Blvd. – Phone: Main 10154."

Mather Field was temporary home for Bay Area pilots W. J. Barrows and Harrison C. Ryker who flew their Fairchild cabin plane on aerial surveying missions in February photographing the highway system between Sacramento and Bakersfield. The Fairchild had a camera mounted downward through the bottom of the fuselage that could take a photo of five-square miles in each frame.

Vance Breese flew one of his newly built passenger planes into Del Paso Airport in early 1928. Breese's airplane was used by a new passenger service, Tri-State Air Lines, which flew between Sacramento and other cities in California. Field manager H. G. Andrews met Breese when he landed in early February.[12]

According to Ray Nicholson there would be a register by March 1, 1928, at the municipal airport office to record every landing aircraft with the names of its pilot and passengers.

H. G. Andrews had two to three queries a week about night flights to San Francisco from Sacramento. He explained the costs and that night flying was more dangerous. When flying to San Francisco at night he flew to Dixon, Fairfield, and Vallejo, using their city lights to guide him. Some who were interested backed out of booking a flight. The route, he said, would be easier once Standard Oil Company finished erecting its beacon on Mt. Diablo.

For airports across America, Sunday was the most important day of the week. Many local residents drove to Del Paso Airport and watched the activities. Commercial pilots sold rides and did enough stunt flying to keep spectators interested and satisfy thrill seeking passengers. Traffic on

Auburn Boulevard got so congested on Sundays state authorities were often called in to keep the cars moving. To alleviate this problem, a request was made to have Auburn Boulevard widened or have the airfield fenced off from the boulevard.[13]

John Lawson, a North Sacramento city official, came forward supporting the fence suggestion but said it must encircle the entire municipal airport in Del Paso Park. He said on Sundays and holidays crowds of spectators walked right up to whirling propellers with no idea of the danger. People used the runway as a shortcut through the park. A surrounding fence, he argued, would keep people off the landing areas and eliminate the menace of motorcycles that made Sundays particularly dangerous on the field. Field manager Andrews agreed the situation was getting out of control and becoming more of a problem than he could handle.[14]

Clarence Young, director of the DOC Aeronautics Branch at Washington, D. C., flew to Mather Field in March 1928 and spent an hour watching a Crissy Field army squadron fly gunnery passes on ground targets. He then boarded an eight-passenger Air Corps Douglas C-1 that shuttled him and a few Crissy Field officers around. The C-1 departed Mather for Reno.[15]

Local pilots and aviation enthusiasts reorganized the Sacramento Aviation Club in early 1928 welcoming 15 new members. Newly elected officers were: Charles Wilkins, president; Henry. G. Andrews, vice president; Elliott Tabor, secretary; and John S. Lawson, treasurer. Charles Lipps and Ingvald Fagerskog were voted in as directors. Airport committee members were: L. D. Packard, chairman; Ken Blaney, E. Funke, Walter Lockhoof, and D. H. Greeley. It was also necessary to pick a committee to qualify the club for admission to the National Aeronautic Association.[16]

H. G. Andrews reported his flying business, Andrews, Nicholson and Morris, had soloed 47 students with 30 more in various stages of training. His company was now a dealer for the Swallow Aircraft Co. They had sold their first Swallow to R. U. St. John, an engineer for Standard Oil Company. Andrews said his company had flown nearly 1,000 passengers since January 1, 1928, and making two cross-country hops a week flying over $6,000,000 of bank clearing paper from Sacramento firms to San Francisco banks. He noted his repair shop had recently overhauled a Waco for John Tremayne of Oroville.

By late March, lights had been installed at the municipal airport—a beacon as well as ceiling and taxi floodlights. The city was contemplating oiling and graveling the dirt runways. During a recent air show attended by 7,500 spectators, many complained about clouds of dust stirred up by aircraft.

Ingvald Fagerskog, whose airfield was across Auburn Boulevard from the municipal airport, had hauled 500 passengers in his new Eaglerock biplane since the beginning of 1928 and soloed 15 flying students in his two Jennies. He sold his third Jenny to a local contractor and was rebuilding another. Fagerskog was associated with Walter Lockhoof, in the dealership for Alexander Eaglerock Aircraft at Sacramento.

Ken Blaney was building flying time daily in his homebuilt OX-5 powered biplane for his commercial license. Ralph Canning another local pilot was getting a lot of flying time in his newly rebuilt and recovered, short-wing Jenny.

EAGLE ROCK AIRPORT had become competition for Del Paso Airport. Originally named Sierra Aircraft (AKA Air Service Airport), Eagle Rock Airport was southeast of Sacramento on Upper Stockton Road. Based on the field was Eagle Rock Airlines, primary agents for Alexander Eaglerock Aircraft in Northern California. Eagle Rock Airlines, by April 1928, had carried 200 passengers since the first of the year and soloed a number of students. The manager of the airport and chief instructor for Eagle Rock Airlines, Chris Meyling, sold three Eaglerocks to local businessmen and planned to deliver them in May. Meyling had a combo-wing Eaglerock and a Hisso Standard for passenger flying and instruction.

Tri-State Air Lines began service from Eagle Rock Airport on March 19, making scheduled round-trip flights between Stockton, Sacramento, and Oakland. R. U. McIntosh, company manager, said the airline was flying Wright Whirlwind powered Fairchild cabin planes. The airline's fees were based on ten cents per mile per passenger.

A cabin Fairchild carrying McIntosh and Tri-State official Major Edwards was met by Sacramento city officials on its arrival from Oakland for the airline's maiden flight. Passengers R. E. Conley, mayor of Sacramento, and Jack Boucher boarded, and the Fairchild continued to Stockton and then Modesto. Tri-State Airlines was the result of an earlier attempt to create an airline known as Valley Air Service by Major J. Paulding Edwards.

A. F. Mickel, a Sacramento commercial pilot, who would soon join Howard Hughes' production of *Hell's Angels* at Oakland, opened a small temporary airfield west of Sacramento. The site he chose was at a very small community called Zero, two miles west of the city on the Davis highway. Mickel reported his passenger hopping business was doing fairly well. His short-wing Eaglerock was painted bright yellow and drew a lot of interest wherever he landed.[17]

All of the plans noted so far were miniscule compared to those of Ohio inventor Robert Condit. Condit announced a planned space departure from Miami Beach, Florida, as a "rocket passenger" to Venus where he expected a "... cordial reception when I get there." He planned to depart as soon as atmospheric conditions were "absolutely perfect." He would leave Earth in a huge rocket fueled by explosives "... more powerful than gunpowder." Condit said, "I believe there is a race on the planet similar to our own people. They may be even more advanced. I expect to find about the same conditions as here, although the climate may be hotter." Condit revealed more about his spacecraft as he "... groomed his torpedo-like craft." Two parachutes attached to the nose would allow him to land "gracefully." "He plans to open a turret on the rocket, and when a peep through a periscope reveals Venus is near, he will strap a parachute on his back and leap out."[18] One thinks Mr. Condit discovered 151-proof Puerto Rican rum while on a side trip from his Miami Beach vacation.

Marie Wilcox, fourteen years old, did some stunt flying with Ingvald Fagerskog over her Arcade School in North Sacramento. Fagerskog had taught Wilcox to fly at the municipal airport. Her exhibition kicked off "At-home Day" in the Arcade District schools. Fagerskog claimed Miss Wilcox was the youngest aviatrix in California. She was five feet tall and weighed 104 pounds.[19]

J. L. Smith, the new manager of Eagle Rock Airport, and Chris Meyling, chief pilot for Eagle Rock Airlines, gave 35 Stanford Junior High School students tours of the airplanes, motors, and hangars at the airport on April 16. The two men gave talks on aviation and meteorology, and afterwards the students' teacher was given an airplane ride.

A third hangar was built at Eagle Rock Airport on the south side of the existing hangars. The hangars adjoined each other forming one large hangar with a smaller hangar on either side. There was a lot of activity at the airport in April. A program of stunt flying and parachute jumping was scheduled for the 22nd.[20]

A security fence was erected around the entire municipal airport at Del Paso Park for the upcoming Sacramento Aircraft Show. Roland Federspeil was in charge of its construction.[21]

Jack Irwin flew to an air show at Mills Field, San Bruno, from Sacramento in his tiny Meteorplane. Its miniscule size attracted a lot of curiosity and interest.

A crew began grading Del Paso Airport. Andrews, Nicholson and Morris graduated two prominent Sacramento men, Curtiss Cutter Jr., head of a local lumber company and real estate developer, and Chauncey Dunn, a local attorney. John S. Lawson of North Sacramento completed his flying course and purchased a Swallow biplane. Andrews flew city manager Bottorff and city airport engineer H. R. Blood to Oakland Municipal Airport to pick up pointers on how to improve Sacramento's municipal airport. H. G. Andrews and Ray Nicholson sheared off a valve head in their International's engine while flying from Oakland to Sacramento. Part of the valve dropped into the cylinder head and was driven through the wall by the piston. The water jacket broke and both men were showered with hot water. They put down without incident on the airfield at Concord.[22]

Grading and leveling Del Paso Airport was finished May 18, 1928. The next day a width of 400 feet was to be oiled 600 feet out from the hangars. Planes could now take off in any direction and several planes could depart at the same time. Boundary lights were installed around the field to make night flying operations safe. The 29 lights were mounted on standards four feet high (!) around the outer edge of the field so pilots could see from altitude the field's boundaries. Red lights were placed in the corners of the field, green lights marked the runways, and white lights marked the intervening space. Floodlights and a beacon had been installed on the roof of the main hangar several months before.[23]

Capital Airlines inaugurated a regular scheduled air service between Sacramento and Oakland on May 15. The new airline's home field was Sacramento's municipal airport, Del Paso Airport, in Del Paso Park.[24] The Sacramento Aircraft Show, an extensive aviation trade show and air show, was scheduled for Del Paso Airport on May 25–27, 1928.[25]

Fig. 37. A team of barnstormers known as Thrash & Herzog demonstrate their wing walking technique over Sacramento in 1923. They were one of the many barnstorming outfits crisscrossing the United States during the barnstorming era following the World War. After about 1921, it is believed city newspapers stopped writing stories about them unless they bought advertising, thus most will forever remain unknown.

CHAPTER 7

Capital Air Lines – The Sacramento Aircraft Show of 1928 – Flying activities at Sacramento airports – Replacing Del Paso Airport – Final years at Eagle Rock Airport

The founding of Capital Air Lines at the municipal airport in Del Paso Park was first announced in April 1928. Initial plans were to fly scheduled routes between Chico, Marysville, Sacramento, Stockton, and the Bay Area with Sacramento as headquarters. The board of directors for the new airline included W. W. Shipley of Redding and R. S. Watkins of Chico.[1]

Capital Air Lines Inc. would fly Breese cabin monoplanes powered by Wright Whirlwind engines. They were to travel twice daily between Del Paso Airport and an airport at Alameda near Oakland. Plans were to eventually have four Breese aircraft flying projected routes to Chico, Redding, and later Lake Tahoe, Yosemite Valley, and Del Monte. The new airline would take over the air service firm of Andrews, Nicholson, and Morris at Del Paso.[2]

Royal Miller, president of Capital Air Lines Inc., had planned to introduce his airline's new six-passenger Breese high-wing monoplane to Sacramento by giving free rides in the new plane at Del Paso Airport on May 20, 1928. Unfortunately, H. G. Andrews, chief pilot, was unable to bring the Breese from the Bay Area in time for his advertised flights. The Breese had been inspected the prior week by a DOC inspector and passed inspection, but the new owners wanted a second inspection before putting the plane in active service. The second inspection made the plane a day late getting to Sacramento. The inspections indicated the Breese was in top condition.[3]

Andrews had the Breese airborne for a publicity flight on the 23rd. He took three Sacramento women up for an "airplane party": Mrs. G. Pollock, Mrs. J. K. Reese, and Mrs. Charles H. Carter. After departing Del Paso and reaching 2,600 feet, Andrews flew wide circles over Sacramento and surrounding farmlands while the ladies played bridge and drank tea.

Capital was to start flying its first route from Del Paso Airport to Oakland Municipal Airport on July 1. Andrews decided a May 24 timing flight would be made to Oakland with company president Miller and officers Charles Wilkins and S. J. McDonogh as passengers.[4]

Sacramento Aviation Club planned to hold the Sacramento Aircraft Show at the municipal airport. In early May, the club's air show committee was meeting three nights a week at the home of Roland Federspiel, who was in charge of the field arrangements. Elliot Tabor was chairman of the reception committee, and Douglas Greely was secretary of the air show committee.

H. G. Andrews made many night flights to study the new lighting arrangement on the municipal airport. With the border lights installation completed, the club had to put up a temporary fence 1,500 feet long. Without it, the DOC inspector would not allow the air show to happen. The public had to be kept from the aircraft during departures and landings at Del Paso Park.

Sacramento city officials revealed in early May a minimum of $200,000 was needed to put the municipal airport into adequate condition. They reported the $18,000 allotted for airport development was spent, and only the lighting installation and 10 percent of grading was finished. They also reported the city was about to lose its airmail service with Boeing Air Transport. The government was closing Mather Field to commercial aircraft. The city had an agreement with Boeing that the municipal airport would be ready for Boeing mail planes by July 1928, but it would not be possible.[5]

Dust at the municipal airport was a serious concern and with the Sacramento Aircraft Show to begin May 25 aero club members complained to city officials. They feared clouds of dust generated from all the airplanes landing and taking off might cause collisions.

Two water trucks were sent three days before the air show began. Unfortunately they only provided partial relief; dust was six inches thick on parts of the airfield. City engineers said there was little more that could be done; there were no funds available for a permanent solution.[6]

The repair shop on the municipal field was doing well. A Jenny belonging

CHAPTER 7

to Clem Lowe of Woodland was returned to him completely reconditioned by the shop. The job took all winter. Lowe, an active pilot in the Woodland area for several years, was one of the few Yolo Fliers Club members who actually flew.

Leo Moore, a former member of the Isleton Aviation Club, traveled to Wichita, Kansas, in early May with one of his flying students, Homer Coffing, to pick up Moore's new Travel Air biplane from the factory. Moore and Coffing flew the plane back to Sacramento via the southern transcontinental route. They travelled 2,700 miles in 29 hours and 45 minutes before landing at Del Paso Airport.[7]

One night in May, Ingvald Fagerskog received a telephone call at midnight from a man requesting an immediate flight to San Jose. A sleepy Fagerskog agreed. A small boy to be operated on for appendicitis wanted to see his father. Charles Lipps brought the father out to Del Paso Airport and at 12:45 AM the three men were airborne. Sixty minutes later, Fagerskog made a perfect landing on an unlighted airfield at San Jose. The father saw his son at the hospital.[8]

THE SACRAMENTO AIRCRAFT SHOW opened before a large crowd of spectators gathered on Del Paso Airport at noon Friday, May 25, 1928. The previous week water wagons worked around the clock soaking the grounds to keep dust down and harden the dirt runways.[9]

Friday's first event of the three-day air show was the arrival of planes from Mills Field, San Bruno, in a race for aircraft powered by Curtiss OX-5

Fig. 38. Del Paso Airport is depicted here during the Sacramento Aircraft Show of May 25-27, 1928. Running across the upper portion of the photo with over a hundred cars parked beside it is Auburn Boulevard. Fagerskog's runway starts at the boulevard and runs diagonally upward to the right and out of the photo. Notice that a space has been left between the parked cars so aircraft from Fagerskog's airport can taxi across Auburn Boulevard to land or depart from Del Paso's longer field.

engines. The air race or derby, as it was called, was won by "Red" Williams flying his International F-17 biplane in one hour and three minutes. Joe Salzman, in a Waco, was second. Williams' prize was $100 cash.[10]

Mills Field's mascot was a cat named Contact and rode with "Red" Williams during the race. The cat was very attached to Williams and flew everywhere with him. The feline was found wandering around Mills Field several months earlier and adopted by local pilots; it soon began hitching rides with them.[11]

George Debois won the last contest of opening day, a dead stick landing competition, with Leo Moore taking second. Late that day, A. M. Bass, the local "Houdini," made a parachute jump while blindfolded and handcuffed.

The next day the air race started from Oakland Municipal Airport. Local pilot "Sandy" Sanders won with a time of 37 minutes in a Lincoln-Page biplane. W. D. "Denny" Wright, also from Oakland, took second in 39 minutes. Sacramentan Ray Nicholson flying a Swallow with a passenger, made it in 42 minutes coming in third. Sanders' win was contested. Some racers believed carrying a passenger was required by the derby rules. Later it was confirmed that, indeed, the rules stated each plane had to carry a passenger. No prize money was awarded.[12]

Even though some events were held on Friday, Saturday was the official opening of the show. At 10:00 AM a static display of airplanes was opened for viewing. At 11:00 student pilots put on flying demonstrations.

Huge numbers of spectators descended on the spectacle in Del Paso Park. The crowd was at its largest at 1:30 for the air race from Oakland. After the race planes arrived on the field, Al Willett, of the California Highway Commission and a charter member of the Sacramento Aviation Club, was flown to 2,500 feet and made his first parachute jump. Afterward he said, "It's sure an awful feeling when the pilot hollers go." At the pilot's command, he stepped out of the plane travelling at 80 mph. Willett's descent was perfect.

A race for planes powered by OX-5 engines started after Willett's jump. It was a four-lap race from the municipal airport to Mather Field and back. Stunt-flying exhibitions by military and civilian pilots filled time between races and other contests. Ingvald Fagerskog skillfully demonstrated a small 400-pound homebuilt airplane, the *Bumblebee*, which he and Donald Pruett built. Miss Christine M. Speichinger, a San Francisco aviatrix, was to do stunt flying during the show, but if she did it went unreported.[13]

Alfred M. Bass' parachute jump late Saturday afternoon was memorable.

Prior to taking off with Leo Moore, Bass was photographed being blindfolded and handcuffed to a wing strut next to his cockpit in Moore's Travel Air by police officer Frank Boniface. After they departed Moore climbed to 3,000 feet over the airport, Bass removed the cuffs and jumped. Dropping away from the aircraft, Bass pulled the D-ring on his chute. It came out of the bag but did not deploy. Bass, still blindfolded, didn't realize he had a problem. The crowd below knew something was wrong; the chute had not opened. In these earlier days of parachuting, it was rare that a parachutist delayed opening his chute. The use of arms and legs to control one's body while falling, as skydivers do today, was unknown then.

Bass later explained because of the blindfold, he hadn't realized how far he had fallen. It was only when he heard an audible groan from the crowd below that he lifted his blindfold and looked up at his canopy. Bass was about 800 feet from the ground. He grabbed the shroud lines, gave them a furious shake, and the canopy popped open at 300 feet. He then fell gently into the side of a tree unhurt. To the crowd it seemed a miracle, Bass had fallen like a bullet for 2,700 feet.

Alfred Bass was a volunteer parachutist at the aircraft show. A member of the Sacramento Aviation Club and a veteran of the World War, Bass worked as a draftsman for the state of California. He lived at 928 H Street in Sacramento and possessed one of the finest collections of aeronautical literature in the United States. He wrote articles about early aviation for *Western Flying* and other periodicals. He was a pioneer experimental flyer. When he was younger, he built and rode in large kites. Later, he built and flew gliders and eventually designed, built, and flew airplanes. He also had experience in ballooning. It was written that probably no one in America had a fuller knowledge of the history of aeronautics, gained from self-experimentation and friendship with the later developers of aircraft, than Mr. Bass.[14]

There were 75 aircraft on the municipal field Saturday. During the three-day show, Major Livingston G. Irving of Dole Race fame and George Noville, Admiral Byrd's flying partner for his famed trans-Atlantic flight, made appearances.[15]

Sunday, the last day of a most successful air show both in attendance and financially, featured many more events. A popular one was a free-for-all race around Sacramento Valley. Lt. T. J. Cushman won in his US Marine Corps Curtiss Falcon biplane powered by a 450hp. Pratt & Whitney Wasp engine. He made the 100-mile race to Marysville, over to Colusa, and back to Sacramento in 59 minutes and 20 seconds. Right on his tail was his commanding officer, Capt. H. D. Campbell, flying another Falcon and arriving 20 seconds later. Cushman was awarded the chamber of commerce's perpetual trophy.

Leo Moore in his Travel Air won the dead stick landing contest and the Sacramento Aviation Club trophy at the final competition. Then all eyes looked skyward for an hour-long exhibition of solo and formation aerobatics as well as battle maneuvers flown by Captain Campbell and Lieutenant Cushman in their Falcons.

No air show in the 1920s was complete without an aerial marriage, and the last day of the Sacramento Aircraft Show was no exception. Rose Churchill, a local woman, and John C. Gregory, of Mayfield Aerial Surveys, were married over the city in Capital Air Lines' Breese six-passenger cabin plane. H. G. Andrews, chief pilot of Capital Air Lines, planned the arrangements. The wedding gave a big boost in publicity for Capital Air Lines. Andrews flew the Breese, and his father H. P. Andrews, a justice of the peace, performed the ceremony. The pilot and a photographer witnessed the wedding.[16]

Sam Purcell, who in 1928 was one of the last Bay Area aviation pioneers from the Exhibition Years still flying, flew from his home field at Redwood City to hop paying passengers at the aircraft show. He was still flying his old 200hp. BMW powered Curtiss R from the Marina Field era.[17]

This three-day event was successful with 40,000 spectators overall. It showcased one of the few commercial aircraft displays in the Sacramento Valley. There were 14 industry exhibitors in the large hangar and adjoining tent on the airport grounds. They were: Standard Oil of California with a working model of their big beacon located near San Francisco; Galt Union High School's aviation department brought an Eaglerock airplane and a display of parts, instruments, and aircraft accessories; Sydney's Aviation Service of San Francisco displayed Resistal flying goggles and Fonda leather flying helmets; General Electric Company and B. B. T. Corporation had a display of airport lighting equipment; Consolidated Instrument Company had an exhibit; and Boeing Air Transport displayed an impressive small display model of their Boeing Model 40A mail plane sitting prominently in one corner of the hangar.[18]

The air show was reasonably safe—two crashes the last day but no one was seriously injured. The first crash happened during the final dead stick landing competition. Leo Moore and Ken Blaney were each landing without power. Moore was first with Blaney following. Moore stopped quicker than Blaney expected. To avoid a wreck, Blaney swerved into the ground smashing his right wing. Fortunately, minutes before the crash, the airfield siren sounded a warning because pilots had been complaining all day about the field not being cleared during their dead stick landings.

In the military free-for-all race to Marysville, Colusa, Williams, Woodland, and return the second crash happened. Lt. N. H. Ives and his observer Capt. H. J. Cooper of the 40th Division, California National Guard Air Service, were in third place behind two Marine Corps Falcons. A fuel or oil line stopped functioning on the Douglas O-2 US Army National Guard observation plane. Ives lost power and banked sharply to avoid a tree in his forced landing. The plane crashed on a wing and hurdled a gulley ripping away its landing gear. The accident occurred one mile north of Del Paso Airport at a spot that would later be the center of McClellan Air Force Base. Both men escaped serious injury. The Liberty powered O-2 was dismantled and trucked to its home base, the National Guard airfield at Griffith Park, Los Angeles.[19] It was one of two National Guard O-2s flown at the show.[20]

P. L. Munkler, used car manager for the Don Lee Company, bought a Standard J-1 with a 140hp. Hisso engine on May 26 from Eagle Rock Airlines. He planned to use it for business and pleasure. That same day, Eagle Rock Airlines' chief pilot Chris Meyling was participating in the dead stick contest over at the municipal airport. Meyling had rescheduled his flying classes at Eagle Rock Field so he could participate in the contests.[21]

The 49er Round Up Rodeo was happening at the state fairgrounds while the Sacramento Aircraft Show was going on at Del Paso Park,. The two rodeo headliners were nationally known cowboy movie star Hoot Gibson, who was also an aviator, and stunt flyer Harold "Daredevil" Lockwood with his parachuting dog.[22]

IN AN AFTERNOON of the first week of June, Walter Lockhoof, named the official North Sacramento Chamber of Commerce aviator, had an unusual accident. He was taxiing across Auburn Boulevard from Fagerskog's airport to the longer municipal field runway and collided with a car driven by N. R. Hekerlie of Oroville. Lockhoof's plane suffered a broken propeller, and the car's roof was smashed. There were no injuries, but it brought up the interesting question of who had the right-of-way—the car or the plane?[23]

Later that month, Lockhoof, known in his hometown as "the flying barber," took the train to Colorado to pick up a new Alexander Eaglerock he just purchased. Arriving in Denver, he learned a fire at the Alexander factory destroyed nearly half the plant and several airframes. Everything remaining was moved to a new factory site in Colorado Springs. He went there and found out his plane wasn't finished; there would be a lengthy delay. All he could do was return to California and wait.[24]

US Marine Corps Squadron Eight spent the summer on temporary duty training at Mather Field. Squadron commander Captain Campbell showed off all eleven new Curtiss Falcon attack planes when the squadron flew Fourth of July celebrations at Sacramento, Davis, Woodland, Roseville, and other Northern California towns. The squadron demonstrated battle formations while simulating bombing and gunnery attacks over Del Paso Airport. Afterward, the Marine planes were put on static display near the runway at Del Paso.

A few days later, Martin Jensen, one of the two pilots who made it to Hawaii in the Dole Race, landed at Mather Field in the *Aloha*, the Breese racer he flew to Hawaii. Marine Corps Capt. H. D. Campbell greeted him. Campbell was temporary base commander of the usually dormant Mather Field for his squadron's summer deployment there in 1928.[25]

Sacramento was the first stop on an aerial goodwill tour of 33 states by Martin Jensen in the *Aloha*. The tour's mission was promoting public interest in aeronautics. Fred Bowerman Jr, Jensen's wife Marguerite, and their sponsor, C. M. Schoening, accompanied Jensen in his Breese.[26]

There were 67 students at Del Paso Airport by the end of July; 32 were students of the Andrews, Nicholson and Morris flying school, and 25 were Ingvald Fagerskog's. Leo Moore had seven students and A. F. Mickel had three. At Eagle Rock Airport, Eagle Rock Air Lines had 18 flying students.[27]

Walter Lockhoof finally took possession of his new Eaglerock August 1. James Mayberry of Golden State Aircraft Company delivered the Eaglerock to Lockhoof in Sacramento. Mayberry successfully sold Eaglerocks for two years. At the time he delivered Lockhoof's plane, he was selling Lincoln-Page aircraft for Golden State. He delivered Lockhoof's plane as part of a previous sale.[28]

By the time Lockhoof's Eaglerock arrived, he had developed his own airport between Sacramento and North Sacramento. It was located on the highway leading into North Sacramento (Del Paso Boulevard) at the North Sacramento city limits on the eastern bank of the American River. He had cleared and leveled a runway running northeast and built a hangar that could shelter two aircraft. *Western Flying* reported Lockhoof Airport as the fifth active airfield in the Sacramento area, and acknowledged Lockhoof's

Fig. 39. Walter Lockhoof with his new Alexander Eaglerock biplane on his airport in North Sacramento directly across Del Paso Boulevard from the old Liberty Iron Works circa 1928.

flying school there. The other four airports were: Mather Field, Sacramento Municipal Airport (AKA Del Paso Airport), Eagle Rock Airport, and possibly the old Irwin Airport.[29]

After a week or two of flying his plane from his new airport, Lockhoof decided to move his plane back to Del Paso Airport. The runway at Lockhoof Airport was not in line with the prevailing winds and he considered the constant crosswind landings an irritation.[30]

Regardless of the crosswinds, North Sacramento had its first aerial guest land at Lockhoof Airport on September 1. E. E. Edwards was on a transcontinental flight from San Francisco to his home state, New York. Not yet 18, Edwards was one of the youngest pilots flying. Lockhoof let Edwards use his hangar for the night.[31]

"Monty" Mouton, DOC chief aviation inspector, made many trips to Del Paso Airport in 1928 inspecting aircraft and testing applicants for pilot's licenses.[32]

By July 1928, the new federal aircraft and pilot licensing regulations were beginning to show results in Sacramento Valley. At Sacramento new private pilot licenses were issued to: R. U. St. John, Roland Federspeil, and J. A. Moliter. Paul S. Schreck was upgraded to a commercial license. Registration numbers were issued to: R. U. St. John for his Swallow; Andrews, Nicolson and Morris, for an International F-17; Ingvald Fagerskog for his

Eaglerock; Thomas A. Stewart for his OX-5 Standard J-1; and Cowan Aviation Co. for a Anzani powered Pruett CAC 1. George B. Vawter and N. Wallace of Arbuckle registered their Thomas Morse Scout, and Oroville's John E. Tremaine (or Tremayne) registered his Waco.[33] J. G. Nall, a DOC aviation inspector, was sent to San Francisco from the East to ease the workload on Mouton.[34]

Early in August a request by Capital Air Lines (by then a charter service and flying school, its scheduled airline service had not succeeded) and the Sacramento Aviation Club to clear a strip of land 1,000 feet wide north of the runway at the municipal airport in Del Paso Park. The proposal caused a storm of protest led by Sacramento City Councilman Martin I. Welsh, a member of the airport committee. They wanted to protect 13 large oak trees and other smaller ones growing along Arcade Creek, the north boundary of Del Paso Park.

Proponents said a strong north wind would curl turbulence over the oak trees and then down towards the ground on the leeward side. Planes at the airport, while taking off to the north could get caught in the curl coming over the taller trees, suddenly lose altitude, and fly into the trees with devastating results.

Councilman Welsh said he had, "... been told by fliers that there is little danger to the local aviators or others acquainted with conditions at the field. These men avoid the pull down [downdraft] of the current over the trees ..." on takeoff by turning just before they reach them and climbing out another direction. "I am told that visiting aviators are always warned by the local men of the condition before they take off." Welsh finished his comments, "I'm for leaving these trees in at least until we are certain whether Del Paso Park is to remain the site of the [municipal] airport." C. H. Bidwell, city councilman and airport committee member, said he would make an inspection of the trees before his decision on the subject. Mayor R. E. Conley, the third committee member, strongly in favor of aviation, wanted the trees removed.[35]

A few days later, the chamber of commerce got involved when a recommendation was made that its board of directors go on record in favor of continuing improvements to the municipal airport in Del Paso Park. The recommendation was tabled until the board could inspect the grounds.

The chamber's airport and industry committee led by Charles E. Wilkins finally made its recommendation based on the following criteria: 1. Del Paso Airport was chosen originally to be the municipal airport because all of the aeronautical experts available, which included the US Army and Navy, the Department of Commerce, and expert aviators unanimously chose the site as ideal. 2. Del Paso Airport was on the east/west government airway and was part of the lighted system on that airway. 3. Del Paso was the only field that complied with all of the requirements set by the airport committee. 4. Del Paso could be improved cheaper than developing any of the other suggested airport sites.

Wilkin's committee eliminated the other sites. An airport site adjoining Mather Field was too far from town and lacked transportation facilities. A Freeport Boulevard site was subject to more fog because its elevation was only 17 feet. Elevation at Del Paso was 70 feet. Property surrounding the Freeport Boulevard site was already subdivided and would surely be developed soon, creating a hazard. The purchase price plus improvements at Freeport Boulevard would cost more than the improvements to Del Paso. A Stockton Boulevard site, at 30-foot elevation, was subject to more fog than Del Paso, and its costs would also exceed those of continuing on at Del Paso.[36]

A few days later airport manager H. G. Andrews escorted members of the Sacramento Realty Board on an inspection tour of Del Paso Airport's northern border to see the trees that local aviators believed were a menace to departing aircraft. Andrews modified the removal request by pointing out only 400 feet through the 13 tall oak trees needed clearing to provide safety. After the tour, the realtors went on record favoring Andrews' modified request.[37]

As a response to councilman Welsh's letter and other letters to the newspapers in favor of not cutting the oak and locust trees at the end of the runway, Elliot Tabor, a Del Paso pilot, wrote a lengthy letter to the editor of the *Sacramento Bee*. He made an excellent case for cutting down the trees by citing the possibility of a pilot having engine failure during takeoff to the north. Engine failure was not an uncommon occurrence in the 1920s. Such a failure would leave the pilot low, slow, and without power. To avoid a stall/spin result, the pilot could not turn to avoid the trees or climb over them; he can only glide downward straight ahead. With the trees there, his only alternatives are either crash into the trees or stall and crash into the ground. If the trees were removed, the pilot could glide onward and make a safer forced landing.

In the same issue Tabor's letter was published, an interview with E. H. Traxler, a Realtor, was featured in the *Bee*. He said careful consideration should be given to the question of whether Del Paso Airport is suitable for being the permanent location of Sacramento's municipal airport. Traxler's concern was based on several days a year winter flooding closed the road going from downtown to the airport. He pointed out when that happens it is necessary to drive southeast to Florin, then head north on roads east of Sacramento to get there. Distance to the airport, which was normally only an eight-mile drive from the city center became, during flood season, a trek of 115 miles. Traxler's single concern may have tipped the scales.[38]

Arcade Farm Center members and the Sacramento County Farm Bureau came out in opposition to cutting down the trees and went even further calling for the removal of the airport to a new location. Their reasoning was the land had been turned over to the city originally for use as a park. The presence of the airport was foreign to that purpose. Others complained of the flooding situation and the commercialization of the park. All agreed the airport subjected park users to danger and discomfort.[39]

Three days later the Sacramento Chamber of Commerce came out with a plan to change the direction of the main runway, lengthen it, and add a crosswind runway eliminating the need to cut down any trees. The Sacramento Aviation Club supported the new plan. The local pilots realized they had opened a can of worms, which could possibly force the relocation of Sacramento's municipal airport. They wanted to keep the location and hoped the controversy they stirred up would go away.[40]

At least three commercial fliers at Del Paso Airport made it known they wanted the city to appoint a new airport manager as a way of solving the municipal airport problem. The fliers, Leo Moore, R. U. St. John, and A. F. Mickel with Moore as their spokesman, urged the city to resume control of the airport with an airport manager directly answerable to the Sacramento city manager. Moore said the city should build additional hangars to protect the aircraft of those pilots who would use the airport if it were under municipal supervision. Moore said he and the others felt since the airport was being leased to the Andrews, Nicholson and Morris Company, the company received preferential treatment from its airport manager Andrews—thus the airport was not truly a municipal airport.

If the airport was under the management of the city, according to Moore, aviators and airplanes in the area would be concentrated at the municipal airport instead of scattered about on the three or four airports currently in use around Sacramento. He reiterated the city must build more hangar space on the Del Paso site; planes currently had to be parked outside, day

Chapter 7   141

and night, at the mercy of the elements, which was detrimental to the planes' fabric, wood, instruments, and engines.[41]

H. G. Andrews and his partners Nicholson and Morris, who held a five-year lease on the airport, offered to surrender their lease for a payment of $5,000. They acknowledged there had been many complaints about their lease holding back development of the airport. They obtained the lease in June 1927 at $25 a month with that monthly fee increased ten dollars each year.[42]

The Sacramento City Council chose a nine-member commission in late August to shape the city's future aviation policies. They would immediately investigate whether the city should continue to use the airport in Del Paso Park, develop it properly, or find a new location.[43]

SIERRA AIRCRAFT COMPANY filed articles of incorporation in June 1928. This time its headquarters was listed as Oakland Municipal Airport. The company was to take over California sales of Alexander Eaglerock aircraft. Albert Hastings was again in charge. Golden State Aircraft Co., the former distributor of Eaglerock aircraft in Northern California, was under the leadership of James L. Mayberry who had switched to selling Lincoln-Page airplanes. Mayberry was top salesman of Eaglerocks in 1926 and 1927. In fact, the company's airport at Sacramento, initially named Sierra Airport, was renamed Mayberry Field for a short time and eventually became Eagle Rock Airport.[44]

The history of Alexander Eaglerock aircraft sales in Northern California is confusing. There were distributorships, sub-distributors, dealers, etc. Lester Lamkin was the first Alexander Eaglerock distributor for Northern California. He acquired the Eaglerock agency in 1925 and was based in the Porterville area at a place called Sunland where he opened his own airport that same year. As a young man in 1917, Lamkin wanted to join the army when America entered the war, and he wanted to fly. To help his chances of getting into the Army Signal Corps Aeronautics Branch, he learned to fly before enlisting. Lamkin enrolled in J. Paulding Edwards' aviation school at San Carlos in 1917 and learned to fly a Standard Model Curtiss Pusher. Afterward he joined the army and was sent to the army's aviation ground school on the University of California campus at Berkeley. After ground school, he was sent to Kelly Field, Texas, where he learned to fly the army way. He recalled, 62 years later, "We didn't know anything about flying, when you come right down to it. We were having men crash and spin in and all kinds of trouble so finally they sent two experts down to teach us how to recover from stalls and spins. I was one of about ten to get training to teach the rest of the instructors."

Lamkin wanted to fight overseas, but was assigned as an instructor pilot. He believed one of the reasons he didn't get to France was a secret dossier kept on him by his roommate in flying school. He claimed his roommate was an intelligence officer posing as a flying cadet, who never seemed to graduate from flying school. He supposedly reported that Lamkin had "pro-German" relatives. Lamkin said, "You can't imagine the hatred in those days, I remember some people who made a few pro-German remarks and they had the whole front of their homes painted with yellow paint."

Lamkin taught others to fly at Kelly Field and later Rich Field at Waco, Texas. After the war he barnstormed occasionally in a Curtiss Jenny when farming near Porterville would allow him time. He was the first in Porterville to own an airplane. William Lester Lamkin held ACA/FAI License No. 1528.[45]

Lamkin sold his Eaglerock distributorship after a couple of years selling "Eaglebricks," as they were derisively referred to. He recalled, "I was way ahead of my time [making] money in aircraft, they were not practical from a commercial standpoint." He quit selling airplanes but kept flying until World War II began. He sold his airplane to actor Randolph Scott in 1942.[46]

James L. Mayberry purchased the Eaglerock distributorship from Lester Lamkin in early 1927. Mayberry did well selling Eaglerock aircraft, and at one time placed a single order for 50 Eaglerocks from the factory.

The Eaglerock was one of the first postwar aircraft designs to enjoy success on the civilian aircraft market. Over 900 were built. By 1925, Curtiss Jennies and Standards were beginning to wear out to such a degree they couldn't be saved economically. The Eaglerock was an early successor to the ubiquitous JN-4. The reason the Alexander Company took a major share of the aircraft market was its introduction to the aircraft industry of the installment payment plan by J. Don Alexander, president of the Eaglerock organization. Time payments were an important key to success of Eaglerock sales.[47]

Eagle Rock Air Lines, Inc. was for a time the Alexander distributor for Northern California. James Mayberry was the man behind the organization. The company operated from Sierra Airport (AKA Eagle Rock Airport) on Upper Stockton Road. Chris Meyling, the company's chief pilot, also managed the airport.[48] Chris Meyling was locally known for a company flight in March 1928 to San Francisco and then down to Los Angeles to pick up photographs for the *Sacramento Bee* of the St. Francis Dam disaster in Southern California.[49]

A week later, Meyling was waiting while his engine was warming up for a flight to Oakland. There was a small crowd of people at the airport fence on Eagle Rock Field. Meyling stepped over to the fence and said he had to make a quick trip to Oakland and back. He asked if anyone was interested in riding along; he had an empty passenger seat, and the ride was free. Mrs. L. Constable volunteered and left with Meyling at 1:00. They were back on the ground at Sacramento by 4:00.[50] Stockton's College of the Pacific signed with Eaglerock Air Lines to teach an aeronautics course for 40 students. Chris Meyling flew to the college on April 10 and began teaching the course.

J. L. Smith, part owner of Eagle Rock Air Lines, reported Walter Hall's April 8 demonstration of parachute jumping at Eagle Rock Field attracted 5,000 people. Smith arranged another demonstration later in the month. This time Ralph Canning, a local musician and aviator, promised to do stunt flying in his plane after Walter Hall made his jumps. The Upper Stockton Road airfield (Sierra Airport/ Eagle Rock Airport) was a little over four miles from the center of Sacramento.[51]

Al Borth of Lodi bought a new Eaglerock from Eagle Rock Air Lines. He traded in his old Curtiss Jenny towards the purchase price. A short time later, Jack Beilby, a Sacramento automobile dealer, was taking lessons from Chris Meyling at Eagle Rock and purchased Borth's Jenny. Beilby hadn't finished his course and with so little experience thought it wise to hire Carl V. Smith to fly him to customer meetings. It was said this was Smith's return to the flying game. He flew as a stuntman with H. G. Andrews several years before. During the war, Smith worked for Curtiss Aeroplane Company at Mather Field. Beilby, originally from Wheatland, quit the auto business and enjoyed a long career as a professional pilot.[52]

Meyling and Ken Kleaver formed a business partnership teaching students and doing charter work in July 1928. They purchased an Eaglerock for their business.[53]

James Mayberry planned a new use for Eagle Rock Airport. His Golden State Aircraft Company was taken over by Consolidated Aircraft of Oakland. As part of the takeover Mayberry planned to open a branch office of Consolidated on Eagle Rock Airport. He claimed the new Oakland branch had 60 students and five planes with 14 more ordered.[54]

Throughout the 1920s, the 1928 telephone directory was the only year with more than one listing in the "Airplane Service and Airport" category. The Sacramento phone book yellow pages had two listings for flying services: ANDREWS, NICHOLSON, & MORRIS – MUNICIPAL AIRPORT (Del Paso), and EAGLE ROCK AIR LINES – 830 L STREET, SACRAMENTO, AND EAGLE ROCK AIRPORT – STOCKTON BOULEVARD. The Eagle Rock Airport block ad stated: SCHOOL OF AVIATION–COMPLETE FLYING COURSE, UNDER SUPERVISION OF LICENSED PILOTS. AERIAL TAXI ANYWHERE – FIVE MILES FROM SACRAMENTO – UPPER STOCKTON BOULEVARD.

In October, Chris Meyling, who hadn't been seen in the Sacramento area for many months, stopped at Eagle Rock Airport on a flight to San Francisco. Meyling, who had always worked from Eagle Rock Airport when he was in Sacramento, was currently flying a Travel Air for the McCloud Aviation Club at McCloud, literally at the base of Mt. Shasta.[55] In December 1928, Meyling made one of his bimonthly flights to Sacramento. He told friends he had a large student business at McCloud including E. N. Bellenger, J. D. Lambari, James Allemanti, Pete Foriveno, and Charles H. Finch. He flew back to McCloud, which had six inches of snow on the airport, and planned on returning to Sacramento in a month or so and remain for the rest of winter.[56]

Chris Meyling and one of his students, Ernest Burging of Weed, were instantly killed when their plane crashed six miles north of Weed in late June 1929. Meyling was said to be living in Dunsmuir at the time.[57]

The last reported activities at Eagle Rock Airport were: Jack Walsh flew into the airport late October 1928 from Oakland to demonstrate a Monocoupe, a high-wing monoplane, for his employer, Goddard Aircraft Company of Oakland. He reported selling several planes. One was sold to Hart's Cafeteria Company. The company used the plane to transport its auditor between Fresno, Modesto, and Sacramento where the company operated cafeterias.[58] Ken Kleaver purchased a new Eaglerock from the Eagle Rock Air Lines dealer after the first of the year. Carl V. Smith, who had been a pilot since 1919, was granted an airplane and engine mechanic's license in February 1929. Smith, who flew out of Eagle Rock Airport, was building flying time for a transport pilot license.[59] In late March 1931, an unnamed pilot in a Waco biplane belonging to Meadows Airways of Bakersfield was running low on gas, found a hole down through the fog, and landed at "old Eagle Rock Airport."[60]

CHAPTER 8

New airlines and flying services – Roseville opens an airport – Del Paso hangs on – New municipal airport sites are studied – The Sacramento Aviation Club – NAA Chapter is formed – New management at Del Paso – The first California Air Tour

Union Air Lines began daily service between Oakland and Sacramento on August 8, 1928. It had been operating on a route between San Francisco and Seattle from March 5 through June 30 carrying 3,900 passengers with no accidents or forced landings.[1]

Sacramento air activity in the months of August and September 1928 included: Royal U. St John who passed the flight test upgrading his license from private to a limited commercial license. His OX-5 Swallow was licensed in the commercial category allowing him to paint the letter C in front of his registration number on the wings and tail. The day St. John flew his test, other pilots at Del Paso did the same. Leo Moore passed his transport pilot's license test, the highest pilot rating achievable, as did John E. Tremaine of Oroville. Roland W. Federspiel, a local flier, passed his private pilot license test. James L. Mayberry got his OX-5, long-wing Eaglerock licensed for commercial work, and Walker P. Inman of Reno did the same for his Hisso Travel Air.[2]

J. L. Maddux, owner of Maddux Airlines, bought Beacon Airways, Inc. and all its assets in August. Beacon operated between San Francisco and Fresno. Maddux would soon be operating to and from those cities in addition to Sacramento and elsewhere in the state.[3]

Don Cardiff, the Monocoupe distributor from Bakersfield, dropped into Del Paso on August 21 in a Monocoupe, which attracted all the pilots on the field who were told he would soon choose a dealer for the Monocoupe at Sacramento.[4]

Del Paso Airport's situation was improved somewhat at no cost to the city. The state highway department reduced the knoll at the north end of the runway by using the dirt to add shoulders along Auburn Boulevard where none existed along the airport boundary.[5]

Curtiss Flying Service, from the Bay Area, provided flying exhibitions for the 1928 California State Fair. On September 9, Curtiss planes flew an exhibition to honor Curtiss Flying Service pilots who had just completed a 4,000-mile air tour of the West.[6]

Boeing Air Transport Company, carrier for the transcontinental airmail from Chicago to San Francisco, notified Sacramento officials in September that unless the municipal airport in Del Paso Park was able to handle their larger aircraft by November 1, Sacramento would be dropped as an airmail stop.

The airway beacon lighting system from Chicago to San Francisco was to be completely operational by November 1. Boeing mail planes would leave the Bay Area at night instead of the following morning. Del Paso Airport was lighted at night, but the runway was in such poor condition planes could not use it in wet weather. The Boeing mail planes had been using Mather Field as its airmail stop for Sacramento, but Mather had no lights for night operations and would have to be abandoned by November 1, thus the ultimatum to Sacramento.

The California Fruit Exchange, based in Sacramento since 1900, immediately notified the chamber of commerce if the city lost transcontinental airmail service the exchange would move its 73 employees and $23,000,000 business to a city that had airmail service. The Sacramento branch of Crane Company, a plumbing supply business, also warned the chamber that airmail service meant thousands of dollars a month for the company, and losing that service would be very serious.

At a special meeting of the new city airport commission, it was agreed the city would not pay the lessees of Del Paso Airport $5,000 to surrender their lease until a permanent airport site was chosen. However, the commission was very anxious to mollify Boeing Air Transport. Someone would be hired to turn the airport lights on both night and day when an aircraft entered the airport's traffic pattern, and they vowed to find a site quickly for a permanent city airport.[7] A. V. Bottorff, the city manager, made an important gesture to Boeing authorizing the immediate expenditure of $15,000

CHAPTER 8   147

to improve Del Paso Airport.[8]

Apparently, such threats either didn't work or weren't even considered when Boeing was dealing with the small city of Reno, Nevada, the next stop to the east on the transcontinental airmail route. Their airmail field was being prepared during the first week of September 1920. Two 1,000-foot runways were being graded and graveled for wet weather. The airmail was first flown into Reno's airport on September 8, 1920. It was four miles south of town on Plumas Street, about two blocks west of South Virginia Street. The runway was on the fifth fairway of today's Washoe County Golf Course near the west side of today's (2017) Peppermill Hotel and Casino. In 1925 the airport was named Blanch Field, properly misnamed for airmail pilot William F. Blanchfield. It should have been named Blanchfield Field, but that would have been awkward. Blanchfield was killed September 1, 1924, while flying the funeral salute for a deceased airmail employee at Elko, Nevada.

Charles Lindbergh landed at Blanch Field in September 1927 during

Fig. 40. Blanch Field at Reno, Nevada, was the U. S. Air Mail Service stop from 1920 until October 1928. The field was uncomfortably short for the Boeing Model 40A and dangerously so for the soon to arrive tri-motor Boeing Model 80A. So BAT purchased its own land for a larger airfield on Plumb Lane. Initially named Hubbard Field it is now Reno-Tahoe International Airport. Leaving the Bay Area Reno was the next airmail stop after Sacramento. Blanch Field is today (2018) Washoe County Golf Course.

his national tour following the Paris flight. When asked his opinion of the Reno airfield by city officials, he said the high altitude 1,000 foot runways were too short for the larger types of mail and passenger planes that would soon be coming; they needed to find a larger field.

Within two months, a new site was found six miles southeast of Reno on Plumb Lane east of South Virginia Street. Boeing Air Transport purchased this 120-acre site in July 1928, and the first plane landed there in late October. First it was named Hubbard Field after the Boeing Company's chief pilot, Eddie Hubbard who led its development.[9] It is now called Reno-Tahoe International Airport. When an airmail and passenger stop was needed at a small, underfunded town, Boeing could step up to the plate, but apparently not in the case of Sacramento.

Jack Casey of Capital Air Service at Del Paso Airport was on Mather Field in September 1928 to meet the Boeing airmail plane (still landing at Mather due to unsatisfactory conditions at Del Paso). Casey was meeting it to see his good friend Ivan Gates of the Gates-Day Aircraft Corporation, a passenger on the Boeing. Gates had turned operation of the Gates Flying Circus over to Clyde Pangborn and was pursuing his new interest: manufacturing the New Standard biplanes.

Capital Air Service signed four new students in September. Three were from surrounding communities: the Brander brothers from Tudor (Yuba City), an unnamed Chinese student, and Jim Lum from Sacramento. The fourth, Harry Merchant was from Reno.[10] Two of Jack Irwin's Stockton customers, H. F. Holt and Fred Booth, licensed their new Irwin MT2 Meteorplane with the DOC.[11]

There was little activity in October at Del Paso. Several pilots were on barnstorming tours so for over a week there were only two or three aircraft on the field. A transient Travel Air, flown by Grover Tyler, landed with magneto problems. After several hours his Whirlwind engine was repaired.

Capital Flying Service ran an advertisement promoting its charter service and flying school. It stated the company used only, "U. S. Government Licensed Planes and Pilots," and its motto was, "Today's Greatest Opportunity—Tomorrow's Biggest Future."[12]

A week later two planes from Perth Amboy, New Jersey, landed at Del Paso flown by Ive McKinney and Warren B. Smith. The two had recently flown in September's National Air Races Transcontinental "B" Race from New York to Los Angeles. Ive McKinney, placed seventeenth in his Whirlwind powered Pacer aircraft, registered X7269. It still carried race number

110 on the fuselage when he arrived at Del Paso. Smith was in his Swallow racer. They had flown up to Oregon after the race to go hunting. They stopped at Sacramento on their way back to New Jersey via the southern transcontinental route.[13]

McKinney was considered a local man because he learned to fly while in the army at Mather Field and did flying work in the Sacramento area four years earlier. Now he was employed by Syracuse Flying Service Inc., and was president of Pacer Aircraft Corporation. Local fliers remembered him as manager of Sierra Aircraft Company in earlier years.

The Seattle-Los Angeles airway would soon be completely lighted with beacons. The San Francisco-Los Angeles portion of that airway was said to have the best weather reporting of any airway in the world.[14]

Harry Culver, president of the California Real Estate Association, stopped in at Del Paso on the ninth from Culver City. Culver was flying a Stinson-Detroiter described as the "nattiest four-passenger monoplane" seen at Del Paso in some time.[15]

DOC inspector Mouton arrived at Del Paso in October in a new Whirlwind Stearman. Mouton visited his mother in Sacramento quite often.[16]

Capital Flying Service sold tickets for Capital Air Lines, a daily scheduled passenger service between Sacramento and San Francisco. The latter's planes left Del Paso every day except Sunday at 8:00 AM and 2:00 PM—landing at Oakland 45 minutes later and then making the return flight. Capital Air Lines, owned by Pickwick Airways, was not affiliated with Capital Flying Service.

Aviation had grown so much as an industry on the West Coast and in the state of California, it became necessary for the Department of Commerce to add another aeronautical inspector to cover the territory north of San Francisco. Dillard Hamilton from Dallas, Texas, got the job.[17] Inspector James G. Nahl covered the territory south of San Francisco; both men worked under E. E. Mouton, who had charge of all territory west of Salt Lake City. Supervisor S. L. Willits from St. Louis would further help Mouton handle his work overload. With these new changes, there would always be a federal inspector in the San Francisco office.

Del Paso flier Ingvald Fagerskog flew to Lake Tahoe on October 31 and made the first landing on the new airfield at Richardson Resort. A. L. Richardson, a resort and stage line owner at Placerville and Lake Tahoe, constructed a 1,765-foot landing strip at the south end of the lake. John S. Lawson of North Sacramento had sent word on the 30th of the completion of Richardson's airstrip. Lawson had been at the lake since the previous spring.[18]

Roseville developed a municipal airport in a large field north of the city on the Kaseberg property. The site had a paved road running along its southern border and was less than a half-mile from Roseville's town center. The terrain around Roseville was mostly level, which could be used for emergency landings. The federal government already had a beacon on the site to mark the transcontinental airway and designated it an emergency landing field. The beacon was mounted on a 50-foot steel tower at the southwest corner of the airport and had a 1.5 million candlepower revolving light. Roseville had yet to make any improvements to the field, which could be used for landings in its natural state. Being located on high ground kept it from flooding. The city's airport committee agreed grading a north-south runway and an east-west runway would improve the site.[19]

November 3-4, 1928, were chosen for the dedication of Roseville's new airport with a large air show organized by Don Castle, the new head of California Association for the Promotion of Aeronautics (CAPA).[20] Castle, who claimed he assisted in dedications of 25 airports in the past year, said Kaseberg Field was one of the finest in Northern California. He described the field as having two runways at right angles with plenty of room for departures. The dedication was well attended and deemed a success; except for a few accidents. According to Castle, the success was due to attendance numbers and the confidence in the safety of flying it instilled in the public.

To make the latter point, he pointed out how Al Willitt demonstrated outstanding piloting skills in an emergency situation. Willitt was landing his Monocoupe during the air show with his passenger, Roseville Air Show Queen Dorothy Keener, when Harold Jensen, 12, ran onto the runway in front of their plane. Willitt swerved to miss the boy and ran off the runway into a barbed wire fence at 45 mph. Neither Willitt nor Keener, were injured, but the propeller was smashed, the landing gear wiped off, and one wingtip was damaged on the Monocoupe.

Castle, still following his disingenuous line of "instilling confidence in the people," described Leo Moore's aerobatic act. "Moore demonstrated to the crowd the various dangers of airplanes that are commonly feared. He zoomed [sic] out of tailspins, looped the loop, sideslipped, and did other stunt flying to demonstrate that flying is safe."

The second accident was more serious. On Sunday, the last day, Walter Lockhoof in his Eaglerock collided with Royal St. John's Swallow while landing. St. John was waiting to take off and Lockhoof was on final approach. Lockhoof was going to land over St. John's plane, but let his Eaglerock, or "Eaglebrick" as they were known, sink too low. He struck the Swallow tearing off its top wing and injuring St. John, who was rushed to a hospital. It was announced his injuries were not life threatening. Royal St. John was a member of the Sacramento Airport Commission. Lockhoof, who was not injured, owned an airport at North Sacramento.[21]

A respectful number of aircraft, ten in all, flew in for the two-day event. Pilots included Leo Moore, Royal St. John, Eddie Shellenbacker, Al Willitt, Ingvald Fagerskog, all from Sacramento, and Walter Lockhoof from North Sacramento, Jerry Andrews from Oakland, and Floyd Nolta from Willows. The Exchange Club of Roseville, Richfield Oil Company, and CAPA put on the air show.

Prior to Lockhoof's crash, Leo Moore won the four-mile pylon race in his yellow and black OX-5 Travel Air biplane, named *Miss Sacramento*. His time was 2 minutes and 13 seconds. Royal St. John was second, and Walter Lockhoof took third. Richfield Oil awarded Leo Moore a silver trophy during a later banquet at the San Carlo Café in Roseville. The managing editor of the *Sacramento Union*, Leslie Davies, was also honored for his interest in aviation.

Lieutenant Kalinski from Crissy Field, San Francisco, flew over the field during the air show and was scheduled to land, but instead he dropped a note stating he had engine problems and was going to Mather Field for repairs. Mrs. Cora M. Woodbridge dropped another note to the spectators at Kaseberg Field announcing she was running for the state assembly.[22]

Don Castle and Byron Lake were caught in a recurring problem. Arrested and jailed in Auburn on November 10, Castle, president of CAPA, and his assistant, Byron Lake, were charged in Roseville for defrauding the DuBarry Hotel. They were held in jail because they couldn't pay the $500 bail set for each of them.[23]

Roseville's American Legion chapter and the Southern Pacific (SP) Railroad, spelled out on the roof of the SP station the air marker R-O-S-E-V-I-L-L-E. W. P. Fuller Company donated the paint.[24]

Several pilots with planes based at Del Paso Airport reported they might move to another airfield once winter rains began. Rain made Del Paso's dirt runway unusable. Some planned to move to Eagle Rock Airport on Upper Stockton Road.[25]

In November 1928, air markers 25-feet long were painted on the roofs of Hotel Land, Hotel Sacramento, and Associated Oil Co. with the city name and an arrow pointing north or to the airport.[26] The Hotel Sacramento also opened an aviation office in the hotel. With the surge in flying activities at the Capital City, it was decided special service should be given to aviators.[27]

Ex-Royal Air Force Wing Commander W. E. Wynn of Maddux Air Lines gave a public lecture at Sacramento's Lubin Elementary School about developing adequate airport facilities. It was intended for those seeking such an airport for Sacramento.[28]

With two pilots hospitalized, three airplanes wrecked at Roseville, and two planes away barnstorming, there was little activity at Del Paso Airport in November.[29]

W. K. Andrews, a new DOC inspector, came to Sacramento in November and gave examinations at the Elks Temple for airplane mechanic's licenses. L. Laine, a mechanic for Del Paso pilot Leo Moore, took the test.[30]

W. J. "Joe" Barrows and the veteran parachutist W. F. Hall, both from the Bay Area, landed at Del Paso in November after being forced down in the Sierra Nevada at a remote airstrip for four days. They had flown an air show at Ely, Nevada, and were flying home when they were caught in a terrible storm over the mountains; forced to land near a sheep camp they were taken in until the storm passed.[31]

Richfield Oil's tri-motor Fokker landed at Del Paso in late November. The enormous plane stayed only long enough to take aboard company officers and then departed for Los Angeles.

The same month, S. J. Kubota, a 25-year-old Japanese aviator, came to Del Paso Park from his Oakland home in a black biplane named *The Rising Sun* with a large red ball painted on the fuselage and Japanese lettering in white. He was seeking financial backing for a first attempt to fly round trip from America to Japan. He would start in early spring with Livingston Irving as his copilot. Kubota said the flight would be paid for by a subscription of Japanese merchants throughout California. He described his plan to fly a tri-motor sesquiplane, being built by an unnamed California aircraft manufacturer, to Japan via Hawaii. The return trip to America would be nonstop from Tokyo to Seattle requiring 65 hours flying time.[32]

City officials issued orders in the press during December that pilots avoid landing at Del Paso Airport due to the bad field conditions. Those orders stopped further progress and development of the airport until summer. Rumors began circulating that a San Francisco firm would be taking over the lease.

A pilot named Peters flew a new Spartan biplane to Sacramento from Los Angeles in December for demonstration to a prospective buyer at Del Paso Airport. Peters arrived during a heavy rainstorm and was unable to find the airport. While circling the area looking for the field, his magnetos got wet, and he had to make a forced landing in a muddy field near North Sacramento. The following morning he was able to take off and land at the municipal airport regardless of its condition. He spent two days making repairs to the Spartan before demonstrating it.[33]

By January 1929, transcontinental airmail planes were still landing at only one site in California's Great Central Valley—Mather Field. From Mather, mail planes would continue west to their terminus at Oakland Municipal Airport. If they were flying east from Mather, their next stop was Hubbard Field at Reno. The air carrier, Boeing Air Transport (BAT), was using Boeing Model 40As to fly the mail.

The Boeing 40A, powered by a 425hp. Pratt & Whitney Wasp engine, carried more than mail. It had a glass-enclosed compartment which seated two passengers just ahead of the pilot's open cockpit. It was a popular means of travel; seats for the airmail planes were booked weeks in advance.

Demand for seating was mounting and Boeing planned to put a dozen new 12-passenger, tri-motor Model 80A biplane airliners on day-to-day transcontinental operations within a few months. A pilot and copilot flew the Model 80A with the copilot or a steward serving lunch. The plane was equipped with hot and cold running water and had an on board lavatory. It could carry one ton of mail and cargo in addition to 12 passengers. D. M. Baker, BAT field manager at Sacramento, reported that in the previous year over 100 passengers had flown out of Sacramento in Boeing Model 40A mail planes.[34]

In January 1929, the Sacramento Airport Commission, formed the previous August, published the first in a series of reports about choosing a suitable site for the city's future municipal airport. A survey was started to determine the prevailing winds and typical weather conditions at four sites under consideration. Instruments were placed at Del Paso Airport; a Stockton Boulevard site; a Freeport Road site; and a site at West Sacramento. The instruments were self-recording and supplied a 24-hour, seven days a week, record of conditions conducive to or accompanied by fog. The US Weather Bureau supervised the survey and included 20 years of Weather Bureau reports for the area. The city was experiencing an unusual amount of fog at the time of the study, which enabled more data to be gathered than would usually be possible.

The problem of temporary lighting for landings had to be addressed. Sacramento would loose airmail service unless a lighted airport was developed to accommodate the upcoming night schedule of the Air Mail Service.

The DOC had lighted the entire transcontinental airway with rotating beacons from Boston to San Francisco. The San Francisco-Reno leg of the airmail route was the final section to be completed. Boeing airmail planes were to be put on a night schedule very soon. It would save one business day to and from New York. The Del Paso Airport could not safely handle the new Boeing Model 80As soon to be put on line because of the small landing area and lack of adequate lighting. Mather Field was again used under a temporary authorization as Sacramento's airmail stop, but, as stated, the lack of landing lights would eliminate Mather for further use once the night flights started.

A last ditch effort by the airport commission succeeded in getting the federal government to permit installation of temporary lighting equipment on Mather Field to allow the mail to stop at Sacramento until a new municipal airport was ready. The commission gave landowners of the four proposed airport sites a questionnaire pertaining to their land and what they expected to be paid for it. After the foggy season ended and the questionnaires studied, the commission would make its recommendation to the city which site should be purchased.[35]

Meanwhile activities at the current municipal airport in Del Paso Park went on as usual—when the January fogs allowed. In mid-month, a high-wing Cessna Airmaster, powered by an Axleson radial engine and flown by R. S. LeRoy, landed at Del Paso. The Axleson motor, which had only been available a short while, was a seven-cylinder radial engine that developed 150hp. Dan Emmett, "the Flying Legislator" departed Del Paso Airport for his home at Santa Paula in January 1929. He would return in his Whirlwind Stearman when the California legislature reconvened in February.

On Sunday, the 20th, a cold north wind blew, but it didn't stop a large crowd from gathering at Del Paso to watch airplanes land and depart.[36] Heavy fog returned a few days later forcing a West Coast Air Transport tri-motor Bach to land at Del Paso after the pilot was unable to find the airport at Corning. The passengers and crew stayed for three hours until the fog lifted. Leo Moore and his mechanic, Earl Bowker, did their best to provide a little hospitality for their surprise guests. Leo scrounged some chairs for the exhausted passengers while Bowker forced the lock on the airport refreshment stand and cooked up an impressive meal for everyone.[37]

R. U. St. John, the Del Paso aviator injured at the Roseville Airport's dedication, was feeling better and soon put the repaired wings back on his Swallow.[38] Nationally known aviatrix, 23-year-old Bobbi Trout who held an endurance flight record of 12 hours and 11 minutes, flew into the municipal airport in late January. Her new record was broken a day after she landed.[39]

J. L. Smith reported another reorganization of the Sacramento Aviation Club; 30 were charter members. At a January meeting, it was agreed a membership drive be started. Members weren't required to be pilots; it was an organization of flying enthusiasts and businessmen formed to promote aviation in Sacramento. Charles Lipps, a Sacramento High School aeronautics instructor, headed a committee to look into forming a junior members' glider club. A separate committee was chosen to ask the California State Fair Commission for special recognition of aviation at the coming state fair.[40] National Aeronautics Association members of the Sacramento chapter formed a glider club and purchased a glider. They planned to build a hangar for their sailplane near White Rock, six miles from the town of Folsom. The club had 20 members who each contributed 25 dollars towards the purchase of the glider.[41] The Sacramento Aviation Club elected a full slate of officers in February. The membership drive opened with Elliot Tabor in charge. James J. Finson of the Hotel Land let the club use a conference room for its meetings every Tuesday.

Los Angeles attorney Lawrence Kelley flew into Del Paso on a quick trip to Sacramento. By train it would have taken him 12 to 14 hours, but his plane made the trip in under four. Tony Miller, an Isleton farmer, transported his farmhands and their tools from one ranch to his other by airplane. The trip by car would have taken four hours, it took 15 minutes in his plane.[42]

Excellent weather for flying in late February brought Sacramento pilots out in force with the most intense activity since summer taking place at Del Paso. The sunshine not only brought out the pilots, it brought paying customers out as well.[43] A growing problem had to be addressed at Del Paso Airport. The warm-up area, where pilots stopped their planes to run up their engines to check magnetos before taking off, needed oil surfacing. To prevent overheating their engines, pilots taking off to the north pointed their planes into the wind during run-up for magneto checks. Dust clouds from the propellers blew directly across Auburn Boulevard into the spectators parking area. The blinding, choking dust drove customers away from the airport and affected traffic on the boulevard, the main east-west highway in and out of Sacramento.

Dan Emmett, the legislator from Santa Paula, kept his Whirlwind Stearman at Del Paso. Local pilots were quite envious of his beautiful big biplane.[44]

Kenneth C. Brown of Sacramento graduated from army flight training at Kelly Field, Texas. He was an alumnus of Sacramento High School and Stanford University. Before being sent to Kelly Field, he trained eight months at March Field near Riverside. Brown was stationed at Crissy Field after leaving Kelly.[45]

Glen and Del Fishback, Sacramento youths, were part of a group who won a local newspaper's model airplane contest. They won a ride with Leo Moore in his Travel Air. The Alhambra Theater provided judges for the contest and was the cohost. The judges were: Herb Meyerinck, music director for the Alhambra; Ray Nicholson, flying trombone player in Meyerinck's orchestra; and Charles Lipps, head of the aviation club at Sacramento High School.[46] Ray Nicholson was a respected commercial pilot at Del Paso; however, he kept his "day job" playing trombone because, as one wag put it, "The biggest danger to pilots in the flying business in those early days was starving to death."

Allan F. Bonnalie, vice president of the San Francisco chapter of the National Aeronautical Association (NAA) came to Sacramento in March to speak to 45 pilots and businessmen at the Hotel Sacramento. Many of those attending wanted to join the NAA, in fact, there were more people than required to become chartered by the NAA. C. E. Wilkins, who presided over the gathering, said an official charter would arrive within the month. Applications were accepted at the next meeting of the Sacramento Aviation Club. An NAA chapter could sponsor any aviation event and get worldwide recognition for any records set. The NAA was the only aeronautical association recognized in America by the Federation Aeronautique Internationale. The NAA had relieved the defunct Aero Club of America (ACA) in 1922 of these duties. The future Sacramento members agreed with the extensive NAA 15-point plan for advancement of aviation in America.[47]

The Sacramento chapter of the NAA was formed with a charter membership of 32 Sacramento Valley pilots and businessmen. Some of the more prominent members were: Ingvald Fagerskog, C. E. Wilkins, E. G. Funke, and L. D. Packard of Sacramento; W. N. Woodson, the "father" of the city of Corning; Dr. Julian P. Johnson, the first aviation business owner of Yuba City; and E. R. Norby, district attorney of Marysville.[48]

After managing the airport in Del Paso Park for ten years, H. G. "Andy" Andrews and his silent financial partner, C. E. Morris, a Grimes farmer, either wanted out or were forced out of their lease of the city airport. City officials made a deal with General Aeronautics Service of San Francisco's Mills Field to lease Del Paso Airport. Morris and Andrews were paying $25 per month for the old lease, which slightly increased over time. The new lessees would pay the city $135 per month. The city promised to pay Morris and Andrews for the improvements made by them during their tenure. Morris wanted $3,500 for the buildings he had erected on the field.

General Aeronautics Service company headquarters with Burdette Palmer president, was on Mills Field at San Bruno.[49] General Aeronautics Service (GAS) took over Del Paso Airport under the current Morris lease the first week of March 1929. It was expected GAS would hammer out a new lease from the city within a month. It is not known if and when that ever happened. Tom Mitchell, vice president of GAS and president of the San Francisco chapter of the NAA, was reputed to be one of those most responsible for the success of San Francisco's city airport, Mills Field. He told the press the same spirit and effort would be given Del Paso Airport.[50]

Beautiful weather and the draw of eight airplanes in the air on a March Sunday brought a record number of visitors to Del Paso Airport. Consequently, the most customers ever taken on hops—about 100—bought a total of 51 passenger flights that day. Several planes were brought over from Mills Field by GAS, which increased the aerial spectacle. New to the field were a Ryan Brougham and a new Waco flown in by A. F. Mickel and W. Stead, both local aviators. Bill Swain, the new Del Paso Airport manager, required local pilots to line up their planes facing Auburn Boulevard so, upon starting, their engine's dust would not be blown into the airport's spectators.[51]

The following activities took place at Del Paso in March: Senator Lyons and his wife made a quick trip to San Francisco in a plane chartered from GAS. H. T. Blunt from the Pacific Coast Air Service at Oakland landed at Del Paso on a flight home from Portland. Roy Meisser, a Sacramento businessman, purchased a used International F-17 biplane for pleasure flying.[52] An ad placed by the new municipal airport lessees appeared in a local newspaper. It announced a new Waco trainer at the airport and emphasized student instruction, ground school training, short passenger hops, and special charter flights to all points of the compass. It mentioned GAS local headquarters being located in the Hotel Sacramento and W. T. Swain as the new field superintendent.[53]

Al Willitt impressed Sunday spectators flying his Monocoupe in and out of the airfield, as did C. F. "Sully" Sullivan flying GAS's green Waco. Sullivan was working at Del Paso permanently as pilot and instructor. He had a lieutenant's commission in the naval reserve and had been flying since 1919. He was experienced in piloting navy bombers, torpedo planes, and contemporary commercial aircraft.[54]

Transient aircraft at Del Paso Airport for the week of March 18 through March 24, 1929, were: On 3/18 – Boeing biplane of Associated Oil Company; passenger-S. Wilson; pilot-G. Dickson; Departed on 3/19. Arrival on 3/19 of a J-5 Waco from Salt Lake City; passengers-A. E. Smith, G. R. Graham; pilot-Weems; Departed 3/20 for Tres Pino. Eaglerock departed on 3/20 for San Francisco; pilot-Ingvald Fagerskog returned same day. On 3/23 OX-5 Waco of GAS arrived from San Francisco; passenger-Donorin; pilot-C. F. Sullivan. On March 24, a total of 47 short hops were made from Del Paso with 96 passengers carried.[55]

E. Burrell Smith and A. E. Cameron from Los Angeles landed their two Whirlwind Eaglerocks at Del Paso on April 2. Both were salesmen in the aviation industry on an extended business trip to all airports in the state of California.

Roland Federspiel, Elliott Tabor, and J. A. Molter had learned to fly under the tutelage of H. G. Andrews, but they signed up with GAS, the new outfit running Del Paso Airport. C. F. Sullivan would be their instructor when needed.[56] Ken Kleaver, who had done much flying out of Sacramento airports, took a job flying for the GAS branch at Modesto in early April.

Dan W. Emmett, the flying legislator, reported the government sale of war surplus "Jennies" at incredibly cheap prices had stunted the growth of aviation for several years after the war. He said there was little doubt those "… condemned planes in the hands, for the most part, of inexperienced pilots did much to retard the public's confidence in aviation."

Airport manager Bill Swain reported that on April 7, a Sunday, 87 passengers went for short hops with 51 takeoffs recorded. On that day, E. V. Vandercook, general manager of GAS, flew up from San Francisco to inspect the airport at Del Paso Park. Others who flew into Del Paso the same day were: Allen Chapman and Frank Reid in a Curtiss JN-4D from Alameda; Jerry Andrews with two passengers in a Royle Airlines Swallow from Alameda; and C. F. Sullivan in a GAS Swallow flew a charter to San Francisco.

Arrivals and departures at the municipal airport for the week of April 8–14, 1929, were: Bill Martin in a Travel Air from Fresno on Tues., 4/9. On 4/10, Royle Air Lines with one passenger and return; Ken Blaney from Stockton Blvd. airport and left for Galt. On 4/12, Ken Blaney in an Eaglerock from Marysville and returned; Virgil Cline in a Lockheed Vega from Mills Field, with T. R. Mitchell, director of GAS as passenger. On April 14, Sunday, 132 passengers were carried on 67 short hops.[57]

Charles E. Wright, a Sacramento businessman, was believed to be leveling a 200-acre property at Twenty-First Avenue and Stockton Boulevard for an airport. Wright was personally supervising the grading and surveying work; however, he insisted the field was being leveled to farm wine grapes.

Further activities at Del Paso Airport in April 1929 were: Charles F. Sullivan, who worked for many months as a pilot for GAS resigned. Wallace Beery, movie star and pilot, flew into Del Paso unexpectedly. He was flying his $20,000 Travel Air monoplane from Red Bluff. After fueling his plane and departing for Los Angeles, Bill Swain realized Beery had given him a Canadian half-dollar in payment for fuel.[58] Ken Blaney and Kermit Parker of Sacramento, students in the aeronautics program at Galt Junior College used a Curtiss Jenny to commute to school from Sacramento to Galt. J. Hosking, head of Sacramento's Peerless Ice Cream, took delivery of a new Whirlwind Stearman from Frank Rose's Metro Air Service at Oakland.[59]

Mutual Aircraft Company, distributors of Ryan aircraft, brought a Ryan Brougham B-3 to Del Paso in late April as a demonstrator. Mr. Schleuder, the company pilot, took Mr. and Mrs. Boyd of Marysville for a demonstration ride in the Ryan. The aircraft was advertised as the sister ship to Lindbergh's *Spirit of St. Louis*.

Edison E. Mouton returned from a trip to Washington, D. C., and announced that five states had been added to the district from which he supervised as chief aeronautics inspector for the DOC. Oregon, Washington, Idaho, Montana, and Wyoming were added to his previous territory of California, Nevada, and Utah.

Del Paso gained a new wind cone courtesy of the Richfield Oil Company, which was installed on the east end of the field. Maddux Air Lines sent a tri-motor Ford to Del Paso flown by Capt. John Gugliametti. He hopped passengers over Lake Tahoe and back, on the first Sunday in May.[60]

Also in late April, Lt. Colonel Gerald C. Brandt, commander of the 91st

Observation Squadron at Crissy Field, led a five-plane flight of army observation aircraft over the state capitol and downtown Sacramento. The Army Air Corps squadron had been temporarily posted to Mather Field for its annual bombing and gunnery training on the range at Mather.[61]

Night flights of airmail planes were going to be inaugurated on the newly lighted transcontinental airway beginning May 1, 1929.[62]

On the night of May 6, the most spectacular crash in the history of the municipal airport at Del Paso Park happened. Harvey Lemcke, an experienced Bay Area professional pilot flew four San Francisco businessmen into Del Paso Airport during the day of the sixth. The passengers were: San Francisco (SF) Supervisor Warren Shannon, SF Supervisor William Stanton, SF deputy city attorney Henry Heidelburg, and superintendent of the SF municipal railway, Fred Boeken. Lemcke was flying a high-wing, single-engine, Lockheed Vega for the charter. The Vega, a new, fast, successful design, had only been in production two years. Famous long distance fliers Wily Post and Amelia Earhart used Lockheed Vegas for many of their record setting flights. The four men were flown to Sacramento for a hearing on a congressional bill that would affect the San Francisco municipal railway. They were to go back home that day.

It was already dark when H. S. McNeil in his taxi took the five men from the Hotel Senator to the airport on Auburn Boulevard. McNeil, standing by airport manager Bill Swain, heard him tell Lemcke to make a turn when, on take off, he reached a certain airport light post. McNeil stayed with Swain to watch the Vega take off. Later he said, "As they reached the light post Swain had described, they kept on going, I called Swain's attention to it. A moment later the big ship had crashed into the billboard."

According to the passengers, the plane had just left the ground when the engine sputtered and quit completely. Lemcke was able to clear the fence between Auburn Boulevard and the airport grounds by about four feet, and then the Vega smashed nose-first into a large roadside billboard. Luckily, the Vega struck the sign in such a way the engine, on the nose of the plane, was torn loose and pushed under the left wing as the plane hit the ground. It was not pushed back into the cockpit where it, probably, would have killed some or all of the occupants. As it was, Heidelburg was flung out a hole in the fuselage. Boeken, Shannon, and Stanton were trapped in the wreckage. Shannon got free and crawled out of the hole in the fuselage dragging Stanton behind him. Lemcke also crawled free then collapsed on the ground. Later at the hospital, the injured victims told reporters they didn't realize how close they came to dying. Shannon said, "It all happened so suddenly we had no time to think of consequences. I remember I held on for dear life and waited for the crash I knew was coming." The Vega suffered considerable damage, but reportedly part of the $14,000 airplane could be salvaged.

McNeil, the taxi driver, had rushed to the crash and administrated first aid, then drove them to the hospital in his taxi. The four businessmen were considered walking wounded and boarded a train and headed for home the next morning. Lemcke had to stay several days in Sutter Hospital due to back injuries.[63] To his credit, Lemcke didn't make the fatal error of trying to turn the aircraft away from the sign. By hitting the sign, much of the energy was taken out of the final impact with the ground plus it caused the engine to be displaced to the side—saving everyone on board. Lemcke, a veteran pilot, had been flying since 1914 and served in Europe during the Great War. Swain said he lost 24 hours of sleep after Lemcke crashed that Monday night. He claimed, tongue-in-cheek, that he was making a new regulation at the airport forbidding any pilot to have an accident after sunset.[64]

Charles Wright finally admitted to the Sacramento Aviation Club he was privately developing an airport at Twenty-First Avenue and Stockton Boulevard. He said how far the development would go depended upon the cooperation and moral support the city gave his project. It was certain he was leveling two runways each 2,500 by 300 feet to be completed by June 1. He invited the aviation club to hold an air show on the field June 1–2. He said it would be possible for the Boeing Air Transport Company to use his field instead of Mather for its mail planes in the near future.[65] Boeing did not use the field, as it wasn't lighted, and it is doubtful there was an air show held there. What became of Wright's airfield is a mystery.

John Wagge flew into Del Paso from Bakersfield in a Travel Air biplane the first week of May 1929.[66] Arrivals and departures at Del Paso May 7–14, 1929, were: On 5/7, a Whirlwind Stearman flown by Bart Stephens, superintendent of Mills Field, arrived from Mills; a Monocoupe came from Mills with Fred McKenly, pilot, and Bill Smith, passenger; Ernie Moe arrived in a Swallow from Yolo Fliers Club; and a Pitcairn Mailwing came from Mills Field flown by Jack Chadbourne. On 5/8, a Travel Air came from McCloud flown by Jim Alaman. On 5/9, a Monocoupe arrived from Mills flown by Bill Smith with Joe O'Hearn as passenger. On 5/10, a Navy Vought from the USS *Lexington*, anchored in SF Bay, landed to refuel. On 5/11, a Travel Air monoplane arrived from Mills Field to pick up Harvey Lemcke, the injured pilot, for return to SF. On 5/12, Sunday, a JN-4D came from Placerville flown by O. G. Harper; a J-5 Eaglerock came from Hollister flown by W. A. Williams; and 42 passenger hops were made. On 5/13, the J-5 Eaglerock left for Medford, Oregon. On May 14, a Templeman Flying Service Travel Air from Mills Field with Don Templeman as pilot landed with one passenger.

Humming Bird Aero, a Nevada corporation, had chosen a location for its plant and offices at 927 Del Paso Boulevard, North Sacramento, in May 1929. Their aircraft was described as more like a dirigible than an airplane. The craft had two huge propellers on the top and bottom of the body, which were supposed to create a vacuum enabling the craft to rise. A propeller on the front of the body would pull the machine forward. The aircraft was to seat 20 passengers. William Vardell said if successful, the aircraft powered by two 400hp. Liberty engines would be able to land anywhere its size would permit. Vardell was listed as company president and general manager with Charlie Bowser secretary-treasurer. As one might imagine, the project soon disappeared into the mists of time.[67]

Emory Bronte, who navigated for Ernie Smith on their flight to Hawaii in 1927, was invited to Sacramento in May by the local chapter of the NAA. Bronte brought with him Marvel Crosson, a popular woman flyer, who had just come from Alaska. Bronte had learned to fly and obtained his license after returning from the famous Smith-Bronte flight to Hawaii. He was hired by Associated Oil Company to pilot their Boeing Model 40A. He made several flights carrying prominent business leaders on sightseeing trips over Sacramento.[68]

At Del Paso Airport, a tractor and scraper spent a week leveling and eliminating rough spots on the landing fields. C. R. Blood, assistant city manager, supervised the work.[69]

Ken K. Kleaver, a well-known Northern California flier moved his base of operations to Del Paso. He had an Eaglerock and was formerly based at Eagle Rock Airport on Upper Stockton Boulevard. Kleaver, in June 1929, would leave for an extended barnstorming tour of Oregon and Washington, then explore his possibilities in the eastern United States. He had flown from various airfields in the north state the previous two years and logged over 1,000 hours of flying. He had received his transport pilot license in January. He contracted to fly in the Fourth of July celebration at Ft. Jones, southwest of Yreka, California.[70]

C. E. Morris, lessee of the municipal airport at Del Paso, bought a JN-4D from S. Salisbury of Walnut Grove and flew the plane to his ranch near

Grimes where he planned to accumulate the flying time required for a limited commercial pilot license.[71]

The General Aeronautic Services company, which had been subleasing the municipal airport, decided in late June they had had enough of the Sacramento aviation scene. The company withdrew its planes and personnel back to Mills Field at San Bruno. Ray Nicholson and Roy Meisser took over operation of the airfield under C. E. Morris' continuing five-year lease. Nicholson and Meisser would operate a flying school and air taxi service. They planned having a mechanic stationed on the field day and night to service transient aircraft.[72]

A plane crash in Sacramento killed Ira Wilkinson and his stepson Charles Wilson on July 1. Wilkinson was an executive of Capital Airways. Pilot of the ill-fated plane was Ross Martin, who also died. Neither the plane nor the pilot was licensed.[73]

Government licensing of pilots and planes began in July 1927, but it would take time to get everyone licensed. There was a de facto grace period while the federal government struggled with its few DOC Aviation Branch inspectors to reach everyone. When someone crashed during this grace period, the press always asked whether the pilot and the plane were licensed. It made the aviation community look bad when a serious accident involved an unlicensed pilot or plane; even though the lack of a license may have had nothing to do with the cause.

The first California Air Tour was to begin at Sacramento on June 1, 1929, and end at San Francisco on the 9th. An air show with air racing was planned to kick off the tour from Mather Field. The air tour was under the auspices of the San Francisco chapter of the NAA. Its purpose was promoting confidence in the safety and reliability of flying from airports in the north state. It was not an air tour like those predating it. Earlier tours, such as the Ford Air Tours which began in 1925, were nearly all handicap races. They were long distance races where the winner was decided not only by time en route, but also by the aircraft engine size, specifications, and capability. The first California Air Tour was run as a series of pylon races held around the state.

At the beginning of the tour at Mather Field, 40 planes took part in three pylon races and a dead stick landing contest. There was usually a stunt flying exhibition.[74] The first event was the 510 cubic inch (cu. in.) race, which was flown around a 15-mile pylon course on Mather Field. All races were flown around this same pylon course. Norman Goddard won this first race, which was essentially for OX-5 powered aircraft. Ray Moore took second and Tom Penfield third. Between races, veteran parachutist Frank Brooks provided thrilling jumps. Brooks, who had been parachuting since 1895 when he was only 11, made a particularly thrilling jump from a plane at 5,000 feet. He opened his parachute and then cut it away falling free again until he opened a second parachute. He cut that chute away and fell free once more before opening a third chute. The audience below was stunned by his performance.

The next race was the 800 cu. in. race (for Wright Whirlwind powered aircraft) won by Virgil Cline in a Pitcairn. Norm Goddard took second in a Waco 10, and Denny Wright was third in his Waco. The last race was the free-for-all for any plane and pilot who wished to enter. Frank Rose won it in a Stearman after the other two contestants were disqualified for touching the ground during the race! Goddard won the dead stick landing contest by landing 99 feet past the mark. Tom Penfield was second at 162 feet, and Al Willitt landed at 189 feet in his Monocoupe for third place.

Members of the Sacramento Aviation Club were responsible for operations at the Mather event. At the Sacramento Hotel during the customary banquet on the closing night of the air show, the main topic of discussion was whether the city should have a new municipal airport. Also during the banquet, the charter for the new Sacramento chapter of the National Aeronautic Association was presented to its members.[75]

Stockton, the next stop on the tour, had only two pylon races. The first was for OX-5 aircraft and the second race was a free-for-all. Norman Goddard, in a Waco, won the OX-5 race with Ray Moore taking second in a Travel Air, and Hinchy was third in a Velie powered Monocoupe. The free-for-all race was won by Virgil Cline in his Pitcairn, powered by a Whirlwind motor with one of the first NACA engine cowlings to appear in the north state. Allan Barrie took second in his Waco, and Frank Rose was third in the Stearman. The next day the tour was in Modesto where Ray Moore won the OX-5 race. Patterson was second in his Travel Air, and Tom Penfield was third in the Robin. Cline, Barrie, and Rose won the free-for-all in the same order as at Stockton.

The tour stopped at Merced and Fresno for more racing, but Los Banos was the final competition stop. There was only one race, and it was the 510 cu. in. (OX-5) catagory. Moore won as usual, but this time Barrie took second and Pat Patterson third. The tour advanced to Monterey, but a rainstorm cancelled the scheduled air show and pylon racing. The pilots all returned to their hangars in Oakland and San Francisco after the storm. The air tour caravan of planes attracted large crowds in every city they visited. In each city, officials and businesses assisted in promoting and carrying out the operations.[76]

At Sacramento, another flying club was organized at Eagle Rock Airport. Ralph Canning had recently taken a lease on the airport and planned to use an Arrow Sport to train members of the new club. Canning said his plan was to accept 30 members into the club. They were to be trained by a licensed pilot under the new regulations now enforced by the DOC.[77]

Homer W. Tatham of Sacramento was a surviving passenger of an airliner crash in the English Channel on June 17, 1929, at 11:33 in the morning. He was flying to Paris in a plane named *City of Ottawa* on business from London when it happened. The airliner was a twin-engine plane of an undisclosed manufacturer and the airline was also unmentioned in his accounts. Tatham reported the channel was uncharacteristically calm, which he believed was the reason only seven people died. He suffered many bruises and cuts on his head plus injuries to his right arm, which hung limp.

Tatham was on his eighth cross channel flight to Paris. He said trouble started when the airliner's right engine quit. Initially, he claimed he wasn't too worried because he had always flown on tri-motor aircraft and thought he was on one then. He tried calming the passengers. But it became clear he was not on a tri-motor and the plane had lost half its power. The pilot was having difficulty keeping the right wing up as the plane rapidly descended.

Little was spoken as everyone struggled to adjust lifebelts. The plane's descent increased rapidly and then came the crash with a surge of seawater rushing into the cabin. "After a few minutes struggling in the water, I climbed aboard the wreckage and we helped the others aboard. The pilot was thrown into the sea when the crash came. How long we stayed on the floating wreckage I do not know, it must have been a quarter of an hour, but seemed like eternity, knowing that others were caught in the cabin and that the plane itself might sink at any moment." A Belgian trawler and a London pilot ship witnessed the crash and came quickly to help. Sailors dove underwater to reach trapped passengers but apparently the wings had folded back over the cabin, and they couldn't be helped. At 3:00 PM Tatham and the other survivors arrived safely at Folkstone.[78]

IN SACRAMENTO THE 1929 California State Fair began its ten-day run on August 31. Three days later, loops, spins, and other aerobatic maneuvers were performed over the fair's racetrack by planes of the Curtiss Flying Service. The three Curtiss aircraft were on a 4,000-mile tour of the United States under the command of Capt. Harry B. Claiborne. Piloting the other two planes were E. B. Wilkins and E. H. Robinson.

The Curtiss tour served dual purposes. First, it was scouting possible sites for new Curtiss sales agencies. They visited 40 cities in the United States and western Canada. The second purpose was gathering information for the DOC Aeronautics Branch. The pilots were to report on flying conditions, present location of landing fields, the adequacy of those landing fields, and any other aeronautical information. The three planes thrilled packed grandstands at the state fair before continuing their tour to Alameda.

A young San Luis Obispo girl was flown to Sacramento to represent her county in the state fair spelling bee. Elsie Louis rode an airplane assembled by students at California Polytechnic School of San Luis Obispo. One of the students piloted her flight.[79] The state fair set aside a special tent for aircraft exhibits. V. W. Hoffman, a member of the state fair committee and a former army pilot was a major influence in acquiring the tent and its exhibits.[80]

C. E. Wilkins, a member of the city's airport commission, was making frequent trips in September to Del Paso Airport.[81] W. A. Andrews, DOC aviation inspector, gave flight exams to: Al Willitt and Ralph Canning for their transport pilot licenses; R. U. St. John for a limited commercial pilot license; and Archy Memler for his private pilot license. C. E. Morris and M. Bannister stopped in at Del Paso in early September, as did Bill Marsh, a mechanic for Sacramento Flying Service who flew to Yosemite for a quick vacation. Robert Weaver bought a Whirlwind Pitcairn biplane, which was to be shipped from the factory. Ray Nicholson would be delivering it.[82]

Jimmie Angel flew a large tri-motor Kreutzer into Del Paso Airport on September 1 carrying six passengers. They were on their way to Reno and stopped to refuel. One of the passengers was James Kreutzer. They stopped at Del Paso two days later on their way back to Los Angeles.[83]

M. Anderson flew into Del Paso with passengers in an Overland Airways plane to attend the grocer's convention. Also, Mr. and Mrs. Jensen and Miss Anneta Anderson arrived in a plane from Lake Tahoe flown by C. C. Allen, formerly of Sacramento. Bert Lavel also flew into the municipal airport in September. He was test pilot for Marchetti Aircraft Corporation. Bill Marsh received his airplane and engine mechanic's license the same month.[84]

Henry F. Blohm and Denison Ayer flew into Del Paso from the Naval Reserve Base at Oakland, and B. B. Smith with J. Kerris landed their Student Prince from Portland en route to Los Angeles in late September. I. W. Galehouse, an ex-World War pilot, flew into Del Paso from San Francisco; he was in a demonstrator for American Eagle Aircraft Company of Kansas City, Kansas.[85]

R. G. Green, a DOC aeronautics inspector, and Ace Bragunier flew into Del Paso on their way to Reno, Nevada, in October. It was as far as they could go by plane—Green had to continue over the Sierra Nevada by train because of a storm at Reno. The same week Herbert L. Clark and Paul San Martino stopped at Del Paso in a new Wright J-6 Travel Air. They were from Mills Field. Local flier Paul Schreck reported he expected to have the aircraft he was building in the air by January.[86]

Franklin Rose, the Stearman distributor for the north state, stopped at Del Paso in October on a flight to Redding. J. E. McCarthy of Detroit and, from Fresno, T. P. Shelton flew into Del Paso in a Curtiss Flying Service plane that month. About the same time, H. L. Blunt demonstrated a new Fairchild KR at Del Paso for the local pilots and allowed some of them to fly it.[87] C. E. Morris arrived at Del Paso from Grimes to check on his fellow lessees and build a little more flight time for his license. Leo Moore flew Mrs. Dorothy Ingram from Oregon into Del Paso in his Romair and went on to Oakland.[88]

Another air show with a crowd of 5,000 was held at Del Paso on Sunday, November 10, 1929, under sponsorship of Ray Nicholson, the new airport manager. There were the usual air races, contests, and stunt flying. Stunt flyer Sig Smith managed the air show and his wife Babe parachuted over Del Paso Park from 10,800 feet to claim a new altitude record. The wind carried her during her long descent to a landing near Carmichael.

Bill Marsh, the assistant airport manager, made a jump from 2,000 feet. Ken Kleaver from Dunsmuir won the three-mile pylon race in his Eaglerock, and Lieutenant Gregg of San Francisco flew an aerobatic exhibition. Later in the day, a motorcycle polo game was held.[89]

A few days after the show, Clyde "Upside Down" Pangborn, the famous stunt flyer, arrived at Del Paso Airport in a Gates-Day New Standard biplane, which he demonstrated for local pilots.[90]

Two weeks later, Carl I. Dixon and John H. Hadigan followed Pangborn to Del Paso Airport. They were test pilots for Gates-Day New Standard Corporation, and were visiting Sacramento before departing California for their factory at Patterson, New Jersey.[91]

Leo Moore and Edsel Newton arranged a meeting at Del Paso Airport for those interested in forming another aviation association in Sacramento.[92] The Sacramento Aero Club began that day on December 12 as an organization of pilot hopefuls with modest incomes. However, due to the economic panic after the stock market crash in October, their new club only existed a few months.[93]

CHAPTER 9

Prominent Sacramento aviators of the 1920s – John Fulton "Jack" Irwin – Henry G. "Andy" Andrews – Ray E. Nicholson – Ingvald Fagerskog – Leo Moore – Walter L. Lockhoof – Jack Beilby – Arthur F. Mickel – Ken Blaney – A. B. Willett

What follows are sketches of the ten most prominent aviators in the Sacramento area during the 1920s. Most of these aviators flew out of the municipal airport at Del Paso Park, although not all were based there. These pilots were the founders of commercial aviation in Sacramento during the postwar and pre-regulation years. They have been mentioned many times prior, but it might clarify their importance with this extended examination of their careers and activities at Del Paso Airport during its final years as Sacramento's first municipal airport.

John "Jack" Fulton Irwin

Regardless of Irwin's claims of having built aeroplanes as far back as 1908 (the first aircraft he built was a glider), *Jane's All The World's Aircraft* for 1927 states that Irwin began building airplanes in 1916. By 1926 his company, the Irwin Aircraft Corporation, was building airplanes at Sacramento on his own airport.

Irwin Airport was on Freeport Boulevard across the street from the current (2017) Sacramento Executive Airport location. In July 1928, the Sacramento Chamber of Commerce favored the Irwin Field location for a new permanent municipal airport.[1] But it was not chosen.

Irwin rarely flew into Del Paso Airport, but in early May 1929, he did land there in a low-wing monoplane he built for Peter Munkler. He had test

Figs. 41, 42. The above two photos taken on the same day depict Del Paso Airport circa 1927. There are only five resident aircraft on the field. In the top photo, the closest aircraft is the Fisk International F-17 of Henry G. Andrews and Ray Nicholson and they are standing by the prop. The next aircraft is a JN-4D Jenny and then an Alexander Eaglerock probably belonging to Walter Lockhoof is next. After the Eaglerock is a Jenny and the last is of unknown make. A small model airplane sits by the unknown make. The lower photo is taken from the opposite direction of the same planes and the camera is looking north in the direction of the airport's prevailing winds.

flown the new plane and was pleased with its handling.

Jack Beilby made a test flight in Munkler's new plane and was irate upon landing. He had taken off and climbed straight out to 1,000 feet and discovered the ailerons did not respond properly to his stick movements. He remained calm and judiciously brought Irwin, his passenger, back to the airport safely. Somehow the aileron cables had been improperly connected.[2]

A new Sacramento municipal airport was opened in April 1930. It was located about five miles south of the city center on Freeport Road, as mentioned right across the road from Jack Irwin's airport, which he had abandoned in 1927 or '28. All references to Sacramento Municipal Airport after April 1930 refer to the Freeport Road (later Boulevard) site.

Jack Irwin, in 1929, reported eight unfilled orders valued at $24,000 from buyers for his biplane and had received numerous requests to open sales agencies in various states.[3] In July 1930, after many test flights in his Meteorplane, Irwin flew the miniature biplane to Oakland for an air show.[4] He assembled the Meteorplane and flew it several times from the new municipal airport in October 1930. He let several of the pilots, who witnessed his flights, fly the Meteorplane. Most commented on how great it flew and how sensitive it was to control. They all liked the plane.[5]

The Irwin Aircraft Company announced in March 1931 a large building was to be built on Watsonville Airport to house an Irwin plant. Claude R. Wilson enticed Jack Irwin to move to Watsonville Airport and succeed him as airport manager. Irwin never built the factory plant, but he did build a few Meteorplanes in the airport's main shop hangar during his tenure there.[6]

It should be noted that today's Sacramento International Airport in the Natomas District is a mile-and-a-half east of Jack Irwin's first flying school located at Target, which if it still existed would be in the flood control bypass for the Sacramento River. Today's international airport is on the east side of the eastern levee of the Sacramento River and out of the flood plain—hopefully.

Henry Gay "Andy" Andrews

H. G. Andrews, born at Red Bluff on May 21, 1895, began flying in 1909 in a homemade glider. Later, he joined Troop B of the First California Cavalry of the US Army and in 1916 he rode with General "Black Jack" Pershing during the Punitive Expedition into Mexico. After the expedition to punish Pancho Villa, Andrews transferred to the Signal Corps Aviation Section and learned to fly the army way. He qualified as a military aviator and was commissioned a lieutenant at Rockwell Field in November 1917. During the war, Andrews instructed flying at Rockwell Field, San Diego, and later at Waco, Texas. He was one of the first six pilots to arrive at Waco's Rich Field where he taught aviators until the war ended. In late December 1918, he returned home to Sacramento on furlough from Rich Field.

Andrews began flying in the Capital City area after leaving the US Army Air Service in March 1919. He had obtained an ACA/FAI license No. 929 and was issued an Army-Navy Air Cognizance Board civilian license No. 823 in July 1919. With a couple of partners, he started the Sacramento Aviation Company that same year, and soon was flying from the Curtiss Oaks flying field and later Del Paso Airport. He barnstormed California and the

Rocky Mountain states for the next year or two then he flew for Walter Varney in the Bay Area in addition to his work at Sacramento. He flew regular scheduled flights for a few months between Sacramento and San Francisco for Capital Airlines in the summer of 1928.

Andrews taught many Chinese students to fly after which they returned to China and flew airmail or for military forces. It was said he developed the method of flying over rice fields to scare off ducks and geese, but others made the same claim. Also he was said to have flown for the movies right after leaving the Air Service and was part of the group of exhibition flyers who made the first plane-to-automobile exchange for movie cameras. The author has found no information to corroborate any of the claims made in this paragraph.[7]

Andrews was best known for the years he was the Del Paso Airport manager and chief pilot for the Andrews, Nicholson, and Morris Flying Service. Curtiss Cutter Jr., a Sacramento businessman, started flying lessons with Andrews February 8, 1928, and after twelve lessons he soloed. He finished instruction in March 1928 and proudly told a reporter flying was the "king of sports."

Andrews also taught North Sacramento businessman John S. Lawson to fly. An exceptional student, Lawson learned quickly and then purchased a new Swallow aircraft.[8] Chauncey Dunn, a local attorney, soloed and completed his course with Andrews, as did Roland Federspiel, who took an advanced flying course. Fred Cooper, another of Andrews' students, was ready to solo by mid-March.[9]

Andy Andrews became vice president of newly established Capital Air Lines Inc. and also supervised maintenance. He went to the Bay Area in May 1928 and picked up a new six-passenger Breese cabin monoplane for the new airline. He test flew the plane and got the paperwork for licensing the Breese, which Capital used on a regular airline route between Sacramento and San Francisco.

Andrews had flown to the Bay Area to pick up the Breese in an International F-17 biplane used as a trainer by the Andrews, Nicholson and Morris company. Upon his return the F-17 went down for a complete overhaul. The fuselage needed to be rebuilt and a new orange and black paint job applied. Landing lights were installed on the plane as more customers were requesting night flights out of Del Paso Airport.[10]

On the weekend of July 7, Andrews was flying the big Breese cabin plane to Redding for taking passengers on short hops at a few dollars each. During one takeoff, the shock absorber shaft fell out of a landing gear leg. The leg and wheel were dangling under the fuselage.

Andrews circled the airfield while planning the safest way to land the crippled new airplane. He decided to sideslip in for a landing on his one good gear leg, holding the opposite wing and damaged gear leg off the ground as long as possible. When that wing finally lost lift and contacted the ground, the Breese pivoted around a half circle in a ground loop. All passengers were unharmed. There was little damage to the plane. The shaft was redesigned and installed in a manner that would never come loose again.

Andrews took Ed Gerber to Redding from Sacramento. They stopped in Red Bluff, Andrew's birthplace, for fuel. They flew a side trip to a favorite fishing spot Andy fished with his father in 1908. It was near Mineral in Tehama County. He landed the Breese on the fine airstrip at Mineral with a runway long enough that Ford Tri-motors landed there. The trip took 32 minutes from Red Bluff. In 1908, it took Andrews and his father two days to get there on horseback. From the air Andy could see the deserted trails of his boyhood memories, an old swimming hole, the area where he used to hunt, even the spot where he shot his first deer, and finally the bottom of the falls, his favorite fishing hole.[11]

Shortly thereafter, Andrews flew Mrs. Alice Taylor to Eugene, Oregon, in the Breese. Later, Andrews used the plane to save California National Bank of Sacramento a day's interest on $2,000,000 in securities by delivering them to San Francisco.

Residents of Sacramento living in the northwestern city limits under Andy's regularly scheduled Capital Air Lines route to San Francisco needed no alarm clocks. The Breese's engine roared to full power every morning at 8:20 as he took off for Mills Field.[12]

Jim Lum, a local Chinese student, signed up with Andrews for a flying course in late August.[13]

The International F-17 which Andrews, Nicholson and Morris Flying Service recently overhauled and painted was severely damaged in a crash in mid-September. To save money, the company hauled the remains to Galt High School where students in its aviation program would rebuild it.[14]

H. G. Andrews started flying for Maddux Airlines in November 1928. After Maddux merged with Transcontinental Air Transport (TAT), he continued flying the Pacific coast route for TAT-Maddux Airlines until March 1930. He transferred to the eastern division of the airline to fly the St. Louis to Columbus route. The airline merged once again, this time with Western Air and became Transcontinental and Western Air, or TWA. Much later, it became Trans-World Airways. Andrews flew the first TWA aircraft out of Newark, New Jersey, on October 25, 1930, loaded with celebrities and airmail.[15] Andrews was back in San Francisco by September 1938 as TWA's assistant superintendent of the Pacific Division.[16]

Andrews quit flying and became the chief dispatcher at Los Angeles International Airport. He ended his career with TWA in management for its division in Taiwan and Burma.

In 1974 Andrews' old friends from Sacramento arranged a reunion at the Cordova Lodge to pay him tribute. Andy gladly attended. He had taught them all to fly at either Del Paso Airport or Irwin Airport.

Among those at the reunion were Ken Blaney, Elliot Tabor, who had arranged the reunion, Paul Schreck, Arthur "Pop" Mickel, Ed Schoenbackler, Albert Lane, Roland Federspiel, Carl Smith, Curtiss Cutter, Frank Bennetts, Archie Memler and Carroll Gay. Everyone agreed Andrews had taught them well and had done all right for himself; at 79 he had survived the most dangerous years in aviation's history. Andrews died on April 12, 1977, in Canoga Park; however, he was buried in Sacramento's East Lawn Cemetery next to his wife and son. Back in the early years of aviation in Northern California his friend and former student, Elliot Tabor, said H. G. Andrews was "… truly Mr. Aviation."[17]

Fig. 43. The Del Paso gang meet with renowned Bay Area aviator and air show announcer William Royle. Third from the left is Ingvald Fagerskog; fifth from the left is Ray Nicholson; first from the right is Leo Moore; third from the right is Henry G. "Andy" Andrews; and fourth from the right is Bill Royle. The location is believed to be Del Paso Airport circa 1928.

Chapter 9

Ray "Nick" E. Nicholson

When Andy Andrews with new partners formed Capital Air Lines in April 1928, Ray Nicholson took over as chief pilot of the Andrews, Nicholson and Morris Flying Service. The partnership became Nicholson and Morris, which was still the lessee at Del Paso. Morris was not a commercial pilot, so Nicholson instructed all students who remained with their flying service.[18] Ray Nicholson flew the company International F-17 to Grimes in July, and Morris rode back with him to Sacramento for business. A. C. Memler made his solo flight after only five hours of dual instruction with Nicholson that same month.[19] In September 1928, Nicholson, instructing under the provisions of his limited commercial license, passed the test for his transport pilot license.[20]

H. G. Andrews became too involved in scheduled airline flying forcing the breakup of the Andrews, Nicholson and Morris Company. Nicholson didn't fly very often for several months until Roy Meisser purchased an International F-17 at Del Paso. Later, Nicholson joined Meisser in a small commercial endeavor to make the plane pay for itself by Nicholson giving flight instruction in the F-17 and also teaching Meisser to fly. Many of Nicholson's students returned and completed their flying courses, which were interrupted when his old company broke up.[21]

Ray Nicholson, now the airport manager, arranged to have a DOC inspector visit Del Paso Airport on May 31 to test Archie Memler and Roy Meisser for their private pilot license.

Del Paso Airport was taken over in August 1929 by a new company, Sacramento Flying Service. Nicholson became their chief pilot gaining several new students with the change of regimes.[22] The stock market crashed in October 1929 and flying at Del Paso began to slow. In January 1930, to make a little cash, Nicholson went on barnstorming tours for weeks at a time. He took along Bill Marsh who served double duty as mechanic and parachute jumper.[23] Nicholson was still flying for Roy Meisser who, by February, acquired a Hisso Travel Air.[24]

Del Paso Airport ceased being the municipal airport in April 1930, but it remained open a few more years. Nick Nicholson continued to fly from there. Nicholson flew to Los Angeles in August 1930 and stayed several days. He was checking out employment possibilities and looking for airplane deals; it was a buyer's market with the deepening Depression.

Robert F. Weaver, owner and manager of the Sacramento Flying Service, returned to Del Paso Field the last week of January 1931. He had been in

Los Angeles looking for a good deal on a cabin plane. He wanted to add to his growing fleet of planes at Del Paso. At the time, he owned a de Havilland Gypsy Moth and a Hisso Travel Air, which his chief pilot, Nicholson, used to hop passengers on Sundays and for flight instruction. Nicholson soloed four students by the end of January: Bud Meredith, George Koshell, Frank Jones, and Edward Sandin. Nicholson had 24 students in training at Del Paso. Sacramento Flying Service acquired two Russell Lobe parachutes so he could teach aerobatics to advanced students. It was and still is against federal regulations to instruct aerobatics without the instructor and student wearing parachutes.[25]

George Koshall, one of Nicholson's students, took his license examination March 17. Nicholson planned to have Bud Meredith ready for his test in April. Ralph Canning temporarily moved his Travel Air from the old Eagle Rock Field to his new base of operations at Del Paso Field.[26] Nicholson reported in April 1931 Frank Jones would be ready for his license test the next time inspector Wiley Wright was in town. A new student, Bill Ganow from Georgetown, was progressing rapidly. Ralph Canning had a good week hopping passengers at Del Paso in his Travel Air.[27] Nicholson left on vacation at Clear Lake in April for a week, and Ralph Canning took his place. Canning returned to Sacramento from Oakland after renewing his transport pilot license.[28]

Sacramento Flying Service students, under Ray Nicholson, showing progress were Jack Selby and Joe Cecchettini. The company's Gypsy Moth was overhauled for an expected busy summer.[29] Selden Parnham, who worked in Sacramento Flying Service's repair shop, soloed. Parnham was a former student of Charles Lipps' aeronautics class at Sacramento High School. Nicholson also soloed Archie Memler in the Gypsy Moth. Memler had 50 hours before he was allowed to fly the Moth. He was learning aerobatics in the Moth to sharpen his skills before taking his private pilot license test.[30]

Hermie King was master of ceremonies at the Hippodrome Theatre in Sacramento. Nick Nicholson and Ralph Canning worked at night as professional musicians in the theater's orchestra. They both hounded King to take flying lessons from Nick until he finally agreed. Another student of Nicholson, Paul Lazzarini who lived on Auburn Boulevard not far from Del Paso Airport, was doing very well by mid-May.[31]

Nicholson and Canning announced in September 1931 they were combining their flight instruction operations. They also planned to move their operations to the new municipal airport on Freeport Boulevard. At the time, Nicholson and Canning used a Commandaire and Blackhawk for advanced instruction. They planned a buying trip to Los Angeles to acquire a training plane with low cruising and landing speeds more suitable for beginners. Nicholson and Canning had trained many local pilots and were close friends since their days at the old airport on Upper Stockton Boulevard in 1925.[32]

At their new headquarters on the new muni airport on Freeport Boulevard, Canning sold his Commandaire to Tony Brazil. He and Nicholson became the local distributor for Switlik parachutes. They added a new Waco F to their fleet, which became very popular with students and short haul passengers. They sold Standard Oil aviation products. Their new flight school had 32 students by November 1931.[33] Nicholson soloed Sacramento Fire Department Capt. Manuel Vierra in January 1932. About that time, Tony Brazil passed tests for his private pilot license. Nathanial Wallace of Woodland, and local men Bill Scarpino, Edwin Sturm, J. A. Wilhoite, and Ed Shepard began lessons with Nicholson and Canning.[34]

Nicholson and Canning put one of their planes back on line in April after having it completely reconditioned. Hilton Lusk, the former airport superintendent, ground looped the plane while landing in a crosswind. He caught the propeller and smashed a wing. He decided it might be time for additional instruction from Nicholson. Don Smith, the new municipal airport superintendent, said Lusk had only a student license. Nicholson was opening a DOC approved repair shop by June 1 in hangar No. 1 with Selden Parnham as chief mechanic. Norman Reinhart from Knight's Landing signed on with Nicholson and Canning in May; at 15 he was one of the youngest flying students in the valley.

Nicholson bought out Ralph Canning in May 1932. He planned to continue operating as before.[35] In late June, Nicholson hired Les Moore and his Fleet from Stockton to help with instruction duties. The Fleet was an excellent trainer with outstanding aerobatic capability and popular with students. Nicholson used his Waco for passenger hops and charter work. Albert Waite, an ex-army pilot who flew overseas during the war, began refresher training with Nick, as did Elwood Hildebrand.[36]

The July heat of the Sacramento Valley forced Nicholson to do all instructing in the early morning. Turbulence could get very uncomfortable as the day wore on. Les Moore (not to be confused with well-known Sacramento commercial flyer Leo Moore) began work with Nicholson's students by the end of the month. Student Floyd Baker was ready for his private license tests.[37] Afterward the DOC inspector scored him 100 percent on the written test and the same for his flying test—quite exceptional. Ed Shepard, Ed Sturm, and John Cook all soloed by the second week of August. Pat Bennett, who took lessons from Nicholson in 1929, returned three years later to complete his training.[38]

In the fall of 1932, Ray Nicholson added a Curtiss Fledgling trainer to his fleet. The plane was a two-place biplane purchased as surplus from the US Navy powered by a 175hp. Challenger engine; it cruised at 85 mph. Ed Anderson, Bud Alderson, Alva Fisher, Henry Yuen, and Ed Wong, all local men, began lessons with Nicholson that fall. Al Waite, a teacher at Sacramento High School, Elwood Hildebrand, who worked for a local title company, and a Sacramento Junior College student, Dave Walker, all soloed and were working towards their private licenses. One of Nicholson's former students, Joe Cechettini, broke his leg in a toboggan accident. He returned to flying with the comment, "It is safer." In late fall Manuel Vierra, Bill Scarpino, and Hildebrand passed their DOC tests for James Peyton, the DOC inspector, and received private licenses. Miss Genevieve Nebeker was ready to take her test on the next exam date.[39] Nicholson hired Woodland pilot Ernie Moe to help with instructing duties.

Nicholson's students formed the Dumbbell Flyer's Club. Its president was required to carry the club's symbol, a gilded dumbbell with wings, when he was on the field. He was supposed to display the dumbbell prominently when going up for a flying lesson. The presidency was awarded to the next student who showed the greatest lack of common sense during his flying training. That temporary president carried the dumbbell until another student pulled the next boneheaded miscalculation.

As the year was ending, old-time local pilot Carl V. Smith began taking dual instruction from Nicholson. Nicholson also soloed service station owner Pat Bennett.[40]

Ingvald Fagerskog

Ingvald Fagerskog was born near Grass Valley in 1895. His family moved to the Sacramento area in 1900. His father, Fridtjof, farmed land where the deactivated McClellan Air Force Base is today. Ingvald was taught to fly by a discharged Great War veteran, name unknown, in 1918.

In August 1928, Ingvald Fagerskog took time off from his business for the opening of deer hunting season. He had been laid up in bed with severe bronchitis for most of the previous month and wasn't sure he could go. He either got better or just went anyway. Avid deer hunters never miss opening day. Fagerskog flew his Eaglerock up to Ukiah in the northern Coast Range of California. He was one of the first aviators in Sacramento who used an airplane to go deer hunting. He did well and returned to Sacramento a short time later, probably with his deer strapped to a wing.[41]

Fagerskog flew out of Del Paso Airport by taxiing across Auburn Boulevard from his own field so often the locals thought he owned it too. He liked the longer runway. In its very early years the airport was a bare open field.[42] A report once credited a Sacramento fuel distributor for painting "Sacramento" on the roof of Ingvald Fagerskog's hangar. The municipal airport at Del Paso Park needed the sign, but had no building on which to paint an identifier.

Fagerskog was from a large local family who worked in many trades. He had been flying from Del Paso Airport since the war ended. He flew from the field long after the first surge of ex-army pilots had skimmed the easy money of ten to fifteen dollars per ride from the local citizenry in 1919 before they moved on.

Fagerskog remained at Del Paso acquiring enough business contacts to survive the postwar economic depression of 1920–21 and the following lean years. In November 1928 a local paper published photographs of Fagerskog handing the film reel of the Hollywood movie *Wings* to Mr. McCurry, Capitol Theater's owner. McCurry wanted to run the movie another week, but his film was promised elsewhere so he had to find another copy and get it to his theater overnight. He located a copy and hired Fagerskog to retrieve it with his Eaglerock from an unnamed city.[43]

Fagerskog flew John S. Lawson of the Sacramento Aviation Club to A. L. Richardson's resort at Lake Tahoe in November, landing on the resort's new runway at the lake. Fagerskog's plane was the first to land there.[44]

Several days after flying the movie reel to Sacramento, Fagerskog applied for a DOC pilot's license, a license for his Eaglerock, and one for his Curtiss Jenny. He got his license six weeks later and his airplanes were licensed at the same time. Now in the bureaucracy, his students were required to take the DOC written exam before they could continue their flying lessons.[45]

Fagerskog sold one of his Jennies to Art Wilson of the Sacramento Police Department. The Jenny was powered by a 140hp. Hisso motor. Ingvald Fagerskog still had two Jennies and an Eaglerock.[46] After the sale, he took off with Sacramento businessman and aviation enthusiast W. A. Hoskins who wanted to buy an airplane. They headed to Tulsa to look at one, but didn't buy it, and were back in little over a week.[47] Franklin Rose and Sam Metzger' Metro Air Service Stearman distributorship at Oakland Airport, sent a Whirlwind Stearman to Del Paso in late February for Hoskins to try. He loved it and bought one, then hired Fagerskog to fly it.

Fagerskog took Lou Moreing on his first flight in early March. Moreing said his ranch in the Natomas District looked very different from the air. The baseball stadium built in 1922 at Riverside and Broadway in Sacramento was named Moreing Field after the wealthy family.

A few days later, Fagerskog received a telephone call from George and Bill Beckstrom in Mendocino County. They needed to get to Chico fast and asked Ingvald to pick them up at Hopland. Ingvald flew the brothers to Chico three hours after they called. It was a seven hour trip by car. After the Chico trip, Fagerskog sold his Eaglerock to Percy Perkins of Placerville.[48]

Fagerskog was thought to have set an instructing record in March 1929, for soloing three flying students. They were: Roy Meisser, who had just bought an International F-17; Percy Perkins, who had just purchased Ingvald's Eaglerock; and J. S. Wakefield of Davis. Later that month, Fagerskog flew to Oroville and back with N. Teramoto.[49]

Fagerskog and his brother-in-law, R. Godard, flew to the rugged Ukiah area for a quick hunting trip in early May. They captured a couple of young wildcats and took them away in Hoskins' new $10,000 Stearman. Not satisfied with abducting two animals, they also added a small pig. It must have been an interesting flight transporting three frightened wildlife to Del Paso in a plane![50] Ingvald flew a passenger to Reno in Hoskins' Stearman soon thereafter. Clearly, Hoskins had leased his Stearman to Ingvald so they both could make money from the acquisition. Two days later Ingvald flew two passengers to San Francisco in the Stearman, and then a couple more to Oakland.[51]

Later in May, Fagerskog announced he was the new Sacramento dealer for Travel Air. He obtained an OX-5 Travel Air biplane to use as a demonstrator at Del Paso Airport. Ingvald piloted W. A. Hoskins in his Stearman to Wichita, Kansas, to look over the new lines of Stearman and Travel Air aircraft. They hoped to acquire a cabin plane, which were popular for charter flights.[52] The flight to Kansas took a little over 15 hours at an average speed of 100 mph. On return they encountered several heavy rainstorms forcing Fagerskog to take the Stearman up to 14,000 feet at times. They left on a Thursday from Del Paso and were back in Sacramento ready for work

Chapter 9

Fig. 44. Ingvald Fagerskog in his new Travel Air 2000 circa 1930. Fagerskog maintained the Ingvald's Comet name with the stars, moon and comet painted on the sides of the fuselage.

by Monday morning. They spent two days in Wichita.[53]

By January 1930, Fagerskog owned two Jennies, a Travel Air, and a displaced wildcat. He kept them all in his hangar on Auburn Boulevard. The wildcat was reported as, "...no respecter of persons," but the Jennies were in good condition after years of flying.[54] Fagerskog's purchase of his Travel Air, named the *Comet II*, was recorded in May 1930. He bought the OX-5 Travel Air 2000 from F. Muller of Hollywood.[55]

Soon after acquiring the *Comet II*, Ingvald flew two passengers to Reno from Del Paso in an hour and 15 minutes. Then he flew Dr. Gundrum to Redding. He made several trips there and back to Colusa with the doctor. Fagerskog reported having 12 flying students.[56]

Fagerskog's Travel Air *Comet II* succeeded his Jenny, the *Comet*. Both planes were painted all black or dark blue with many different sized bright yellow stars all over the fuselage. A similarly colored comet was painted just below the rear cockpit on the fuselage, and on the vertical stabilizer and rudder of the Jenny were the letters "rides," and below that the price "$2.50," all in the same bright yellow colors. This paint job was a little creepy and reminds one of Van Gogh's *The Starry Night*. It was not typical of colorful paint jobs seen on a few other barnstormer's Jennies. Most barnstormers didn't have the money to paint their planes fancy colors; they were left as the military had painted them.[57]

Fagerskog flew two passengers to Los Angeles August 1, 1930, in

Hoskin's Stearman. They left Del Paso at 6:30 AM and Ingvald Fagerskog returned that afternoon at 2:25.[58]

Eddie Schoenbackler, one of Fagerskog's students, passed his exam for a transport pilot license in November 1932.[59]

An interesting perspective of Ingvald Fagerskog was given by Marie Wilcox Hill. In 1927 Wilcox may have been the youngest female flyer in the state and, possibly, the country. She began taking flying lessons from Ingvald at age 14. She was in the eighth grade at Arcade School in North Sacramento. The story of her becoming a pilot began in 1925 when her parents decided to move out into "the country." They moved into a house near Ingvald's private airstrip on Auburn Boulevard. Across the street was Del Paso Airport, the location today (2017) of Haggin Oaks Golf Course. Not long after Hill and her family moved in near the airport, Fagerskog boarded with them.

Hill recalled Fagerskog asking her if she would like to learn to fly. He told her he would teach her for free. In later years, when she was "older and wiser," she decided Fagerskog gave her free lessons because teaching a girl in grade school, who was only five feet tall, had great publicity value to him. (In aviation there was a very sexist belief that if a woman could learn to fly men would believe it was easy and flock to the sport.)

Marie used a school composition book as her pilot's logbook, writing in pencil about her beginning lesson, "Thursday, Nov. 24, 1927, Thanksgiving Day. I had my first lesson at 9:15 in the morning instructed by Ingvald Fagerskog." Her logbook held the records of her 13 flying lessons each lasting a half hour. Learning to fly was thought to be quite an achievement for a young woman in those early days, but Marie didn't think so until she read the first articles written about her in local newspapers. She began to feel important and enjoyed her new fame. She became the envy of classmates at Arcade School.

To fly, Marie needed pillows to reach the rudder peddles with her feet. Fagerskog gave her lessons in a JN-4D. She remembered she had to "... fly with my head sticking out the side because I couldn't see over the top of the cockpit." Marie and Ingvald married a short time later, but the short-lived union ended in divorce. They had two children, James and Joyce. Marie gave up flying in 1932 because of her children. Of the experience she later said, "I wasn't all that enthusiastic about it really." She said her aerial exploits had all been Fagerskog's idea.

She thought it humorous she had a student license and could already do loops and spins, but Ingvald was, "... very protective of his property. He wouldn't let me fly alone." The only time she was alone with the plane's controls was at air shows when Fagerskog crawled out of the cockpit and walked on the wings, but he was always in the cockpit for takeoffs and landings.[60]

Marie claimed Fagerskog was the first to seed rice from an airplane in the Sacramento area, which may or may not be true. This author has been unable to discover any dates when Fagerskog began ag-flying. That he did seed rice is undeniable; Vince Vanderford, a prominent rice farmer near Yuba City, remembered Fagerskog aerial seeding his father's rice fields.[61]

Fagerskog operated a flying school 20 years on his own airfield across the street from Del Paso Park. Of his exploits, the two that brought him the most publicity were in the early twenties when he landed his plane on Del Paso Boulevard in North Sacramento dressed as Santa Claus. The other was when he flew photographs of Charles Lindbergh in Paris after the Atlantic flight in May 1927. Ingvald flew the photos from Denver to Sacramento for the local newspapers.

Fagerskog flew until almost the day he died at home in Carmichael, a suburb of Sacramento, in October 1955, where he lived with his wife Dorothy.[62]

Leo Moore

Leo Moore was a long time member of the Sacramento aviation community and a fixture at the municipal field in Del Paso Park. In July 1928, he was hired to fly night aerobatics above the Alhambra Boulevard district for Independence Day festivities. Between 8:30 and 9:00 PM Moore flew a routine with bright flares streaming from his plane. He also fired off rockets, which raced through the air and could be seen for miles around.[63] A few days later, Moore flew a new propeller to Colusa for a pilot who had damaged his on July the Fourth. Leo picked up a tailwind and made it from Del Paso to Colusa in 29 minutes in his Travel Air 2000, which had recently been christened *Miss Sacramento* by Miss Alberta Staff who broke an empty champagne bottle on the propeller hub.[64]

Moore held another christening of *Miss Sacramento* the next week. Mrs. Wilbur Clark of Reno rechristened the plane, again with a champagne bottle. Afterwards Leo flew his brother Dr. Glen Moore to visit a friend in Fairfield.[65]

Leo Moore made a hair-raising flight from Reno in July 1928. He took off from Blanch Field in a dense fog, which became thicker as he climbed over the Sierra Nevada en route to Sacramento. Flying blind near mountain peaks was not a healthy thing to do, and suddenly, looking down, he spotted an opening in the fog. He was about to dive through it when a large plane coming from the opposite direction punched up through the hole almost colliding with Moore's Travel Air. He banked hard to avoid hitting the interloper, momentarily losing his bearings, but he quickly identified Donner Lake as he passed over. He banked hard again to clear a mountainside and kept climbing. He flew into a blizzard at 10,000 feet and continued maneuvering until the he broke out of the storm clouds into clear blue sky.[66]

Alma Rubens, a popular movie actress, was being filmed in a scene for the movie *Showboat* at Sacramento during July 1928. She was on one of the sternwheeler riverboats that cruised the Sacramento River between the Capital City and the Bay Area. Miss Rubens being very air-minded for the '20s spent much of her time off camera at Del Paso Airport in the front seat of *Miss Sacramento*. Leo Moore took her on several flights around Northern California. She had fallen in love with flying and even thought about returning to Hollywood in Moore's plane when the shoot was over.[67]

Moore removed the OX-5 engine from his Travel Air in August for a complete overhaul. Andrews, Nicholson and Morris Co. very generously loaned him an OX-5 from their International F-17.[68] He flew an aerobatic exhibition at Marysville celebrating the opening of Cheim Airport on August 25, 1928, and flew in various contests that day.[69]

In early September, Moore took and passed his transport pilot license test. On the twenty-first he headed north from Del Paso in *Miss Sacramento* on a barnstorming tour anticipated to last several weeks. He wrote to friends at his home field in early October, "… the folks out in the 'sticks' of Oregon are going strong for airplane rides at three dollars a throw." He returned to Sacramento a week later with minor damage to a wing.[70] He made arrangements with the aeronautical program at Galt High School to fix the wing, overhaul the entire airplane, and paint it.[71] The students painted *Miss Sacramento*'s wings orange and her fuselage black. They finished by the end of October. To break in his newly refurbished plane, Leo and his brother Glen flew to Klamath Falls, Oregon, on the 30th to visit family and friends; he would make many flights there in the future.[72]

Moore flew at the dedication of Kaseberg Field in Roseville on November 8 winning the four-mile pylon race in 2 minutes and 13 seconds. When he returned to Del Paso that night, he wiped out his landing gear attempting to land. He said the accident was caused by defective material in the axle.

Two days later he departed for Klamath Falls in his repaired plane.[73] Leo barnstormed California, Washington, and Oregon sporadically from September through November 1928; then decided to settle down and start a flying school at Del Paso Airport.[74]

Moore demonstrated *Miss Sacramento* in late November for the Sacramento High School aeronautics class and their teacher Charles Lipps during their visit to Del Paso Airport. Moore explained aircraft construction, design techniques, and talked about aircraft engine care and repair. He put each student in the cockpit to show how the controls functioned. The field trip was arranged by W. H. Hockin, district manager of Richfield Oil.[75]

Moore spent most of the first week of December at Oroville giving those who attended the Orange and Olive Exposition a chance to view the area from above. Upon his return to Del Paso Airport he learned he had temporarily been put in charge of managing it until it was decided whether Del Paso would become the city's permanent municipal airport.[76] A local paper reported Moore was, "... mothering the field along in an effort to retain some semblance of airplane facilities."

On Sunday, December 16, many spectators came to Del Paso Airport to watch "Reckless Rosie" parachute from Moore's Travel Air.[77] After the rainy season and with the runway dry, crowds began gathering Sundays again to watch the flying. Those brave enough with a few extra dollars in their pockets would go up for a short hop. On March 3, 1929, a Sunday, Leo had a banner day hopping passengers. He carried 35 on short hops, and Ingvald Fagerskog got his share of the action hauling 27.

The week before, Moore borrowed a tractor with a scraper on it and leveled a good runway where he could hop passengers safely on a farmer's grain field near Placerville in the Sierra Nevada. All went well until the wind changed as it often did in the mountainous countryside. Leo had to scrape out another runway in a different direction. He paid the farmer more than his grain loss was worth to use the field.[78]

Moore replaced his OX-5 with a spare while his primary engine was overhauled once more. During this overhaul, he had his plane fitted with night flying equipment.[79]

It was almost April when the Galt High School aviation department hired Moore to be its ground school instructor. He assured everyone at Del Paso Airport he would still be spending Sundays hopping passengers in *Miss Sacramento* even though he moved his family to Galt, 22 miles south of Sacramento.[80] Moore purchased another OX-5 spare for his Travel Air in April. Several charter flights had been lost because his plane's engine was undergoing overhaul.[81]

In July, Moore returned with *Miss Sacramento* to Del Paso for the summer months while Galt High School was out for summer vacation. He planned to do commercial flying and instruction until classes began at Galt in the fall.[82] Moore acquired a Romair biplane with a Whirlwind J-5 engine and, once again, barnstormed the northwestern states returning to Sacramento in September 1929.

The 220hp. Wright engine, referred to by the aviation press as the Whirlwind by the mid to late 1920s, and by the 1930s and afterward it was simply called the J-5. Extremely dependable, it was a technological leap above the Curtiss OX-5 and the Liberty engines it replaced. *Janes All The World's Aircraft* of 1927 stated the exhaust valves were of the salt-cooled type, which "completely eliminates overheating." When it came on the market it was expensive, but it was every pilot's dream to have his plane powered by a Wright J-5. It was the single most important element in the success of the early long distance flights made by Lindbergh, Goebel, Byrd, and others.[83]

By January 1930, Moore was back at Del Paso Airport for the winter. Shocking press reports of a mismanagement scandal revealed the nationally renowned Galt High School and Junior College aeronautics program was financially devastated. The principal, William Rutherford, was fired and the aeronautics program was dismantled. By September Moore was out of his teaching job, but he had *Miss Sacramento*, which had been completely overhauled and newly fitted with blind flying gear. Again he went barnstorming through five states. After the New Year, he was back instructing and managing Del Paso Airport, which now had 12 aircraft based on the field.[84] Also about this time Moore contracted to make an aerial survey of Reno.[85]

Leo Moore was one of the oldest commercial pilots in Northern California with more cross-country flying time than most pilots in the business. He flew his J-5 Romair biplane out of Del Paso, and in February made two dangerous flights to Oakland in the fog without incident. He was teaching his brother to fly and had been making many flights throughout the north and central state, as well as regular flights to Klamath Falls.[86]

Moore was one of four aviators contracted to hop passengers for the weekend of the Frog Jump Celebration at Angels Camp in May. In addition to the traditional frog jumping contests, a dead stick landing contest was held at the local airstrip. Moore won a $50 first prize stopping only inches

Chapter 9

past the line. He had shut down his engine at 1,000 feet prior to landing. Jeff Warren, also from Del Paso, flew three passengers to Angels Camp for the frog jump in a Buhl Air Sedan cabin biplane.[87] A few weeks later, Moore flew to Napa Airport for an air show. He took first place there in the dead stick landing event.[88]

In August 1930, Leo Moore moved to the newly completed Sacramento Municipal Airport on Freeport Boulevard. Western Aircraft Distributors, a new company, hired him to fly for them.[89] Moore's job at the new airport did not last long; the Depression was hurting everyone. He decided somehow that Angels Camp looked better for him and his family, so they moved there. By January 1931 the economy was worsening, so he and his family moved back to Sacramento, and he, once again, was hopping passengers out of Del Paso Airport on Sundays.[90]

In January 1932, Moore began flying for Ryan Air Service at the new municipal airport. Ryan made plans for Moore to fly five passengers at a time in a Ryan Brougham over Lake Tahoe on sightseeing trips.[91] Carl Van Meter, a mechanic for Century-Pacific Air Lines, was soloed by Moore in late January. Van Meter only had his student license a week when he soloed after just three-and a-half hours of instruction. He set a record for the shortest flying time to solo.[92]

Snow was causing problems in the Sierra during February. Moore was hired to drop supplies to a snowbound work camp at Lake Bowman. The weather had been abysmal for a week keeping most planes on the ground at the new airport. A few pilots were able to get up for advanced flight instruction, but not many hours were flown. On a Sunday with bad flying weather, Moore got a call requesting a charter flight. A Japanese couple did not want to wait the three-day requirement to get married in California, so Leo flew them to Reno in the Ryan. He climbed to 16,000 feet before escaping the summit haze on his return flight.[93]

Moore had a busy day the third week of July 1932. He picked up J. G. Rohan at Sacramento Muni at 3:05 PM and flew him to Reno. He returned at 5:25 PM, refueled the plane, and took off for Mills Field at 6:20. He returned to Sacramento via Stockton at 7:35—a total of 425 air miles covered in 4.5 hours.[94]

Leo Moore, 85, went west on October 11, 1983. He had a heart attack working in his small sewing machine repair shop on Del Paso Boulevard in North Sacramento. His obituary reported he had opened the shop only two months before; he was an eternal optimist. The obituary said he began flying in the early 1920s by driving his horse and wagon into Bakersfield in 1923 and trading them for a Curtiss Jenny plus three flying lessons. He managed the old Sacramento municipal airport at Del Paso Park for a short time and was one of the first pilots in Sacramento to get his transport pilot license. He won numerous trophies for air racing and dead stick landing contests with his plane, *Miss Sacramento*, in the 1920s and '30s. While in Sacramento, he taught aeronautics at Galt High School and was an official pilot for the California Association for the Promotion of Aeronautics.

He moved to Alaska in the 1930s and did some bush flying. He said he was with Wiley Post and Will Rogers the night before their fatal crash in 1935. He remained in Alaska until 1941 when he moved back to the states and was commissioned a captain in the US Army Air Corps in 1942. He ferried Bell P-39s and other military aircraft from Great Falls, Montana, to Fairbanks, Alaska, where they were handed over to Russian pilots and flown into Russia under the Lend Lease Program that aided our allies in World War II.

After the war, Leo opened a sewing machine shop in Oak Park, Sacramento. He later returned to Alaska, briefly, and then settled for good in Sacramento. He flew *Sacramento Bee* photographer Bob Hundsecker on many aerial photography assignments well into the 1950s.[95]

Walter L. Lockhoof

Walter Lockhoof was born in Pennsylvania and came to Sacramento from Vancouver, B. C., and Washington state. He had worked as a barber on passenger ships in that area. He owned his barbershop in North Sacramento and in 1921 built the Nite Hawk Building. It was said to be the first two-story structure in North Sacramento. He also constructed what became North Sacramento's Grand Theater in 1925. He operated it first as an open-air movie theater during the summer months. He bought an Alexander Eaglerock biplane after learning to fly in 1928 and was thereafter referred to as "The Flying Barber."

Much has been mentioned already about Walter Lockhoof, especially his prominence in the city of North Sacramento and his aviation roots with Ingvald Fagerskog and the airports on Auburn Boulevard. Also covered was the founding of his own airport at the western end of Del Paso Boulevard near the American River. Lockhoof had ties to Del Paso Airport and stayed there after most of the permanent party moved to the new municipal airport when it opened in April 1930.

CHAPTER 9

After he soloed, Lockhoof flew his family to Los Banos in his Eaglerock to visit friends in September 1928. He bought a Russell Lobe parachute to use in air show work.[96] Lockhoof began venturing out from Sacramento in October on short barnstorming flights. In Marysville, he and Rose Cahill, his parachutist, carried out one of their most egregious stunts. Cahill parachuted over downtown Marysville; shocking the city's residents. She was arrested after getting snagged in a tall tree. Lockhoof landed at Cheim Field, the local airport, to pick her up and was also arrested. Rose became known in the Sacramento area as "Reckless Rosie" for her daring stunts.[97]

November 1928 was a disastrous month for Lockhoof. On the fourth, as mentioned earlier, he collided with Royal St. John's parked airplane while landing at Kaseberg Field during the Roseville airport's dedication air show. St. John made an attempt to grab Lockhoof's wingtip and spin the Eaglerock away from his plane. He failed and suffered some broken ribs for his efforts. The top right wing of St. John's Swallow biplane was destroyed, and Lockhoof's Eaglerock was damaged.[98]

One week after his wreck at the air show, Lockhoof had another accident that nearly killed him and his passengers. On Sunday, November 11, Lockhoof and two passengers were flying at 1,000 feet above Del Paso Airport. He pulled his just-repaired Eaglerock straight up into a vertical maneuver. At the peak of his climb, he threw the plane into a bank, according to G. T. Lundy, assistant manager of the airport. It went into a spin. When Lockhoof tried to recover from a normal nose down spin, it went flat on him. In Lockhoof's "flat spin," the nose came up towards the horizon and the airplane spun like a falling pinwheel, striking the ground in that same flat attitude. Most of the force from the crash was straight down on the bodies of the pilot and passengers, breaking the backs of Lockhoof and Melvin Thompson. A third passenger, Mr. Webber, suffered only minor injuries. Lockhoof's Eaglerock was destroyed.

The crash site was 200 yards north of the airport boundary between Arcade Creek and Del Paso Airport. Airport personnel and the usual Sunday visitors witnessed the crash and rushed over to pull the men out. Lockhoof and Webber were sent to Sutter Hospital and Thompson to Sacramento County Hospital. Everyone survived but a long recuperative time was necessary for Lockhoof and probably Thompson who was a logger.

G. T. Lundy told the press the accident was due to Lockhoof's overconfidence in his ability. Lundy claimed Lockhoof had less than 100 hours of solo time. Lockhoof had never gotten a government pilot's license nor had his plane been government certified as airworthy. Lundy said federal inspectors had on several occasions talked to Lockhoof attempting to get him licensed. Aviation regulations that went into effect in 1927 prohibited any pilot from stunt flying with passengers over airports or populated areas. With his accident at Roseville the week before, Lockhoof was definitely in hot water with the DOC Aeronautics Branch.

It should be noted that enforcement of the new federal aviation regulations began July 1, 1927, and it took quite a while to get all of the pilots flying in the United States licensed and their planes inspected. Lockhoof was either stuck in, or enjoying, the license limbo going on in the nation. Technically he was violating regulations for flying without a license in his unlicensed Eaglerock. He was in violation for accepting pay for hopping passengers, stunt flying, and dropping parachute jumpers without the proper license. He was in violation for stunting over Del Paso Airport and stunt flying with passengers without parachutes. He was in trouble with the DOC aviation branch for at least five violations[99]

Lockhoof was still recuperating at home in late January 1930. In March, over a year-and a-half after his crash, he made his first public outing. He attended a meeting of the aviation club at the Hotel Sacramento. Standing with a cane, he replied that he expected to be back flying soon.[100] There is some doubt that he ever flew after his devastating crash. It was reported he passed the physical exam for a transport pilot license and was going to fly the smallest plane in the valley. He said it had a wingspan of 24 feet by 14 feet long. It weighed 500 pounds, was powered by an Anzani motor, and was named the *Sunfish*. Whether he ever flew again is speculative.[101] Lockhoof died in December 1966 at age 77 in Sacramento.[102]

Jack Beilby

Jack Beilby and Ralph Canning formed a partnership in July 1928 after selling their two Jennies and jointly purchasing a new Alexander Eaglerock.[103] Shortly after the Eaglerock was delivered, Canning and Beilby learned why it is not wise to start an airplane in an enclosed hangar. They propped their new plane in their hangar at Eagle Rock Airport on Stockton Boulevard, not realizing the throttle was full forward. With a roar it lurched into the side of the hangar smashing a wing. Their partnership was off to an ominous start.[104]

Jack Beilby, a Sacramento businessman, soloed the Eaglerock in October under the instruction of his partner, Canning. The following month they made a flight in the Eaglerock from Eagle Rock Airport to Fresno in an hour and 35 minutes.[105] By the end of April 1929, Beilby and Canning were training their first flying student, A. E. Mautby.[106] Beilby flew the Eaglerock to San Francisco in early June on a business trip. A week later he advertised in the local newspaper that a flying club in Sacramento had a few memberships available to the "right men."[107]

Beilby flew to Stockton in late June where he passed the DOC tests administrated by DOC inspector William K. Andrews, Jr. for his transport pilot license. Three months later Beilby was hired as the Sacramento Valley sales manager for Travel Air dealer D. C. Warren of Oakland.[108] Warren wanted Jack Beilby to be based at the municipal airport in Del Paso Park, so Beilbly transferred operations in October from Eagle Rock Field. His sales territory was from Sacramento to the Oregon border, and he was given a Travel Air biplane to cover it.[109] In late fall Beilby delivered a Hisso Travel Air to Sacramento resident Roy Meisser.[110]

Jack Beilby and Leo Moore flew to Colusa for its airport opening May 31–June 1, 1930.[111] The following weekend Beilby flew a new Curtiss Robin to Napa for another air show. Curtiss-Wright, the growing airport chain conglomerate, purchased Travel Air and several other smaller aircraft companies and overnight D. C. Warren became a Curtiss-Wright distributor. After the air show at Napa, Beilby made a weeklong tour of the Sacramento Valley as the new Curtiss-Wright sales representative for the territory.[112]

Beilby and Canning kept their side business hopping passengers on quick sightseeing trips over Sacramento. In October they and another partner, Federolf (Federspiel?), sold their OX-5 Eaglerock to Hobday and Gold of Galt. Beilby then bought a Travel Air 2000 biplane from D. C. Warren, his employer. Beilby's friend, Roy Meisser, sold his Travel Air 3000 to Robert F. Weaver, manager of the Del Paso Airport.[113]

Forrest E. Bennett purchased a four-place, high-wing, cabin monoplane built by Mono Aircraft Inc. of Moline, Illinois, in late 1930. Beilby was hired to fly the plane, which was based at the new municipal airport. By February 1931, Beilby was giving local folks rides over their neighborhood homes three at a time. The aircraft model was the Monocoach. A Wright J-5 motor or a J-6 provided enough power for the Monocoach to perform well with a full load of passengers. Mono aircraft were usually painted an attractive black and orange color scheme at the factory. This same company built the popular and speedy "Monocoupe." The Monocoach was one of the best four-place, single-engine designs on the market; however, during the

Depression at $8,000 each less than two dozen were built.[114]

With improving weather in March, Beilby, piloting Bennett's Monocoach, was able to fly six hours from the new municipal airport. On April 10, Beilby flew three passengers to the Bay Area in the Monocoach.[115] Night flying equipment was installed on Bennett's Monocoach and Bob Laurin's Travel Air biplane in the late spring. Aircraft lights were powered by a small propeller driven generator. Beilby flew night hops over Sacramento and Buzz Slingsby did the same in Laurin's biplane.[116]

Jack Beilby, who learned to fly in 1927, joined Varney in June 1931 boosting his career to a new level. He started scheduled flights on a new route from Marysville to Fresno with stops in between. According to reports, he was the first Sacramento pilot to fly a scheduled airline flight out of Sacramento on June 22. (It seems that Andy Andrews, making such flights for Capital Air Lines in June 1928, had been forgotten by reporters.) Varney Airlines connected with an airliner from Century Pacific Airlines at Fresno twice a day.

Beilby was an aircraft salesman in addition to flying for Varney.[117] The Marysville route was eventually shut down for lack of customers, so Varney transferred Beilby to Los Angeles where he flew the popular Lockheed Orions for Varney Speed Lanes.[118]

Following his retirement from a long career of flying for airlines, "Smiling Jack" Beilby was a fixture at Grand Central Air Terminal in Glendale working as maintenance manager for Grand Central Aircraft Company. Jack Beilby passed on in November 1975.[119]

Arthur Franklin Mickel

Arthur Mickel was accumulating flying hours in August 1928 to meet the requirements for a transport pilot license and refurbishing his Eaglerock the *Yellow Canary* to get it licensed. He installed lights to make it legal for night use.[120] The Auburn Aero Club chose Mickel to be its chief pilot, however the government landing field at Auburn was not completed. Mickel stayed in Sacramento giving flying instruction.[121]

Mickel helped found a new business, Capital Flying Service, in September. Mickel was chief pilot, Harry Merchant was company manager, and Jack Casy business manager. Mickel acquired a black Travel Air with a 180hp. Hisso engine. The company provided flight instruction and air taxi service from Del Paso Airport. In October Paul Schreck was hired as company mechanic having just received his DOC mechanic's license a few days

CHAPTER 9

earlier. Capital Flying Service also became Sacramento's Travel Air dealer and acquired another Travel Air soon after.[122]

Mickel spent a lot time getting used to flying the Hisso Travel Air and honing his aerobatic skills until it seemed to those who rode with him he had mastered the plane. The new flying school signed up two students in September, Elliott Tabor and W. K. Cates.[123] Later, Capital Flying Service "invaded" Marysville. On a Sunday, Mickel flew an aerobatic exhibition, hauled "Reckless Rosalie" to 2,000 feet for her parachute jump, and then hopped 115 passengers.

"Reckless Rosalie" Evans was one of the few female parachutists based in Northern California.[124] The next Sunday Mickel flew to Colusa, repeated his performance, and took 80 passengers on short hops.[125]

Mickel signed on with Howard Hughes' Caddo Company in October 1928 to fly in Hughes' aviation epic, *Hell's Angels*. Filming began in 1927 in the Los Angeles area, but due to the introduction of sound in moviemaking and a lack of clouds in the Los Angeles area, Hughes still filmed flight scenes throughout 1928. He moved to Oakland Municipal Airport late in 1928 for the weather conditions and propensity of clouds in the Bay Area. Hughes hired a number of aviators from Northern California, not all of his Southern California pilots could come with him.

A. F. Mickel was the only pilot from Sacramento to fly in *Hell's Angels*. He flew to Oakland in November to start working and by November 7 had flown three dogfights portraying a German flying ace. Owning a Travel Air was an advantage getting the job. The Travel Air, with its distinctive tail section and "elephant ear" wingtips, was very similar in appearance to the German Fokker D. VII fighter of the Great War. Another contributing factor to getting hired was Mickel's aerobatic experience. Mickel gained considerable dog fighting experience flying with other north state pilots such as Bert Heringer, a Bay Area tri-motor pilot, and "Wee Willie" Willingham of Oakland, who were also flying in the film.

It took several storms at Oakland to provide Hughes the puffball cumulus clouds he wanted as a backdrop for scenes. Clouds gave the audience a sense of the plane's speed that is lost filming in clear skies. Hughes' Caddo Company finished the movie's Oakland shoot the first week of January 1929, but Mickel didn't return to Sacramento until February 24.[126]

Mickel left the Sacramento area a month later to fly for Calahan Flying Service at Visalia. It was only a temporary job, and he was back in Sacramento shortly.[127] Percival Perkins hired Mickel to fly his Alexander

Eaglerock out of Placerville Airport in June.[128]

The Yuba-Sutter Flying Club at Marysville's Cheim Field hired Mickel as flying instructor for a while, but by February 1930 he returned to Del Paso flying Homer Coffing's Travel Air. Mickel remained active at Del Paso a few more years.[129]

It was said that A. F. Mickel made an early airmail flight into Reno, but the claim is unsubstantiated. His main occupation was the wholesale produce business from 1946 until 1984. For excitement, he drove hardtop auto racers in the 1950s and early '60s. He was known as the oldest hardtop race driver in America. About flying, he once said in the 1970s that, "My bag was stunt flying." He loved the excitement of doing aerobatics in his Travel Air. Mickel, always the adrenalin junkie, made his first parachute jump at the age of 75. He went west in August 1989 at age 88.

Ken Blaney

Ken Blaney took his first airplane ride in 1920 at age 15. A group of ex-army aviators were barnstorming through Sacramento and Ken got to ride in a Jenny. He became enamored with flying and was determined it would be his life's work. Jack Irwin, a friend of Blaney's, gave him some lessons in a Standard J-1 in 1925. Before he soloed, the Standard was involved in an accident. Blaney bought the wreck from Irwin for $300 to rebuild it.

It took a year-and-a-half, but he was able to restore the plane to flying condition in his parents' garage. Ken's mother sewed the fabric covering for the wings with her pedal-powered sewing machine. Once it was ready to fly, Blaney hired H. G. Andrews for additional dual instruction so Blaney could solo on December 21, 1927.[130]

In August 1928 Blaney began rebuilding a Curtiss Jenny. It would have special wings similar to his Standard. The rebuild took a little longer than expected, but he was in the air by November. Blaney brought the Jenny to Del Paso Airport in January for a new paint job.[131]

Blaney and a friend, Kermit Parker, were featured in newspaper reports that they were the only students in America commuting to school in an airplane. Both were enrolled in Galt Junior College of Aeronautics. They flew the Jenny on school days from Sacramento and landed at the Galt school airport 15 minutes later. They attended aviation school at Galt, never missing a day due to bad weather and never having a forced landing. (With the fog that develops in that area in December and January, their claim was quite an accomplishment.) Both were pilots and cadet corps corporals at

CHAPTER 9   195

the school.¹³²

Blaney learned navigation, meteorology, and aircraft and engine maintenance to qualify for both DOC pilot and mechanic licenses while in the Galt aeronautics program. On weekends Blaney worked as a brakeman on the Sacramento Northern Railroad run between Sacramento and Chico to pay for his aeronautical education.

When Blaney had 100 hours of flying time, he obtained DOC private pilot license No. 5416. He had the minimum flying time of 200 hours for his transport pilot license by June 1929.

H. G. Andrews, who was flying tri-motor Ford transports for Maddux Airlines out of Glendale, sent Blaney a telegram in August 1929 informing him Maddux would soon be hiring a number of copilots who had to be both pilot and mechanic qualified. Maddux hired Blaney as a "mate" to help with the maintenance of one Ford airliner registered NC9641.

Blaney's first flight as a Maddux copilot/mechanic was from Glendale to San Diego and on to Agua Caliente with pilot Milo Campbell. On takeoff Blaney put his hands on the control wheel to "follow through" Campbell's control movements during the departure. Campbell slapped his hands hard and Blaney learned that one never touched the plane's controls without the pilot's permission. Maddux Airlines merged with Transcontinental Air Transport (TAT) in late 1929. At the time, Blaney was copilot on the Glendale to Clovis, New Mexico, leg of the transcontinental run. The pilot laid over at Winslow, Arizona, for the return trip, but the copilot joined the new captain and went all the way to Clovis. It was a long day for Blaney.

Blaney was made a reserve captain after a check ride in June 1930. Based at Waynoka, Oklahoma, he had 400 hours solo and 1,000 hours as copilot. He didn't fly much as a reserve captain. In a good month, he only got about 40 hours.

When the TAT, Maddux, and Western merge took place, Blaney was moved back to copilot. Transcontinental and Western Airlines began flying the entire distance across America, no longer transferring passengers to rail service at night. The airline began using the single-engine Northrop Alpha in March 1931 to carry mail across the United States. Blaney's boss, Jack Frye, insisted Alpha pilots have at least 1,000 hours of solo time. Blaney was out of luck; he had only 600 hours, 200 as a Ford captain. It didn't matter that he had over 1,000 hours as a copilot.

Blaney wanted his captain's position back and fly the Alphas. The only way he could was wait until he accrued the additional hours with the airline or buy an airplane and get the hours on his own. In June 1931 as the Depression worsened, Blaney purchased a two seat Monocoupe. During his two-week vacation, he flew out to Stockton and returned by the southern route through Barstow, Tucson, and El Paso. He gave ten dollar airplane rides at several stops along the way all the while building his flying hours. When his vacation ended he showed Jack Frye his gas receipts to substantiate an additional 160 hours of new solo time to his logbook. Frye was impressed and cleared Blaney to fly the single-engine Northrop Alpha. Blaney then alternated between copiloting Fords and piloting Alphas. He also served as a night airmail dispatcher and mail clerk.

In April 1932, Blaney took his next vacation and flew his Monocoupe west once more. Included was a trip to Las Vegas where he married his fiancee Dorothy. He saved his receipts again for Jack Frye and boosted his solo time to 1,200 hours. He was based at Saint Louis flying as reserve pilot on east and west runs and continued working as night mail dispatcher. He kept his Monocoupe in the TWA hangar at Saint Louis.

One day in June 1932, Blaney found a red tag on his Monocoupe. A steel fitting on the landing struts at the fuselage was bent, and a DOC inspector grounded the airplane until it was fixed. Blaney hoisted the airplane with a ¾-inch cotton rope draped over a tree limb and removed the landing gear. While he working under the airplane the rope broke, and a welded steel tube in the fuselage came across his back pinning his chest to the floor between his legs; he had been in a sitting position under the airplane. Two boys heard his cries for help and lifted the 800-pound plane high enough for him to crawl out. An ambulance rushed Blaney to the hospital.

At first doctors expected Blaney to live only a few weeks; his back was broken. He spent two months in the Saint Louis hospital in a full body cast and nine more after it was removed. His pregnant wife and his mother moved to a house near the hospital. In January 1933, Blaney's son Bruce was born in the same hospital. In May, Blaney was discharged from the hospital in a wheelchair; his flying days were over.

Blaney became a dedicated ham radio operator and developed as an outstanding radio repairman opening a repair shop in Sacramento. For over 30 years, he drove a specially equipped car with all hand controls. In the 1980s, Blaney said his medical costs through the years were huge, but thanks to Jack Frye, who argued his case at the time of the accident, he was eligible for Workmen's Compensation. As one historian wrote, Blaney's life was one of courage and determination. He passed on September 19, 1989.[133]

A. B. Willett

Al Willett acquired the Monocoupe agency for the Sacramento region in October 1928. He was also employed with the California Highway Department (now Caltrans) and became a respected aviator in the Sacramento area.[134] Willett bought his own Monocoupe, which was a two-place, high-wing monoplane powered by a Velie engine that consumed barely four gallons of gas per hour. He took delivery at Mills Field, San Bruno, and flew it to Sacramento in just over an hour. He planned to use the plane for air taxi work and flight instruction on weekends.[135] Willett's sales territory included Sacramento, Placer, and Yolo counties.

Willett started flying during the Great War as an Air Service cadet in 1917. He took primary flying training at Rich Field, Waco, Texas, then went to Ellington Field at Houston for advanced training. He returned to Rich Field as an instructor pilot after being commissioned a lieutenant. After the war ended, Willett bought a Jenny, which he flew several years. He served the bridge department of the state highway commission at Sacramento for nearly eight years, and enjoyed a lot of recreational flying.[136] In December 1928, Willett's Del Paso Airport hangar was completed, he moved in and established his Monocoupe agency. The following six weeks were wetter than usual and the airport too muddy for Willett to fly. By the last week of February, it dried enough for Willett to get around the north state demonstrating his new Monocoupe for potential customers.[137]

Al Willett passed his examinations for a transport pilot license with DOC inspector William Andrews in September 1929. This author has been unable to determine whether Willett was successful in airplane sales in the looming atmosphere of the Great Depression, and has found little else about his life.[138]

Fig. 45. At Sacramento Municipal Airport on Freeport Boulevard, a Cessna C-34 of the Brown Flying Service taxis for departure circa 1936. This Cessna was the forerunner of the thousands of general aviation Cessna high-wing light aircraft built following World War II.

Fig. 46. Del Paso Airport was Sacramento's municipal airport from 1919 until 1930. It was located on Auburn Boulevard near the dead end of Fulton Ave. Today the airport grounds are part of Haggin Oaks Golf Course. This photo was taken during the Sacramento Aircraft Show May 25-27, 1928. Notice Ingvald Fagerskog's runway in the top right quadrant of the photo running diagonally out of the picture.

CHAPTER 10

A new municipal airport on Freeport Boulevard – Airwar over the Sacramento Valley – A grand airport dedication – New flying businesses on a new airport – Aircraft movements at the new airport – Sacramento flying activities for 1931 through 1933

The Sacramento Airport Commission reported in October 1928 it would make an immediate survey of all available airport sites around the city in an effort to finally decide where to locate a new municipal airport. Only sites large enough to accommodate the multi-engine transports like those being built by Fokker, Ford, Stinson, and Boeing would be considered.

Airport commissioners making the decision were C. E. Wilkins, chairman; R. U. St. John, vice chairman; Jens Petersen, W. B. Jenkins, William Robbins, Lou Brayton, E. W. Vandercook, and J. A. Molter.[1]

The commissioners surveyed eighteen sites over nine months. Four were favored most: Del Paso Airport; Upper Stockton Road near the location of Eagle Rock Airport; Freeport Boulevard across from the old Irwin Airport; and one in West Sacramento.[2]

The Sacramento City Council in July 1929 unanimously approved the commission's final recommendation for the new municipal airport at a 232-acre site on the Sugget property next to Freeport Boulevard, south of the city. The city took an option to buy the site for $80,000 in ten equal payments.

Boeing Air Transport brought O. C. Richerson, its western division superintendent, to inspect the site and he found it outstanding. Boeing was anxious to land its planes closer to the city center than Mather Field to stimulate passenger interest and possibly erect a hangar on the new airport if the city would reimburse the company when public funds became available.

Sacramento was already the northern terminus for a Western Coast Air Lines Travel Air cabin plane flown by Jerry Andrews six days a week the length of the Great Central Valley landing at Fresno, Modesto, Stockton, and Sacramento. The company's headquarters were at Fresno where its passengers connected with Maddux Airlines to proceed south to Los Angeles.[3] After work started on the new airport site, prominent citizens of the Capital City were flown over it in Standard Oil Company's tri-motor Ford.[4] J. W. McCrillis in a Monocoupe was one of the first pilots to land on the site at Twenty-First Street Road, later renamed Freeport Boulevard. McCrillis, a pilot for West American Air Schools, had flown in from Oakland Municipal Airport. He was photographed in a discussion with airport commissioner E. V. Vandercook, possibly explaining why he landed in the middle of a construction project.[5] Chairman Wilkins reported in January 1930 the commission would spend money left over from the airport appropriation to improve runway drainage. The airport could not officially open until this was completed. However, he said, a large cabin plane had made a recent landing.

An 80 by 60-foot hangar was finished on the site and fifteen 600-watt lights were erected for night work. It rained the first week of January, but the main runway dried rapidly; it was 2,000 by 250 feet.[6] W. E. Garey flew onto the new site in a Union Oil Company aircraft February 8. A Travel Air piloted by L. Bishop from Valley Flying Service of Fresno flew in. Al Pilgrim landed a Waco there, also in February.[7]

An access road was built leading to the hangar area from Freeport Boulevard. The latest in fueling pits was installed by Standard Oil Company. The airfield was ready to land aircraft by mid-February and would be fully operational in a short time. After beacons were installed, Boeing Air Transport began flying airmail to and from the new airport.

Roland Federspiel, who learned to fly at Del Paso Airport with H. G. Andrews, moved his Swallow to the new airport in February.[8] Late February and early March 1930 brought heavy rains to the area, but work wasn't halted on the airport. Flying was impossible, but work continued on the drainage system. The city council made a supreme effort to maintain funding for completion.[9]

THE FIRST PROVISIONAL Wing of the US Army Air Corps, commanded by Brig. General William E. Gilmore, assembled at Mather Field east of

Fig. 47. An open house was held on April 3, 1930, at Mather Field to mark the beginning of the Army Air Corps' 1930 Air Maneuvers. Dubbed a mimic air war by the newspapers, flying operations out of Mather took place over much of Northern California. At the open house, this author's great grandfather, George W. Herr, one of Sacramento's few surviving Civil War veterans, was a guest of honor.

Sacramento for the Air Corps' annual air maneuvers in April 1930. Approximately a quarter of America's Army Air Corps aircraft flew to the airfield. Newspapers called the maneuvers "mimic warfare." For the first two-and-a-half weeks of April, aerial warfare between the Blue and Red Forces was fought in the skies of Northern California. On the night of April 17, the Red Forces who were attacking Sacramento Valley towns flew to the Bay Area and attacked San Jose. All of their targets were defended by pursuit planes of the Blue Forces.[10]

San Francisco was "bombed" next and then Modesto. On April 21, Red aircraft attacked targets as far south as Oakdale and as far north as Marysville. Blue defenders engaged the attackers. Sailboats from the San Francisco Yacht Club represented a massive Red fleet of warships. They were theoretically destroyed just beyond the Golden Gate as they approached San Francisco Bay by an aerial armada of Blue Force bombers and pursuit planes.[11]

The First Provisional Wing departed Mather Field on April 25 for Fresno, then went to March Field at Riverside to continue the war games over California. Only the 91st Observation Squadron from Crissy Field remained at Mather. On May 1, the official end of the Air Corps maneuvers, the 91st Squadron returned to San Francisco.[12] Over 160 army warplanes came to Northern California for the "mimic warfare" of April 1930. The largest aerial formations since the Great War were seen over the Great Central Valley. Not until World War II would such a massive aerial spectacle be seen again. During their time in the valley, Army Air Corps aviators took part in air shows at airports between war games.

THE OFFICIAL OPENING and dedication of the new Sacramento Municipal Airport (Sac Muni) was April 12–13, 1930. It was referred to as Sutterville Aerodrome while it was being built, but never after it opened. It was Sacramento Municipal Airport. The opening coincided with the Army Air Corps' air maneuvers, thus a large number of aircraft were involved. Aerial exhibitions and flying contests were held with military and civilian planes participating, but the army competed against civilians in only a few contests. Prizes were awarded by local National Aeronautics Association members who judged the contests.

Over 60,000 area residents attended the opening. The dedication ceremony started early on the 12th as three tri-motor transports landed. Politicians and the entire Sacramento Airport Commission emerged from the transports—and the show began.

At the opening dedication ceremony, General Gilmore, commander of the army's aerial war games, commended the city for developing the new airport and choosing a location and design that could easily be expanded in the future. E. E. Mouton, chief DOC Aeronautics Branch inspector for the area, in his short speech agreed with the general's sentiments.

At noon on Saturday, the Army Air Corps kicked off the air show with more than 100 aircraft taking part in formation flights, simulated bombing attacks, strafing runs, laying smoke screens, dog fights, and aerobatic exhibitions. Lieutenant Roland Birnn, the Air Corps' announcer, described in detail the maneuvers being executed and how they were used in wartime. One demonstration that particularly thrilled spectators was three squadrons of pursuit planes repeatedly attacking a large force of bombers all flying below 100 feet. The bombers made three separate bombing runs over the airport. All attacks were carried out with the precision of a drill team. Lieutenants Woodring and Hopkins from Rockwell Field flew a half-hour demonstration of dogfighting and aerobatics.

Chapter 10

After demonstrating their military flying prowess, two air races were held for army fliers in the late afternoon. The first, a race for pursuit (fighter) planes, was won by Lt. P. E. Shanahan in a Boeing P-12 from the First Pursuit Squadron of Selfridge Field, Michigan. Lieutenant E. D. Graves of the 95th Pursuit Squadron at Rockwell Field, San Diego, took second place and Lt. A. R. Maxwell from the same base was third. Later in the day, Capt. Frank Hackett of the 2nd Bombardment Squadron from Langley Field, Virginia, won the bomber race with Lt. E. M. Day of the same squadron taking second. Lieutenant W. C. Kingsbury of the 14th Bombardment Squadron at Rockwell Field finished third.

It is interesting to note the dominance of Curtiss aircraft in the Army Air Corps. For the 1930 air maneuvers at least half of the aircraft involved were built by the Curtiss company. Those Curtiss aircraft were the: Curtiss P-1C pursuit plane, Curtiss 0-1E observation plane, Curtiss A-3B attack plane, and the Curtiss B-2 Condor bomber. Other Air Corps aircraft used were the Boeing P-12 pursuit plane and the Keystone (a Curtiss subsidiary by then) LB-6&7s.

The Sunday air show turned from military flying to civilian flying and to the more commercial aspects of the opening. Civilian airplanes competed in the dead stick landing contest; a race to 4,000 feet; an OX-5 race; Whirlwind engine race, and a free-for-all race. Winners received cash prizes. Harry Abbott of Berkeley won the dead stick landing contest in a Travel Air, and Les Oranges from Stockton, in a Fleet, was second. Ingvald Fagerskog was third in his Travel Air. John Penfield from Stockton won the OX-5 race in a Curtiss Robin with D. C. Warren of Oakland in a Travel Air taking second and Leo Moore third. W. H. DeVries from Visalia won the race for 100hp. aircraft in an Eaglerock. Ray Moore in a Pitcairn won the Whirlwind race. Leo Nomis from Los Angeles was second in a Travel Air and D. C. Warren took third in a Travel Air.

Bad weather had halted morning flights, but the weather improved and the full slate of civilian events were successfully held. One critic judged Sunday just an average air show with a lot of civilian planes flying and not nearly as interesting as the army's performance. There were long periods of dead time while commercial pilots hopped passengers, and the air races were cut short due to rain. Lieutenant Harold Bundy of the 95th Pursuit Squadron, in a Boeing P-12, won the altitude race (time to climb). Denny Wright of Oakland came in second in a Waco and D. C. Warren took third in a Travel Air. Lieutenant Bundy provided an unexpected thrill for the crowd when he dove for the finish line at over 200 mph. He pulled up too slowly from his dive and struck the ground shearing off his landing gear. He managed to stagger back into the air and continue flying. He circled a nearby field and crash landed with no landing gear. His plane skidded on its belly and eventually flipped over. Bundy walked away with only a broken bone in his hand. His mother saw the crash. Bundy, from San Jose, had been a football star at Santa Clara College.

Bundy's crash was the second of the day. A Hollywood movie pilot, Leo Nomis, was landing a Warner Brothers' Travel Air when his wheels hit a soft spot in the runway; the plane went up on its nose, damaging the prop. Nomis replaced the propeller and took second in the race for Whirlwind (810 cu. in.) powered planes; the final event of the two-day celebration.[13]

PILOT'S LICENSES WERE approved for Forrest Earle Bennett and William A. Swain by DOC inspector William Andrews in April 1930. West

Fig. 48. The new Sacramento Municipal Airport (today's Sacramento Executive Airport) was opened on April 12-13, 1930 at the same time the Army Air Corps' 1930 Air Maneuvers were taking place from Mather Field – 12 miles to the east of Sacramento. This photo shows the last day of the opening celebration. Freeport Boulevard runs diagonally across the lower left portion of the photo. The new airport is on the east side of the boulevard. Where all the cars are parked on the west side of the boulevard was the location in 1926 of Irwin Airport.

America Air Schools employed both men at the new municipal airport. Bennett was field manager and Swain was head mechanic. Al Harris, chief pilot for West America, was their instructor.[14]

R. U. St. John, a Sacramento engineer and pilot, replaced Lynn Schloss, engineer in charge of construction at a new Bay Area airport—said to be a million dollar project. St. John had been construction manager for the Standard Oil Company at Sacramento. He supervised a 440- by 120-foot hangar at Alameda's new San Francisco Bay Airdrome. The fireproof building was scheduled for completion in May.[15]

Hilton F. Lusk was hired in April by Boeing School of Aeronautics to head the company's ground school training program at Oakland Airport. He had been teaching aeronautics at the College of the Pacific in Stockton the past two years. He took part in organizing aeronautical courses at the college (now known as University of the Pacific). Lusk would spend a year with Boeing, then move to Sacramento Junior (now City) College to lead their aeronautical department.[16]

The following entries denote aircraft movements taking place at Sacramento during the third week of May 1930: Charles Cooley flew his boss, Franklin W. Wakefield of San Francisco, into Sacramento Municipal Airport in a J-5 Eaglerock. They were en route to Rocklin. Lieutenants Wallen and Caroll flew into the municipal airport in a California Army National Guard plane to attend to state business. Two US Navy Boeings and a Boeing airmail plane also landed during the week.

The most active flight school during the first two months of Sacramento Municipal Airport was West America Air Schools, Ltd. Its advanced flying students were: B. D. Lock, Jeff Diff, Dale Hunter, George Haney, Ross Martin, Ed Helm, and Jack Ross.

Flying into the new airport in mid-May were Dewey Ashford and Bill Brander of the Yuba-Sutter Flying Club from Marysville. They came for their license tests with DOC inspector William K. Andrews. Members of a local glider club led by M. E. Coulter met at a spot in the foothills east of Sacramento to fly the club's glider.[17] The next week DOC inspector Bill Andrews visited the airport to give license tests. H. L. Blunt landed in a Fairchild monoplane demonstrator. He was on a sales tour around the state for the company. Ray Crawford landed with two passengers in a Travel Air cabin plane belonging to Overland Airways of San Francisco. They spent the night in Sacramento and returned the next day.

That same week Jack Frye, former president of the Aero Corporation of

Fig. 49. An Air Ferries Loening Air Yacht C2C amphibian biplane lands on the Sacramento River in 1930 near what today is called Old Sacramento.

California and Standard Airlines, flew up from Los Angeles with his wife aboard a Loening amphibian. Air Ferries Inc., of San Francisco, owned the plane and managing partners Sam Metzger and J. Tynan ordered the flight. Frye and his wife were guests of Air Ferries and part of a plan to start an air service to Sacramento from the Bay Area. The amphibian landed in the Sacramento River then took off and landed at the new airport.

E. W. Whiting, flying an experimental aircraft, landed at the municipal airport and stayed several hours. Two young men who worked for Douglas Aircraft Company built Whiting's airplane. Whiting had flown to Seattle on business and was returning home in Burbank.[18] Al Harris from Oakland Airport became the new chief instructor for West America Air Schools at Sacramento Municipal Airport.[19]

Sacramento residents were asked to vote yes on a bond issue in the June 1930 election to take advantage of the "great growth of aviation." It was explained that voting for the bond issuance would not raise taxes, it would be to raise the city's annual airport revenue from nearly $10,000 to a little over $30,000 per year. Passing the bond issue would add five more large hangars and various other buildings to the single large hangar on the airport.[20] The voters rejected it. Effects of the stock market crash and ensuing panic had, by June 1930, demoralized the public to such an extent that voting to approve funds for any community project was out of the question.

Due to great flying weather in June the following flights were made at Sacramento's airport: Harvey Lemcke, pilot of the spectacular night crash of the Lockheed Vega at Del Paso Airport in 1928, had been hired by Fuller Paint Company to fly the company's plane. He made short flights for five days to prepare for his duties.[21] Ken Kleaver of Weed landed his Hisso Eaglerock. He was on his way to Quincy for an air show.[22] Peter Rinehart and Gilbert Anderson left Sacramento for Los Angeles to search for a suitable training plane for their new business at Sacramento Municipal Airport. They were associated with the Clover Flying Service. An Air Ferries' Loening from San Francisco landed at Sacramento Municipal Airport, once again. Bill Andrews, DOC aviation inspector, was at the airport giving exams to pilots and students for their licenses and license upgrades.[23]

Bob West, a Hollywood stuntman, was planning two parachute jumps at an air show featuring his parachuting and was to be joined by George N. Mitchell in a double wing-walking stunt. Mitchell, an experienced parachutist and wing-walker, had a reputation as an aerial stuntman going back to 1925 when he did stunts with Jimmie Angel at local air shows.

Jack Elliott of Elliott & Duck Flying Service at Oakland Municipal Airport flew a group of baseball fans to Sacramento from the Bay Area for a night game and returned to Oakland after the game. Jeff Warren, of Clover Flying Service at the Sacramento Municipal Airport, made a number of charter flights carrying passengers on business trips around the Great Central Valley and to Oakland. Pete Rinehart returned from Los Angeles in a Swallow he acquired for the Clover Flying Service. The plane would be added to the company's stable of aircraft used for primary instruction. George N. Mitchell was head of instruction for Clover. He was a licensed ground instructor and taught aerodynamics at Western College of Aeronautics in Los Angeles for a year.[24]

Jack Elliott flew another planeload of passengers to Sacramento from Oakland and returned with them. Sergeants Smith and Bobuliski from the army airfield at Galveston, Texas, landed at Sac Muni. They were touring the country testing a new type of radio.[25]

Flying activities for July 1930 in the Sacramento area were as follows: George N. Mitchell of Clover Flying Service, the only mixed aviation training school in Sacramento, was recruiting students. Mitchell was formerly field manager for Summit Aircraft Company at Mills Field. Mitchell had been active in all branches of aviation since 1921. He claimed graduating 234 students from ground school when he worked for Western College of Aeronautics. He was the holder of mechanic's license No. 78 out of 8,000 issued at the time, and said he had an instructor's license No.170.

Paul San Martino flew a Travel Air from Marysville to Sac Muni where he picked up a passenger and flew him to Mills Field. Jeff Warren of Clover Flying Service flew its cabin biplane, a Buhl Air Sedan, to Yuba City and back to Sacramento on business. Another Clover pilot, Pete Rinehart, flew Mr. and Mrs. Terrell to Chico and back in their own plane, the Buhl Airsedan named the *Angeleno*.[26]

Henry T. Hurley, an Oakland flying school operator, filed suit against the city of Sacramento seeking $7,075 damages for an airplane crash at the municipal airport on May 14. Jack Jordan, the surviving pilot, claimed the airport lights were turned off before he cleared the field during a night takeoff causing him to hit two service stations. Results of the suit are unknown.[27]

Pete Rinehart flew the Terrells and their guests to Los Angeles over the Fourth of July in the *Angeleno*. George Mitchell quit working for Clover Flying Service and began operating a Swallow trainer on his own. Jeff Warren continued flying the Buhl Airsedan for Clover Flying Service. He made several charter flights to the Bay Area in early July.[28]

Jean Harlow, one of Hollywood's most famous stars of the period, flew into Sacramento en route to Seattle where she was appearing for the premiere of Howard Hughes' movie *Hell's Angels*. She was the film's female lead. J. B. Alexander, who reportedly was in charge of most flying for the film, landed the Fairchild monoplane at Sacramento for fuel.

A Washington-Alaska Airways Lockheed Vega flown by a Mr. Phillips landed at Sac Muni with two passengers. They were en route to Alaska from Burbank. Lieutenant Walker from Selfridge Field arrived at Sacramento in a Curtiss Falcon on a flight from Los Angeles to Seattle. His ultimate destination was Selfridge Field.[29]

The Boeing Air Transport Company's hangar construction was delayed over a legal issue about who owned the land under it. The problem was solved when a new contract for the land purchase of Sacramento Municipal Airport was quickly drawn up by Sacramento City Manager Dean's office and submitted to Dr. A. H. Suggett of San Francisco, the original land owner. It was found that in the old contract a portion of the field slated for immediate improvement would not actually become a possession of the city for several more years under the parcel purchase contract originally entered into by the city with Dr. Suggett.[30]

Some of the notable flights at the municipal airport in August were: J. B. Alexander of Hollywood who once again flew into the airport in a cabin Fairchild with his wife and M. Hall en route to Seattle. Vance Breese landed a Lockheed Air Express belonging to Detroit Aircraft Corporation for fuel. He was flying a passenger from Burbank to Portland.[31] Ralph Canning was racking up more hours in the Sacramento Flying Club's Travel Air with other members of the club doing the same. Jack Beilby made a flight to Fresno.[32]

Hilton Lusk, ground school director at Boeing School of Aeronautics at Oakland Airport, resigned and was appointed head of the aeronautics department at Sacramento Junior College. Allan Bonnallie replaced Lusk at the Boeing School.[33]

Roland B. "Pete" Rinehart, who flew the Terrells' *Angeleno* commercially from Sacramento Municipal Airport all summer in 1930 had, in July 1929, flown huge circles over Grand Central Air Terminal at Glendale in an attempt to set a new endurance record. He and his partner Loren W. Mendell were hoping to stay up for 1,000 hours. They didn't make it, but they did set a new record of 246 hours and 43 minutes in the *Angeleno*.[34]

The following were notable flights made at Sacramento Municipal Airport during the fall of 1930: R. U. St. John took time off from his duties as manger of the San Francisco Bay Airdrome at Alameda to fly his Eaglerock to Sacramento the last week of September. Jerry Andrews landed at Sac Muni in a Fleet biplane the same week. He was flying home to Oakland after participating in an air show at Marysville's Cheim Field.

The Standard Oil tri-motor Ford landed at Sacramento on its way to San Francisco after partaking in the Marysville show. George Pope, another participant at Marysville, stopped off on his way to Fresno.[35] Roscoe Turner and the Gilmore Oil mascot, Leo the Lion, landed at the municipal field in his record-setting Lockheed Vega on October 21. They were going to points north from Los Angeles.[36]

Organized air tours began in the mid-1920s to stimulate community interest in flying and creation of airports throughout California. Air tours by large caravans of aircraft brought a burst of business to communities with recently developed airports.

The second California Air Tour began October 29, 1930. It included 35 airplanes from airports around the state flown by notable aviators. The tour assembled at United Airport in Los Angeles where pilots started a five-day tour to 23 airports around the state and ended November 2 at the Los Angeles Municipal Airport. This, the most successful, tour visited Santa Paula, Santa Maria, Salinas, San Francisco, Oakland, Santa Rosa, Red Bluff, Marysville, Sacramento, Stockton, Modesto, Merced, Fresno, Strathmore, Visalia, Bakersfield, Lancaster, Indio, Yuma, El Centro, and San Diego.[37]

Mrs. West, wife of "Wild Bob" West, parachuted over Sacramento from 3,000 feet in November. She and her husband barnstormed the northwest states during the summer and fall. They were in Sacramento several weeks then returned home to Hollywood so Mr. West could resume working as a stuntman for movies.[38] Mrs. West said if the weather is good she would make a double parachute jump the next week at Sacramento Muni. She would open two chutes and ride them both down.

Jeff Warren quit flying for Clover Flying Service at Sac Muni to join a pilot named Slager moving to Los Angeles for the rest of the year. Slager had operated a Travel Air out of Sacramento Municipal for several months. He said weather was better at LA in the winter and there would be more flying work.[39]

As previously mentioned, construction of the Boeing hangar had been put on hold. The existing hangar and buildings on the new airport were slated to be moved to satisfy a newly revised purchase agreement for the airport land. With no hangar at the new airport yet, Boeing Air Transport (BAT) continued operating from its original Sacramento mail stop at Mather Field. It was allowed to operate from the government airfield because it was the sole Western carrier of transcontinental airmail service for federal government mail.

A bizarre incident at Mather Field involving a BAT airliner happened December 1, 1930. The large tri-motor Boeing Model 80A biplane, flown by Harry Huking, landed on its first stop after leaving Oakland Airport, its western terminus. As soon as the transport rolled to a stop, night mechanic Ralph B. Meyers began loading mail while Huking kept the engines running. Thinking the mail transfer was completed, Huking began his take off for Reno, unaware Meyers was still on the wing. Meyers was too shocked to jump off as the Boeing started moving. He stood with one foot in the foothold of the lower wing and one hand gripping the handle on the mail compartment door. He thought his best option was hanging on with all his might.

In seconds Huking was off and climbing on his way over the Sierra Nevada. The Boeing gradually increased its speed and altitude. Slipstream and

Fig. 50. A tri-motor Boeing Model 80A biplane airliner of Boeing Air Transport is shown here over the Sacramento River circa 1930.

propwash were tearing at Meyer's clothes. He lost his hat, the buckle came off his coat, and he was freezing. Ten miles from Mather, Meyers was able to shift his position slightly, enabling him to tap on the nearest passenger window.

A new employee, "plane matron" Miss Olette Hasle, heard him tapping and told Huking a passenger was on the wing. Huking gently turned the plane around toward Mather Field without losing Mr. Meyers and landed. Meyers thankfully climbed off the wing—quite numbed by the cold but unhurt.[40]

The north-south runway at Sac Muni was ready for surfacing, and the crosswind runway was ready for packing and rolling. Moving the hangar and other buildings to an area closer to the edge of the field had begun.[41] While the large aircraft hangar was being moved closer to Freeport Boulevard and its foundation floor poured, workers erected a large tent to house airplanes.[42]

All nine members of the Sacramento Airport Commission submitted their resignations in a joint letter to the Sacramento City Council on December 4, 1930. It was a simple formality as the city council voted to abolish the commission. The commission had done its job choosing a new site for the airport and had it up and running. The city council did not look favorably on commissions and had set a pattern of abolishing them as soon as possible.[43]

Another large hangar 150 by 125 feet was scheduled for construction in December. Landscaping hangars, a parking lot, and a new entrance road

Fig. 51. At the new Sacramento Municipal Airport the Boeing Air Transport hangar, at the top left of this photo, had to be built on the portion of the airport site already paid for by the airport commission, so the entire airport construction plans including the large hangar already built had to be moved closer to Freeport Boulevard as one can see when comparing this circa 1932 photo to the photo on page 204 of the opening weekend in 1930.

was also scheduled. Freeport Boulevard would be widened to a three-lane highway as far south as the airport. This improvement was to be funded in the next city budget.[44]

West America Air Schools moved its headquarters from Sacramento back to Oakland Municipal Airport for the winter. Company manager E. A. McMullen reported weather conditions were better there during winter. Actually, the new municipal airport was in chaos with the hangar and buildings being moved and runways being hard surfaced. Business opportunities were better in the Oakland area with its larger population base.[45]

Overland Airways started a scheduled service from Sac Muni with three trips a day to Oakland. It began the first week of January 1931 with planes landing at San Francisco Bay Airdrome at Alameda. It cost five dollars for a one-way flight.[46]

General contractor J. R. Reeves employed 20 full-time men installing drainage pipes at the Sacramento airport in January. Recent rains formed pools on the oil soaked runways making them hazardous. Workers graded the parking lot and entrance road, spread crushed rock on the road, and packed it down.[47] The area south of the road was leveled later in January and a concrete apron for the existing hangar on the field was poured. Construction of the Boeing Air Transport hangar would begin soon.

Marston Campbell, head of Overland Airways, flew into Sacramento

CHAPTER 10

with his chief pilot, Clayton Allen. Campbell reported Overland Airways carried 75 passengers its first week of operation. Del Hay flew in from Oakland in a Fleet biplane, as did Lieutenant Cooper from Crissy Field. Cooper was flying an Army Douglas. Art Wilson reported his Travel Air biplane was currently hangared on the new airport.[48]

Construction of the Boeing hangar got under way and the lighting system was laid. Drainage ditches throughout the new airfield were completed with the exception of one connecting Willow Slough.[49]

A tri-motor Kreutzer on a survey flight from San Diego to Seattle landed at Sacramento Muni early the next month. They identified themselves as officers and employees of Pacific Air and Steamship Company. Syd Neighbors and William Mathews were directors of the company. With them were employees Jeff Warren, a former Sacramento pilot; Tommy Thompson, pilot; and Cliff Soule, mechanic.

Mr. Neighbors said their mission was examining airports along the route Pacific Air and Steamship Company was allegedly exploring for a possible new airline. Already incorporated into Pacific Airways and Steamship Company was British Columbia Airways Ltd., he said, which supposedly operated a triangular route between Seattle, Victoria, and Vancouver. He claimed his company held contracts to fly airmail between the United States and various Central American republics. He also said Joseph L. Gianelli of Hamilton City would be the local governor for the planned airline service. After refueling the tri-motor, they departed for Medford but developed engine trouble and landed at Cheim Field in Marysville for repairs and spent the night.[50]

A month later Neighbors returned to Sacramento. He proposed a Chico–Sacramento airline, First National Airways of America, Ltd., a division of Pacific Airways and Steamship Co., routing between Chico-Marysville-Sacramento-Oakland and back. Operations were to begin mid-March. Neighbors also claimed that within 60 days his company would open air express service from Oakland to Reno. Pilots Jeff Warren and Gene Tigar, who were known in Sacramento, were affiliated with Neighbor's company. Warren was slated to be assistant manager of operations, and J. L. Costello the general traffic manager.[51]

Syd Neighbor's companies never existed. One must suppose his story was cover for another enterprise—possibly the creation of Consolidated Airlines, which occurred a short time later. Gene Tigar would fly for Consolidated.

TRAVELLING BY CAR, DOC inspector Wiley Wright stopped at the municipal airport in February. He gave Paul San Martino of Oakland his test for a transport pilot license.

Overland Airways was doing well carrying passengers from Sacramento to the Bay Area. The airline's plane was seen several times arriving at the airport with a full load of passengers, and departing for the Bay Area with a full load.[52]

Mervin Smith, president of Gibralter Auto Club, flew into Sacramento Muni in February aboard Gilpin Airways' cabin Fairchild flown by Jack Slaybaugh. Smith and five men who came with him went uptown to the governor's office. They were in Sacramento to secure a promise from Governor Rolph that he would come to an air meet in Los Angeles. It was a charity event with proceeds to benefit the unemployed.[53]

Although Sacramento Muni was in a chaotic state with construction going on, it appeared flying activities were barely affected. Airport officials hoped future crowds similar to the one which thronged to the airfield on February 22, wouldn't be discouraged by the field's temporary disarray.

Pete Reinhart returned from a trip to Texas in F. W. Terrell's Stinson in late February. Another Stinson, belonging to Mrs. William Randolph Hearst, landed about the same time with pilot Hargrove at the controls.[54]

Notable arrivals at Sacramento Muni in March 1931 were as follows: a Stearman came from Rankin Air Service at Oakland; a special caravan of planes sponsored by the San Francisco Junior Chamber of Commerce came to "sell" aviation to the legislature; and a tri-motor Ford belonging to Western Pacific Air Freighters arrived from Seattle with 2,300 pounds of fish en route to Oakland.

B. G. Chandler and his wife arrived from Santa Ana in their Stinson. Ray Nicholson flew a passenger to Clear Lake from Del Paso Airport.

Mrs. Florence Lowe Barnes (not yet called "Pancho" by the press) on March 1, 1931, set a new women's record flying from Los Angeles to Sacramento in 2 hours and 40 minutes and returning in 2 hours and 12 minutes. Governor Rolph presented her with a trophy as "America's Fastest Woman Flyer" at the Capitol on March 2. The trophy was for setting a record of 196 mph during a speed run over Los Angeles Municipal Airport on August 4, 1930.[55]

Concrete for the Boeing hangar floor had been poured. Runway surfaces hardened in the warm weather and the ground absorbed oil with a positive result for planes no longer being drenched in oil upon touching down.[56] April 2 was the deadline for bids to erect the second hangar (Boeing's) at Sacramento Municipal Airport. The structure was estimated to cost $50,000.[58] The hangar needed to be finished before Boeing Air Transport could move its operations from Mather Field.

DOC inspector Wiley Wright arrived at Sacramento Muni in March to check various planes on the field preparatory to relicensing. Bob Laurin's especially interested Wright; Laurin had just given the plane a thorough overhaul intending to use it for instruction. George Koshell and J. W. Terrell passed their pilot license tests with Wright later that month.[59] Kermit Parker, who would become professor in aeronautics at Sacramento Junior College, graduated from the Boeing School of Aeronautics at Oakland in March.[57]

Overland Airways shut down operations a few days to repair some planes. On March 31, service was resumed between San Francisco Bay Airdrome and Sacramento.

Operations for the last week of March were comparatively light, as shown by the following arrivals at the municipal airport: E. J. Williams of the Inland Aviation Club arrived from Kansas City, Missouri; Dave Postle arrived in a Fairchild from New York; William K. Scott brought a passenger up from Los Angeles in a Stearman; Ray Crawford in a Varney Air Lines Stinson flew in with three passengers; Buzz Slingsby came up from Elk Grove in a Commandaire; and Forrest Bennett flew a charter to the Bay Area in his Monocoach.

Pete Reinhart, who had been J. W. Terrell's pilot, moved on to Los Angeles. Terrell received his pilot's license and no longer needed Reinhart.[60] Forrest Earle Bennett, Shell Oil rep at Sac Muni, installed a windsock on top of a grain silo three miles southwest of the airport.[61]

Arrivals in the first week of April 1931 included: Denny Wright from Oakland in a Travel Air; Jack Cardiff from Bakersfield in a Monocoupe; Ray Joseph from Martinez in a Curtiss Robin; Phil Brush from San Francisco in a Boeing; Harry Ogden from Los Angeles in an Odgen Osprey; Ruy Feliz from Petaluma in a Monocoupe; Earl Kelly from Redding in a Pitcairn; and S. Pastal from San Jose in a Fairchild. Each of the aforementioned were carrying at least one passenger. Others arriving that week were: N. C. Orr from San Jose in a Fairchild; E. Allen from Los Angeles in a Northrop; R. U. St. John from San Francisco in a Swallow; S. F. Carey, Union Oil, from San Francisco in a Travel Air; and H. L. Weaver from Stockton in a Stinson.[62]

Shell Oil Company generated much activity in early April when Ralph

Becket flew Selwyn Eddy, district manager, to Redding in a company Stearman. John Macready, who made the first nonstop transcontinental flight across America in 1924, now working for Shell, flew a company Lockheed to Sacramento the same month.

Workers broke ground on the new larger hangar at Sacramento Municipal Airport in late April. Work on the Boeing hangar was to be completed in early May.[63] There were complaints about costs exceeding the $150,000 bond issue approved last June. An additional $10,000 had been approved recently plus another $7,699 after that.

City manager James S. Dean remained firmly dedicated to building a first class airport, and the city council continued to support him. Airport contracts for grading, leveling, a drainage system, the Boeing hangar, a city hangar, lighting, and extras cost a total of $124,532.[64]

Dan Emmett, the "flying legislator," flew home in early May. Jack Beilby took a four-day charter for Dr. Thomas R. Haig in Bennett's Monocoach; flying daily to Palo Alto.[65]

Joe Decetis was given the DOC exam for his private license the previous week by DOC inspector Billie Moore, and Art Wilson had his Travel Air relicensed by Moore the same day.

Travel Air distributor D. C. Warren created much interest landing at Sacramento Muni after a quick flight from San Francisco Bay Airdrome. He was flying his special low-wing Travel Air racer in which he had won a number of air races around the state.[66]

In early May 1931 the municipal airport was a hive of activity. Preparations were being made for the arrival of a Goodyear blimp, one of many owned by the nationally known rubber company. Airport construction was still in full swing when several commercial pilots announced their intended use of the new airport as headquarters for their flight schools. Buzz Slingsby reported he was training six students in his Commandaire at the new airport. Jack Beilby said he was supervising work there for others. Bob Laurin announced his plane was recently refurbished for student instruction. His wife had recently soloed and was working towards taking her DOC exam. C. W. Bear was one of several individuals interested in starting an airport restaurant. He wanted to set up a food stand at the field for the blimp's visit to gauge the crowd's reaction to food service at the airport.[67]

In May the drilling of a 16-inch water well began as part of the plan to erect a new hangar. Slabs for both the new hangar and the administration building were poured. The rest of the work concentrated on completing the heart of the airport—the electrical substation. Night lighting would become available, making for a safer airport 24 hours a day.[68]

Harold F. Brown stopped at the municipal airport in May while ferrying a new Spartan biplane to Cheim Field. He had flown from the Spartan factory at Tulsa. R. H. Dickinson accompanied Brown in a loose formation flying a new Spartan monoplane.[69]

Hilton F. Lusk, the aeronautics professor at Sacramento Junior College, took a second job as superintendent of the Sacramento Municipal Airport on June 1, 1931. Bill Cortopassi in his Commandaire successfully passed his exam for a private license in early June. He was tested by DOC inspector James Payton in Sacramento.[70]

BOEING AIR TRANSPORT began its first regularly scheduled airmail flights from Sacramento Muni on the night of June 3, 1931, departing at 9:20 for Chicago. Sacramento postmaster Harold McCurry reported thousands of airmail letters were stamped and posted for that eastbound mail plane.[71] The westbound plane arrived at 5:10 AM. Before then, BAT flights used Mather Field. The official inauguration of Boeing's service from Sacramento Municipal Airport was June 7 in observance of "Boeing Day." Federal, state, and company officials gave speeches and a Boeing Model 80A tri-motor biplane airliner was on display. The official inauguration flight was piloted by Don Broughton. A copilot and a stewardess made up the rest of his crew.[72]

The day before BAT's inaugural flight, Amelia Earhart landed a little after noon with her mechanic Edwin DeVaught in what she thought was the first autogiro to land in California. It turned out that Johnny Miller beat her by two weeks. Their autogiros were built by Pitcairn-Cierva Autogiro Company of America.

Arthur S. Dudley, secretary of the Sacramento chamber of commerce, and other local officials met Earhart at the airport and took her to lunch at the Senator Hotel. She told them that the day before on her way to Reno from the east, she was forced to land the autogiro on a government emergency landing field 21 miles from Lovelock. After sitting in the plane for two hours waiting out a dust storm of extreme intensity, a group of local miners arrived by automobile and escorted them into Lovelock. After a short wait, they took off for Reno and stayed overnight. She said their flight from New York was a test flight to prove the practicality of autogiro aircraft. She intended to make the first transcontinental autogiro flight and was able to get the Beech Nut chewing gum company to supply the autogiro. The autogiro was still experimental, she said, but she was confident her flight was a successful test. She planned to fly on to Los Angeles after spending a night in Oakland.[73]

A week later on her return east, Earhart crashed during takeoff from Abilene, Texas. Neither she nor her mechanic were injured, however the aircraft was heavily damaged. They left Abilene immediately by train for Oklahoma City to pick up another Pitcairn autogiro being flown from the factory at Willow Grove, Pennsylvania a suburb of Philadelphia. Here the story becomes murky. Another source implies her round-trip flight ended with the crash in Texas.[74]

A few months later, J. P. Lukens flew another Pitcairn autogiro into Sacramento Municipal Airport for the purposes of demonstrating the odd-shaped aircraft to the public. The machine was described by the press as a "... coverless umbrella-like fan, which supports the ship in the air [and] attracts much attention as people fail to comprehend what makes it revolve. The fan is motor operated only while the ship is preparing to take off and from that time on revolves at a constant speed regardless of the [forward] speed of the ship." Lukens, Pitcairn company pilot, was invited to fly the aircraft out to Mather Field by the army so its officers could inspect the odd machine. The autogiro used whirling rotor blades for lift like a helicopter, but its biggest drawback was its inability to hover.[75]

By July 1 Ray Nicholson, previously based at Del Paso Airport, was operating a de Havilland Moth from the municipal airport on Freeport Boulevard.[76]

Ten airliners landed daily by July 1931 at the new airport. They belonged to Boeing Air Transport, Varney Speed Lines, and Overland Air Lines. Boeing and Varney were subsidiaries of the recently formed United Air Lines. According to a 1931 survey of Pacific coast states by the publishers of the Standard Oil Company directory of airports, the number of airports in Pacific coast states had increased by 300 percent. The 1927 inaugural directory listed 125 airports; four years later there were 475.[77]

Ken Kleaver noted night hops were becoming more popular at the new airport. He made four flights in one night. Earl Bennett said his night flights had also increased.[78]

Les McClasky, operating out of the old Del Paso Airport under the name of Sacramento Flying Service, reported in late July a group of dentists and doctors had organized the Medico-Dental Flying Club with 25 members, and his school would be giving them instruction. Once hangar No. 3 of the new airport was completed, he would be opening an aircraft repair shop and a parts store offering Curtiss-Wright products including airplanes.[79] This newest hangar was expected to be ready in August and would include new administration offices.[80]

Aero Digest reported, "...the new Sacramento Municipal Airport, one of the best airports on the Pacific coast, [was] five miles south of town with no obstructions on any side. New hangars of concrete and steel are nearly finished as well as an administration building. The flying field is level with three wide runways, each two thousand feet long. ... A few miles north of town is the privately owned ... airport operated by Ingvald Fagerskog as a flying school and commercial flying field. Directly across the highway is the old Sacramento [Del Paso] Airport now the field of the Sacramento Flying Service."[81]

Hangar No. 3 was still several days from completion as August began. The original field office was moved behind the airport beacon and possibly rented out as a restaurant. A new field office was quickly being constructed on the site of the old office.[82] Plans for the office specified an observation tower with full view of the entire airport grounds. On top of the tower a large orange light was to serve the same purpose visually, as a siren did audibly—warning pilots of the immediate landing or departure of an aircraft. Use of this light was unique in airport procedure. The DOC wanted to know if it was successful at increasing airport safety.[83]

William Terrell and his wife left the airport in their Stinson for the Bay Area in early August.[84] Ralph Canning reported Tony Brazil and Floyd Baker had signed on with him for flight instruction in late August. Brazil soloed after only ten days of instruction, and Baker, who signed on only ten days before, was expected to solo within the week. Canning was training them in a Commandaire at the municipal airport.[85]

Appointing a new airport superintendent to replace incumbent Hilton Lusk was expected in September, as was the beginning of air service by Century-Pacific Air Lines between Sacramento and the Bay Area.[86]

Early September 1931 was, once again, time for the California State Fair in Agricultural Park at Broadway and Stockton Boulevard with headliner "Spud" Manning parachuting daily. For the fair flights between Sacramento and the Bay Area increased. Varney Air Lines flew five planes on schedule to and from Sacramento while Century-Pacific doubled its flights to the fair.

Donald B. Smith, the new muni superintendent, reported air traffic was on the uptick during the fair.[87] Smith soon left on a fact-finding tour to the Bay Area to see how other airports handled the daily problems of air traffic, repair shops, and hangar usage. His first stop was San Francisco Bay Airdrome in Alameda as a guest of R. U. St. John, the airport's manager. Prior to his trip, Smith flew to Woodland with Ivor Witney. An instructor for Summit Flying Service of Sacramento, Witney had a dozen students. Three of those students, Harry Trayham, Rex Buckles, and Leslie Morris lived in Woodland. Witney gave lessons there once a week.

Les McClaskey, unable to get space in new hangar No. 3, took half of hangar No. 1 at Sac Muni where he moved his repair shop from Del Paso Airport. After a layout change of his rental space, he planned to sell Curtiss-Wright products. He already had room to repair airframes and engines and was refurbishing Bob Laurin's plane for the coming winter season. Sacramento Junior College flying club was to be taught by McClaskey's Sacramento Flying Service.[88]

Sacramento was becoming the regional aviation hub. Daily, 22 aircraft were arriving and departing from Sac Muni. Three airlines were using the airport for regularly scheduled flights. Three businesses employing five commercial pilots were flying short hops and longer charter flights from the airport in addition to giving flight instruction. An aircraft repair station was on site, 11 private planes were based there, and five to eight transient airplanes flew in daily.[89]

Don Smith reported 1,800 gallons of used crankcase oil was obtained from local service stations and garages to spread on runways and taxiways. In addition, Standard Oil Company delivered and spread 550 gallons of unmarketable heavy fuel oil. Runways were improved by the application of hot oil. It held dust down and hardened surfaces for winter use. Good weather allowed maximum oil penetration into the soil.[90]

On October 27, G. Wilbur Cornelius from Glendale flew into Sac Muni in his "Free Wing" aircraft. The airplane had movable, self-adjusting wings, and Cornelius claimed it was the safest airplane in the world. He made takeoffs with his hands out of the cockpit above his head. He demonstrated the plane for Major Clarence Tinker, commandant of Mather Field.[91]

The three airlines flying to and from Sacramento by the end of October 1931 were: United Air Lines, Century Pacific Lines, and Varney Speed Lanes. United, at that time the largest airline in the world, was flying Boeing Model 40A three-place mailplanes, twice daily, on the transcontinental run to Chicago. Harold Newman was the local company manager. Century Pacific flew ten-passenger tri-motor monoplanes to the Bay Area and points south with four daily flights. A. W. Kimball was its local passenger agent. Varney Speed Lanes was flying the fast single-engine Lockheed Orions into Sacramento. The Orion carried six passengers. Varney made six daily flights between Sacramento and San Francisco Bay Airdrome at Alameda. Richard Brown was Varney's local ticket agent. BAT now United Air Lines had the Boeing hangar on the field, Century Pacific was located in the new hangar No. 3, and Varney had an office in the airport administration building.[92]

Commercial pilots working from the municipal airport in 1931 were: Buzz Slingsby flying F. Earle Bennett's Monocoach; Bob Laurin with his two-place Travel Air; Ralph Canning flying a Waco F; and Ray Nicholson in his two-place Commandaire. Summit Flying Service of San Francisco had a two-place Fleet at Sacramento flown by Ivor Witney.

Three other airports were known to be in use at this time in the Sacramento area—Mather Field, Del Paso Field, and Ingvald Fagerskog's airport. There were no reports of flying activity at Eagle Rock Airport or any other field east of the municipal airport. Eagle Rock may have fallen into disuse with the opening of Sacramento Municipal Airport.

Henry Gastman of Auburn flew for his pilot's license test in Summit's Fleet and Albert Mock from Folsom, a student of Bob Laurin's, also took his test ride. Laurin reported Howard Connolly was getting additional flying time in the Travel Air.[93]

In November 1931 storms brought heavy rains to Sacramento, but runway damage at the municipal airport seemed minimal. Don Smith reported a few soft spots in the runways but could be repaired, although heavy consistency of the soil runways and taxiways prohibited deep penetration of oil. The hard surface of the runways only averaged 5/8 inch in crust thickness. Several local pilots were afraid future storms would severely damage the runways making landings for any aircraft dangerous, especially heavier planes. They wanted to see disking, harrowing, and surfacing with sand and crushed rock followed by vast amounts of oil applied to harden the runways.[94] Landing pilots reported other soft spots. When the rain stopped, the city engineer's office exhaustively inspected and repaired the damage using gravel to build up wet spots to prevent harming an unfortunate aviator.[95]

Special flights were arranged in November to take passengers from Sacramento to Palo Alto for the popular Stanford-Cal football game. Two planes were booked for the day. Some fans were accommodated on earlier flights.[96] Fifty people were flown to Mills Field, by Century Pacific Lines. From Mills Field at San Bruno, it was 20 miles by bus to Stanford Stadium.[97]

Despite bad flying weather in November there was no decrease in receipts at the municipal airport compared to October. Don Smith reported 76 transient aircraft hauling 50 passengers landed in November. Fourteen stayed overnight.[98]

Sacramento Municipal Airport was socked in with fog during early December. Two Bay Area couples, who flew into Sacramento hoping to get to Reno and get married were unable to fly further. One couple proceeded to Reno by train. What happened to the other couple is a mystery. Second thoughts—perhaps?[99] Century Pacific reported express (freight) hauling by airplane was gradually catching on as a popular shipping method.[100]

Two new Douglas bombers (possibly B-7s) landed at Sac Muni in December evoking considerable interest to local pilots. They were powered by supercharged 600hp. Curtiss Conqueror engines, liquid-cooled with a specially developed fluid (antifreeze) that had a high boiling point and low freezing point. Lieutenant E. B. Bobzien piloted one of them. Riding with him was Col. F. H. Dengler, G-2 officer for the Ninth Corps Area, which included Sacramento. Lieutenant Bobzien said his bomber had a top speed of 165 mph and was liked by pilots. However, he mentioned military pilots were frustrated because some new commercial planes, like the Lockheed Orion, outran them with ease.[101]

Hubert McGinnis signed on as a new student with Canning and Nicholson. Dick Pardee of Dixon was building time in their Waco for his private license. Hilton F. Lusk accepted two students, Henry Cody and Francis Pope. Carl Smith, a Great War pilot, was planning fly a Waco to familiarize himself with modern aircraft and take the DOC private pilot license test.[102]

Heavy rains in late December once again tested the Sacramento Municipal Airport runways. The commercial fliers based there praised the drainage system, which relieved an incredible amount of overflow. Some trouble spots caused by previous rains were cited as a failure of the resurfacing. City employees went back to work on them. After considerable effort, the surfaces could support trucks hauling rock, and the problems were considered fixed.[103]

DOC chief inspector Edison E. Mouton visited the airport a few days after Christmas to inspect work done on Joe DeCetis' Ryan Brougham and other aircraft. He praised the city's foresight in creating such an airport for the region. Frank Jones needed cross-country dual instruction before taking the test for a limited commercial license. He hired Ivor Witney and Summit Flying Service's Fleet. They had left for Reno on December 21 and had an uneventful flight. The return flight didn't go as well. After flying 100 miles, bad weather forced them back to Reno. They secured the plane and returned to Sacramento by train. Witney said the cold was barely tolerable when they pushed the Fleet to 11,500 feet to get over the Sierra Nevada.[104]

Dana Thompson, manager of Summit, flew into Sacramento December 29 in another Fleet. He left it at the municipal airport and went to Reno by train to retrieve the stranded Fleet. But continuing bad weather prevented him from bringing the Fleet home. Finally, Ivor Witney went to Reno January 4, 1932, and brought the stranded Fleet back.[105]

Because of bad weather, flying activity was minimal in the Sacramento Valley; only five transient pilots registered at the municipal airport for the week preceding December 30: H. W. Parker of Susanville, H. L. Stadley of Alameda, Harold F. Brown of Marysville, Edison E. Mouton of Oakland, and Dana Thompson from Mills Field.[106]

Ernie Smith and Emory Bronte, who in July 1927 were the first civilians to fly to Hawaii, came to Sacramento for a visit. They were in an Associated Oil Company plane, Bronte's employer. Smith was a Transcontinental and Western Air pilot, and he flew a route in the eastern United States. He said weather east of the Rockies was generally bad, and he really enjoyed flying with Bronte in California. He complimented superintendent Don Smith on the great work done creating the new municipal airport.[107]

By mid-January 1932, better weather in the Sacramento Valley resulted in more business for local commercial flyers. Students were able to get back in the air. Leo Moore's aerial tours of the high Sierra Nevada got off to a good start on January 10. Airline companies increased business, particularly United Air Lines with its new decreased fares.[108]

"Several heavy storms and much rainfall failed to cause our runways to show any great distress," reported superintendent Don Smith. "It served to assure us that our underground drainage system is functioning satisfactorily. Several transport pilots using our port during the month commented that runways at Sacramento Municipal Airport were in the best condition of any in the state but one—United Airport at Burbank."[109]

THE NATIONAL AIRWAY beacons were critical for safely flying into and out of the Sacramento Valley at night over the Sierra Nevada. Heavy snows during the winter of 1932 were particularly hard on the airway beacon tenders in western Nevada. W. J. Majors, a 60-year-old caretaker of the emergency field at Buffalo Valley, was without food for three days and nights after a heavy snowstorm prevented delivery of his supplies. Some DOC and the Nevada Highway Department employees eventually broke a trail to his cabin. Walter Dolan, caretaker of the emergency field at Battle Mountain, had to fight his way through deep snow for three days after his car stalled 32 miles from the station. He continued on skis but only made about ten miles a day.[110]

Winter brought tragedy the night of February 2. John W. Sharpnack, a veteran airmail pilot, was killed. His Boeing Model 40B airmail plane crashed and burned after encountering a freak midnight snowstorm near Rio Vista. Will L. Campbell, a Pacific Air Transport pilot, found the crash site after a prolonged search. He attempted to land nearby and was slightly injured when his plane flipped onto its back during landing.[111]

In February, supplies were flown to a group of Nevada Irrigation District employees snowed in at Camp 19 on the west end of Bowman Lake, west of Donner Summit. The decision to use an airplane to resupply the dozen men was made by district manager William Durbrow. Durbrow calculated the cost of a pack train of snowshoe transportation was more expensive than air transportation, plus it would take longer. The irrigation district hired Kimball Flying Service to help, and Leo Moore was to make the flight. Kimball's high-wing Stinson cabin plane was perfect for the job. It would involve dangerous close-in maneuvering to drop 1,600 pounds of fresh and smoked meats, small bags of sugar, canned goods including milk, and newspapers were to be dropped in 50 pound packages with long red streamers to mark their locations.

Moore had to approach the dam at the lower end of Bowman Lake at an altitude lower than the dam's top, drop the supplies, climb sharply to get through an 85-foot gap at the top of the dam, make a spiraling turn over the lake, pass through a 125-foot gap at the other end of the dam, glide down over the camp, drop more supplies, and repeat the same series of maneuvers. The job took four flights. Camp superintendent J. A. Kelleher said all supplies were recovered in good condition.[112]

Kimball's Flying Service had ten students at the beginning of March and reported their little Aeronca C-3 logged 700 flights in 25 days. Les McClaskey planned to operate a mobile aircraft repair shop. He sold a Curtiss Robin to Norboe and Slingsby in March. Buzz Slingsby and Paul Norboe had just opened a business for charter flights and instruction. They were offering special rates for round trip flights to Reno in their Pitcairn biplane. The improving weather allowed Ken Kleaver to haul 20 passengers on short hops in Joe DeCetis' Ryan Brougham on the last Sunday in February. Bob Laurin flew 14 passengers in his Spartan biplane that same day.[113] The good weather in March increased the number of airline passengers flying out of Sacramento Municipal Airport. Don Smith had community chest laborers cleaning up the airport grounds, leveling areas for lawns, and planting shrubs in front of the big hangars. Century Pacific Lines missed only one flight due to bad weather during the last 20 days.

A. W. Kimball flew charter flights to Mokelumne Hill and Reno the week of March 23. Leo Moore, a Kimball pilot, in his company's little Aeronca C-3 training plane flew some spins, loops, and rolls, then flew upside down for the Sunday municipal airport crowd.[114]

Superintendent Don Smith inaugurated formation flights over Sacramento by the commercial pilots using the municipal airport. They were flown on the last Sunday of March to stimulate more interest at the new airport. The flights resulted in a large crowd gathering at the airfield, and a lucrative day of passenger hopping was had by the commercial pilots on the field. Smith promised more formation flights at the airport on the next Sunday with radio programs and announcements over the airport's loudspeaker.[115]

Smith reported an increase of transient traffic in March due to better weather. He said 83 airplanes other than scheduled airline transports landed with 84 passengers. Local pilots claimed a considerable increase in their business over March of the previous year.[116]

Selden Parnham, 19, received his DOC aviation mechanic's license after studying engine repair and construction with Ray Nicholson. The latter believed Parnham was one of the youngest to get the license. Parnham planned to try for his private pilot license on the next exam date. Frank Baker, a student with Canning and Nicholson, would also be taking his exam then. Nicholson's other students at Sac Muni were William Ganow of Georgetown, who had recently passed his tests for a pilot's license and William R. Schandhals, a former World War pilot.[117]

The new airport restaurant opened in celebration of Sacramento Municipal Airport achieving a US Department of Commerce A1A rating. Commercial operators at the field planned to stage demonstrations of aerial techniques used to train student pilots. Don Smith arranged the April 20, 1932, air show starting at 1:00 with Harold "Buzz" Slingsby demonstrating aerial target flying by cutting strips of paper (usually a toilet paper roll thrown out the window) with his propeller. Bob Laurin of the L and M Flying Service would demonstrate a particular flying technique; Leo Moore of the Kimball Flying Service would demonstrate educational techniques, which were actually aerobatic maneuvers; Ray Nicholson of Canning and Nicholson Flying Service would demonstrate blind flying with his cockpit covered and using only instruments for references; and Ivor Witney of the Summit Flying Service would demonstrate spins as taught to students. An air race was planned to finish out the show.[118]

Hilton F. Lusk, professor of aeronautics at Sacramento Junior College, published his textbook, *Aeronautic Fundamentals And Their Application*, in May. It was a popular book used in the college's aeronautics program many years.[119]

In April, 96 airplanes carrying 92 passengers landed at Sac Muni and 12 transient aircraft remained overnight.[120]

In May 1932 the municipal airport city staff were: Don Smith, Bert Bachman, F. Earle Bennett, and D. R. Swalley. With the exception of Don Smith, the superintendent, they wore uniforms consisting of a military style visor cap, white shirt, long tie and grey pants. Smith was always in a business suit. One of the employees, Forrest Earle Bennett, was owner of the Monocoach cabin plane flown on many commercial flights out of Sacramento Muni by various commercial pilots.

Don Smith posted new airport regulations on May 11. They included a ban on stunt flying and air work over the municipal airport without exclusive permission from the superintendent. Smoking was banned in all hangars and it was illegal to start any fires on the airport grounds. Use of blowtorches was prohibited. Another new mandate was that of an exclusive calm wind runway. When winds were calm, all aircraft were to take off from the north end of the main runway. Also was the rule that all aircraft flying into the airport must fly over the field and make a left turn before landing with approaches made at least 1,000 feet to the leeward side of the landing field.[121]

DOC inspector James Peyton flew into the municipal field to give license tests to two students. The flight test portions were to be flown in a Meteor airplane powered by a Kinner K-5 engine. Louis F. Vremsak, president and general manager of Western Aero Corp., Ltd. of Santa Barbara where the Meteor was built, flew the plane into Sacramento. The students were Gene Hughes, a rancher from Folsom and a student with Kimball, and Robert Barnett from Roseville who had been a student of Ingvald Fagerskog's flying school at Del Paso Airport; both students passed. The Meteor used was not Jack Irwin's Meteorplane, but a different factory-built, high-wing, monoplane design with a cruising speed of 105 mph, a top speed of 125 mph, and a landing speed of 45 mph.[122]

The USS *Akron*, one of the largest dirigibles in the world, flew over the state capitol about 10:30 AM, May 20, 1932. The giant Zepplin-type airship belonged to the US Navy.

Office workers spotted the airship on its first visit to Sacramento from the 14th floor of the California State Life Building at 9:55. They said it was so far away it looked like a football, but by 10:30 it was over the capitol. It circled the eastern residential area of the city returning to overfly the capitol again. Tens of thousands of Sacramentans were awed by the airship's 785-foot length.

Eight engines powered the *Akron*. The *Los Angeles* and the *Graf Zepplin*, two other well-known giant airships of the day, were each powered by only five engines. The *Akron* could lift 91 tons of useful load, whereas the *Los Angeles* and *Graf Zepplin* could lift only 30 tons and 45 tons respectively. The *Akron* had a range of 11,000 miles unrefueled, and the *Los Angeles* had a range of 4,000 miles. The *Graf Zepplin* could travel 6,000 miles unrefueled.

On the day it flew over the capitol, the *Akron* had stopped first in the Bay Area to pick up 20 newsmen making a total of 89 souls on board. The newsmen were from the Sacramento Valley and the Bay Area. During the publicity flight up through the valley and over various towns, the newsmen were allowed to examine the airship's interior. They inspected the engines mounted on the inside of the airship powering long drive shafts connected to the propellers mounted outside the skin of the dirigible. The passengers also examined the large open area on the bottom interior of the airship where Curtiss F2C "skyhook" fighter planes were carried. The fighters had been left at Sunnyvale during this tour.

While passing over the capitol, the crew dropped a weighted message bag that landed on the grounds with a story of the flight written by a *Sacramento Bee* reporter for the evening edition. Then the *Akron* turned northwest and disappeared up the valley to visit more towns.[123]

COMMERCIAL OPERATORS FLEW several charter flights at Sacramento

Muni the first week of June. Among the transient registrations that week was J. B. Jaynes, who flew in with E. L. Yuravich. Both were DOC airline inspectors. They were inspecting airports along the route from the East.[124] Don Smith documented 109 planes, other than scheduled airline flights, landing. He also noted the new surfacing on the entrance to the airport, oiling of the parking area, the lengthening of the east-west runway, the blading and dragging of all the runways, and the increasing business at the new airport café. Before leaving, the DOC inspectors suggested the other two runways be extended another 500 feet. They asked the airport to experiment with runway lighting, such as using torches for boundary markers.[125]

Sundays in June featured impromptu air shows, attracting good attendance to the municipal airport.[126]

On the Fourth of July, another air show was held as was one of many events happening around Sacramento. An estimated 6,000 people attended. Longtime resident commercial pilot Leo Moore opened the show with a demonstration of a dead stick landing. All flying businesses operating at the field participated. Pilots flew stunts to demonstrate aspects of flight training. Moore's dead stick landing showed what happens when an engine quits. Buzz Slingsby demonstrated a target drop to simulate an aviator dropping a message to someone on the ground.

Army lieutenants Dorsett, Dotzen, and Lee from Mather Field flew the Air Corps' Boeing P-12 pursuit planes for the crowd. Their formation maneuvers included power dives, double snap rolls, and loops. Evalan Earle featured a bathing beauty parade followed by a model airplane contest judged by college instructor Hilton Lusk. Summit Flying Service pilots Janet Knight and Tommy Thompson performed stunt flying followed by six military aircraft flying over in formation.

The finale was Charles "Red" Jensen jumping from 4,000 feet wearing two parachutes. He landed safely in a nearby field. Arriving from Los Angeles, Thor Polson, formerly from Mills Field, ground looped his airplane Saturday. He attempted to land downwind but ran out of runway at the southern end. His landing gear was wiped off and he lost a wingtip. Neither he nor his female passenger was hurt.[127]

Franklin L. Jones, a resident of Sacramento, was killed trying to land a Fleet biplane in a Haskins Valley meadow at Buck's Lake in the Sierra Nevada on July 6. Jones rented the Fleet from Dana Thompson's Summit Flying School at Sac Muni.[128]

The DOC equipped emergency airports at Concord, Livermore,

Chapter 10

Auburn, Donner Summit, Truckee, and Fernly with voice apparatuses (radios) to provide planes nearing the sites with weather reports. This augmented the voice system already in place for Boeing Air Transport at Oakland, Sacramento, and Reno in addition to the high-powered DOC stations at Oakland and Reno. These last high-powered DOC stations gave all radio equipped aircraft and the general public weather reports. Harold Newman, Boeing agent at Sacramento, said DOC recommended the municipal field install a Page Teletype machine. It would receive weather reports in the same manner as newspapers handled Associated Press wire reports; in addition the machine would transmit a weather map to the airport every three hours.

Captain Edison E. Mouton, DOC Aeronautics Branch supervising inspector of the Eighth Aeronautical District with headquarters at Oakland Airport, reported to Mather Field on July 18 for two weeks of active duty with the Army 316th Observation Squadron. Mouton's civilian job with the DOC was to enforce federal aviation regulations in eight Western states and the Territory of Alaska. He had flown 6,500 hours while serving 22 months in France as an Air Service test pilot, seven years flying the mail, and five years with the DOC.[129]

A seven-place cabin Travel Air was sold by R. P. Bowman of the D. C. Warren Co. at Oakland to Bob Hancock. This plane was one of those used by Overland Airways to pioneer air service to the San Francisco Bay Airdrome from Sacramento.[130]

July provided the municipal airport with the heaviest monthly transient aircraft travel of the year: 100 aircraft carrying 108 passengers and the pilots landed on the field.[131]

Newly resurfaced, Freeport Boulevard reopened from Sacramento's city limits providing an outstanding drive to the airfield. The surface was five inches thick laid directly on the old concrete pad, forming a strong paved highway. Also, telephone lines were lowered six feet and hazard lights were installed on the east-west runway to minimize danger to landing planes.[132]

An air show sponsored by the Sacramento Veterans of Foreign Wars was held August 22, 1932. Ten thousand spectators turned out. It started with a parade at 1:00 led by the VFW Drum Corps, and then the flying began. Mather Field lieutenants Hotzen, Rea, and Schmidt gave an exhibition of formation flying and dive-bombing in their Boeing P-12 pursuits. Dana "Tommy" Thompson of Summit Flying Schools flew aerobatics in a Fleet trainer. The crowd saw a demonstration of a new Lockheed Vega air ambulance with an exhibition of "Trusty," a life-saving invention which unloaded four passengers simultaneously from a plane via parachutes.

Featured were parachute jumps by "Spud" Manning, one of the nation's top parachutists in the 1930s. He began with a jump that ended just five feet from the center of the airfield. Later, Manning was hauled to 10,000 feet and from there free-fell 8,000 feet before opening his chute. Few parachutists at the time did this type of jump. Manning claimed himself the world record holder for delayed-opening parachute jumps.[133]

A class in aircraft propulsion opened in hangar No. 1 during September. Hilton Lusk taught it as an extension class of Sacramento Junior College. The college had recently received $68,000 worth of obsolete equipment from the navy for shop instruction. The first class had 17 students divided into four teams to work on the equipment.[134]

The first Stinson R-4 Junior came to Sacramento drawing a large crowd as it circled the airport. The Cord Company pilot, John Kelley, lowered the retractable landing gear and landed the cabin airplane. It was an advanced design for the times. A 240hp. Lycoming powered the four-place aircraft giving it a top speed of 145 mph. It had an electric starter, radio, and landing lights. Kelley with Stinson West Coast representative Ralph Johnson allowed local operator A. W. Kimball to fly the plane; then they departed for Marysville.[135]

Les Bowman flew a Waco C, four-place, cabin biplane into Sacramento in late October. Bowman the north state distributor for Stearman, Lockheed, and Waco airplanes was based in Alameda. With Bowman was his wife Marty Bowman, a well-known aviatrix; Joe Hargrove, Bowman's sales manager; and E. Bottimore of Hearld. They were flying a new Waco demonstrator to various airports in the Sacramento Valley. It was equipped with radio, landing lights, and electrically discharged flares. Powered by a 210hp. Continental, the plane cruised at 120 mph. The biplane could climb 1,160 feet per minute, and its motor burned 11 gallons of gas per hour. Its range was 700 miles, and it was priced at $7,000.

Don Smith reported as of November 1, there were 13 airplanes permanently based at Sac Muni. This number included a Fleet trainer which H. L. Newman, the Boeing agent, had just purchased for his personal use. The local pilots rigged a net across the concrete apron between hangars one and three creating a tennis court for their exercise regimen. It was easily taken down and did not interfere with aircraft movements.[136] An illuminated wind tee was installed in the late fall. Don Smith soloed the first week of

November; his instructor was Ray Nicholson.

On the first Sunday of November, Leo Moore flew an exhibition demonstrating the excellent maneuverability of the Fleet trainers belonging to Kimball Flying Service. Also that day, Richfield Oil Company's Fokker Trimotor pilot, Tom Fowler, gave rides over the city to state, county, and city officials.[137]

Don Smith reported that from July 1 to September 30, 14,100 gallons of gasoline and 250 gallons of oil were purchased at Sacramento Municipal Airport. He informed the chamber of commerce that 1,080 transport flights arrived and departed with 2,500 passengers each way at the airport; 323 transient nonscheduled flights with 298 passengers used the field, and 360 sightseeing or short hops with 720 passengers were made during the period. There were 4,590 departures including those for student training. Improvements to the airport during that same period included lengthening one runway an additional 1,150 feet and another by 350 feet. Also 40,000 gallons of oil were dumped on the runways and a new fence was installed.[138] The DOC transferred Alfred Smith, an aeronautics inspector, to the West Coast from the East.[139]

In December foul foggy weather shut down most flying. On the 19th, all Varney flights were cancelled, and no private planes could get up. Visibility was down to 100 feet at the airport. Don Smith reported Boeing mail planes were still landing on the field if there was any chance at all of landing. Smith said the runway surface was holding up well even after recent heavy rains. It was much better than the bogs that had formed in December the previous year. A flight by John Gugliametti in a United Boeing Model 40B mail plane demonstrated the Boeing System's technique for landing on the fog-covered municipal airport on December 20.

Gugliametti made his usual radio call 20 minutes out from the airport. He made his final call three miles east of Sacramento. Harold L. Newman, the United agent, called him back when his plane was within radio range. Newman told the pilot the fog layer topped out at 1,900 feet and reached down to 600 feet above the airport. He mentioned other air traffic in the area and where they were in relation to the runways. Gugliametti then put the Boeing into a spiraling descent from his cruising altitude at 2,500 until he punched out of the fog at 600 feet. The airport siren sounded a warning to all other pilots that an aircraft was about to land, and they should yield the right-of-way; not that anyone was trying to fly that day. Gugliametti could see the runway once he dropped below the fog layer and landed. He maintained stability and direction in the fog using instruments, mainly his turn and bank indicator, artificial horizon, and an audible sound from a radio beacon. After dropping off the mail, he departed for Oakland with much of the flight spent climbing up through the fog layer. After breaking out of the fog, he called Newman and reported the altitude he entered the fog and the altitude he left it. He had two passengers in the small cabin of the Boeing, and he sat in an open cockpit behind them.[140]

The weather at the end of December stopped most private flying at the municipal airport and resulted in many interruptions of the Varney airline schedule. United Air Lines, however, suffered practically no interruptions and schedules were closely maintained.

Paul Norboe reported his Pitcairn biplane had undergone a complete overhaul by mechanic Charles "Red" Jensen.[141] When weather conditions improved in January 1933, DOC inspector James Peyton passed six Sacramento pilots for their private pilot licenses: Al Waite, Carl Smith, Pat Bennett, Charles Overhouse, David Walker, and Karl Harder.[142]

In June 1933, Trans-Air Company established a daily express service between the San Francisco Bay Area, Sacramento, Marysville, and other cities in the valley flying a Curtiss Thrush. Trans-Air was located on Curtiss-Wright Airport at Alameda, also known as Alameda Airport. Its president was George McCallum.[143]

Pacific Seaboard Air Lines, about which little is known, began advertising in Sacramento newspapers in October 1933. Pacific Seaboard claimed to be the eighth largest airline in America. Three daily flights were offered between Mills Field and Sacramento. A one-way ticket cost $4.50; a round-trip was $7.20. It is doubtful this airline lasted longer than two months.[144]

Ken Kleaver, a Yreka commercial pilot formerly from Sacramento, was hired by Arthur Thompson to fly him to Sacramento to see his mother who was suddenly stricken with a serious illness. Thompson, visiting Dunsmuir, was called in the middle of the night and told there might not be much time left to see her. Kleaver and Thompson left Dunsmuir at 2:00 AM. At 3:00 near Marysville, Kleaver thought he might be running low on fuel. He circled Cheim Field hoping someone would turn on lights at the airfield and he could land. After circling a few times, the aircraft caught the attention of a police car. Officers turned their spotlight on the plane then rushed to the airport to turn on the large runway floodlight. On the ground Kleaver discovered he had adequate fuel and immediately took off for Sacramento, landing a half hour later.[145]

An air show was held at Sacramento Municipal Airport in late October 1933 under the direction of airport superintendent Don Smith. The United States was four years into the Depression, and the economy was reflected in the makeup of the show. There was no money for professional parachute jumpers or professional stunt flyers; local pilots flew for free. In fact, all who flew were noncommercial aviators with one exception, Leo Moore. Moore made the obligatory parachute jump, a traditional stunt at every air show in the 1920s and '30s—a tradition that continues to this day.

Only one race for OX-5 powered airplanes was held. There were ten other events including: spiral and spot landing, mock (flour) bombing, balloon busting, aerial target practice, and a figure-eight contest. Of the thirty or so contestants, two female pilots entered, Miss Pansy Bowen and Genevive Nebeker. Male pilots were: Seldon Parnham, Boyd Collier, Leo Moore, Ernie Moe, Dave Walker, Joe Duncan, Carl Smith, and Tex Hudson.

The show had a decent turnout of about 2,000. Seldon Parnham, an aviation mechanic, took three first places in the day's events including the most prestigious Clunie Trophy for his precision flying. Ernie Moe beat out three other pilots to win the OX-5 race, which was considered the only money-making event of the air show. Genevieve Nebeker, competing against male pilots, won third place in three events. Pansy Bowen flew an aerobatic exhibition, and Leo Moore made his parachute jump from 2,500 feet landing safely outside the airport boundary.[146]

Fig. 52. Prominent north state aviator Ken Kleaver (on the right) stands next to Clarence and then Al Bielefeld (far left). They had just made a flight in Kleaver's Eaglerock over Mt. Shasta in August 1930.

Fig. 53. A twin-engine Curtiss Kingbird at Sacramento Muni in September 1931. This eight-passenger airliner was purchased for Consolidated Air Lines.

Fig. 54. The Navy's USS *Akron* dirigible as it departs Oakland for a publicity tour up the Sacramento Valley on May 20, 1932. The large Zepplin-type dirigible flew over the state capitol and dropped a message to reporters on the ground.

CHAPTER 11

Commercial flying at the new municipal airport – Forrest Earle Bennett – Bob Laurin – Harold G. "Buzz" Slingsby – Summit Flying Service – Kimball Flying Service – Capital Airlines Inc. – Boeing Air Transport – Pacific Air Transport – Century Pacific Lines Ltd. – Consolidated Air Lines – Varney Air Lines

The following professional aviators, commercial flying services, and scheduled airlines were the first aviation businesses to work from the new Sacramento Municipal Airport on Freeport Boulevard at Sacramento. Most have been previously mentioned; however, this chapter gives a more precise chronological account of each entity's activities at the airport during its first two years of operation.

Forrest Earle Bennett

Bennett was a member of the Sacramento Municipal Airport service staff when it opened in April 1930. Soon after he began working there, he purchased a high-wing, four-place Monocoach to rent to local commercial pilots for charter flights. The Monocoach became available for charter work in June 1930. In early July, Bennett announced he had been logging time in his Monocoach towards taking the test for a limited commercial license.[1]

Pete Rinehart, flying the Monocoach; Captain McCrillis, in a West America Waco; and Buzz Slingsby, flying his Travel Air, gave passengers night rides over Sacramento in July. Jack Beilby flew Bennett's Monocoach to Reno in February 1931 on a charter flight.[2] In April, local contractor Charles Wilkins came to the field at 10:00 on a Saturday morning with a construction bid that was due at Vallejo City Hall by 11:00. Beilby, in the Monocoach, got him there with time to spare.[3] Bennett reported his

Monocoach would be back in Sacramento by the end of May; it was at Oakland for an overhaul.[4]

Bennett rented his Monocoach to Roscoe Turner of national air racing fame. Turner at the time was flying for the Gilmore Oil Company and in late June needed to make a trip to Arbuckle. Buzz Slingsby was Bennett's pilot for the trip. It seems Turner wasn't yet famous enough for Bennett to turn him loose alone with the Monocoach.[5]

Spectators and local airmen watched with keen interest as skis and other supplies were loaded into the Monocoach in November. It was flown to a snowbound work camp of Campbell Construction Company employees in the Sierra Nevada. With Slingsby again at the controls, the supplies were dropped onto the snow for the trapped men on Echo Summit at lower Echo Lake to retrieve. Walter W. Campbell sponsored the flight.[6]

Bennett hired a new pilot to fly his Monocoach in March 1932. Dale Hunter had a transport pilot license and was a Boeing School of Aeronautics graduate. He would later enjoy fleeting fame setting endurance records.[7] Business was particularly good for Bennett the first week of April. His pilot had been hopping a lot of passengers as warm weather brought large crowds to the airport on weekends.[8] Bennett reported, two weeks later, business was still fair despite adverse weather conditions.[9]

Dale Hunter said weekend business was exceptional in June.[10] Hunter, Bennett's new pilot, age 26, was a native of Sacramento. His was a "local boy makes good" story. His education through junior college took place in Sacramento. He started flying in 1929 at a local flying school that went out of business after he received his private license. He continued his education at the Boeing School of Aeronautics in Oakland and earned his transport pilot license plus a rating as a master aviation mechanic. At the Boeing school, students making bone-headed mistakes received the bronze-winged Jackass Award, which Hunter received more than a few times.[11]

Bob Laurin

In September 1929, Bob Laurin removed the motor from his Jenny and hauled it to the aeronautics class at Roseville High School for repairs.[12] He flew to Stockton in April 1931 for his transport pilot license test with an inspector scheduled to stop there.[13]

In Bob Laurin's plane, Jack Beilby flew a passenger from the municipal airport to Elk Grove in 15 minutes to be at the bedside of his dying mother.[14] Eva Baily Laurin, Bob's wife, was building solo hours in her husband's

Travel Air at Sac Muni to qualify for her license test.[15] Mrs. Laurin, with 30 hours to her credit, passed the test and received her license in September 1931.[16]

In November Eva Laurin flew her husband's Travel Air back to Sacramento from Palo Alto where minor repair work had been done to the plane. After getting his plane back, Bob made a charter flight to the Bay Area and another to Marysville.[17]

Laurin's Travel Air was damaged in a forced landing in January 1932. He began negotiating for a new airplane, and traded his Travel Air for a new Spartan biplane.[18] On Sunday March 6, 1932, Laurin hopped 32 passengers in his Spartan at Sac Muni after which there were no further aviation news reports concerning Laurin.[19]

Harold G. "Buzz" Slingsby

Manager of the Air Taxi Service Company, Buzz Slingsby announced in February 1930 his firm would make the municipal airport on Freeport Boulevard its headquarters when the airport opened. The company operated two Eaglerocks for charter work and flight instruction. At the time, the planes were based at Eagle Rock Airport on Upper Stockton Road. Slingsby had reserved space in a large hangar on the new airport.[20]

Slingsby flew to Napa on a Saturday in June 1930 and returned to Sacramento. The next day he flew to Quincy and back.[21] In July Slingsby pulled the OX-5 motor off his Travel Air and replaced it with a rebuilt OX-5.[22]

Buzz Slingsby and Charles Kendell staged an unusual race at the new municipal airport in August. He flew his Travel Air and Kendell drove a racing car. The race was a half-mile long and began from a standing start. The airplane beat the car three consecutive times, but only by a few feet.[23]

In November Slingsby purchased a new Whirlwind Pitacairn biplane. After being away several weeks, Buzz surprised everyone when he landed in his new plane. He flew it over the snow-capped Sierra Nevada to Reno a few days later.[24]

Slingsby purchased a Whirlwind Stearman a month later from Michael C. Casserly of San Francisco. It is believed Slingsby brokered the sale for someone else.[25] Slingsby, partnered with W. H. Cortopassi and purchased an OX-5 Commandaire biplane from William S. Orvis of Wilton. Slingsby used this plane exclusively for flight instruction at Sac Muni.[26] Joe Decetis, a Slingsby student, learned to fly in the Commandaire and in late May passed his DOC test for a private pilot license.[27] In November 1930,

Slingsby made his aforementioned flight to lower Echo Lake and dropped supplies to snowbound construction workers.[28]

Paul Norboe partnered with Slingsby in the Pitcairn purchase. Buzz Slingsby returned it to Sacramento in December after repairs in San Francisco.[29] Slingsby made several flights in Bennett's Monocoach from the municipal airport on the first Sunday of March 1932. He also flew several passengers in his Pitcairn, and on the eighth he flew a charter to Dunsmuir.[30] Slingsby and Norboe leased the original field construction office at Sac Muni in April. The office was moved to a new location just north of hangar No. 3. It would serve Valley Air Lines; Slingsby and Norboe's new company. Their air service would feature charter flights to most areas in the state at prices only slightly higher than railroad fares.[31]

Valley Air Lines flew a charter to Reno in late April, according to Slingsby. The Pitcairn was put in the shop for overhaul and would be ready for the summer season.[32] Slingsby reported in May a considerable increase in night charter flights to the Bay Area. Warmer weather made night flying attractive to customers.[33] Valley Air Lines made two charter flights to the Bay Area and one to Ely, Nevada, which involved a 420-mile, three-and-a half-hour flight ending in a four-day stay at Oroville for a convention in May.[34]

Buzz Slingsby leased space at Sac Muni in July to house a Lockheed Vega, a five-place, high-wing, cabin plane. The Vega, powered by a Whirlwind J-5, cruised at 125 mph and topped out at 160. Later in the month, Slingsby began retrofitting the Vega as an aerial ambulance. It would carry a stretcher and three seated passengers, who would be able to give medical attention to a patient in flight. A survey indicated enough demand for the service to make it commercially viable.[35]

Valley Air Lines' aerial ambulance was demonstrated publicly during a routine weekend air show at the municipal airport in October.[36] The company reported in December 1932 only three flights were missed in five months of daily operations—because of weather—on its Stockton-San Francisco-Sacramento route. Only Buzz Slingsby, chief pilot for Valley Air, was allowed to fly the speedy Vega.

Summit Flying Service

Summit Aircraft Company, as it was first known, got its OX-5 International F-17 licensed at the company headquarters on Mills Field at San Bruno. The company reorganized as Summit Flying Service in September 1931. Claiming the honor of being the largest aviation school in the West,

Summit announced opening its first branch school at Sacramento Municipal Airport.[38]

Miss Janet Knight, an accomplished aviatrix with a limited commercial license, was chosen to head the branch's ground school instruction with Dana "Tommy" Thompson, a noted Pacific coast professional pilot, handling flight instruction. He would commute from Mills Field, San Francisco's municipal airport at San Bruno.

Lack of hangar space on the municipal field prevented Summit from opening its office and facilities, but the first training plane, a Fleet from Mills Field, arrived to begin immediate operations. It was an open cockpit biplane powered by a 125hp. Kinner engine; nimble and well suited for aerobatic training. The Summit school on Mills Field was training 50 students when the Sacramento branch was opened. Twenty of the students flew to Sacramento for an impromptu air meet to celebrate the new branch with a proper opening. One student, Ruth Marshall, was said to be one of the few commercially licensed women pilots in the Bay Area at the time.

Janet Knight told the press Sacramento was picked to be its first Summit branch because "... this city's future as an aviation crossroads is assured." The school would, according to Miss Knight, serve students from all of Northern California, but she said more branches might be opened at other locations in the region.

At the time of the branch opening, the following ad ran in the *Sacramento Bee*: "Summit Flying School San Francisco's Biggest and Best Equipped School Is Announcing the Establishment of a Sacramento Branch Thursday, September 17, 1931, bringing to the airminded [sic] young men and women the chance to learn to fly and pay as you learn. You can learn for as little as $10 a week – no sum of money down. Dual instruction is $17.50 per hour, solo time is $12.50 an hour in the finest army type Fleet trainers money can buy ... See Miss Knight at the Municipal Airfield Tuesday, Wednesday, Thursday, during the day and at the Senator Hotel desk during the evening and arrange for a free demonstration lesson."[39]

Ivor Witney, a Summit instructor, reported Grafton Reed of Auburn passed his tests for a private pilot license. This was the same Grafton Reed who was chief mechanic on the Friesley Falcon airliner built at Gridley in 1921. Julio Lorenzo, a Sacramento Filipino student, signed on to learn to fly with Witney. Once he received his license, he planned to return to the Philippines and pursue work as a commercial pilot.[40] In November Witney was getting Kenneth Yost and O. W. Castle ready for their private license tests.[41]

Witney reported Summit was about to move into an office leased in hangar No. 3. He also said Chester Hatch, who recently failed his test for a private license, was about ready to ride with a DOC inspector again.[42] A Summit official announced Frank Jones passed his flight test with DOC inspector James Peyton in early December.[43]

The bad weather that fouled Ivor Witney's flight to Reno and stranded the company's Fleet there in early January 1932 continued for weeks.[44] Herbert Pope of Davis signed on with Summit as a new student, and Henry Gastman from Auburn passed his private license test in February. The runways at the municipal airport suffered through heavy rains but survived in good condition. A few soft spots were drained and reinforced with gravel to stop any reoccurrence.[45]

Summit acquired six new students at Grass Valley and planned to start teaching there as soon as the runway dried enough to use. Summit also reported a plan to possibly expand operations at Grass Valley.[46]

During the last Sunday of February, a great crowd showed up at Sacramento Muni and made it the best day to date for passenger hopping. Summit's Dana Thompson gave the spectators a treat when he put a few of his advanced students through aerobatic maneuvers. The spins and inverted flying drew their exhortations.[47]

Dorothy Burkhart, a noted athlete from Sacramento, began flying lessons in March with newly incorporated Summit Flying Schools, Ltd. Dana Thompson, president of the company, traveled to Los Angeles to pick up a new Fleet DeLuxe model.[48]

Four Summit training planes were flown in formation over Grass Valley on March 20 bringing attention to its operations starting soon at Grass Valley Airport. Student pilots flew two of them.[49]

At Sacramento Ivor Witney reported Thomas Whittmore, a theater manager; Gordon Weber; and Jack Smith, all from Auburn, began flight instruction with Summit.[50] W. R. Schanhals, C. W. Castle, Ted Elsen, Carl Danatti, Elmer DaRosa and E. J. Mickle, student pilots with Summit, took their tests with DOC inspector James Peyton for private pilot licenses on April 27.

Ruth Pittenger of Auburn, L. Christensen of Marysville, and C. Wesley Reed signed on late April with Summit.[51] Dr. L. M. Marsh, an Auburn physician, signed up for flight instruction; his wife planned to at a later date. Also from Auburn, Ed Jones and Al Backman registered as students.[52]

Summit Flying Schools held an informal dance in the reception room of hangar No. 3 on June 4 in Sacramento. Janet Knight, who had been instructing at Mills Field, flew in for the dance, as did flight students from the Bay Area, Woodland, Auburn, and Grass Valley.

At Sacramento, Dana Thompson reported new students Jack Lewis, a miner; Ralph Wilson, a theater manager; and Carlos McGuire from the Nevada County surveyor's office. Manley Green of North Sacramento also signed on. Thompson confirmed he would soon be teaching a blind flying course.[53] Gordon Ball passed his private pilot license test the first week of June.

In June, Dana Thompson confirmed Sacramento Municipal Airport would be Summit Flying Schools' headquarters because facilities and service were the best in the area. He put Janet Knight in charge of training at Mills Field. Thompson took five Sacramento students up for night instruction as a large group of spectators assembled to watch Boeing transcontinental planes land and depart, something many local residents enjoyed. Airport superintendent Don Smith was one of the night flying students subjected to a spin and a couple wingovers. He said he couldn't tell the difference between airport lights and the Big Dipper during maneauvers.[54]

In late June, Charles Sands and Frank Freeman of Auburn signed with Summit. Students Grafton Reed, Owen Castle, and Frank Jones were passed for solo night flying. Janet Knight flew from Mills Field to Grass Valley to help teaching its weekly class.[55] Ivor Witney, former Summit instructor who was probably laid off due to declining enrollment, was rehired to take over Thompson's teaching while he tended to business in the south state.[56]

Summit took possession of the Pitcairn owned by Paul Norboe and flown by Buzz Slingsby. The company planned to completely overhaul it and use it for charter flights and passenger hops.[57]

Ivor Witney was born in San Francisco to Mr. and Mrs. W. W. Witney. He began flying lessons in 1928 at Mills Field with "Red" Williams in a Curtiss Jenny and got his private license. In 1931 he upgraded to a transport pilot license. By August 1932, he had flown 500 hours without an accident. Many Northern Californians took flight instruction from Witney during his lengthy career in the Bay Area and Sacramento. Elmer DaRosa and Owen Castle tried for their licenses on August 2. DaRosa passed, but Castle did not. Witney and Dana Thompson had trained them.

Summit completed a contract to fly a fireworks display in the Bay Area during a Shriner's convention. Inspector Peyton of the DOC oversaw the exhibition.[58]

Summit's president Dana Thompson was also a lieutenant in the Marine Corps Reserve. He expected to transfer to the Marine Aviation Reserve as soon as the new unit was organized.[59] Thompson flew a Fleet trainer to Sacramento to replace a Summit training plane damaged at the municipal airport by an airplane whose pilot lost control.

Ivor Witney reported Owen Castle, an auto parts salesman; Adolph Gemignani, a local businessman; and Henry Cody, of Bogota, Colombia; all passed their private license tests. Harold. L. Newman, the Boeing agent, reinstated his lapsed license in July. His reinstatement training was under Witney's direction. Newman later purchased his own plane and kept it at Sacramento Muni.[60] Dustin Clark, a Sacramento insurance agent, took lessons from Witney through Summit. Karl Harder, another Summit student, took his private license test in November.[61]

Dana "Tommy" Thompson died September 13, 1933, in a crash at Bellaire, six miles south of Dixon. He was flying from Mills Field to inspect Summit's branch. Janet Knight took over Summit's Sacramento branch shortly after his death.[62]

Kimball Flying Service

Leo Moore, a popular Sacramento flier, announced in January 1932 the formation of a new flying school, Kimball Flying Service, at Sacramento Municipal Airport. A. Weston Kimball, the Century-Pacific agent at Sacramento, was the owner. Moore was hired as chief pilot.

Moore flew a new Aeronca C-3 to Sacramento for the Kimball flying school. The very small, two-place, "flying bathtub," as it was known, had a 40hp. air-cooled engine, and made the trip through rain, snow, high winds, and fog from Saugus in 5 ½ hours.

Leo Moore was formerly an aeronautics instructor at Galt Union High School and Junior College with over 3,000 hours. He would fly Kimball's Ryan Brougham on special Sunday charter trips over the Sierra Nevada and Lake Tahoe.[63]

Superintendent Don Smith announced the Sacramento airport had nearly run out of hangar room with the lease of office space in hangar No. 3 to Kimball Flying Service. The only space left unused was in hangar No. 1, half of which was leased by Sacramento Junior College for a class studying aircraft engines.[64]

A. W. Kimball reported 320 flights had been flown in the C-3 since his company took delivery of the diminutive plane. Having great passenger visibility, it became popular for charter flights. Kimball had to turn down flights to San Jose, Reno, and Stockton during bad weather.[65] In February Kimball acquired a second airplane for charter flights. It was a four-place, high-wing Stinson cabin plane to be used for charter work and flight instruction.

Stinson company pilot Todd Crutchfield delivered the plane to Sacramento. It was a later model of the Varney Air Lines' Stinson used on their Sacramento–San Francisco route. The plane was luxuriously appointed and its balloon tires made for softer landings. It replaced the Ryan Brougham on charters over the Sierra Nevada and Lake Tahoe.[66]

Kimball's Aeronca and Stinson offered for service in the Sacramento area became the subject of conversation around the airport. Both planes were new designs.[67] Leo Moore flew the little C-3 to Mokelumne Hill with no problem getting in and out of the short airfield. The C-3 and the Stinson made many flights there on Sunday, March 6.[68]

In April, Kimball hired William W. Lawrence as traffic manager to schedule the type of flying desired by customers and students, and employed former Century Pacific mechanic Carl Van Meter. Moonlight flights were keeping his staff busy, said Kimball.[69] Kimball's Chinese students declared their homeland was far behind the West in aviation technology, and they hoped to serve China as airmail pilots rather than army pilots.[70]

Ted Ward, a Kimball student, passed his private license test at Oakland. Also in early May, Harry Stewart of Grass Valley signed on with Kimball.[71] J. A. Hudson, a local restaurateur, and Gene Hughes, a Sacramento rancher, took their license tests in May.

Leo Moore raced a speedboat in Kimball's small Aeronca C-3 at a local boating regatta on May 8, 1932. Later that day Moore flew the C-3 to Shingle Springs for a local picnic.[72]

Kimball's Bill Lawrence reported Charles H. Dye of Mather Field enrolled in June for instruction. Since starting business on January 15, Kimball had carried 1,700 passengers while making 3,000 takeoffs and landings without incidents.[73]

Leo Moore flew the Stinson to Alturas with businessmen Claude M. Adams and G. R. Johnson. After their return, he took R. R. Baker, vice president of the Modoc County Bank in Alturas, to San Francisco. Moore later took Baker back to Sacramento. It was Baker's first flight, and he loved the experience. Moore said Alturas Airport was close to excellent trout fishing and was anxious for more charter flights to the area.[74] A. B. Stribling and Howard Bendix, both local, signed on with Kimball in July.[75] Cheung A'Sik of Walnut Grove was the first Asian student to learn to fly with Kimball. Cheung planned to get his transport license then return to China and fly mail.[76]

Katherine H. Maritsas of Sacramento, a student at Kimball Flying Service, planned to train until she passed her transport pilot license. Leo Moore gave her her first flying lesson on June 14. Two days later, she soloed with only 4 hours and 45 minutes of dual instruction![77]

Kimball returned in August from a six-week trip to the East. He visited aviation businesses and facilities including Curtiss-Wright at Buffalo, New York, where Curtiss military planes were tested at speeds of over 200 mph.[78]

Les Moore (not Leo Moore), a former Stockton aviator, allowed Kimball use of his Fleet for student instruction. This gave the company three aircraft for training students in all aspects of flying including advanced aerobatics.[79] Kimball acquired a new Lockheed Vega in late September; it was one of the fastest four-place cabin planes on the market. It was popular with the public, mainly because the famous Wiley Post set several records in his Vega, named the *Winnie Mae*, and Amelia Earhart had flown to fame in her record-setting Vega. Kimball's Vega was chartered for three trips its first week on the line. The plane was kept at the Kimball facility on Sacramento Municipal Airport.[80]

Superintendent Donald Smith was photographed at Sac Muni in October congratulating Cheung Sik as one of the first Chinese students to receive a private pilot license in Northern California. Moore said Sik's limited English made his achievement even more impressive. Also in the photo were three new Chinese students H. J. Yuen, Wong Sing, and Bill Choy looking on proudly. They had just taken their first flying lessons in the Kimball Aeronca C-3 parked behind them in the photo.[81]

Leo Moore planned an aerobatic exhibition for November 6, 1932, at the municipal airport. He would demonstrate the maneuverability of the Fleet biplane in use by Kimball Flying Service. Les Moore, owner of this particular Fleet, had flown it to Sacramento from Palo Alto Airport. A throng of people had gathered for their Sunday outing. Martin Senn and Leo Lachner, both advanced flying students would soon take their private license tests. Also that month, Fred Pinnegar signed on with Kimball;[82] Leo Lachner passed his flight test; and Ernie Moe, a commercial pilot from Woodland, assisted Kimball Flying Service as a relief pilot and flying instructor.[83]

CHAPTER II 245

Martin Senn passed his flight test in December for a DOC inspector at Sac Muni.[84] Also A. W. Kimball flew the Lockheed Vega to the south state to be retrofitted to transport orchids from Los Angeles to New York for a new 24-hour service.[85]

Capital Airlines Inc.

The Air Commerce Act of 1926 went into effect January 1, 1927 (enforcement started July 1, 1927), finally giving the federal government the authority to regulate airports, aircraft, and aviators. Most importantly, the Act made airmail, airfreight, and passenger airline flying insurable commercial businesses.

The first scheduled Sacramento passenger service based at a municipal airport was Capital Airlines Inc. in mid-1928 when the airline was formed at Del Paso Airport. Royal Miller, W. I. Elliott, C. E. Wilkins and H. G. Andrews founded it and purchased a Breese cabin monoplane.

In July 1928, a one by three-inch box ad was run in the *Sacramento Bee*: "Ride The Air – Tri Weekly Schedule – Sacramento – Oakland – 45 Minute Service – Fare $10 One Way – Tuesday, Thursday, Saturday Leave Municipal Airport Sacramento 8 AM Arrive Oakland 8:45 AM – Leave Oakland Airport 2 PM Arrive Sacramento 2:45 PM – Special trips to all parts by appointment – 4-passenger Cabin Monoplane Equipment – Government Licensed Planes – Government Transport Licensed Pilots. Capital Airlines Inc. – Municipal Airport – Phone Main 1751."[86]

The Breese was kept busy in July on regular runs three times a week between Sacramento and Oakland. It was also used for short hops between scheduled flights. To improve performance, a steel propeller was installed on the Breese.[87] Capital had gone into service with its schedule timed so Capital could serve as a "feeder line" for other transport lines (non-schedule) operating to and from other municipal airports.[88] H. G. Andrews was chief pilot.

In August 1928, Capital Air Lines was acquired by Union Air Line Inc., which in turn was owned by majority stockholders in Pickwick Stage Lines and West Coast Air Transport Company. The latter operated a daily air service between Seattle and Portland and a triweekly service between Seattle and San Francisco.

It was understood Capital would maintain its name and H. G. Andrews would stay on as the local manager. The only changes were triweekly service was changed to daily and instead of flying to Oakland Municipal Airport from Sacramento, the planes would fly to Mills Field on the San Francisco side of the bay.[89]

Union Air Line started service, through its newly acquired Capital Airlines, with a respectable prior record. From March 5 to June 30, the toughest flying period of the year with rain and snow over the mountains of the Pacific Northwest, two of Union's planes flew 125,000 air miles in 1,150 flying hours, hauling 2,906 paid passengers between Seattle and San Francisco without a forced landing or accident.[90] A flight from Sacramento in the Union Air Line Breese, still flown by H. G. Andrews, would land at Mills Field in time to connect with the Los Angeles and Portland-Seattle planes of West Coast Air Transport. Ground transportation from Mills Field to Bay Area destinations was provided by Pickwick Stage Line taxis.[91]

These were the same routes to the same termini Harold Friesley and Charles McHenry Pond had hoped to fly their airliners, the Friesley Falcon (Portland–San Francisco) and the Curtiss Eagle (San Francisco–Los Angeles) in 1921.

For passenger service on the West Coast, Union Air Lines, Maddux Air Lines, and British Airways (*sic*) came to an agreement providing through airline service.[92]

Capital Airlines, Union Air Lines' subsidiary, was doing excellent business on passenger runs from Sacramento to San Francisco in August. H. G. Andrews reported an average of three-and-a-half passengers per trip.[93] Capital Flying Service, which also operated out of Del Paso Municipal Airport, was appointed as Sacramento's ticket agent for Capital Airlines, which was flying daily service between Del Paso and San Francisco. Jack Casey, business manager for Capital Flying Service, announced this new ticket service for Capital Airlines.[94]

In November an ad ran in a local paper: "Capital Air Lines [*sic*] – Union Air Lines, Owners and Operators –Leaves Sacramento at 8 AM and 3 PM [daily] Flying Time one hour – Visit San Francisco and return same day – Fare: One Way $8 – Round Trip $15."[95]

Boeing Air Transport / United Air Lines

When Boeing Air Transport (BAT) was awarded transcontinental CAM 18 (Contract Air Mail Route 18) between Oakland and Chicago in January 1927, the municipal airport at Del Paso Park was not in good enough shape to accommodate the larger Boeing mailplanes, so the US Army Air Corps granted Boeing's request that Mather Field be Sacramento's airmail terminal on the Reno–Sacto–SF leg of CAM 18. Boeing used Mather until Sac Muni opened April 1930 on Freeport Boulevard.

Boeing Air Transport began carrying passengers in the two-seat cabin of their new Boeing Model 40A soon after the company's start-up July 1, 1927. BAT began using 12-passenger, tri-motor Boeing Model 80A biplane transports in late 1928. Mather Field became the first passenger terminal for scheduled transcontinental airline service from the Sacramento Valley. Boeing Air Transport has been mentioned many times previously for the western half of transcontinental airmail service; the following information further describes Boeing's activities in the north state while flying the CAM 18 route.[96]

Good weather in February 1928 brought army planes to Mather Field from Crissy Field almost daily to use the bombing and machine gun ranges at Mather. While this cacophony was taking place, Boeing's mail planes were landing at Mather twice a day on the San Francisco–Chicago route.[97]

Claire Vance, who flew the Reno to San Francisco leg of the transcontinental route, liked to keep his passengers informed as they passed over an interesting landmark. He had a telephone installed in the two-seat passenger cabin of his Boeing Model 40A and identified landmarks from his open cockpit above the cabin. Passengers were given maps to follow their route, but usually the maps only confused them.[98]

J. J. Jacobs, a Sacramento automobile dealer, arranged a flight to the Studebaker factory at South Bend, Indiana, in late summer on a transcontinental BAT mail plane.[99]

The California Fruit Exchange and a plumbing supplier, the Crane Company, told the Sacramento Chamber of Commerce that if the city failed to improve the airport at Del Paso Park or to develop a new airfield for Boeing Air Transport, they would close their Sacramento plants and move to a new location where transcontinental airmail was available. Fast communication was mandatory to maintain their businesses success. If Sacramento lost the airmail service, they would be forced to use telegraph service and incur prohibitive costs. The chamber did not consider these as idle threats by the Fruit Exchange, a $20,000,000-a-year industry. Their concern was Boeing would stop flying into Mather Field because it was unlighted; Boeing was to begin making through night flights once the transcontinental lighted airway system was completed in the fall of 1928.[100] O. C. Richerson, field superintendent at Oakland Municipal Airport for Boeing Air Transport, helped the city of Sacramento plan for a new municipal airport.[101]

Claire Vance, the pilot on BAT's San Francisco (Oakland) to Reno run, told a reporter while waiting for his plane to be loaded with mail at Mather Field, he had made 1,700 trips over the "hump" (Sierra Nevada) as he called it. He said, "Accounts of terrific downdrafts over the hump were mostly fables. Sometimes, when there is an east wind blowing during the winter months, my plane drops a few feet over the western slopes of the mountains. The prevailing winds, however, are west, and they cause downdrafts over the Reno Valley foothills. In neither case are we much concerned about them." Vance said he always tried to fly under a storm in the mountains, but if he couldn't fly under it safely, he would fly over the storm if cloud build-ups weren't too high.[102]

At the beginning of 1929, Boeing Air Transport was still flying the single-engine Model 40A biplanes on the Oakland (SF)–Sacramento–Reno run. The mail exchange at Mather usually went as follows: when the incoming plane stopped rolling a mail truck rushed across the field and backed up to the cockpit. The field manager jumped onto the big biplane's lower wing and retrieved the airmail pouch from the forward mail compartment destined for Sacramento and its surrounding towns. The mail truck driver handed the field manager the outgoing pouch for points east, which he put into the compartment. The pilot, standing in his seat to stretch his legs, would sit down, fasten his seat belt, get a last minute weather report from the field manager, then push the throttle forward and was off to his next stop—Reno.

The glass enclosed two-seat passenger compartment, just forward of the pilot's open cockpit, was usually full; the popularity of these flights was increasing weekly, and these few seats were booked on mail planes weeks in advance. With passenger bookings increasing, Boeing announced it would begin using Model 80A 12-passenger, tri-motor transports within the next several weeks.[103]

Vance was asked by BAT to fly a transport from San Francisco to Mexico City. It was a harrowing flight. Fighting fierce storms and bad weather all the way, he was forced down once and later had to climb above 16,000 feet to get over mountains en route.[104]

The Boeing Model 80As began flying into Mather Field at the end of May 1929. Two of the 12-passenger transports landed daily. The eastbound plane arrived at 8:50 AM, and the westbound plane landed at 2:30 PM. Boeing field manager Dayton Baker said many folks were taking advantage of the new faster service to and from the Bay Area. Nightly planes landed from

San Francisco at 8:50 PM and 2:30 AM from Reno. They carried only mail; early on, no passengers were carried on night flights.[105]

By October 1, 1929, Clair Vance and Burr Winslow had flown close to 2,000 trips each over the hump in the Model 40A on the Reno to Sacramento leg.[106] Boeing announced in November, its two West Coast airlines, Boeing Air Transport and Pacific Air Transport, had a total of 42 aircraft on the company's mail routes, which were being flown by 63 pilots.[107]

In December, BAT reported the company had put more of the larger tri-motor Model 80As on airmail runs to handle the Christmas overload. The Boeing Model 80A could carry 18 passengers when not carrying mail, but only carried 12 when loaded with 500 pounds of mail. Ten Model 80As were being tested on the transcontinental run by late April 1930. The big airliner had reclining chairs, allowing the passengers to sleep during flights. On the flight east, the Model 80As left Oakland at 8:00 PM and arrived at Chicago the next day at 6:00 PM. Passengers had to change planes at Cheyenne. All of the Model 80As were radio equipped and a chain of radio stations was established across the continent; pilots were in communication with ground stations at all times.[108]

When weather conditions were bad over the Donner/Truckee Summit route, the mail planes used a more northern route known as the Walker Pass route. It is an emergency route that can be flown at lower altitudes, but it is longer. From Reno this emergency route goes over Susanville, Westwood, and Corning then down the west side of the Sacramento Valley and on to Oakland.[109]

Pacific Air Transport (PAT), a subsidiary of Boeing Air Transport, had six founding pilots still flying for the company by May 1930: Arthur Starbuck, Charlie Bowman, Ralph Virden, Russell Cunningham, Heber Miller, and Grover Tyler. They had flown 3,125,000 miles over the company's mail route from Seattle-San Francisco-Los Angeles. They had flown 18,000 hours as Pacific coast mailmen. Veteran pilots E. L. Remlin, Al Gilhausen, F. A. Donaldson, Johnny C. Johnston, and Harry Crandall soon joined PAT.[110] Pilots' salaries on airmail and passenger routes were $300 to $850 per month in the latter half of 1929 and the first half of 1930. The average salary for the same pilot was $550 by September 1930. It had been $463.51 in early 1929. Engine and airframe mechanics were paid between $125 and $185 per month by September 1930.[111]

Ralph Virden, PAT's longest serving pilot, logged 6,000 hours on September 9, 1930. He learned to fly in 1920 and joined PAT in 1926 flying

Ryan M-1 mail planes up and down the coast, as PAT pioneered Pacific coast airmail service. Virden stayed with the company when it was taken over by the Boeing System in 1928. He had flown over sixty different types of airplanes during his career.[112]

Pacific Air Transport purchased West Coast Air Transport in March 1931. P. G. Johnson, president of Boeing, told the press PAT would receive all of West Coast Air Transport's tri-motor planes, equipment, and flying personnel. Operations of daily passenger service between San Francisco and Seattle would continue, as would overnight mail and passenger service between San Diego and Seattle.[113]

Luppen and Hawley, electrical contractors, were working employees overtime at Sacramento Municipal Airport on Freeport Boulevard the end of May to get an electrical substation up and running so night flying could begin. Inauguration of Boeing Air Transport service to and from Sacramento Municipal Airport was contingent upon workable night lighting, according to Boeing rep Harold L. Newman. He said June 3, 1931, was chosen for the start of Boeing air service. An enormous floodlight was installed between Freeport Boulevard and the runway some distance north of the original hangar No. 1 location. It would light up the airfield for landings. As soon as an aircraft touched down the floodlight was turned off and the taxiway lights were turned on to lower the electric bill.

Flying over the field or during landing, an airliner would be given a signal from the Boeing field representative that there were passengers to pick up. The same process was used for mail pick up. Weather reporting equipment and a ceiling projection unit would soon be installed at the Boeing hangar.[114]

At long last, Boeing Air Transport began using Sacramento Municipal Airport as its base of operations instead of Mather Field. BAT pilot Don Broughton made the first in-service landing in a company Model 80A on the night of June 3, 1931. The Model 80A, powered by three 525hp. Pratt & Whitney Wasp engines, was used on Boeing's half of the transcontinental route, San Francisco (Oakland)–Chicago.

The time required to fly to Chicago from Sacramento in a Model 80A was 21 hours. All Boeing or its subsidiaries' planes flying into and out of Sacramento were radio equipped by June 1931. The planes of Pacific Air Transport flying from Seattle to San Diego; those of Varney Lines on the Salt Lake to Seattle via Boise and Portland route; and Boeing Air Transport (eventually all merged into United Air Lines) were using radios tuned to the same wave length. Each plane was given a unique time on the hour to report to ground stations and avoid transmissions being stepped on. The Department of Commerce transmitted reports throughout the United States about weather, ceiling, visibility, and any other pertinent information at 40 minutes past the hour starting at Oakland and terminating at Reno. At 25 minutes past the hour, a report was received starting at Salt Lake City and terminating at Reno. Every three hours a general summary of weather was transmitted. Once every six hours soundings of the upper air were made to determine wind directions and velocities. The first sounding was taken at 700 feet, then 1,400 feet and thereafter every 600 feet. This helped pilots know which altitude might find helping winds. The weather reports were received and sent with Teletype (TTY) machines, similar to those used by the Associated Press, to company weather reporting stations printed on conventional ticker tape to be relayed by radio to the airline pilots.[115]

Boeing Air Transport, from the first day they were flying from Sacramento, made it clear that passenger safety was its primary objective and even though its planes were equipped with every modern flight instrument, pilots were forbidden to engage in "blind flying," (later known as instrument flying) while carrying passengers. To underscore that point, it was reported in mid-June an eastbound airliner climbed 15,000 feet to get above the clouds for better visibility. On another day, a pilot tried the same thing but returned to Sacramento when he was unable to ascend above the clouds. He crossed the Sierra Nevada after the weather improved. However, a pilot carrying only mail might be asked to fly on instruments to complete his flight.

Spectators were arriving nightly at the municipal airport to watch BAT planes land and take off on their regular schedules. As many as a thousand people would watch the big planes on warm summer evenings.[116] After BAT and PAT were renamed United Air Lines, UAL was awarded a new route in the East in July 1931. United's daily routes totaled 35,000 miles. It was the most miles of any airline in the world, pushing out Lufthansa for the title of number one in route miles.[117]

Harold Newman, Boeing System manager at Sac Muni, returned from vacationing in the East late in August 1931. He toured several factories and brought back a lot of useful technological information to share with city officials. He described a new radio system for police cars to Sacramento Police Chief William Hallanan.[118]

Pacific Air Transport was one of the first commercial airlines in the nation. It shared the honor as the oldest airline to fly a regular schedule on the Pacific coast with Western Air Express. PAT made two round trips daily with a schedule totaling 1,750,000 miles flown annually on its Seattle to San Francisco route.[119] United Air Lines aircraft took over PAT's routes between Seattle and San Diego but quit landing at Sacramento after the first of the year as planned.

Harold Newman reported unforeseen delays were holding up inauguration of the new service. When the service begins, Newman said, there would be a reduction in time for the transcontinental trip. Boeing was planning to use a new low-wing bomber type of plane with a cruising speed of 180 mph. The plane was undergoing further testing. Newman was referring to the Boeing Model 247, which was based on the company's B-9 bomber design. The twin engine 247 was the world's first modern airliner.[120]

In January 1932, an attempt was made to stimulate more passenger business; United Air Lines dropped its prices. Newman reported a one-way ticket to Reno was lowered to $6.66, and the round trip cut to $11.98. The one-way fare to Chicago was reduced to $135 from $150. Fare to New York was dropped to $160 from $200.

The eastbound Boeing Model 80A landed at Sacramento on January 5. It was the first of its type to use the airfield since the heavy rains. It was loaded near capacity, and the runways held. Larger planes were required because passengers on flights to the East were increasing dramatically.[121]

United Air Lines pilot John W. Sharpnack was killed February 2, 1932, when his Boeing Model 40B crashed near the town of Rio Vista during a freak snowstorm. Sharpnack carried 203 pounds of mail and no passengers. Searching from the air, Pacific Air Transport pilot Will L. Campbell found the crash site the following day. He landed next to the crash and his plane flipped over. Campbell was unhurt but, unfortunately, nothing could be done for Sharpnack whose plane burned on impact.[122]

April 1932 flying activities at Sacramento Muni were as follows: Newman, the UAL agent, stated there had been a crush of business the last 30 days. The previous week, UAL tri-motor transports were flying at near capacity with local demand increasing. It was the heaviest passenger demand ever experienced by the Boeing System at Sacramento.[123] Additional UAL Boeing 80As were brought on line in late April.[124]

Unusually late storms over the hump in April had Boeing employees wondering what to expect; the weather had disrupted all trans-mountain air service. Varney's airline was working at full capacity and occasionally forced to double up on some schedules to accommodate additional passengers.[125] Newman reported blind flying test runs were undertaken by UAL from Sacramento Municipal Airport in May.[126] UAL reported a flight to Detroit from Sacramento would take less time than before. Passengers leaving Sacramento at 10:35 AM Monday would arrive in Detroit at 12:35 PM on Tuesday.[127]

Ralph Meyers, radio repairman for Boeing at Sacramento, was hospitalized in San Francisco after being struck on the arm by a spinning propeller. His arm was paralyzed, requiring the care of a specialist.[128]

Radio engineers upgraded UAL office radio equipment in July, giving it maximum efficiency. A four aerial system was installed providing use of the various wavelengths for Pacific Air Transport and the other subsidiaries that made up UAL.[129]

December brought a severe cold spell, which had little effect on transcontinental airmail service over the Sierra Nevada hump. Newman said airmail was rerouted by train only once during the record cold. Temperatures as low as 44 degrees below zero did cause problems in Nevada. Temperatures in UAL airliners were reported as fair and maintained at comfortable levels.[130]

Claire Kinsey Vance, considered a legendary figure by colleagues, crashed fatally on his UAL airmail run December 17, 1932. Many local commercial pilots, upon learning Vance was overdue, took off to search immediately led by Harold Newman hoping Vance might have survived a crash. They searched between Sacramento and Rio Vista with no luck. The group included Ivor Witney of the Summit flying school; Ray Nicholson and Ernie Moe of the Nicholson school, and Leo Moore of the Kimball flying school. Pilots all reported dangerous situations they got into while attempting to avoid the ground fog, which raised and lowered around them as they searched. They knew forced landings in the soup could have deadly consequences, but their personal risk was forgotten when considering Vance's greater need.

Vance had departed Oakland at 11:45 PM on his eastbound airmail run to Reno. Later it was learned his plane failed to clear Rocky Ridge near Danville by ten feet. It was the last mountain ridge he needed to clear before reaching the Great Central Valley and on to his next stop at Sacramento. Wes Moreau, a commercial pilot from Oakland Airport, flying one of 20 planes looking for Vance, found the charred remains of Vance's plane the next day; Vance was only minutes from Oakland Airport.[131]

J. A. Rose, traffic manager for UAL at Sacramento for several years, was transferred in late 1934 to Oakland. There he would continue to be in charge of the Sacramento, Oakland, and Reno territory. Al Everett from Oklahoma replaced him as operations manager at Sacramento.[132]

Century Pacific Lines Ltd.

Century Pacific, founded by the owner of Auburn Motor Company E. L. Cord, began airline service on July 3, 1931. The airline set a passenger carrying record of over 10,000 passengers hauled in its first two months of service. All revenue was from passenger and freight service; it had no airmail contract. During early operations, the airline lured customers from competitors by selling seats on its tri-motor Stinsons at less than train fares. The airline served San Diego, Los Angeles, Bakersfield, Fresno, San Jose, Oakland, San Francisco, and Sacramento. Century Pacific eventually extended service to Arizona.[133]

A scenic route reflected in the airline's new schedule started on October 3 between San Francisco and Los Angeles. The 7:00 AM flight leaving Sacramento proceeded to San Francisco Bay Airdrome at Alameda; then on to Mills Field across the bay; then San Jose, Salinas, Santa Maria, and on to Los Angeles, landing at 1:00 PM. Century Pacific also began running special flights to accommodate fans attending University of California and Stanford football games. Special buses would meet the planes and shuttle passengers to the stadium.[134]

A. W. Kimball, Sacramento agent for Century Pacific, returned to work late in November from the East after a family funeral. Kimball married Johanna "Dodie" Blewett, a noted championship swimmer, in December at Los Angeles. He was the son of Alonzo Kimball, the New York artist and illustrator. A. W. Kimball started learning to fly and after six hours of dual instruction from Sacramento's Summit Flying School, he soloed.

Century Pacific expanded the number of flights between Sacramento and San Francisco with planes departing Sacramento five times daily between 8:00 AM, and 5:00 PM. The planes returned from Mill's Field between 9:15 AM and 7:15 PM.[135] Jack Hewson, a Century Pacific pilot, completed 5,000 hours of transport flying without an accident. Hewson learned to fly during the Great War and had served at Rockwell Field, San Diego, as a flight instructor. Several years after the war he flew for Transcontinental Air Transport then Century Pacific hired him for the route between Sacramento and Los Angeles.

Many of Century Pacific's passengers were elderly and A. W. Kimball was concerned about them. For example, he said James Anderson, an invalid from Sacramento, waited with his nurse four days for weather to improve so he could fly to Los Angeles on a Century Pacific airliner.[136]

Century Pacific loaded one of its planes to capacity with a vaudeville troupe after their show in Sacramento and flew them to the Bay Area for their next engagement.[137]

Century Pacific reported an increase in business between Sacramento and Los Angeles. They also announced an extension of air service to El Paso, Texas.[138] On April 1 the airline inaugurated additional stops in the Great Central Valley between Sacramento and Fresno. One plane a day would fly each way and connect with the southbound plane from Fresno. A Los Angeles bound customer would arrive an hour earlier than before. Century Pacific stationed Frederick McKinley at Sacramento to fly regularly between Sacramento and San Francisco to eliminate service interruptions, which occurred the previous winter when bad weather held up airliners in Southern California. Century Pacific employees, A. Weston Kimball and Carl Van Meter, a mechanic, received private licenses during a visit to Sacramento by DOC inspector James Payton.[139]

Century Pacific discontinued air service between Sacramento and San Francisco in April 1932. As a result, Varney Air Lines, operating fast Lockheed Orions between Sacramento and Los Angeles, increased business on that route. On April 15, Varney found it necessary to add two additional planes each direction between Sacramento and San Francisco.[140] In addition to cutting fares below railroad rates, Century Pacific's E. L. Cord also cut pilots' and other employees' salaries drastically. In February 1932, the pilots went out on strike after the newly founded Air Line Pilots Association protested pilots being controlled as if they were bus drivers.

Century Pacific failed mainly because the Department of Commerce allegedly disliked the way Cord was running the airline and refused to award him a mail contract, which might have saved the airline. In April 1932, Cord traded his airline assets to the Aviation Corporation for a large cache of American Airways stock.[141]

Consolidated Air Lines

Beverly Gilmore, president of Consolidated Air Lines, and Sterling Boller, the air lines' chief pilot, stopped off at the Colusa Air Show on May 30, 1930, en route to Montague in Shasta County. Consolidated Air Lines (CAL) was planning to start scheduled passenger and airmail service from as far south as Fresno to possibly as far north as Montague with stops at

Stockton and Sacramento. Gilmore and Boller arrived at Sacramento the first week of June. They hired Jeff Warren of Clover Flying Service at Sacramento to take them to the Napa Air Show on June 7 in his Buhl Airsedan on another promotional flight for CAL, then return to Sacramento.[142]

CAL completed plans in early June for the airline to start flying by mid-month from Redding to San Francisco with several stops in between. The airline arranged for a central office in downtown Sacramento and a field office on the new municipal airport.[143]

Consolidated was unable to get started until Sunday, September 14, 1930, when Sterling Boller flew the inaugural flight from Sacramento to Oakland in 43 minutes. He carried C. E. Wilkins, Sacramento Mayor C. H. S. Bidwell, and A. S. Dudley. Boller probably flew CAL's eight-passenger Fokker Super Universal on this maiden flight. At Oakland, the three dignitaries boarded an Air Ferries Loening amphibian and made the six-minute flight across the bay to San Francisco's Ferry Building.[144]

A tri-motor Ford was part of CAL's stable of aircraft. Their 14-passenger Ford transport flew from Sacramento to Marysville on September 25 with several city officials aboard for the inaugural flight of scheduled air service between the two cities.[145]

Consolidated Air Lines would make connections with Western Air Express, Maddux-TAT, and the Air Ferries shuttle planes at San Francisco Bay Airdrome, Alameda, on a regular schedule. CAL's planes were flying from Marysville to Alameda with one stop at Sacramento Municipal Airport.[146]

By April 1931, Consolidated Air Lines had called it quits; the Depression was too much to withstand. CAL pilots had been flying a five passenger Curtiss Kingbird because they couldn't possibly fill the 14 seats in the Ford. With only two Wright Whirlwinds burning gasoline, the Kingbird was cheaper to fly. Going out of business, CAL liquidated its aircraft. In April the Kingbird was sold to A. M. Dinsmore of Oakland for an unknown price.[147] The tri-motor Ford had already been sold. By February 1931 it was being flown by Western Pacific Air Freight and on February 23, 1931, it landed at Sacramento en route to Oakland loaded with 3,000 pounds of dressed chickens from Boise, Idaho. Monte H. Lukov was president and general manager of Western Pacific Air Freight. Charles Rector flew the Ford with copilot Ray Moore.[148]

Varney Air Lines

Varney Air Lines opened a new route between Sacramento Municipal

Airport and the San Francisco Bay Airdrome at Alameda on April 6, 1931, and carried its first passenger on the route. Varney would operate three aircraft daily, leaving Alameda at 9:00 AM, 1:00 PM and 5:00 PM and returning at 10:00 AM, 2:00 PM and 6:00 PM. The fare was $7.50. Their service included a taxicab picking the customer up at his home in Sacramento and delivering him to the municipal airport. From there he was flown to Alameda to meet the Air Ferries amphibian, which transported him across the bay to San Francisco's pier No. 5 in six minutes.

Clayton Allen, former chief pilot of Overland Airways, and Joe Taff pioneered this route as pilots for Walter Varney's speedy air service.[149] Varney used the Boeing hangar at Sacramento Municipal Airport as its passenger terminal.[150] Charles E. Wilkins was named the Varney district traffic manager for the entire Sacramento Valley.[151]

Varney extended service from Marysville, Sacramento, and San Francisco to Stockton, and Modesto by April 1931.[152] Varney Air Lines and its subsidiary, Overland Airways, were operating six aircraft between Sacramento and the Bay Area by the first week of May. Varney personnel also operated the Standard Oil fueling station at the municipal airport with Jack Beilby in charge.[153] Varney soon expanded service to Reno and Fresno from the Bay Area in late July.[154] Two Varney airliners began service through the Sacramento and San Joaquin valleys on July 21. This route extension of the entire Great Central Valley connected the Boeing System at Sacramento with Century Pacific airlines at Fresno.

Hilton F. Lusk, superintendent of the municipal airport, represented Sacramento on the inaugural flight of the Great Central Valley route, joining Walter T. Varney as passengers on a Varney airliner flown by Jack Beilby. Lusk told the press it was possible to take an airliner from San Diego directly to Sacramento by transferring to a Varney plane at Fresno. At Stockton and Modesto, a reception committee of the city mayors and officials met the two Varney planes. Company executive Franklin Rose was pilot of the second Varney airliner.[155] One week later, Varney announced cancelling the Sacramento to Fresno route due to lack of customer interest. The run to Marysville was also stopped temporarily, however it was planned both routes would be restarted in the future.[156]

The Sacramento office for Varney announced in October Varney Speed Lanes had finally settled on its north-south routes. It would run seven round trips daily from Alameda to Sacramento and two trips daily from Alameda to Grand Central Airport at Glendale. The trip from the bay to

Sacramento would take 25 minutes and the trip to Los Angeles would take 1 hour and 58 minutes.

The unusually fast, low-wing Lockheed Orion airliner was powered by a single 475hp. Wasp engine. The sleek planes were white with a maroon stripe down the fuselage sides. Varney personnel dressed in uniforms of the same colors. The fare was $25 one-way to Glendale from San Francisco Bay Airdrome or $45 round-trip. The customer was rebated ten cents per minute for every minute late on the Glendale run only. The Orions were radio equipped with communication between all planes possible at any time.[157] The new Orions were placed in service by Varney on routes between Sacramento-Alameda-Los Angeles, and proved so popular Varney was unable to seat everyone who sought them the first week of operations. The planes were departing full those initial flights.[158] Varney Speed Lanes took delivery of two additional Lockheed Orions in November. The Varney Company was said to have an option on all Orions built by the factory at the time.[159] Due to bad weather in December, Varney was carrying passengers around 65 percent capacity, but claimed flying at least one plane a day regardless of severe weather.

Varney announced in January 1932 they would have two Sikorsky amphibians to replace the Air Ferries Ltd. Company, which suspended operations on January 1.[160] In March, Varney Speed Lanes added two more round trips to the daily schedule between Alameda and Los Angeles. The company was still making six round trips daily to Sacramento.[161]

W. P. Thomas, express manager for Varney, visited Sacramento Municipal Airport in March to make it known air transportation was the quickest way possible to move freight. He also wanted everyone to know that mostly Varney customers used the air ferries crossing San Francisco Bay; there was little room for anyone else.[162]

Franklin Rose, president of Varney, announced in April extra flights would be added to certain Sunday schedules at Sacramento Municipal Airport. These extra flights were due, he said, to expected upcoming better weather leading to increases in service.[163]

Norman Word, formerly of San Francisco Bay Airdrome, replaced Dick Brown as the Varney agent at Sacramento. Brown was sent back to ground personnel at San Francisco Bay Airdrome.[164]

Varney Speed Lanes added two more flights per day between Sacramento and San Francisco Bay Airdrome on May 15. This gave Sac Muni eight-plane-per-day service on a 90-minute schedule. The Sacramento Varney agent, reported that 828 passengers flew from Sacramento to the Bay Area in April achieving 79 percent capacity on Varney planes.[165] Vic Hoganson, a former Air Ferries pilot, was transferred to an Orion on the Varney air shuttle from Sacramento Muni to Alameda in June.[166]

Varney added an 8:00 PM flight to the Bay Area daily except Saturday in late June. The plane was for freight delivery and had room for three passengers on return flights.[167] George Buck, who had flown for Walter Varney when Varney started his airmail service from Elko to Pasco and Salt Lake in 1925, was placed in charge of the Sacramento office of Varney Speed Lanes. He replaced Norman Word who was transferred to Alameda.[168]

Passenger ticket sales for Varney Speed Lanes was so heavy during the last weekend of July 1932 company president Franklin Rose had to pilot one schedule; no one else was available.[169] Roscoe Behan, general traffic manager of Varney, and Rose made an inspection trip to Sacramento on August 9, 1932, in a Stinson Junior. After conferring with George Buck, they flew to Crissy Field, satisfied knowing increased passenger demand was being handled adequately.[170]

Fig. 55. The tri-motor Kreutzer Air Coach K-3 was used for Pacific coast corporate and company travel in the early 1930s.

Fig. 56. A tri-motor Bach Air Yacht 3-CT-8 airliner like those used by West Coast Air Transport.

Fig. 57. The most popular airliner of the late 1920s through the early '30s was the Ford Tri-motor. This Ford 4-AT-19 transport belonged to Standard Oil Company. The man in the photo is aviator Albert Lane standing next to his Cord automobile.

Fig. 58. Sacramento aviatrice Avis Sutfin Bielefeld, an early member of the Ninety-Nines, is shown here in a Fleet trainer at Sacramento Municipal Airport in 1935.

CHAPTER 12

Women in aviation – Sacramento's Avis Bielefeld – Sacramento flying activities 1936 and beyond – B-17s at Sacramento Muni in 1937 – Del Paso Airport's final years

Greater numbers of women were getting involved in aviation by the 1930s. They were preceded by famous aviatrices Blanche Stuart Scott, Harriet Quimby, and a handful of others during the Exhibition Years then came Amelia Earhart, Elinor Smith, and Louise Thaden (to name a few) in the late 1920s. Women were grabbing headlines with record-setting flights, making it clear flying was not just for men.

Three national women's flying organizations existed by 1933 dedicated to encouraging women's involvement in aviation: the Ninety-Nines, the Betsy Ross Corps, and the Women's Air Reserve.

First came the Ninety-Nines in December 1929 at Long Island, New York. By August 1932, the group was 260 members strong. For membership there were two requirements: applicants had to be female and possess a Department of Commerce pilot's license. Dues were two dollars a year, and initiation fee was one dollar. There were no other assessments. Women from outside the United States could join with a valid license.

Vice president Louise Thaden wrote in 1932, "We have tried, and I think succeeded, in making the Ninety-Nines a broad group in activities, purpose and organization. A purely civilian group, with no aspirations to be anything else, we are nevertheless prepared to answer any call for work that might be put to us in an emergency. It is strongly felt that there are as yet too few women pilots to have efforts duplicated by overlapping groups. Therefore, we have endeavored to keep the activities of the Ninety-Nines as broad as possible."[1]

As to the Ninety-Nines' philosophy, Amelia Earhart, president, said, "... the Ninety-Nines may be one of those agencies which will help at least one segment of women to become individuals—industrially, mentally and spiritually. This they should strive for in spite of failures which might tend to discourage them."[2]

There was some revising of the name early in the group's creation. *Western Flying* reported in March 1930, "The Eighty-Sixes, a national organization of licensed women pilots, has been organized in New York City. The name signifies the number who attended the first meeting. Sectional chairmen, making up the board, are: for New England, Joan Fay Shankle; New York, Opel Logan Kunz; southeastern states, Mary C. Alexander; Pennsylvania and Michigan, Louise McPhetridge Thaden; Ohio, Blanche Noyes; the mid-west, Phobe Omlie; Texas, Margaret Thomas, and the far west, Gladys O'Donnell [sic]."[3] An additional 13 names were added to the list of charter members and the group renamed itself the Ninety-Nines.

The Betsy Ross Corps, created May 9, 1931, was a national patriotic society of licensed women pilots founded in the interest of national defense under the direction of Opal Kunz, founder and first national commander. The Betsy Ross Corps was intended to act as an auxiliary air corps, an idea, to which its founders claimed the US Army and Navy were sympathetic. A member of the Betsy Ross Corps had to be female and a "certified" American citizen holding a DOC pilot's license. She had to take an oath to uphold and defend the Constitution of the United States; to maintain law and order; to foster 100 percent Americanism; to inculcate a sense of individual obligation to the community, state and nation; and to assist in any and all matters pertaining to the welfare and advancement of the Betsy Ross Corps. The official uniform of the Betsy Ross Corps included a belted military tan coat and beret. The winged insignia of the corps was fixed to their coat lapels and beret. Membership grew from a handful to just over 100 by 1932.

Commanding officers of the western corps areas were Dorothy Lyon, Kansas City, Missouri, VIII Corps Area; and Pansy Bowen, Visalia, California, IX Corps Area. Other national officers were: Opal Kunz, founder; Peggy Remey, national commander; Althea Murphy, Laura Morgan, Mary Goodrich, Manila Davis, Eleanor McRae, and Mary Swanson.

THE THIRD ORGANIZATION of women pilots was the Women's Air Reserve, which first met in California on October 1, 1931. W.A.R., as it was known, was not a club in any way. There were no social activities provided for by rules or regulations. There were no dues or assessments. Eligibility for membership was quite stringent. A woman must be serious, purposeful, and willing to contribute to the betterment and "upbuilding" [sic] of the organization before her name was even proposed. Headquarters for W.A.R. was in the Reserve Officers' Clubhouse at the Army Reserve Air Base in Long Beach.

Florence "Pancho" Lowe Barnes was the commanding officer. La Velle Sweely was squadron commander; Mildred Morgan, chairman of the rating board and officer in charge of public relations; Eileen Curley and Viola Neal in charge of the Medical Corps; Valentine Sprague, financial secretary; Elizabeth Inwood, drill master in charge of physical education; Peggy Sherman, mess officer; with Anona Hansen, Alice Jane Kelley and Patty Willis as adjutants. Eastern flyers Louise Thaden, Blanche Noyes, and Jean La Rene became members; however, the entire group was not expected to go national until the end of 1933.[4]

Only the Ninety-Nines organization has withstood the sands of time and is still in existence, in fact, it is thriving. At this point in the history of north state aviation, we follow the path of a Sacramento Valley member of the Ninety-Nines through the years 1934 to 1939.

AVIS SUTFIN BIELEFELD was born in Yuba County August 1904 to Willis A. Sutfin and Elizabeth Hamon Sutfin of Linda. She graduated from Marysville High School where she was active in school sports, particularly basketball. She excelled at typing and won a statewide typing competition. Approaching her 32nd birthday, Avis had achieved her dream in life—learning to fly—and in 1936 she joined the Ninety-Nines.

Later, Avis wrote about flying and her life, "I learned to fly because I've always wanted to, ever since I can remember. When I was just a small child I'd often dream of it, not in an airplane, for I'd never seen one, but by jumping off a cliff and spreading my arms, or some such fantastic way. And when my mother told me if I'd be a very good girl all year I would get what I wished for most on Christmas Day. I wished long and fervently to be able to fly. When Christmas Day dawned and no wings had sprouted or other means appeared for me to—well, I *knew* there wasn't any Santa Claus!

"As I grew up, there was no money for flying, and so other things claimed my attention. When I was finally earning a goodly salary of my own, friends and family and fiancé thought it was too dangerous and foolish. So I got married. And when I watched an airplane soaring and turning and diving high up in the blue, tears would fill my eyes. After five years of this, we dissolved the marriage. Then I decided that I'd do the one thing I'd always wanted to do—fly. I did (it) on a Depression salary of $85 a month to support myself and (partially) my small son. I took out adequate insurance to protect him, then proceeded to spend $30 or more monthly for flying. It was worth every hardship! The ecstasy of my first flying lesson, when I knew I was actually at last learning to fly, was the thrill that comes once in a lifetime. Now, after three years, I am very happily married. My husband is also a pilot and my son, not (yet) seven, is quite sure he too, will be an aviator."

Avis took her first flying lesson in March 1934 and obtained her student pilot license soon after. In the fall of 1935, she took an airplane repair and construction class from instructor William Sullivan at Sacramento Junior College's hangar on the municipal airport. Having moved to Sacramento some years before, Avis was working for the California Division of Highways when she got amateur pilot license No. 34314 in April 1936. She took her tests for the license from DOC inspector Charles Walker. This license was a second stage in the process of obtaining a private pilot license in the 1930s. The amateur pilot license was discontinued in the late '30s.

Avis was taught to fly by Ivor Witney in a Fleet open-cockpit biplane, registered NC626M. Witney began his career as a flight instructor at Sacramento Municipal Airport with the Summit Flying School. By the time Avis came along, he had partnered with Jerry Barker to form Barker and Witney, Inc., a new flying school.

While working towards her license at Barker and Witney's flying school, Avis met Al Bielefeld, taking instruction from Barker and Witney Inc. to get his license reinstated. Licenses in the early years of DOC regulation had to be renewed regularly and his had lapsed. The two dated and Avis became Mrs. C. A. Bielefeld in September 1935.[5]

Five women student pilots of Barker and Witney, Inc. were featured in a *Sacramento Union* photo layout. Under the somewhat dubious headline, WOMEN DESERT BRIDE FOR PARACHUTES, were excellent photos of Avis, Genevieve Nebeker, Mrs. Frank Elmer, Dorothy Jones, Katherine Maritsas, and Mrs. E. W. Beach.[6]

Two male students at the Barker and Witney flying school took flight tests with DOC inspector Walker the same day as Avis. They were: Wellington "Duke" Harbaugh, a wholesale grocer's representative who passed his private pilot license test, and William Chow, a local Chinese student

CHAPTER 12   265

Fig. 59. Avis Sutfin Bielefeld and Ivor Witney, her flying instructor, stand next to a Barker and Witney Flying School Fleet Model 2 at Sacramento Municipal Airport in 1935. It was said a pilot could do anything in a Fleet and was only limited by capability and guts.

who passed his test.[7]

Avis logged a total of 60 hours and 20 minutes flying time by the time she took her private license exams. Having passed her tests on August 27, 1936, her logbook recorded a flurry of passenger-carrying flights the following months.[8]

Not long after Avis got her license a terrible accident at the airport deeply affected the pilots of the Barker and Witney flying school. During an air show on October 4, 1936, G. E. "Jerry" Barker died flying an aerobatic exhibition for 25,000 spectators at Sacramento Municipal Airport. Barker had entered an outside loop in his company Fleet trainer at 1,500 feet. At the bottom of the loop, he flew into the ground just outside the eastern boundary of the airport.

The outside loop maneuver was a very difficult maneuver for both pilot and aircraft to achieve in the 1930s. It took much physical strength on the pilot's part to make an airplane fly inverted (outside) maneuvers. Airplanes of the day were not designed for such maneuvers. The airplane's wing was asymmetrical having more camber (curve) on top of the airfoil than on the bottom, which created lift more easily while flying inside maneuvers (a right-side up flying attitude rather than an upside down attitude). To execute an outside loop requiring less arm strength from the pilot, the airplane needed a more symmetrical airfoil having some curve on the bottom of the airfoil to create more lift when the plane is flying inverted (upside down).

The Fleet trainer was manufactured with a Clark Y-15 airfoil. The thick heavily constructed airfoil with a slight curve on its underside allowed a flight instructor of average aerobatic competency to safely complete an outside loop. However, any type of flying, particularly aerobatics close to the ground, requires a healthy pilot, and Jerry Barker was not in good shape. He had been convalescing after three weeks of illness. An hour before he took off for his routine, Barker told Mrs. Elmo Teed, wife of one of his flying students, he felt terrible. He told his partner Ivor Witney, earlier in the day, he didn't think he would fly for the air show.

Barker changed his mind and flew in the 15-mile air race placing third. He then immediately went up to start his aerobatic routine flying two sets of maneuvers. His first series of stunts included an outside loop, which he completed with some difficulty; his engine was missing according to observers. However, during the inverted part of a maneuver he would have expected his engine to miss and cut out due to fuel starvation. Don Smith, airport manager, discounted motor trouble as cause of the crash. He felt Barker may have passed out from the physical strain (g-force) and his illness, causing him to collapse at the controls. Barker was overheard just before leaving the ground on his last flight: "Do you think it is worth it? I don't feel like getting up there again, but my name is on the program and the crowd has to have its show."

Barker, a native of Grass Valley, learned to fly in 1929 at Mills Field, San Bruno, and received his transport pilot license at Sacramento in 1931. He returned to Mills Field for a short time and came back to Sacramento in 1933 as manager of Summit Flying School. By 1934 he partnered with Ivor Witney in their flying school. Barker and his wife lived in an apartment on the airport.[9]

Avis and the rest of the airport community were devastated over the loss of Barker. Avis was particularly sad. Jerry Barker had occasionally signed her logbook for flights, and he crashed in the plane Avis had done all of her flying—the Fleet Model 2 registered NC626M.[10]

In the late 1930s, government flight regulations required a private pilot to renew his or her pilot's license each year, which Avis did in August

Fig. 60. The instructors and women student pilots of the Barker and Witney Flying School are shown here at Sacramento Municipal Airport in 1935. Standing from the left are: Ivor Witney, Avis Sutfin Bielefeld, Jerry Barker, and Dorothy Jones; sitting in front from the left are Genevieve Nebeker and Mrs. E. W. Beach. Not in the picture were Mrs. Frank Elmer, Katherine Maritsas, and Mrs. Elmo Teed

1937.[11] Avis and her husband Al Bielefeld, a rancher at Clarksburg, owned a four-place cabin plane which they flew until World War II began. In early 1942, all civilian flying was prohibited within 175 miles of the Pacific coast. The prohibition lasted the duration of the war.

A member of Avis' family later wrote, "When World War II came and many women were ferrying war planes to England, they came to Avis and asked her to participate. Could she? The call to pilot so many different types of planes was a once-in-a-lifetime opportunity—one she had dreamed of! She had a husband and three small children—who would care for them and raise the children if something happened to her? Her smallest was just a few months old. Her decision was to choose her family over her dream. She declined, and it was the hardest decision she ever had to make. It nearly broke her heart not to participate. Tears would come to her eyes nearly 40 years later, as she related the story to her children." Avis Sutfin Bielefeld passed on in September 1981.[12]

During World War II (WWII) the women referred to above were members of the WASPs, the Women Air Force Service Pilots; they ferried military aircraft, instructed flying cadets, towed targets, and carried out other noncombat military missions during the war.

By taking over these noncombat duties, American and British women pilots released large numbers of their male counterparts for frontline aerial combat. Russian women during WWII were allowed to fly combat missions and some became fighter "aces" downing five or more German aircraft.

Turkish president Mustafa Kemal Atatürk's daughter Gocen Sabihi, Turkey's most famous aviatrix, was photographed posing with her new Vultee warplane in 1939. She was a wing commander in the Turkish Air Force and took part in campaigns against uprisings in western Turkey. This would make Sabihi the first woman to fly combat missions in the era of World War II.[13]

The Sacramento air show of early October 1936 mentioned above was held to demonstrate skills of flight instructors at schools on Sacramento Municipal Airport. The Sacramento Junior Chamber of Commerce and the Sacramento Chapter of the National Aeronautics Association were sponsors. Official starter for events was Harold F. Brown, general manager of Consolidated Air Lines and an important figure in the development of commercial aviation in Yuba, Sutter, and Sacramento counties.

Floyd Baker opened the show with a demonstration of cutting rolls of toilet paper unfurled from altitude with his wings. Next was a demonstration by Hilton Lusk and A. E. Waite that in today's world seems incredibly outrageous: how to shoot eagles from an airplane. This practice was actual commercial work for sheep ranchers who paid a bounty for the dead birds. They claimed eagles carried off their newborn lambs.

Dale Hunter then flew an aerobatic demonstration in a light cabin plane followed by other pilots showing off the latest commercial aircraft. Next was a parachute jump by Gordon Baugh, an aerobatic routine by Pansy Bowen, and what today would be called a "Crazy Cub Act" by Walter Browne; the wild aerobatic act started when a "drunken farmer" fell into an empty Piper Cub whose engine was running and took off.

Contests started after the flying exhibitions. The first was flour bombing followed by pylon races. Next came Jerry Barker's ill-fated advanced aerobatic demonstration. After he crashed, officials cancelled the rest of the show, and Charles "Red" Jensen was unable to give his crop dusting

Chapter 12

demonstration. Nor did Ivor Witney demonstrate his precision flying routine. Vernon Heaton did not perform his trick flying act and Fran Merry was unable to carry out a planned parachute jump.[14] Barker's fatal crash marked a decline in organized air shows in the Sacramento area until after World War II.

On August 12, 1937, it was reported a squadron of US Army Air Corps bombers from Langley Field, Virginia, would land in Sacramento late in the day or after dark. The bombers arrived just before 11:00 PM. They circled over the city nearly an hour before the pilots landed their massive four-engine planes at Sacramento Municipal Airport. While the nine YB-17s, called Flying Fortresses, circled the city wrapped in darkness, 5,000 people assembled at the airport to watch them come in. There was a mile of parked cars along Freeport Boulevard from which they walked to the airport entrance.

The crowd was in awe of the Flying Fortresses. They had never seen a four-engine airplane, much less nine of them. They watched as Arthur S. Dudley, head of the Sacramento Chamber of Commerce, greeted Maj. Gen. Frank M. Andrews, officer in charge of the mission from Langley, and Lt. Col. Robert Olds, commander of this unique squadron of bombers of the future.

The squadron was preceded by two army transport aircraft, an attack plane, and a Martin B-10 bomber, which arrived in the afternoon. They came from Hamilton Field, the new Army Air Corps base in Marin County north of San Francisco. From the planes emerged troops who set up camp at Sac Muni for the aircrews of the incoming YB-17s.

The Flying Fortresses had taken off from Oakland Municipal Airport after noon on the 12th for maneuvers over the Pacific Ocean. The crews reported covering approximately 600 miles before landing at Sacramento. They landed at Sacramento instead of returning to Oakland because fog had settled in over the Bay Area.

The YB-17 squadron departed Sacramento August 13 at 9:00 AM for more exercises in a secret location. Before leaving, several pilots and navigators told service employees at Sac Muni the runways and taxiways were in perfect condition for heavy airplanes. One officer said the Sacramento airport was superior to airports in the Bay Area. The bombers took off and circled the city many times as they assembled into battle formation. Spectators stared in wonder at the shiny new 20-ton bombers with wings that spread 105 feet. Each carried a crew of nine and was armed with five machine guns. They cruised at 200 mph.¹⁵

The above was all the public knew about the aerial maneuvers off the coast of California August 12–14, 1937. More of what happened those three days was revealed decades later.

The August maneuvers off the California coast were joint exercises of the US Navy and the Army Air Corps. They were officially known as Joint Air Exercise Number Four, but would later be known as the Utah Exercise. The Air Corps was given 24 hours to find the battleship *Utah*. It was cruising off the coast between San Francisco and Los Angeles. Once found, the YB-17s were to drop water bombs on it. Rules of the exercise did not allow the Air Corps to look for the *Utah*. The bomber pilots had to rely on the navy to give them the ship's position.

The YB-17s under the command of Lt. Col. Robin Olds were led to the position by the best navigator in the Air Corps, Lt. Curtiss LeMay. After a full day of flying to the navy's coordinates and not finding the *Utah*, the squadron returned to Oakland from which they departed many hours before on August 12. But Oakland was socked in by evening fog—so prevalent in the Bay Area during summer—they flew inland to Sacramento and landed about midnight.

It was decided to repeat the exercise with not much time left until the 24-hour deadline. Before the squadron departed for another attempt to bomb the *Utah* early in the morning, Lieutenant LeMay suspected the navy had given the squadron the wrong coordinates. Lt. Colonel Olds confirmed LeMay's suspicion prior to takeoff. The navy admitted the information was wrong. LeMay told Olds they had been off course by 60 miles.

On the second attempt, the navy reported the wrong position, but the Air Corps, knowing the navy had pulled the same trick, had its bombers fan out and they found the *Utah*. The squadron hit the battleship with water bombs just minutes before the deadline. The navy was furious its ship was found and bombed. The exercise was carried out once more and the *Utah* was bombed again, making the navy more agitated and full of excuses why the bombers were successful. The navy used its sway in Washington and had the exercise results classified top secret.¹⁶

Donald Smith issued angry statements to the Department of Commerce in June 1938 after the DOC refused to allow the new Douglas DC-3 airliners to operate from Sacramento Municipal Airport. Smith accused the

Fig. 61. A squadron of YB-17s landed at Sacramento Municipal Airport in August 1937 after Hamilton Field was closed due to fog during a joint army-navy exercise off the Northern California coast.

DOC of being influenced by DC-3 airline pilots who, upon departing Bay Area airports for the East, did not want to lose altitude to land at Sacramento before climbing over the Sierra Nevada.[17]

Sacramento voters passed a bond issue August 3, 1938, approving $143,000 to hard surface the three main runways. The Public Works Administration of the federal government would provide additional funds needed to finish the project. Don Smith reported that, "Sacramento Airport is not only at the crossroads of air travel on the West Coast but is also the first port west of the [Sierra Nevada]. It will particularly service transcontinental ships when the San Francisco area is fogged in and when heavy storms in the mountains require a landing in a location where clear weather almost always [exists]."

At the time of the bond passage, 35 airplanes parked permanently at Sac Muni, six of them were commercial.[18] Sacramento Municipal Airport soldiered on through World War II as a US Army Air Force secondary fighter base to defend the nation against possible invasion of the West Coast by the Japanese. It's thriving today as Sacramento Executive Airport operated by Sacramento County and is home to many private and business aircraft. Airline traffic was rerouted in October 1967 to Sacramento International

Airport, nine miles north of the city. The new international airport is about a mile east of the Sacramento area's first purpose built landing field at Target, circa 1910–12.

FLYING ACTIVITY CONTINUED at Del Paso Airport in 1930 after the new municipal airport on Freeport Boulevard opened. Clyde "Upside-Down" Pangborn flew into Del Paso from New York City in January 1930. He was demonstrating the New Standard biplane throughout Northern California on behalf of his old flying circus partner, Ivan Gates. Gates was manufacturing the New Standard in his New Jersey Gates-Day Aircraft Company factory.[19]

J. A. Jarvis and R. Franz, Waco aircraft dealers, were operating from Del Paso Airport in early January 1930. Typically for this time of year bad weather slowed air traffic but activity was expected to pick up by the middle of the month. Royal U. St. John kept his Swallow at Del Paso Airport after being elected president of the Sacramento Aviation Club.[20] Homer D. Coffing logged 70 hours in his new Travel Air at Del Paso. He needed 200 before he could take his transport pilot license test in the spring. He was waiting for the weather to improve. Paul Schreck became Del Paso Airport's manager and purchased a new International F-17 biplane. Schreck, taught to fly by H. G. Andrews years before, was known as an excellent pilot.

A New York pilot, J. C. McTadyer, came in from Lakeport and landed at Del Paso Airport the first week of January. His plane was an experimental design with a Warner motor. He studied the regional weather reports and took off for Oakland. A representative from West America Flying School landed at Del Paso in a Waco the same week.[21] Dick Smith flew an Eaglerock from Oakland in February, as did Ed Wagner in his Fairchild from the Stockton airport.

On February 9, 1930, approximately 8,000 people visited Del Paso Airport and watched the Sunday activities. The "Great Diavolo" jumped from 3,500 feet and dropped to 1,500 before opening his chute. Leo Moore was one of the aerobatic pilots flying stunts. The local pilots were busy selling rides to spectators.[22] The "Great Diavolo" jumped for another crowd two weeks later.

Paul Schreck opened an airplane repair shop at Del Paso. He overhauled F. Retteratch's Swallow so it could be certified for a DOC license. Schreck planned to get his limited commercial license soon and eventually his transport pilot license.

E. E. Mouton of the DOC arrived in a Whirlwind Stearman to test students and inspect planes for airworthiness licenses. Yuba-Sutter Flying Club pilots arrived from Cheim Field, Marysville, for license testing. Ken Kleaver was at Del Paso having the upper wing on his Hisso Eaglerock repaired.

C. E. Morris, the lessee of the Del Paso airport, visited the field in mid-February. Being from Grimes, he may have flown together with H. F. Ritchey of Grimes who also visited the field. Ritchey had 170 hours and planned to get his transport pilot license.

During the second week of February, the following pilots and passengers landed at Del Paso Airport: E. E. La Parle in a Fairchild for the Parker Pen Co.; Clay Fisher in a Travel Air from Santa Rosa; pilot Rutherford in an Eaglerock from Modesto; F. Don Carlos in an International from Bakersfield; Ed Wagner in a Fairchild from Stockton; Frank Moore in a Waco for the Lowe Motor Co.; Frank Rose in a Stearman for Varney Air Lines; R. P. Bowman in a Travel Air from Oakland; and R. E. Dickerson in a Stinson from Fresno.[23]

The DOC announced in September 1930 that eight stations would soon be established throughout the United States for flight-testing pilot applicants and aircraft licensing by DOC inspectors. Los Angeles and Oakland Municipal airports would be the West Coast inspection sites.[24]

On one Sunday in September, the Sacramento Glider Club members demonstrated their method for teaching new glider pilots. They pulled a glider around Del Paso Airport behind an automobile never allowing the glider to leave the ground. This let the student familiarize himself with the controls.[25]

Robert F. Weaver took delivery of a de Havilland Gypsy Moth biplane on September 22. It was added to the fleet of the Sacramento Flying Service on Del Paso Airport. Weaver would use the Moth for student and commercial flights.[26] In addition to the Moth, the Sacramento Flying Service had a Hisso Travel Air for school use.[27]

Although Robert Weaver was the new proprietor of Del Paso Airport and manager of the Sacramento Flying Service on the airport, he did not have a pilot's license. He began practice flights in his new Gypsy Moth and disclosed his goal to take the flight test on November 29.[28] The de Havilland Gypsy Moth biplane was a successful English design built under license in the United States for the American market.

Ray Nicholson, chief pilot for Sacramento Flying Service, had his Hisso

Travel Air equipped with a new type of pneumatic tire, making landing and takeoffs in wet weather from muddy fields safer.[29]

Herald rancher W. W. Bottimore gave his son Ebner Quiggle Bottimore, who had a landing strip on his father's ranch, a four-passenger Stinson Detroiter. The young man had qualified as a pilot. The Detroiter was powered by a nine-cylinder, 210hp. Lycoming, air-cooled radial engine and cruised at 103 mph with a top speed of 125.

The Sacramento High School Glider Club sometimes flew from Del Paso Airport. Membership was limited to students actually building an airplane or glider, and 12 joined. Aviation class instructor Charles Lipps mentored the club. In late October 1930 Jack Williams was elected its president; Jack Renwick, vice president; Talbert Spanhoff, treasurer; and Fred Wong, secretary. Renwick, 16, made his first solo in a powered plane at Del Paso Airport that month.[30]

The first Northern California soaring meet was planned for November 23, 1930, at Livermore Airport under the auspices of the Western Inter-Club Glider Association at their monthly meeting. The association, representing 16 Northern California glider clubs, invited other gliding organizations. Twenty gliders were expected to participate in amateur contests and soaring demonstrations. At its planning meeting, the association's technical committee, led by C. S. Terry, was instructed association officers were to investigate the Salinas accident that killed glider pilot Louis Martella, age 23.[31]

Among the area's power plane community, Glenn Vanderford flew from his own airfield at Rio Linda in the early 1930s.[32] Sacramento's Karl Harder learned to fly at Del Paso Airport in an OX-5 Standard J-1 and an OX-5 Waco in the early 1930s.[33] Miss Josephine Black signed on with the Sacramento Flying Service to learn to fly.[34]

ROBERT WEAVER OF THE Sacramento Flying Service (SFS) returned to Del Paso on February 3, 1931, after visiting Quincy. He said he might start a pilot instruction class at the Quincy airport. Plumas County officials were planning extensive improvements including leveling, lengthening runways, and constructing a drainage system.

Sacramento Flying Service's chief pilot, Ray Nicholson, tried on a new 28-foot diameter Russell Lobe parachute in early February and climbed into the Gypsy Moth's cockpit. He realized there wasn't room to safely handle the controls. SFS planned to replace two 28-foot chutes with 24-foot chutes.[35]

Chapter 12

Robert Weaver crashed the SFS's Hisso Travel Air near Georgetown in the Sierra Nevada. Weaver and Ray Nicholson flew to Oakland on February 16 for Nicholson to renew his license and Weaver to report details of his "crackup" to DOC inspector Bill Moore. W. C. Ganow, who trucked Weaver's wrecked Travel Air back to Del Paso from Georgetown, visited the airport on February 17 and declared he would be taking flying lessons from SFS soon.[36]

Sacramento Flying Service's advanced students drew a large crowd February 22, 1931, with aerobatic exhibitions over Del Paso Airport.[37] Weaver's wrecked Travel Air had been traded for a new Fleet and was hauled away from Del Paso on March 2.[38] Weaver planned taking delivery of the new biplane trainer on March 7. Marion McKeen, Waco distributor from Los Angeles, landed at Del Paso March 17. Robert Weaver's plans to acquire new planes for SFS at Del Paso seemed to be coming together.[39] He reported SFS signed on E. W. Adams of Nevada City as a new student. Weaver made two trips to Quincy in April. One only took 55 minutes setting a local speed record.[40]

The unbelievable happened the following month. Robert F. Weaver, proprietor of the Sacramento Flying Service, robbed a bank in Sparks, Nevada, May 29, 1931. Ray Nicholson, chief pilot for SFS, told reporters Weaver went to Los Angeles on May 9 to buy another plane for the business. A few days before the robbery, he received a telegram from Weaver stating he was sick and his Sacramento return would be delayed. Associates at SFS said company money was available to Weaver on deposit, and there was no obvious motive for him to rob a bank although Weaver's wife, Loretta, had been granted a divorce on May 25. Losing his marriage may have caused a mental breakdown resulting in this bizarre act.

Acting alone, Weaver robbed $415 from the Bank of Sparks. He was shot in the arm by police chief Fred Morris while escaping. Sheriff's deputies and Reno and Sparks police found him two hours after the robbery in a cabin near Reno. Weaver refused to surrender and threatened to shoot anyone who came in. Tear gas bombs were sent for, but Weaver surrendered before they arrived. Another report said the tear gas bombs were used and forced him out of the cabin. Sheriff Russell Trathem took him into custody.

Of all his mistakes, the worst was robbing a bank in Nevada whose state legislature had just passed a law making the penalty for bank robbery death or life in prison. Weaver was sentenced then extradited to Macon, Georgia, for a parole violation prior to the bank robbery.[41]

Les McClaskey stepped up to replace Robert Weaver managing Sacramento Flying Service. Ray Nicholson was still chief pilot when SFS took on two new students, Dr. Earl Nesbitt and Arthur Lear. McClaskey and Frank Jones flew to Stockton to take tests for their pilot's licenses, but were denied. They claimed the denials were because they were outside their home territory, which they said was a new ruling from the DOC. McClaskey reported he was relocating Sacramento Flying Service to the new municipal airport on Freeport Boulevard very soon. He installed lights on the Gypsy Moth for night instruction from the lighted new municipal airport.

Dr. G. M. Kennedy of Fair Oaks had a Curtiss Junior at Del Paso and was learning to fly in August 1931 from Fred Munro, his personal pilot. Paul Schreck relicensed his International biplane and Ray Nicholson renewed his pilot's license that same month. All these pilots were based at Del Paso Airport.[42]

After the opening of Sacramento Municipal Airport on Freeport Boulevard in April 1930, activity declined annually at Del Paso. With most flight instruction taking place at the new airport, all that was left at Del Paso was Ingvald Fagerskog taxiing across Auburn Boulevard to use the longer runway for his heavily laden airplane's new purpose—crop dusting. How long he was allowed to use the Del Paso site is unknown.

Operations at Del Paso Airport probably ceased by September 8, 1936, the groundbreaking ceremony day for the United States Army Air Corps' newest airfield named Sacramento Air Depot, later renamed McClellan Air Force Base.[43]

Del Paso Airport was a mile or less from the threshold of Sacramento Air Depot's main north-south runway. Flying would definitely have stopped at Del Paso by November 15, 1938, the day the Air Depot began repair work on aircraft flown in by Army Air Corps pilots.[44]

The decommissioned McClellan Air Force Base is now known as McClellan Airfield and is located in McClellan Park, an industrial park. The main runway and a hangar are used (in 2017) as a base of operations for US Coast Guard Lockheed C-130 patrol planes. During the forest fire season, commercial borate bombers use the airfield.

Fig.62.

Part II. Early Aviation in Colusa and Glenn Counties

CHAPTER 13

Agricultural flying history – Chasing ducks – Duck patrol in 1920 – Moffett and Hunt in Glenn County – Seeding and dusting crops in the north state – Colonel Livingston Irving – Merced-Wawona Air Lines and Frank Gallison

In Colusa and Glenn counties, a major rice farming region in the north state, aviation's progress is found by examining the flying activities at the only two cities with significant population: Colusa, the county seat of Colusa County, and Willows, the county seat of Glenn County. In 1939 the former had a population of 2,116 and the latter 2,024. When commercial agricultural flying began in Glenn and Colusa counties in 1919, after the Great War, the population of these two cities was even less.[1] During that first year after the war, gypsy pilots from the San Francisco Bay Area and Sacramento pioneered commercial flying in the two counties when they barnstormed the northwestern Sacramento Valley hopping passengers for money. The majority of them were ex-army aviators.

Technically, the Army Air Service carried out the first agricultural flying in California with its forest fire patrols beginning in June 1919 after the Great War. They were protecting a most valuable crop—the timber forests.

In late summer 1919, the state's first commercial agricultural flying began in the rice growing districts when airplanes were used to scare waterfowl away from rice fields—saving a considerable amount of the crop usually lost to hungry migrating ducks and geese. Using the ubiquitous Curtiss JN-4 Jennies or Standard J-1s, two very similar appearing wartime training planes, veterans kept mud hens, ducks, geese, and even blackbirds out of rice farmers' fields. This work of "chasing ducks" out of farmers' fields conceived the birth of a new category of professional flying: agricultural flying.

Duck patrol work lasted only a couple years, however in 1929 aerial dusting of crops began in the Sacramento Valley and seeding rice by airplanes started the following year. Over the years the work was known as: seeding by air, aerial dusting, crop-dusting, aerial application, and today its called ag-flying.

USING AIRPLANES TO chase waterfowl out of rice fields wasn't a method purposely developed by the US Army Air Service, but it was responsible for the result. The airplane's effect on waterfowl came about during the war in the rice fields around Gerstner Field, a Lake Charles, Louisiana, Army Air Service training base. Flying instructors noticed ducks stayed away from flooded rice fields surrounding the army base during flight training. When flights stopped, due to weather or a change in scheduling, the birds returned to the fields. Some astute ex-army pilots thought flying regular patrols over the rice fields of California during the critical weeks after planting and flooding would have the same effect. Many pilots roaming the north state in their Jennies could only find work barnstorming with dangerous stunts and endless passenger hops. Duck patrols emerged as a new and marginally safer alternative work for them.[2]

The Army Air Service carried out the first experiments in crop-dusting after the war in the summer of 1921. The Air Service was looking for new ways to utilize their planes and pilots to encourage the citizenry and legislators to appropriate funds for maintaining its strength. Congress wanted to cut funding to the bone. Some in the Air Service thought it might be cut completely. The army needed to find useful peacetime work to convince legislators and the civilian population of the Air Service's value. Missions it took on were forest fire patrol, aerial photography, mapping, and border patrol.

Air Service Lt. John A. Macready carried out America's earliest known crop-dusting experiments on August 31, 1921. Macready, at the time, was chief of the flying section at McCook Field, Dayton, Ohio. He was a test pilot, and McCook Field was the early equivalent of a flight test center like Edwards Air Force Base is today. Macready's target for this experimental dusting mission was the catalpa sphinx moth larva infesting a farmer's catalpa tree grove near Troy, Ohio. Unless eradicated, the bugs would defoliate and kill the trees.

Etienne Dormoy, a French engineer working for the army at McCook, designed and built a hopper from which powdered lead arsenate could be dispensed. He joined Macready on this first flight in a Curtiss Jenny. Dormoy operated a hand crank on the hopper mounted to the side of the fuselage. Once over the grove of catalpa trees Dormoy started cranking. Fifty-four seconds later the dust was dispensed. Macready and Dormoy's experiment was judged a complete success.[3]

Lieutenant Macready would make more successful "first" flights in the future for the Army Air Service and later for Shell Oil Company. Dormoy went on to design and build the world's smallest airplane.

The Air Service was called upon in early 1922 to carry out further crop dusting experiments at Tallulah, Louisiana, for Dr. Bert R. Coad, head of the Delta Laboratory. There, Air Service personnel using two Curtiss Jennies and a de Havilland DH-4B, developed suitable equipment and dusting techniques to combat the destructive boll weevil and other insects attacking the valuable cotton crop.[4]

To try and determine the identity of the first civilian pilot to dust, spray, or seed from an airplane is nearly impossible. In Northern California, local legends and myths abound as to who seeded or dusted first. It is easier to determine who was not first amongst those who claimed or were attributed that honor.

Even Macready's flight may not have been first. Martin Kronberg, director of training at the Agricultural Aviation Academy in Minden, Nevada, gave an interview in 1964 in which he claimed Franklin Rose, the notable Oakland aviator, made flights in 1918 and 1919 in the San Francisco Bay Area that involved aerial application of pesticides. Corroborating evidence to support this claim has yet to be found.[5]

California's first rice crop was planted in Butte County in 1912. A Mr. Christensen planted 12 acres. Rice growing caught on with other farmers and the acreage expanded each year thereafter. By 1916 blackbirds, jackrabbits, and ducks had become the scourge of rice crops. What rice seed the blackbirds and rabbits didn't eat at planting time, ducks wallowed out and ate after the fields were flooded. Farmers professed they were going to protect their rice crops regardless of fish and game laws. One farmer who reported blackbirds used his scarecrows to roost on and the birds were costing him $100 a day said, "I'm going to kill them. ... Ducks no longer migrate to the north, but make their home during the hatching season in the rice fields during the summer. If anybody wants to kill ducks this fall and winter send them to my ranch. I'll let them have free hunting grounds ... wild ducks and wild blackbirds, together with jackrabbits and cottontails are a pest to rice growers."[6]

Not everyone agreed with the rice growers. After the Great War, a report was written by federal game wardens appointed to investigate the necessity of California rice growers killing waterfowl to protect their crops. Growers had been issued special permits allowing them to kill the birds. The report stated that in only three cases birds actually damaged the yield. Farmers adamantly disagreed. The California Fish and Game Commission told them they must have absolute proof of the damage or they would be subject to arrest if they abused the privilege. Along with this notification, a demonstration was given by the commission to show the effectiveness of bombs and black powder in driving ducks away.[7]

Growers were concerned about the consequence of shooting ducks without absolute proof of crop damage, so they hired airplanes to chase the birds away. They telegrammed their assemblymen protesting the Fish and Game Commission nullifying their recently issued special permits. The main flyway for ducks and geese was further west and did not affect Butte County growers as badly as those in Colusa and Glenn counties. But Butte County rice growers said they would cooperate with Colusa and Glenn growers in hiring aircraft to drive waterfowl from the rice fields.[8]

OGLE MERWIN, AFTER barnstorming in Butte County, was one of the earliest aviators to fly duck patrols there. He flew for a Sacramento aviation company lead by E. H. Pendleton and Frank W. McManus at Del Paso Airport. It is believed McManus was the instigator of most duck patrols in Northern California during 1919, the first year of the patrols. Even if McManus came up with the idea of chasing ducks with airplanes in the Sacramento Valley, it was Edmund J. Moffett, who purchased or leased McManus' airplanes and hired the pilots who began flying duck patrols in Colusa and Glenn counties.

Ed Moffett was originally from Woodland in Yolo County. As a young man, he hoped to fly in the Great War and joined a naval aviation unit, but not as a pilot. In April 1918, as a member of a naval reserve training unit at San Pedro, he left the family business, Moffett Sales Company of Woodland, and went on active duty with the navy.

After the war, Moffett returned to Woodland and began looking for a way to make it in aviation. He didn't fly, so he became an aviation entrepreneur. He financed planes and organized pilots to work under his management. He began with the duck patrols then worked his way into barnstorming and the air show business. He would be more successful with his duck patrols than organizing air shows. He made one last stab at the aviation limelight in the spring of 1927 when he organized Ernie Smith's first attempt to fly to Hawaii and later Robert Fowler's unsuccessful attempt to enter the Dole Race. (For more on Moffett, Smith, and Fowler, see chapters nine and ten in this author's book, *Aviation in Northern California 1910–1939 Volume II*.)

Moffett had signed up growers with 15,000 acres of rice to patrol by August 1919. He convinced them repeated low-level airplane flights over their fields would protect crops from damage by ducks, mud hens, and geese that landed in their flooded fields. His planes would drive the birds elsewhere.[9] H. O. Jacobson, director of the Pacific Rice Growers' Association, told a reporter that 15 to 200 planes might be employed to drive all of the ducks out of the Sacramento Valley. There would be a cooperative campaign to protect rice crops from the ravages of waterfowl in the valley. This belief was supported by the experience of growers in the Lake Charles area of Louisiana where army planes had driven "every duck out of the country."[10]

One of the first pilots Ed Moffett had hired for duck patrol was J. M. Fetters, an ex-army flier who was recently at Oroville with his mechanic Berger Johnson in a Curtiss Jenny owned by Frank McManus. Fetters, assisted by his tour manager and advance man E. H. Pendleton, was barnstorming up the valley from his Del Paso Airport home base.[11] Moffett had just acquired two of the Jennies originally built by Liberty Iron Works that McManus was

Fig. 63. Edmund J. Moffett (on the right) was the duck patrol impresario of Colusa and Glenn counties in 1919–1920. Here he is talking with Ernest L. Smith prior to Smith's attempt to be the first to fly to Hawaii. Moffett was manger of that failed attempt and was fired. During his second attempt, Smith crash landed on Molokai and survived to be the first civilian pilot to make it to the islands.

refurbishing for resale at Del Paso. McManus advised Moffett how to use the planes for duck patrols.[12]

Although Moffett had several thousand acres under contract, he was concerned that Japanese and East Indian growers who hadn't signed contracts would benefit from the patrols without paying for them. They farmed rice acreage between some farmers who signed.[13]

Moffett received a valuable endorsement in October from Mr. Christensen of Christensen & Burmeister Farms of Willows. Christensen, a pioneer grower, reported his company had five large tracts of rice, the largest 1,200 acres, and damage done by ducks during the previous season amounted to $40,000. He had tried all methods to rid the waterfowl and nothing worked. Christensen opposed slaughtering wild game and allowing them to rot on the ground; shotguns would never be used on his fields. So he hired Ed Moffett's duck patrol for the 1919 rice season. Moffett, known to many of the farmers because of his earlier auto battery business in Woodland, was his last resort to get ducks off his fields. Christensen paid Moffett fifty cents an acre to patrol his rice fields.

Christensen later claimed the airplane patrols worked. His fields escaped damage from the waterfowl. "You could go out to our rice fields any day or night this season and not see a dozen ducks. Moffett's scheme has done more than I anticipated and I hope that he receives more encouragement than he has been getting. Every rice man should secure his services, then there would be no more ducks in the country. They would be driven to other parts of the state. This method is more humane than shooting, to which I am opposed. I am not telling you this as an advertisement but to tell the rice growers my experience and how to rid the country of the pests without wantonly slaughtering them."[14]

Passengers riding the Sacramento Northern interurban commuter train on its early morning run to Woodland in October were treated to an exhibition of the duck patrol chasing waterfowl from the rice fields. A patrol plane overtook the electric train near Riverbank and flew beside it through the rice fields of the Conway Tract, diving down on clusters of ducks every few hundred feet. Huge clouds of the birds could be seen scattering from feeding in the rice fields. It was claimed the value of patrols was beyond question to anyone who witnessed them. The Conway growers had established a morning patrol and enjoyed a great measure of success.[15]

Ed Moffett, now head of the Moffett Aero Patrol, said in October it was, "a daily occurrence for planes to fly into large bands of ducks, killing some and wounding others." A reporter who rode in the passenger seat on one patrol wrote they, "... encountered one bunch of ducks where eight of them became entangled in the ship's wires in the course of a very few seconds and were finally dislodged by the wind created by the speed of the ship and propeller, the birds falling lifeless off of the wings of the ship to the rice fields below." So much for the airplane patrols being more humane than shooting. But Moffett was doing well; he had just signed the Western Rice Company to a contract for duck patrols.[16]

It seems inconceivable an airplane could hit so many ducks and not be brought down by damage to its wings and propeller. The reason these pilots could get away with so many bird strikes may have been the low speed Jennies and Standards cruised in these early days of flying. The patrol planes cruised at 60 mph and a duck, trying to fly away from the plane at 20 mph lowers the impact speed. If a modern day aircraft hits a duck, it is at a speed of 100 to 300 mph. The damage is often severe and at times fatal for the people on board.

Ogle Merwin was one of the first to suffer a crash while on duck patrol. He was flying over the Parrott Grant rice fields (Llano Seco today), just east of the Sacramento River in Butte County when his Jenny lost power. He was only five feet above ground and dropped like a rock into the flooded field. The plane was severely damaged, and Merwin suffered facial injuries. The damaged Jenny, which belonged to Frank McManus, was dragged from the Parrott rice field by a Caterpillar track-layer tractor.[17]

If flying a Jenny five feet above ground smashing into dozens of ducks and knowing you're flying an airplane that cruises at 60 mph and stalls at 40 mph wasn't dangerous enough, the rice growers were begging for night flights. It wasn't enough for them to have patrol flights carried out in daylight; they wanted the waterfowl off their fields at night as well. It was still early in the airplane's technological development and planes had no electrical systems to power lights for such dangerous low-level flights. Charlie Stoffer, one of Ed Moffett's pilots in the first season of duck patrols, was convinced probably by Moffett, the ex-battery salesman, to install two lights shining to the front on Moffett's plane and a searchlight to allow him to avoid hitting ducks, while patrolling the rice fields in total darkness. Stoffer was sure his initial effort was the first "commercial" night flight made in the United States. Unfortunately, it did not go well.

Stoffer and his mechanic installed a heavy storage battery in Moffett's plane to power its three lights. On October 20, 1919, Stoffer took off at

8:00 PM climbing out over Willows. He turned south for the rice fields with a north wind blowing at gale force. He reached the Culver Ranch very quickly and flew his patrol. Once he chased the birds away, he set course for home directly into the north wind. It took an hour-and-a-half for him to reach Willows, but a mile out from reaching the airfield he ran out of gas. He was at 2,000 feet when the noise up front stopped. He didn't know what was under him as he brought the plane down for a dead stick landing. Nearing ground, he switched on the searchlight. He was about to land in the old central canal, which was protected by a barbed wire fence. He had just enough airspeed left to ease the plane over the fence and make a safe landing. Stoffer later told a reporter, "It was the narrowest escape I ever had." Gasoline was brought out to his plane, and he continued on to his home field, a mile west of Willows.[18]

Eight months later, Charlie Stoffer was involved in a horrendous accident near Vallejo. He had recently purchased a four-place Lincoln-Standard for $7,000 and was making a trial flight. He took his father; a friend, Joseph Siveris; and eight-year-old Josephine Siveris along on the flight. Shortly before noon, Stoffer's plane fell 300 feet out of control and crashed. Stoffer was removed from the wreckage unconscious. Stoffer's father and the girl were dead; Joseph Siveris died a short time later. Stoffer upon waking went temporarily insane when told what happened.

A newspaper report of the accident stated Stoffer came to Willows a year before and gave many townspeople their first airplane rides. Also that he had flown for Moffett's duck patrol and was known as a brave pilot who made several risky flights in the Willows area. It stated his plane caught fire near Vallejo, almost a year before the above accident, and that he narrowly escaped.[19]

Dick Grace's Buzzards were a squadron of Hollywood movie fliers formed to fill in for film work after Howard Hughes hired nearly all of the experienced Los Angeles area stunt pilots to fly exclusively for his film, *Hell's Angels*.[20] Charlie Stoffer joined the Buzzards in 1928 with Bond Spencer, the Friesley Falcon's designer, builder, and test pilot, and Del Hay, who would do early ag-flying in the Sacramento area.

THE 1919 DUCK patrol season ended late October. Ogle Merwin, preparing to return to Sacramento, had McManus' Jenny repaired and his own affairs in order. He declared that while flying at the Parrott Grant Ranch, "We successfully kept that large rice area free from ducks for nearly a month.

The story told by some that a duck will become accustomed to an airplane is told without thought. It would be just as sensible to say a man will become accustomed to being shot through the head with a loaded gun. The plane runs into flocks of ducks, killing the birds by the score. Ducks fly fast, but not fast enough to escape an airplane."

With that last comment, Merwin strapped a 30-pound fish he caught that morning in the Sacramento River and two suitcases to the fuselage of the Jenny outside the pilot's cockpit and took off for home at Sacramento.[21]

Word had spread to aviators throughout the state by April 1920 that there were steady flying jobs with money to be made chasing ducks in the rice growing counties of Sacramento Valley. The hub for the duck patrols in the north valley rice growing community was Willows.[22] The Moffett Duck Patrol emerged as one of the most successful enterprises pursuing this new niche of flying. The patrol made two trips daily, flying very low and scaring ducks from fields. At the time, there were so many ducks migrating through the region they could destroy 40 acres of rice in one night. Rice was worth $450 an acre.

Edmund J. Moffett, duck patrol organizer, turned the business over to his brother, William Moffett, and Irwin Hunt for the 1920 season. Ed Moffett was pursuing air show bookings using some of the same pilots and planes as the duck patrol. From time to time William Moffett seemed to prefer spelling his last name Moffitt with an i.[23]

A few patrol aviators coming to Willows to chase ducks and money would become famous. The one who became most famous was Australian flier Charles Kingsford-Smith who, even then, had set his sights on establishing great records in long-distance flying. Another was Clyde Pangborn who became famous as an air show pilot performing with Lowell Yerex. Pangborn joined the Gates Flying Circus as chief pilot. After eight years of flying for Yerex and Ivan Gates, Pangborn started his own flying circus called The Flying Fleet. But in 1920 Pangborn, like Kingsford-Smith, alternated between barnstorming work and chasing ducks in Colusa and Glenn counties for the 1920 rate of a dollar an acre.[24] Ogle Merwin didn't return for the 1920 season. Jay M. Fetters, who flew for Ed Moffett during the 1919 season, started his own patrol competing with the Moffett Aero Service.

Moffett and Hunt came up with new marketing ideas for the 1920 season and expanded their company. Charles Kingsford-Smith was assigned a Curtiss Jenny belonging to Moffett and Hunt, and was told he could barnstorm around Northern California until the duck patrols began in August.

It is likely he had to pay Moffett and Hunt Company rent from a portion of his barnstorming proceeds. Kingsford-Smith ended up Yuba City broke and out of barnstorming prospects in early April 1920. He stayed about a month as a squatter on a makeshift landing field in Jackson Bottoms while trying to cultivate flying work in the community.

William Moffett and Irwin Hunt leased an Avro 504K or two from Bob Fowler's Fowler Airplane Corporation of San Francisco on May 21, 1920. Fowler procured Avros from Interallied Aircraft Corporation of Toronto and New York.[25] This trainer was the type of machine Kingsford-Smith spent many hours flying in Britain during the war. He had recently flown one in Hollywood for a brief attempt at film work.

Orvar "Swede" Meyerhoffer flew a new Varney Lincoln-Standard into the Moffett Airplane Company's airfield a mile west of Willows on May 24, 1920. The airfield was on Devenpeck Ranch where Moffett had a hangar. Meyerhoffer said the Lincoln-Standard could carry two passengers and a pilot and made several claims of his flying prowess. One, which could have been true, was he had made more forced landings without an accident than any other pilot in the world! A modest fellow, he also said he had been in the air longer than any three pilots in the United States. Meyerhoffer spent an entire Sunday teaching a Moffett and Hunt Company pilot the finer points of flying the Lincoln-Standard. Meyerhoffer took C. Burmeister, the rice grower, for a ride in the new plane and climbed to 10,000 feet for a good view.[26]

Moffett and Hunt acquired more airplanes in May. Irwin Hunt flew to Woodland May 25 from Oakland to visit his parents, Mr. and Mrs. Alvis Hunt, in another newly acquired $7,000 Lincoln-Standard biplane. He was ferrying to Willows for use on duck patrols during the upcoming season beginning August 15. The big biplane, powered by a Hisso motor, seated three, which was profitable for Hunt as he made several passenger hops over Woodland before leaving.[27]

Hunt told a Marysville reporter a slightly different story about the Lincoln-Standard. He said he was acquiring the Lincoln-Standard for Willows Aviation Company, an organization formed to slaughter ducks when they threaten rice growers crops. The duck patrol's company name was confusing. It had been referred to as Moffett Aircraft Co., Moffett and Hunt Co., and now Willows Aviation Company.[28]

Ed Moffett was organizing more air shows. He had Charles Kingsford-Smith fly an Avro 504K to Sacramento on June 23, 1920, to take part in an air show and race at South Curtiss Oaks Field. The event, a fund-raiser for the American War Mothers of Sacramento, turned into a mess and ended up costing the War Mothers money. According to an historical accounting about long distance flyers of the interwar years, Kingsford-Smith flew for the Moffett-Starkey Aero Circus, and its manager ran off without paying the pilots. The story could have been referring to the American War Mothers Air Show in which Kingsford-Smith and Edmund J. Moffett took part.[29]

Moffett and Hunt Co. announced duck patrols would begin as scheduled August 15 over several thousand acres. Six airplanes where needed to patrol all the acreage they had signed up. They had three committed by mid-July. One plane was on the field at Willows and the other two were in Oregon. Irwin Hunt had arrived in Willows from Oregon on the fourteenth just so he could fly with Howard Smith that day to San Francisco and pick up a rebuilt Curtiss Jenney.[30]

The Moffett and Hunt Co. duck patrol suffered severe setbacks before the 1920 patrols even got started. Meyerhoffer was on a barnstorming tour in the north state to pick up some extra money. Prior to the tour he was demonstrating the plane to potential buyers for his primary employer Walter Varney, the Redwood City distributor for Lincoln-Standard aircraft. Meyerhoffer had been at Willows flying the new plane for Moffett and Hunt Co. the week before he left for Oregon. Swede Meyerhoffer was mortally injured on July 17 at McArthur, California, near the Oregon state line.[31]

Six weeks later Irwin Hunt was arrested and jailed in Willows just after he returned from a barnstorming tour through southern Oregon. He had written a $130 check to a garage mechanic in Lakeview, Oregon, for engine repairs. He was unaware his partner William Moffett had emptied the company's checking account to purchase another plane for the duck patrol. Hunt spent a night in jail and was released on bail. He deposited a large sum in the checking account to get the whole mess straightened out, but it took a week to dismiss the charges.[32] Hunt filed suit against the garage for malicious prosecution and demanded $5,000 in damages. He said he put money into his checking account soon enough to cover the check. He claimed the mechanic filed charges because he was angry Hunt signed a contract to fly an exhibition at a local fair that he was interested in.[33]

Irwin Hunt got into trouble with the law once again in the summer of 1925 for an alleged burglary of a Napa home. He flew to Napa from Woodland the morning of his trial scheduled for that afternoon. At noon Hunt took Raymond Asedo, captain of the Napa County traffic officers, for an airplane ride. The wing of his plane collapsed at 1,000 feet, and the plane burst into flames! Both men were killed; Asedo was 28 and Hunt, 23.[34] Hunt was reported to be the son of a millionaire. He was only 18 when he went into partnership with William Moffett in the duck patrol business.

A LOCAL RICE grower reportedly learned to fly in the fall of 1920 and though his name wasn't mentioned in the newspaper article it is believed he was Mr. Holly Culver, a Willows rice grower who learned to fly about this time.[35]

Bud Coffee from the Bay Area landed at Moffett's airfield west of Willows the evening of July 21, 1920. His mission was delivering the *San Francisco Call* to Willows in the early evening instead of 10:30 PM, its usual overland arrival time. Coffee was flying a Lincoln-Standard biplane with a 220hp. Hisso. His passenger was Mrs. Bonnie Glessier, publicity director for the Palace Hotel of San Francisco; she was enjoying the first days of her vacation after which she returned to San Francisco by train.

Coffee's flight was said to be the first time newspapers were delivered to Willows by airplane. He flew on to Red Bluff to deliver more papers and then Westwood to perform exhibition flights under the auspices of the Red River Lumber Company.

When Coffee landed at Moffett's airfield, a pilot drove out to look at the big biplane. He was surprised to meet Coffee whom he had known during the war.[36] Bud Coffee had built a good reputation flying in Northern California. He was hired by the Jacuzzi brothers to fly their J-7 monoplane. The following year, he was killed flying the J-7 when the wings came off near Modesto, his hometown.

In late July, the *Willows Daily Journal* published a 3 x 11-inch ad across the top of page five screaming, "Rice Men THE DUCKS ARE DANGEROUS Better be Safe than Sorry Have Your Rice Fields Patrolled By MOFFITT–HUNT AIRPLANE CO.   Day and Night Flights   For Particulars communicate with W. I. MOFFITT [sic], Palace Hotel, Phone 282, Willows, Cal."[37]

Moffitt and Hunt bought a Lincoln-Standard from the Walter Varney Airplane Co. of Redwood City in August 1920.[38] Moffett and Hunt aircraft were patrolling rice fields twice a day by September 1. On a flight the night before, moonlight made it seem as bright as day and the pilot had no problem covering his allotted territory. He also had a bright searchlight mounted on his plane. The waterfowl preferred moonlit nights to feed in the rice fields. They would wallow out and mash down the standing rice, then strip it of the grain. In one night, ducks could ruin acres of rice at a single location. With the farmer's popguns causing an uproar and airplanes overhead, the ducks usually stayed away for a night.[39]

The next day a competing duck patrol operating from Willows and led by Jay M. Fetters was praised in a front-page article of the Willows newspaper. Fetters had flown duck patrol for Ed Moffett the previous season. For the 1920 season, he formed his own patrol and signed contracts to patrol 10,000 acres for two flights per day. During the moonlit nights when the waterfowl did the most damage, Fetters planned nightly patrols. Since he was then competing with Moffett and Hunt, he could not use their airfield. He used a landing strip on Holly Culver's property. Culver, a flying farmer, made a small machine shop near his airstrip available to Fetters for repairs when necessary. Fetters flew duck patrols six hours a day because there were twice as many ducks as the year before. Fetters also flew his customers to inspect their rice crop and monitor growth. Nightly duck patrols weren't a problem for Fetters. In 1919, he had made what he claimed was the first night flight across the Sierra Nevada; from Carson City to Sacramento.[40]

AVIATOR ARTHUR RAYMOND Borne and his wife rented a room in the Willows home of Mrs. Alice Davis as did another aviator, whose name was reported only as Smith. Borne came home around 9:00 the night of September 28, 1920, but his wife wasn't there. He immediately became enraged and screamed curses throughout the home. When she finally came home, Borne "... upbraided her in the vilest epithets that could be hurled against a woman and accused her of improper conduct." She declared her innocence but was met by a series of "stunning and savage blows, which greatly disfigured the helpless wife." Borne, however, was just getting started.

During the assault, pilot Smith of the Moffett and Hunt Co. duck patrol arrived at the boarding house where he also had a room. Borne stopped assaulting his wife and accused Smith of trying to take his wife. He accused Smith of the filthiest actions and ranted like a "wild man." Borne's wife, clad only in a sheet, slipped out of the house during the confrontation and took refuge at the Crystal Baths.

Smith tried to assure Borne nothing illicit occurred and he hadn't ever given the woman "undue attention." As Smith gave his explanation, Borne became even more furious. He ran to an adjoining room, came back with a shotgun, and pointed it at Smith. He gave him three minutes to confess, but Smith said he had nothing to confess. Borne pressed the gun against Smith and worked the action. A shotgun shell got stuck in the action, possibly preventing murder. Frustrated with the jammed gun, Borne used it to club Smith over the head two or three times. Smith was stunned and unable to defend himself. He was momentarily immobilized. When he regained his senses, he told Borne to put down the shotgun and he would fight him. Borne wouldn't drop the weapon and Smith, drifting in and out of consciousness, fell to the ground as police officers arrived and hauled Borne to jail. Sheriff Newt Power and the district attorney discussed charges to be filed against Borne.

Smith had an excellent reputation and friends said there was no reason for Borne's attack. Smith sustained a deep scalp wound, a broken finger, facial abrasions, and bruising. Before the attack, Borne and Smith had been best friends and got along well.[41] Borne appeared before Judge L. P. Farnham on October 4 and pled guilty to a single charge of disturbing the peace. Considering he beat his wife and Smith, it is hard to understand why he was let off so lightly.[42] The only Smith known to be flying for Moffett and Hunt in September 1920 was Charles Kingsford-Smith.

Kingsford-Smith departed America and walked down the gangway at Sydney Harbor, Australia, on January 11, 1921. Seven years later, he returned to California to become the first to fly across the Pacific Ocean from California to Australia in his tri-motor Fokker, the *Southern Cross*.

In October 1920 a journalist, Mr. Hogg, came to Willows to write a story about the duck patrols based there. Hogg's assistants were Paul Gott and O. W. H. Pratt from the Yolo Fliers Club at Woodland.[43]

The duck patrols of Moffett and Hunt Co., Ogle Merwin, and J. M. Fetters had disappeared by 1921. Fish and Game authorities were unhappy with the volume of ducks killed by the patrols. The end of the patrols was a direct response to a movie newsreel film by Richard Done, photographer Louis Hutt, Lt. Harry Halverson, and commercial aviator J. M. Fetters. They produced a newsreel of Fetters making passes over a rice field on October 16, 1920. It showed his airplane flying into immense flocks of ducks killing and wounding hundreds with the propeller and wings. Louis Hutt had also written a series of magazine articles on the thrill of hunting ducks by airplane. Washington received a firestorm of letters protesting this cruelty and an agent was sent to California to investigate. Charles S. Hauser, head of the Fish and Game Department, filed a complaint with

Wallace Sheppard, the United States commissioner. The four were charged for hunting ducks with airplanes in violation of the migratory bird act.[44] Even though legal action ended the duck patrols, airplanes and helicopters were still being used to scare birds off rice fields, more humanely of course, through the 1960s.

TRACY FARMER A. Grunauer hired Fauna W. Farris, an aviator from Stockton, to sow winter wheat from his airplane in January 1923. This date is the earliest reference to aerial crop seeding on a farmer's field this author has found. But, was it the first? The initial newspaper report of this application method suggests not. It stated, "Just to keep the pace set by some farmers in the Tulare section, Abe Grunauer, extensive land owner and president of the Fabian-Grunauer Company here, announced today that ... he will sow to barley his large ranch near here with an airplane. The ranch to be seeded in this novel way is known as the 'adobe ranch.'"[45] This quote suggests aerial seeding may have been done before January 1923 at Tulare in the San Joaquin Valley. Sowing Grunauer's farm with an airplane was an experiment to prove the feasibility of aerial application when fields were too wet for the usual sowing with a machine pulled by a team of horses. Only 30 acres were sown in this aerial experiment.

FARRIS, THE PILOT, felt the experiment was a success but said a larger plane carrying 1,000 pounds of seed would be much better than the ex-military plane (JN-4 or Standard J-1) he flew. Farris could only carry 225 to 250 pounds per trip requiring him to land often. He had a hopper built and installed it in the front cockpit of his plane. He manipulated a lever from his seat in the rear cockpit to release the seed, and the prop wash distributed it over a 50-foot swath. Farris flew into the wind while seeding. A sandy unplowed landing field was chosen a half-mile away to operate from. Farris used the same plane for seeding that he trained students and hopped passengers at Stockton Center Airport (also known as Farris Field) over the past few years.

Farris thought the cost of aerial seeding could be reduced to less than a dollar an acre. The Tracy experiment was carried out on such a small scale the cost was considerably higher. Grunauer told the reporter it cost approximately 37 cents per acre to sow the same field by ground methods. He said he was happy with the results of the experiment. He believed a great future was at hand for aviators planting and caring for crops with airplanes. Farris was reflecting the struggle aviators were experiencing to find useful work for their airplanes at this early stage of the technology.[45]

The Grunauer/Farris seeding of winter wheat in 1923 was recorded in the *Stockton Daily Evening Record*, possibly the earliest report of aerial seeding in California's Great Central Valley. It was only an experiment. The first commercial seeding flights were claimed later by Frank Gallison of Merced; Floyd "Speed" Nolta of Willows; Sacramento's Leo Moore and Ingvald Fagerskog; and Herb Weggers of Woodland—however, Fauna W. Farris preceded them all.[46]

If it is a question of who was the first pilot to sow *rice* by air in the Great Central Valley, the honor goes to Frank Gallison of Merced who seeded rice from the air the spring of 1929 in the San Joaquin Valley.[47]

Many people in the Sacramento area believe the legend of Charles T. "Red" Jensen, which was posted in the foyer of the administration building at Sacramento's Executive Airport. For many years, this display plus an article published in *Sport Flying* made Jensen out to be the father of agricultural aviation in Northern California. The legend makes many claims about his early flying days in the 1920s and '30s, which defy credibility.

Charlie Jensen's legend simply doesn't jibe with his life's timeline. As the legend goes, Jensen's first exposure to flying was washing airplanes for aviators at Mather Field in exchange for rides during World War I. Jensen was six years old when army aviators began flying at Mather in 1918! The war ended four months later.

The legend claimed Jensen made his first parachute jump at age 14 during the air show dedication for the opening of Colusa Airport. Jensen reported using an assumed name so his father wouldn't find out about the jump. Research reveals he did make the parachute jump at the Colusa opening. He used the pseudonym "Red" Sullivan and made the jump during the three-day air show. The only problems with the story are the dates. The air show was held May 30–June 1, 1930. Charlie Jensen was then 18. His legend claimed General Billy Mitchell gave a dedicatory speech. That never happened; Mitchell was not at Colusa's airport opening. As far as keeping anything from his father, his jump was reported under his correct name four days later in a Sacramento newspaper. It was an interesting report of Jensen's first jump; he jumped from 3,500 feet like a veteran jumper. It also stated his regular job was a mechanic for Leo Moore, the well-known Sacramento commercial pilot who was soon doing ag-flying work. Moore flew in the air show at Colusa, and it was probably his Travel Air from which Jensen

CHAPTER 13

jumped. The legend claims by age 18 Jensen had sold Howard Hughes four Travel Airs to be used in the movie *Hell's Angels* and had flown in the movie himself.[48] If he flew in *Hell's Angels*, sold Howard Hughes four Travel Airs, and started his own ag-flying business by 1930 (Jensen's business card reads, "Since 1930") why was he still working for Leo Moore?

One possibly credible claim of his early flying days was that he obtained the DOC Aeronautic Branch's aircraft mechanic's license No. 1 by age 18.[49] It has been written Jensen was a crop duster in the late 1920s yet his business card said "Since 1930." If he had flown crops in the '20s it would have been ground breaking and noted in newspapers and aviation periodicals of the day. His obituary says he died in 1980 at 68, which means he was born in 1912, thus he was 15 in 1927. Howard Hughes began filming *Hell's Angels* in 1927 and finished the aerial shooting in January 1929. How is it possible a 15-year-old could possess four Travel Airs for sale to Howard Hughes and then fly in his movie?[50] There is no doubt Charlie Jensen made many contributions to agricultural aviation, borate and water bombing of forest fires, and helicopter rescue following World War II, but the claims made before the war are suspect. Available facts do not support them, and date and age comparisons make them implausible.

During the 1920s and through the mid-1930s aviation trade magazines and daily newspapers printed the movements of pilots and their planes. There was much reporting on the aviation community in the Sacramento area. The two main newspapers published weekly aviation columns reporting movements of private and commercial flights, particularly the latter. After exhaustive research, the previously cited and following reports are the only prewar newspaper and trade magazine entries about Charles Jensen this author has found.

On July 4, 1932, Charlie "Red" Jensen was reported making a parachute jump from 4,000 feet during an air show at Sacramento Municipal Airport. In December 1932, Paul Norboe reported mechanic Red Jensen did a complete overhaul of Norboe's Pitcairn biplane. Finally, there was an actual report that tied Jensen to ag-flying. In October 1936, Jensen was supposed to fly a crop dusting demonstration during the air show at Sacramento Municipal Airport, but due to Jerry Barker's crash Jensen's demonstration was cancelled.[51]

Moving on to other early reports of aerial crop application: there was an April 1929 article in the Turlock newspaper, a short blurb reporting that the state's first licensed "crop-dusting" airplane was ready to begin service.

Pacific Aerodusting Company of Southern California owned the plane and added it to the company's fleet to begin operating over large farms in the Los Angeles area. The short article implies Pacific Aerodusting Company may have been working in this endeavor for a year or two since it already had planes adapted for dusting.[52]

Livingston Gilson Irving was the first pilot to fly insect killing dust on crops in the north state. (Unless the story of Frank Rose's dusting experiment right after the Great War is true.)

Irving was born in San Francisco in 1895 and educated in local schools. He attended the University of California at Berkeley from 1914 to 1917. During the Great War, he joined the US Army Signal Corps as a private. He was sent to the School of Military Aeronautics at Berkeley for ground school training and on to North Island, later named Rockwell Field, for flight training. In November 1917, as second lieutenant, he was sent to France for advanced flight training at the Third Aviation Instruction Center, at Issodun and Cazeaux, France, which he completed in April 1918. First assigned to a French squadron, he transferred to the American 103rd Aero Squadron, Third Pursuit Group, Allied Expeditionary Force (AEF) in August 1918. By September, he was flying combat in a Spad XIII in the skies of France. He was awarded the Distinguished Service Cross and the Croix de Guerre while fighting Germans. He downed four enemy planes but only received official credit for one. It has been written he was a member of the Lafayette Flying Corps during the World War, but he is not mentioned in a definitive publication about the corps that lists all 273 of those illustrious fliers. If he served in a French uniform, he should be included in the Lafayette Flying Corps.

After the war, he worked for Standard Oil and later the Paraffine Company. He returned to flying and entered the Dole Race to Hawaii in 1927. He flew the Breese high-wing monoplane "Pabco Flyer." He was the only Dole contestant having the navigational skills to be allowed to enter the race without a navigator. He made two takeoff attempts at the Dole Race on August 16, 1927, but couldn't get into the air. He wrecked his plane in a bad crash on his second attempt.

After the Dole Race debacle, Irving founded Aviation Activities Inc., based at Oakland Municipal Airport. He introduced crop dusting to Northern California, seeded rice, and gave flying instruction. He was a pioneer in Bay Area commercial aviation. Irving returned to duty during World War II. After the war, he was promoted to colonel in the Air Force Reserve and

Chapter 13

was active with the 349th Fighter Bomber Wing. He retired as an aircraft inspector at Alameda Naval Air Station (former site of the San Francisco Bay Airdrome and Alameda Airport) in 1963.[53]

Livingston Irving began dusting crops in the Sacramento Valley on July 30, 1929, at a site in Sutter County near Meridian. Dusting beans or any other crop from the air had never been done in the Sacramento Valley. Western Sulphur Industries Corporation wanted Irving to demonstrate to valley farmers that it could be done. Western Sulphur Industries claimed it had already promoted crop dusting of citrus groves, mainly oranges, in Southern California according to company representative R. J. Frisbee. That begs the question: who did the first crop dusting in Southern California and, thus, was first in the state? Where and when did they do it?

Irving had come to Hotel Marysville July 26 with Western Sulphur Industries' representative, R. J. Frisbee, to discuss his upcoming demonstration of crop dusting with local farmers. Frisbee was organizing the dusting of beans in the area.[54] The first site to be dusted was Alwood McKeehan's ranch, 15 miles west of Yuba City near Tarke Station, and six miles east of Meridian off the Tahoe-Ukiah Highway (now Highway 20). Agricultural Aviation Activities Company, owned and operated by chief pilot Livingston Irving, would execute the dusting demonstration for Western Sulphur Industries. Nicknamed "Jimmie," Irving did all of the flying for this notable demonstration. It was reported Irving's company had been recently formed to carry out crop dusting throughout the United States. The company name was an appended version of Irving's previous business, Aviation Activities Inc.

Many Yuba and Sutter county bean growers were waiting at McKeehan's ranch to witness the demonstration. Unfortunately, during his flight north from Oakland, the fuel line broke on Irving's Eaglerock. He had to make a forced landing near Davis to repair it and was late to his demonstration. The crowd dwindled to a half-dozen who watched Irving in his Eaglerock fly the sulphur onto the bean field.

Irving's black Eaglerock biplane, powered by a 220hp. Hisso was specially equipped with a hopper, which would leave a 55-foot wide swath of sulphur dust behind the plane when activated. Eight trips were required for the demonstration; each trip laid down a half-mile long swath. It took 18 minutes to dust the 30 acres. Turbulent air forced Irving to fly a little higher than he liked, ten to twelve feet instead of six to eight feet. The result was the swath widened from the higher altitude. The dust was a sulphur compound very effective against aphids and red spiders. Several Western Sulphur Industries Company officials also witnessed the inauguration of bean dusting by airplane. Among them were Courtney L. Moore, M. M. Smith, and Burdett Palmer, a noted flier who was serving with Irving on the company's technical committee.

Reportedly, Irving had signed contracts for 10,000 acres of bean growers' land to be dusted and more would probably be signed before the day was over. Western Sulphur official C. L. Moore told the gathering his company had obtained control of the basic patents covering dusting from airplanes and plans were afoot to form a well-capitalized company to carry out all sorts of crop dusting and seeding from airplanes. Moore also spoke of the company's plan to use a dusting fleet of specially built Stearman aircraft, each powered by a 300hp. Wright Whirlwind motor.

The front cockpit of Irving's Hisso Eaglerock was transformed into cargo space which allowed the plane to carry 700 pounds of sulphur dust each trip.[55] By August 18, Irving had dusted 1,000 acres of beans and prunes in Sutter and Colusa counties. W. B. Meinert alternated with Irving flying the Eaglerock. Each trip was flown below ten feet at a speed of 95 mph. Following the McKeehan farm demonstration the two pilots dusted 11 orchards and bean fields in District 70 by the 18th. Irving reported dusting 165 acres on J. L. Browning's farm in 2 hours and 22 minutes, not including time for landing, loading, and takeoffs.

Dusting was done best in early morning when light dew covered plants and trees. Calm air was necessary—wind stopped all work. In the still air, the dust was hurled out evenly, catching the air stream from the propeller as it was released from the hopper in the front cockpit. The pilot controlled the dust by manipulating a release valve mounted next to his seat in the rear cockpit.

The first fields and orchards dusted by Irving in the District 70 area, near Tarke Station and the town of Meridian, were those of McKeehan, J. L. Browning, J. Clark, V. Vanderford, Ferguson, Wachter, Sanborn, Ettl, Pattison, Andriotti, and R. S. Faxon.[56]

Later in August, Irving's planes finished dusting bean fields for red spider in west Sutter County and then moved across the Sacramento River to Colusa County to begin dusting prune orchards near Grimes. Faxon Ranch was the first to use airplane dusting to control red spider on prunes. Irving was the pilot. He spread 700 pounds of sulphur dust on the 60-acre prune orchard in half-an-hour. It took just one flight.

Chapter 13

Allen H. Rhodes claimed to have flown for Livingston Irving seeding rice in Northern California in the 1920s. Forty years afterwards when he told author Brian R. Baker of his ag-flying his memory for exact dates was nonexistent. He said he flew a Whirlwind J-4 powered Waco for Irving, which would have probably put him in the picture at a later date than 1929 when Irving had only an inexpensive Hisso Eaglerock for ag-work. A J-4 Waco was an expensive machine.[57]

Frank Gallison's Merced-Wawona Air Lines carried out the first Sacramento Valley rice seeding flights in the spring of 1930. Merced-Wawona sent sales representative W. N. Morgan to Gridley the first week of March 1930 to interview rice growers and explain how his company could plant their rice seed with airplanes and why planes were a better way to plant. It would cost them one dollar per acre and the grower had to provide a reasonably smooth landing strip 2,000 feet long and 200 feet wide. Other growers' fields would be seeded from the same landing strip. He said this method would save the growers time. He told them the company, during 1929 in the San Joaquin Valley, had flown on 48 tons of rice seed with one plane in 27 hours. By flying at 200 feet it was possible to plant a crop on ground that could not otherwise have been seeded. After the discussions at Gridley, Morgan signed a contract with O. H. Vanderford, a large rice grower. Reportedly, Vanderford was the first grower in Butte County to have his rice seeded by airplane.[58]

Representatives of the Royal Aero Corporation of Los Angeles also showed up in Gridley in March 1930 to convince local farmers the advantages of aerial dusting to control crop-eating insects. Frank Barber was the company's chief pilot. Company reps claimed he pioneered the development of crop dusting at an undisclosed date and place for the US government. Despite their claim, Livingston Irving had already been dusting in the region for a year.[59]

On April 20, 1930, the first rice seed to be planted in the Sacramento Valley by airplane was spread on the Rathbun brothers 2,000-acre property near Williams in Colusa County. Frank Gallison's Merced-Wawona Air Lines flew the rice seed onto the Rathbuns' fields in two specially equipped aircraft. Colusa County grower S. T. Johnson was having Gallison's planes sow his rice seed the next week.[60]

Some of the smaller rice growers in Glenn County complained they wouldn't follow Rathbun's lead until the cost per acre was reduced. This was their conclusion after W. N. Morgan approached them to sign up with the

Merced-Wawona Company. They calculated that in addition to the dollar an acre cost, they had to build a mile long runway (not true), have the land surveyed, staked in 60-foot sections, and flooded. Additionally, the grower had to pay the wages of the "sack swamper" (the rice seed loader). One large Glenn County rice grower estimated seeding by airplane would cost him $1.75 an acre when everything was paid for. Morgan countered that sowing by air caused a more even planting and saved much seed. Rathun's was the first time aerial planting was tried in Colusa and Glenn counties, and everyone was observing the results carefully.[61]

On April 24, 1930, Merced-Wawona Company moved two airplanes, a Waco and a Fairchild, to O. H. Vanderford's ranch west of Gridley. Vanderford had a 2,000 x 200-foot landing strip ready for them. The two planes were each powered by 300hp. Whirlwind engines and had been modified for rice seeding by the Fairchild Company. They would be seeding 250 acres on Vanderford's ranch and 350 acres on the Frank Hatch property leased to Vanderford. Seeding began on the day they arrived.[62] The *Sacramento Bee* reported the Butte County rice-seeding project. It stated some of the land seeded belonged to Owens and his son. It also reported Vanderford and Adams had land near Sacramento that was seeded by Merced-Wawona Air Lines the week before.[63]

Two unnamed pilots dusted a 170-acre field of walnuts, prunes, and

Fig. 64. In this Merced-Wawona Airlines Waco 10, owner/pilot Frank Gallison carries out the first aerial rice seeding in Northern California for Butte County rancher O. H. Vanderford on April 24, 1930.

grapes on the Williamson property near Sacramento July 29, 1930. They used sulphur to stop the red spiders from devouring the crops. It was reported the pilots were the first to do this in the Sacramento Valley, but Livingston Irving preceded them by almost a year with his flights near Meridian.[64]

Frank Gallison planted trout by air in some of the inaccessible Sierra Nevada lakes for game warden A. J. Brown of Mariposa in September 1930. Gallison and Brown loaded four containers of young trout and flew over a group of small lakes near Wawona. Brown would open a container, attach a small parachute, and drop it overboard. He watched the container drift slowly through the air into the lake and sink. An opening in the top allowed the fish to escape the container. Brown believed the experiment was so successful it would be repeated on a larger scale where it was impossible to truck young fish to high altitude lakes.[65]

Gallison was an owner and chief pilot of Merced-Wawona Air Lines, and L. F. Tedrow was his partner and extra pilot. In the spring of 1929, these two men carried out an experimental flying job that would forever change how rice would be farmed in California.

The story of the first seeding of rice by airplane begins after growers in the Merced area suffered an abnormally dry year. As a result, they needed to plant their rice early. In those days, the rice was planted on dry ground so rice broadcasting machines, pulled by horses or tractors, could get into the fields and plant. After planting, the fields were flooded. Using this technique, an entire section of 640 acres owned by Crocker-Huffman Land and Water Company of California had sprouted by early May. The rice seed was just growing roots when clouds of migratory waterfowl descended. These birds fly over the valleys annually heading north to spend the summer. Usually they arrive before the rice starts to grow. But, with the early planting, tender rice shoots were plentiful, and the birds stayed until all the rice was eaten before flying on north.

E. S. Murchie, assistant manager for the Crocker-Huffman company, got together with Tom McSwain, a land and water engineer. They looked over the wasteland that was recently a rice field. The company had spent over $10,000 in preparation, seeding, and watering the field. Now, there wasn't a nickel's worth of rice left.

They agreed it would be impossible to get the rice broadcasters back into the wet fields. To seed by hand would take an army of men and delay the harvest into the rainy season—the replacement crop could be lost. They thought of another possibility, and weren't sure it had ever been done.

Rice seed grows better when it is sown in water than on dry ground. Murchie was a modern farm manager open to experimenting. The destroyed crop cost $15 per acre to establish. After discussing their options, Murchie and McSwain decided to gamble $1,000. It was worth the risk if it yielded a crop. They agreed to try seeding by airplane. They drove to Merced Airport and spoke with Frank Gallison and L. F. Tedrow of Merced-Wawona Air Lines.

After talking with Murchie and McSwain, the two pilots realized the future possibilities of the project, particularly if it was successful. The 640 acres they were to seed might lead to 6,000 acres next season and a lot more in the northern rice counties.

Gallison and Tedrow after checking around heard about a plane used to seed grain fields nearby some years before, the Farris/Grunauer experiment no doubt, but no one could remember enough about it to help them modify their airplane for the job.

After conferring with Murchie and McSwain, they bought sheet metal and reinforced the floor of the front cockpit in their long-wing Eaglerock, the larger of their two planes. Through this steel sheet and the fuselage floor, they put two four-inch lengths of stovepipe forming a double spout. "The spouts were closed with a single length of smooth board which was hinged to the pipes themselves. The inside of the cockpit was lined with canvas, and a canvas cover was fitted over the top to prevent seed from being blown back (into the pilot's cockpit) by the propeller blast. From the board cover on the spouts, a cord ran into the rear cockpit and attached to a trigger control beside the pilot. The material and labor cost $50."[66]

Murchie and McSwain prepared a landing strip beside their rice field. The four men figured the Eaglerock would carry 500 pounds of seed. Gallison, piloting the plane, calculated that with the 90hp. OX-5 engine in his Eaglerock, he would need 2,000 feet of runway to get off the ground. A runway of 2,400 feet was developed, and a loading area was established 400 feet from the threshold of the runway. Gallison planned to land short on the runway and coast up to the loading area where sacks of rice seed would be loaded into the front cockpit by three men known as swampers.

Flying began in May and took three days. Gallison flew 27 hours making 160 round trips sowing 48 tons of rice seed. Flying at 70 mph he covered 1,900 air miles. The growers paid $648 for the plane and pilot. They paid the swampers $48.50, and grading the landing field cost $173.90. The rice company also provided four flagmen to stand at intervals on the field

Chapter 13

along surveyed lines, so the pilot could fly a true course on each pass down the field. Cost of the flagmen and the surveying was $100.65. Total for the job was $970.55. Afterward McSwain declared, "Never in all my experience have I seen a theory work out so perfectly in practice." They produced a crop—not just a lesser crop— a full crop worth $64,000!

Frank Gallison and Tedrow immediately started plans to promote rice seeding for the following growing season and making changes to their hopper design. They needed a different plane to expand into crop dusting. Gallison, looking out at the vineyards surrounding the airport, told a reporter, "I am going to experiment this year with grape dusting. There are thousands of acres of grapes grown in this county, and they have to be dusted twice a year. I don't see any reason why it cannot be done more economically from an airplane." He also had another idea for the big cattle ranches in the Merced area. They "could use their own plane profitably just for making trips between home and town and for scouting over their cattle ranges. A lot of farming could be done from the air. I think we have opened up a whole new business field for aviation."

Earlier, Murchie had reported, "It cost us about $1.50 an acre to seed that land by airplane, which is just twice what it costs by ordinary methods. But the advantages of airplane seeding appear to be so great that the extra cost means nothing. If our crop is successful and all indications are that it will be I am certain that the airplane will be adopted generally for this purpose." To support this commercial experiment in rice seeding, the rice experimental station at Biggs in Butte County released a report finding rice dropped in water germinates best and the percentage of yield from this type of seeding is expected to be much higher than the old method of dry seeding. Sowing in water had been found to hasten rice maturity by seven to ten days.[67]

Murchie was right on with his prediction that airplanes would be adopted for planting rice. The Crocker-Huffman experiment story ran in nearly every newspaper in the Great Central Valley. For the next rice season in the spring and summer of 1930, close to a dozen different flying outfits sprung up in, or moved to, the rice growing counties, hoping to sign growers to seeding contracts. It was a lucrative alternative for barnstorming fliers, an occupation rapidly disappearing. Unfortunately, crop dusting was more dangerous than barnstorming, but at least no innocent passengers were at risk.

Frank Gallison was one of the lucky crop dusting pilots; he survived the multiple dangers of ag-flying and lived 77 years. Before he learned to fly, he drove a mail truck between El Portal and Merced. He began flying in 1925 and gained his transport license in 1927. After he learned to fly, Gallison moved to Merced and developed Merced Airport with Lou Foote. Their business was named Merced-Wawona Air Line. It was created to fly passengers and mail to and from Yosemite Park. This was in the early days when airplanes were allowed to fly into the park, which had its own airport. The Crocker-Huffman experiment changed Gallison's life and opened a new lucrative market for his and others' aviation businesses. During World War II, Gallison was in the Air Corps Reserve at Eagle Field, seven miles south of Dos Palos, serving as a flight instructor. After the war, he purchased a small airport at Dos Palos, near the Merced County line, and started another crop dusting service there. He sold that airport in 1962. In 1969, he was honored at the Merced Antique Fly-In with a citation from the Federal Aviation Administration (FAA). It recognized his special service to the armed forces during World War II and for valuable counsel and service to the FAA throughout his career. The citation described him as a pioneer aviator, aviation mechanic, and airmail pilot. He was credited as an early barnstormer, and the first person to seed rice by air. Frank Gallison went west in January 1978.[68]

An interesting and tragic sidebar to Frank Gallison's story concerns Lou Foote, his partner in the founding of the Merced Municipal Airport and the creation of Merced-Wawona Air Lines.

After considerable effort, Lou Foote, a Turlock auto mechanic and pilot who ran a garage on South Center Street, established the first airport at Turlock in 1927. His hangar and runway were located at the south end of Orange Street where he gave many rides and taught several flying students.

In the early months of 1928, Foote pulled up stakes and moved to Merced where he and Frank Gallison founded the Merced Airport and started Merced-Wawona Air Lines. In August 1928, Lou Foote disappeared mysteriously from Merced leaving his partner, Gallison, to run their new airport and flying business alone. Worse still, Foote abandoned his wife and young daughter in Merced—they didn't know where he had gone. He allegedly ran off with another woman.

Foote was rocketed from obscurity on March 17, 1929, after he crashed a Colonial Airways tri-motor Ford just after takeoff from the Newark, New Jersey, airport. Fourteen people were killed in what headlines declared the worst accident in American aviation history. Foote suffered severe injuries. Only he and one passenger, who was sitting in the copilot's seat next to him, survived (copilots weren't required for sightseeing trips).

To make matters worse, the woman Foote allegedly ran off from Merced with was now married to him or at least posing as his wife to reporters at his hospital bedside. His marital status was questioned. Comments from both wives became front-page material for the Turlock newspaper.

Cause of Foote's crash was loss of power in one or both wing engines on the tri-motor. The fuselage engine lacked horsepower to keep the fully loaded Ford airborne. Foote correctly did not try to turn back to the runway. He kept the plane flying straight ahead as it was losing altitude. He didn't have enough airspeed to get over a loaded railroad car in his path. The railroad car wiped most of the passenger compartment off the Ford's big high-wing, killing everyone behind the pilot's cockpit.[69]

Over the next several weeks, two more multi-engine airliners would go down in what was a brutal period in early airline history. On March 23, the huge twin-engine Sikorsky transport being used in Howard Hughes' movie *Hell's Angels* to represent a Great War German Gotha bomber, crashed during filming with the loss of one crew member.[70]

The third crash occurred April 21, 1929. It was again tragic and somewhat ironic. Maurice H. Murphy, a Bay Area aviation pioneer, was piloting a Maddux Air Lines tri-motor Ford near east San Diego en route to Phoenix with two passengers aboard when an army pursuit plane collided with his plane killing everyone on board.[71] The irony of this midair collision was Maurice Murphy was known in earlier years on the barnstorming circuit as Loop-The-Loop Murphy, because he was said to have made a flight from San Francisco to Los Angeles looping the whole way. The army pilot who collided with the Ford misjudged a loop he was making around Murphy's airliner.

IT WASN'T LONG after Lou Foote left Merced that Frank Gallison took on a new partner, L. F. Tedrow. In their efforts to expand the Merced-Wawona Air Lines, Gallison, as manager of the company, completed negotiations to take over Lou Foote's airport on Orange Street at the southern city limits of Turlock. Merced-Wawona would have control of the 1,300-foot runway and Foote's old hangar. Gallison's company beat out negotiations that had been going on for a long time between Turlock officials and Archer Beardsly's Independent Flying School of Oakland for the Turlock airfield.

Gallison planned to have a flight school up and running by the beginning of June. He reported he would be moving a new three-place OX-5 Waco biplane onto the field as soon as the Turlock runway was graded. Once established, the Merced-Wawona Air Lines flying school at Turlock would be the only licensed flying school in Stanislaus County.[72]

Frank Gallison and L. F. Tedrow operated the Merced Airport; however, Richfield Oil Company now owned the airport property and probably fueling rights. The two men ran the airport under the auspices of their company, Merced-Wawona Air Lines. Rice planting and student instruction were their principal activities. They had a Stinson operating in May 1930, and more new equipment was being purchased in time for the eventual inauguration of Merced-Wawona Air Lines to be held the coming summer. The Merced-Yosemite Glider Club with W. L. Winton as president also used the airport.[73]

The Curtiss-Wright Flying Service had purchased many airports across America. Today, they would be called an airport franchise chain. Curtiss-Wright (C-W) Flying Service officials announced in May 1930 crop dusting operations would begin at their San Joaquin Valley airport and their Orange County airfield. Paul C. Jackson was named supervisor of all crop dusting activities for C-W. Benjamin J. Busch, sales director of the company's Los Angeles base, reported C-W had contracted with Western Sulphur Industries and Agricultural Chemical Works to supply all the chemicals used for dusting crops.[74] Curtiss-Wright sought to follow up on its expansion into crop dusting by appointing Modesto's Frank Galligan (not Frank Gallison) and Leslie Brisbin of Rutherford as special representatives for the company's crop dusting service. C-W had four planes operating in the San Joaquin Valley and a fifth in reserve for immediate service in Orange County. E. J. Bond was put in charge of all valley operations with Paul Jackson as overall head of C-W agricultural operations.[75]

Royal Aero Corporation was also engaged in crop dusting activities in the San Joaquin Valley by May 1930. The corporation was a subsidiary of Western College of Aeronautics and known as Western Dusters. The Western College of Aeronautics had recently moved to its new site at Culver City in Southern California.[76]

THE AIRPLANE HAD established itself as a necessity for Butte County farmers seeding rice on large tracts of land and dusting to control pests in the numerous southern county orchards. Its importance led to plans being discussed to establish an airport at Gridley for the dusting outfits to use as a base of operations.[77] Dusting many different crops increased considerably during the summer of 1930 in the Sacramento area.[78]

E. J. Kron transferred half-ownership in his long-wing OX-5 Eaglerock from M. R. Nicholaus to L. W. Olsen in September 1930. O. H. Vanderford and Walter Owen hired Kron to fly their new crop dusting airplane over their crops west of Gridley.[79]

Frank Galligan, wrote a long article for *Pacific Flyer* that big farm producers would be depending exclusively on airplanes to eradicate crop pests. Many aircraft were going to be needed for the 1931 growing season, he wrote. Dusting in the San Joaquin Valley in 1930 had been a large-scale successful experiment—55,000 acres were dusted. Acreage consisted of fruit trees, grapes, beans, alfalfa, tomatoes, and cotton. Galligan claimed farmers would need 750,000 acres dusted in 1931. He described the pests to be eradicated, the types of aircraft needed, how planes would have to be equipped, and the piloting skills necessary for crop dusting. Galligan's article was obviously meant to influence pilots in favor of Curtiss-Wright airplanes, which, of course, Mr. Galligan would gladly sell them. But, in reality, the clarion call for crop dusting planes and pilots only succeeded in crowding the job market for ag-pilots.[80]

WHEN EXAMINING AUTOBIOGRAPHICAL and often even biographical information about aviators, it is sometimes better to use the earliest information found, before legend creep occurs. Glenn Martin is a perfect example. A biographical article about him very early on in an aviation trade magazine made no claims of him making California's first successful powered flight at Santa Ana in August 1909. It stated that after the Dominguez Air Meet of January 1910, Martin made his first successful flights. This information had to have come directly from him as he was a relatively unknown aviation figure before the 1912 article was published.

There have been claims that Floyd "Speed" Nolta was the first to seed rice by airplane in California. The most egregious, published in 2010, claimed Nolta did it in 1919! This author must go with the earliest information when researching that claim. Reporter Charles J. Gleeson wrote an article about Floyd Nolta for the 60th anniversary issue of the *Willows Journal* in 1937. Based on an interview with Nolta, Gleeson gave an honest, unbiased account of Nolta's early flying career. He began his article, "Seven years ago a young Willows man attached his newly devised seed sower to an antiquated war-type plane[probably a Jenny] and went into the farm flying business... [as] Willows Flying Service." That man was Floyd Nolta who Gleeson said graduated from an army aviation school as a mechanic. A job he did for the duck patrols for the two years after the war. Nolta, in 1927, was still a garage mechanic "when farming began to take wings" with the introduction of aerial dusting of cotton fields in Texas." Two years later [1929] Frank Gallison of Merced made aviation history with the first rice planting [in Northern California]. Gallison's success fired Nolta's ambition. All of his spare time now went into flying, to give him sufficient hours in the air for a transport license.... In the spring of 1930 [Nolta] was ready to try out his new [aerial seeding] scheme." This earliest 1937 example of Floyd Nolta's biography does not support the claim in a 1986 publication that gave a fanciful story of Nolta's early flying career and that he seeded rice by air in 1928.

Regardless of whether Nolta began seeding rice in 1930 or even 1931, he definitely started seeding in the Glenn-Colusa rice country before any other local pilots from Glenn, Colusa, Butte, Sutter and Yuba counties. He eventually would seed not only rice, but wheat, alfalfa, corn, and oats. For several years during the rice growing season he had one of his planes patrol the fields to scare off marauding mud hens, ducks, and geese.

In 1936 a sheep rancher asked Nolta for help eradicating eagles that were killing lambs in his flocks in the western Glenn County mountain region. Nolta went out in one of his planes with another of his crew manning a shotgun in the passenger seat. It was dangerous flying over timberlands and into canyons where engine failure could have extreme results. The work was successful; they killed many eagles. In fact, the work was so successful they were called on the next year to do the same down in the valley where eagles were said to be feeding on lambs, pigs, and turkeys.

A conversation by this author with Guy "Speed" Hughes of Yuba City confirms Nolta's eagle eradications. Hughes claimed he manned the shotgun riding in a Piper J-3 Cub with Nolta over the Sutter Buttes.[81] Killing eagles was legal with a predator eradication permit from fish and game officials.

Floyd Nolta and his brother, Dale, did much of the rice seeding and dusting work in Glenn and Colusa counties for many years. They have passed on, but the business, ran by Dale's son Greg, continued on for decades. The Noltas were pioneers in water bombing forest fires. Both were very active members in the San Francisco Hangar of the Quiet Birdmen. The annual duck dinner they provided the QBs was always a memorable occasion.[82]

CHAPTER 14

The rice season of 1931 – Early flying attempts at Colusa – Chadwick Thompson flies duck hunters – Colusans choose an airport site – Colusa Airport dedication

There were several new rice seeding and crop dusting businesses offering their services to growers in Northern California's rice heartland of Glenn and Colusa counties in 1931. Large highly organized dusting companies came from Oakland, Merced, Modesto, and even as far away as Los Angeles. Smaller crop dusting outfits were getting started in Butte, Sutter, Yuba, Yolo, Glenn, and Sacramento counties. Harold F. Brown reported in late January 1931 he had signed contracts for seeding over 5,000 acres in Colusa County for spring planting.[1]

Brown had been a flying instructor in Yuba, Sutter, and Colusa counties since 1927. He started a small flying club at Colusa and was already known to many of the rice farmers, giving him an inside track for local ag-flying.

Valley Dusting Service completed its Travel Air rebuild for ag-flying in March 1931. Frank Parkinson and Harold Tarter would fly it from Orange Brothers Airport at Stockton.[2] Hawke Crop Dusting Company was another company that became a leader in ag-flying operations and equipment. Founded by E. R. Hawke at Modesto, the company was totally committed to ag-flying and built its own crop dusting plane—a big, high-wing monoplane powered by a 330hp. Whirlwind engine. H. S. Tharp redesigned and engineered the plane from an original design built by Art "Pop" Wilde of Aircraft Industries Inc., a company founded in January 1928 at Oakland Airport. In those early days before Hawke was involved, the plane was known as the Sierra, a four-place cabin plane similar to the Ryan Brougham.

Hawke bought Aircraft Industries Inc. in 1929 and moved it to Modesto. The company was renamed Hawke Crop Dusting Co. employing pilots O. W. Pilgrim, Bob Streif, Norman Brown, and R. O. Clark.

The plane, after it was redesigned as a crop duster, could carry a large load of dust or seed, which enabled Hawke to lower ag-work operational costs. The company's chief pilot, O. W. Pilgrim, who test flew the plane was said to have flown crop dusters for four years, but there were no details given as to where Pilgrim gained this experience.[3] By early March 1931, Hawke Crop Dusting had several thousand acres of rice land signed up for the season.[4]

Also in March, Frank Gallison of Merced-Wawona Air Lines was a weekend guest of O. H. Vanderford, a grower with extensive rice land in the Gridley area of Butte County. After Gallison flew his Waco north to stay with Vanderford, the grower signed contracts with Merced-Wawona Air Lines for seeding 2,000 acres in southern Butte County.[5]

H. S. Tharp, operations manager for Hawke, reported in April the company had signed contracts to seed 50,000 acres of rice land. Hawke had three planes operating and another three, like the *Sierra* derivative, being built in the company's Modesto factory. By April 1931, the factory at Modesto Airport employed 21 men.[6]

The Gridley area's rice crop planted by airplanes in the spring of 1931 yielded the earliest harvest in the history of Northern California rice production.[7]

In California, due to the rapid growth of agricultural aerial application—commonly known as crop dusting—state agricultural commissioners met at Fresno in August with representatives of the crop dusting businesses to discuss the industry's rapid expansion. The result of their meeting was scheduling another one the following month at Santa Barbara to recommend regulations for crop dusting. At Fresno, the crop dusting companies claimed to be in full accord with authorities that wanted to draw up uniform practices for ag-flying operators. These operators were already co-operating with the California Department of Entomology in their dusting experiments. Both parties were seeking the most effective methods of aerial application. The businesses represented at Fresno included: Aero Dusting Company of Los Angeles, Hawke Crop Dusting Company, Curtiss-Wright Flying Service, and Valley Dusting Company.[8]

Seeding rice with airplanes was an established practice by April 1931 in Colusa and Butte counties. Crop dusting companies working in this region

CHAPTER 14

used a landing strip on E. C. Hughes' ranch as a base of operations. Each pilot with his plane would seed about 300 acres of rice land daily. The pilots received 75 cents per acre and gas. They would depart in the cool dense air of early morning, their hoppers loaded with five sacks of seed, but by afternoon the warmer, less dense, air allowed them to carry only three-and-a-half sacks.

In early April 1931, Livingston G. Irving gave an extensive aerial demonstration at Chico for a group of farmers and orchardists to familiarize them with distribution of synthetic nitrogen fertilizer. He was trying to convince them an airplane could distribute fertilizer at less than a dollar an acre. At Pittsburg, Milton Robertson of Alameda signed contracts to dust the orchards in the Diablo Valley section of the Oakley district.[9]

Livingston Irving dusted 100 acres of peach trees in an hour on the Jackson Diggs property south of Yuba City in May. He was dusting for twig borer and mildew using a mixture of sulphur and lead arsenate. He only had to land once to refill his plane's hopper. R. H. Klamt, farm adviser for Sutter County, watched the dusting and reported all of the trees were adequately covered.[10]

C. A. "Al" Polk, a pilot for Livingston Irving's company, crash landed at 6:00 AM while dusting a peach orchard at Jackson Diggs on July 1. He was flying from east to west at 100 mph, four feet above the trees, and when he reached the west end of his pass, his engine quit. He immediately dove for the ground and crash-landed in an alfalfa field nearby. Polk injured his back and suffered minor cuts and bruises. He was driven to Irving's Colusa headquarters and received medical treatment.[11]

Al Polk had left Irving's employ by the summer of 1932 and began flying for Hawke Crop Dusting Company. In August 1932, he was dusting a large field of honeydew melons for Miller-Cummings, west of Gridley. He put on quite a show for a gathering of spectators. His flying technique demonstrated a high degree of skill. Watching the former army pilot speeding along over the melons with a trail of dust stretching out behind the plane made many spectators sure he was going to crash. Polk was in the process of exterminating millions of melon beetles. He charged the farmer three cents per pound for spreading the poison over the vines. Between 25 and 30 pounds of the poison were required for each acre dusted. The farmer also had to buy the dust.[12]

C. A. "Al" Polk was killed dusting sulphur on the Aldrich property at Hughson in July 1937. He was still flying for Hawke Crop Dusting in their duster, Hawke No. 3. The Hawke Nos. 1–3 were all crop dusting versions of the older modified *Sierra* design.[13]

Ray Nicholson of Sacramento signed contracts to seed rice on 10,000 acres in the Sutter Basin during the 1933 rice season. His plane could distribute 600 pounds of seed in six minutes. Planting would begin on April 1.[14] Leo Moore and Ingvald Fagerskog of Sacramento were also ag-flying in north state rice counties during these early days.

In July 1933, working at Gridley for fruit grower W. P. Harkey, Floyd "Speed" Nolta of Willows dusted grapes and prunes with sulphur to control mildew.[15]

Elmer "Joe" DeRosa was flying sulphur on to the Pieratt brothers' bean field—a wide expanse of level ground south of Marysville's Cheim Airport in an early morning of September 1934. He finished a hopper load and landed to refill it. During takeoff, his wings struck the guy wire of a power pole as he passed it. The plane's controls were damaged to the extent he had no control. The plane stayed in the air a short distance then nose-dived into the center of the bean field. Ray Nicholson, who owned the plane and for whom DeRosa was flying, was working as DeRosa's loader and flagman. He saw DeRosa go down and summoned the landowner who called Lipp & Sullivan's ambulance. DeRosa was taken to Rideout Hospital in Marysville. He suffered broken bones, cuts, and bruises, but survived; the plane was demolished.[16]

Louis Vremsak, a mining engineer and aviator, made his headquarters at Cheim Airport during the rice season of 1934. He engaged in crop dusting and seeding for two months using his own airplane. A year later, while working for a mining company in Mexico, he was kidnapped and held underground three weeks in Zacatecas state until freed by Mexican federal troops.[17]

In April 1935, Jack Aulthouse, a commercial pilot who had done lots of ag-flying in the upper Sacramento Valley the previous few years, crashed and died instantly while crop dusting a few miles south of Gilroy.[18]

Floyd Nolta completed his fifth year of seeding on June 15, 1935. He was said to have planted 25,000 acres of rice that year. Owner of three planes, Nolta began sowing rice April 10 in Glenn, Colusa, and Butte counties. He employed two assistants. The rice was seeded in standing water, eliminating loss to blackbirds, which devoured the seed when sown on dry ground His three planes worked through rice seeding season without a serious mishap, according to Nolta.[19]

Chapter 14

George Boyd Jr., a Yuba City ag-pilot who had been working throughout the Sacramento Valley for the Oakland based Independent Crop Dusting Company, was sent by the company to the Midwest to introduce the California system of planting and dusting crops from the air.[20] The company hired airplane mechanic Tom Webdell in June 1936 who worked for Dudley Cunningham and Bill Brander at Marysville's Cheim Airport (more commonly known as Cheim Field). He went with Boyd to Chicago as an assistant on his first assignment. They would spend two months there then fly back to Oakland.[21]

Walter Owen and O. H. Vanderford, Butte County growers, bought their own plane intending to seed and dust their own crops and those of their neighbors'. Ed Kron, a duster pilot from Turlock, would fly their plane when needed.[22]

In early May 1936, Vremsak Agricultural Air Service of Los Angeles sent a large crop dusting plane to Cheim Field to be on station for any rice work contracted in Yuba, Sutter, Glenn, and Colusa counties. Del Hay piloted the big plane, which was the first tri-motor Kreutzer Air Coach built. The three low horsepower engines had been removed and one 330hp. Whirlwind was mounted on the nose of the plane. It could carry one ton of dust or rice seed in a single load.[23] The Vremsak Kreutzer crop duster was completely destroyed in late August near Robbins in the Sutter Basin. Pilot Ed Grant was dusting bean fields for Bolen and Pachmayer Farms. He had just loaded dust in the hopper and taken off when the Whirlwind quit. The plane was too low and slow to maneuver; it just dropped onto the ground. The hopper full of sulphur ignited from blazing gasoline, which destroyed the plane valued at $8,000. It is believed Grant escaped in time.[24]

According to Sutter County pilot, Guy "Speed" Hughes, George Curtiss Quick, a crop dusting pioneer who started dusting cotton in Texas as early as 1925, came to the Yuba-Sutter area to dust peaches on a regular schedule throughout the 1930s. As a teenager, Hughes, worked for Quick as a loader and flagman when Quick flew into the area each year from Arizona.[25] Quick had moved from Texas to Arizona in the 1930s and set up a crop dusting business in Phoenix with Tom Allen Scott.[26]

Hughes described an incident about Quick in the Yuba City area around 1938 dusting peaches. A family, dressed in their Sunday best, were changing a flat tire on their car. Curtiss Quick was dusting the orchard next to the road where they stopped. He was incensed they stopped in the direct path he had to dust, so he dove on the family who were staring wide-eyed at the plane diving towards them. He dumped the remainder of his sulphur load on them; transforming the family into ghost-like figurines. Quick thought it was funny, but it's doubtful anyone agreed.[27]

After World War II, numerous crop dusting businesses popped up all around the state. Thousands of ex-military pilots, who came out of the war with the desire to fly commercially, wanted flying jobs. Airline jobs filled quickly, so some former military pilots went into crop dusting work. The availability of Stearman PT-17 biplane trainers on the war surplus market gave these new ag-flying businesses a cheap source of aircraft well suited for their needs. Most military flyers had flown the PT-17 in primary training during the war and knew the plane well. They quickly removed the PT-17's 220hp. engine and installed a 450hp. Pratt & Whitney, usually off a war surplus BT-13 trainer—a plane no one wanted after the war. With the Pratt & Whitney on the Stearman, a near perfect crop duster was created.

Many in the aviation community believe that crop dusting began after WWII, but the preceding pages show that not to be true. It started long before.

COLUSA COUNTY WAS lightly populated in the early 1900s. As stated above, as late as 1939 there were just over 2,000 people in Colusa, the county's largest town. Low population was typical of towns on the west side of the Sacramento Valley. The gold seekers of the 1850s created the population centers on the east side of the valley near the gold they sought in the creeks and rivers of the Sierra Nevada.

The city of Colusa sits on the southern bank of the Sacramento River. In the early 20th century the city celebrated the river with an annual water carnival. For the 1911 carnival, locals were clamoring for a flying exhibition. Such exhibitions had been occurring in many towns on the east side of the valley for over a year. Colusans, on the west side of the valley, decided it was time they saw an aeroplane fly.

L. R. Boedefeld, secretary of the executive committee of the Colusa Water Carnival, traveled to San Francisco in March 1911 to arrange for an aviator to fly for the water carnival in May. Even as early as March 1911, there were at least three San Francisco businesses that might provide flying exhibitions: Eames Tricycle Co., Paterson Aeroplane Co., and California Aero Manufacturing and Supply Co. Mr. Boedefeld chose the latter. Boedefeld was shown around its shops and saw a dirigible, gliders, and possibly two aeroplanes being built. Company manager and part owner Roy Scott said there were aviators available to fly at Colusa. If the water carnival committee wanted to make the arrangements.[28]

Boedefeld returned and the committee worked on making arrangements to bring an aeroplane and aviator to Colusa. They hired C. C. Walker whom Bodefeld had been told (erroneously) was the best aviator in all of the Bay Area.[29] The committee directed Bodefeld to sign a contract with California Aero Manufacturing and Supply Company for one successful flight per day during the carnival. Roy Scott promised to send one aeroplane and two experienced aviators.[30] Boedefeld returned to San Francisco to close the deal. It turned out Walker was not available. Perhaps he had not returned from his tour of Asia where he flew exhibitions. Or, maybe Walker quit flying, which he did, date unknown, shortly after returning from his tour.

With less than a week until the water carnival, Boedefeld signed a contract with Ivy Baldwin, an aeronaut, who had only recently began flying heavier-than-air machines. Baldwin was making aeroplane flights for a fair at Hanford in the San Joaquin Valley. He made several successful flights in his Standard Model Curtiss (Pusher). His plane would be shipped directly to Colusa Junction from Hanford on an express train. He was supposed to arrive at Colusa by rail with his aeroplane May 28, 1911. Bodefeld would arrange to have the aeroplane hauled from Colusa Junction to Colusa.[31]

Ivy Baldwin was supposed to sign a contract on May 27 to fly for the water carnival on the 28th and 29th. It was to be Colusa County's first aeroplane flight.[32] It never happened.

Boedefeld received a telegram from Roy Scott the evening of the 26th that Baldwin had crashed and wrecked his Curtiss. He suffered injuries. Boedefeld shot off a telegram requesting a replacement, to which Scott replied he already tried and was unsuccessful. There wasn't enough time to find a replacement and get him to Colusa, said Scott. Boedefeld told him to keep trying. "Do the best you can. I will have to leave town if you don't." Scott couldn't find anyone, but it's doubtful Boedefeld left town.

The water carnival committee seemed jinxed getting a "birdman" to fly at Colusa. Its first choice, C. C. Walker, was unexpectedly unavailable, supposedly his replacement choice was killed in a crash which destroyed his plane in Los Angeles, and Ivy Baldwin, Scott's third selection to fly at Colusa, crashed at Hanford two weeks later. At least this was the local newspaper's explanation why the carnival had no flying exhibition. This author has been unable to confirm anyone was killed in a flying accident at Los Angeles in mid-May 1911.

The *San Francisco Call* reported differently: Captain Ivy Baldwin took sick and was unable to fly at Hanford. Baldwin and his aeroplane did not make it to the Colusa Water Carnival. "In a last attempt to fulfill the contract for aviation exhibitions [at Hanford], a mechanic for the sick Baldwin attempted to fly in his [Baldwin's] plane this afternoon [May 27], but when ten feet above ground the big Curtiss biplane shot to the earth, damaging it beyond repair."

Water carnival executive committee secretary Boedefeld, after receiving Roy Scott's wire of Baldwin's supposed injuries, became skeptical, especially after reading the *Call* report. Boedefeld wired the official in charge of the Hanford event to find out which story was true. J. J. Spitzer wired back, "Yes, machine wrecked but Baldwin not injured." This entire story of Baldwin's plane being wrecked and the various wires back and forth, plus the *Call* report, were all published in the Colusa paper to dispel the notion held by many Colusans that Boedefeld promised aeroplane flight just to lure people to the water carnival. Boedefeld obviously wanted Colusa residents to know what happened and that the committee made every effort prodding Roy Scott to find a replacement for Baldwin. Unfortunately, Scott failed.

The first aeroplane flights in Colusa County are believed by this author to have taken place at Arbuckle on October 6-7, 1916. Sam Purcell, a Bay Area aviation pioneer, was signed to fly for the Arbuckle Almond Festival by Arbuckle resident D. S. Nelson in late September. Even though it rained heavily during the festival, it was reported the aviation flights were a success.

Lyman W. Doty, an aviator born in Biggs and trained to fly at the Christofferson Aviation School, as was his sister, Jeanette Doty, made an early flight in Colusa County during the first week of June 1917. Lyman flew an exhibition in his Curtiss Pusher biplane at the Odd Fellows Picnic at Grimes. Doty shipped his Curtiss to Arbuckle where he unloaded his machine from the train and assembled it. He then flew it to Grimes where he later flew an exhibition. Afterward he flew back to Arbuckle and loaded his plane on a train and returned to the Bay Area.[33]

THERE WAS NOTABLE aerial activity in Colusa County after the Great War—especially the duck patrols of 1919 and 1920.

Captain Chadwick Thompson, a Bay Area sea captain, loved to hunt ducks at his hunting club on rice land near Colusa. Thompson took up aviation as a sport in 1923, and in 1925 he began flying around the state to lodge meetings, draymen's conventions, and his hunting club.

One day in late 1927 or early '28, Thompson crashed taking off from his grain field, which also served as his makeshift airfield near Richmond in the Bay Area. The field was precarious at best; a high power line stretched across it. Thompson had overloaded his plane with shotguns, boots, ammunition, a hunting partner, his pilot, and himself. Despite the dangerous conditions, his pilot took off from a wet runway and hit the power lines. The plane, type unknown, crashed and burned, but everyone escaped with moderate to minor burns. They were lucky. The good citizens of Richmond were not; their power was out for many hours.

Captain Thompson, while in the hospital recovering from his burns, thought back to the days following the building of San Francisco's yacht harbor (next to Marina Green today). Its construction and opening brought about an enormous surge in local yacht racing. He decided the same thing might happen for the sport of flying if he opened an airport on the eastern side of the bay. Once out of the hospital, he began searching the East Bay for a site within a short streetcar ride from his home. He found land next to the Alameda mole and leased a tract of 65 acres from the city of Alameda to build an airport for his personal use and a few friends, should they take up flying. After Charles Lindbergh's flight across the Atlantic, Americans became enthralled with flying. It was then Thompson realized his airport should be open to everyone. He bought more tidelands to expand his airport. Once built it became Alameda Airport and later usurped by Alameda Naval Air Station.[34]

There was some misunderstanding when Chad Thompson began offering air service to the duck hunting gun clubs around Colusa. *Pacific Flyer* found itself duty bound to publish an article explaining to those who misunderstood what Thompson was offering Bay Area duck hunters. The article explained that airplanes carrying the duck hunters did not actually kill the ducks, and hunters riding in the planes were not allowed by law to shoot ducks from airplanes. Game laws prohibited shooting migratory birds from any gasoline propelled vehicle.

Hundreds of duck hunters living in the Bay Area knew (in 1928) that to hunt ducks in the Colusa area, they would have to travel by automobile more than half a day from San Francisco. Duck clubs were often rice fields flooded after the harvest to attract waterfowl. Some clubs developed airstrips enabling an avid Bay Area hunter to make the 100-mile trip from Alameda Airport to his duck club at Colusa in at most two hours.

Captain Thompson was a pioneer flying hunter. Others began following his example and numerous charter flights were flown to Colusa and Glenn County rice fields. The Alameda Airport air taxi services' specialty was flying into and out of those gun clubs.[35] Thompson hired Milo Campbell of Royle Air Lines to fly him and two friends to Colusa to hunt. The November 1928 charter flight was the first to Colusa's gun clubs.[36]

Bay Area commercial air taxi (charter) companies flying into the Colusa gun clubs by the fall of 1928 were Royle Air Lines and Pacific Coast Air Service. Joe Barrows, a Pacific Coast Air Service pilot, flew J. V. Gifford, a Bay Area banker from Oakland Municipal Airport to the Colusa gun clubs. In three hours they had flown from Oakland, hunted near Colusa, and on return each had a limit of ducks.[37]

Colusa's postmaster, Grover Power, a pilot during the Great War, gave a talk to the Marysville Lions Club about aviation in January 1929. He expounded on John Montgomery as the "father of aviation," which is believed by few today.[38]

The success of the Willows Airport dedication June 1, 1929, in Glenn County stirred the Colusa city airport committee to move the community towards choosing an airport location. Committeemen R. Grover Power, Fred McCormac, and H. J. Doty took the lead promoting an airport for Colusa; Doty, representing the American Legion, and McCormac, a leading aviation enthusiast, met with Royle Air Lines' A. E. Wagner, a commercial pilot and stunt flyer who organized the Willows Airport opening. They wanted information about a new airport's needs.[39]

A brush fire broke out on George Ash's ranch near Arbuckle in southwestern Colusa County in June 1929. It started in the center of a 400-acre barley field; how it started was a mystery since the center of the field was a quarter mile from any road and nearly a half-mile from the Pacific Highway. It was finally deduced the cause must have been from the formation flight of eight airplanes flying over the barley field just before the fire was reported. Possibly a piece of burning carbon fell from the exhaust system of one of the aircraft.[40] Another theory, which should have been considered, was a lit cigarette. Many pilots in the days of open cockpits were very adept at lighting up while cruising at 65 to a 100 mph.

The city of Colusa placed a revolving beacon atop its water tower in early 1929. It was for advertising and not aviation claimed city officials. Local aviators complained it was being confused with federal airway beacons, which were placed at ten-mile intervals through Colusa County and up the state. Since the beacon was installed as an advertising device, no permit to operate

CHAPTER 14

it was applied for. The government notified the city council a permit had to be obtained, and the city must operate the beacon all night not just part of the night, as was the current practice. The city couldn't decide on a plan other than turning the beacon off.[41]

THE COLUSA AIRPORT committee decided a new airport, located southwest of town on the Colusa-Williams Highway, was to be dedicated with a big air show planned for June 1929. The committee had its eye on an existing landing strip known as Slaughterhouse Field, previously used on occasion by itinerant aviators. In the 1980s and '90s a company known as Pirelli Cable Co. operated from this location.

When Fred McCormac met with A. E. Wagner, an air show promoter, he was told a contract would be sent immediately. Once signed, Wagner would come to Colusa three weeks before the celebration to generate interest in the event. Wagner promised at least eight to ten planes from Oakland would fly to the Colusa Airport opening. He would put on an air show even bigger than the one at Willows. He promised parachute jumps, air races, stunt flying, and other events.[42]

There were problems, probably financial, that made the dedication announcement a bit premature. On July 11, 1929, a report in the local paper declared the entire airport proposal a dead issue. The airport committee met all of the provisions required by the city council including obtaining an individual to take charge of the airfield. However, one of the interested parties in the airport project decided to pull his support and the project died. The newspaper chastised the community stating, "There is something sadly lacking in this community when progressive moves like these are defeated. Some day Colusa will need that airport for airmail, air passengers, or freight service. Maybe the matter will come up again next year. Colusa always lives in hopes."

In the same issue of the *Colusa Daily Sun*, it was reported Robert Peebles, president of Interstate Airlines, Inc., a flying school, toured the Colusa area with Fred McCormac. They were looking at possible landing fields near the city but found none suitable. Peebles said if they had found one, he would have sent two planes up to hop passengers on the following weekend. He also volunteered to help to promote local interest in a new airport.[43]

George Vawter of Arbuckle announced in March 1930, he was bringing his Swallow biplane to Slaughterhouse Field at Colusa to give a free ride to anyone who wanted to go up. He had a reason for his offer. Vawter was

Colusa County's only entrant in the *Woodland Daily Democrat's* Airplane Derby. The derby was a promotion for the *Democrat* to increase subscribers. It awarded the winner a new $3,560 Waco biplane as prize. Vawter could win the Waco by signing up the most subscribers. If a passenger taking a free ride on the following Sunday agreed to buy a subscription, Vawter would give him or her a long ride over Colusa. If not, the passenger got only a short hop.

It was apparent the airport committee had returned the airport project to the city council's review. The Slaughterhouse Field site was accepted and three-day airport dedication events were planned for May 30, 1930.

The first action taken towards the dedication was painting COLUSA in large letters on the roof of Farmers Warehouse, a property of the Sacramento River Navigation Company located north of the city waterworks. Shell Oil Company provided painters and Fuller Paint Company donated the paint. Fred McCormac was in charge of the painting project and organizing the air show for the airport opening.[44]

On April 14, the runway turf was mowed and Shell Oil employees erected a windsock (wind indicator) on the field in preparation for May's dedication events.[45]

Three days later two large formations of Army Air Corps bombers numbering 67 aircraft flew over Colusa at 9:10 AM en route to "destroy" the Willows Airport. The two formations, one high and one low, were part of the 1930 Army Air Corps Maneuvers originating from Mather Field and comprised of twin-engine heavy bombers; single-engine pursuit planes; attack planes; and observation aircraft. Approximately one-quarter of all Army Air Corps aircraft were assembled at Mather for a mock air war. The Air Corps command had established "domes of security" over Colusa, Colusa Junction, Oroville, Marysville, Butte, Ione, and Stockton. The planes were said to be in constant radio contact with their headquarters at Mather.[46]

MANY MEMBERS OF the Yuba City chapter of the National Aeronautics Association (NAA) were asked to help with timing and judging contests at Colusa Airport's dedication air show.[47] Of the pilots performing at Colusa, would be Harry W. Abbott, known as the "Little Colonel." Abbott had received the rank of colonel from China's leader Dr. Sun Yat-sen while flying in the Chinese air force.

Abbott had taken up aerial stunts when he was young and under the tutelage of his father, a Cheyenne Indian named Mad Wolf. Mad Wolf became

Chapter 14

an expert balloonist and parachutist known by his non-native name, Wayne Abbott. Abbott partnered with his son Harry in stunt exhibitions. During the Great War, Harry Abbott served the US Navy in submarines. In 1917 he learned to fly at Seal Beach. After a few years of barnstorming, he trained Chinese pilots at Courtland, as previously mentioned, and flew in China for Sun Yat-sen. He resigned after extended service and pursued a commercial flying career in China. Longing to return to the states, he chose Mills Field, San Bruno, as his home field. For a while he did mechanic work for various pilots. He later started a flight school and returned to stunt flying. Abbott was one of only three pilots on the Pacific coast who did an outside loop in his stunt routine. It was believed he would perform one at the Colusa Air Show. He was expected to fly into Colusa Airport Thursday evening, May 29, with a squadron of planes from the Bay Area.[48]

On Tuesday, the second day of Colusa's Airport Week as the *Colusa Sun* dubbed it, aerial activity began to increase at Colusa's, soon-to-be-dedicated new airport. A Standard Oil tri-motor Boeing Model 80A biplane landed on the freshly graded runway. Sydney S. Chadderton, an official of Standard Oil, stepped from the transport. He came to inspect the airfield to determine if it would be safe for the Standard Oil planes not only for the dedication air show but for all future operations. Chadderton gave his official approval and assured Colusa officials Standard Oil would send one of their large planes to participate in the dedication.

R. E. Jellison, representing Varney, arrived May 28 with his wife in their Kitty Hawk biplane. Jellison got out of his plane and complimented the Colusa officials for the wonderful job they did developing the airport. He told them the airport "... will be given national recognition as one of the air centers of the West." He said Varney Company would be sending $100,000 worth of airplanes to fly in the air show. Varney also sent a Bowlus glider to Colusa to be flown during the three-day weekend program beginning Friday, May 30. The glider, built by Harvey Bowlus, arrived Friday afternoon. Frank Hawks had flown an exact copy across the United States towed behind a powered aircraft advertising Texaco products. This glider was the same model used by Charles and Anne Lindbergh in Southern California when Mrs. Lindbergh carried out her first solo flight in an aircraft. The glider was assembled and displayed in front of the Colusa courthouse to be seen by the many visitors who came for the airport dedication.[49]

During Airport Week, the Colusa Theater was showing *Young Eagles* starring Buddy Rogers—billed as one of the greatest airplane movies ever made (not so). Bill Royle was master of ceremonies for the flying events. Monty Mouton and D. C. Warren, both from the Bay Area, represented the NAA, and A. E. Wagner from Royle Airlines organized the flying events.[50] George N. Mitchell and Charles J. Warren flew to Colusa from the Bay Area on Thursday in a five-place Buhl Airsedan to be used for long distance passenger rides during the three-day air show.[51]

Friday, opening day, the schedule of events was as follows:
10:00 AM–Formation flight over cemeteries, dropping flowers for Memorial Day ceremonies in conjunction with activities of American Legion posts
12:30 PM–Parachute jump by Walter Hall
1:00 PM–Dedication ceremony, Standard Oil's Ford Tri-motor lands with Colusa officials
1:30 PM–The welcoming address by Albert L. Sheets, US District Attorney, who would be flown into Colusa Airport by Pete Rinehart in the *Angeleno*, the plane Rinehart and Lorrin Mendell broke the endurance record at Los Angeles. Also riding in the plane would be Charles Wilkins, chairman of the Sacramento Airport Committee with Mr. and Mrs. Terrell, owners of the *Angeleno*.
2:00 PM–Dead stick landing contest–A contestant would cut his motor at 1,500 feet and glide to a landing at the line.
2:15 PM–Passenger carrying–Scenic tours to Snow Mountain, Sutter Buttes and Clear Lake
2:15 PM–Formation flying and speed tests by Associated Oil Co. and Union Oil Co.
3:00 PM–Pylon race for planes with up to 110hp.
3:15 PM–Passenger carrying same as 2:15 PM
4:00 PM–Stunt Flying by Harry Abbott, Gene LeGault, Franklin Rose and others
4:30 PM–Passenger carrying and local and scenic tours until sundown
6:00 PM–Parachute jump by Claudia Griffith, a 17-year-old local high school girl
Saturday and Sunday the schedule was planned to be the same with some additions and some deletions.
On Saturday there was a contest of model airplanes put on

by the Yuba City chapter of the NAA added to the events. At 8:00 PM there was to be an aviator's ball held at the prune packing plant in Colusa. There were $50 airplane rides given out as prizes on Saturday. On Sunday, events were to be the same with the addition of a demonstration flight by John A. Macready in the Shell Oil Company's Lockheed Sirius monoplane, a sister ship of the plane Lindbergh had recently flown for a transcontinental record.[52]

VARNEY PILOT R. E. Jellison, as part of the Aviation Week activities, met at the Hotel Riverside with local enthusiasts who wanted to start a glider club. He advised them on the best way to do that.[53]

The *Colusa Daily Sun* reported, "The city is decorated with hundreds of flags and the citizens are tansed [sic] as they await the opening of 'Our airport.' As the hour nears the bands will strike out and the phone and telegraph wires of many news services will inform the world that Colusa, California, has taken its place on the pages of aviation history."[54] A. E. Wagner announced 31 airplanes had registered.

JUST AFTER 1:00, the Standard Oil tri-motor Ford sped down the runway breaking a ribbon held by Miss Virgina Starkweather and Miss Dorothy Coleman officially opening the Colusa Airport. The rest of the day went as scheduled. The only exception was the addition of "Red Sullivan" making his first parachute jump instead of the 17-year-old high school girl scheduled to jump. Sullivan told a reporter he had flown 450 times but never made a jump. The young girl's jump was rescheduled for Sunday, the last day of the air show. In actuality "Red Sullivan" was Charles T. "Red" Jensen, an 18-year-old airplane mechanic from Sacramento, and it was his first jump. He was working for Leo Moore, a commercial flyer at Sacramento Municipal Airport.

Wagner reported on Saturday that 150 to 200 Colusans had taken airplane rides to Snow Mountain, the Sutter Buttes, and Clear Lake. During Memorial Day services at the Catholic cemetery, 12 planes from the air show circled the grounds.

It turns out, R. E. Jellison, encouraged the following people to form a soaring club: Jackson King, Temple Jeffries, Mike O'Hair, Verbal Mayberry, H. Ward, Woodrow Humburg, Richard Fender, and E. M. Hampton, all from Colusa. From Sycamore, Sydney Stinchfield and Frank Dunham signed up as did C. Morely from Marysville. Later during Aviation Week, Jellison encouraged additional enthusiasts in forming the club. They were: Francis Steidlmayer, Joe Willoh, Harold Taws, L. Schlosser, K. Keller, Beston Gordon, Bill Stokes, L. Middlecamp, Claude Cotter, Ham Graham, Charles Martin, L. A. Stevens, Ned Lewis, and Alfred Abreu. The rest of Colusa Glider Club's history is a mystery, as is the Arbuckle Glider Club that tried to form a year or two earlier. Jellison, who brought the Bowlus glider to the dedication celebration, tried twice to make lengthy flights in the glider but discovered there was little "up" air at Colusa to generate lift. Colusans saw only a few seconds of glider flight after it was launched.[55]

The fastest air race during the three days happened Sunday afternoon. It was a free for all race for any aircraft with up to 225hp. Four airplanes took part in the competition set on an irregular 15-mile course of sharp turns and several laps. Frank Rose from the Varney Company of Oakland won in a Viking Kittyhawk biplane. Varney was distributor for the Kittyhawk, one of the seven planes Varney Company brought to Colusa for display, races, and passenger carrying.[56] G. Darbarn of Nome, Alaska, surprised those at Sunday's show when he made an unscheduled call on the city. He was flying down the coast on business and decided to slip over the Coast Range to visit friends who were flying in the dedication events.

After the three-day celebration ended, it was determined 4,000 spectators attended the first day, 1,200 on Saturday, and 5,000 on Sunday. Aviators gave great credit to Colusa for a well-run opening. They singled out Fred McCormac, Temple Crane, and Arch Davison with special praise.[57] Jeff Warren and George Mitchell of the Clover Flying Service flew home to the Bay Area Sunday evening with their passengers Betty May Ketly and Ola Chapmenn.[58]

No accidents marred the celebration although Sunday, during his jump Walter Hall delayed opening his chute and faked a struggle to get it open, which led many to believe he was going to be killed. It was just an added thrill—Hall landed safely.

E. E. Mouton, DOC chief aviation inspector, dropped in on the proceedings Sunday and complimented Colusa for a successful show and its new long level airfield. It was still not possible on Monday to determine how much money was made, but A. E. Wagner assured everyone all the bills were covered, and the airport was free and clear.[59]

When Colusa Airport opened, the runway was a half-mile long on a north–south heading, and a quarter-mile wide. It was located two miles

CHAPTER 14   323

Fig. 65. The site of Colusa's first airport is depicted in this 2002 photo. It was dedicated with a three-day air show beginning on May 30, 1930. Sacramento's Charles "Red" Jensen, 18, made a parachute jump there for the air show. The current Colusa Airport is out of the picture and several miles to the right. The Sutter Buttes are at the top of the photo.

southwest of the city on the road to Williams (now Highway 20). The 80 acres of airport land was leased by the city for $750 a year. The ground was already level, and once the hay crop was removed a few days before the dedication nothing needed to be done to prepare it for the air show.[60] Grover Powers, the Colusa postmaster, a Great War pilot, and an aviation enthusiast, spoke in November to the Rotary Club of Marysville about the advantages of the new municipal airport.[61]

Leslie J. Nickels of Arbuckle bought an OX-5 Curtiss Robin in December from W. Austin Denehie of Los Angeles. In March 1931, Michael O'Hair and Alfred Abreu, both from Colusa, passed their private license tests for DOC inspector, Wiley B. Wright. Harold F. Brown had taught the two members of a Colusa flying club to fly. The club had purchased a plane for training.[62]

Members of the Yuba-Sutter Flying Club purchased a new Spartan biplane and were anxiously awaiting its arrival from the factory. After it was delivered, the club's old Spartan was sold to the Colusa flying club. Harold F. Brown, instructor for both clubs, taught part time at the new Colusa Airport and part time at Cheim Field in Marysville.

L. R. Zumwalt and Noel Helphenstine of Colusa flew to Oakland as passengers of Harold Brown on a Saturday in late March 1931. The trip took 50 minutes. The return next morning was against a stiff north wind that took much longer. A group of Colusa student pilots were eagerly waiting for their flying lessons with Brown upon his return.

Harold Frederick Brown was born January 17, 1905. Raised in Oakland, he enlisted in the Army Air Corps circa 1927 and was sent to Kelly Field in Texas for flight training. He was in a training group of 100 men of which only 7 graduated. Brown was the top of the class. In April 1929 he crashed while flying an Air Corps observation plane in Southern California. His observer, Lt. Harry Doyle, suffered a broken shoulder. The plane crashed because of a broken gas line. Brown resigned from the Air Corps in August 1929. In 1930 he was an airport manager living in Montebello. In early 1930 a passenger Brown was flying tried to commit suicide by jumping out of the plane. Brown threw the plane into a steep bank, which forced his passenger against the fuselage. Brown grabbed his leg and threw the man into the front seat. He tried to jump again, and Brown stunned him with a blow to the head with a fire extinguisher then made a safe landing. In 1935 after his and John Wagge's Consolidated Air Lines went bankrupt, Brown went back into the military. He joined the Marine Corps Reserve. By 1951 he was a full colonel in the Marines, retiring from the Corps in 1961. He passed on in July 1966. (For much more on Brown see the author's book, *Aviation in Northern California 1910–1939 Volume I*.)[63]

After federal government airport grants became available in December 1933, airport committee head Fred McCormac said Colusa was selected to receive a $5,000 grant to improve the airport. The sticking point was the city had to own the land the airport was on, and it didn't. McCormac and Adolphus Ahlf led a drive for the city to purchase the land, but their efforts were unsuccessful.

CHAPTER 15

Albert Lane – A Korean flying school – Postwar barnstormers – Willows Airport established – Willows Airport dedication– Orland's airports – Glenn County flying activities

There were other flying activities in Glenn County besides duck patrols, crop dusting, and rice seeding. Albert "Bert" Lane, born in 1908 at Willows, built a small Chanute type glider in 1921 and made short flights off the roof of his father's barn. Lane had four brothers, and of the five, Bert, Glen, and Stan learned to fly. Bert had a long career as a professional pilot. He flew for Speed Nolta in the early 1930s doing ag-work. Later, he and Gorge Boyd of Yuba City took over the Independent Crop Dusting Company, a pioneer ag-flying company that originated in San Francisco. During World War II he was a production line test pilot for Curtiss-Wright.[1]

One of the earliest aviation enterprises at Willows was a flying school organized by a Korean rice farmer named Kim in 1920. Mr. Kim prepared an airfield and housing for Korean flying students on land he purchased next to the Quint district schoolhouse, which he rented to use as an aviation ground school. The Quint schoolhouse sat unused from dwindling enrollment of local children. The Korean student pilots also received physical training, and learned English at the schoolhouse.

Mr. and Mrs. Kim acquired the land and its schoolhouse in January 1920. Mrs. Kim, who spoke flawless English, explained to S. M. Chaney, Glenn County superintendent of schools, she and her husband wished to continue to use Quint schoolhouse and train young Koreans to learn to fly. The Kims claimed their students wanted to learn American culture and language so they could fly for America if the nation was ever drawn into another war. Chaney put the proposition up for discussion with the Quint school trustees and they readily consented to the idea.

Mr. Kim had recently purchased a home in Willows, then he and his family moved into it from Colusa County where Mr. Kim worked for several years growing rice. He made a fortune and was a leader in the Korean community. Mrs. Kim had originally said there would be 100 students at the flying school, but that number was reduced to 15 later. It was also revealed later that once the Koreans learned to fly, they would be sent back to Korea and, at the proper time, they were to help take their country back from the Japanese.

Mr. Kim hired a flying instructor, and a staff of ground instructors was employed. Three airplanes, war surplus Jennies, were purchased and would arrive any day. A runway with hangars was developed. Two mechanics were hired to maintain the planes.[2]

Within a few days after the newspaper reported the Korean flying school being established, a complaint written to the paper from the president of the Fourteen Counties Protective Association demanded an interview with a reporter. The president railed against the flying school as being part of the "Asiatic" menace in the state. He demanded the state legislature and Governor Stephens act immediately and ranted on about Asians evading California's land laws, etc.[3]

On March 1 it was reported that Kim's flying school was part of the Korean Independence Movement launched a year earlier. The school trained Korean pilots who would be used if war between Korea and Japan broke out. These facts were frankly admitted in an interview at Sacramento with Col. Palin K. Law, a Korean officer and patriot.

Law declared young Koreans were already being trained at Frank Bryant's Redwood Aviation School at Redwood City and, after finishing their course in March, they would offer to serve as instructors at the new school in Willows. Law explained all of the students at the new school were volunteers from California's Korean families. The school, he said, would depend upon personal interest and financial support from California's Korean community. He scoffed at the idea the school would be using only 40 acres of land. He said a wealthy Korean farmer and his American companion (the Kims) promised 3,000 acres of land for the project.

Colonel Law stated, "If the same young men later see fit to take part in a campaign to secure the independence of Korea, the trouble would not come in America but in Asia, and I don't see why the people of America should object to the school." He also said there were plans to start aviation schools in China. March 1 was the anniversary of the independence movement and hundreds of Koreans from Northern California gathered at Sacramento to celebrate. Law travelled from Willows to join them.[4]

By the end of June, the number of Korean flying students at Quint had doubled to 30. The students were absorbing lessons in aviation ground school, military tactics, and English. They were eager to help their countrymen avoid the grasp of an expanding Japan. Almost three months passed before the first airplane landed at Quint school's adjoining airfield. Everyone was overjoyed with the new plane arriving from Redwood City; it was either a Curtiss Jenny or a Standard J-1. The Hall-Scott Motor Car Company of Oakland built the engine. Mr. Kim hired Henry "Happy" Bryant to fly it to Willows. Bryant, the brother of Frank Bryant of Redwood Aviation School, agreed to stay and work as an instructor pilot.[5]

Two days after ferrying the first plane to Willows, Happy Bryant flew a second one onto the Quint District landing field. Three Korean graduates from Redwood Aviation School were chosen to assist Bryant with flying instruction: Young S. Lee, Peter Ohu, and Charles Lee.[6]

The Associated Screen News Company of San Francisco planned to film a number of Kinograms depicting the Quint district Korean flying school. The school attracted national attention since its founding. The film company's Maurice Blache arrived at Willows and went immediately to the site. He had arranged to not only document the flying school but also the farms and land surrounding the airfield. The Kinograms would be shown in every state in the nation.[7]

An employment bureau manager in Willows, A. E. Chandler, planned to fly over the small Fallen Leaf Lake near Lake Tahoe to photograph winter conditions. Chandler, formerly an instructor at the Quint District aviation field, said part of his plan was to use an airplane from the Korean flying school and take a Korean pilot with him.[8]

BARNSTORMING GYPSY AVIATORS made their way up through Glenn County from the Bay Area and Los Angeles after the Great War. In the spring of 1920, the Mattley Aircraft Company of San Francisco had J. A. Eldridge, an ex-army aviator, fly O. H. Mattley, the company manager, to Willows on a barnstorming tour. Eldridge had been a flying instructor in France during the war and gave safe and sane rides to anyone who wished to pay. If aerobatics was requested, he would do that, too. It was said Eldridge invented some of the maneuvers taught to Army Air Service pilots for use in combat. Eldridge began hopping passengers at Willows on March 18 in his plane, named *The Lark*. He remained in Willows for two days giving rides.[9]

In August 1919, the Mills Orchard Company of Glenn County announced its farm manager would be observing conditions of its orchards from an airplane. Inspections that took days by automobile would only take hours in an airplane.[10]

H. G. Andrews, who flew for the state fair in 1919, signed a contract to fly for the Glenn County Fair at Orland. Andrews, flying for Sacramento Aviation Company, would bring two aircraft.[11] The Sacramento Aviation Company signed another contract at the same time to fly for the three-day Arbuckle Almond Festival; again, H. G. Andrews would do the flying.[12]

The Glenn County Fair ran six days from September 22–27, 1919. The Sacramento Aviation Company brought Miss Tiny (actually Ethel) Broadwick to parachute jump during the fair, and H. G. Andrews would do stunt flying on Thursday at 3:30 over the fairgrounds. The aviation field was a mile east of the fairgrounds at Orland and from there the company would be giving airplane rides daily during the fair's run.[13]

Miss Broadwick jumped from Andrew's Jenny causing quite a thrill for the spectators on the 26th. A Chico reporter wrote an eloquent description of the jump: "Advertised to flirt with death, Miss Ethel Broadwick made her act come nearer the truth than was meant yesterday when she jumped from an airplane in a parachute before six thousand onlookers at the Orland fair and was knocked unconscious when she was dashed against an automobile when she reached earth." Broadwick jumped at 2,000 feet. Her chute, weighing only five pounds, had a single wood slat for a seat. She landed outside the fairgrounds on the radiator of an automobile.

The crowd quickly rushed to her aid; her limp body was placed in an automobile and taken to Orland where she recovered consciousness. She was bruised and had an ugly cut, but was otherwise all right.

That particular day was Chico Day at the fair. One hundred cars drove from Chico, 19 miles east of Orland. After the cars gathered at Stonyford Creek Bridge, they formed a long procession with the Chico High School band in the lead and, "… took Orland by storm." Andrew's airplane escorted the procession and glided low over the band to listen as it sounded out to everyone at the fair that Chico had arrived.[14]

Dr. Salter of Williams in Colusa County updated his mode of transportation for house calls. His old "flivver" was too slow, so when he had to travel

CHAPTER 15   329

Fig. 66. Clyde "Upside Down" Pangborn was hired to fly aerobatics for the 1920 Glenn County Fair at Orland, but first he had to lead a parade down Colusa Street in that city.

long distances he used an airplane. In March 1920, he made a flying house call at Stonyford and then flew to another patient at Mills Orchards on the Sacramento River in Glenn County.[15]

A flying business performed a novel advertising exhibition in Willows. At noon April 10, 1920, an aviator named Williams flew his Jenny at 2,000 feet over the public park that fronted Del Monte Emporium, a men's clothing store. Abe Plato, sitting in the passenger seat, threw promotional dodgers (leaflets) out for the surprised spectators below. When Plato ran out of dodgers, Williams began flying stunts. Then Plato jumped out of the airplane and descended by parachute, landing on the roof of a business near the park. The gimmick caught everyone's attention.

It is believed Moffett Aero Service carried out this job, as the parachutist was supposed to be a man named Moffitt. William Moffitt occasionally spelled his last name this way instead of with an "e" like his brother Edmund Moffett. The two owned the aero service. The plan was to have the parachutist descend wearing a pair of Carhart overalls, and the first person to touch him after he landed would receive a new pair of Carharts. Moffitt backed out of the jump for reasons unknown. Since Plato landed on a roof, it is unknown if anybody made the touch. All children who turned in the dodgers at the Del Monte Emporium were given a free soda.[16]

The Varney Company of Redwood City sent a Lincoln-Standard,

three-place biplane to Willows and gave rides May 26–27, 1920. Varney pilot Cloyd Clevenger flew passengers at $10 a person for safe and sane flights and $15 to $20 for aerobatic rides.[17]

ALBERT "BERT" LANE began constructing a biplane in 1925 very similar to a Curtiss Jenny. He studied every book and magazine he could find about airplane construction for years prior to this project. Bert learned a lot about woodworking from his father L. L. Lane, a cabinetmaker. Another advantage for building his plane was access to his father's cabinet shop. Bert called Sacramento pilot H. G. Andrews to inspect the finished product. He pronounced it perfect, then made the inaugural flight from a landing field near Willows grammar school. It went well with no mishaps. A 90hp. OX-5 engine powered the airplane.[18] Bert Lane's first flight in his biplane was July 2, 1926.[19]

Standard Oil Company of California decided to both promote its gasoline and aid aviators by painting air markers in huge block letters on roofs of its company buildings in the many towns Standard Oil had distributors. The air markers were visible for miles, enabling aviators to determine their location without having to land and ask directions.

Rooftop air markers not only named towns, they usually included arrows pointing north and/or the direction to the local airfield. Pilots of the military services, the airmail service, and civilian fliers agreed the signs were a critical aid. The Ninth Corps Army headquarters at the Presidio in San Francisco issued the following statement: "This project is of inestimable value to aeronautics. Had our cities been so marked with these aerial signboards in earlier days, many pilots who became lost in fog or rain, and were killed in consequence, would be alive today. It is of infinitely greater importance to the flier than to the motorist to know exactly where he is, as the motorist may stop anywhere and ask the way, and this of course is impossible to the aviator. Now, with these valuable guides to aid him, he can, if lost, pick up his true bearing and go to a field that he knows or return to his starting point." Above the newspaper article reporting this story was a photo of the air marker painted on the Standard Oil building in Orland.[20]

Bert Lane began spending weekends at Oroville in August 1926. He stayed with his brother L. E. Lane, the owner of Lane's Electric Shop. Bert would hop passengers on occasion from one of the few level landing fields he and his brothers found just south of Hutchinson Lumber Company (possibly old Riley Field).[21] In March 1927, Bert Lane returned to Willows in a new three-place Standard, which he had flown over Bechtel Baseball Field at Oroville to drop the first ball of the Sacramento Valley League baseball season on March 20.[22] Lane became airport manager of Stockton Municipal Airport in August. He flew to Willows later that month and took his grandmother Clementine Biddlecome, age 88, for her first airplane ride.[23]

Lee Schoenhair, a Willows aviator, became a major competitor in national air racing. His photograph appeared in the September 1928 *Aero Digest* as a top contender in the transcontinental Bendix Race, part of the National Air Races. At the time, *Aero Digest* was a most important aviation trade magazine in America.[24]

G. R. Fitzgerald of DOC Airways Division spoke to the Willows Kiwanis Club in 1928 advising the town to establish a permanent municipal airport. He said if the town failed to do so, the government would establish an emergency field and new DOC regulations would prohibit commercial planes from using the field for anything other than an emergency. If commercial flights couldn't use the field, Willows would be eliminated from commercial routes. It was an obvious advantage for a city to establish its own airport for everyone to use. He said a minimum of 80 acres were needed, and there was an ideal site southeast of town.[25]

S. S. Boggs of the DOC Airways Division selected an 80- to 100-acre tract of land just west of Willows city limits as the best site for a municipal airport. The property's northern boundary was Willows-Elder Creek Highway. The city and county were expected to approve Boggs' selection, and each agreed to put up half of the $4,000 cost of land. The federal government agreed to spend $7,000 on the airport for necessary equipment to make it a suitable airport for government and commercial airplanes. Included in this sum would be the purchase and installation of a revolving beacon, airfield perimeter lights, and two large gasoline tanks. Boggs said Willows would be on the main Pacific coast air route. He said the government was installing airway beacons at ten-mile intervals between San Francisco and Seattle, and there was to be a lighted airport every 40 miles. Boggs explained the installations would result in tremendous development of aviation throughout the region. In a short time, scores of planes would be flying over the area each day, and an airport at Willows would see a lot of use. He inferred mail planes would stop at Willows quite often.[26]

The Pacific Gas and Electric Company office in the Colusa County town of Williams received an order in May from the federal government to run an electric line out to the government landing field developed on the Salter property, south of Williams. An airway beacon and lights down one side of the airfield were to be installed soon, making night flying on the west side of the valley safer. Salter Field was one of nine emergency landing fields in the Sacramento Valley located on the San Francisco–Seattle airway established by the DOC.[27]

On July 10, Glenn County's board of supervisors moved to buy a tract of land for the county airport.[28] Mayor George R. Freeman received a proposal in July for the federal government to take over the local airport at Willows. Under terms of the proposal, any aircraft, including commercial planes, would be permitted to use the airport.[29] Another report on August 15 stated the city of Willows would soon purchase the airport site.[30]

Lieutenant Trit and a passenger landed at Del Paso Airport in December on a duck hunting trip to Willows. Trit was flying an army aircraft from March Field at Riverside.[31]

Floyd Nolta, a local aviation enthusiast, was appointed as overseer of the new Willows Airport on February 13, 1929. At the same time, the county surveyor was told by the Glenn County board of supervisors to inscribe "Willows" with white crushed rock in letters four feet wide and fifty feet long as a locator on the airport.[32]

At Orland in northern Glenn County, Al Hastings, president of Sierra Aircraft Corporation, landed for a visit in March. He met with Carl Franke and John Wright, part of the aviation committee of the Orland Exchange Club, to inspect two landing field sites. He wanted a field to establish another Sierra Aircraft Co. flying school. They located one immediately; it was east of the Masterson place on the southeast corner of Orland; the other location was unnamed.[33] Hastings returned to Orland three days later with Paul Nelson, manager of the National Theater in Chico. Their plan was to select an airport location. It is unknown if they did.[34]

There was an airport in the Orland area that always welcomed fliers. Miss Nora Simpson established it on her ranch ten miles west of Orland. Three buttes were nearby and her airfield was located on the west side of the longest one. The Associated Oil Co. painted an arrow pointing to the field on the roof of her ranch house. This airport site is probably located underwater at the bottom of Black Butte Reservoir today.[35]

A second airport was established at Willows south of the government emergency landing field. It was a privately owned airport, probably named for the manager, Freman Retteruth, who built a hangar there. Harold

CHAPTER 15

Ritchey kept his three-place Swallow there.[36]

Bert Lane was flying at Willows for Floyd Nolta in early 1929. Later he joined Clayton Allen in a flying business at Stockton Airport where he became airport manager.

On March 18, an air show and air race were held at Stockton. Clayton Allen won the race in his Hisso Swallow in 8.5 minutes. Bert Lane took second and J. M. Nightengale in a Travel Air was third. Peter Bodkin, flying a Waco, and Cliff Werle in a Jenny were also in the race. Clayton Allen flew a demonstration in a Heath Parasol. Les Oranges did stunt flying in his Waco. Robert Six organized the air show assisted by James Wrench and Edward Wagner. Six would one day head Continental Air Lines.[37]

WILLOWS AIRPORT WAS dedicated June 1–2, 1929, after the Memorial Day celebration. A. E. Wagner of Royle Air Lines at Oakland organized the air show. Wagner organized most of the new airport dedication shows in the north state between 1929 and 1930. He was hired because his employer, Royle Air Lines, always sent 6 to 12 airplanes from East Bay airports to the events; practically guaranteeing a successful show.

On Thursday afternoon and Friday morning prior to the weekend air show, a plane from Royle Air Lines arrived at Colusa and gave free rides to generate added interest in the Willows Air Show. At the same time, Floyd Nolta flew to various north valley towns and gave free rides to stimulate additional interest. This same activity took place at Willows and Orland on Friday afternoon. Willows merchants and Royle Air Lines paid for the free plane rides.[38]

Dedication ceremonies kicked off with a parade in the Willows town center featuring Willows and Princeton high school bands. Pedestrians were admitted free, but a 50-cent parking fee was charged to defray overall expenses. Each car received a 20 percent discount coupon for airplane rides. No one was allowed to park along the highway for quite a distance on either side of the airport to discourage freeloaders. Bob Boyd, a local photographer, filmed the parade, air show, and other occurrences over the weekend.

The new airport at Willows was considered one of the better airports in the north state, and it surprised fly-in visitors by its size. Purchased jointly by the city and county, it spread over 160 acres adjacent to the city. It was designated a federal emergency landing field with crosswind runways. The main runway was 3,200 feet long.[39]

On Saturday morning, first day of the dedication, three Army Air Corps planes from Crissy Field, San Francisco, arrived ahead of schedule at 9:30. More planes arrived later than anticipated due to bad weather at their airports. Free airplane rides were flown over Willows shortly before a "monster parade" opened the two-day dedication events.

With the arrival of the first 20 airplanes, the official ceremony got under way about 3:00. George R. Freeman, known as the "father" of the airport, introduced the speakers and also spoke. He noted the increased interest in aviation that had developed in Willows the past several years. He introduced local citizens who were pioneers establishing an airport at Willows: Floyd Nolta, William Durbrow, the Willows Board of Trustees, and the Glenn County supervisors. Warren Woodson of Corning, the pioneer of aviation development in northern Sacramento Valley, was the first speaker Freeman introduced. Next, W. H. Cotrell of the Richfield Oil Company spoke on behalf of the visiting fliers. He mentioned the biggest handicap to the growth of aviation was the lack of adequate landing fields throughout the country. Freeman introduced some of the visiting transport pilots: Dudley Steele of Richfield Oil; A. R. French of Standard Oil; Bob Allen of Standard Oil; Shirley Brush; and Ray Crawford of Overland Airways.

Ray Crawford was flying Overland Airways' six-passenger cabin plane Saturday and Sunday with L. H. Tryon, a major stockholder in the company and also a local wool buyer, accompanying him. Tryon owned a lot of land in Glenn County and had been purchasing wool a number of years.

Other aircraft visiting were: A Ryan Brougham, a cabin Travel Air, two Whirlwind Stearmans, a Hisso Waco, three Eaglerocks, a Swallow, an American Eagle, and two Curtiss Standards.[40]

Herb Kraft won the air race to Colusa on Saturday with Jerry Andrews taking second and Captain Doolittle third. An aviators' ball was held at Green Mill that evening. It turned into one of the most successful events of the two-day celebration. The aviators were introduced to everyone attending and ten people won airplane rides.

Sunday morning Jerry Andrews won the race to Chico. One report claimed Floyd Nolta won the race to Colusa carrying two passengers, Lowell Stark and a young woman. In an unusual move, local people were allowed to ride along during the air races for a price, of course. There were several planes in each race so some of the local folks enjoyed the thrill of riding along during an actual air race. It wasn't too dangerous because it was a distance race not a pylon race. Ingvald Fagerskog from Sacramento's Del Paso

Airport blew a tire on landing Sunday causing some excitement but little actual damage.

There was one serious accident, but luckily no one was killed or even badly injured. Herb Kraft, son of an Oakland millionaire, lost the lower right wing off his biplane. He was giving a ride to William Feeny and Henry Pahlin. They were at 1,800 feet when the wing left the airplane. That wing had been repaired after a mishap nearly a year before. Kraft immediately looked for a place to land; he still had some control but could only turn left. The plane was badly crippled, and it would try to go into a spin with any change in attitude or airspeed. Kraft wanted to land in a stubble field but was unable to turn right towards it, so he was forced to pick another spot.

A report in *Pacific Flyer* stated, "Kraft was able to keep the plane spiraling to the left to break the fall and succeeded miraculously from allowing the plane to go into a spin. He planned his last turn so that he would be headed into the wind, thinking that he could keep it straight, as he landed by doing this. But again it started to spin, and Kraft's plan was only partly successful. It was successful enough to save the lives of everyone in the plane, but not enough to prevent severe damage to the plane." The wing that left the airplane floated lazily down after the spiraling aircraft. The plane glided nearly two miles before crash landing in a barley field north of Willows. It hit with great force in a landing attitude and went over on its back. After being pulled from the wreckage, Palin hurried back to the airport and went for another 15-minute ride. It was estimated the cost to repair the plane's damage would be about $2,500. Kraft had crash-landed the plane near a location known as the Eucalyptus Grove at Willows. Feeny, a prominent local rancher, sustained a gash on his forehead, and the others were bruised, but that was all.[41]

Very few aviators without parachutes have survived the loss of a wing in flight. Kraft and his passengers only survived because they were in a biplane with the undamaged upper wing and two left wings providing a stabilizing effect and still giving minimum roll control.

Total attendance for the two days was over 12,000. Lots of people had purchased airplane rides and enjoyed flying. The celebration was considered a success from the moment the three Air Corps planes burst on the scene Saturday morning until the last event Sunday afternoon, a parachute jump. Walter Hall was to parachute jump both days but was unable to get to Willows Saturday, so he jumped twice Sunday.

Event organizer A. E. Wagner said Willows had definitely put itself on the air map. Everyone was so pleased with the successful air show it was suggested the event become an annual occurrence, which it did. However, they changed the date from June to September.

Lee Schoenhair, the son of a prominent Glenn County landowner, departed from an airport in Los Angeles at 3:41 am June 22, 1929, flying a Lockheed Vega. He was making an attempt to set a new nonstop speed record between Los Angeles and New York. Shortly after he took off, the Fresno chief of police told United Press reporters he was holding a warrant for Schoenhair's arrest on a charge of passing a fictitious check for $125. Schoenhair wrote the check to a jeweler in Fresno for a wristwatch. Shoenhair arrived in New York, but only stayed to refuel. He had to get back in the air for his attempt to lower the record going the opposite direction. He failed to set a new record.[42]

Harry E. Ahlstrom, mechanic for the federal government's beacon light on Willows Airport, was promoted in July and transferred to care for the beacon on Goat Island (now Yerba Buena Island) in San Francisco Bay. This island would one day anchor Treasure Island and the San Francisco Bay Bridge. W. M. Howard whose previous assignment had been caring for the beacon at Las Vegas, replaced Ahlstrom at Willows.[43]

Floyd Nolta placed an ad in *Western Flying* to sell his Jenny in August 1929. It stated the JN-4D had new linen fabric throughout the airframe, its Curtiss OX-5 motor had all steel valves, the motor turned 1450 rpm, the Jenny was in A-1 condition, and it's a good plane to build hours for a license. The owner was selling because he was getting a new plane. The ad ended with his name F. H. Nolta, Willows Airport, California.[44]

Floyd Nolta enrolled a dozen students at Willows. He was instructing at several Sacramento Valley airports totaling 27 flying students at Willows, Corning, Red Bluff, and Orland.

A 15-month lease for the property on which Colusa Airport was located was signed with an option for an extension according to Frank L. Clayton of the airport committee. If the city bought the property, the money spent on leasing would be credited towards the purchase price.

Orland painted its town name across the roof of a local warehouse in large letters 135 feet long. The paint was chrome yellow on a black background, as recommended by the Department of Commerce.[45]

Harry Claiborne, leader of the Curtiss Flying Service Squadron, landed at Willows in September 1929. He complimented the city's airport and

Chapter 15

encouraged the local chamber of commerce to continue improvements until it was rated a first-class airport.[46]

Bert Lane, originally from Willows, was hired by Paul Marchetti to handle the instructing duties at Marchetti's new flying school at Mills Field, San Francisco. Lane, holder of a transport pilot license and manager of the Stockton Airport, had his own flying school at Stockton. He had over six years flying experience when Marchetti hired him in July.[47] By November Lane was test pilot for Marchetti Motor Patents of San Francisco. He also was flying several hours a week in the Golden Bear aircraft built by Neilson Steel Aircraft Corporation of Berkeley. The plane was similar to a Ryan Brougham. The previous company pilot of the Neilson plane, Harry Abbott, had rolled, looped, and stunted the plane during early test flights.[48]

George Freeman of Willows announced the designated intermediate airport on the Pacific coast airway was available to any transient aircraft. Department of Commerce wouldn't allow commercial operators to be established there, however charter companies could fly passengers in and out of Willows Airport. Visiting duck hunters were also allowed to use it.[49]

Six months after the airport dedication, a smaller air show was held at Willows the weekend of December 1, 1929. Participating Sacramento fliers were: Noel Shadoan, Ken Kleaver, Ingvald Fagerskog, James O'Connor, Jack Beilby, Eddie Schoenbacker, Percy Perkins, William Marsh, and Ray Nicholson, manager of the Del Paso Airport.[50]

Robert W. Short and his wife, both pilots from Los Angeles, were following the airmail plane from Spokane to Oakland on January 3, 1930. Engine failure forced them to land on the government field at Willows. They spent the night at the Hotel Barton and continued on to Oakland by train.[51]

The Achean Club of Willows painted an air marker on the roof of the Ellis J. Levy building in letters 15 feet high and half a block long. An arrow alongside pointed towards the airport.[52]

Floyd Nolta was sworn in as Glenn County's first flying cop in April 1930 as an unpaid special deputy sheriff. He would enforce newly passed state aviation laws, stop reckless flying, and inspect licenses for conformance with state law. State aviation laws were rarely enforced because federal law, enforced by the DOC Aeronautics Branch, superseded them.[53]

CHAPTER 16

The 1930 Army Air Corps Maneuvers – Floyd Nolta, the Willows Airport manager –Flying activities at Willows – Willows Air Show of 1933 – A larger air show in 1935 – A better air show in 1937 – The best and last air show of the 1930s

Fig. 67. For the open house air show at the beginning of the April 1930 Air Maneuvers, a large formation of heavy bombers makes a pass and review flight for the thousands of civilians who came out to Mather Field for the show. Curtiss B-2 and Keystone LB-6s and 7s were the heavy bombers used during the maneuvers. A quarter of the nation's Army Air Corps assembled at Mather for the simulated air war.

On April 17, 1930, the Willows newspaper headlined the "GREATEST SIGHT IN HISTORY HERE ... Willows thrilled to the greatest sight in its history this morning when 66 army planes from Mather Field ..." attacked the Willows Airport, as part of the Army Air Corps' Air Maneuvers of 1930. The purpose of the anticipated mock war was to destroy important strategic points in Glenn County. The airport was one such target and Butte City Warehouse another. No one had ever seen anything that could compare to large twin-engine bombers flying high over the airport and their town on mock bombing runs. The entire attack took only 15 minutes and left the locals awestruck. Theoretically the Air Corps destroyed not only the airport but also the northern half of town. When finished, the planes turned east to attack Gridley and then south to hit Marysville.

A crowd of 800 gathered at the Willows airport; businesses closed temporarily and schools suspended classes to watch the attack. Of the 66 Army Air Corps aircraft flying over the city, there were 12 heavy bombers, 27 attack planes, and 27 pursuit planes. Other planes to the east and southeast formed "domes of security" over Oroville, Colusa Junction, and Butte City, and were seen from housetops.

The morning of the attack a single plane flew over the city at 9:15 to scout. Preceding the approaching attack force, it came from the northeast, circled the airport, and broke off to the southeast. The heavy bombers were sighted flying towards the airport in perfect formation. From the east and the south, pursuit and attack planes made their entrance low over the airport with their engines screaming. Heavy bombers flew over at high altitude dropping imaginary bombs. There seemed to be planes flying simultaneously towards the airport from every direction. They were so low spectators could make out the faces of pilots and crew. Some attackers were only 50 feet above ground. The planes came directly from Mather Field, hesitating at Colusa for a quick attack on the railroad system.

In eastern Glenn County the aircraft came together for an attack that lasted five minutes as bombers "destroyed" Butte City Warehouse, the largest warehouse in the interior of California. Residents in the vicinity were treated to a spectacle of combat flying by pursuit planes. Advance warning of the coming attacks came late in the day, before hundreds of people rushed to the sites to watch. After the attack force left the northern counties, it flew to Yolo County and "blew up" the Woodland Reservoir.

A press release revealed attacking formations would visit the San Francisco Bay Area around 6:00 PM guided by a robot (automatic) pilot. The next day would bring Air Corps formations maneuvering over Santa Clara Valley.[1] In late April, the Air Corps armada transferred from Mather Field,

CHAPTER 16   341

and the large formations of bombers, fighters, and attack planes were no longer seen in the skies of Sacramento Valley. They had been over the valley about three weeks. After brief stays in the Bay Area and Southern California, the squadrons returned to their home bases scattered throughout the nation.

FLOYD NOLTA, CARETAKER of the new airport at Willows, reported in late May that 35 airplanes had stopped there. More would have stopped if there had been a gas pump on the field. Unfortunately, local oil companies were totally unwilling to install a pump while the government retained control of the field. Fueling airplanes was accomplished by sending a fuel truck from a local gasoline distributor upon request.

Three planes landed one May weekend, according to Nolta, including an army aircraft flown by Lt. C. F. Pond on a flight from Portland to San Diego. He stopped for fuel. Ted Lowe and friends flew in from San Francisco, and Ed Wagner flew up from Stockton. Three army planes flying over Willows to the north were believed to be returning home from maneuvers near San Diego.[2]

Bert Lane flew to Colusa in his Travel Air for the Colusa Airport dedication on May 29.[3]

Department of Commerce officials let it be known that Willows Airport would no longer be government supported if it weren't improved.[4]

Leland Peoples of San Francisco sold his Hisso Travel Air 3000 to Floyd Nolta and E. M. Lederer of Willows in late August 1930.[5]

Frank Zeman, a parachute jumper from Willows narrowly escaped death on September 12, 1930. He was jumping from a Spartan biplane flown by Harold F. Brown that originated at Sutter Air Terminal, a Yuba City airport, for a large public barbecue at College City in nearby Colusa County.

At 3,000 feet Zeman stepped out of the cockpit onto the lower wing in preparation. Zeman was using one of Brown's parachutes in addition to his own. Unfortunately the harness on the outer parachute wasn't fastened properly and blew off in the slipstream as he stepped out. It tore loose then pulled down under his elbows. Zeman realized he could not reach the latch. If he jumped using his inner parachute, he could break his shoulders.

Brown was flying as slow as he dared, but it was still very fast. In an instant the force of the slipstream tore Zeman's legs out from under him, and for a few seconds he was hanging from the side of the plane by one hand. He quickly managed to wrap a leg around one of the wing struts and got back on the wing. Brown descended immediately, landing with Zeman still on the wing. He clamped the parachute harnesses together and they took off for another attempt. At 1,000 feet the motor coughed, and they couldn't ascend further. They gave up trying and landed. Zeman's actions went totally unnoticed by the crowd at the barbecue.[6]

The DOC officially notified Willows the airport lighting equipment would be removed and the airport stricken from the department's official airways documents unless the field was improved. The Achean Club promised to create better drainage and develop a 1,500 x 500-foot runway.

The Achean Club and the American Legion's plans to make improvements were put on hold because the government sent a team of inspectors to Willows to examine not only its airport, but also the landing field used on the Harlan Ranch northeast of Willows, which had a gravel base and was more usable in the winter than the government field, which had poor drainage. During winter, the government field was a mire of mud while the Harlan Ranch field remained in excellent condition.

After inspecting both airfields, it was unknown what the team recommended, but clearly there would be extensive improvements to the government field soon. Floyd Nolta, caretaker of the field, told the two service organizations the government was "... considering grading and graveling the field and installing drains."[7]

In late October 1930, Nolta was called to confer with DOC engineers and learned the government was going to spend $600 to improve Willows Airport as a part of the airways program. The county promised to donate gravel for the runway and loan equipment to fill in a troublesome low corner of the landing area.[8] The airfield was graded and smoothed by city and county equipment under the direction of DOC engineer John Beardslee in November.[9]

Floyd Nolta flew T. K. Boles, a geologist for the Ohio Oil Company, on an aerial survey of the northern Sacramento Valley in late January 1931. Boles was gathering data on oil possibilities. They covered the territory between Maxwell and Redding.[10]

Arrangements for airport committees of the American Legion and Achaen Club to assume operation of the government airport at Willows were completed the evening of June 23, 1932. Assumption of control was

Chapter 16

planned for July 1. The committees were still haggling with PG&E over power rates for border lights around the field. The government got a rate of eight dollars a month; the best the airport committees were offered was $22 per month. The committees decided to lease Standard Oil Company exclusive rights to furnish gas and oil at the airport for five years. Standard Oil agreed to pay $300 in advance for the privilege.

A small northwest corner of the field, which was somehow missed in the original transaction, had to be purchased by the airport committees; it could be purchased for payment of delinquent taxes in the amount of ten dollars. The American Legion and the Achaens would lease the airport land from the city and county, which jointly owned the property, and they would lease the border lights from the government. The government would sublease from the clubs a small strip of ground surrounding the beacon light, which it would continue to operate at its own expense.[11]

The superintendent of lighthouses at San Francisco, Mr. H. W. Rhodes, approved the leases for the government in September 1932. Under the new lease agreement, the airfield could now be used as a base for commercial operations. Before, the airfield was used for emergencies only. Floyd Nolta would continue as airport manager.[12]

A large grain fire in the Willows area burned over three miles on four ranches, destroying 175 tons of hay and over 250 tons of grain. It was blamed on a low flying airmail plane, which may have blown a hot piece of carbon out its exhaust system, or the pilot threw out a lighted cigarette butt.

A second fire started when a cigarette was thrown from a car driving past the airport. It started in a stubble field very near Floyd Nolta's hangar on Willows Airport. Nolta came close to losing his plane. Both fires were on the Fourth of July.[13]

Following the May 1929 Willows Airport opening celebration, it has been said the city held an air show every September until the start of World War II. It was the only Sacramento Valley airport to do this annually.

This author hasn't found any record of air shows during the first few years after the airport's dedication, but there was one in September 1933; the first year of local airport control. In the morning of September 8, three planes piloted by Floyd Nolta, Al Brien, and Glenn Lane departed Willows to Sacramento Valley towns promoting the air show at Willows on the ninth and tenth. They dropped leaflets advertising the air show along with two tickets among the leaflets for free airplane rides.

The Saturday air show schedule was planned as follows: An air parade led by a cabin plane with the air queen and two maids-in-waiting aboard would kick off the events. Denny Wright from Oakland would perform aerobatics, followed by an aerial dogfight. Next was a free-for-all five-mile air race around a circular course. Then Walter Hall would free-fall from 6,000 feet and open his chute at 1,000 feet.

On Sunday, Walter Hall would open the show at 11:00 with parachute stunts. Then five planes piloted by women of the Ninety-Nines would have a flour-bombing contest. Next an aerial combat between Mike Doolin and Sandy DeRenzo was planned. Then Thor "Smokey" Polson would skywrite at 15,000 feet. Throughout the day several pilots would give passengers lengthy rides not just the usual short hops.[14]

Air shows rarely go as planned; unforeseen circumstances force changes in schedules and participants. On Saturday Bill Royle announced Claude Swanson was replacing the great Walter Hall as parachutist for the Willows Air Show. Hall had duties elsewhere. Royle said Swanson would try to break the world's record, if he could find a pilot who could take him to 15,000 feet. Royle also said Denny Wright and Eddie Edison would be amazing to watch as they flew an aerial dogfight.

A dozen airplanes and pilots were registered at Willows by Saturday noon according to air show chairman, Bob Smith, who also announced the formation of army aircraft scheduled to arrive at noon would not be there until 2:00. The six-plane formation was supposed to circle Sacramento before coming to Willows. Flying activity was going strong by Saturday afternoon. Newly arrived planes were lined up on display with their pilots offering special prices for rides. An aviators' ball at Blue Gum Lodge Saturday night would be the biggest dance of the year at Willows.

All aspects of the two-day event were successful. Thousands watched air races, parachute jumps, army formation flights, and dogfights. On Sunday, Thor Polson climbed to 15,000 feet and wrote UNION 76 to everyone's delight. Six locals took long rides to Clear Lake the same day and many more had shorter rides around Glenn County. After Bill Royle left at 4:00 for another engagement, air show chairman Smith took over as air boss. Smith reported 23 airplanes came to Willows for the air show, which he declared a financial success[15]

There was a 1934 Willows Air Carnival, but none of the usual periodicals reported it. Only through a mention in the advertising for the 1935 show do we know that one took place in 1934.

Before 1935, the annual air show at Willows was called an air carnival, an ambiguous term replaced with the more precise term: air show. The 1935 annual Willows Air Show ran September 14–15. A promotional article published two days before described some interesting entrants. It wasn't unusual for pre-show articles about local air shows to smack of wishful thinking by the organizers or dubious teasers about noted performers who never arrived and probably were never invited.

Floyd Nolta said 40 aircraft would participate. He identified some of the planes and pilots coming: a tri-motor Fokker from Scenic Airways of Sacramento; an Aeronca C-2 "flying bathtub" from Eureka; and possibly a glider from Marysville. "Smokey" Poulson of San Francisco was to skywrite. E. E. "Monte" Mouton was bringing a Staggerwing Beechcraft from the Bay Area. With a 220 mph cruising speed, the Beech would be the fastest plane on the field. A cabin Waco was being flown in by factory representative Les Bowman, accompanied by his wife and daughter. His wife had a transport license and their daughter, 15, had soloed two years before, making her one of the youngest pilots in the country.

United Airlines was expected to send a passenger transport, and Boeing School of Aeronautics planned to send a plane and pilots to demonstrate the art of "blind flying." A Porterfield high-wing, cabin monoplane, the latest low-priced light plane to hit the market, was to be flown up from Sacramento. Dan Best of Woodland was bringing his new Stearman, and a large gaggle of army planes were expected.

Slim Perratt of Grass Valley was flying a Vultee V-1A, all-metal, low-wing airliner to the show. The Vultee was used to carry a half-million dollars of heavily guarded gold to San Francisco each week from the Idaho-Maryland mine near Grass Valley.[16]

Harry Middleton left his job as top mechanic for Aerovias Centrales at Grand Central Air Terminal in Glendale to work for Idaho-Maryland Mining Company at Grass Valley. He maintained their modern Vultee V-1A, which was originally built by Cord. Middleton eventually settled at Loma Rica in Butte County, but his expertise was well known in the aviation community throughout the Sacramento Valley. The Idaho-Maryland Mining Company always used the most modern airplanes available for their gold shipments. It wasn't long before the company sold the Vultee and bought a twin-engine Lockheed 10, which Middleton also kept in top flying condition. The mining company's airfield is now the Grass Valley airport.[17]

The day before the 1935 Willows show, Floyd Nolta, Dale Nolta, Glenn Danley, and Joan Bush flew over Sacramento Valley towns and dropped leaflets advertising the event. The Willows newspaper published an ad with a photograph of the Scenic Airways tri-motor Fokker and text that stated for only $1.50 one could go for a moonlight ride in the big modern tri-motor transport.[18]

Although the crowd numbered a record-breaking 6,500, the first day was a blowout—it rained. However, 52 airplanes were on the field, which was said to be twice that of the 1934 show. Bad weather kept at least a dozen more away. Les Bowman, the Waco dealer, was stuck on the ground at Portland due to fog, as were a gaggle of army planes coming from Crissy Field. Two planes flown by Dr. Adams and Bill Randall battled fog and made it down from Klamath Falls.

Sunday a modified air show program pleased the crowd. The most impressive act was Smokey Poulson's skywriting. He climbed to 14,000 feet and smoked out messages in 300-foot letters readable as far away as Butte County. Harry Sham of Oakland won the free-for-all race in his Travel Air with Monte Mouton taking second in the Staggerwing Beechcraft, and A. B. Spreckles, of the well-known sugar company, flew a Luscombe to third place. Dewey Ashford of Yuba City kept the crowd on edge with stunt flying, and Dwight Clark of Oakland made a delayed opening parachute jump. Floyd Nolta gave an excellent exhibition of crop dusting and rice seeding. There were no accidents either day of the show.

Sunday evening a $350 Shell Oil fireworks display was set off followed by an aviators' ball at Memorial Hall in Willows. The fireworks display was a crowd pleaser seen by an estimated 7,500 spectators on the airport and thousands more around the area. Ranchers up to 18 miles away could see the starbursts.[19]

THE ACHAEN CLUB and the local American Legion post, two organizations controlling the Willows airport, met in September 1936. Robert E. Boyd, chairman of the clubs' airport committee announced plans to build an additional hangar and oil the runways. Boyd and Floyd Nolta, owner of Willows Flying Service, also attended the meeting and spoke to them about arrangements for the annual air show to be held on the upcoming weekend of September 19–20.[20]

On Saturday the 19th, planes began arriving for the annual Willows Air Show, which officials claimed would be the biggest air meet in local history. Fair weather was predicted for both days. Thirty planes arrived by afternoon. First to land were eight army aircraft from the new Army Air Corps base in Marin County, Hamilton Field.

Bomb dropping (flour bombs), a model airplane exhibit and contest, and exhibition flying were on the program for early afternoon both days. Formation flying and parachute jumps were held late afternoons. The first day's program would conclude with an aviators' ball at Memorial Hall serenaded by an eleven-piece orchestra.

Pre-show advertisements suggested most of the air show features were scheduled for Sunday such as: stunt flying, crop dusting and seeding demonstrations, air racing, skywriting by Smokey Poulson, and precision parachute jumping by Dwight "Suicide" Clark. Then there was to be an exhibition of glider flying by Marysville's Herb Keeler, considered one of the best glider pilots on the Pacific coast; blind flying was scheduled featuring Johnny Martin in a specially modified ship sent by Oakland's Boeing School of Aeronautics. The show would end Sunday night with the free Shell Oil fireworks display.

There was supposed to be a new Martin bomber (B-10) and a new fast pursuit design among the eight planes from Hamilton Field. There would be a sister ship of the plane that won the Bendix Trophy at the National Air Races, and Frank Spreckles, the sugar millionaire from San Francisco, would bring the Luscombe monoplane in which he won the Ruth Chatterton Derby by flying from Cleveland to San Diego during the recent National Air Races.

A special public address system was installed and Don Smith, superintendent of the Sacramento Municipal Airport, was announcer.[21]

Consolidated Airlines would bring a new Fokker monoplane to the show flown by the company president, Harold F. Brown. This Fokker was a Super Universal then in use by the airline. Frank Rose, of the San Francisco Bay Airdrome and former president of Varney Speed Lanes, was to bring a new Stinson monoplane. In addition to the Staggerwing Beechcraft flown in by Monty Mouton, another Beechcraft of the same design was to be flown to the show by Fred C. Talbot. Also, there were to be other new designs coming; the most varied designs ever to land at Willows.[22]

The above information all came from promotional articles about the 1936 Willows Annual Air Show. The following is what *actually* happened.

The 1936 Willows Air Show broke all attendance records for the annual event; but only 3,500 people attended the flying events; 450 couples attended the aviators' ball. Over 8,000 came to the airport that night for the Shell Oil fireworks display. Some people in cars were unable to find parking on the airport or in the vicinity. They had to drive a mile and park at the golf course to watch. There were 78 airplanes attending; 23 more than the previous year's air show.

Monte Mouton of San Francisco, sometimes flying more than 200 mph in a Beechcraft, won the show's free-for-all race. Bill Ong, Beechcraft factory pilot and noted national racing pilot, took second in a Beech, and Harry Sham of Oakland was third.

The only mishap was Saturday afternoon. After touching down for a landing, Smokey Poulson collided with George Schmitz of Oakland who was preparing to take off. Schmitz suffered a cut over one eye and both planes were damaged.

Aerial Crop Dusting Service from Marysville gave an exhibition of crop dusting. Bill Ong flew a special display of speed flying in a very fast Beechcraft Staggerwing. Dwight "Suicide" Clark made a parachute jump. George Meyers, chief pilot of the Boeing School of Aeronautics, and student Johnny Martin of Willows amazed the audience with blind flying (instrument flying). Martin's cockpit was entirely enclosed with no outside view. Instructor Meyers sat in the open cockpit as safety pilot.

Herb Keeler an aeronautics instructor at Yuba Junior College, Marysville, was at the field with his glider on display drawing a lot of interest; it was a Grenau-8 glider designed by Wolf Hirth of Germany. Keeler was known as an authority on soaring. He spent a few summers in Los Angeles building gliders for Hawley Bowlus.

Fifteen female pilots from around the state flew in to watch the air show. Lester Pierce of Eureka flew an exhibition of upside-down flying, known today as inverted flying. Hundreds of people paid for airplane rides, and the demand for rides became intense as sunset approached. Pilots had to turn people away as the sun went down.[23]

In July 1937 plans were being worked out for the next annual Willows Air Show in September. The slogan for the air show was "Bigger and Better."

Ray Varney, a pioneer Bay Area pilot now a Glenn County commercial pilot, was back on the job after two weeks' active duty with the navy. He held a US Navy flying officer's rating. Dale Nolta, Floyd's brother, was flying over the Holmes and Wing ranches with Frank Merrill, as observer, in Shasta County looking for a herd of lost sheep. Floyd "Speed" Nolta was spending the Fourth of July holiday flying and celebrating at Eureka. Mrs. Nolta drove up with a friend to meet him. George Jansen, Andy Johnson, and Eddie Kotes, all high school students, were taking instruction at Willows

Flying Service.

Johnny Martin, the student at Boeing School of Aeronautics from Willows who flew the blind flying demo during the 1936 air show, was flying the route between Cheyenne and Salt Lake City for United Airlines by July 1937.[24]

The Willows Annual Air Show was an established event in the Sacramento Valley by 1936. The number of airplanes attending increased yearly since the first air show opened the airport in 1929. It attracted several thousand people each year—more than any 1930's flying event north of Oakland.

The September 25–26, 1937, air show was, as usual, well planned, organized, and ready to handle record crowds. It was living up to its claim of being the "Best in the West." Hotels and campgrounds were nearly sold out by prior reservations.

A new type of parachutist, Manus "Mickey" Morgan, a bat-wing jumper was hired and was expected to be the highlight of the show. The 26-year-old from Sioux Falls, South Dakota, belonged to the famed "Red Devils Squadron" of aerial stunt performers was to give the Pacific coast its first viewing of bat-wing flying. Morgan used wings eight-feet long strapped to his body. He had been doing aerial stunts since 1930.

Morgan hadn't done stunts for eight weeks after breaking his collarbone during a bat-wing jump at Fairbault, Minnesota. He talked about his other bat-wing mishaps. Once he got tangled in his parachute but managed to right things and land safely. At Grand Rapids, he almost landed on the horns of a large buck deer. For his Willows bat-wing routine, he would leave the airplane at 10,000 feet doing rolls and loops until opening his chute at 1,000 feet. Only Morgan and one other jumper in the country, he told a reporter, were using bat-wings, and that fellow was recently killed during a jump.

The first day was to open in the afternoon with a model airplane contest and close with a sportsmen's air race from San Francisco to Willows. Many of the locals felt Saturday's big event was the dance that night. Its theme was a "Night in the Clouds."

Sunday's program would include races, stunt flying, bomb dropping, exhibitions by Dorothy Barden, a north state parachutist well known for her jump skills, and Dolores Guinther, a stunt flyer from San Francisco. Miss Guinther operated her own flying service at San Francisco Bay Airdrome, Alameda, where her five airplanes were based.[25]

The new Beechcraft Model 17 Staggerwing, the apotheosis of biplane design, would be well represented at the air show. Jerry Andrews would fly one up from the Bay Area for passenger hops. Monte Mouton and Jack Anweiler would each be racing Beech Staggerwings. Chris Sauer of Chico would demonstrate his anti-blowout car tire by having it punctured with a shotgun as he drove 65 mph. A new "foolproof" airplane design built by Stearman-Hammond, was to be exhibited. The flying Fullers, of paint manufacturing fame, were bringing several of their fast racing planes. Frank Fuller had recently won the Los Angeles to Cleveland Bendix Trophy at the National Air Races. Dana Fuller was arriving in his Stinson cabin plane. His sister, Dorothy Dorst, was arriving in a new Waco. She was one of the few women holding a blind flying rating.

The air show would end Sunday night with spectacular fireworks fired from an airplane flown by Ivor Witney of Sacramento and an exhibition by an illuminated airplane carrying electric sign letters five feet high.[26]

Actual events brought great thrills for a crowd estimated between 5,000 and 6,000 spectators on Sunday. Officials didn't have an accurate assessment of the crowd, but were sure it was one-fourth larger than 1936.

As planned, the following stunts were successfully carried out: bat-wing flying by Mickey Morgan; parachuting by Dorothy Barden; Dolores Guinther's stunt flying; and the anti-blowout demonstration by Chris Sauer. Air races and crop dusting exhibitions also were flown well and safely.

Harry Sham, of Oakland won the free-for-all race with Jack Antweiler of San Francisco placing second and Jerry Andrews of San Francisco taking third. Ray Varney of Willows won the bomb dropping contest and the paper-cutting contest with Vern Heaton of Woodland placing second in the latter. Lee Porter and Dale Nolta of Willows finished at the same instant in the light plane race with Porter winning the deciding coin toss.

Field judges for races and contests were: Franklin Rose of San Francisco, J. Adamson of San Francisco, Frank Moore of Sacramento, and Dewey Ashford of Yuba City. It was estimated 75 to 100 planes flew in for the show. Once again, passenger hopping planes were unable to handle the rush of people wanting rides late Sunday afternoon. Crowd control got out of hand several times holding up events until the landing areas could be cleared in the interest of safety. Seven events, including a free-for-all stunt-flying contest, had to be cancelled for lack of time. Crowd control got out of hand, which delayed the schedule. Floyd Nolta and Sacramento's Don Smith shared announcing duties.[27]

The next month, several visitors landed at Willows Airport: Paul Johnson, chief pilot of R. P. Bowman Company from the San Francisco Bay Airdrome in a new Stearman-Hammond design; W. H. Clyde of San Francisco flying a new Beechcraft Staggerwing; Larry Martin of Oroville in a cabin Waco; and Don McKinnon of Chico flying a Curtiss Robin. Willows Air Service hired Andy Johnson who had been building time in the company's Fleet biplane.

Willows Flying Service pilots reported they were flying to Corning for the October 1937 weekend air show at Woodson Airport.[28]

The 1938 Willows Air Show date was set for September 24-25. The annual air shows became the town's biggest event each year. It generated an economic boost for Willows' businesses. The Saturday night aviators' ball was advertised as, "Always the BIGGEST DANCE of the year." The importance of the 1938 event was evidenced by the largest newspaper ad in the air show's history being published in the *Willows Journal*.[29]

The air show lived up to its motto "Bigger and Better" in 1938. A first class aerobatic pilot, Joe Lewis, was hired for the stunt-flying portion. Lewis was a Hollywood stunt pilot and reputed as one of the best. He had 7,000 hours flying time of which 700 were aerobatic. The National Air Races at Cleveland could not provide a better aerobatic act than Joe Lewis. His specialty was flying an all-metal low-wing Ryan ST, upside down, ten feet above the ground and doing outside loops. Lewis would be the highlight and most expensive act in the air show's history.

Floyd Nolta, who served in the Army Air Service during the Great War as a mechanic, and Ray Varney, a Navy Reserve pilot, flew to San Francisco to confirm that barring any last minute changes the military would send planes to the Willows Air Show. The fire fighting aircraft exhibition was predicted the next favorite act after Lewis."[30]

To promote the air show further, instead of sending just three airplanes to various Northern California towns as before, a caravan of 30 decorated automobiles would show up with Dale Nolta overhead in a company Fleet trainer skywriting "Air Show." The lead car used a loud speaker and a phonograph to provide music announcing the parade's entry. The cars stopped at city centers and the air show master of ceremonies gave pep talks to encourage attendance.[31]

Some of the more unusual planes and pilots expected at Willows for the 1938 show were: George P. Fuller, the San Francisco paint executive, in his twin-engine Lockheed; Charles LaJotte in the Gilmore Oil Company's

Lockheed; the Shell Oil aircraft flown by Bob Adamson; Union Oil's plane flown by Warren Carey, an official at the recent Cleveland National Air Races who would be officiating the Willows show.

Frank Rose was bringing a new Stinson from San Francisco, and Jack Wing of Gerber would bring a new Porterfield. Both were examples of high-wing cabin monoplanes capturing the aircraft market in the late 1930s. Featured stunt pilot Joe Lewis brought two cabin planes in addition to his Ryan ST aerobatic aircraft. His extra airplanes would be used to hop passengers during the show. Lewis declared to the Achaean Club before dinner on Friday night at Kline's, "I'm just as good as others doing the same thing though I won't say I'm any better." [32]

New bleachers were built for the comfort of spectators, and a high wire fence was installed to control the crowd, preventing problems similar to those a year ago.[33] Warham Singh Gravell, one of the few East Indian pilots in the nation, was scheduled to make a parachute jump during the show.

The Sunday program entertained an estimated 4,000 spectators. One hundred airplanes arrived for the show. Many felt the sensational flying of Joe Lewis was worth the price of admission alone.

The two air races were crowd pleasers. Dale Nolta won by a nose in the light plane race with Glenn Danley of Marysville taking second. The free-for-all race was nose-to-nose between Floyd Nolta and Harry Sham with the latter eking out a win. Ray Varney took third place. An exhibition of rice seeding and crop dusting, presumably by the Noltas, along with Gravell's parachute drop were also highlights of the day.

Joe Lewis gave an unforgettable experience to everyone with his incredible aerobatics, equal to none—even in the movies. Lewis flew upside down close to the ground according to reports. He did the hammerhead maneuver in which the plane goes straight up until out of airspeed, it pivots, then comes straight down. The double snap roll and the Immelman turn were performed with ease leaving the crowd sure they saw everything possible in stunt flying.

Following the evening fireworks display, Dwight Clark made an illuminated parachute jump to conclude the weekend.[34] The 1938 Willows Air Show achieved a program of the highest quality.

Unfortunately, Joe Lewis died two weeks later performing at Woodson Airport for the Corning Air Show October 9, 1938. Dale Nolta acted heroically chopping through the metal fuselage of Lewis' Ryan ST to get Lewis out of the burning wreckage. Sadly, Lewis died shortly after arriving at a Red Bluff hospital. Nolta's shirt was singed and his finger was cut deeply while pulling Lewis from the burning plane.

Despite the trauma Nolta just experienced, that same day he took Dwight Clark up for his parachute jump. Clark talked to him continuously as they climbed to jump altitude. Clark seemed nervous, and Nolta said he had to circle the jump point twice before Clark was ready. He couldn't understand Clark because of engine noise. As Clark rose to make his jump he shook hands with Nolta, bailed out, and executed his delayed drop. Somehow, the force from the chute opening broke his neck in midair! He survived the landing and was talking on the way to the hospital, but Dwight Clark died after he arrived.[35]

Scenes for *Stand Up And Fight* starring Wallace Beery and Robert Taylor were filmed near Chico in September 1938 along Diamond Match Company's railroad spur running from Stirling City and Butte Meadows in the Sierra Nevada. Floyd Nolta flew the film stock, each week it was shot, from Chico to San Francisco where it was transferred to an airliner going to Los Angeles. Actor Errol Flynn often hired Nolta to fly him around the north state during his stay shooting *Robin Hood* in Chico the same year.[36]

THE ANNUAL WILLOWS Air Show had grown to be recognized as the largest air show in Northern California. Pilots who returned every year told officials it was the best one on the Pacific coast. A valuable asset to the Willows community, businesses reaped thousands of dollars a year, which multiplied throughout the area. Very little profit was made on the air show itself, and any profit gained was spent on airport upkeep.[37]

The 1939 air show planning started August 22. The executive committee of Floyd Nolta, Robert Roland, W. E. Gagen, and Robert E. Boyd chose Capt. Charles Steele as general chairman of the event. One of Steele's first duties was negotiating with world champion aerobatic ace "Tex" Rankin to be the air show's featured stunt flyer. Several local people had raved about his performance at the opening of the 1939 San Francisco World's Fair.[38] He agreed to fly for both days of the air show.

FOR MANY YEARS the Noltas were known as the "flying family of Willows," but in the summer of 1939 the Ottersons would share the title. On August 24, Lee Otterson completed his solo flight at Willows Airport. Lee's dad, Bert Otterson, was studying for his private license. Bert already owned an airplane, which he kept at Willows Airport. His brother, L. S. "Babe"

Otterson, possessed a private license.[39]

Five aircraft from Willows Airport landed in Corning at Woodson Airport for an air show Sunday, August 20, 1939. The planes and pilots were: George Jansen flying a Fleet; Babe Otterson also flying a Fleet; and Ray Varney, who flew there in a Travel Air, was one of the featured aerobatic acts. Dale Nolta arrived in a Willows Flying Service Travel Air, and Al Bryant flew in from Chico.[40]

Sacramento Valley pilots gathered at Willows on the evening of August 28 to hear CAA inspector Richard Lees Jr. from Oakland speak about new standardized regulations for flying instruction being put into effect throughout the country. The pilots from out of town who came for the talk were Byron Johnson, J. W. Phillips, Sam Smith, and James Wiseman—all from Oroville; J. E. Leonard, Garrison Patrick, and Don MacKinnon from Chico; Mr. and Mrs. J. E. Hunter and Mr. and Mrs. Lester Pierce of Eureka; Glenn Danley and Bill Brander of Marysville; Wally Stryker of Weaverville; Gene Graham of Willits; and L. H. McCurley from Corning.[41]

By August 31, the flying activity at Willows Airport during the previous seven days was as follows: Ray Varney returned from Los Angeles where he took Clyde Devinna and Richard Rossen, MGM film directors who had been working on the film *Balalaika* at Chico for the past two weeks; George Jansen flew to Sacramento on Tuesday; Floyd Nolta flew over forest areas at Mt. Shasta on fire duty; and A. Webster, a Stanford professor, landed at Willows on the 30th en route to Montague from Palo Alto.[42]

Dale Nolta, who opened a gas station at Willows in 1938, celebrated its first anniversary of business on September 1, 1939.[43]

THE WILLOWS AIR SHOW of 1939 would take place on September 23-24.[44] Evelyn Burleson of Albany, Oregon, was signed to fly for the upcoming Willows Air Show. She was one of the few women in America who held a transport pilot license. Floyd Nolta and Ray Varney spent the first weekend of September in the Bay Area arranging for army and navy aircraft to attend the show.[45]

By mid-morning September 9, Ernest Clark and Robert Donnell had been in the air 88 hours—they were shooting for a record of 720 nonstop hours. Arrangements were made for them to carry out aerial refueling over Willows if they were still flying during the air show, according to their flight director Charles Branstetter. They failed the endurance record attempt.[46]

On September 9, Willows Mayor Charles S. Schmidt issued a

CHAPTER 16

proclamation setting aside September 11–24, 1939, for the observance of Air Progress in Willows.[47] Aircraft sales distributors, most of whom were located in the Bay Area, would be bringing their newest models to Willows for display before and during the air show. Frank Rose would bring a Stinson Model 105, Monte Mouton, a new Beechcraft Staggerwing and a new Luscombe; R. P. Bowman, a new Waco; and Duck Air Service was bringing the latest Taylorcraft. Bowman was also bringing a Stearman-Hammond and Duck was also bringing its tri-motor Stinson used for forest service work. Bill Fillmore was bringing a new Ryan. All these dealers were based at Oakland.[48]

Willows Air Show management revealed they would be paying Tex Rankin $700 per performance during the two day run.[49]

Two window displays in Willows advertised the air show and told the story of various aviation enthusiasts. One display, in the Glenn grocery store, showed aviation maps belonging to Raymond Fong who possessed an amateur pilot license, and at one time had dreams of flying and fighting for the Chinese Air Force until US government officials "thought otherwise." Fong was a Willows aviator. Poland's Stationery Store had a second display of photos of famous flying personalities including Johnny Martin, formerly of Willows, standing by the United Airlines transport he was currently flying.[50]

A photo and article appeared in the Willows paper showing Tex Rankin standing next to his aerobatic Ryan ST aircraft with 26 trophies cascading from the Ryan's wing. The article described Rankin's exploits to date. "Tex Rankin, world's champion stunt flier, who has been signed for the Willows Air Show this year, may not look like Clark Gable, but he has doubled for him. Rankin was the 'Gable' film fans saw doing the difficult aerial stunts in *Test Pilot* and has been the double also in *Too Hot To Handle*, *Sky Giant*, *Road To Reno*, *Men With Wings*, *Made For Each Other*, *The Woman I Loved*, *The Sun Never Sets*, and *Stunt Pilot* among others." Tex Rankin would be flying a Great Lakes biplane at the Willows Air Show. Rankin had written several flying textbooks and had been flying for 23 years. He was an instructor during the Great War, and later made the first nonstop flight from Vancouver, B. C., to Agua Caliente, Mexico. He was one of the first airmail pilots in Idaho and Oregon, and developed the "Rankin System of Flying," used by aviation schools throughout the country.

He won a championship world title in aerobatics competing against famous fliers such as Germany's Ernst Udet and Captain Papana of Rumania.

Rankin did stunts most pilots of the day couldn't even imagine. Many thought it was impossible to recover from the deadly flat spin. Rankin not only recovered from it, he purposely performed it upside-down. An inverted flat spin was an amazing feat at the time.[51]

Tex Rankin planned to use his extensive repertoire of aerobatic maneuvers at Willows to entice those spectators who would normally only come Saturday to return on Sunday. On Saturday his maneuvers were publicized in the order he would perform them. They were: full power spin, pirouette roll, one-and-a-half snap roll stopping upside down, inverted snap roll, double snap roll, Clarke roll, hesitation roll, jitterbug zoom, inside Cuban eight, flying on side (knife edge flight), reversible slow rolls, diving and climbing slow rolls, and wing over to side slip landing.

On Sunday only, Tex would perform his signature outside maneuvers in the following order: inverted flat spin, vertical figure eight, outside loop, outside Cuban eight, two inside loops within a loop, square loop, low slow roll, flaming geyser, one-and-a-half slow roll straight down and the same straight up, upside down speed dash, upside down climbing spiral, upside down figure eight, and chandelle zoom to side slip landing.

At a dinner for Achaean Club members the night before the air show, Tex Rankin praised Floyd Nolta and Ray Varney for their outstanding reputation as flight instructors. He said, "With teachers like Floyd Nolta and Ray Varney, no one should have any trouble learning to fly within three weeks with half-hour lessons at a time. Willows is fortunate to have two such good instructors."

Reportedly, cameras would be barred from the air show at the request of US Navy officials. Three of its latest designs would be there. The public could walk right up to them, as long as they didn't take photos.[52] World War II had started in Europe weeks before the air show, and war jitters had the military a bit on edge and cautious.

The 1939 Willows Air Show was ushered in on Saturday with the roar of 1,000hp. engines of three navy Curtiss scout bombers flying in formation over the airport and city. As soon as the bombers landed, special deputies were placed to guard the planes, and the order prohibiting cameras was repeated. Tex Rankin and bat-wing parachute jumper Walter Miller, both reported to have performed at the Cleveland National Air Races, were on deck and ready to go. Light plane races and hare and hound races were scheduled for Saturday afternoon. The aviators' ball and banquet were planned for Saturday night at Willows Memorial Hall.

The ball started with a grand march led by Capt. Charles Steele, chairman of the event, and Mrs. A. J. Baker, worthy matron of the Marshall Chapter, O. E. S. The ball was attended by over 1,500; it was the first dance of the fall season. All porches around the Memorial Hall were screened and chairs provided for the comfort of dancers. A popular dance orchestra from Oroville, the All-Stars, provided music [53]

The air show brought in a bigger crowd than ever and was accident-free. There was no rain, however adverse weather affected some plans. Evelyn Burelson, the stunt-flyer, was grounded by rain in Albany, Oregon. Walter Miller, the bat-wing jumper, was ready to perform, but the two DOC inspectors present advised officials to cut his act because of a "still south wind."

Tex Rankin was the hit of the air show. The slow talking flier from Spokane gave two thrilling performances a day with aerobatics the likes of which had never been seen in the Sacramento Valley. Veteran pilots who understood the difficultly of his maneuvers were even more excited watching his routine.

On Sunday, the navy pilots in three new scout bombers demonstrated flawless formation flying and screaming dive bomber attacks. Lieutenant Ed Walter led Lt. James Edgar and Ensign Balch, a cousin of Glenn resident Tom Balch. Prior to their flight, Lieutenant Walter complained to Ray Varney the local naval reserve contact that a lot of people were crowding around the three navy aircraft. Varney said US Army Capt. Charles Steele, who was in charge of the entire air show, would take care of the problem. A little later, Walter was back in Varney's face complaining the army was doing such a good job guarding the aircraft they wouldn't let him get to his own plane.

Next, Varney took off with two other Willows Flying Service pilots and they came back over the airport in a shallow dive. Passing over the airport boundary, Ray Varney rolled his biplane upside down and with his colleagues still in close formation passed in front of a stunned crowd applauding with excitement. Following the three planes, a formation of six high-wing Aeronca monoplanes belonging to Pierce Flying Service and the Eureka Flying Club, all from Eureka, passed in front of the crowd.

Dale Nolta won the aerial foxhunt, also known as a hare and hound race, on both days. Monte Mouton won the race for airplanes with motors of 65hp. or less in his Luscombe. Lester Pierce of Eureka took second in an Aeronca. Bill Brander of Marysville won the race for planes with 100hp. or less in a Porterfield. Mouton was second in his Luscombe, and Ray Varney was third in a Fleet. Twelve planes were supposed to arrive from Oregon, but weather grounded them.

To illustrate the importance of the Willows Air Show to aviation in Northern California, the register of pilots who attended the two-day event in 1939 reads like a who's who of the movers and shakers of aviation in the San Francisco Bay Area and the Sacramento Valley prior to World War II. They were: W. Last, John Allen, and Frank Nervino of Alameda; J. E. Leonard and John D. Fay from Chico; J. L. Perrine and L. O. McCurley of Corning; Andy Christiansen, Tony Mora, Les Pierce, Andy Camilli, Frank Emenegger, Quentin Jeffers, R. Meyers, Andy Castalotti, E. J. Wright, Gilbert Moore, Lloyd Larsen, and Les Teagarden from Eureka; Frank Bruman from Fairfield; Glenn Danley, Tom Bowles, John Bowles, Bert Lefevre, Earl Stoner, Adolph Del Pero, Robert Clarke, Ferne Beale, Bill Brander, and Ernie Williams from Marysville; Ed Sandin, Norman Wagner, Doc DeNeal, Bill Weiss, and R. Young from Nevada City; K. Whitsit, J. Morel, Harry Sham, Henri Chang, Tom Harned, Joe Dawson, E. H. Walter, M. Balch, J. O. Edgar, James Henderson, John Murphy, G. Murphy, E. B. Osler, C. S. McBrier, and H. W. Elliott from Oakland; Joe Kula of Orland; J. W. Philipps from Oroville; L. Harvey Long and M. Smith of Palo Alto; Dave Lewis and Bill White from Portland, Oregon; E. V. Wing of Red Bluff; Mr. Fernsted, N. H. Harvey, Virginia and Bart Woodruff, L. Brown, Frank Wolf, Jimmie Sallee, Stanley Wilson, Earl Weaver, Mr. Magli, and Mike Novarro from Redding; Don Smith, W. J. Thompson, Ted Hoffman, Ray Gundlach, B. Criten, C. K. Puthhaber, Shigeo Nakano, J. Schunacho, E. Clark, E. Garside, L. Weatherhead, P. R. Anderson, J. Leedy, Irwin DeRosa, Adolph Gunigani, and E. E. Hughes from Sacramento; Charles Burkhart of San Carlos; G. C. Shrash and Russell Rice from Santa Cruz; James and Agnes Duncan, R. Partelow, Edward Hulett, L. Nicholson, Bill Ridenour, S. N. Parmalee, C. Bray and Edison E. Mouton from San Francisco; Cecil Landis of Shasta City; W. Stryker of Weaverville; Vernon Heaton of Woodland; and Slim Davis of Yuba City.[54]

The north state rain finally reached Willows on Monday, and 15 planes had to wait for a break before they could go home.

WITH THE WAR beginning in Europe, it was obvious to many the United States would be pulled in at some future time. The danger of America being drawn into the war and the necessity of providing aircraft for countries that would surely be allies caused an increase in the production of aircraft and training of aviators. Once America was in the war, pilots throughout

California scattered to aircraft factories as test pilots like Bert Lane. Some like Sherman Perkins ferried aircraft to Alaska for the Russians. Some went into the Army Air Corps, like Floyd Nolta, or opened military flight training schools like Tex Rankin. His flying school at Tulare trained over 10,000 pilots for the Army Air Corps during WWII. The time for air shows was over and in September 1940 Willows Airport was recommended as a training field for the government Civilian Flight Training Program (CFTP), a non-collegiate course in flying to train civilian pilots for possible future military service.[55]

As a postscript about Tex Rankin, the author's father, Ted Herr, went for a demonstration flight at Marysville's Alicia Airport in a Republic Seabee amphibian with Tex Rankin in the summer of 1947 shortly before Rankin was killed in the same plane while giving a demonstration ride at Klamath Falls, Oregon.[56]

Fig. 68. At Mather Field, near Sacramento, an Army Air Corps LB-7 twin-engine heavy bomber is being refueled during the Air Maneuvers of 1930.

Fig. 69. An Army Air Corps experiment of night photography taken during the April 1930 Air Maneuvers at Mather Field reveals the words "Welcome Lindy," which were painted on the tarmac for Charles Lindbergh's visit to Sacramento in September 1927.

Part III. Early Flying in Tehama, Shasta, and Yolo Counties

CHAPTER 17

Corning's first airport – Warren Woodson develops an airport – Ben Torrey, airport manager – Pacific Air Transport and West Coast Air Transport choose Corning – Fuel stop for the famous – Corning's first air show – Ben Torrey does it all – Torrey's final days – The Corning Air Show jinx

Seven de Havilland DH-4 Army Air Service bombers raucously brought flying to the attention of Corning residents in June 1921. The bombers circled Corning in battle formation with their engines snarling and landed on a makeshift airfield prepared at the northwest corner of the small Tehama County town. The refurbished, single-engine, biplane bombers of the Ninth Aero Squadron were under the command of Lt. John Morgan. The DHs were flown up to Corning from their base at Mather Field. The 160-acre airfield had been scraped and leveled by local workers. Wooden barracks were built and a well drilled to supply water for the aircrews and their planes. These Army Air Service crews were assigned to patrol forests of the Sierra Nevada, the Siskiyou Mountains, and the Coast Range to spot forest fires. For the 1921 fire season, Corning was chosen as the northern terminus for forest patrol aircraft in the north state with Mather Field as the southern terminus.

The Air Service crews operating from Corning spotted numerous forest fires the summer of 1921. Unfortunately, few Corning residents knew anything of the fires army pilots discovered. What they did know was the DH-4's noisy Liberty engines stopped their chickens from laying eggs, and women saw their linens and clothing drying on clotheslines turned brown from clouds of dust blown around by airplanes landing and departing the powdery dirt runway.

Warren N. Woodson, "The Father of Corning," in 1926 would establish a new permanent airport north of the northeast corner of Corning, a town site laid out in a square. He developed a runway and built a hangar. The north wind, which often blew at a steady 15 to 30 mph from the north-northwest, would blow dust kicked up by the airplane's propellers away from the city instead of diagonally—directly into the city, as the army forest patrols did in 1921.

The Air Service at Corning in 1921 and the story of the forest fire patrols are covered extensively in the author's book, *Aviation in Northern California 1910–1939 Volume II*. Oroville was the state's first northern terminus for army forest patrols that began in 1919. The northern terminus was extended further north to Red Bluff in 1920 and then to Corning for the 1921 fire season.

Woodson was a staunch aviation enthusiast, but he was not a pilot. The

Fig. 70. Corning Airport AKA Woodson Field (in 1990) is located in the center right of the photo, one mile northeast of the town. It has been in continuous operation since it was opened in 1926. The only other airports in Northern California to exceed that record are: Benton Field, opened in 1919; Woodland-Watts (Yolo Fliers Club Field), opened in 1920; and Mather Field, opened in 1918. The first airport opened at Corning on the northwest corner of town and was developed for the army forest fire patrol in 1921.

site Woodson chose for the city's permanent airport was first used as a landing ground when Art Starbuck, a Pacific Air Transport pilot flying airmail, made a quick landing in 1926 to relieve himself on his mail route from Portland to San Francisco.[1]

Corning's airport, Woodson Field, has incorrectly been called the oldest airport in the north state. It was located one mile north of the railroad station with a landing strip 2,000 by 600 feet.[2] When Woodson developed the airport in 1926, there were only a handful of permanent civilian airports in the north state including: Del Paso Airport at Sacramento; Durant Field at Oakland; Redwood Airport at Redwood City; Garden City Airport in San Jose; Richmond Airport; Benton Field at Redding, and Yolo Fliers Club Field at Woodland. With the exception of the last two, those sites were no longer in use by 1937. Today, Woodson Field is still Corning's airport in the same location as its founding in 1926. With the exception of the airport at Woodland and Benton Field at Redding, which is the oldest airport in the north state, no other active civilian airport in the Bay Area or the Sacramento Valley can make that claim. To be fair, it must be said the runway at Yolo Fliers Club Field at Woodland, founded in 1919, fell into disrepair and was so dangerous few pilots landed there during the early Depression years. It has been said Woodson Field was the first municipal airport constructed in Northern California. Even that is not true. Del Paso Airport, considered Sacramento's first municipal airport, had been in existence since 1919 as had the Redding airport later named Benton Field in 1928. Woodland's Yolo Fliers Club Field, now known as Woodland-Watts Airport, was opened in 1920. Oakland's Durant Field was created in 1919 and Redwood Airport at Redwood City in 1916. Marina Field, San Francisco's first municipal airport was in operation by 1919.

A YEAR AFTER the army's forest patrol had begun their flights from the airfield on the northwest corner of Corning, residents were excited to learn the Gates Flying Circus was coming to Round-Up Ranch, east of nearby Vina, in May 1922 to put on an air show. Air shows put on by Ivan Gates had been held to great acclaim at Crissy Field, Mather Field, and Fresno.

Wesley May, Gates' parachutist, would jump from 5,000 feet and drop a 1,000 feet or more before opening his chute. Lowell Yerex was known for his crazy aerobatic maneuvers. Best of all was Clyde "Upside Down" Pangborn who became legend for his inverted flying stunts rarely done in 1922.[3] Pangborn was well known in the area for his Glenn County Fair exhibition at Orland in 1920. He taxied his Jenny up Colusa Street in the parade opening the fair.[4]

Other Gates Flying Circus pilots at Round-Up Ranch's May 14 air show were Joe Dawson and Bill Morris, veteran pilots from Marina Field, San Francisco and other Bay Area fliers Cloyd Clevenger, Dick Doane, and Mike Doolin. Chico Pyramid of the Sciots, a fraternal organization, organized the air show. The location was also known as the Bennet and Bell Ranch located between Chico and Red Bluff.[5]

In September 1925 Ned Torrey of Corning, having completed his hitch in Uncle Sam's Air Service, bought a three-seat biplane (probably a Standard J-1) from a government surplus sale. Ned was the brother of future Corning airport manager, Ben Torrey.

By January 1927, the Klamath Air Service Company of Klamath Falls, Oregon, was operating Woodson Field at Corning. The manager, Jess E. Hart, was considered Corning's pioneer aviator. Klamath Air Service merged with Bill Waterhouse's Waterhouse Aircraft, Inc. to manufacture the Waterhouse Cruzair, a Ryan M-1 mailplane clone. Warren Woodson wanted aircraft manufacturing at Corning. By fall 1927, the venture went bust and Klamath went bankrupt after selling its Cruzair and an engineless Romair biplane to satisfy a loan from Woodson's Bank of Corning. The creditors got a 17 percent court settlement on September 26, 1927.[6] Two months later, an ad appeared in *Western Flying* stating: "Corning Cal. Airport – An ideal location for airplane factory or assembling plant... 240 acres in field ... town of 2,500 people ...1.5 hours from San Francisco, 1 hour from Sacramento ... 1.5 to 2 hours from Medford. W. N. Woodson, Secretary of Corning Chamber of Commerce."[7]

Ben Torrey was hired by Warren Woodson to manage Corning Airport, also known as Woodson Field, on September 19, 1927. In a position he would hold for over ten years, he became the heart and soul of the airfield. When Torrey took over, Corning was the best available fuel stop on the San Francisco to Seattle route for Pacific Air Transport airmail pilots and soon the airliners of West Coast Air Transport.

Torrey was born in Milan, Missouri, on May 6, 1896. His family came to California in 1906 and eventually settled in Corning. In 1911 Torrey, 15, joined the navy and served three years. He began working in 1916 as an apprentice machinist and mechanic for the Hall-Scott Motor Company at Fifth and Snyder streets in Berkeley. He was an Army Air Service mechanic during the Great War at Camp Lewis in Washington. After the war, he transferred to the flying school at Mather Field and flew in its Ninth Aero Squadron during 1920–1921. He left the Army Air Service and returned to working for Hall-Scott.

Torrey partnered with W. A. "Sandy" Sanders in a flying business and airport on the northern end of Bay Farm Island. Sanders opened his airport on Bay Farm Island in 1920, which was barren except for a few truck farms on the northwestern section of the island. Sanders, joined a short time later by Torrey, acquired use of an old barn on the island and used it to hangar his airplanes. The location was such an ideal spot for an airport the two men went before the Alameda Chamber of Commerce to see if Alameda would develop a proper airport there but couldn't persuade them. The central and southern part of Bay Farm Island would become Oakland Municipal Airport in 1927.

At Corning Torrey was granted a Department of Commerce, Aeronautics Branch (DOC) airplane and engine mechanic license in 1927, possibly the earliest one issued in the northern Sacramento Valley. On April 21, 1927, Torrey completed the construction of what he thought was the first airplane built in Northern California following the conclusion of the Great War. In June 1930, Torrey was granted his transport pilot license.[8]

The DOC rated Corning Airport as a permanent commercial airport in late 1927. A description of the airport listed its elevation as 272 feet and 1.5 miles from the Corning business district. Rectangular in shape it had two runways with good drainage. There were 30-foot power poles on the south and east sides of the field. A 100-foot landing circle marked the center of the field. CORNING AIRPORT was written in six-foot letters on the roof of the hangar. There was a wind cone mounted on a 50-foot movable pipe, and lights for safe night landings. On the field were: oil and gas service, fire apparatus, guard quarters, transportation to town, telephone, repair facilities, and one hangar measuring 120 feet by 40 feet by 12 feet. A 24-inch beacon was planned for construction in the spring. The airport was near the Pacific Highway, the Southern Pacific Railway from San Francisco to Seattle, and four miles west of the Sacramento River.[9]

On a flight to Corning from an undisclosed airport in January 1928, A. B. McKenzie and passenger Phil Hobson, unknowingly lost a wheel from their American Eagle on takeoff. A phone call from their departure field was made to Corning and Ben Torrey signaled the plane on arrival. They landeded safely with minimal damage.[10]

Warren Woodson visited Sacramento in February and told everyone he met about the excellent airport facilities at Corning and at Mineral near Mt. Lassen. He was positive the two airports would become popular stops for transient pilots.[11] The schedule for West Coast Air Transport, a new airline flying passengers and mail between Seattle, Tacoma, Chehalis, Portland, Medford, Corning, and San Francisco was: Monday, Wednesday, and Friday, planes would arrive at 2:45 PM and on Tuesday, Thursday, and Saturday planes would leave Corning at 9:30 AM. The fare from Corning to San Francisco was $12.[12]

Woodson spoke to the Oroville Rotary Club in April about the importance of an airport for every city and town in the state. He said a town would be sidetracked in importance in the future if it didn't have an airport. It would be the same as having no railroad stop. He also suggested that parents give their children maps of the Sacramento Valley and put them on airplanes to see major parts of the valley from on high.[13]

Jerry Andrews and Herb Mathison of Royle Airlines closed a deal in June at Corning for the purchase of three Swallow airplanes, two powered by Hissos and the third by an OX-5.[14]

The airport at Mineral near the base of Mt. Lassen was on the estate of W. E. Gerber of Sacramento. The local folks thought it was a wonderful sight to watch the Standard Oil tri-motor Ford land in such beautiful surroundings. When the Ford came to Mineral, it was usually carrying W. J. Hanna from San Francisco, he was vice president of Standard Oil Company of California. He used the Ford often to travel from San Francisco to his summer home at Morgan Springs near Mineral in Tehama County.

The 1928 Ford Reliability Air Tour designated Corning a stop for fuel and lunch during its July national tour. It was an honor for Corning to be chosen as part of this famous air race around the United States. Well-known names in American aviation flew in the Ford Reliability Tours of 1925–1931. The tours' mission statement was defined before its first tour in 1925, "… to end the dominance of the military [in aviation] and the emphasis on thrills and stunt flying, [and] demonstrate the reliability of travel by air on a predetermined schedule regardless of intermediate ground facilities."[15]

At least 26 tour planes would arrive at Corning on July 16, 1928, including famous aviators Frank Hawks, Eddie Stinson, Al Henley, William Brock, Vance Breese, Lee Schoenhair, George Haldeman, Cloyd Clevenger, Phoebe Omlie, and Ben O. Howard. Among the six pilots of the accompanying support planes (not contestants) were Martin Jensen and Emory

Bronte.[16]

Woodson, in a letter to tour manager Ray Cooper, assured Corning's readiness at whatever hour the planes arrived. There would be chilled melon, sandwiches, jars of Corning's world famous olives, and cool or hot drinks for the pilots. Corning women would serve everything in the hangar. He added that all city stores and businesses would close their doors from 9:00 AM to 2:00 PM. so that all of the townspeople could watch the planes land.

Rotary Club volunteers would observe the planes and be field officials. The field was marked per Ford Tour instructions. Standard Oil would have eight fuel trucks on the field. Woodson confirmed people were coming from towns and communities all around the north valley. He told Cooper to warn everyone the temperature would probably be over 100 degrees. He also asked Cooper to phone upon arrival in San Francisco and approximate the time the first tour aircraft would arrive in Corning so he could coordinate the events. He ended his letter: "Corning will be happy to greet, serve and regale you."[17]

The event started in early morning when Capt. R. G. Breen landed with tour referee Collins from the US Army Air Service headquarters at Wright Field, Dayton, Ohio. Their huge tri-motor Fokker and Ford support transports were lined up first on the field next to a Waco with "Baby Ruth" printed on its fuselage. They prepared for the tour planes to arrive from San Francisco. A crowd of 7,500 to 10,000 had assembled.

The first competitor arriving was a Lockheed Vega monoplane flown by Robert Canwell in 1 hour and 12 minutes. Next came Al Henley in a Ryan Brougham, Henley had been in the Dole Race to Hawaii. Twenty-four planes landed that day. Twenty-six had started the tour at Detroit on June 30, but four dropped out and two were added. Mrs. Phoebe Omlie in her Monocoupe 70 was forced down at Marfa, Texas, but the determined pilot borrowed a plane and continued. Aircraft started leaving Corning at 10:30 at one-minute intervals for Medford.

Mrs. Omlie was delayed at Mills Field because her mechanic accidently shattered her propeller. She hired another mechanic, found another propeller, and reached Corning at 11:30 after everyone had taken off for Oregon. She refueled and left immediately, hoping to catch up. Dan Robinson, flying plane No. 5, a Curtiss Robin, broke his tailskid attempting to take off from Corning. He was delayed for repairs.

Beginning with Captain Breen's arrival at Woodson Field, the planes extended out a half-mile on final approach to the airport. Upon landing, a referee directed every movement of the plane until it was parked on the line in front of spectators. Each plane was inspected and a record of its condition and time of arrival was noted. After the inspection, the pilot was released for lunch. The local Rotary Club handled all these details efficiently. Referee Collins complimented the outstanding job done by the community. The 1928 tour was the only one of the seven annual Ford tours flown to the West Coast. The others toured the Midwest, the East, and the South.

Other Corning activities in July 1928 were: the DOC issued Ben Torrey a registration number for his Hall-Scott powered, Curtiss JN-4.[18] Ted Campbell, Beacon Airways manager at San Francisco, reported Beacon was considering making Corning a stop for a new air service. It would cut hundreds of miles from transcontinental flight for passengers wanting to go from Reno to points north of Sacramento. The plan was not adopted.[19]

Frank W. Anderline, formerly with Pacific Air Transport, became the "Lone Eagle" (one of Lindbergh's many nicknames) of the Portland–Yakima Airline in July. The airline was part of (Tex) Rankin Flying Service of Portland, Oregon.[20] Anderline, while flying for Rankin, crashed taking off from Corning Airport on August 10 after trying to climb too quickly.[21] He was pulled from the wreckage unconscious and suffering from severe shock and possible internal injuries. His plane hit a "hot air pocket" (downdraft) at 150 feet. Witnesses said the plane took off normally and was climbing steadily when it hit the air pocket, then nose-dived into the ground. The plane was destroyed. There were no passengers.

Anderline regained consciousness, but the Corning doctor sent him to Enloe Hospital at Chico in the Westfall ambulance with Dr. Moulton accompanying him. Judge T. K. Kelly of Minneapolis, Minnesota, had flown the airplane shortly before Anderline crashed and said it was running fine when he flew it. Anderline had no life threatening injuries when examined the next morning.[22] He continued flying for Rankin several years. Later he became a West Coast Air Transport captain and finally a United Air Lines captain, a position he held until World War II.[23]

Warren Woodson established the airport at Mineral. Its elevation was 5,000 feet and had a 4,200-foot runway.[24] However, Woodson's airport at Corning was described as one of the nation's best considering the size of the community. One of the pioneer airfields in Northern California, it was only five minutes by car to the town's Hotel Maywood. By 1928, the field had a runway a mile long and 2,000 feet wide. Its hangar could accommodate three airplanes, and the overhang would shelter three more. Restrooms and showers were on site, and there was a room for the caretaker. A skilled mechanic was also available. Warren Woodson spent a lot of time and money enhancing the airport's reputation.[25]

A West Coast Air Transport tri-motor Bach airliner carrying six passengers and two pilots departed Corning November 3, 1928. Captain L. C. Goldsmith got lost in fog and they crashed near De Sabla Reservoir in mountainous eastern Butte County. He, copilot N. B. Evans, and all the passengers aboard the airliner survived. (There is a detailed description of the crash and rescue of the survivors in this author's book *Golden Wings Over the Feather River*.)[26]

West Coast Air Transport, a subsidiary of Pickwick Airways, would begin operating from Portland to San Francisco in December. Another subsidiary of Pickwick, Capital Air Service, operated planes twice a day between Sacramento and San Francisco. Capital planes pick up passengers on transcontinental planes with connections to California's southern cities at San Francisco and would meet those with connections to northern cities at Corning and fly them to their destinations.[27]

Corning's pioneer aviator, Jess Hart, was chosen to make an unusual charter flight for his new employer Maddux Air Lines in March 1929. Hollywood's royal couple, Mary Pickford and Douglas Fairbanks, wanted an airliner to fly them over the battlefield of a Mexican revolution near the Texas/Mexico border. Jess Hart with Stewart Wilkinson as copilot, would fly the party in one of the Maddux tri-motor Fords. In addition to the glamorous couple, accompanying guests were their daughter Gwendolyn Pickford Fairbanks, Mr. and Mrs. John Fairbanks, Mr. and Mrs. Schalif, and Lillian Gish. The Maddux Ford departed Glendale's Grand Central Air Terminal with its eight passengers, Sunday, March 23 and landed at Phoenix, Arizona, that afternoon following a flight along the Mexican border. After spending the night in Phoenix, the party was flown to El Paso, Texas, and spent the day cruising above the war zone. The next day they made a side trip over the Grand Canyon and the Painted Desert area. They returned to Los Angeles about March 27.[28]

This last revolution in Mexico was known as the Cristiados War. It was dangerous to be flying a Ford transport over the battlefield. The Mexican government had aircraft over the battle sites and were opposed by planes flown by mercenary pilots, which included a few Americans. One would hope the Maddux Ford remained on the American side of the Rio Grande to view the battlefield from above El Paso.[29]

In March with weather improving at Corning, Ben Torrey and Floyd Nolta spent a Sunday giving flying instruction and hopping passengers at Woodson Field. Nolta taught five students, and Torrey spent the afternoon flying passengers. Nolta's students were Charles Cramp and Paul Hobson of Corning; Milton Finch from El Camino; and Judge Stryker. Leo Mello, formerly of the Army Air Service and a member of the Army Reserve, took a short lesson to brush up on his flying. Torrey would be training students and hopping passengers on Sundays that summer.[30] Ben Torrey had 15 students by April, and the latest to sign on were his brother Ned, Elgie Stillwell of Gerber, and Art Smith. If enrollment stayed the same or increased, lessons would have to be given twice a week.[31]

D. E. Little established a weather reporting station for the lower Sacramento Valley airways in April. Little was a chief meteorologist for the DOC. A telegraph printer was installed at Corning Airport to receive reports from the central station. Instruments to record and report local weather conditions data were planned for the airport.[32]

Warren Woodson was presented with an engraved certificate from the Daniel Guggenheim Fund for the Promotion of Aeronautics in May 1929 for his part in making Corning Airport a necessary element of the nationwide system of aerial transportation. Reporting his award, the newspaper stated Woodson "... had a hunch some three years ago, when he began the development of the field..."; lending proof that Woodson developed the airfield in 1926 not 1925 or 1924 as stated in later reports concerning Corning Airport's history. It explained further that Woodson had 750 yards of gravel hauled in for the runways after the ground was leveled and graded. Earl Kelly an aviator from Redding told the Rotary Club when the award was announced, Corning Airport was the safest airport north of Oakland Municipal. He said no other airport north of Oakland had a powered gas pump while Corning had three: Union Oil, Richfield Oil, and Standard Oil. These were each capable of pumping 20 gallons a minute, allowing transports to refuel quickly. Tri-motor Bachs refueled in ten minutes. Ben Torrey, field mechanic and airport manager, was noted for repairing the Bachs' persistent magneto problems fast and get them flying again. A blackboard was mounted on the side of the shop hangar with current weather reports furnished by phone from the DOC for departing aviators.

In May, planes were landing with passengers who boarded a small local plane to take them up and land beside the best trout streams in the mountains, all within 25 minutes from the time their feet touched ground at

Corning.³³

Maddux Air Lines put out a press release on May 8, 1929, that the public could see Mt. Lassen, the only active volcano in the United States, from a Maddux airliner. Maddux sent one of its Fords to Corning to give rides over the volcano. Maddux claimed to be the oldest airline in the state, and that their experienced pilots flew the finest aircraft.³⁴

W. E. Wynn, vice president of operations for the Sierra Pacific Air Transit Company, reported that due to problems in getting delivery of their amphibian aircraft, operations would not be starting in the Great Central Valley. The is no evidence the airline ever got started.³⁵

Ruth Elder, one of the best-known of women pilots in America, flew into Corning late on June 19. She was training for the first National Women's Air Derby of 1929, a cross-country air race starting in August at Clover Field, Santa Monica, and ending in Cleveland, Ohio. She told Ben Torrey the nation's top female pilots would take part in what was later named the Powder-Puff Derby.

In September 1927, Elder tried to cross the Atlantic with George Halderman in a Whirlwind powered Stinson monoplane. They took off for Paris from Mitchell Field, New York. After 22 hours over the Atlantic and fighting a heavy storm for the last seven hours, engine problems brought them down. They splashed down near a freighter and were saved by its crew. As it was hoisted aboard in the heavy seas, the Stinson was wrecked against the side of the ship. They had flown within 300 miles of Paris and even though they landed in the sea, they were still given a great welcome upon arrival. It was said to have rivaled Lindbergh's reception. Their attempt came after Chamberlin and Levine had already made a successful second crossing.

Ruth Elder and Jim Granger, the Pacific coast distributor of Swallow Aircraft, had recently flown to Seattle stopping in Corning on June 8 for gas and lunch. They stayed in Corning on their way back to the south state. Miss Elder told a Corning reporter after a swim in Hotel Maywood's pool, she enjoyed her hotel swim much more than the one in the Atlantic on her flight to Paris. After her swim, she took her Swallow biplane up for an impromptu solo exhibition. Miss Elder kindly posed for several photographs, which would be available for purchase at Franklin's Studio. Both flyers were impressed with Corning Airport and the hospitality shown them The pair left on June 20 and said they would stop again when in the area.³⁶

Roy DeHaven and passenger Fern "Speed" Durand crashed an OX-5 Standard into an olive orchard just after departing the southwest boundary of Corning Airport about 10:30 AM on July 26. They had flown from their Red Bluff home field to Corning on business. After takeoff, at 150 feet, the OX-5 began missing. Losing airspeed and facing high-tension power lines directly ahead, De Haven turned to the right towards the orchard. Unfortunately the plane slowed even more in the turn, went into a spin, and crashed turning end-for-end. Both men were shaken, but only received minor scratches and bruises. Only the engine and instruments could be salvaged. Its owners were Gus Johnson and Roy DeHaven from Red Bluff. Three months earlier, this same aircraft crashed only 200 feet from DeHaven's crash site. Volney Chadwick of Red Bluff was flying it. [37]

A tri-motor Kreutzer Air Coach owned by Mar-Jones Mining Company landed at Corning on July 27. The pilot and his three passengers were inspecting the Northwest for mining possibilities. A Fairchild aerial photo plane landed at Corning the same day. Frank Moore, its pilot, and H. N. Guernsy observed the field from the air and decided to land. They had flown up to Corning to make an aerial map of an area known as Morgan Springs. R. W. Hanna, vice president of Standard Oil, had purchased the property and was completely renovating the famous old resort that was enjoyed by Tehama County citizens since the 1860s. State highways and airways were giving new life to the mountain regions.[38]

Jim Granger granted Ben Torrey the northern territory dealership of Swallow airplanes. The Speed Johnson Flying School at San Mateo was distributor for the central portion of the state, and Granger handled Southern California sales.[39]

West Coast Air Transport Co. sent official word to Corning Airport on July 31, 1929, that starting August 10 both its north and southbound planes would be flying in and out of Corning Airport. The company, purchased by Western Air Express, was operating tri-motor Bachs. The Bachs would only be used on the northern route between Portland and Seattle. New tri-motor Fokkers with more powerful engines would handle passenger loads from Portland to points south. Fokkers could carry more passengers than the Bachs, now operating at full capacity.[40]

David S. Ingalls, assistant secretary of the navy, spent November 5, 1929, in the Bay Area inspecting a proposed site at Sunnyvale for a new dirigible landing field for the Pacific coast. The following day, his pilot Lieutenant Cuddahy landed Ingall's tri-motor transport at Corning. Ingall's party included: E. L. Johnson, a business associate; Lt. Commander Molten; Lt. Cuddahy, the pilot; plus a copilot and a mechanic all from Washington, D.

C. The trimotor was refueled and the crew took on a cargo of Maywood's Sevillano olives, Corning avocados, and two dozen Hotel Maywood sandwiches. Big Ben Torrey at the Corning hangar snapped a good picture of the party of high flyers. It was later said, "Dollars do drop from the sky into Corning's pockets."[41]

Corning's runways needed more gravel to handle heavy transports like Ingall's and West Coast Air Transport's for the upcoming winter. The residents wanted to uphold Corning's good relationship with the aviation community and maintain the reputation Warren Woodson had fostered through his own efforts and money. It was decided December 3 would be Gravel Day. Everyone with a truck, pick-up, or wagon was to show up at the nearby gravel quarry and haul gravel to the airport all day. Corning businesses closed so everyone who wanted to help out could. One hundred fifty men shoveled 458 loads of gravel on to the runway, spreading it evenly. The nine yards of gravel hauled to the airport were worth $1,350. Every man who handled a shovel or drove a truck, and every woman who made sandwiches for the volunteers, got his or her name published in the Corning newspaper the next day. Gravel Day was the community's Christmas present to the airport.[42]

In June 1930, a dozen people saw Henry Lechen's cry for help as he was swept down the Sacramento River. They thought he was joking. He went into the rapids below the highway bridge at Red Bluff and disappeared. Sheriff Hull at Red Bluff immediately called Ben Torrey in Corning and asked him to make an aerial search for Lechen's body. Torrey came right away but never found a trace of Lechen.[43]

Mineral Airport was a busy site on Fourth of July weekend; planes were coming and going continuously. A dozen airplanes were on field all day Sunday. The airfield, established by Warren Woodson, was known as the Battle Creek Bowl. It was a dried up lake bed, which left a large, smooth, level meadow.[44]

CORNING CELEBRATED ITS official airport opening October 4–5, 1930, with an air show on Sunday. Saturday was arrival day, which also brought out crowds. Before landing, three army observation biplanes under command of Crissy Field flight surgeon Major Marsh, passed over the field in a demonstration of formation flying with their Curtiss Conqueror engines roaring. Several lieutenants tagged along as passengers. Airplane rides were given both days at five dollars for five-minutes, an eternity for the less brave. Hawkers had customers lined up, and no time was wasted loading and unloading passengers. An aviators' ball that night at Idyllwild Dance Hall across the river was well attended.

Thirty-one planes were on the field Sunday for the air show. Chief attractions were aerobatic exhibitions by Bob Streif of Redding and Joe Hicks from Chico thrilling the crowd with fancy flying. In his rush to get into the air for his performance, Ben Torrey forgot to close the baggage compartment on his plane. After Torrey climbed to ten thousand feet, he rolled the plane upside-down, and a flurry of tools fell out, which luckily didn't hit anyone on the ground. He did every maneuver he could think of including inverted flying, spins, loops, and a dead stick landing. It is amazing he thought it safe to do aerobatics with loose tools in the compartment.

A pylon air race at 4:00 over a triangular course ended in a tie for first place; Joe Hicks and Bob Streif split the $250 purse. The final event featured Hollywood's Firpo Zeman jumping from Speed Nolta's plane. Once clear of the plane, he pulled the ripcord and nothing happened. He jerked it a second time successfully, allowing him to float safely to the ground.

A reporter wrote of Sunday's stunt flying as being, "... too frequent, rapid and intricate ..." for him to describe. His description of the planes was they "... wallow around in the air like a porpoise wallows around in San Francisco Bay." Arthur Wilcox, owner of a large cattle ranch some distance from the field, hired a visiting Fleet airplane to take him over his ranch, which he had never seen from the air. His flight took an hour. The air show ended at 6:00 accident free and a success. An estimated 2,000 automobiles came through the airport gates Sunday, yielding several thousand spectators.[45]

CORNING AIRPORT MANAGER Ben Torrey acquired a Pitcairn Sport Mailplane in April 1931. He kept it in the airport hangar to use for charter work. It carried two passengers, was powered by a Whirlwind, and had a top speed of 147 mph.[46]

Tex Rankin and Dorothy Hester, holders of the world outside loop records, were hired as the featured flyers for the Sunday, June 7, 1931, air show at Corning. Rankin held the record with 76 consecutive outside loops, and Hester the women's record with 23. Two weeks before her Corning exhibition, Dorothy Hester, 19, set a new record of 56 consecutive inverted barrel rolls over a span of 1.5 hours at the Omaha Air Races. A number of notable pilots and planes would be coming to the June air show said Ben Torrey, who was organizing it.[47]

Over 4,000 people came to that second annual air show and were mesmerized from the opening stunts until it closed late in the day. Tex Rankin and his protégé, Dorothy Hester, were the stars among the exhibition flyers at the show.[48] Army Air Corps Lieutenant Kingham of Mather Field was forced to bail out of his Boeing P-12 pursuit plane during his second appearance of the day, after it went out of control at 1,500 feet a few miles from the field.[49]

The DOC Airways Division in January 1932 obtained a ten-year lease for the Corning Airport to be operated as an intermediate landing field on the northern airmail route. Further improvements would be made by the government.[50] Warren Nicholas Woodson celebrated his 69th birthday August 30, 1932. The "Daddy of Corning" practically sprinted into the road to pick up a package in the middle of Solano Street just a few feet from his office, dropped from an airplane by Ben Torrey. In it was a scroll from all his business friends who signed their names congratulating him on his birthday. Woodson was deeply touched by the gesture.[51]

Many Sacramento Valley commercial pilots struggled through the Great Depression putting food on the table and keeping their flying business alive. Ben Torrey took every flying job that came his way, some of which were illegal and even repugnant. Torrey's airport was in a farming and ranching community and farmers and ranchers generated most of the income earned by the rest of the community. If farmers or ranchers needed a service only an airplane could provide, Ben would move heaven or hell to provide it for them.

Following are some notable aerial activities at Corning the summer of 1932. On June 30 Ben Torrey's rowboat, painted chrome yellow inside, was stolen. Torrey made a 10-minute flight down the Sacramento River and found his boat 2.5 miles south of the Woodson Bridge. It was on a sand bar along the west bank. A week before, Torrey spent 25 minutes searching for Hugh Martin's missing rowboat, which he discovered eight miles down river.[52]

On July 5, Torrey flew his Waco 10 to Sacramento on business and pleasure.[53] Three weeks later he departed Corning Airport in the Waco heading east for Loyalton in Sierra County to meet up with Miss Esther McCollum. She would join him in her Kinner powered Consolidated Fleet biplane for the rest of their journey to Pyramid Lake, Nevada, and the two planes would search for the body of a Berkeley woman who disappeared while fishing. They never located it, but later Native Americans from the nearby reservation dragged the lake with barbed wire and found the body.[54]

A newspaper reported, "Ben Torrey, Corning's aerial hunter, brought in a live golden eagle Saturday afternoon after a flight over the Sutfin property." At 4:15 PM on a Saturday, Torrey received a telephone call from Omar E. Sutfin who told Ben a big eagle was preying on his lambs. Torrey took off in his plane, and 35 minutes later returned to Woodson Field with the eagle, which had an eight-foot wing spread. He spotted the big bird near a barn on Sutfin's ranch and chased it out into an open place before firing. The eagle was stunned by the shot and fell to the ground. Torrey landed, bound up the eagle's claws, and took off again for the airport. Wool found clinging to the claws of the eagle showed it had been carrying off lambs.[55]

Hollywood movie star Wallace Beery accompanied by his wife landed at Corning in August 1932 in his red Bellanca monoplane powered by a 425hp. Wasp engine. While the plane was being fueled, they went into Corning for breakfast and were off for Los Angeles an hour later.[56]

Ben Torrey made arrangements in late August to relay weather reports from the Pacific Airways Teletype service at Corning to airport operators at Chico, Red Bluff, Oroville, Willows, and Orland.[57] Torrey flew to Lincoln with two passengers on September 11. One of them, Walter Correa, went to visit his parents in Newcastle. After visiting Correa's parents, the three men departed for Corning as darkness fell. Suddenly and unexpectedly the engine quit, forcing Torrey to crash land. Realizing the plane was overdue, E. J. Lawrence found Torrey and his passengers uninjured and brought them to Corning. The Corning Airport floodlights had been turned on by Lucius Preble for Torrey's return, but his plane ran out of gas and crashed on the way back.

Torrey said later someone had stolen four gallons of gas while his plane was parked at Lincoln. He should have had enough gas for 1 hour and 45 minutes. He didn't explain how he happened to crash north of Corning when Lincoln was southeast. Could he have been lost in the darkness and burned up his fuel looking for the airport?[58]

Every effort was made to make Corning Airport financially self-sufficient during the Depression. This included raising crops on ground not used for landing aircraft. The first crop taken off the airport was eight tons of hay harvested earlier in the summer by Warren Woodson. The airport's second crop that season was harvested in early October 1932 by Ben Torrey. Without any fertilizer, he grew giant sunflowers. The seeds were used to feed Torrey's carrier pigeons kept in the airport hangar.⁵⁹

Torrey received a call October 16 from the manager of State Theater in Red Bluff. He asked Torrey to fly to Sacramento and pick up the film scheduled to show that day. *The Vanishing Frontier* had been flown from San Francisco to Sacramento on Varney Air Lines but failed to make connections to Red Bluff. Torrey and Walter Correa departed as soon as possible in Torrey's Waco. With a strong tailwind they made it to Sacramento in 1 hour and 3 minutes. Returning to Red Bluff took 1 hour and 35 minutes. The film was delivered 20 minutes before the afternoon show time.⁶⁰

Ben Torrey had to fly to Sacramento in November. He placed an ad in the Corning newspaper stating, "Wanted – Three passengers to fly to Sacramento and return Sunday in six-place Ryan monoplane. Fare ten dollars each round-trip. Ben Torrey, Corning Airport." He obviously hoped to cover expenses by turning the trip into a paying charter flight.⁶¹

Torrey went to Sacramento to pick up the leased Ryan to use November 13 when he was to return to the capital, pick up Governor James Rolph, Jr., and bring him to Corning to give a speech officially opening the rotary drilling action for the first new test hole for gas or oil in the area. Tehama Petroleum Corporation would be drilling for El Claro Oil and Gas Company on a site 21 miles southwest of Corning on the Masterson property. It was estimated 5,000 people would attend the celebration. Ben Torrey needed the Ryan Brougham's six-seat passenger capacity to haul the governor and his entourage to Corning.⁶²

Corning had the largest lighted airport north of the Golden Gate in January 1933. The boundary was lit approximately one mile on each side. Ben Torrey flipped the switch that illuminated the entire government-leased airfield for the first time on the night of January 24. Power poles on the east side of the airport and the north and east ends of the hangar had red obstruction lights in addition to the boundary lights.⁶³

Ben Torrey flew his brother Ned and four friends in Ben's newly acquired Ryan Brougham to Howell's Camp in the Coast Range February 5. They saw snow up to the eaves on the cabins indicating heavy fresh snowfall. They returned to Corning by way of the Lowery District and saw oil wells: Heavy No. 2, Marker No. 1, and Scharr No. 1. Upon returning to Corning, Mrs. Gupton joined the party and Torrey flew them over Red Bluff, Los Robles, Los Molinos, and Vina.

Torrey spent ten days doing a major overhaul of the OX-5 high compression engine in his Waco 10. He increased the horsepower from 105 to

115.[64] Returning from Alameda on a February night, Ben Torrey reported he could see Corning Airport's boundary lights from 16 miles out.[65]

On a Sunday in February 1933, W. R. Brewer, president of the El Claro Oil Co., asked Torrey to fly his publicity director, E. M. Martin, and the *Los Angeles Examiner* financial editor to San Francisco Bay Airdrome to make connections with the TWA Ford flying the Alameda to Los Angeles route. The two men were driven from Willows to Corning and departed in Torrey's Waco at 2:30. The flight to Alameda only took 1 hour and 36 minutes. He was back in Corning at 6:55 pm.[66]

An unusual charter flight was requested in March 1933. Four men, whom Torrey would not identify, hired the Ryan Brougham for a flight to Sacramento. Prohibition had been repealed and the men wanted to go to Sacramento where the first legal beer in the north state would be poured on April 4. Ben declared the Ryan would be named *Steam Beer Special* for the occasion.[67]

John A. Macready had to crash land his Shell Oil Lockheed Orion a half-mile east of Corning Airport after running out of fuel. He was attempting to glide dead stick to the airport but ran out of airspeed and altitude. Macready was flying from Portland to San Francisco in one of the fastest passenger planes on the West Coast. Top speed was 270 mph and landing speed was 75 mph. He did a masterful job handling the crash landing. He wiped the wings off in an old almond orchard taking out nine trees, but walked away unhurt. Macready, head of Shell Oil's aviation department, left the plane in Ben Torrey's care directing him to dismantle what was left of the plane and ship it to Burbank for rebuilding. Torrey said the Orion was valued at $35,000 and had $7,000 to $10,000 of damage, all covered by insurance.[68]

E. E. Johnson, traffic manager of United Air Lines, appointed Ben Torrey in May as representative for UAL, which qualified him to make ticket reservations for any point in the United States served by the company and connecting air lines. Corning was the only California airport north of Sacramento where this service could be rendered. From Sacramento, a UAL plane could make the transcontinental trip in 28 flying hours, approximately one-third the time it took a passenger train. Johnson had been the traffic manager for West Coast Air Transport Company, which began operations out of Corning Airport five-and-a-half years before Torrey's appointment.[69]

Torrey donated a 10-foot wind cone to Mineral Airport. It was taken to Mineral the first week in June and installed by Frank Becker.[70] E. M.

Patterson, manager of Fig Leaf Swimming Pool, broke his hip stepping in a ditch on the Fourth of July. Ben Torrey flew Patterson with a nurse to Los Angeles for treatment by a specialist.[71]

Earl Lee Kelly went up with Torrey for dual instruction and reacquainted himself with flying. He hadn't flown for 11 months. Kelly owned the first Waco purchased in the Sacramento Valley. He bought it in Redding in 1928 and wanted to fly it again.[72]

A new operating schedule for lights at Woodson Field became effective in late August 1933. As a cost-cutting move, boundary lights would come on at 1:00 AM and go off at sunup. Boeing 40B passenger/mail planes overflew Corning at 1:00 AM and around sunrise. Boeing and the DOC agreed to make these changes. Previously, southbound mail plane passed over at midnight and the northbound at 5:30 AM—all the lights were on then from sundown to sunup.[73] Due to more cost cutting by the US government, because of another economic dip during the Depression, two airways observers were laid off from the reporting station on Woodson Field September 15, 1933. The weather Teletype was shut down when Lucius E. Preble and Al Smith, the weather observers, were laid off. Ben Torrey said he would still be making weather observations privately and such observations would be made at other airports privately. The reports, he said, would still be reported by telephone, rather than Teletype.[74]

Torrey purchased a Ryan Brougham for his Corning business. It arrived early in October. The plane was powered by a Whirlwind engine that developed 325hp. It carried 100 gallons of gasoline and had a cruising range of 625 miles. Its cruising speed was 105 mph, top speed was 135 mph, and it could climb 900 feet per minute. The Ryan could be reconfigured as an ambulance. This factor gave Corning the best-equipped air service in the Sacramento Valley north of the Capital City. The plane was to be used exclusively for fast long flights. The Ryan was also fitted for photo work. It could carry more passengers than the Waco 10 Torrey had been flying for charter work, which now would be used mainly for student instruction.[75]

Lighting schedule at Corning Airport was rearranged in April 1934. They were used on a cost saving scheme in which they were turned on by the approach, landing, and departure of aircraft. They were no longer turned on for a six- to eight-hour block of time. The 76-foot rotating beacon tower was painted bright red and white by Joe Hicks, former Chico airport manager, and Lloyd Waterman of the DOC paint brigade.[76]

In June 1934, the following report concerning the ducks and geese used to guard the Corning Airport was published locally: "Some thoughtful and generously-minded person donated a batch of grape mash sometime Sunday evening at the airport leaving said mash at the northeast corner of the hangar." That night the guard ducks and Epsom and Pluto, the goose members of the team, ate the mash and got very drunk. Torrey said afterward they were not willing to go back to their regular barley rations, and he had to sugar coat the barley with enough mash to get them to eat. By the next morning the lead duck, Sam, had things pretty well under control with the exception of "Brown-eyes" who refused to be quieted because someone had walked on her toes during their mash party.[77]

Torrey painted the underside of his Waco's lower wings with, "Metzger for Senator" in early August and flew over towns in Metzger's senatorial district. Speed O'Donovan of Orland had chartered Torrey's plane for a flight to Sacramento and Martin Hulshizer of Orland went along as a passenger.[78]

A SOMBER NEWSPAPER article came out August 1934. It reported northern Sacramento Valley aviation pioneers dying one by one and not from natural causes. Volney Chadwick, a former Tehama County flyer who had moved from Los Molinos to Red Bluff, was killed while ferrying a plane to Morgan Hill. Gus Johnson, Chadwick's successor at Red Bluff, died when his plane spun in over his home field. By August 24, there was no commercial pilot at Red Bluff Airport. At Redding, "Ollie" Rose, who operated two commercial planes from Benton Field and provided Shasta County with aerial transportation, was "washed out" in 1932 while carrying two passengers over the Redding Airport resulting in no licensed pilot at Redding. At Chico, Willis "Billy" Welschke who worked hard to get his transport pilot license, was killed in a motorcycle accident east of Mt. Shasta City. As of August 1934 there was no one at Chico qualified to provide commercial aerial transportation to and from the city. At Willows, it was reported Speed Nolta left to work at Chicago, leaving the town without a commercial pilot.

Corning's Ben Torrey saved the day for quickly needed aerial transportation at Red Bluff, Chico, Willows, and his hometown. He was ready to go whenever the phone rang. For seven years, he had been flying any plane he was asked to fly and wherever he was paid to fly it. "Caution has been his middle name." The newspaper report concluded Corning was proud that her native son had survived in the dangerous profession he had chosen and that he had remained to provide air service for the northern Sacramento Valley.[79]

CHAPTER 17

YOUNG DON SAYLES of Corning graduated from the Boeing School of Aeronautics as an aviation mechanic at the end of August, and bought the three-place Travel Air that belonged to the late Willis Welschke of Chico. Earlier in the spring of 1934, Ben Torrey gave Sayles four hours of dual instruction and planned to continue teaching him in the newly purchased Travel Air until Sayles passed his private pilot license tests. Sayles' Travel Air had a 185hp. Challenger engine with a top speed of 135 mph and cruised at 105 mph. It could climb at 850 feet per minute. Its fuel tanks held 70 gallons of gasoline. Torrey accompanied Sayles to Chico to finalize the purchase from Welschke's father. Torrey then flew the plane to Woodson Field.[80]

One Sunday about 4:00 AM, Pacific Air Transport's northbound trimotor airliner began circling over Corning. To those on the ground, it was thought to be either off course, or its pilot wanted to land due to the nasty weather. Ben Torrey telephoned the Redding weather station explaining the situation to the person in charge, and he radioed the pilot telling him his position and estimated altitude based on Ben's phone call. The pilot continued to circle over Corning at reduced throttle settings until the weather improved and then continued northbound to Medford from Oakland. This incident was the second in a week in which bad weather caused a plane to circle over Corning until Torrey called Redding to help the pilot.[81]

Ben Torrey was the son of Mrs. Lillian Torrey of Corning. He married a Seattle nurse, Della De Boise, in November 1934 at Corning. They took off in Torrey's airplane for a short honeymoon following the ceremony then moved into a comfortable apartment at the airport, which Torrey had prepared.[82]

Corning postmaster Ray Siler suffered an appendicitis attack May 1, 1935. Ben Torrey rushed him to San Francisco for an operation at the Fort Miley Veteran's Hospital where he soon recovered.[83] Torrey, a pilot for the forest fire patrol in 1925, ironically, was burning tall grass on the Corning Airport in July 1935, he lost control and the fire swept northward toward Richfield burning 40 acres. The rural Corning and Red Bluff fire departments put it out before it reached structures.[84]

Torrey reported on July 27, 1935, recent improvements to Woodson Field put the airport in better shape than it had been since opening nine years before. Inspector Hugh Brewster of the DOC Aeronautics Branch relicensed Torrey's Waco at Willows in July; it was good until August 1936. Brewster had flown to Willows in a new DOC Stinson monoplane.[85]

The annual Corning Air Show was held before a crowd estimated between 4,500 and 7,000 on Sunday, October 20, 1935. Thirty-nine aircraft arrived at Woodson Field. The Corning Mt. Raisner Post of the American Legion sponsored it. Ben Torrey was air show manager, and Royal St. John from the San Francisco Bay Airdrome was the air show judge. Don Smith, manager of Sacramento Municipal Airport, was the show's announcer.

Torrey won the aerial bombardment (flour bombing) contest flying his Waco against Al Resse of Guerneville, Glenn Danley, Lee Moran, and Al Bryan from Willows. Next, Oakland's Dwight Clark parachuted from Resse's Travel Air at 3,000 feet.

With the free-for-all race about ready to start, Tex Hudson of Sacramento flew an aerobatic routine but had a problem at 3,500 feet. His plane went into a flat spin from which he was unable to recover. He took to his parachute, but hit the ground hard due to the strong wind. Hudson needed help collapsing the parachute in the high wind after his hard landing. The crowd rushed out to the crash, forcing the four remaining events to be cancelled. His plane was destroyed. Despite the cancellations, Ben Torrey declared the air show the best ever staged in Northern California.[86]

A 52 mph northeast gale hit Corning the last week of October and damaged the Woodson Field hangar. The sheet metal roof blew away at 9:45 PM forcing Ben Torrey out of his hangar apartment and to dress outside the building. Airplanes inside the hangar were undamaged. Torrey had braced the building earlier with heavy timbers, which prevented further damage, although it was twisted out of position by the storm.

A number of trees in Corning were toppled. Parts of Sacramento Valley suffered severe damage from the winds.[87] Hangar damage was around $1,000.

In December strong southeast winds reaching 53 mph hit the north state, but no damage occurred at the Corning airport. The highest recorded wind at Corning Airport was in February 1931; it was a southeast wind of 58 mph.[88]

Ben Torrey secured membership of 20 ranchers in the Eagle Club of the Squaw Hollow, Henleyville, Flournoy, and Paskenta districts. He wanted to begin his eagle eradication plan. The birds, which could have an eight-foot wingspan, were said to carry off ranchers' lambs and turkeys.

In January 1936 Ben Hershey, a Williams aviator and prominent rancher flew into Woodson Field to visit Torrey. He was in his OX-5 "Travelrock," as he referred to his Travel Air. He had signed up 14 sheep and turkey ranchers for the Eagle Club. Torrey said more eagles could be found on ridge tops and treetops in the foothill districts, 15 miles west of Corning.[89]

Chet Flournoy, a prominent rancher, telephoned Ben Torrey on February 5, 1936, from the Flournoy District and told him two large coyotes were doing considerable damage to his sheep flock. The coyotes were seen about eight miles west of Corning in a large open area. He offered Torrey a $20 bounty for each one Torrey shot from his plane. That was in addition to the county bounty on coyotes of four dollars for males and eight dollars for females.

Torrey took off immediately with Harold Merrill as gunner. The hunt was on. Both coyotes were spotted in the red hills standing by a recently killed sheep. Torrey maneuvered close enough for Merrill to kill one, but the other escaped. They took the corpse to Corning where several hundred people viewed it. Some sheepherders claimed it was the biggest coyote they ever saw.[90]

Bill Wallace, chief pilot for Moreau Flying Service at Oakland Airport, flew into Woodson Field in a Great Lakes biplane with his passenger millionaire lumberman H. M. Luilliwitz. They were going to Klamath Falls, but forced to land because of bad weather. Ben Torrey drove them to Klamath Falls in his car.[91] Ken Clark and his copilot flew a tri-motor Ford to Watsonville March 1. The tri-motor had been parked at Corning Airport since February 16 due to weather conditions.

Speed Nolta and Joe Bush of Willows paid Ben Torrey a visit on March 1. They were flying Nolta's J-5 Travel Air. Les Bowman, the Bay Area Waco dealer, landed at Corning in a new Waco a few days later. Dale Fry, Red Bluff airport manager, landed March 5 with one of his students, Paul Schramm. The pair stopped for fuel while en route from Chico to Red Bluff in an OX-5 American Eagle borrowed from a Mr. Kennedy. Virgil Coenen hired Ben Torrey on March 7 to fly him over seven oil wells being drilled in the Corning area so he could photograph them.[92]

On June 6, 1936, the *Sacramento Bee* published a letter to the editor written by W. A. Brandenburger. The subject was hunting condors and eagles. The letter read as follows: "Sir: I warmly appreciated your editorial in the interest of preserving the California Condor. ... What a desolate world it will be for our children's children, if they are never to feel the thrill of seeing an eagle soar the mountain tops?

"These are now rapidly being exterminated by airplane pilots as witness a recent news dispatch from Willows reporting that Fred [sic] Nolta, a Willows flier, boasted that he had killed 38 eagles only to be chagrined to learn that Ben Torrey, a flier of Corning, has 160 eagles to his 'credit.' Their vaunted prowess looks pitiable when viewed from the standpoint of keeping this small world of ours interesting and preserving its esthetic heritage for coming generations ... such acts will excite, not admiration but execration. W. A. Brandenburger"

Even though wildlife conservation laws were nonexistent, insufficient, or just ignored, the killing of these raptors did not go unnoticed by vigilant citizens.

On the other side of the argument, Ben Torrey landed in the limelight of the national farm magazine, *Country Home*. The September 1936 issue had a paragraph complimenting him for his shooting skills in his crusade against eagles and coyotes to protect the flocks of Tehama County sheep ranchers.[93]

BEN TORREY REPLACED the fabric on his Waco 10 in September assisted by "Skeet" Flournoy, David Hughes, Donald De Fries, and Arthur Austin, all air-minded young men from the Corning community. Torrey, in addition to being a licensed commercial pilot, also held airplane and engine mechanic's license 4083, issued in October 1927. The DOC registration on Torrey's Waco was NC 3724.[94]

Colonel Walter Harvey, a retired US Army officer, was staying in a mountain cabin 25 miles west of Paskenta, Tehama County, in late January 1937. His cabin was on the south range of Thomas Creek Canyon. Reportedly, he lived alone deep in the mountains for his health. He was a 73-year-old, shell-shocked, Great War veteran and had run out of supplies. An unusually heavy snowfall prevented him from getting more.

Huge snowdrifts kept at least one rescue pack train of horses from helping Harvey. It was decided Ben Torrey would air-drop supplies to the colonel. Torrey gathered 200 pounds of food and supplies at Woodson Field. He was ready to go but had to wait for the weather to break. Ned Cooper, a trapper, left Harvey two weeks' of supplies, but that was five weeks ago.

On February 14, 1937, Torrey could make a quick flight over Harvey's cabin on the Petersen property five miles southwest of Bald Rock Ranger Station, which was only open during summer. From 6,500 feet, Torrey saw no signs of life at the cabin, and snow was up to the tops of fence posts by the cabin. Ben couldn't stay long; wind over the mountains was blowing at 70 mph causing excess fuel consumption. He would try again after the wind subsided.

Chapter 17

It is unclear whether he was able to get there the next day, but he definitely got there soon because Colonel Harvey talked about it after he finally escaped the woods on March 11: "Ben Torrey's airplane flying over my cabin dropping supplies was the most welcome sight I have ever seen. I was on short rations, being low on coffee, bacon and tobacco. The first day that the airplane came over I heard it but didn't try to flag it down as I realized the danger of flying low in the canyon with a gale blowing."

Harvey did not hear radio messages from a Chico broadcasting station telling him Ben Torrey would return and drop eight sacks of provisions. However, "I stood out where I could spot each sack as it was dropped from the plane. Then I found all of them. One was completely buried in the snow and I found it after the snow had melted. Only one sack was damaged, but not seriously. It contained a pail of lard and canned goods and fell on a stump hidden by snow. I found the sack containing cigarettes first and then the one with my mail inside. They were the two things I wanted most."

Snowdrifts around his cabin were 10 to 15 feet deep. The temperature was below zero when Torrey dropped the supplies. Colonel Harvey came up with a method that would enable him to retrieve the packages, he called it "planking." Taking two one-by-twelve planks, Harvey used them as sort of a pontoon bridge to travel over the deep snow. In spite of all precautions, he made one misstep and slipped up to his neck in deep snow.

Telling his adventure, he only laughed in a jolly way and seemed none the worse for his unusual experience of being marooned. He had been gassed during the Great War; not shell-shocked as first reported. It was for his lungs that he lived in the higher altitude of the Coast Range. He said during the 15 years he'd lived in the mountains, he'd never been away from town more than five weeks at a time. Being marooned kept him from attending to important business dealings in February. Reportedly, he was hale and hearty and looked far younger than his years. Colonel Harvey had ridden out from his cabin to Paskenta on his own horse. Ned Cooper, Paskenta trapper and cattleman, had made his usual trip to Harvey's cabin on March 10 with monthly supplies. When he came back to Paskenta the next day, Harvey rode out from his cabin with him.[95]

Soon after the wind event of October 1935, work started on a new hangar at Corning's Woodson Field. It would house eight airplanes in a 140 by 40-foot enclosure. Warren Woodson stated that several new improvements were incorporated into its construction that were not in the old 1926 hangar wrecked in the wind. The most important being an especially heavy concrete foundation to which the hangar was anchored.[96]

The owner of Corning Motor Supply, Lyle Perrine, purchased a Curtiss-Wright Junior from John Martin of Willows in June 1937. Perrine was taking flying lessons from Ben Torrey and soon soloed. He had 2 hours and 35 minutes total solo flying time when he took his new Curtiss for a flight around the Corning area. He had been in the air only 10 minutes when his three-cylinder, 45hp. Szekely motor began missing badly. He throttled back and made a forced landing with no damage to himself or his plane in a grain field a half-mile north of Lover's Lane, just outside Corning.

He checked over his motor and determined it was too late to fix the plane so he left, came back the following morning, made the repairs, then flew back to the airport. Torrey complimented Perrine, a military dispatch messenger in France during the war, on the remarkable way he handled the situation.[97]

THE ANNUAL CORNING AIR SHOW of 1937 was scheduled for Sunday, October 24. It would have the usual stunt flying, air races, and flour-bombing contest plus a hog calling contest and a turkey catch. An aviators' ball would be held the night before across the river at Idyllwild.

The hog-calling contest is self explanatory, but the turkey catch was something new. Five turkeys would be released from the 75-foot airport beacon tower, and whoever caught one with his bare hands could keep the bird. It was later decided to release the turkeys from an airplane over the airport. (Is this where they got the idea for the infamous turkey drop skit on the TV show *WKRP*?) Another new feature in the air show was Chris Sauer's demonstration of his new anti-blowout car tire. Lloyd Langille of Chico drove a car at 70 mph past a man with a shotgun who shot Sauer's tire causing it to burst without endangering the car or occupant. Langille kept the car perfectly straight and under control. For the show Ray Varney from Willows would perform aerobatics, and Speed Nolta was to bring a formation of seven planes from Willows.[98]

Ben Torrey's fuel line broke on the engine of his Waco October 20 while instructing Lloyd Gray. The engine quit over Vina and Torrey glided towards Corning landing dead stick about three miles from the airport in a field near Frank Moller's ranch about 6:00 PM. No one was injured and other than a shattered propeller there was no other damage to the plane.[99]

On December 18, 1937, it was reported Ben Torrey, who managed

Chapter 17

Woodson Field for ten years, signed a contract to manage the Red Bluff Airport for the next decade. No reason was given as to why Torrey was leaving. It was a loss for the airport and the community.[100]

Woodson Field suffered another major setback in March 1938. A 65 mph wind destroyed the new hangar. The high wind damaged two planes, one of them quite severely. A newspaper photo showed a Curtiss Junior (probably Lyle Perrine's) that had been picked up by the wind, blown over a fence, and dropped upside down on the ground. Another plane had its fabric ripped completely off the airframe. The photo caption claimed airport co-manager, L. V. Turner, owned the Curtiss Junior, but it still had Corning Motor Supply painted on the vertical stabilizer. L. H. McCurley, the other co-manager, and his brother escaped from the hangar, where they were sleeping, as the roof blew off but before the walls collapsed.[101]

BEN TORREY HAD WORKED hard helping Red Bluff secure the United Air Lines contract. He was happy to hear his ambition would soon be realized. His allegiance to United Air Lines in its move to Red Bluff may have been the reason he left Corning so abruptly in December 1937.

On July 20, 1938, Corning, Red Bluff, and the rest of the northern Sacramento Valley aviation community suffered a tremendous loss. Ben Torrey died in a flying accident. He was giving lessons to student Jack Baskins, 19, of Red Bluff when their two-place cabin plane crashed four miles from Red Bluff about 6:00 in the evening. According to witnesses it appeared the plane encountered a severe downdraft and went out of control. No official reason was given, and it was not known whether Torrey or Baskins was the pilot in command.

The plane had been delivered to Red Bluff airport for local residents Courtney Bovee, Ira Wilson, and Lester McGrew early that fateful day. Torrey took it for a test flight and told the three it was the "sweetest flying" plane he had ever flown. He took student pilot Victor Werlhoff for a short flight. Then McGrew made a few preliminary test flights before Torrey and Baskins' final flight.

The make of the plane was unreported, its registration number was NC15280, and in a crash photo the rudder appears to this author as that of a Waco. The crash was on the old Schoenfeld property about two miles south of Bidwell Airport; one-third mile southwest of Matt Pimentel's ranch.[102]

The American Legion Raisner Post No. 45 gave Ben Torrey a military funeral with buglers and a rifle salute. His casket was covered with an American flag, which was presented to his family. Planes from Willows and Corning circled Sunset Hill Cemetery with Ray Varney and Speed Nolta leading the formation, which included L. H. McCurley and Lewis Turner from Corning.[103]

CORNING HELD ITS eighth annual Corning Air Show October 9, 1938. During the earlier portion of the air show, Dale Nolta easily won the light plane race with Ray Varney taking second. Glenn Danley won the flour bombing, and Nolta took second. Ray Varney did stunt flying and some skywriting. Speed Nolta was air show announcer.[104]

Bad luck plagued the aviation community that afternoon as previously mentioned. Star performers aerobatic pilot Joe Lewis and veteran parachutist Dwight Clark were both killed in separate accidents a half-hour apart in front of the audience of 4,500. E. E Hughes, CAA (later FAA) inspector for the air show, cancelled the rest of the day's flying events.

Parachutist Dorothy Barden and veteran Willows stunt pilot Ray Varney let it be known they were unafraid of any supposed jinx on Corning's air shows and would demonstrate their lack of fear by participating in the next year's show August 27, 1939.[105] Unfortunately the jinx continued. At the 1939 air show, two people were injured in a landing accident mid-show. A cabin plane flown by Elliott F. Dobbins, 23, ground looped during landing and flipped onto its back. Passengers Merle Baker of Chico, 20, and James Holland of Corning, 21, suffered minor injuries. Pilot Dobbins, who held a transport pilot license, passengers Vince Merande of Chico, 20, and Andrew Wheeler, of Corning, 16, were unhurt.

CAA inspector E. E. Hughes once again cancelled a Corning air show but not because of the accident. He cancelled because spectators rushed onto the field to get a better look at the damaged plane and refused to leave the wreck so the show could continue. This was the last notable aviation occurrence at Corning in the 1930s.[106]

CHAPTER 18

Didier Masson makes first flight in Tehama County – Red Bluff fire patrol base –Gates Flying Circus at the Round-Up – Lindbergh circles Red Bluff – "Aces Up" at the county fair – Red Bluff flying activities – The Gordon and Stryker airplane – Red Bluff loses airport managers

Didier Masson made the first aeroplane flight in Tehama County at Red Bluff on April 12, 1912. He took off from the city's first generation airport, the fairgrounds racetrack. Masson was a mechanician and spare pilot for his French countryman, Louis Paulhan, whom he accompanied from France for the January 1910 Los Angeles International Air Meet in the Dominguez Hills. Paulhan then went on an exhibition tour to a few American cities but soon returned to France frustrated by court injunctions for infringement of the Wright brothers' patent. Didier Masson stayed in America and went on his own exhibition tour.

Masson and his aeroplanes arrived in Red Bluff by rail on April 11, "… accompanied by a small army of mechanicians and assistants," led by chief engineer (mechanic) W. E. Gibson. A crowd gathered at the rail stop and watched as Masson's machines were unloaded, then followed the heavily loaded wagons to the fairgrounds where assembling began. Masson told a reporter it was a perfect day for flying and his flights should meet everyone's expectations. Miss Henrietta Lee was chosen by the faculty and students of Red Bluff High School to fly with Masson.[1]

After Masson's 1912 flight, little flying activity was reported in the Red Bluff area until the Great War. After the United States entered the war April 6, 1917, several Tehama County men joined the Army Signal Corps' Aviation Section, which became the Army Air Service. The choice was unfortunate for Red Bluff's Lt. Robinson E. Bidwell. On August 2, 1918, during a cross-country training flight from Love Field near Dallas, Texas, his Curtiss Jenny caught fire at 2,000 feet, nine miles south of Dallas. He guided his burning plane down to 500 feet. There he jumped from the plane to avoid burning to death and without a parachute he died on impact. American military aviators did not have access to parachutes during the Great War.[2] In the terminal building at Red Bluff Municipal Airport during the 1990s a display stated the airport was named Bidwell Field for Second Lieutenant Bidwell, the first Red Bluff serviceman to lose his life in the Great War.

Red Bluff residents read a July 30, 1919, local newspaper report their city would soon have airplane passenger service to Sacramento. Planes would take passengers from Red Bluff to Sacramento for ten dollars Wednesdays and Thursdays. E. H. Pendleton of the Sacramento Aviation Company at Del Paso Airport in Sacramento was coming to Red Bluff to make the arrangements. His plans for passenger service to Sacramento were premature. It would take years for the necessary infrastructure to be developed for successful scheduled passenger service in the Sacramento Valley.[3]

DAILY FOREST FIRE patrols by Army Air Service aircraft were responsible for the majority of air traffic in Shasta, Tehama, and Butte counties from 1919 through 1921. Fire patrols were the impetus for developing the first airports in those counties. They influenced thought about the possibilities, importance, and even the necessity of having access to flying service locally.

The Army Air Service fire patrol came to Tehama County in September 1919 when Lt. E. C. Kiel landed his DH-4 at Red Bluff. Colonel Henry H. "Hap" Arnold, Lieutenant Kiel's commander at Crissy Field, had ordered him to find a suitable landing field for the northern terminus of the army's fire patrol planes in Northern California. Their current terminus was a Redding airfield at the end of West Placer Street. Its runway was uncomfortably short for their DH-4s, and the locals were not acting fast enough to improve the situation. Arnold wanted all fire patrol aircraft and personnel out of Redding by September 17. Kiel found a new site at Red Bluff where town officials and residents were glad to help the army protect the nation's forests. On the 17th, the entire squadron moved to Red Bluff and managed to keep its DH-4 patrols on duty without missing a single flight. The pilots were positive about moving to the new field. It was spacious, level, and without surrounding mountains to complicate arrivals and departures. The

Army Air Service finished the 1919 fire season using Red Bluff as its northern terminus and returned to Mather Field when the season ended on the last day of October.[4]

In June 1920, the DH-4s returned to Red Bluff for another active fire patrol season. In 1921 the patrol gave up the Red Bluff base as its northern terminus to operate from a new airfield at the northwest corner of Corning. There were no Air Service fire patrols in 1922 and 1923. In 1923, the pilot of an Air Service photo reconnaissance plane was looking for a possible future landing field at Red Bluff. He found the old fire patrol landing field, but the locals had abandoned it and plowed the ground so he had to look elsewhere.[5]

The first lawsuit in Tehama County for which an automobile owner sued an airplane owner for damages sustained in a collision was filed in April 1920. W. W. Ackerman, postmaster of Gerber, was the plaintiff and O. H. Mattley, aviator, was the defendant. The case concerned the right-of-way between aerial and ground vehicles. In the early 1920s, roads in isolated mountainous areas were often the only level safe surface to fly from. Aakerman claimed his car was parked alongside the road and during takeoff Mattley misjudged his distance and tore the top off Ackerman's car. Ackerman sought damages of $256. Who prevailed is a mystery.[6]

The annual Northern California Roundup, sponsored by the Chico Pyramid No.17 of the A. O. E. Sciots, was to be held Sunday, May 14, 1922, near Vina on property midway between Red Bluff and Chico belonging to the Bennett and Bell Ranch. Usually a rodeo, this time the event was an air circus (air show). It was the first air circus in the region since the Great War ended.[7]

The fliers were pioneers of the famous Gates Flying Circus. Ivan R. Gates, a Bay Area aviation impresario of the Exhibition Years, and Lowell Yerex, a World War veteran from the British Royal Flying Corps, assembled the group. Gates managed the group and handled public relations promotional work. He called himself the director-general of the outfit and led everyone to believe he was the boss. Actually, Lowell Yerex controlled the purse strings but preferred Gates receive all of the attention, which left Yerex free to fly. Another who shaped the organization was chief pilot Clyde "Upside Down" Pangborn.

Ivan Gates had announced on May 10 he secured permission from Col. H. H. Arnold for the appearance at the Roundup of DH-4 bombers from Crissy Field.

Lowell Yerex did his clown aerobatic act at Vina. Ivan Gates claimed Yerex was a 12-victory ace from the Great War in press releases, but Yerex admitted to Clyde Pangborn his military career had been short. He had enlisted in the Royal Flying Corps but was shot down and captured by Germans. He spent the rest of the war in prison camp.

Pangborn was billed as the first pilot to fly an airplane upside down even though Gates knew Lincoln Beachey had done it years before. But Pangborn would fly a Jenny or Standard J-1 upside down until the engine quit from fuel starvation due to gravity feed fuel tanks.

The other pilots who flew for Gates during the Vina air circus were Joe Dawson, Cloyd Clevenger, Dick Doane, Mike Doolin, and Bill Morris. All were professional aviators from Marina Field in San Francisco.

Sciots from all around the north state were heading to the ranch. They were advised to arrive early and bring picnic baskets to enjoy noon hour under the beautiful oak trees prevalent on the rodeo grounds. The grounds were said to have once been home to Ishi, the last Yahi to live outside captivity, during his tribal years. Admission was one dollar. The two-and-half-hour "sky vaudeville" (air show) would start at 3:00 PM May 14.[8]

William "Bill" Morris was Gates' partner in an earlier enterprise from 1912 to about 1916. They were supplying aviators for flying exhibitions in Northern California. There is a contract extant under the Gates-Morris Company letterhead for Thaddeus Kerns of Chico to fly an exhibition in 1913; it was displayed at the Chico Air Museum in 2013.

By May 1922, the Gates Flying Circus had already lost its first wing walker and parachutist, Jinx Jenkins. Before Jenkins was killed at a Crissy Field air show in 1921, Wesley May telegrammed Gates he wanted the job of their current wing walker when he got killed. Parachutists of the day seemed to know—it was not *if*, but *when*—you would die in the dangerous profession, yet they jumped anyway. Performing at Mather Field in March 1922, Wes May thrilled and amazed a crowd of 20,000 by leaping through the air from one plane to another, then climbing from a speeding automobile into an airplane overhead; this was followed by hanging by his toes from every perch on the airplane. His finale was a 5,000-foot drop before opening his parachute.

THERE WERE FEW REPORTS of notable aerial activity during the years 1923–1926 at Red Bluff, but on May 13, 1927, James Mayberry of Fresno and Floyd Keadle of Red Bluff flew a three-seat Alexander Eaglerock to

Mount Lassen accompanied by a Mr. Davis of the Ford garage in Red Bluff. Theodore Bent of Modesto and Keadle purchased a pair of three-seat Eaglerocks with plans to make Red Bluff their base for commercial work. The planes were to be the nucleus for a new airport in Red Bluff on which the American Legion would construct its post building.[9]

Floyd Keadle, 33, was taken to Sisters' Hospital with multiple fractures of his left arm. He had made a forced landing at Redding after his engine quit on June 5. While hand cranking the propeller to get back in the air, he left the throttle wide open. When the engine started, the plane jumped forward, and the propeller struck his arm. Despite a broken arm, he grabbed the wing, jumped into the cockpit and shut off the engine avoiding damage to the plane. Shasta County traffic officer Goodlow took Keadle to the hospital. Keadle operated a commercial passenger service and had been flying in the area several days.[10]

Aviation committees of the American Legion and Red Bluff Chamber of Commerce met on July 17 to discuss the location and construction of a new airfield. Due to an airport being developed at Mineral, interest in an airfield for Red Bluff had been rekindled. Several locations were under consideration. A recent speech given at Susanville by A. H. Dudley, secretary of the Sacramento Chamber of Commerce, about the importance of a city airport increased the interest.[11]

The old Red Bluff Airport was mentioned in a new booklet titled *Airplane Landing Fields of the Pacific Coast* published by Standard Oil Company.[12]

Lieutenant Allen was flying a new type of military plane and had to make an emergency landing at Proberta's Jackson Field. He hit a ditch at the side of the field and turned over. The plane sustained considerable damage but Allen, on a flight from San Diego to Vancouver, was uninjured. Driving his car on the highway paralleling the airfield, Red Bluff physician I. R. Tremain accelerated rapidly to avoid colliding with Allen's plane as it came to rest a short distance from the road.[13]

Members of the Mt. Lassen post of the American Legion, led by commander Stan Gordon, marked off a large landing circle in the center of the as-yet-unnamed Red Bluff airfield. The reason for the markings was National Air Derby racers from Mills Field, San Francisco to Spokane, Washington, were expected to arrive on September 21. Arrangements were made to have fuel and oil on the field in addition to a large water tank wagon. A special ground handler was hired to take care of the racers as they landed.

Red Bluff was designated an official stop for aviators making their way to Spokane.[14]

CHARLES LINDBERGH CIRCLED low over Red Bluff on September 16, 1927. He was on a national tour of all 48 states in the Ryan *Spirit of St. Louis*. He left Portland at 6:55 AM, and just after noon Lindbergh appeared over Red Bluff. He was banking above Main Street and waving greetings to the hundreds of people gathered below. He leaned out of the cabin so people waving back could see him. It was reported, "A short distance south of Pine Street the air hero made a sharp turn and flew around the city hall where the fire bell was clanging in his honor. He again passed over Main Street and dropped a message on Main near Pine Street to the people of Red Bluff." Lindbergh turned again to the west and circled near the high school. He made a third pass over Main Street banking his plane with the wings almost perpendicular to the ground; the inscription *Spirit of St. Louis* on the Ryan's nose could easily be seen from below. He rolled to an upright attitude and assumed a course southward to San Francisco.

Lindbergh's message to Red Bluff read: "Greetings— To the City of Red Bluff: Aboard *Spirit of St. Louis* On Tour, Because of the limited time and the extensive itinerary of the tour of the United States now in progress to encourage popular interest in aeronautics, it is impossible for the *Spirit of St. Louis* to land in your city.

"This message from the air, however, is sent you to express our sincere appreciation of your interest in the tour and in the promotion and expansion of commercial aeronautics in the United States ... if each and every citizen in the United States cherishes an interest in flying and gives his earnest support to the air mail service and the establishment of airports and similar facilities ... [it] will result in America's taking its rightful place within a very short time as the world leader in commercial flying."

The message was signed Charles A. Lindbergh, and endorsed by Harry F. Guggenheim, president of the Daniel Guggenheim Fund for the Promotion of Aeronautics, and by William P. MacCracken, Jr., assistant secretary for aeronautics, Department of Commerce (DOC).

Two days before Lindbergh circled Red Bluff, Donald E. Kehoe, Lindbergh's assistant and pilot of his support plane, telegrammed the *Red Bluff Daily News* that Colonel Lindbergh would drop the above message over Red Bluff during his circling fly-by. Many citizens of Red Bluff believed the message would be dropped on the local airfield, and a great number gathered there. However, he dropped it on Main Street.

An oil salesman was determined to retrieve the message and take it to his hometown of Redding. He grabbed hold of Lindbergh's message, but *Red Bluff Daily News* editor Don Foster convinced him it was intended for the people of Red Bluff and, after much debate, the salesman handed it to Foster.

Lindbergh's arrival times over Northern California towns on his way to San Francisco were: Hilt 10:35 AM; Montague, 10:36; Dunsmuir, 11:10; east of Redding, 11:37; Red Bluff, 12:08 PM; Hamilton City, 12:31; and arrival over the Ferry Building in San Francisco at 1:25.[15]

ACCORDING TO A September 16 press release the National Air Derby cross-country race from New York to Spokane had 50 entrants. Eighteen were entered in the Class "A" race for larger planes and 32 planes entered the Class "B" race. These two events started at Roosevelt Field on September 23 and 24, 1927. A related simultaneous race called the Pacific Coast Air Derby from San Francisco to Spokane signed up six entries in the "B" race and five in the "A" race, according to National Air Derby headquarters.[16] The racers were to be at Mills Field no later than 9:00 AM on the 20th, the race was to start the morning of the 21st.[17]

Fig. 71. A day or two after Charles Lindbergh circled city hall at Red Bluff on September 16, 1927, during his national tour of the 48 states, his Ryan monoplane, the *Spirit of St. Louis*, was parked overnight at Mather Field while he attended various official functions in Sacramento. Notice the chalk letters under the Ryan as it sits on a concrete hangar threshold. The letters spell "WELCOME LINDY" a nickname Lindbergh hated. The letters were still there during the April 1930 Air Maneuvers.

Two unrelated crashes happened September 19 near Red Bluff. Gus Johnson with passenger Leo Wahl was flying a Curtiss biplane in the first plane crash. They had just departed Red Bluff at an altitude of 150 feet when a control wire to the ailerons broke. The plane went into three successive spins then nose-dived into the ground. Johnson cut his chin on the cowling, but other than that he and Wahl only suffered a severe shake-up. The landing gear was torn off and the lower wings destroyed. The other crash that day was a Swallow flown by its owner R. W. Martland, managing editor of the *Pacific Radiator* of Oakland. His passengers were Noel Dowe and William Richel. After developing engine problems, Martland attempted to land on rough ground, three miles east of Red Bluff. His aircraft was heavily damaged but his passengers were only shaken up a bit. The prop, landing gear, and one wing were damaged. The plane was towed into an enclosure next to Walbridge Garage for repair. Martland and his passengers were going to Spokane to watch the finish of the National and Pacific Coast Air Derbies.

Immediately after Gus Johnson's crash, two planes passed over Red Bluff Airport. One, *The City of Roses* flown by James Rhinehardt with his mother riding along, landed to help the victims. Rhinehardt was entered in the Pacific Coast Air Derby. It was decided the pilot's mother would return to Spokane by airmail plane. The other plane was *The City of Vancouver* flown by airmail pilot Vernon Brookwalter. He was also entered in the Pacific Coast Air Derby. His sister was aboard as passenger. Both pilots were flying Travel Air monoplanes and on their way to San Francisco for the race start to Spokane.[18] On September 21 the race started before dawn at Mills Field. Two hundred spectators gathered at Red Bluff Airport a little after 6:00 AM to watch the derby racers land and refuel, but only one, Arthur A. Borne, landed. He landed at 7:34, took on 20 gallons of fuel and departed at 7:38 in his Brown monoplane racer. Eight planes were sighted flying over the airport towards Spokane. Most were too high to be identified as race planes.

The San Francisco to Spokane Pacific Coast Air Derby 650-mile race started just before dawn at Mills Field on September 21. Floodlights lit the runways. The weather was perfect. Eleven planes were competing in two classes. Race officials warned pilots before takeoff to not do any aerobatics or take any unnecessary risks. The planes were required to make a fuel stop at Medford, which explained why only one racer, Borne, stopped at Red Bluff for fuel.[19]

N. C. Lippiatt won the Pacific Coast Air Derby beating Lee Schoenhair by 34 minutes to win first place and $1,500.[20] Arthur Borne, who landed at Red Bluff for fuel, encountered fog and was forced to land in a farmer's field damaging his plane in the process. Vernon Brookwalter also had to make a forced landing and walked to nearby Eugene, Oregon.[21]

C. W. "Speed" Holman of St. Paul won first place and $10,000 flying the National Air Derby. His time from New York to Spokane was 19 hours and 43 minutes. Second place and $5,000 went to E. E. Ballough of Chicago. Eight of the 15 planes that started in New York made it to Spokane on September 21.[22]

After the races, Jack Irwin passed through Red Bluff on September 28 with his little single-place Meteorplane strapped to the top of his touring car. He had hauled his little plane to Spokane to fly in the pylon races to be held there, but while test flying his plane he struck some rough ground during the landing and wiped off his landing gear and was unable to compete. He had built his plane at Sacramento.[23]

Red Bluff voters were asked to approve a $23,000 bond issue in the April 1928 municipal elections to finance the purchase of land for a permanent airport at Red Bluff. The bond issue passed by a vote of five to one. With the money in hand, the temporary airport was purchased and became the permanent airport named Bidwell Field.[24]

In April, Frank Gordon, Robert Stryker, and Charles Stryker were building *Miss Tehama*, an airplane of their own design, at their shop in Los Molinos.[25]

The federal government announced Red Bluff would soon have its own flashing airway beacon at Bidwell Airport. It was part of the project to erect beacons along the San Francisco-Seattle Airway. In the Sacramento Valley, beacons would go up at Capay, Willows, and Williams. Boundary lights and beacons would go up at Woodson Field, Corning, and Bidwell Field at Red Bluff.[26]

Air activities at Red Bluff for the summer of 1928 were as follows: Floyd Keadle reported the Portland Aerial Circus he attended in August was a success.[27] Volney Chadwick flew up and down the Sacramento River searching for the body of Roy Karsten, a Red Bluff boy who drowned with his brother in August.[28] Grading and scraping operations at Bidwell Airport were completed on August 3, and a broad expanse of smooth landing ground was prepared. A DOC inspector was requested to lay out runways.[29]

The Tehama County Fair of September 13–15 featured Aces Up, a flying circus from Oakland. It showcased Bay Area aviators including Ernie

Smith, the first civilian pilot to fly from the mainland to Hawaii, and parachutists.[30] Aces Up was under the direction of the ubiquitous A. E. Wagner from Royle Airlines at Oakland. The Red Bluff Achaeans arranged this air show and developed a 52-acre plot next to the fairgrounds as a landing field for the flying circus.

A. E. Wagner scheduled air races of 100-mile, 50-mile, and 25-mile lengths. Several Aces Up pilots were ex-Army Air Service fliers, and some had flown the airmail. There were four-, five-, and six-passenger planes at the fairgrounds landing field giving rides to whomever could pay. Aces Up had carried 4,200 passengers on flights from Oakland Airport the past year and claimed no accidents.[31]

Aces Up's slogan was, "Safety in flying." Its members were: Nelson "Jenks" (AKA Jinx) Jenkins, a former night flying instructor with the Army Air Service; Jack Ness; George Heddinger, a former Air Service and airmail pilot; Frank Rose, a former Air Service pilot during the war who later flew airmail; Ed DeLarm, who claimed being the first Native American pilot; Jerry Andrews; Ed Greer; and W. D. "Denny" Wright. Three of the airplanes flown by Aces Up pilots were: a Monocoupe with a 95hp. Velie motor; a Waco biplane with a 180hp. Hisso; and a Travel Air biplane with a 150hp. Hisso. Featured parachutist was Warren F. Hall who had 660 jumps prior to jumping at the Tehama County Fair.[32]

On the first day of the fair, Aces Up pilots flew a 50-mile race around Gerber, Corning, Vina, Los Molinos, and along the foothills to a point east of the grandstands. There they turned in a dash to the fairgrounds and flew three times around the one-mile racetrack to determine the winner. Something unusual was each pilot carried two paying passengers except the Monocoupe, which could only carry one. Pilots and passengers in the competition were: Mr. and Mrs. John M. Moore flying with Volney Chadwick; George Growney and Hugh Sisson flew with pilot "Pat" Patterson; Don McLaughlin and Bert Bell were with Jenks Jenkins; Harry Lee and Don Smith flew with Bob Barber; Craig Hamilton and L. Newberg flew with Buck Bucklin, and Claude Gordon flew in the Monocoupe with an unnamed pilot.[33]

EARL LEE KELLY of Redding became one of the first Rotarians to visit a neighbor city's Rotary Club meeting in an airplane. He flew to Red Bluff in his new Waco with Al Pilgrim as pilot. After the meeting he took Earle Brown, manager of Tehama Title Company, with them to San Francisco.[34]

Chapter 18   399

The new airport at Mineral near Lassen Volcanic National Park was developed through the generosity of W. E. Gerber of Sacramento, R. W. Hanna of San Francisco, and W. N. Woodson of Corning.[35]

The airport at Red Bluff was officially named Bidwell Airport and described in September 1928 as located 1.5 miles southwest of Red Bluff, on a wide, open plain. It was acquired under the state law passed by the legislature in 1927 allowing cities to own airport property outside the city limits. The government provided its large beacon light because the field is on the federal airway. Weather bureau records show this locality almost entirely free from winter fog, making all-year flying safe. The government weather bureau office on the airport provided information to pilots.[36]

Volney Chadwick of Red Bluff earned his transport pilot license in October 1928. He had about 500 flying hours at the time mostly in his Waco.[37] Elmer Chadwick of Red Bluff, N. Hansen of Montague, and Robert Strief of Redding, all received their private pilot licenses on the same October day from J. T. Nall, DOC aviation inspector.[38]

The city of Red Bluff announced it was taking possession of Bidwell Airport as of January 1929. The city had paid $1,279 for the 75-acre airfield to an unnamed seller. It had been graded and leveled, and the DOC had already approved it as an airport. Funds had been approved by voters in the April 1928 municipal election, but were not forthcoming until January.[39]

Three revolving beacons of two million candlepower each were set on towers in Tehama County in 1928. They marked part of the Pacific Airway between Suisun and Redding. The towers were erected on the El Camino Rancho, Bidwell Airport, and Hickman's ranch at Hooker. The last airway beacon tower to the north was at Anderson about 10 miles south of Redding in Shasta County. The Anderson tower carried the number 17 indicating to a pilot he was 170 miles from Oakland Airport. At night, its number flashed in code by small red lights near the beacon tower. A large No. 17 visible to fliers was painted on the concrete arrow at the tower's base. A light sensitive automatic instrument controlled by daylight and darkness activated the lights. This instrument was so sensitive to any change in visibility, even fog would activate the lights.[40]

Gordon and Stryker Aircraft Company of Los Molinos was building not only its own monoplane design, which was in the experimental stage, but also rebuilding a Waco 10 for owner Ed Bragdon of Red Bluff.[41] Frank Gordon and the Stryker brothers were rapidly finishing construction of the first airplane to be designed and built in Tehama County. The monoplane, powered by a 180hp. Hisso engine, held three passengers. Frank Gordon, who served in the Army Air Service during the Great War, designed the plane. He upgraded from the usual wood and fabric aircraft construction and built the wing's leading edges of aluminum.[42] The National Air and Space Museum recognizes the Gordon and Stryker airplane as the Gordon A-3 monoplane built in 1929 by the Gordon Aircraft Company of Red Bluff.[43]

Raines Griffin, who would become a prominent Red Bluff aviator, made his solo flight in March after six hours of dual instruction at Oakland Airport where Griffin was taking lessons.[44]

D. E. Little, superintending meteorologist for the Department of Commerce Aeronautics Branch, had the Red Bluff weather reporting station completely up and running by April 1929.[45] The lumber and other construction materials had been purchased for building a hangar and caretaker's cottage at Bidwell Airport. Airport development moved slowly until the money from airport bonds approved in 1928 finally became available and improvements progressed.[46]

Frank Gordon and the Stryker brothers finished *Miss Tehama* and on the morning of July 27, 1929, Gus Johnson took her up for her first test flight from Bidwell Airport. Before takeoff, Johnson was in the cockpit gunning the throttle repeatedly. Suddenly, the plane jumped the wheel chocks and its tail went up forcing the propeller tips downward catching loose gravel before the tail came back down. About a third of an inch was ground off the propeller tips. Upon inspection it was determined the prop was not damaged badly, and Johnson could take off. The plane made a run of about 150 feet and jumped into the air at a sharp angle. He was airborne for half-an-hour and made a perfect landing. He reported the plane handled well and was fast.[47]

Volney Chadwick from Red Bluff, 23, was killed August 12, 1929, flying over the town of Morgan Hill, south of San Francisco Bay. Chadwick had completed a test flight to Watsonville and was returning to Oakland against a strong headwind. Witnesses said a wing crumpled against the side of the fuselage as he passed over Morgan Hill. The plane swerved to one side, then dove into a farmer's field at terrific speed. The right wing tore loose at 2,000 feet near Morgan Hill. They said the pilot was not stunt flying; he was flying straight and level towards Oakland. The wing was found a considerable distance from the crash site.

Chadwick received his pilot's license in October 1928 and had almost

CHAPTER 18 401

1,000 hours of experience. The crash was blamed on structural failure. His mother and sister brought him to the Chadwicks' former home in Elk Creek for burial. Volney graduated from Los Molinos High School in 1926 and attended Heald's College in Sacramento. After college he took flying lessons at Sacramento's municipal airport in Del Paso Park from H. G. Andrews, formerly from Red Bluff. Chadwick moved to Red Bluff and for months flew an old Standard J-1 biplane in which he made 14 forced landings. He hoped to gain a 1,000 hours and land a job flying tri-motor airliners. When he died, Chadwick was flying for the Morgan Aircraft Company of Oakland. His job was test flying consigned aircraft and demonstrating them for prospective buyers.[48]

In late summer of 1929, Frank Gordon, of *Miss Tehama* fame, was hired as superintendent of Bidwell Airport. He was also on-site professional pilot and mechanic. Today we would call him the airport FBO or fixed base operator. He had a two year contract and lived on the airport. The local airport committee recommended Gordon for the job.[49]

Construction of the first Bidwell Airport hangar was well under way by October 1929. The 100 by 40-foot concrete floor was finished the month before.[50] The new three-plane hangar, the caretaker's cottage, and the Pacific Airways Beacon No. 17, were all in place by the end of November. The field was 2,700 x 1,400 feet; a wider field wasn't needed because most landings were to the north or south. Prevailing winds came from the north or the south 98 percent of the time.[51] The last hazard to landing at Bidwell Airport, also called Bidwell Field, was eliminated after PG&E moved the high power lines near the northern end of the field underground. Wesley Holt, a local aviation enthusiast, obtained the new right-of-way for them.[52]

Residents of Red Bluff were offered free airplane rides in Fuller Paint Company's Pitcairn biplane on June 19, 1930. W. P. Fuller authorized the rides, and his company pilot, Harvey Lemcke, made the flights. The rides were 15 minutes each with over a dozen people taking advantage of the offer. Fuller and his family, many of whom were aviators, were dedicated flying enthusiasts.[53] Also in June, requests were made to Transcontinental Air Transport and Maddux Airline pilots by the DOC to report by radio any forest fires they saw on their daily routes.[54]

John "Slim" Davis, who replaced Frank Gordon as Bidwell Airport FBO, was admitted to Sister's Hospital in Red Bluff December 1, 1930, with a broken left arm, a severely bruised left shoulder, and numerous other bruises. Davis crashed his old JN-4 biplane on Orrie Breese's ranch in Antelope

Valley and nearly destroyed it. The JN had previously crashed many times.

Davis had spent that afternoon flying over Red Bluff and the district east of the Sacramento River. He was returning to Bidwell Field and decided to buzz Breese's strawberry patch. Reportedly, Davis dove low several times flying over the Antelope District attracting the attention of residents. Several saw him crash and rushed to the site expecting to find the pilot dead. He was taken to the hospital and was said to be doing well the following day. Ben Torrey, the voluntary deputy state aviation inspector for the district, investigated and reported Davis violated state and federal aviation regulations by flying the old Jenny.

Torrey announced the public could help stop these kind of crashes by reporting to authorities any airplanes without the letters N, NC, or X preceding the large registration numbers painted on the underside of the wings. Without exception, licensed pilots were required to fly only planes with legal letters before the number. Torrey told a reporter it was against the law to fly below 1,000 feet over any city or town.[55] By 1930, Jennies from the Great War were so worn out and dangerous, the only way some pilots could be stopped from flying them was when an overzealous DOC inspector sawed the fuselage in half!

Slim Davis gave up managing Bidwell Field in early 1931 after crashing the old Jenny. He became a crop duster pilot later in his career, and after World War II he owned a crop dusting airfield and business two miles west of Colusa. The landing strip and hangars are still there, and as of 2012 Davis' airport was still on the FAA's San Francisco Sectional air map.

This author was visiting a farmer who lived across the road from Davis' landing field one day in the 1970s. They watched a Stearman PT-17 make a wide "bomber pattern" and gingerly land at Davis' airport. The PT-17, a World War II biplane trainer, had been converted into a crop duster, which was common after the war. The pilot was seeding rice fields immediately around the Davis landing strip. The PT made several trips, and the pilot kept making huge circular patterns when he turned the Stearman for each seeding pass and when landing to get more seed. It seemed he never banked more than 10 degrees in turnarounds, which is very unusual for crop dusting and seeding work. Finally this author asked the farmer, who was flying the Stearman? "Oh that's just old Slim Davis," he replied. "He still insists on seeding his own rice fields. He can't see much. He's legally blind, but there he is."[56]

Raines Griffin, originally from Winters, took over as FBO of Bidwell

Field in March 1931. He gave flying lessons there and at Redding. He purchased a Kinner powered Fleet biplane from the factory that same month for instructing.[57] In April he led a flying circus performing additional thrills for rodeo fans at the Red Bluff Roundup. Griffin joined Marshal Seagrave, "Bantie" Bannister, John Waage, and Harold F. Brown, who brought their planes from as far south as Oakland to put on a very professional exhibition at the roundup.[58]

Beginning July 14, 27 boundary lights, two floodlights for field illumination, two smaller floodlights for the field sign, and a wind cone were being installed at Bidwell Field.[59]

Mildred Mae Haekstra of Red Bluff, 16, was making great progress at Bidwell Field learning from Raines Griffin to fly. By July, she was making solo flights as long as 40 minutes.[60] Norman Krebeer, manager of the Red Bluff School of Aeronautics, offered Red Bluff Union High School an aviation ground school course for the upcoming school year to benefit the large number of students taking lessons from Griffin at the airport. Krebeer wanted the same opportunities made available to the high school students.[61]

Bidwell Airport, by October 1931, added a crosswind runway which gave the two runways an "L" shape. They were now 2,800 feet and 2,000 feet in length. The field, on the airway beacon route for Seattle, had floodlights, boundary lights, and 24-hour service.[62]

Bidwell Airport's administration building caught fire on New Year's Eve. Raines Griffen saw a small fire just above the telephone in the building and quickly put it out with a fire extinguisher. He thought there was some sort of electrical problem and that he had taken care of it. Thinking the fire was out, he went out to check the hangar, then a few minutes later he looked back and saw the administration building ablaze. He and another man tried putting the fire out, but it was out of control and destroyed the building. It had been built by volunteer labor and would cost nearly $1,000 dollars to replace. Plans were made to rebuild.[63]

A formation of 15 small planes was expected to land at Bidwell Airport May 29, 1932. It was part of an advertising campaign promoting the Los Angeles Olympics. The planes were going to visit airports at Bishop, Reno, Red Bluff, Eureka, Oakland, and Fresno. Afterwards they would travel to Oregon and Washington. The pilots were accompanied by US Olympic swimmers who swam exhibitions at each city.[64]

Raines Griffin wrecked his plane flying over the Sacramento River boat races on June 12. He swept low along the race course then turned and started to climb over a hill north of George Sutton's place at the upper end of the course. His plane couldn't climb fast enough to clear the hill and crashed between two trees. He suffered a slight cut on his face His passenger, local student pilot Cecil Landers, came away with facial cuts and a broken rib. The left wings were torn off the fuselage, the right wings were entwined in the tree branches, and the wooden propeller was shattered. The crash ended Griffen's flying career and employment as Bidwell Field's airport manager due, no doubt, to his violation of DOC regulations against low flying over a populated public event.[65]

A Lockheed Vega flown by Harry Ashe landed at Bidwell Field August 10 carrying William Gibbs McAdoo of Los Angeles. McAdoo was the former secretary of the US Treasury and a candidate for the Democratic nomination of US senator. He was going to campaign at the Hotel Tremont then fly to his next destination on a whirlwind speaking tour. He was supposed to be at Red Bluff 50 minutes sooner but had difficulty getting away from Marysville. Part of his speech severely criticized the Smoot-Hawley tariff bill, a protective measure creating a wall against exportation of American farm products and causing resentment among foreign nations. Many experts believe the Smoot-Hawley Bill was a major reason America was slow to recover from the October 1929 stock market crash.[66]

Gus Johnson, a noted Red Bluff aviator, 26, became the next manager of Bidwell Field. He succumbed to the "jinx" that befell the previous three managers of Red Bluff's airport, except his results were fatal. His plane went into a dive from an altitude of 600 feet and crashed, killing Johnson and seriously injuring passenger Henry Schafer. Johnson was flying a Consolidated Fleet biplane owned by Associated Air Services. The Fleet had recently been inspected by the DOC and relicensed. Johnson, however, was not licensed and it was against federal regulations for him to be flying a licensed airplane. Ben Torrey, deputy DOC inspector, told Red Bluff's sheriff Floyd Hull to keep the plane intact so chief inspector E. E. Mouton could thoroughly investigate.

The airport managers job at Bidwell Field was jinxed. The first one hired was Frank Gordon, who took office in 1929, but because he quit flying for some unknown reason he was unable to make money as a pilot and couldn't exist on what he made as a mechanic. He gave up the job before his two-year contract was up. The second manager, Slim Davis, crashed in December 1930. Due to his injuries and with his only plane destroyed he had to give up the airport job. Raines Griffin, the third manager, had a career ending

CHAPTER 18

crash in June 1932, and the fourth manager, Gus Johnson, was killed in a crash in January 1933.

In addition to the jinxed airport job, Gus Johnson crashed his Jenny in September 1927. Slim Davis bought the remains, rebuilt the Jenny, and destroyed it in a job ending crash.[67]

An incorrect newspaper article stated Gus Johnson succeeded Volney Chadwick, as Bidwell Field manager, which implied Chadwick survived the crash at Morgan Hill—he did not.[68]

Richard Rasmussen, a Red Bluff aviator, had his OX-5 Commandaire biplane parked at Bidwell Field in 1936.[69] That same year Dale Fry, a later Red Bluff airport manager, was giving flight instruction to Paul Schramm of Corning in an American Eagle monoplane belonging to Pacific Coast Airways mechanic Mr. Kennedy of Redding.[70]

As previously mentioned, in March 1938 gale force winds struck Bidwell Field. Ben Torrey, Red Bluff's newest airport manager, was awakened around 2:15 AM by the disturbance. He went outside to check the hangar and open its doors to allow the wind to pass through the building, rather than blow it down. He couldn't budge them, so he forced all four open with his car. One of the planes inside the hangar was blown several feet into the air before Torrey could tie it down. Torrey estimated the winds at 65 mph.[71]

As we learned in Chapter 17, Ben T. Torrey was killed in a crash July 20, 1938. His passenger Jack Baskins also died. Ben Torrey was, without a doubt, the best known and one of the most respected aviators in the north state. It was the final jinx for Red Bluff airport managers in the 1930s. Torrey, who had managed Woodson Field at Corning for ten years, had taken over as airport manager of Bidwell Field only a year before he died.[72]

Fig. 72. John "Slim" Davis was airport manager of Red Bluff's Bidwell Field in 1930. He crashed his Jenny and lost the manager's job, but he survived. Other managers of the airport in those early years were not so lucky.

CHAPTER 19

Captain Moore and his dirigible over Redding – Frank Bryant and Roy Francis fly first – Air Service fire patrols – Pendleton and Merwin barnstorm Redding – John W. Benton – Flying activities in Shasta County from 1927 – Redding chooses an airport site – Benton Field dedication activities

In 1909, before the first aeroplane flew successfully in California, a balloon exhibition in the Shasta County town of Redding during its Fourth of July celebration may have had a negative impact on the townspeoples' attitudes about aeronautical endeavors. After each day's baseball game during the three-day celebration, Captain James Moore was scheduled to make an ascension in his dirigible *America*. He would leave the ground at a 45-degree angle and, between 600 and 1,000 feet, level off and circle the Redding courthouse, proceed south to the end of Market Street and return over the east side of town.

Some people complained that if they didn't buy a ticket for the day's events they couldn't witness the dirigible leaving ground. That was not true. After the late Saturday ball game of July 3, 1909, the gates were thrown open. There was no charge to watch the dirigible depart from Redding's Recreation Park.[1] Everyone was excited; the flight was the feature of the day. The dirigible had been up and ready to fly with only a few minor details to be corrected by Captain Moore.

As Captain Moore prepared to climb onto the dirigible's riding car and to begin his carefully planned flight over the city, he yelled out to the crowd gathered around his airship a bold yet unfortunate statement, "Here's for a successful fly or a trip to Hades." That was his plan, but someone once said, "When man makes plans, God laughs."

Ten minutes later: Moore was lying on the ground mutilated and mortally injured underneath the airship's riding car. The giant silken bag was consumed by flames. What remained lay only a few yards from the car. Milton Mygatt, a spectator knocked down by the concussion of the gas bag exploding, was lying nearby with a broken thigh from being trampled by the crowd fleeing the exploded dirigible.

A reporter described what happened during the first flight of a controllable airship in the northern Sacramento Valley, "... The ship would not retain an even keel position and Moore was climbing up to better balance it. At this moment ... it was noticed that the rapidly revolving propeller was cutting into the oiled silk gasbag. [A.M.] Short and two bystanders yelled to Moore. Moore saw it and was endeavoring to reach the motor to shut off the power, when the horrified spectators saw a burst of flame, and ... the car and the man turning over and over in its fall to earth, some thirty to forty feet [below].

"The concussion and the rush of heat from the fierce blaze reached the crowd, which had surged around the dirigible before its ascent, and those out of reach of the danger zone watched with horror as they saw ... Moore, the [aeronaut], and Milton Mygatt, a carpenter of Redding, aged 78 years ... badly injured and ... immediately [taken] to the St. Caroline Hospital."

Four hospital doctors worked on Moore and Mygatt. Moore had little chance of surviving. Doctors tended to him four hours. At 9:00 PM he regained consciousness and talked a few minutes with his half brother, A. M. Short. At 11:45, seven hours after the crash, he died. Milton Mygatt was in very serious condition for 24 hours then began showing improvement. It was believed he would recover.

The Redding newspaper quashed rumors that Moore was too inexperienced to be performing. It had proof Moore made over 200 ascensions. He had just installed the new riding car under his dirigible, which was his undoing. Its propeller was too long, and when the bag sagged as it does under certain conditions, the propeller chewed into it and 10,000 cubic feet of hydrogen gas exploded. Moore was in the center of the explosion. There was no way a body could survive the trauma. He was 40 years old. Earlier in the year the same situation happened in Davenport, Iowa, but that time he was able to reach the motor quickly and shut it off.

A special news report from Los Angeles published in the *Redding Courier Free Press* stated the dirigible *America* lost at Redding was the sister ship of one lost in the mountains north of Pasadena with a party of five men aboard a few months before. Its aeronaut was Captain Mueller, and it was one of two airships brought to Los Angeles to take part in a transcontinental race, but failed because neither could get over the Sierra Nevada. Captain Moore came to Los Angeles in 1908 from Memphis, Tennessee, where a series of his exhibitions were quickly stopped when a festive (drunk) band of picnickers at a summer park riddled his dirigible with bullets. Moore said that was the second such mishap that happened to his airships.

The people in Redding only knew Capt. James Moore a few days, they didn't know his was a stage name. Most professional balloonists and dirigible aeronauts of the day went by a nom de théâtre. Anytime there were large amounts of cash involved, it was handy to use an assumed name in the ballooning business. On occasion balloonists couldn't fly because of dangerous winds, and spectators often got very angry when the flight they paid to see was cancelled. So, balloonists frequently left town unexpectedly—usually without paying their hotel bills, etc. An alias sometimes helped them avoid the resulting bill collections by local sheriffs. Moore's real name was James Louk Caufield.[2]

Citizens of Redding grew cautious of airmen after the horrific accident and discovery that its aeronaut worked under an assumed name. Undoubtedly "Captain Moore" was paid an up-front fee before his ascension and, as the accident happened at the beginning of Moore's first flight, Redding officials received nothing for it.

Seven months later, Col. Frank "Millionaire" Johnson was touring the Sacramento Valley in his Standard Model Curtiss biplane, performing at times pathetic "first flights" for valley towns. When Johnson performed Chico's "first flight," Joseph Lorenz, a Redding hotel owner visiting Chico, negotiated with Johnson to make a "first flight" at Redding the following week. After seeing him fly no more than 10 to 40 feet above ground, Lorenz told Johnson he would have to guarantee a flight at an altitude of at least 100 feet at Redding to get paid. Johnson refused the terms and Redding waited nearly two years to see an aeroplane over its city.[3]

Redding's first aeroplane flight was on January 6, 1912. Aviators Frank Bryant and Roy Francis had their two aeroplanes shipped by rail from the San Francisco Bay Area to Redding's Recreation Park. About 200 people gathered to watch the aeroplanes being assembled, and were treated to a flying preview of what they could expect the following day. The aviators' manager, J. T. McTarnahan, had Recreation Park workers remove 60 feet of the wooden fence surrounding the park so the aviators could take off and land safely.

Roy Francis took off, leaving the ground 100 feet before reaching the new opening in the wooden fence, and flew north to Reid's Ferry. There he turned toward the courthouse and circled it descending lower over south Redding. Eventually Francis flew back over the business district and landed near his starting point in the park. He was in the air for three or four minutes flying as high as 450 feet at over 50 mph. The newspaper acknowledged the "first flight" and encouraged its readers to come out to see the two aviators fly their exhibitions the next day. "Weather will make no difference," the paper stated. "The aviation 'goes,' rain or shine." Well, almost.[4]

It turned out weather did make a difference. The planes could not fly Sunday, January 7, because the weather was so bad. The aviators were ready to fly, but city officials asked them not to because the weather would keep many spectators away. The aviators agreed. It wasn't until the following Thursday, January 11, they were able to perform their exhibitions; the first ever at Redding. When the newspaper reported that at 9:00 AM the aviators would fly at the park in the afternoon, an impromptu holiday was declared throughout the city. Most stores and businesses posted signs they would be closed from 1:00 to 3:30 PM. Four hundred spectators gathered at the park and another 600 gathered on North Street Bridge, housetops, telegraph poles, and railroad berms.

Roy Francis made the historic first flight in his Gage biplane. The spectators were attentive but, unexpectedly, did not crowd in on his takeoff path. Most spectators were not knowledgable enough in the early days to realize they had to allow open space ahead of an aeroplane. It needed to run along the ground 300 or 400 feet to reach flying speed. Sometimes those in charge failed to provide enough security to keep people out of the way.[5]

The newspaper described Francis' plane as a "Wright biplane," an astute description but technically wrong. Francis was flying a newly constructed Gage biplane, which he recently acquired. When this plane was later rebuilt, it was called a Francis-Gage biplane. It was one of the very few early designs that copied the Wright brothers' method of dual propellers powered by a single engine through the use of long lengths of bicycle chains transferring engine power to the propellers. Later Roy Francis referred to his plane as a Francis biplane, which cut the original designer and builder Jay Gage, out of the picture completely.[6]

The Standard Model Curtiss (Pusher) biplane design was the basis for the majority of successful self-built aeroplanes in Northern California and the rest of the nation during aviation's Exhibition Years (1909–1914). The next most copied designs were the French Farman biplane and, in lesser numbers, the Bleriot XI monoplane.

After leaving the ground for Redding's first exhibition flight, Francis climbed to 1,500 feet in 15 minutes, then descended to a perfect landing in the very center of the makeshift aviation field. Within seconds, 200 people crowded around him to shake his hand. The first to grasp him was his friend the accompanying aviator Frank Bryant.

After congratulating Francis, Bryant began preparing his Standard Model Curtiss copy for flight. He took off from the park at 3:00 and flew up the Sacramento River five miles, then turned back towards the park when his engine began running rough. The announcer was claiming Bryant was traveling at more than a mile a minute, then his Curtiss dropped out of sight. Speculation began immediately that he crashed into the river. Autos, buggies, and bicycles full of people rushed for the river to see the wreckage. From the top of the hill, a mile from the park, the Curtiss could be seen sitting in a plowed field on the Baker Ranch with Bryant calmly walking around inspecting his plane. Bryant had fixed his engine problems in 35 minutes. Soon he and Francis were flying around the park simultaneously.[7] They promised on Sunday, January 14, to step up their exhibition with more daring stunts such as a contest for altitude records, close and quick landings, and bomb throwing.[8]

H. W. "Ed" Blakely flew the next flying exhibition at Redding in its typical summer heat of 110 degrees during June 1913. On his test flight, he hit a fence just after sundown. He had no injuries and with little damage to his Standard Model Curtiss he was able to fly the next day.[9]

THERE WAS LITTLE notable flying activity reported in Redding before the Great War. However, after the war in mid-1919, the Army Air Service joined with the US Forestry Service to protect the timberlands of California, Oregon, and Washington from forest fires. The methods devised by these two government services would utilize Army Air Service planes and pilots carrying Forestry Service observers to spot and report any forest fires they discovered during daily patrols. (For a detailed description of the Air Service forest fire patrols please see Chapter Ten in the author's book *Golden Wings Over The Feather River*.)

Lieutenant E. E. Newbig (or Neubig), in a DH-4, landed at Redding July 22, 1919, on his return from Eugene. Newbig had landed at Redding a few days earlier with his passenger Robert E. Smith, director of the war loan organization of the Twelfth Federal Reserve District. They were flying to Seattle with a million dollars in $100 and $1,000 savings certificates just issued by the Treasury in Washington, D. C. At Seattle, the certificates were to be placed for transport on a steamship to Alaska. After arriving in Portland, it was decided Mr. Smith should travel on to Seattle by train, probably do to weather. Turning back for Eugene, Lieutenant Newbig got lost twice and made a wide detour to get back on course. He was flying at 110 mph and took three hours and ten minutes to reach Redding.[10] Newbig set a new round trip speed record from Mather Field to Portland, and back. He averaged 98 mph flying the 1,070 miles in 10 hours and 55 minutes. On landing at Redding Newbig reported a large forest fire burning between Roseberg and Grants Pass, Oregon.[11]

A. S. Jones was in Redding on June 28 scouting for a field to land a JN-4 that would be coming soon to give paying locals their first airplane rides.[12] He found a field by the Sacramento River on property owned by Bill Menzel.

E. H. Pendleton, director of aviation for Sacramento's municipal airport at Del Paso Park, and Ogle Merwin, an ex-army flyer and flight instructor, arrived at Redding on August 1 in a JN-4 to give airplane rides for three days. C. E. Bennet of Chico Contracting Company sent a scraper to Menzel's field the day before to level a landing strip for Merwin. The operator created an ideal landing field 1,400 by 40 feet.

R. Walthers was the first to ride with Merwin, and Tom Mulhern went next. Pendleton told a reporter every city, especially Redding—the valley's last stop before encountering the northern mountain range—should have a municipal airport.[13] Pendleton planned to mark the field before he went back to Sacramento so it could easily be found from the air.

Two-dozen people went for hops with Merwin in his Jenny on August 2. Merwin said interest was so great he decided to stay until the middle of the week to make sure everyone who wanted got a ride.[14] On the third, Merwin took Milton Heryford Jr., a rancher, over his land near Millville. The flight took 32 minutes. They flew just 50 feet above the farm buildings so Heryford could see his family gathered in front of his home. Merwin declared he was the first farmer in Northern California to see his own farm from the air. However, Merwin had told a farmer in Butte County the same thing just a week or two before.[15]

Leslie Jones, an Anderson businessman, demonstrated air-mindedness

CHAPTER 19   413

when he hired a plane, probably Merwin's, to scatter leaflets over town advertising his store's big moving sale. He believed he was the first merchant in Northern California to use an aeroplane for advertising.

Pendleton and Merwin flew on to Sisson and Weed from Redding to sell more plane rides. Their venture to Siskiyou County towns was hampered by strong winds coming off Mt. Shasta. At Weed, Merwin reported he couldn't get his Jenny higher than 20 feet above the surrounding treetops, making it too dangerous to fly. He said, "The winds [downdrafts] were so strong from the mountain that machines are unable to get above the currents." He returned to Redding and landed on the new airfield at West Placer Street. This new airport would eventually be designated Benton Field and serve as Redding's municipal airport for many years. A much larger municipal airport now exists on the east side of the Sacramento River and serves as the primary Redding airport. Benton, located on the west side of the river, is still in use as of 2018.[16]

On Wednesday morning, September 17, 1919, the Army Air Service issued an order that all its personnel, planes, and equipment were to leave the

Fig. 73. Benton Field at Redding is located in the lower right of this 1995 photo. It was developed by the city in 1919 for the army's forest fire patrol. It was occupied briefly by the fire patrol and judged inadequate. The army abandoned the field for a better airfield at Red Bluff. Benton Field named for the late Lt. John Benton in 1929 by then had been expanded into a first class airport.

airport and move to a new airfield at Red Bluff. The army had abandoned Redding by the following day. Air Service planes flew fire patrols from the Redding airfield between mid-June and mid-September. For the remainder of the fire season, patrols were flown from Red Bluff.[17]

Redding's Benton Field namesake was John William Benton born November 27, 1897, at Manton. His parents were Thomas Hart Benton (not the famous artist) and Kate (Lennon) Benton. He graduated from a Redding grammar school and Redding High School and attended University of California at Berkeley. In late 1917 he joined the Army Air Service and was sent to Rockwell Field, San Diego, for flight instruction. In August 1918 he began pursuit training and was assigned as a pursuit flying instructor at Rockwell Field in October 1918.

Benton left the Air Service February 1919 and joined Robert G. "Bob" Fowler's Airway Development and Service Company, which had an airfield in western San Francisco. While working for Fowler he flew Walter T. Varney's Bristol Air Tourers for potential buyers.[18]

Sometimes when he demonstrated the Bristol for Varney Air Service, Benton was able to visit his Redding hometown. On February 11, 1920, Benton arrived in Redding at 3:07 PM, circled town, then landed with two passengers: H. Benton, his brother, and F. C. Heron. All three were employees of Airway Development and Service Company. At noon they left Redwood City in Varney's Bristol Tourer leased to Bob Fowler. They made it to Redding in three hours. The next day Benton was hopping passengers for ten dollars a head; for a little more he would throw in some aerobatics.[19] He was hopping his passengers at Johnson Hill airfield on West Placer Street in Redding. He took up Mrs. Nora Ashfield, 85, who loved every minute including several stunts thrown in to spice up her ride. Jimmie Wood and his family enjoyed an airplane party flying together with Benton. Benton hopped 35 passengers that day.[20]

Benton left for Redwood City two days later after hopping passengers for a week. He took two Redding passengers, Dr. C. W. Bryant and Byron Wicket who had won the tickets to the Bay Area. A. L. Watson, manager of Lorenz Hotel, had the town crier (mayor) Bill Menzel raffle them off. It would be Wicket's first ride. Bryant had flown frequently with Benton.[21] They covered the distance of 238 miles to Varney Field at Redwood City in 2 hours and 30 minutes; a record time due to high altitude flying and a strong tailwind.[22]

Johnny Benton flew a nonstop charter to Reno on April 29, 1920, in a

Chapter 19

175hp. Curtiss, probably one of Curtiss' new Oriole biplanes. The flight ended in a serious landing accident. Benton hit a stone wall and his Curtiss swapped ends injuring both passengers. Reportedly, the accident was due to a poor landing field and a misunderstanding of the landing signals. It was the Reno airport's third accident that week.[23]

The Reno airport in September 1920 would be used for the first transcontinental airmail flight by a US Air Mail Service plane. It was small and required an expert pilot like those who flew airmail to land safely. Charles Lindbergh landed there September 19, 1927, during his national air tour of the United States. He complained the airfield was too small. For that reason and others, another site was soon developed named Hubbard Field, which is now Reno-Tahoe International Airport.[24] The airport, an unnamed airmail field, when Benton crashed there was named Blanch Field in 1924 after recently deceased airmail pilot, William F. Blanchfield.

BACK AT REDDING, an unnamed barnstormer ran a newspaper ad on August 19, 1920, "Fly With Me – Airplane passengers carried over Redding; 15 min. ride by army trained pilot $10 up and down at old government aviation field on Johnson Hill." The same ad appeared two days later with the price lowered to five dollars.[25]

Aviators Marion Miller and Charles West departed Redding August 21. They were caught by darkness and had to land on the Kneeland prairie where they spent a cold night at high elevation surrounded by mountains. They arrived at Eureka the following day damaging their plane upon landing. The two men suffered no injuries.[26]

James R. Hennessy arrived at Redding August 26 from San Diego. He had been advanced $1,500 by Harry Fisher to buy an airplane from government surplus sources. Hennessy stopped making payments to Fisher on the loan. Fisher learned Hennessy was there and notified the Redding sheriff to hold the plane until he got there. Two days later Hennessy was back in possession of the plane and everyone was satisfied it had been a simple misunderstanding.[27]

MAJOR GEORGE H. BRETT and Lt. W. S. Goldborough from Crissy Field stopped at Redding on their way back to San Francisco from Seattle June 29, 1923. They were finishing a mapping mission of the aerial route between Seattle and San Diego. The map would serve aviators like road maps did motorists. Major Brett was noting convenient fields for landings and sketching the topography. He wrote of probable weather conditions and other essentials aviators would need. Redding would become an important stop for pilots flying into and out of Sacramento Valley. Major Brett requested power lines near the airport at Redding be moved back. Pacific Gas and Electric Company agreed to do it. "Inn stations" or overnight landing fields on the San Diego–Seattle route would be Los Angeles, Bakersfield, Fresno, Stockton, Sacramento, San Francisco, Redding, Medford, Eugene, Vancouver, and Seattle.[28]

Civilian flying jobs right after the war were scarce for the many ex-military pilots. Making a living from barnstorming, the only available work for ex-military pilots, was described as "feast and famine" with an excess of the latter. John Benton reenlisted in the Army Air Service September 1920 at his former job, flight instructing at March Field near Riverside. In February 1921 he transferred to pursuit flying at Kelly Field, Texas, for three years; 1924 found him stationed at Crissy Field, San Francisco.[29]

While landing at Redding, Major Brett hit a car driven by California State Assemblyman Dr. Earnest Dozier. Brett was reported dodging high-tension power lines as he was landing; his plane, probably a DH-4 from Crissy Field, hit the ground at a faster speed than anticipated. Brett yelled at the car, "Get out of the road. I am coming." Dozier had begun to comply when the plane struck him from behind. No one was injured, but the rear of the car was dented and its soft top ripped. The airplane's wing was damaged and a tire punctured.[30]

Lieutenants Oakley G. Kelly and H. C. Miller, Air Service aviators, were forced to land at Redding on December 28, 1924, due to heavy fog. They were returning to Vancouver, Washington, after a mission to Crissy Field. They fought fog and snow for an hour in a wasted attempt to climb over the Siskiyou Mountains north of Redding. They decided it would be wiser to turn back and lay over in Redding until conditions improved. On a trip down the coast from Vancouver a week before, weather forced them to divert and stop overnight in Marysville, causing reports to go out they were lost[31] Earlier in 1924, Kelly had made the first nonstop transcontinental flight across the United States with Capt. John Macready in a single-engine Fokker T-1 overloaded with extra fuel.

First Lieutenant John W. Benton returned to Crissy Field in September 1926 from duty at Fort Lewis, Washington, where he spent two weeks as an aerial artillery observer. To his surprise, he was chosen to fly as relief pilot on one of the five Loening OA-1A amphibian aircraft that would fly a goodwill tour of South America's continental coastline.³²

The US Army Air Corps Pan-American Goodwill Tour departed Kelly Field, San Antonio, December 21, 1926. Weather plagued the fliers from the beginning, but the aircraft performed well with few problems. However, several of the 400hp. Liberty engines powering the Loenings reached their overhaul time and had to be replaced during the tour.

The tour would be John Benton's final mission. He was killed on February 26, 1927, over Argentina in a midair collision. His Loening, named the *Detroit*, was commanded by Capt. Clinton F. Woolsey with Benton as relief pilot. The other Loening, *New York*, was flown by flight commander Maj. Herbert A. Dargue and relief pilot Lt. Ennis C. Whitehead.

The accident happened over Palomar Field, a few miles from Buenos Aires. The five Loenings had just broken formation to move into single file for landing and the *Detroit* turned into the *New York* instead of away from it on the break. The planes locked wings and spun like two hawks with their talons in a death grip fighting all the way to the ground. Major Dargue and Lieutenant Whitehead bailed out safely, but Captain Woolsey and Lieutenant Benton could not escape. Cause of the accident was never established. Fatigue from the long flight might have been a factor.³³

The ex-fire patrol airfield on Johnson Hill, off West Placer Street at Redding, was officially named Benton Field in July 1929. Local folks started calling it Benton Field soon after John died in 1927. It is still in use today.³⁴

THE FOLLOWING PARAGRAPHS chronicle notable aviators and flying activities at Redding and around the north state from 1927 through 1932: Lieutenant Jack Ram on April 19, 1927, was flying a de Havilland DH-4 from Sacramento to Corning and, after darkness fell, lost his way. He landed in the dark at Benton Field but hit an uprooted oak tree on the edge of the airfield.³⁵ Floyd Keadle a well-known north state professional pilot was hopping passengers at Benton Field and broke his arm while propping his airplane in June.³⁶

Redding would have a perfect airport once changes were made to Benton Field. Starting in the fall of 1927 the landing surface was expanded to 2,500 by 2,000 feet. By April 1928, it was one of the largest airfields in the north state. The city had purchased the entire block adjoining Benton Field to increase its size.³⁷ This allowed West Coast Air Transport airliners to use Benton as an emergency stop on its new Seattle to Los Angeles route.³⁸

Montague, 80 miles north of Redding, purchased a 420-acre parcel that adjoined town for a municipal airport in March 1928.[39]

In late May 1928, Jimmy Young, a Chinese parachutist, made his 116th jump at a Benton Field air show. It nearly was his last. Young's parachute jump was billed the "crowning feature" of the show. He leaped from 2,000 feet and pulled the ripcord, but the chute did not open. After falling 1,000 feet it finally opened but with such force the chute's pack ripped open breaking most of the 12 shroud lines. Those left saved Young's life. H. S. Salisbury of Lassen View Airways told the story to a local reporter. He said the chute was similar to ones used by military aviators. But, he said, Young's chute had been in use five years, and his prolonged drop before opening was too much of a strain on old shroud lines.[40]

Less than a week later, Reed Vowles, an instructor for Lassen View Airways on Benton Field, was giving a third lesson in the company's Eaglerock to John B. McColl, a Redding confectioner. The engine quit as the pair were flying into a strong north wind on final approach to land. Against the wind and without power, they could not reach the runway and crashed three-quarters-of-a-mile south of Benton Field. McColl was flying the Eaglerock when they lost power and Vowles took over the controls. The plane was seriously damaged, but the men sustained non-life-threatening injuries.[41]

Tehama County pilot Floyd Keadle won the dead stick landing contest at the Portland Air Carnival on June 10. He brought his Eaglerock down eleven feet, seven inches from the line with a "dead" engine. Keadle received the Valentine Gephart Trophy and $50 cash prize.[42]

The town of Jerome used a laundry service from Klamath Falls that flew in, picked up dirty laundry, and dropped it off clean every few days in July.[43]

Martin Jensen, second place winner of the Dole Race to Hawaii, landed in Redding on Monday, July 7, 1928. He was on a goodwill tour to 33 states. First, he arrived flying his Dole Race plane, the *Aloha*, in Sacramento shortly before noon on Friday. A formation of Marine aircraft based temporarily at Mather Field met and escorted him to the airport where he met with city officials. From there he proceeded to Redding, then on to Oregon.[44]

Following a two-hour-and-15-minute flight to Mineral from San Francisco in Standard Oil's tri-motor Ford, W. J. Hanna filed an application in July with the US National Parks Commission for permission to construct an airport there. Several Air Corps officers from Crissy Field and other aviators had shown an interest in flying to Mineral on weekend trips to spend time in "… the glorious mountains of Lassen National Park." Park officials

CHAPTER 19

requested approval for the plan from the commission with the understanding no park money would be available for a modern hangar and a campaign would have to be made to acquire funds to do finishing work on the field.[45]

Two hundred spectators who gathered at Benton Field on Sunday, July 8, to watch flying operations were shocked seeing a wheel hanging off the gear leg of Capital Air Lines' six-passenger Breese cabin monoplane after it took off. A pin had dropped out of the shock absorber allowing the right wheel to hang loose off the landing gear leg, rendering it useless. Luckily for everyone involved, Henry G. "Andy" Andrews was flying the Breese that day. Andrews was one of, if not *the* most experienced pilot in the north state. When he reached 1,000 feet, Andrews saw the dangling wheel and decided to land as soon as possible. Witnesses were concerned about the pilot and passengers, Mr. and Mrs. J. F. Nielsen and Harold Junkans, all from Redding.

Andrews told the passengers to "hold tight to your places" and began a wide descending turn preparing to land at Benton Field. On final approach, very close to the ground, he banked to the left at a slight angle in a sideslip and touched down first on the good left wheel. He held the plane in that position during rollout until the wing lost lift and dropped to the ground. The plane suffered only slight damage. The pin was replaced and within the hour they were flying again.[46]

Mrs. H. S. Salisbury, wife of the Lassen View Airways proprietor, flew with a salesman for Aero Corporation, S. B. Smith, to Oakland on July 21. They stopped along the way at Corning, Chico, and Marysville. Wallace Martin, a Redding pilot, ordered a new Eaglerock from Lassen View Airways, dealers for the Alexander Aircraft Co. Martin planned to use his new plane barnstorming the northwest.[47]

Pilots at Benton Field received weather reports for the first time on July 24, 1928, given by meteorologist E. M. Jones of the US Weather Bureau. This service would become a necessity during the winter storms over Mt. Shasta and the Siskiyou Mountains.[48]

Ira M. Powell, a Redding pilot, purchased a new OX-5 Swallow from Royle Airlines at Oakland Airport.[49]

Floyd Keadle took second place in the Swan Island to Silverton, Oregon, July 1928 cross-country air race in his Eaglerock. He won the looping contest. He and Tex Rankin won first place in the relay race at the Swan Island Airport air show in Portland.[50]

Earl Lee Kelly, former mayor of Redding, went to Los Angeles with his pilot, Al Pilgrim, to take delivery of a new Waco in August 1928. Upon return, he claimed being the only private plane owner in Redding.

In the early years when airplanes were more of a novelty than a means of transportation, city councilman William Menzel owned an airplane and kept it on his land across the river from where Benton Field was eventually developed. After the Great War the first Army Air Service planes that visited Redding had landed on Menzel's property.[51]

Al Pilgrim, a Shasta County commercial pilot, broke a landing gear strut on takeoff from Benton Field in August. He felt the biplane lurch during takeoff roll, and he knew what happened. He climbed to 400 feet and leveled off, then he turned the control stick over to his passenger, L. Lloyd MacCalay. If MacCalay was not a pilot, he became one very quickly. Pilgrim climbed out of the cockpit, walked out to the leading edge of the lower wing, looked under the wing at the landing gear strut, and saw the strut was broken. He climbed down on the landing gear and was able to repair the strut well enough to land the plane safely without damage.[52]

The Shasta Aircraft Company of Redding became the north state dealer for American Aircraft Corporation in August. Floyd Keadle passed his transport pilot license test in September 1928.[53] H. S. Salisbury, manager of Lassen View Airways, sent a telegram from Lakeview, Oregon, to his office at Benton Field stating the company plane he was flying had been badly damaged in a collision with another unnamed aircraft during an air meet there. Salisbury had flown the plane to Lakeview earlier in the week. Al

Fig. 74.

Chapter 19

Fig. 75. These two photos were found labeled Art Starbuck at Enterprise Field circa 1927-28. Starbuck landed his Pacific Air Transport Ryan M-1 airplane named *San Francisco* on Enterprise Field at Redding for more fuel probably due to strong headwinds. Enterprise Field was directly across the Sacramento River from Benton Field and was renamed Enterprise Sky Park before it was closed forever. It is believed to have once been the private airport of Redding city councilman William Menzel. Army aviators occasionally used this Menzel property in 1918-19 before Benton site was expanded.

Pilgrim flew Earl Kelly's new Waco, also to Lakeview, for the September meet to earn money making passenger hops. Duane Fountain of Redding went along with Pilgrim to do a parachute jump at the close of the meet.[54]

West Coast Air Transport requested a hangar be built at Benton Field large enough to park an airliner overnight. The city council discussed the matter and concluded it would cost $5,000. They tabled the request. The council approved a new weather bureau building costing $4,000. A new $100 aviation business license was discussed. It would be required of all aviation businesses making Benton Field their base of operations. Companies flying into Benton to drop off or pick up passengers did not have to pay, nor did student aviators.[55] Earl Kelly complained the license fee was too high. The city council said the high fee would keep out-of-town barnstormers off Benton Field. This matter was also tabled.[56]

West Coast Air Transport announced it would start air service between Seattle and some Sacramento Valley towns on September 10. Mr. and Mrs. J. Harry Brown of Olinda purchased the first round-trip tickets to Seattle sold in Shasta County from Mr. Roycroft, local agent for the Pickwick Company, owners of the airline.[57]

Emory B. Bronte stopped in Redding with Raymond J. Little and S. S. Boggs. They were on a flight from Seattle to San Francisco, September 6, in a new Boeing Model 40A recently purchased by Associated Oil, Bronte's employer. Bronte told Redding officials Benton Field was the finest airport between Sacramento and Portland.[58]

A gathering of local aviation enthusiasts got a thrill on September 10 seeing the Richfield tri-motor Fokker transport land at Benton Field. The Fokker was on a trip from Seattle to Sacramento. While at Redding, the big plane was used to give rides to VIPs. Tom Fowler was the pilot with John Yates, copilot. C. M. Fuller, a company VP came along as spokesman.[59]

Duane Fountain parachuted from Earl Kelly's Waco at Benton Field on September 18.[60]

The Mt. Shasta Airport was located four miles north of Mt. Shasta. The US Forest Service constructed it as an emergency field for the Air Service forest fire patrols circa 1919. In the center of an 80-acre parcel of land was a runway 2,100 x 900 feet running southeast to northwest. The Forest Service planned to do more work on the field later in the year. During the fall, winter, and spring, it was free from fog and prevailing winds were southeast or northwest. These conditions made the field one of the best in the Mt. Shasta region. The airfield was a half-mile west of Black Butte and the Pacific Highway and 300 yards east of the Southern Pacific Railroad line.[61]

Union Air Lines notified Redding officials its plans to begin operations at Redding in September 1928. Union had bought out Capital Air Lines and West Coast Air Transport. Union also said if a hangar wasn't built at Benton Field they might make Corning their north valley stop instead, which is exactly what they did.[62]

Al Pilgrim was hand propping Earl Kelly's Waco at Montague. It "kicked back" and broke his arm. Pilgrim wrenched his other arm at the same time. Kelly said there was nothing out of the ordinary about the incident—airplane engines kick back just like "cranky" automobile engines. It was quite common for Ford Model T engines to kick back, and if the person turning the crank had his thumb wrapped around the crank it could easily get broken. The safe way to crank was not loop the thumb over the handle. The injury did not interfere with Pilgrim continuing to fly Kelly's Waco.[63]

A *Sacramento Bee* report on "Airport Facilities In Superior California Towns" described Benton Field in 1928. The gist of the information was the field was half-mile long from north to south and a quarter-mile wide from east to west. Aviators reported they could land in any direction due to the large size and smoothness of the field. Equally important was the airport's proximity to the business center of Redding. The airfield was on a plateau known as Johnson's Hill or Placer Street Hill, a half-mile from the center of town. The field's surface had been scarified and then rolled. Aircraft could approach the field from all sides at low altitude. PG&E had moved a power line to a safe distance from the north end of the field. Telephone wires were also moved, and the government's airway rotating beacon was located at the northeast corner of the field. The field had not been marked yet but would be to accommodate night flying. It was so large and smooth it hardly seemed necessary to mark it; the beacon was flashing right there on the field.[64]

Six people in Redding earned pilot's licenses in October 1928. They were: R. J. "Bob" Strief, H. S. Salisbury, Lloyd McCaulty, Earl L. Kelly, D. Fountain, and Miss Gladys Lane.[65] Earl Lee Kelly sold his Waco in March 1929 to a pilot in San Francisco.[66]

The US Weather Bureau moved from downtown Redding to a new building adjacent to Benton Field in the southwestern part of the city. Julius C. Smith, meteorologist in charge, had two assistants. They started meteorological balloon activity immediately.[67]

Floyd Keadle organized several local citizens and businessmen at Alturas in Modoc County. Keadle planned to buy a Travel Air 2000 in which to instruct the group. It is unknown whether Keadle bought the plane or if the club was a success. Keadle was reportedly killed flying for rebel forces in Mexico in mid-April during the Cristiados War, but he was not. He did say later he flew a combat plane for several weeks with the rebels, who paid him $250 a day.[68]

Royle Air Lines planned to give away ten airplane rides during the

Benton Airport dedication air show July 6–7, 1929. Royle offered excursions to Mt. Lassen, as well as short hops around the airport. Royle pilots would be flying a Ryan Brougham and a Fokker Universal for excursions, and a Wright J-6 Travel Air for short hops.[69] Pylon races were planned for the dedication as was a cross-country race called the Yellowstone Air Derby. Robert J. Strief, a commercial pilot who got his start in aviation at Benton Field, was the first to register for the pylon races and would fly a Travel Air biplane. When Strief stopped at Benton Field to register, he said the Benton air show poster and accompanying entry blanks left at Bay Area airports encouraged several Oakland fliers to enter the air races. Strief entered the Redding contests representing a Vallejo flying school, his current employer. The racing committee believed Strief would be a crowd favorite; he learned to fly with Earl Lee Kelly at Benton Field. Strief and Earl Kelly planned going to the Stockton air show on July Fourth to lure pilots to Redding July 6–7 and compete in Benton's air derby and pylon races.[70]

Bob Valentine was responsible for Redding's thousands of spectators attending the cross-country air derby on Sunday afternoon listening to a direct radio hookup between Redding and Boise over W7AGK Boise, and W6DTK at downtown Redding, and W6ATQ Redding at the airfield with Chris Bechtle at the microphone. Boise folks would hear the beginning of the Yellowstone Air Derby and Redding would hear Boise reports of the racers landing. The entire Redding Air Show would be broadcast from Benton Field. It was planned for Redding Mayor Grenwoldt to greet the Boise mayor and report the name of the flyer, his plane, and his takeoff time. The mayor of Boise was expected to do the same, as racers landed at his end. Mrs. Zelma Benton, widow of Lt. John W. Benton, arrived at Redding on July 2 from San Francisco with her two children to watch the July 6 dedication and the unveiling of a tablet erected on the airport in his memory.[71]

Saturday, July 6, 12:25 PM, the official dedication of Benton Field, Redding's municipal airport, began with an eight-plane formation from Crissy Field thundering over the city at low altitude. There were five Douglas O-2 observation planes, one Loening amphibian, one cargo plane, and one transport plane (probably both Douglas C-1s), in the large army formation. In the planes were: Colonel and Mrs. G. C. Brandt, base commander of Crissy Field, Lieutenant and Mrs. Hargrove, captains Myers, Frye, White, and Jenkins, lieutenants Hansen, Sandborn, Bourdeaux, Pettis, Myer, and five enlisted men.

After the planes landed, the speeches began. One recalled Redding's first air show with the dirigible spectacle on the Fourth of July, 1909. The Redding newspaper reminded everyone that many Northern Californians came to Redding for that first air show because city officials had the vision to collect by popular subscription $7,000 to bring in the famous aeronaut James Moore. (Neither the newspaper nor anyone else mentioned the fact that Moore was killed at the beginning of his first flight and the whole affair was a failed exhibition.)

The paper went on to describe the next 20 years in the city of Redding as "... a struggle with a people gradually growing air-minded. For years, meeting after meeting ... called by the chamber of commerce for studying ways and means for securing an aviation field for Redding. Time after time, the project almost died, but always to be revived by R. M. Saeltzer, whose vision for the advancement of aviation was greatly in advance of his time." The paper mentioned that in 1927 the city council bought 420 acres on Johnson Hill for a sum of $8,500. The city had a 432-acre airport at an approximate investment of $12,000 by July 1929.

By 2:00 o'clock, over 20 airplanes sat on the field—the eight army aircraft plus the following civilian pilots, their employers, and their planes: Vic Hogan, Royle Air Lines, Ryan Brougham; Ray Crawford, Overland Airways, Travel Air; Ray Varney, Humbolt Air Service, Fokker; Frank Rose, Whirlwind Stearman; Harvey Lemcke, Pitcairn; Fletcher Walker Jr., Whirlwind Travel Air; Joe Barrows, Fairchild; Charles Sullivan, Whirlwind Travel Air; Jimmie Purinton, Hisso Travel Air; Bob Strief, OX5 Travel Air; R. U. St. John, OX5 Swallow; Al French, Standard Oil, tri-motor Ford; and an unnamed pilot, Union Oil, Eaglerock Bullet. Captain A. B. McDaniels, who was with John Benton during his last flight on the South American Good Will Tour, was there in an Air Corps Loening amphibian.

The day's last event was the ribbon cutting, which stretched across the runway threshold. A big Standard Oil tri-motor flown by Al French roared down the runway at five feet traveling 130 mph, cut the ribbon. Then French pulled the airliner up and over spectators, guests, and VIPs as his crew dropped flowers on everyone. Riding in the Ford airliner were Menzel and Gronwoldt, other city councilmen, and several VIPs. The festivities ended with a Saturday night aviators' ball at Diestelhorst Pavilion where tickets for 16 free airplane rides on Sunday were given out. The Achaean Club reported it took in $400 at the ball.[72]

Sunday morning at 9:00, Royal U. St. John was official starter for the Yellowstone Air Derby, but it did not happen. The derby, also known as the

Redding-Boise Air Derby, was cancelled at the last minute. Redding officials cried foul, as did the pilots who signed up to race, albeit at the last minute.

There were only two airplanes on the field Saturday morning at Benton Field powered by OX-5 motors, which were required for the Yellowstone Air Derby. To attract more entrants, a rule change had to be made to open the race to planes with engines of any horsepower, but even with the rule change, there were few additional entrants. Other pilots who could have raced but wouldn't complained the prize money wasn't enough to even cover their costs to race. By Saturday night, only four pilots had entered the race: Frank Rose, Joe Barrows, Fletcher Walker Jr., and Harvey Lemke. Some pilots from Los Angeles and Portland wired vague promises to be there to start the next morning.

On Saturday night, Boise officials declared if there weren't enough planes for a "bona fide" race they would withdraw from the event. A short time later, W. P. Lockwood, manager of the Boise Chamber of Commerce, whose members subscribed one-third of the $1,500 prize money, learned Saturday evening only 3 of the 16 planes on the field at Redding were willing to start. Cyril C. Thompson, Idaho governor of the NAA and head of the committee in Boise, advised them to pull out of the race, which they did.[73]

The next morning, instead of starting the air derby at 9:00, Royal St. John had to tell contestants the city of Boise refused to put up its $500 share of prize money, and due to their unsportsmanlike behavior the air derby was cancelled. Redding citizens simply couldn't believe Boise officials would act in such a manner. It was certainly the primary topic of conversation that Sunday morning, but the news did not hinder the air show or the dedication of Benton Field.

The dead stick landing contest was a popular event Sunday. W. R. Hansen landed his monoplane just six feet, six inches past the line. It was said to have been the first time a monoplane ever won (a doubtful claim) a dead stick contest. His prize was $75. Jimmie Purinton took second place, winning $40, and L. C. Orange of Stockton was third, winning $25.

The first race was for aircraft with engines of 510 cubic inches (OX-5s). Clayton Allen of Stockton won the 15-mile event in six and a half minutes in an OX-5 Travel Air owned by Bob Six, who rode as copilot. He took home $125. Ken Kleaver of Dunsmir placed second winning $100, and R. L. Rideout tied for third with W. R. Hansen of Weed for a $50 prize, but both were disqualified: Rideout for not rounding a pylon properly, and Hansen for cutting in.

CHAPTER 19   427

The day's second race was restricted to engines of 800 cubic inches (Whirlwind). Harvey Lemcke of San Francisco won the $200 first prize in a Pitcairn biplane. His time was four minutes and 50 seconds, with a speed of 180 mph. L. C. Orange won second for $150. His Whirlwind Travel Air was clocked at 165 mph. Franklin Rose took third at 158 mph in his Whirlwind Stearman for $75 cash.

The final events were parachute jumps. Walter Hall from the Bay Area surprised the crowd when both of his chutes deployed at the same time. Hall, who had made over 2,000 jumps, reported his second chute opened by mistake. Duane Fountain, a Redding man, made a fine jump and came down directly in front of the spectators.

The eight-plane army flight entertained everyone both days with formation changes and battle maneuvers. The city's street crew worked constantly both days watering the grounds to keep dust down. There were 31 airplanes on the field the final day. Mrs. Amanda H. Boyer may have enjoyed the air show more than anyone. The 85-year-old joined a few friends for her first airplane ride. In a comfortable cabin plane, they flew over the crater of Mt. Lassen. In 1850 she had traveled across the plains in a covered wagon and wanted "... to fly before I go to the angels." She came 25 miles from Ono to witness the Benton Field dedication.

Despite Boise pulling out, the celebration was successful. Only government licensed planes and pilots had been allowed to participate in the air show. There were no accidents the entire two days of competition and exhibitions.[74]

THE SISKIYOU COUNTY Board of Supervisors was considering the land at the old Mott Railroad Station between Mt. Shasta and Dunsmuir for development as an airport in July 1929. The property was under consideration several months by the board. It had multiple owners. The district attorney made it clear if the money was appropriated and the owners couldn't agree on a price it would be condemned.[75]

The rotating beacon lights on the federal airway were so powerful aviators were finally able to fly over the Mt. Shasta region and Siskiyou Mountains at night. On dark nights the beacons could be seen for 80 miles. Beacons provided a continuous path of flashing lights to follow as long as visibility was good.[76]

Pilots flying the Oakland to Portland route in winter weather usually attempted to follow the Sacramento Canyon from Redding to the summit, which was a different route than they took in clear weather. Sometimes a pilot was uncertain about which was the best course based on weather conditions. In December 1929 an airmail plane circled Dunsmuir 30 minutes until the pilot decided which course, then he climbed through the clouds and proceeded to Portland.[77]

In March 1931 the Redding airport committee announced the Pacific Air Transport short-wave radiotelephone transmission apparatus at Benton Field had begun broadcasting weather information to pilots flying the San Francisco to Seattle route.[78] The committee also reported several companies were considering locating commercial flying businesses on Benton Airport. The committee recommended filling and leveling on the east side of the airport, and draining a certain section of the runway. These improvements were advised so the city could bid for a stop on a rumored daily passenger service to be started by Pacific Air Transport.[79]

Ollie Rose, a Redding pilot, and Mr. and Mrs. George Halcomb, prominent Redding residents, were killed when their plane went into a spin at 200 feet and crashed just outside the boundary of Benton Field on July 7, 1932. The plane began burning after impact and no one escaped. Airport attendants attempted to pull the victims from the plane, but were driven back by the flames. The three on board had been in the air for an hour flying over very rough country searching for Halcomb's brother, Thomas, who had been missing for two days. Thomas Halcomb had been ill and it was thought he wandered off and got lost.

Witnesses said the motor on Rose's plane was turned off or throttled down at 200 feet. It was believed this was done to make a quick turn or a turn to landing at Benton Field. The noise of the motor died down when the plane went into the spin and crashed before Rose could recover. George Halcomb, 25, and his wife, 20, were survived by a three-month-old child. Ollie Rose, 45, was survived by his wife.

The coroner's July 9 inquest ruled their deaths were from asphyxiation caused by carbon dioxide gas in an accidental airplane crash. There was an indication that efforts were made by the pilot to save themselves from disaster in testimony given by witnesses near the scene. The airplane entered the pattern for a landing at Benton Field. The motor was idled, and when the plane began to fall into the spin Rose increased power in an effort to get out of the spin. There was no structural defect contributing to the crash in the opinion of James N. Peyton, DOC inspector from Oakland, who conducted the official accident investigation on the day before the inquest.[80]

CHAPTER 19   429

REDDING'S NEXT AVIATION event of note was an air show in the fall of 1939, held after several years without one. There were stunt flying exhibitions by Dale Fry, Don Hemsted, and William Withrow, Benton Field's airport manager. Harry Munday, Earl Weaver, and Ray Varney won the aerial contests and 17 airplanes flew in for the show.[81]

Fig. 76. Little is known about this US Mail flight sponsored by the Chamber of Commerce of Redding, Weaverville, and Fall River Mills.

Fig. 77. Albert Lane with his first airplane, a Standard J-1 with an OX-5 motor; His father, L. L. Lane is in the front cockpit. The location is probably Willows.

Fig. 78. On March 17, 1935, Harold F. Brown and John Wagge flew supplies in this Fokker Super Universal to snowbound miners in the Sierra Nevada. The man in the white shirt and tie is believed to be Brown or Wagge. This plane belonged to Consolidated Air Lines and was flown to the miners from Cheim Field at Marysville.

CHAPTER 20

Frank Johnson makes Woodland's first flight – Ivy Baldwin races a train – Thad Kerns flies an exhibition – Woodland's wartime airport – Charlie Stoffer barnstorms Woodland – The Yolo Fliers Club – O. H. Pratt – Yolo Fliers Club has first air meet – Flier Club Floral Festival Air Meet – William Sanborn killed flying the mail – Best Field – Ernie Moe

Colonel Frank "Millionaire" Johnson introduced aeroplane flight to the residents of Yolo County on March 13, 1910, at Woodland. He made five low short flights from the fence-enclosed racetrack. His audience that afternoon numbered about 800 inside the fence with the same number in the cheap seats outside the enclosure, which may have been the reason Johnson never climbed above the surrounding oak trees. He flew so low the trees and even the fence enclosure hid his plane from view.

Johnson flew a Standard Model Curtiss (Pusher) he bought at the Curtiss Factory in Hammondsport, New York, from Glenn Curtiss in late 1909. Flying lessons were included in the sale, but not many. Johnson was still getting lessons from Curtiss after the plane was brought to California for the Los Angeles International Air Meet of January 1910 in the Dominguez Hills. Curtiss competed in several events at the meet, but Johnson did not fly in the meet. He did ride with Curtiss during a passenger carrying event. With the meet over, Johnson took possession of his aeroplane, one of several that Curtiss and his team of aviators would fly for the meet. Johnson shipped it from the meet by rail to the Bay Area. He ordered eight more Curtiss Pushers and claimed he was the Northern California representative for the Herring-Curtiss Aeroplane Company.

Johnson practiced flying the rest of January in the Bay Area, then entrained for Marysville and introduced aeroplane flight to the Sacramento Valley. After making the valley's "first flight" in Marysville February 12, 1910, he made "first flights" for the communities of Chico, Stockton, and on March 13 he was in Woodland. His Curtiss was assembled and ready to fly on the 13th at the Woodland racetrack, but something was bothering him. After a long delay, he ordered the Curtiss moved outside the track into a large grain field on the north side of the track. From there he made five exhibition flights that were low and short; his longest flight of the day was barely a half-mile. They were all straight-line flights with no turns. He landed and his crew turned him around on the ground and he flew back. On his fifth and final flight, he crossed over the fence enclosure and landed on the track barely clearing the fence. The crowd was not happy.[1]

An account of Johnson's first flight at Woodland was written by eyewitness Will Weider 60 years after the flight. The passage of time had dimmed his recollection somewhat, but he gave an honest appraisal of Woodland's first flights, even if slightly inaccurate about the number of flights. He described the location, "If North Cleveland Street terminating at Kentucky Avenue (then known as Racetrack Road) continued on northward, this hypothetical line ... would establish the west side boundary of the old Woodland racetrack grounds. A total of sixty acres to the north and east from this west line with Kentucky Avenue as the south boundary, was largely occupied by rows of horse barns bordering the south and west, the one-mile oval track, the grandstands," faced east towards the track.

Weider wrote of a deep voiced man screaming through a megaphone from the back of an open automobile driving around Woodland, "At the racetrack! At the racetrack! You'll find out – You'll find out – Colonel Johnson, the birdman will fly. You'll find out at the race track next Sunday at 2 PM."

The young Weider couldn't find out how Johnson got the rank of colonel. He wrote that Johnson didn't fly the plane to Woodland; he disassembled it at Stockton, shipped it by train in crates, and there he and his mechanics reassembled it for flight. On the 13th, a crowd of 1,600 gathered at the track. Those inside the fence paid 50 cents to watch. At first, Johnson's engine failed to start, but the mechanics eventually got it running. Johnson then made a grand entry by strutting from a nearby horse barn to his Curtiss as the spinning propeller blew dust over everyone close. He bowed to the crowd, donned his goggles, and using a small ladder prepared to climb into his seat, but the engine quit. Johnson decided to move the biplane to the field northwest of the track for spectators to have a better view.

People were getting restless and an uneasy feeling permeated the event. Finally, Johnson got his engine restarted and took off. Rising to 20 feet, he flew 200 yards, and landed. "Some flight!" was the crowd's response. Johnson's second flight was as lame as the first. On his third and final flight, Johnson took off from the stubble field and landed immediately inside the track enclosure.

Some praised his efforts, but others thought it wasn't worth the price of admission. One said, "The whole damn thing was a rank frost."[2]

THOMAS WHITE, A YOLO COUNTY farmer who lived near Knights Landing, saw a fire burning on his property in late February 1910. He quickly put it out and discovered the remains of a large balloon. No one was around, and he had no idea where it came from.[3]

In the summer of 1910 Capt. Ivy Baldwin, (AKA William Ivy) best known as an aeronaut, gave up exhibition ballooning for a while and learned to fly an aeroplane "... to make some real money." The same remark was made by Lincoln Beachey when he gave up exhibition ballooning to become America's top exhibition flier.[4]

For a week in late July 1910, Ivy Baldwin made aeroplane flights in his Curtiss copy from his Yolo County camp at Swingle to Webster's Station.

Ivy wanted to audition for the Fiesta of the Dawn of Gold, which would be a part of September's California State Fair. He needed the festival committee to watch him fly at Swingle, a rail stop a few miles west of the Sacramento River on a road that today parallels Interstate 80. Ivy was hoping to get an exhibition contract for the same $2,000 per day he believed Charles K. Hamilton was going to be paid for flying at the fair.[5]

Even though this flight has been covered briefly at the end of the first chapter about early aviation in Sacramento. It is covered in more detail here as it was an important event in Yolo County's early flying history.

On August 11, Baldwin raced a passenger train from Webster Station to Sheep Camp. Sheep Camp was the next rail stop two miles west on the Southern Pacific line between Sacramento and Davis. The race was declared a tie. Ivy challenged the decision pointing out he had to deviate from the two-mile railroad path and flew three-and-a-half miles. Reports of the race stated it was "... the most spectacular race ever held in Superior California and created a great deal of excitement among the passengers on the train." Ivy competed with the train just to have an opponent to race against. It is doubtful the railroad company knew about his plans to race their train. He came up with the idea to publicly demonstrate his perfect control over the machine, which he had flown above the tule cattails of Yolo County for several weeks. Gus Jamieson, Ivy's assistant at Swingle, described the race in a interview, "Captain Baldwin maintained a speed of more than fifty miles per hour, was on an average of sixty feet from the earth, and reached a height of 200 feet near the finish of the race. Contrary winds," said Jamieson, "caused Baldwin to circle from his course and to lose ground, otherwise the aeroplane would have finished first at Sheep Camp instead of running a tie heat." Ivy planned to race the scheduled train every day until the state fair started, but that was just an idle boast.[6]

Ivy Baldwin failed to convince the festival committee to give him a "big money" contract for the fair. He never had another chance to try. He also underestimated the importance of Hamilton's national reputation as the most exciting exhibition flyer in America until Lincoln Beachey surpassed him.

It is believed Ivy did fly some exhibition flights in Northern California under the auspices of the California Aeroplane Manufacturing and Supply Company. However on May 27, 1911, company manager Roy Scott had to cancel Ivy Baldwin's agreement to fly in Colusa May 28 and 29. Scott claimed Ivy crashed his Curtiss that day at Hanford during an exhibition. Actually, Ivy's mechanic crashed the plane while attempting to fly it because Ivy was sick. It wasn't long until Ivy gave up flying his aeroplane and returned to ballooning, a much safer profession. He moved to Denver where he finished out his exhibition career as an aeronaut.[7]

Thaddeus Kerns arrived at Woodland November 31, 1911, by rail with his disassembled aeroplane. His manager from San Francisco, Ted Orr, accompanied the young aviator. Orr, formerly of Woodland, was assisting Kerns in arranging a program of events for an exhibition he was scheduled to fly at 2:30 on Sunday, December 3, at Woodland's racetrack. Admission was 50 cents and kids under six were allowed free.

On Thursday morning, the day he arrived in Woodland, Kerns carted his plane to the racetrack. Before the close of the day, it was assembled and ready for inspection. He had invited the public to come out and examine his Curtiss copy. It was the third plane he built, he told a reporter, and he made a number of successful flights with it. Despite his youth, Kerns had been experimenting with flight for many years in Chico, his hometown. "He has made ten successful flights ranging from three to ten miles," wrote a reporter. "Though possessing supreme confidence in his ability to fly under any ordinary circumstances, he is a very modest young man, and creates a very favorable impression."[8]

On the scheduled day of his exhibition, 17-year-old Kerns walked out to his Curtiss at 2:30 and began tuning his engine. He carefully inspected every part of the plane. At 3:00 he was ready and he climbed onto the seat. After the mechanic spun the prop, the Curtiss began rolling down the track gaining speed; near the three-quarter turn Kerns raised the nose and lifted off the track. The biplane kept climbing straight out from the racetrack on a northerly heading.

Briefly blocked from view by nearby trees, Kerns took the plane to the southeast corner of Yolo Orchards two miles away. He turned to follow a county road back until he was opposite the racetrack. Turning again, he flew over the grandstand full with spectators at 100 feet. They cheered as he passed over, and he waved. Kerns continued across the track enclosure from the north and gradually began his descent; landing 300 feet east of the judge's stand in a clover patch. The only mishap was minor, a broken wire and loose stay, caused from the rough landing ground. He was roundly congratulated and as cool after the flight as he had been before. He went about his work in a businesslike manner; a demeanor that made him a hit with everyone. Unlike those of Frank Johnson, his flight was a grand success.

He completed about a six-mile flight overall, and it appeared he could have stayed up longer. As stated, he built the aircraft himself. On close inspection it appeared crude to one reporter, and not too strong, but his control of the machine was never in question. It was understood Kerns was making exhibition flights to earn money and build himself a first class aeroplane. Those at Woodland considered themselves fortunate to see him fly. As usual in these early Exhibition Years, people stood outside the racetrack willing to watch Kerns risk his life, but unwilling to pay him 50 cents to do so. In their defense, some residents of Woodland were skeptical the young boy could fly and did not want to get "stung" as they had been when Frank Johnson made his anemic flights the year before.[9]

During the Great War, aviators from Mather Field flew over Woodland on July 4, 1918, and landed at the city's newly developed airfield named Webber Field for the property owner, Mrs. Bertha Webber. The JN-4Ds had landed just before the parade, marking one of the most memorable Fourth of July celebrations ever held in Woodland.

Webber Field, an 80-acre airfield one mile west of town, was leased by the Army Air Service for flying cadets from Mather Field as a destination for cross-country training flights. Lt. S. W. Harkins, the assistant officer in charge of flying at Mather Field, had accepted the lease for the Air Service on June 29, 1918. He informed the local newspaper that the senior civilian flying instructor is Charles McHenry Pond.

On August 4, Capt. Jones and Lt. Niles landed at Webber Field after a cross-country flight from Mather Field. Ten days later three Jennies landed on a cross-country flight from Mather – Marysville – Colusa – Arbuckle – Woodland. Before returning to Mather they discussed the erection of a service station for the transient army planes with Woodland city officials. On September 11, Lt. Post arrived at Webber Field on a flight from Mather. Upon checking the engine of his Jenny, he discovered a broken file jammed in the engine. He suspected a pro-German mechanic or an I.W.W. (International Workers of the World were anti-war zealots during WWI) follower at Mather put the file there. Two days later, a cadet from Mather on a training flight made a forced landing in a wheat field north of Esparto. For security purposes he had to sleep with his plane until an army recovery crew arrived the next morning.

On September 19, Mather fliers landed on Webber Field. The night watchman/field caretaker Mr. Hoffman told them he repainted the air marker on the field in addition to removing the flagpole and having a telephone installed.

On September 28, army Jennies visited every city in Yolo County. The aircrews threw out leaflets urging citizens to buy Liberty Bonds. These bonds were to finance the costs of Americans fighting the Great War.

On December 2, an army Jenny crashed into a tree while flying in the fog near Knights Landing.

AFTER THE WAR, ex-Air Service Lt. Charles Stoffer was one of the first barnstormers to stop at Woodland. Stoffer visited Woodland July 12, 1919, by train and made the rounds of the city with Fred Shaffer of the Woodland Board of Trade. Stoffer visited the office of the *Woodland Daily Democrat* and told a reporter he would be bringing his airplane to Woodland July 16 to give rides for a nominal fee from Beamer Park.[10] The newspaper received several telephone calls on the 16th asking when Stoffer would be arriving from Sacramento. An airplane had flown over Woodland the day before, and locals were convinced it was Stoffer making an inspection flight of the city.[11]

Chapter 20

On July 17, Stoffer arrived at Woodland a day late and took his first passenger, Kathleen Burk of the *Daily Democrat*'s editorial staff, for the day's first airplane ride, which she planned to write about for the afternoon edition. Miss Burk had written she would be riding in a Curtiss aeroplane belonging to the Eagle Aviation Company of Sacramento. Stoffer's JN-4D remained on a landing strip in Beamer Park at Woodland for several days to give airplane rides.

His Jenny was originally from Mather Field and in top condition for passenger hops. Stoffer, a former instructor pilot at Ellington Field, Texas, would be assisted by W. B. Randall and Ernest Illing, who came by car prior to Stoffer's arrival. Randall was Stoffer's mechanic, and Illing would sell rides and help passengers in and out of the Jenny. Miss Burke reported Stoffer failed to keep his original arrival date on the 16th because his mechanic had to check ... every inch of celluloid canvas [fabric] and test every nut and screw to insure the greatest safety" for his passengers at Woodland. Miss Burke had waxed poetic about the wonder and beauty of flight until the engine began running rough and Stoffer put the JN down in farmer Deaner's field, a mile from their starting point. Then she wrote about the "two hours wait under the glaring sun while mechanic ... Randall toiled over the trouble and then once again ..." they were flying. This time her flight lasted 20 minutes at a height of 2,000 feet cruising at 75 mph over "Woodland the Beautiful."[12]

Later in the day, Reva Shaffer went up with Stoffer for a 20-minute ride over Davis and Woodland. Stoffer gave her thrills with a few steep turns. After he brought her down, Bob Huston and Leonard Wooster went up with Stoffer. O. W. H. Pratt, a Woodland realtor, went for a 20-minute hop. He was profoundly struck by the beauty and thrill of flying and hired Stoffer to fly him to Sacramento the next day. Pratt was enthralled with flying.

During a lull in passenger hopping on July 18, Stoffer and Fred Shaffer took a car to look for a better landing field to use for passenger hops. Stoffer was not satisfied with Beamer Park. He got permission to use Webber's field west of town; he agreed to use that part of the field furthest from the Webber home. This may have been the same landing site used by Mather Field cadets during the war.[13]

Many residents who rode with Stoffer at Woodland showed interest in purchasing an airplane. Those most interested were: O. W. H. Pratt, W. R. Fait, Arthur Huston Jr., and W. A. Bloodworth. Their interest was such that the Earl Cooper Company, West Coast distributor for the Curtiss

Aeroplane Company, sent vice president C. E. Foote, L. A. Moore manager of Cooper's Sacramento branch, and R. C. Poor of the Barney Oldfield Tire Company to Woodland for interviews with the prospective buyers. Stoffer remarked at the time, "Woodlanders are real sports. Many places we have been, but few where the people are so interested in aviation. We expect to sell a couple of planes here."

Three days later civilian pilot O. C. Rice was flying from Sacramento to Woodland with a young soldier as passenger, J. Zeuhlke. Zeuhlke begged a ride when learning where Rice was going. Five miles northwest of Sacramento, Rice developed engine trouble requiring an immediate landing in the Natomas area. This was pretty much standard operating procedure when flying Jennies and Standards after the war. As Rice repaired his engine, several children from a nearby farm gathered around the plane and began climbing on it and into the cockpit. Reportedly one of them turned on the magneto switch, and someone else moved the propeller causing it to kick over starting the engine. Jennies had no brakes so it rolled forward and the prop struck Zeuhlke who was standing in front of the plane. The prop threw him 25 feet into the air and was killed instantly. Rice was standing to the side and not injured.[14]

AFTER O. W. H. PRATT's ride with Charlie Stoffer, all he could talk about for a month was flying. He dreamed about it and thrived on everything having to do with airplanes, aviators, and flying. Pratt organized enough aviation enthusiasts in Yolo County to form the Yolo Fliers Club.

The primary purpose of the club was the promotion of a local social organization composed of persons owning aeronautical machines for personal use. Advancement of the development of aeronautics, aerial navigation, and kindred sciences were its secondary purposes. A clubhouse, hangars, and assorted buildings to be used for the assembly and repair of aircraft by professional mechanics were to be built and maintained by the club. Pratt's further efforts were the facilitation of the club owning and maintaining its own real property conveniently located within a reasonable distance from the city of Woodland. A clubhouse, bowling alleys, and a swimming pool might be built. He wanted athletics, indoor and outdoor, to be encouraged and teams to be formed for competition in baseball, bowling, swimming, boxing, fencing, and flying.

Creation of the Yolo Fliers Club gave Woodland and Yolo County the prestige of having organized the first aero country club in Northern

California. Allowing non-residents memberships, territory from the Oregon state line south to San Francisco would be linked to the Woodland community in the new sport of flying. The country club planned to affiliate with the Aero Club of America (ACA), the nexus of American flying organizations. This would link them with the world organization, the Federation Aeronautique Internationale (FAI) in France, and aero clubs in every important American city.

By maintaining an airport at Woodland, the club would become a point of call for military and airmail pilots. Members of the Pacific Aero Club, the Western Aero Association, the Aero Club of the Northwest, and the Aeronautical Society of California, both flying and non flyers, would be welcome. A local newspaper article expressed hope Woodland would be a planned stop for various aerial tours projected by the Aerial League, and a landing place for passenger planes the Aerial League planned to send out over the United States in 1920. (This author has been unable to corroborate existence of the Aerial League.)

The club planned to make honorary members of famous American men including President Woodrow Wilson, Admiral Sims, and General "Black Jack" Pershing. It also planned to spend $30,000 on five hangars, a repair shop, a clubhouse, a Curtiss JN-4 training plane, and an airfield.[15]

The Yolo Fliers Club incorporation documents were drawn up and ready for filing in early September 1919 at Sacramento. It was not organized for profit, but a membership fee was set to raise funds for carrying out the club's plans. The charter members, all from Woodland, were: A. C. Huston, lawyer; J. W. Monroe, sheriff; H. S. Summers, merchant; W. B. Stoddard, farmer; J. B. Maurath, merchant; O. W. H. Pratt, real estate broker; Forrest A. Plant, lawyer; Charles H. Christal, physician; Winfield H. Arata, merchant; and Emil K. Kraft, merchant.[16]

At Pratt's office in Woodland, September 28, A. C. Huston was elected president and chairman of the board of governors of the Yolo Fliers Club. It was the club's third regular meeting. Pratt was chosen first vice president, Sheriff Monroe second vice president, Floyd Tuttle of the Bank of Yolo, treasurer, and Emil Kraft, secretary. Fully organized and incorporated, the club received and accepted an option on 617 acres of land west of Woodland, known as Wolfskill's place, owned by Sieferman brothers. It became the club's home.

Some by-laws needed changes; the most important involved membership. Membership would be limited to 200 with a fee of $100 each. It was later increased to 300 with the next 100 memberships $150 each. New lists of eligible members were prepared.[17]

Charles Broadwick, noted parachute maker, parachutist, and aeronaut, came to Woodland in October 1919 to put on an exhibition at Beamer Park. Broadwick had been performing aerial exhibitions for 33 years. He started out by ascending in hot air balloons, and was one of the first parachutists to make night jumps. His current "wives" or "daughters" (they were billed at various times as one or the other) also made balloon ascents for him, leaping out in parachutes. Broadwick's women, all parachutists, jumped from 2,000 to 6,000 feet at Woodland.

Broadwick claimed he never broke a bone in ten years due to the perfection of his parachutes. Prior to then he broke almost every bone in his body at one time or another. At his Woodland exhibition, he reported his "daughter" Ethel would jump from an airplane, her specialty. She was going to step off the wing of H. G. Andrews' JN-4 at 2,000 feet, traveling at 60 mph. Her parachute pack weighed only five pounds. After her jump Andrews would do aerobatics for the crowd below.[18] (For more on the Broadwicks, see chapter five in Herr's *Aviation in Northern California Volume I.*)

Andrews advertised airplane rides in a Woodland newspaper stating the first person to go up would save five dollars. The ad also mentioned he flew exhibitions at the state fair the previous month.[19]

The Yolo Fliers Club signed the papers purchasing the Wolfskill property from the Sieferman brothers. Located on the Woodland-Madison Highway, it consisted of 300 acres of rolling grain land and 300 acres heavily forested with large beautiful oak trees. The sellers received $5,000 in the first payment with the second payment of $10,000 due on November 5, and the undisclosed balance payable on December 22, 1919. There was an ideal site for the clubhouse on a knoll about 200 feet off the highway with a commanding view of many miles of orchard and grain land. The clubhouse grounds, golf course, and airfield would use 150 acres of Wolfskill. The club planned to sell off the rest.

The club signed up 94 members during its membership drive in October 1919.[20] It sold 148 acres of the original 617 for $31,000. It was very desirable farmland between Moore's Ditch and Cache Creek.[21] Even though wives of members enjoyed the same privileges as their husbands, Miss Mathilde Leland wanted her own membership. Women and men could join. She signed up with O. H. Pratt and became the Yolo Fliers Club's first female member.[22] The Fliers' Club signed its 100th member and had collected

Chapter 20   441

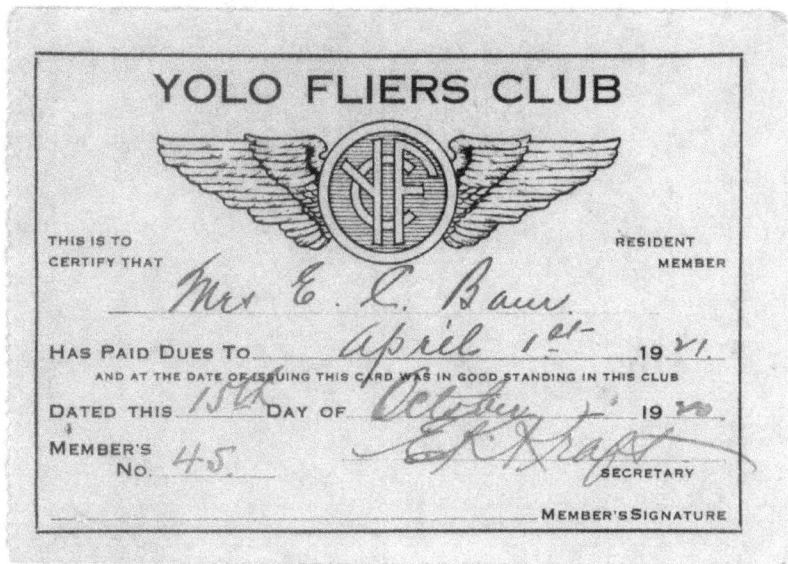

Fig. 79. Mrs. E. L. Baur's membership card for the Yolo Fliers Club is depicted here. She joined on October 15, 1920, and was the club's 45th member. The price to join then was $100, which is the equivalent of $2400 in 2016.

$10,000 in membership fees by October 31, 1919. The local newspaper listed all 100 members.[23] By April 1920 with a change to the by-laws the Yolo Fliers Club had 600 members; 200 from outside the Woodland area and the rest local.[24]

Moses McGrew was awarded the contract to level, roll, and develop the airfield. O. H. Pratt, in June, sent plans for the Yolo Fliers Club airfield to Captain Balsley, secretary of the Pacific Aeronautical Association and its president, Rutherford Pates. Pratt sent the same to Col. H. H. Arnold, commander of aviation for the Western Department of the Army Air Service at the Presidio in San Francisco.[25]

Christopher V. Pickup, a pilot for R. C. "Cliff" Durant's aviation business at Durant Field, Oakland, notified Woodland officials he would be bringing a three-passenger Standard biplane to Woodland the third week of June to give $10 passenger rides to anyone interested.[26]

On June 18 a message was received stating Colonel Arnold and Major Spatz from Crissy Field would be flying in on the 27th to inspect and approve the Yolo Fliers Club airfield to accept military flights. Reportedly this would be the first civilian airfield approved for Air Service operations in Northern California by the war department. The airfield had two

Fig. 80. Yolo Fliers Club Field shown in this 1995 photo is now known as Woodland-Watts Airport. The Yolo Fliers Club buildings are seen just peeking out from under the wing strut of the author's Bellanca Decathlon and the club's golf course west of the runway is plainly visible.

runways, a north-south runway 500 feet by 2,000 long and an east-west runway of the same dimensions being rushed to completion. O. H. Pratt reported there would probably be other airplanes on the field during Arnold's inspection. He contacted Robert Fowler, manager of Airway Development and Service Company in San Francisco, who told Pratt he would send Monte Mouton in one of his company's LeRhone rotary powered Avro 504Ks. The Airway Avros were British training planes modified to carry a pilot and

CHAPTER 20   443

two passengers. Cliff Durant notified Pratt he would be sending one three-passenger plane, and possibly three more planes if they were back from San Diego in time; another airfield opening was happening there.[27]

The date of Colonel Arnold's inspection and acceptance was moved to Sunday, August 22, 1920. It was planned to make the inspection day an air meet, which is the equivalent of a fly-in and air show in today's aeronautical jargon. Air racing was also thrown into the mix. It would be the first such air meet in Northern California and only the second in the entire state.[28]

On June 25, Chris Pickup and passenger O. H. Pratt, flew a three-place Standard from Durant Field to Yolo Fliers Club Field in 50 minutes. After inspecting the field, Pickup said it was the best one in the state owned by a club. He offered to act as the advance man for the club spreading the word amongst the aviation community to help make the upcoming August air meet the greatest in the state.[29]

Fourteen aircraft flew into Yolo Fliers Club Field for the north state's first postwar air meet on August 22, 1920. Between 2,500 and 3,000 spectators arrived in 750 to 1,000 automobiles. There was only one injury accident that day. Berkeley aviator Joseph Desaulles, who flew his own plane in for the meet, mangled his little finger when he got too close to a whirling propeller. At Woodland Sanitarium, Dr. Fairchild had to amputate it.

Speeches were given while planes were arriving in the morning, and four of the monster oaks on the club grounds were each dedicated to one of the four high-ranking officers who attended: Col. Hap Arnold, Maj. Carl Spatz, Maj. Reed Chambers, and the French ace, M. Deckert. Lunch was served to visiting pilots, their assistants, and special guests. After lunch stunt flying and passenger hops were carried out by several pilots who flew in for the day. Wesley P. Johnson, a reporter for *Auto and Aerial News* of San Francisco, told a local reporter the Fliers Club Field was one of the best in the state. After the runways and grounds were planted in grass, the airport would be without equal due to the huge level ground protected from treacherous winds by low rolling hills to the north, he said.

Early Sunday six Liberty powered de Havilland DH-4s from Mather Field flew over Woodland in battle formation and landed at Yolo Fliers Club Field. Captain Walsh led the squadron. Initially, it was planned for five DHs to fly over, but at the last minute Cadet Jennings, flying a fire patrol mission, wanted to be in it and joined the formation. Dan Davison, an ex-airmail pilot, flying a Curtiss Oriole for the Earl Cooper Company, followed the DH formation in and landed. Davison was carrying passengers J. H. Roxstall of the Hall-Scott Motor Company and I. E. Elm from San Francisco. Reed Chambers arrived flying an Italian Ansaldo A.300, called a Balilla, that belonged to R. C. "Cliff" Durant. (The famous WWI 26-victory ace, Eddie Rickenbacker, would use Durant's Ansaldo during the year he spent in the Bay Area managing the Sheridan automobile line for General Motors.) The Ansaldo was said to be a 200 mph aircraft, but in actuality its top speed was 150–160 mph; it carried a pilot and one passenger with an SVA engine of 300hp. Hall-Scott Motor Company sent a German Fokker D-7 equipped with their latest 200hp. engine, flown by French WWI ace, M. Deckert.

Two JN-4s were kept busy all day hopping passengers for ten dollars each. The Jenny pilots were Fauna W. Farris of Stockton and George Purington whose home was unknown. The Walter T. Varney Company of Redwood City sent a new three-place Lincoln Standard to the Woodland event. The big biplane plane proved to be very popular.

Another postwar Standard J-1 at the meet was the Pacific Standard, flown from the factory in Los Angeles. The Pacific Standard biplane was modified and remanufactured by Pacific Airplane and Supply Company of Los Angeles. Head of the company, noted aviator Emory Rodgers, flew it to Woodland with a journalist friend John Edward Hogg as his passenger. Rodgers knew Hogg's penchant for camping and asked Hogg to bring his camping gear. They stopped to camp along the way to Woodland and on

Fig. 81. A Jenny used for hopping passengers at Yolo Fliers Club Field during the official opening air meet on August 22, 1920.

Emory Rogers loading up for a trip to Woodland. THE ACE was well represented at the opening of the new field at Woodland.

Fig. 82. Emory Rogers, a prominent Southern California aviator, loads his Pacific Standard biplane for an aerial camping trip from Los Angeles to the air meet that would open Yolo Fliers Club Field. It was the first post-war air meet held in Northern California.

Fig. 83. Roger's Pacific Standard at Yolo Fliers Club Field on August 22, 1920. The Pacific Standard was a post-war version of the wartime Standard J-1 training plane.

the way back to Los Angeles. Hogg's two-part article about their trek was published in the September and November 1920 issues of *The Ace*. The two set up their tent and cooking stove beside their plane, fascinating people at the air meet. They answered many questions throughout the day about aerial camping.

Unfortunately, activities at the air meet were under-reported due to the crash of one of the visiting aircraft on its return to the Bay Area that Sunday evening. The crash superseded all other news for the day. Clifford B. Prodger, age 30, was piloting the ill-fated aircraft. Earlier in the day at Woodland, he performed aerobatics flying a Bristol F.2B, a Great War fighter-bomber that had been converted into a three-passenger plane named the Tourer. With him at Woodland were two passengers, Gus Jamison and John C. Nelson The plane was a demonstrator for Walter T. Varney's flying business at Redwood City Airport. Cliff Prodger had over 6,000 flying hours. Prodger's primary employer was Arbon-Bristol Aeroplane Company, a Canadian aircraft sales company that imported the planes from Britain. Prodger and his passengers had just returned to Redwood City Airport from the Yolo air meet and decided to make one more flight before sunset with Jamison and Nelson. Prodger decided the flight would be an aerobatic demonstration, which was a typical occurrence on Sundays along with passenger hopping at most airfields across the United States. Augustine "Gus" J. Jamison, 32, was an ex-instructor for Redwood Aviation, and John C.

Fig. 84. A Walter T. Varney Co. Bristol Tourer, which was a converted wartime F.2B fighter-bomber, could carry three to five people depending on the model. Clifford B. Prodger flew it up to Woodland from Varney Field at Redwood City for the air meet on August 22, 1920. Upon his return to Redwood City that afternoon, Prodger and his two passengers were killed while flying an aerobatic exhibition over Varney Field.

Nelson, 30, was a Firestone tire representative from San Francisco. With his two passengers aboard, Prodger had flown 15-minutes of aerobatic exhibition when he fell into a flat spin and didn't have enough altitude to recover. All three aboard were killed in the crash. It was believed a passenger grabbed the control stick and wouldn't let go, as the two sticks were found bent out of line with one another.

During the war, Prodger, an American from Montana, had been a test pilot for the British Royal Flying Corps. He set a record for the most number of passengers taken aloft in one plane. In early 1919, after packing 42 passengers into a Handley Page 400, a twin-engine heavy bomber, he was able to get it off the ground for a short flight.[30]

It was tacitly agreed in the aviation community that the Woodland air meet was going to be a showcase event for aircraft builders on the West Coast. One of the planes was the Hall Scott L-6 powered Standard belonging to George F. Stephenson. Stephenson had his pilot Frank Clark(e) fly him from Los Angeles to Oakland and then on to Woodland for the meet.[31]

The Yolo Fliers Club made plans in February 1921 to spend about $125,000 during the new year constructing golf links, a swimming pool, the first rooms of the clubhouse, two hangars, and a reservoir. To date the club had purchased 617 acres, built a landing field, drilled a water well, laid out a golf course, and improved the entrance to the grounds. There were at the time 359 members.[32]

INTEREST WAS STILL high among the Yolo Fliers Club members to promote aviation in Yolo County and the Sacramento Valley. Another air meet was scheduled for Yolo Fliers Club Field as part of the Woodland Floral

Fig. 85. Clifford B. Prodger, an American, had been a test pilot for the British during the Great War. He set a record in 1919 for the most passengers taken aloft after he stuffed 42 people into a Handley Page 400 heavy bomber and went for short flight. He is shown here shortly after that flight. He was flying the Bristol Tourer that crashed at Redwood City in August 1920.

Festival, a three-day event ending May 7, 1921. The Fliers Club air meet would take place on Saturday, the seventh. It was a benefit for the American Legion and was well publicized throughout the state.[33]

THE OFFICIAL SCHEDULE for the "Second Annual Aeronautical Show and Race Meet" on Saturday, May 7 was:

> 10:00 AM – Assembled ships of low horsepower will leave the landing field and form an Aerial Parade over the city of Woodland: Duration of flight, 15 minutes, then Maurice "Loop-the-Loop" Murphy from Marina Field, San Francisco, to skywrite his name over the field.
> 10:30 AM – Start of the Altitude Record Flight.
> 10:35 AM – Start of Class "D" race for airplanes equipped with OX-5 engines, 10 laps of 3.33 miles each. Approximate flying time 30 minutes.
> 11:00 AM – Inspection of planes. Passenger hops. Moving picture filming.
> 12:00 NOON – Lunch for air meet guests followed by reception for Eddie Rickenbacker and VIPs.
> 1:15 PM – Stunt flying by Frank Clarke, Los Angeles' most famous moving picture aviator.
> 1:30 PM – Start of Class "C" race for Standards equipped with 150hp. Hissos and 200hp. Hall-Scott L-6 engines. Mr. Clarke challenges them all, entering the field with a 125hp. Hall-Scott Four. The Aero Club of Southern California reports the betting is two to one he will, by his daring form of flying, win this race against planes of greater power.
> 2:00 PM – Special demonstration flight by the monster 12-passenger Friesley airliner, the largest plane ever constructed west of the Rocky Mountains.
> 2:00 PM – Special demonstration of the JL-6 all-metal plane. This cabin plane will carry passengers who desire to ride without helmets and in groups. – Inspection of displays – Passenger rides.
> 2:45 PM – Start of the Class "B" race for high-powered planes. This race includes the Jacuzzi monoplane and other unusual planes; 14 laps of 3.34 miles each. Duration approx. 25 minutes.

3:30 PM – Start of the Class "A" race for the fastest aircraft in the West. This includes the [Ansaldo] S.V.A., entered by James Otis of San Francisco, the LePere Special, entered by Leslie C. Brand of Glendale, and the Fokker D. 7, to be flown by Frank Clarke and entered by the Hall-Scott Motor Co. of Berkeley. Fourteen laps of 3.34 miles each. Duration 17 minutes.

4:00 PM – Aerial Combat between Frank Clarke and Eddie Rickenbacker, both flying scout planes – Stunt program by "Loop-the-Loop" Murphy, who will attempt to break the looping record for the United States. – Passenger carrying by the JL-6 all metal, enclosed cabin plane and other open cockpit planes. Field cleared of racing ships for one-half hour.

5:00 PM – Yolo Fliers Classic. The three fastest planes of the day, winners of the previous races, will be pitted against each other for a first prize of life membership in the Yolo Fliers Club (valuation $1,000) and time officially taken by a representative of the Aero Club of America for a Pacific coast record. – Judges – Col. H. H. Arnold, commander of the Air Service for the Ninth Corps Area at San Francisco; Maj. B. M. Atkinson, commander of Mather Field; Mr. Eddie Rickenbacker, America's foremost ace; Starter – George B. Harrison, Aero Club of Southern California.

UNFORTUNATELY THE ABOVE schedule was thrown out due to a large storm extending from the middle of San Joaquin Valley to Los Angeles. Many of the guests and contestants mentioned above were weathered in and could not get off the ground to compete in Woodland. The few who left before the storm arrived in Woodland the day before, and even fewer fought through the storm in new planes with more powerful engines, making it to Yolo Fliers Club Field on Sunday morning. The air meet was extended over Sunday, so some semblance of the original schedule could be followed after the weather passed.

One of those who made it through the storm was L. C. Brand in his luxurious LePere Special built by Waldo Waterman for the hefty price of $30,000 ($750,000 in today's dollars); he arrived on the field at noon Sunday. His pilot, Gilbert "Bud" Budwig made the flight nonstop from Los

Angeles to Woodland in five hours.[34] The LePere Special was officially designated the Waterman Model 3L-400. L. C. Brand, the owner, named it *Tioga Eagle*. The plane was built from plans acquired by Brand from the Army Air Service test center at McCook Field, Dayton, Ohio. To power the LePere, Brand spent $2,500 right after the armistice for one of the first war surplus Liberty engines to come on the civilian market. Waterman customized the army design for Brand, but he admitted the finished plane was 90 percent true to the original plans. Packard had built 27 of the LePere biplanes for the Air Service prior to the end of the war when most military aircraft production contracts were cancelled.

Waterman extended the LePere wingspan four feet and widened the fuselage for two passengers to sit comfortably in the rear cockpit. He added fuel capacity, allowing Brand to reach his summer home at Mono Lake and return to Glendale on one tankfull. Waterman nickel plated all exposed fittings on the biplane and gave the mahogany plywood fuselage skin a piano finish. A small icebox was installed in the passenger cockpit, and the LePere had one of the first electric starters ever installed on an airplane. Brand used the LePere quite a lot then sold it to Donald Douglas, who in 1925 presented it as a gift to Capt. Lowell Smith for his extraordinary effort in leading the US Army's Around-the-World Flight.[35]

Fig. 86. Col. Henry H. "Hap" Arnold on the left stands with L. C. Brand (center) and a third officer believed to be Major B. M. Atkinson. Behind them sits Brand's LePere Special, which he named the *Tioga Eagle*. This was a scratch built copy of the top U. S. Air Service fighter plane of 1919. This luxurious three-seat modified LePere copy was built by Waldo Waterman and was designated the Waterman Model 3L-400. The photo was taken at Yolo Fliers Club Field during the "Second Annual Aeronautical Show and Race Meet" on May 7, 1921.

Frank Clarke, flying his 125hp. Canuck (a Canadian built JN-4) won the Class A and C races at Woodland by a close margin over planes having 180 to 220hp. motors because of his daring tight turns around the pylons. The Class A Race was over a triangular course of 22 miles, which he completed in 12 minutes. Brand took credit for second place in the Class A Race even though his pilot, Budwig, did the flying. There were several pilots flying aerobatic exhibitions during the day. Frank Clarke held the crowd spellbound by flying upside down and performing other hair-raising maneuvers. Maurice "Loop-the-Loop" Murphy wrote his name over the field through various skywriting maneuvers, which the crowd enjoyed. After seeing pilots like Murphy do his maneuvers with such seeming ease, many spectators took advantage of airplane rides being offered. New planes on static display were popular with the crowd especially the big Friesley Falcon, the twin-engine, 12-passenger transport built near Gridley in Butte County. Brand's LePere Special was a hit with spectators, as was Clarke's Fokker D-7. The display of the high-wing Jacuzzi J-7 cabin monoplane and the all-metal, low-wing Junkers-Larsen JL-6 monoplane saw much foot traffic.

Reportedly at Sunday night's aviators ball, Eddie Rickenbacker was awarded a gold life membership card in the Yolo Fliers Club. The reporter obviously was not there as Captain Eddie didn't make it to Woodland for the air meet. Club officials were disappointed. Reed Chambers, Rickenbacker's good friend from the 94th Aero Squadron during the war, explained Rick's plane was tuned up at Durant Field in Oakland and ready to go, but his train from the East was late and Rickenbacker couldn't get to Woodland in time.

An estimated 2,000 to 4,000 people came to watch 28 planes arrive for the meet. Irving Hunt, a local pilot, was on the field every minute of the meet. He did more flying and passenger hopping than the rest of the planes combined. Roy Francis, now nationally known due to the press hyping his attempted 1919 transcontinental flight in an Air Service Martin MB-1 heavy bomber, flew the Friesley Falcon down from Gridley carrying ten passengers to watch the meet as the new airliner sat on display for the crowd to inspect.[36]

Clyde Pangborn flew into Fliers Field for the air meet; he described those who were there later to a friend who wrote his biography. Pangborn confirmed that Col. Arnold, Reed Chambers, Frank (Spook) Clarke, and Gil Budwig were there, and he said Matty Laird was also there from his Midwest hometown with his "Speedwing" airplane. Laird brought George

E. "Buck" Weaver to demonstrate the new plane. Weaver would found the Weaver Aviation Company and build the popular WACO (pronounced Wahco not Wayco) biplanes. Pangborn mentioned others at the meet: Emory Rogers, Lt. Johnny Benton, Capt. Lowell Smith, Lt. Halverson, and the Jacuzzi brothers; Monte Mouton, who had flown the first transcontinental air mail into Marina Field. Mick Doolin, who later managed San Francisco's municipal airport, Mills Field; and Walter T. Varney, the airmail and airline pioneer, were all there. Pangborn told how, during the air races, Matty Laird's "Speedwing" crushed the competition, which were a Fokker D-7, an Ansaldo Ballila, a Curtiss Eagle, DH-4s, modified Standards, and JN-4s. Pangborn flew in one of the races and won $50 for second place.[37]

MRS. GERTRUDE FREEMAN, 85, wife of the late Major F. S. Freeman of Woodland, as mentioned in chapter five, took her first airplane ride May 23, 1923, satisfying a lifelong dream. She had experienced all of the early forms of transportation going back to the oxcart used by the pioneers who came to California.[38]

Yolo Fliers Club Field, also known as Woodland Airport, was listed in *Western Flying's* 1926 annual airport directory as west of Woodland; a landing tee in the center of the airfield; and runways 1,500 feet long and 1,000 feet wide with accommodations on the field.[39] By March 1927 the field had deteriorated from non-use, and local editorials chided the city for not funding the airport thus depriving the city of income, the prestige of air travelers, and commerce.[40]

The Yolo County town of Winters lost one of its favorite sons April 15, 1927. William E. Sanborn was killed flying airmail in Idaho. Sanborn had been a Varney Air Lines airmail pilot for about a year. He was an Army Air Service veteran of the war and a popular young man in Winters. Known around town as "Pilot Bill," Sanborn was carrying 100 pounds of mail in one of Varney's Whirlwind powered Swallow biplanes when he departed Salt Lake City. Seven miles north of King Hill, Idaho, he ran into strong headwinds and was seen flying at only 200 feet. People on the ground saw him climb, then turn and quickly crash. Nearby ranch hands found him dead in the cockpit. The crash site was memorialized with a crude marker, still visible in the 1970s. He was buried with military honors in the Winters cemetery with Walter Varney in attendance.[41]

J. Paulding Edwards, vice president and engineer for Valley Air Services, bought a 96-acre plot of land in the Yolo County town of West Sacramento

CHAPTER 20   453

on Riverbank Road. He planned to build an aircraft factory with its own airport on the grounds. There is no evidence a factory was ever built nor an airport developed on the site.[42] During the Great War, Edwards did develop an airport and flying school at San Carlos in the Bay Area.

In June 1927, the efforts of former Woodland resident Edmund J. Moffett and his involvement in Ernie Smith's first attempt to fly to Hawaii, were headline news in newspapers of the Great Central Valley and the Bay Area.

Vance Breese, who spent the summer of 1925 flying out of Yolo Fliers Club Field, later took up aircraft design and construction. He built many aircraft, two of which were entered in the Dole Race to Hawaii, one was crashed at the race start by Livingston G. Irving, and the other took second place with Martin Jensen at the controls.[43]

A group of Los Angeles aviation enthusiasts laid claim in July 1927 to have created the first country club for fliers in the world. Yolo citizens set up a howl of objections. They sent a dispatch to the Los Angeles "Flying Falcons" organization reminding them members of the Yolo Fliers Club opened the first such country club in 1919. The Los Angeles group's club site was actually in the southern San Joaquin Valley, 20 miles north of Bakersfield and a lengthy flight from Los Angeles.

Yolo Fliers Club members admitted their organization had evolved into a golf club, but its members were still in full support of aviation. Although the club had only one active flying member, Clem Lowe, it claimed having one of the best airfields in the region. The members said plans were being undertaken to extend the field for bigger aircraft and fulfill the federal requirements for a first class airport.[44]

In late July, the Standard Oil Company of California's guide to landing fields of the Pacific coast listed 145 useable landing fields in the Western states. Of those, 95 were permanent, and 50 were listed as emergency or temporary airfields only. Woodland's Yolo Fliers Club Field was listed as follows: "Permanent, a small L shaped field – 1500 feet x 500 feet north and south, 800 feet x 200 feet east and west with a white circle marker. Four-and-a-half miles west of town; Five miles west of Standard Oil Plant marked Woodland. Golf clubhouse on right, surface fair and soft when very wet."[45]

An army aircraft of unknown type crashed on Yolo Fliers Club Field July 31 destroying its landing gear. The aircrew, lieutenants Melton and Willit, were not seriously injured.[46] A week later two men speeding through the night with wings from the wrecked plane lashed to the sides of their roadster were apprehended by the police near Stockton. The police forced them to return the wings to the field, which was quite a distance. There was no arrest; it seemed to be a misunderstanding over their taking the wings. The two men claimed to have "heard a report" in their hometown of Monterey that the plane was a total wreck, and the wings, which they thought might be salvageable, were to be destroyed.

When the men first arrived at the airfield to get the wings, they were told by Lieutenant Thompson who was sent from Crissy Field to repair the plane and fly it back, that the wings were not to be taken. Thompson was summoned elsewhere for a short time. He returned and the men and wings were gone. Thompson immediately called Constable Hillhouse reporting the theft, and Hillhouse notified surrounding cities with an alarm.

After returning the wings, the men were not charged, and their names weren't revealed. It was known one of them was a Monterey garage man and an ex-serviceman.[47]

The Army Air Corps at Crissy Field notified O. W. H. Pratt it was declaring the Yolo Fliers Club airfield unsafe. It was not properly marked for aviators unfamiliar with its poor condition, and the field needed to be leveled because it was too dangerous for pilots who had never landed there. Two accidents to army planes had occurred there in recent past. Pratt was told the situation could have been avoided if the field was in better condition.

Unfortunately the club was unable to fund redevelopment and maintenance. Some residents said the board of supervisors should realize commercial aviation was making huge strides, thus the city and county should make every effort to accommodate fliers with proper facilities. The Air Corps favorably reported the hospitality of Yolo Fliers Club, and they believed orders prohibiting army planes from landing there would be lifted as soon as some minor corrections were made. In August 1927, several Dole Race entrants were dismayed to learn Yolo Fliers Club Field was not in good condition. They were making test flights to various towns around California and would have included Woodland if it were not for negative army reports.

Clem Lowe, a clever local pilot who was familiar with the landing field, had no difficulty steering his plane to those sections of the runway that allowed a safe takeoff or landing. However, he conceded strangers to the field might have problems during landings.[48]

Charles F. Vieu of Yolo County was planning a trip to San Diego in August to examine a new Ryan for possible purchase. He had been interested in flying since a memorable ride with the late William Sanborn in an to attempt to restore his hearing. After a dive of several thousand feet with Sanborn at the controls, Vieu, who had been almost totally deaf, could once again hear normally. Vieu had flown in a plane on several occasions and wanted to become a pilot.[49]

A Woodland favorite entrant for the upcoming Dole Race to Hawaii in mid-August was Livingston Irving. He was popular with local residents because of his participation in the 1921 air meet at Yolo Fliers Club Field.[50]

A bound booklet was received by the Woodland public library in late September entitled, *In Memoriam Lieutenant William Edward Sanborn, 1897–1927.* It was a brief biography of the Yolo County pilot killed flying the airmail for Varney Air Lines.[51]

Supervisor Frank Edson made a motion in June 1928 for a committee of supervisors to meet with a committee of city council members and a third committee of local businessmen to discuss financing the airport's revitalization. While Edson was making his motion to the board of supervisors, Herbert Kraft of Oakland damaged his Stearman landing at Fliers Club Field.[52] The club made elaborate plans for their airfield, but lacked funding according to a November 1928 report. They put the plans off until 1930. Members claimed their club was founded with the idea that eventually somewhere in the wide expanse west of Woodland another airport would be built.

There were more than 200 acres in the Fliers Club's approximate 450 acre tract exclusive of the golf course and the clubhouse. Of the 200 acres, there were more than 100 acres of level ground to build a first-class airport. The implication was the federal or state government should build a new airport—after all, the federal government was paying for construction of an emergency airfield near Capay near the 60-foot tall airway beacon.[53] In December 1928, the government beacon was turned on near the Capay emergency landing field constructed on 70 acres belonging to Wyatt G. Duncan in the Capay Valley of Yolo County. It was built to aid pilots flying the airway from Portland to San Francisco. Pacific Air Transport pilots derived the most benefit from the beacons; they flew airmail twice daily in each direction.[54]

Harry Crandall, a Pacific Air Transport pilot, was unable to see the beacons one morning in January 1929. He left San Francisco and ran into a fog bank immediately. He was forced to fly on the deck keeping landmarks in sight. As he approached Zamora near Woodland, a large tree suddenly appeared in his flight path. Before he could react, one wing struck it. Luckily, the plane held together while Crandall shut down his engine and landed in a farmer's field. Upon inspection, he discovered the tree did little damage and within several hours he made repairs and got on his way. The accident happened about 6:00 AM. Crandall was carrying only mail; no passengers were in danger.[55]

The following are notable aviation activities in Yolo County from 1929 through 1933. Carl Hansen of Woodland completed his flying course at Oakland Polytechnic College of Engineering. He passed his tests for a government pilot's license and received his diploma from the engineering school as an airplane and engine mechanic.[56] By April 1929 Woodland had its own flying club. The club owned a Swallow biplane that, during the last week of April, Ernie Moe flew from Woodland to the Sacramento municipal airport in Del Paso Park.[57] Vance Breese, a noted Bay Area aviator and airplane builder, with his wife flew into Fliers Club Field on Sunday, May 5. They intended to pay a surprise visit to Clem Lowe, a Yolo County grape grower and aviator. Breese was a flying student of Lowe's in 1925 at Yolo County. The Breeses were on their way to Portland for an airport opening.[58] The *Woodland Daily Democrat* announced a subscription drive in which the winner could win a new Waco 10 plus three hundred dollars in flying lessons.[59]

Pat Patterson of Oakland made an emergency landing in a grain field just south of Yolo Fliers Club Field on June 16. His biplane flipped over on touch down. Patterson lost two teeth and suffered minor cuts to his head; his passengers, Arthur Williams and James Dieudonne, both from Woodland, suffered minor cuts and bruises. According to the passengers, the engine seized at 500 feet. Patterson maintained control of the plane, gliding to the ground with a dead engine. His landing would not have been a problem except for a giant oak tree and high-voltage power lines. Patterson had a choice of landing over the heads of motorists parked around the grounds at the Fliers Club, or hitting the tree and power lines. He decided on a third option and landed off the airport in the nearby grain field.

L. J. Boldt of Oakland, owner of the biplane, was on the field that day with Patterson. The damage estimated at $1,200 was not covered by insurance. Three of the plane's four wing panels and the landing gear of Boldt's plane were damaged. Boldt, Patterson, and Jack Link, all from Oakland, took the plane apart during the night and shipped it back to Oakland for repair. Link reported Patterson had a good day making passenger hops before the accident, which he said was a minor annoyance. The accident did not disrupt him, his friends from Oakland, and Ernie Moe, a local aviator;

Chapter 20

all did good business flying passengers in their planes that day.[60]

Glenn Atterbury, formerly of Woodland, was planning distribution of stock in an aviation syndicate known as the Sierra Pacific Air Transit. Plans were to form an air service from Yolo County and other Northern California towns to San Francisco carrying mail, freight, and passengers. A. A. Clark was company president. The validity of this endeavor seems doubtful to this author. Practically every well-known financier and aviation personality in the state was listed as being on the board of directors, the advisory board, or the company's technical committee of the unknown aviation syndicate.[61]

Several Woodland service clubs and civic organizations announced in July they were planning to make improvements on Fliers Club Field in the near future. Those organizations estimated it would take about $1,100 to put the airfield in first class condition. The funds would cover removal of a tree obstructing the landing approach to one of the runways and the grading and surfacing of both runways. It also included filling a gully at one end of the field. It is unknown whether these improvements were made.[62]

H. R. Cook opened a commercial flying service at Woodland's Fliers Club Field in May 1930. H. H. Weggers and Ernest P. Moe, both of whom had recently acquired their transport pilot licenses, joined Cook in the new enterprise. Cook acquired the Northern California distributorship for Lincoln-Page aircraft. In the process, he purchased an OX-5 Lincoln-Page P-3 and an OX-5 Lincoln-Page PT for immediate delivery from Dycer Airport in Los Angeles. Cook stated he would be adding a Lincoln-Page PTK to his stable of aircraft on Fliers Club Field within a few weeks.[63]

CLYDE "UPSIDE-DOWN" PANGBORN brought his "Flying Fleet" air circus to Woodland for an air show and passenger hopping on July 3–4, 1930. The two-day event was at Best Field on Dan Best's farm (Today The Maples farm is at Highway 113 and Best Ranch Road—Best Field was on the south side of Best Ranch Road across from The Maples farmhouse.), one mile north of Woodland.

Pangborn, once a partner in Ivan Gates' flying circus, was now in partnership with Hugh Herndon Jr. They had another pilot flying with them, Ray Baumgartner. Pangborn and Herndon had purchased three airplanes (Standard J-1s or Jennies) from the recently bankrupt Empire Air Circus and painted them an eye-catching green and gold. They had just flown in an air show at Laramie, Wyoming, then proceeded directly to Woodland,

Fig. 87. Dan Best beside his Stearman C-3 circa 1931. Behind the Stearman is the hangar at Best Field, which served as Woodland's airport when Yolo Fliers Club Field fell into disrepair during the early Depression years. Notice the name of the Best estate, the "Maples," on the hangar roof.

a favorite destination of Pangborn's. He had participated in the Yolo Fliers Club meet of 1921, and he and Herndon had flown an air show at Woodland in the fall of 1929. They had done well financially and decided to give the area another try. After the Woodland show, they were planning to swing northward through Oregon and Washington. Since forming the Flying Fleet they visited 60 cities and performed 100 exhibitions. With DOC pressure mounting on barnstormers, Pangborn finally gave up barnstorming after his Flying Fleet performed at Palo Alto Airport in February 1931.

However for the 1930 three-day celebration at Best Field near Woodland the Flying Fleet would sweep over the city in battle formation and then each pilot would break off and go into his aerobatic routine. Each afternoon there would be aerobatics with an emphasis on upside-down (inverted) flying. Airplane rides were given for extremely low prices. Each day's activities would end with a parachute jump in the evening.

After the battle formation flight at noon, and before the pilots each went into a stunt-flying routine, they threw out copies of the *Woodland Daily Democrat* some of which contained tickets for a free airplane ride. There was no charge for admission at Best Field and no parking fees. Many folks from

Woodland remembered the Flying Fleet from its visit in the fall of 1929 just after Pangborn formed the group. To illustrate how low prices for barnstormer hops had dropped, the ad for Pangborn's Flying Fleet July Fourth 1930 air show in the Woodland newspaper read, "FLY for $1.00 with The Flying Fleet" In 1919 hops cost ten dollars a person; by 1921 they were five dollars; the 1924 price was two-fifty; then a penny-a-pound; and finally by 1930 the Depression price was one dollar a ride.[64]

A commercial flying school opened on Yolo Fliers Club Field in June 1930 run by Cook, Weggers and Ernie Moe. Ten students signed on: Louis Giminez, John Hanson, Wallace Huston, Leonard Cook, D. Richards, L. F. Thomas, Curtis Hanson, Nathanial Wallace, Harold Marley, and Dan Radcliffe. In addition to teaching these students, the three instructors did any commercial flying job offered.[65] In 1930 the three started crop dusting and seeding operations in the Woodland and Knights Landing area. They joined several other flying businesses in the Sacramento Valley as pioneers in ag-flying.

The name of Cook's flying business at Fliers Club Field was Woodland Flying Service. His newspaper ad stated he used approved-type training planes and lessons were five dollars each. Passenger and cross-country flights were available. The July 7, 1930, newspaper ad said nothing about crop seeding or dusting.[66] One of Woodland Flying Service's first commercial jobs was dropping 10,000 leaflets advertising the new Buddy Rogers flying movie, *Young Eagles*, opening at the National Theater in Woodland. Weggers and Moe dropped 2,000 more over Winters, Esparto, Madison, Yolo, and Knights Landing. One hundred included free tickets to the movie. Their planes displayed the movie title painted on the underside of the wings.[67]

In early July 1930, it was believed Charles Kingsford-Smith would stop at Woodland on his flight from New York to Oakland in the now famous tri-motor Fokker, *Southern Cross*. In 1920, Kingsford-Smith and Irwin Hunt had flown over the rice fields near Knights Landing for Edmund J. Moffett's duck patrol. The locals were disappointed when he did not stop.[68]

Woodland Airport, as Fliers Club Field gradually became known, had a busy day the first Sunday of November 1930. Thirty passengers purchased short hops over the field setting a record. Pete Borello, from Kirksville in Sutter County, flew his plane into Woodland. Mr. M. Thompson of Dixon visited Woodland in a plane he purchased from Woodland's Clem Lowe. Francis Gallagher of Kirksville brought his plane over to Woodland, as did

George Vawter of Arbuckle who was showing off his new Curtiss Robin purchased the week before in Los Angeles.

Ernie Moe and Herb Weggers were now managers of Woodland Airport.[69] They finally organized a flying club starting that November. Its ten members each bought one-tenth interest in an airplane to be used by them for instruction and flying the required number of hours to qualify for a private pilot license. At the time Moe and Weggers were reported busy giving instruction and flying charters from Woodland Airport.[70] No mention had been made in local newspapers or aviation trade magazines yet of Moe and Weggers doing crop seeding or dusting in 1930.

In December Gilbert Anderson of Woodland purchased an OX-5 Swallow from Thomas Fredrick and Claude Trader of San Diego.[71] In April 1931, Woodland dealer H. R. Cook sold an OX-5 Lincoln-Page to his own business, which was run by Ernie Moe, Herb Weggers, and himself at Woodland Airport. He also sold an OX-5 Lincoln-Page to C. C. Smith of Princeton.[72]

Dan Best of Woodland, holder of a limited commercial license for the

Fig. 88. Dan Best with his Stearman C-3 at Best Field, one mile north of Woodland. Dan's father, C. L. Best consolidated his business, the C. L. Best Gas Traction Company, with the Holt Caterpillar Company in the spring of 1925 to form today's Caterpillar Tractor Company, one of the most successful companies in America.

past year, took the DOC exams from aviation inspector James Peyton on November 3, 1931, and earned his transport pilot license. Best, born in San Leandro, living in Piedmont and Woodland, first owned a Stearman C-3 then a Staggerwing Beechcraft C17B, registered NC16439.[73]

On December 10, 1932, Santa Claus arrived from the North Pole in an airplane flown by Harry Trayham. He landed at 1:30 on the west side of Woodland and taxied up Court Street with Sea and Boy Scouts acting as an honor guard. The Woodland High School marching band followed playing Christmas songs. At Fourth Street, the parade turned onto Main and traveled down the boulevard to the city Christmas tree at First and Main; there the party began. Precautions were taken to protect citizens from the plane's spinning propeller when it taxied down Main Street. In addition to the scouts, local traffic officers were on duty and county law enforcement provided crowd control.[74] Another report claimed Sacramento pilot Ivor Witney flew Santa Claus to Woodland, then taxied Santa up Main Street in a Fleet biplane. Santa was a guest of the Woodland Merchants Association. Permission from the DOC was given for the stunt.[75]

Charles W. Bird, a Woodland youth, invented an adjustable pitch airplane propeller and received patent pending papers from Washington, D. C., in June 1933. Bird explained the pitch of the prop was adjusted by the pilot pulling a lever, which would automatically enable the propeller to adjust for thinner air at altitude. He also said the prop could act as a brake when an airplane was rolling out on landing, and it could be used to back the airplane up while taxiing.[76]

THE WOODLAND FALL Fiesta had a new attraction added to its celebration. Local aviators announced an air show in conjunction with the October 7–8, 1933, festival. They planned to have stunt flying, an autogiro, military aircraft, and a parachute jump each day.

Dan Best offered his flying field north of Woodland once again for the air show. A small admission fee was charged spectators to get onto the field; the money was used to build a permanent hangar for local aviators. Some of the money earned from passenger hopping over the city during the air show went into the new hangar fund. Besides Best, the following aviators and air enthusiasts were responsible for organizing the air show: W. H. Hazeman, Vernon G. Heaton, Rex Buckles, Leslie Morris, Mark Edgar, and Harold Marley. These pilots assisted the chamber of commerce by distributing leaflets from an airplane throughout the county advertising the Fall

Fiesta schedule.[77]

Dan Best and his good friend, Harry Trayham, flew to Bay Area airports on September 28 to encourage pilots to attend the Woodland air show. They visited airports in Alameda, Oakland, and San Bruno. A number of the pilots said they would come, including Joe Hargrove of Hargrove Air Service who said he would be happy to attend.[78]

On September 30, George Creel, Western States Administrator of the National Recovery Administration (NRA), was flown into Fliers Club Field from the Bay Area by Shirley Brush to participate in a NRA Day celebration and Blue Eagle (NRA symbol) parade at Woodland.[79]

Dan Best dropped green and white leaflets on Woodland and nearby communities on the fourth. Finding a green leaflet entitled one to a free airplane ride.[80]

Yolo Fliers Club added two more pictures to its clubhouse Hall of Fame. One depicted Admiral Richard E. Byrd, the polar explorer. The poster size photograph carried greetings to club members with his autograph. The other photo was Capt. Lester Maitland and Capt. Albert Hegenberger, the first pilots to fly from the mainland to Hawaii. It came from the US Army and carried both aviator's autographs. The club's Hall of Fame was rapidly growing with large photographs of famous American aviators.[81] Even though most of those in the Hall of Fame never visited Yolo Fliers Club Field, it is an impressive collection of photos which remain on display at the clubhouse to this day.

The air show at Woodland's Best Field was a success in every way. Over 1,500 people attended and 200 went for airplane rides. Sacramento's Charlie "Red" Jensen was a huge hit with his parachute jump from 4,000 feet. Dan Best won the air race against Bay Area pilots, Harry Sham, Denny Wright, and Phil Worley. Henry Krines was the sole Woodland entrant in the motorcycle events. Sacramento motorcycle clubs raced and fielded a motorcycle polo match between exhibition flights. J. Brandt flew an autogiro up from Oakland and demonstrated the curious looking machine—one of the most interesting performances of the day. Brandt later flew several passenger hops with the autogiro. In addition to Brandt, the following pilots gave passenger rides: Phil Worley, Harry Sham, Denny Wright, Dan Best, and Floyd Nolta. The entire event was held without an injury. Enough money was made to pay for a new hangar on Best Field resulting in local aviators thanking the merchants and everyone who supported the show.

Woodland's Ernie Moe was hired by Valley Air Lines to fly a Boeing passenger biplane from Sacramento to San Francisco five times a day. He also made one night flight every 24 hours delivering a San Francisco newspaper to Modesto, Stockton, and Sacramento.[82]

Plans for the American Legion membership drive at Woodland were completed on October 26 after Dudley Steele, state aeronautic committee chairman for the American Legion, landed at Best Field to meet with local commander Fred McGrew and membership chairman Harold McCollom. The three conferred, then Steele's plane departed. Chet Elliott would fly into Best Field on November 12, pick up the final membership cards, and rush them to Oakland. The local legionnaires would extend every effort during the membership drive to secure the full quota from the local American Legion post before Elliott arrived.[83]

Al Davis, brother of L. F. Davis of Woodland, was killed on the night of November 9. The Boeing Model 80A tri-motor airliner he was flying crashed into a hill a mile-and-a-half from Swan Island Airport at Portland, Oregon. Three passengers died. Copilot H. B. Woodworth and four passengers were injured. Stewardess Libby Wurgaft was uninjured. Davis was flying the Seattle to Oakland run for Boeing Air Transport and was scheduled to stop at Sacramento.[84]

Yolo Fliers Club held its annual meeting to elect directors on November 13; it was reported membership was down to 116. Sixty-three were local residents and the rest were mostly associate members from out of town.[85]

DAN BEST PULLED off a spectacular stunt December 2, 1933, at Knights Landing. The old railway bridge over the Sacramento River, converted for automobile use, was replaced with a new bridge. Supervisor Frank Edson lobbied hard for the upgrade for many years. Yuba City engineer Ed Von Geldren designed the bascule bridge, which still connects Sutter County to Yolo County on Highway 113, once known as Knights Landing Highway. The opening celebration was a big event for both counties featuring concerts, baseball, boating events, a dedication ceremony, ribbon cutting, many speeches, and then—best of all—Dan Best flew under the new bridge.

Best received approval on November 29 from the DOC to go ahead. Three days later he carried out the stunt. He had 200 feet of clearance for the 35-foot wingspan but only 35 feet of clearance between the bottom of the bridge and the river, so the bridge was slightly raised. Best later told a reporter, "It was just a case of sneaking in over the trees, leveling off the ship about eight or ten feet above the water and then getting back into the air

Fig. 89. Dan Best is depicted here flying under the new bridge over the Sacramento River at Knights Landing. He did this twice during the opening celebration for the bridge on December 2, 1933.

before the ship came too close to the trees and power lines on the other side. I would estimate the speed of the ship at about 120 miles per hour when it went under the bridge. There was plenty of clearance on the sides. ... It was a case of either making the effort safely or cracking up, and I was praying that everything would go all right. After the first time under the bridge, it was simple, and ... I did it a second time." About 1,500 people attended the dedication and witnessed Best's two flights under the bridge. They were further entertained by Best, C. A. Wulff, and Vernon Heaton who put on a stunt flying exhibition and ribbon cutting (toilet paper rolls) demonstration. Passenger rides were sold all day long followed by a 9:00 o'clock dance held in Knight's Landing.[86]

THE WOODLAND CHAMBER of Commerce informed the city council in December there was federal grant money available to cities for building or improving the nation's airports. There was $5,000 available per city to employ 50 people. But it was discovered the city didn't own the Yolo Fliers Club airport property and for this reason Woodland could not get a grant.[87]

Veteran Woodland pilot E. Clem Lowe announced at the end of December he was running for constable of Woodland. His experience of working ten years as a lawman for the Western Pacific and Southern Pacific Railroad companies and his time as a Yolo County deputy sheriff qualified him for the job. He was the son of Woodland pioneers Mr. and Mrs. Thomas R. Lowe. Lowe graduated from Woodland High School and lived in Woodland most of his life. An avid flier and member of the Yolo Fliers Club, he was a Woodland aviation pioneer. He was not elected sheriff but he was made a deputy sheriff in the mid-1930s.[88]

In June 1934, the new hangar was dedicated at Best Field followed by an air show. Carl E. Wulff, chosen as chairman of the air show by local pilots, organized the event. The new hangar was built with money raised by local pilots at previous air shows.[89]

Ernie Moe was wrangling wild horses with an airplane in the Nevada desert the summer of 1934. During this dangerous low-flying endeavor, the Woodland commercial pilot worked with pilots Jerry Barker, Charles Kendall, and Albert E. Waite.[90]

The Aviation Country Club of Northern California made a fly out to Woodland April 16, 1939. Some of the pilots involved were Mr. and Mrs. Carl Vanderford, Foster and Paul McMullen, and Mildred Rose.[91]

Yolo County residents with land for sale between Davis and Woodland on Highway 99W were asked to contact the Woodland Chamber of Commerce. Ross Norrington, a member of the chamber's land committee reported options for a 640-acre tract were being sought for an unspecified project. The committee found few available sights according to Norrington.[92] This is believed to be a military airfield site search that culminated in the construction of the World War II airfield known today as the Winters/Davis/Woodland Airport or more commonly known as Yolo International Airport. It is located on Road 95, seven miles south of the Yolo Fliers Club Field. The Fliers Club Field was later known as Woodland Airport and now is known as Woodland-Watts Airport. During World War II, Yolo International Airport was used by the Army Air Force for training and as a secondary base should Japanese invade the West Coast.

IN MAY 1941, Ernest P. Moe was back in Woodland visiting his family. He had been in Santa Monica in December 1939 looking for work as a flier. He had a transport pilot license and secured a job with Lowell Yerex flying transports in Central America. Yerex was Clyde Pangborn's old friend from their days with the Gates Flying Circus. When Ernie Moe went to work for Yerex at Tegucigalpa, Honduras, on January 1, 1940, Yerex was managing a Central American airline he created a couple years before called Transportes

Aereos Centro-Americanos. It was known throughout Mexico and Central America as TACA. The company's motto was, "TACA flies anything anywhere." It hauled mainly mail and freight.

Ernie Moe joined TACA when the airline started its second year as the lifeline for the La Luz gold mine at Siuna, Nicaragua. This lifeline would continue five more years. Drag Lines, trucks, D-6 Caterpillar tractors, ore crushers, two-ton ore carts, etc. were disassembled and the pieces were loaded into Ford 5-AT tri-motor transports and delivered to the mine. A total of 30,000 tons was flown to the mine over six years.[93]

Moe returned to California in April 1941. He had flown thousands of miles over vast jungles and small pro-American countries. He noticed the war in Europe made all Central American countries aware of Germany's threat to their freedom if Hitler were to win. Moe, in an interview with his hometown newspaper, reported not only what he noticed, but added it was common knowledge the Nazis were collecting useful intelligence while operating Sociedad Colombo–Alemana de Transportes Aereos (SCADTA) Airline out of Columbia.

Moe said, "[It] was the dream of every pilot in Central America to return to the United States to fly. Pilots flying for TACA have fine ratings, but it is difficult to keep them there. Pay is good and all that. However, the boys feel there are more opportunities at home especially in the field of aeronautics." He went on to say, "The TACA line was established in 1932 by Lowell Yerex of New Zealand. Today (1941), the line is a rival of Pan-American in Central America and has 14 Ford tri-motor planes in service along with approximately 25 other airplanes." Moe flew one of these transports for about 100 hours a month. His flights between San Salvador and Costa Rica boosted his total flying time to 4,500 hours.

Moe was born in Woodland in 1908 and remained in Yolo County until he was 17. Then he worked in and out of town until 1927. He began flying with Herb Weggers and Clem Lowe at Woodland. Weggers, Moe's closest friend, in 1941 was still giving flying lessons but was more engaged in planting rice by airplane. Moe did that for a while in the early '30s; he helped Weggers become an ag-flying pioneer in Northern California. During his interview, Moe said he was planning to leave for Los Angeles. He was up for the military draft and thought he might enlist before he was called up. He also wanted to ferry bombers from Canada to England. He said the pay was good and the nine-hour flights were only dangerous during the last hour. He said there were three ex-TACA pilots in service ferrying planes

Chapter 20

to England.[94]

On May 21, 1941, Moe was reported at the Woodland Clinic in critical condition with a mysterious illness. He was stricken on the 20th and taken to the clinic by ambulance where his condition worsened. Members of his family were isolated as a precaution.[95] The next day his condition was unchanged; he was unconscious with a high fever. Moe had recently returned from Central America. The day before he fell ill, Lockheed had offered him an important flying job. Ernie Moe died May 23, 1941, from a form of meningitis.

Moe had planned to visit the Los Angeles family of one of his friends killed flying in Central America. He had some of his friend's personal belongings with him, and he had arranged a meeting with the family. That never happened. Moe was one of the early pilots at Yolo Fliers Club Field. He was admired for his many fine qualities and was a great loss to Woodland and the Sacramento Valley aviation community.[96]

This is the third book of a trilogy that concludes what, in the beginning, was a single work tentatively titled, *Northern Wings Over The Golden State: A History of Early Aviation in Northern California 1910–1939*. Due to the extent of detailed information required to describe the early history of airplane flight in the significantly populated counties of Northern California, meaning those of the Bay Area and the Sacramento Valley, it became necessary to break the work into three volumes of a publishable size. If information is desired about the progress of aviation technology in the north state, such as: who were the notable aviators in those significant areas; where were their first airports; who made the first flights in the cities and towns; when did notable flights take place; what aircraft were used; who built those machines; and what effects did this amazing new technology have on Northern Californians; it would be necessary to read not only this book but also this author's *Aviation in Northern California 1910–1939 Volume I*, a history of early flight in the San Francisco Bay Area and *Aviation in Northern California 1910–1939 Volume II*, a history of early aviation in Yuba, Sutter, and Butte counties, those Sacramento Valley counties not covered in this book.

Fig. 90. Another view of the Bristol Tourer parked on Yolo Fliers Club Field on August 22, 1920, during the air meet held there. Clifford Prodger flew the plane there and later in the day crashed at his Redwood City home field killing himself and his two passengers. He had been flying an aerobatic exhibition over the field when he crashed.

Fig. 91. Shown here in August 1920 is the Pacific Standard flown from Los Angeles to Yolo Fliers Club Field by Emory Rogers with John Hogg as his passenger. They made it an aerial camping trip.

Endnote
ABBREVIATIONS

Abbreviation -- Magazine or Journal

AAHS Journal -- American Aviation Historical Society Journal
AAM -- American Aviation Magazine
AAW -- Aerial Age and Aerial Age Weekly
A CUR -- Air Currents Magazine
AD -- Aero Digest Magazine
Aero -- Aero Magazine (As of July 1912 Aero became Aero & Hydro)
Aero & Hydro -- Aero and Hydro Magazine
Aeronautics -- Aeronautics Magazine
Air and Space -- Air and Space Magazine
Aviation -- Aviation Magazine
PA -- Popular Aviation Magazine
PAN -- Pacific Airport News
SHSJ -- Sacramento Historical Society Journal
PF -- Pacific Flyer Magazine
SPF -- Sport Flying Magazine
The Ace -- The Ace Magazine
WF -- Western Flying Magazine

Abbreviation -- Newspapers

BWN -- Biggs Weekly News
CDS -- Colusa Daily Sun
CG -- Concord Gazette
CH -- Colusa Herald
CO -- Corning Observer
CR -- Chico Record
COR -- Corning Republican
GAH -- Galt Herald
GH -- Gridley Herald
GNP -- Glendale News Press
HT -- Humbolt Times
IVP -- Imperial Valley Press
LMRR -- Los Molinos River Rambler
MA -- Marysville Appeal
MAD -- Marysville Appeal Democrat
MD -- Marysville Democrat
MJ -- Marin Journal
MNH -- Modesto New Herald
MSS -- Merced Sun Star

MT -- Marin Tocsin
NEG -- Nevada Evening Gazette (Reno)
NSJ -- North Sacramento Journal
ODR -- Oroville Daily Register
OMR -- Oroville Mercury Register
OT -- Oakland Tribune
PR -- Porterville Recorder
RBDN -- Red Bluff Daily News
RCD -- Redwood City Democrat
RCFP -- Redding Courier Free Press
RDC -- Redding Daily Courier
RDI -- Richmond Daily Independent
SB -- Sacramento Bee
SCF -- Sutter County Farmer
SCIF -- Sutter County Independent Farmer
SDER -- Stockton Daily Evening Record
SDI -- Stockton Daily Independent
SF Call -- San Francisco Call Bulletin
SF Ch -- San Francisco Chronicle
SF Ex -- San Francisco Examiner
SRPD -- Santa Rosa Press Democrat
SU -- Sacramento Union
TDJ -- Turlock Daily Journal
WDD -- Woodland Daily Democrat
WDJ -- Willows Daily Journal
WDR -- Woodland Daily Register
WJ -- Willows Journal
WM -- Woodland Mail

ENDNOTES

Chapter 1

1. *SU*, Apr. 24, 1909.
2. *SU*, Apr. 20, 1909.
3. *SU*, Apr. 20 & 25, 1909; Raymond, *AAHS Journal*, Spring 1985, p. 66.
4. *SU*, Apr. 22, 1909.
5. *SU*, Apr. 22 & 25, 1909; *SB*, Apr. 22 &25, 1909.
6. *SU*, Apr. 25, 1909; *SB*, Apr. 25, 1909.
7. *SU*, Apr. 26, 1909.
8. *SU*, Apr. 24, 1909.
9. Couch, p. 534; Robinson, *AAHS Journal*, Summer 1976, pp. 84-91.
10. Couch, p. 507.
11. Robinson, *AAHS Journal*, Summer 1976, pp. 84-91.
12. Couch, p. 528.
13. Robinson, *AAHS Journal*, Summer 1976, pp. 84-91.
14. Couch, p. 528.
15. Ibid.
16. Raymond, *AAHS Journal*, Spring 1985, p. 66.
17. *SB*, Jan. 20, 1910.
18. *SB*, Jan. 31, 1910.
19. *SB*, Jan. 29, 1910; *SB*, Feb. 1, 1910; *Aeronautics*, Jan. 1910, p. 28. *SU*, Feb. 2, 1910.
20. *SU*, Feb. 2, 1910; *SB*, Feb. 2, 1910.
21. *SB*, Feb. 2, 1910.
22. *SB*, Feb. 11, 1910.
23. *SU*, Feb. 13-14, 1910.
24. *Aeronautics*, Mar. 1910, p. 99; *Aeronautics*, June 1910, p. 202; *Aeronautics*, July 1910, p. 280
25. *SB*, Apr. 8, 1910; *Aeronautics*, June 1910, p. 202; *Aeronautics*, July 1910, p. 280; California Aviation Company Papers, Box 2494 & Box 2498.
26. *SU*, Apr. 6, 1910.
27. *OT*, Apr. 2, 1910.
28. *SB*, Apr. 8, 1910.
29. *SU*, Apr. 16, 1910.
30. *SU*, Apr. 17, 1910.
31. *SU*, Apr. 18, 1910; *SB*, Apr. 18, 1910.
32. *Aeronautics*, Mar. 1910, p. 89.
33. *Aeronautics*, May 1910, p. 163.
34. *SB*, Apr. 20, 1910.
35. *MJ*, Apr. 7, 1910; *SF Call*, Apr. 4, 1910; *MT*, June 21, 1910.
36. *SF Call*, May 30, 1910.
37. *SB*, June 2, 1910.
38. *SB*, July 11, 1910.
39. *SB*, July 21, 1910.
40. *SB*, July 26, 1910; Villard, p. 75.
41. *SB*, July 28, 1910.
42. Crouch, p. 524-527.
43. Military Museum of the California National Guard, Sacramento, CA, Wall Poster.
44. *SB*, Aug. 6, 1910.
45. *SB*, Aug. 11, 1910; *SU*, Aug. 9, 1910.
46. *SB*, Aug. 13, 1910.
47. Ibid.
48. *SB*, Aug. 13-15, 1910.

Chapter 2

1. Roseberry, pp. 44-45, 224; Gardner, p. 76.
2. *SU*, Aug. 31, 1910; Roseberry, pp. 228, 281, 285.
3. *SU*, Sept. 1, 1910.
4. *SU*, Sept. 4, 1910.
5. *SU*, Sept. 5, 1910.
6. *SU*, Sept. 6, 1910.
7. *SU*, Sept. 7, 1910.
8. *SU*, Sept. 8, 1910.
9. *SRPD*, Sept. 9-11, 1910; Villard, p. 76.
10. *SU*, Sept. 9, 1910.
11. *SU*, Sept. 10, 1910.
12. *SRPD*, Sept. 11, 1910; *SU*, Sept. 12, 1910.
13. *SU*, Sept. 12-14, 1910.
14. *SU*, Sept. 22 & 25, 1910.
15. *SU*, Sept. 26, 1910.
16. Roseberry, p. 290.
17. Roseberry, p. 293.
18. *SU*, Jan. 27, 1911.
19. *SU*, Feb. 5, 1911.
20. *SU*, Feb. 6, 1911.

21. Ibid.
22. *SU*, Dec. 14 & 16, 1911; *SB*, Jan. 20, 1934; *SU*, Aug. 29, 1911; *SU*, Nov. 21, 1911.
23. *SU*, Dec. 16, 1911; *Aero*, Jan. 20, 1912, p. 322; *Aero*, May 25, 1912, p. 201, Robinson, p. 59.
24. Ibid.
25. Ibid.
26. *SU*, Dec. 17, 1911.
27. California Aviation Co. Papers, Box 2498; Roseberry, p. 314; *SB*, Jan. 20, 1934; *SU*, June 2, 1913.
28. Harp, Major Leland, "Biography of Joseph L. Cato," http:// www.rcooper.0catch.com.htm
29. Lewis, p. 61.
30. *Aero*, Dec. 30, 1911, p. 258.
31. *Aero*, Jan. 27, 1912, p. 346.
32. Cummins, p. 28; *SB*, Mar. 1, 1912; Glenshaw, *Air and Space*, April/May, 2008, p. 55.
33. *SB*, Mar. 1, 1912.
34. *SB*, Mar. 2, 1912.
35. *Aero*, Mar. 16, 1912, p. 479; *SB*, Mar. 4, 1912; *SU*, Mar. 3, 1912.
36. *Aero*, Mar. 30, 1912, p. 521; *SU*, Mar. 27, 1912; *SU*, Apr. 23, 1912; *SU*, Apr. 28, 1912.
37. *Aero and Hydro*, Sept. 7, 1912, p. 505; *SU*, May 1, 1914.
38. *Aero*, May 11, 1912, p. 143.
39. Hatfield, p. 32.
40. *SU*, Apr. 18, 1913; *SU*, Mar. 18, 1913.
41. *SU*, Apr. 17, 1913.
42. *SU*, Apr. 18, 1913.
43. *SU*, Apr. 20-21, 1913; *Aero and Hydro*, Apr. 13, 1913, p. 21; *Aero and Hydro*, May 3, 1913, p. 86.
44. *Aero and Hydro*, May 3, 1913, p. 86; *Aero and Hydro*, May 17, 1913, p. 143.
45. *CR*, June 29, 1913; *SU*, Dec. 21, 1913.
46. *Aero and Hydro*, Sept. 13, 1913, p. 455.
47. Ibid.
48. *SU*, Nov. 17, 1913.
49. Ibid.
50. *SU*, Nov. 18 & 30, 1913;
51. *SU*, Nov. 30, 1913.
52. *SU*, Dec. 2-3, 1913.
53. *OMR*, Dec. 2, 1913.
54. *OMR*, Dec. 3, 1913.
55. *OMR*, Dec. 4, 1913.
56. *OMR*, Dec. 5, 1913.
57. *OMR*, Dec. 11, 1913.
58. *OMR*, Dec. 30, 1913; *SU*, Dec. 24, 1913.
59. *SB*, Oct. 19, 1914.
60. *SB*. Oct. 19, 1913; *SU*, Oct. 16-19, 1914; Marrero, p. 78.
61. Harwood and Fogel, p. 116; *SU*, Sept. 2, 1916; *SF Call*, Sept. 6&7, 1905.
62. *SU*, Sept. 3, 1916.
63. *SB*, Sept. 5, 1916.
64. *SU*, Sept. 5, 1916.
65. *SU*, Sept. 6, 1916.
66. *SU*, Sept. 7, 1916.
67. *SU*, Sept. 8, 1916.
68. *SU*, Sept. 14, 1916.
69. *SF Ch*, Apr. 13, 1917.

Chapter 3

1. *SB*, Sept. 8, 1917.
2. *SB*, Sept. 10, 1917.
3. *SB*, Sept. 12, 1917.
4. *SB*, Sept. 13, 1917.
5. *SB*, June 27, 1923; *SB*, Mar. 6, 1918; Henley, *SHSJ*, Vol. 3 No. 2 & 3, p. 36; *WF*, Mar. 1930, p.60-62.
6. *SB*, Sept. 9, 1918; *SB*, June 27, 1923.
7. *SB*. June 27, 1923.
8. *SB*, Mar. 6, 1918.
9. *SB*, Sept. 5, 1918; Lincke, pp. 102-103.
10. Lincke, pp. 102-103; *SB*, Sept. 9, 1918.
11. Bowers, pp. 168-169; Moore, Clyde, Interview, Jan. 2000.
12. *SB*, Mar. 6, 1918.
13. *SB*, Mar. 13, 1918.
14. Kemper, Lt. Seymour, "History of Mather Field 1918-1938," Unpublished, 1944, pp. 1-2; Unknown author, Mather AFB, "Sacramento Saga," No date, pp. 1-2, Sacramento Archives and Collection Center.
15. Kemper, "History of Mather . . .", p. 2; Unknown, "Sacramento Saga," p. 1.
16. Ibid
17. *Air Currents*, Dec. 1918, p. 13.
18. *SB*, Sept. 5 & 9, 1918.
19. *SB*, Sept. 7, 1918.
20. Kemper, "History of Mather . . .," pp. 1-2; *Air Currents*, Dec. 1918, p. 13; Lord, *A Sacramento Saga*, p. 344.
21. *AAW*, Nov. 22, 1915, pp. 225 & 228; *AAW*, July 3, 1916, p. 474.
22. Gordon, p. 453.
23. *SB*, Mar. 8, 1919.
24. Gardner, p. 86.
25. *AAW*, Nov. 25, 1918, p. 561.
26. Billman, *Sport Aviation*, Feb. 1977, pp. 58-60; *SU*, Sept. 23, 1916.
27. *MJ*, Nov. 4, 1961.
28. Billman, *Sport Aviation*, Feb. 1977, pp. 61-63.
29. Grey, pp. 252b-253b.

ENDNOTES 473

30. Billman, *Sport Aviation*, Feb. 1977, pp. 57-65.

Chapter 4

1. *Air Currents*, Dec. 1918, p. 18.
2. *SB*, Mar. 22 & 24, 1919.
3. *Air Currents*, Dec. 1918, p. 10.
4. *MD*, May 8, 1919.
5. *SB*, Mar. 22, 1919; Schonberger, p. 25; *SRPD*, Feb. 18, 1911.Endnoteabbreviations
6. *MD*, May 10, 1919.
7. *MD*, May 19, 1919.
8. *SB*, July 3, 1919.
9. *SB*, June 4, 1919; *SB*, July 3, 1919.
10. *SB*, July 4, 1919.
11. *SB*, July 8 & 14, 1919.
12. *SB*, July 17, 1919.
13. *SB*, July 29, 1919
14. *SB*, Aug. 5, 1919.
15. *SB*, Aug. 13, 1919; *CR*, Aug. 16, 1919; *CR*, Aug. 14, 1919.
16. *SU*, Sept. 19, 1919; *SU*, Sept. 24, 1919; *SU*, Sept. 2, 1919.
17. *SU*, Sept. 5, 1919.
18. *OMR*, Aug. 12, 1919.
19. *SU*, Sept. 8, 1919.
20. *AAW*, Sept. 22, 1919, p. 51.
21. *MD*, Aug. 1, 1919.
22. Murphy, p. 57.
23. *SU*, Sept. 18, 1919.
24. *SU*, Sept. 19, 1919.
25. *SB*, June 16, 1920; *SU*, Feb. 29, 1920.
26. *SB*, June 17, 1920.
27. *SB*, June 23, 1920; *WDJ*, June 26, 1920.
28. *SB*, June 26, 1920; *SU*, June 26, 1920.
29. *SU*, June 27, 1920.
30. *SB*, June 29, 1920.
31. *SF Ex*, Sept. 11, 1920.
32. *SU*, Sept. 23, 1919.
33. *SU*, Sept. 24, 1919.
34. *SU*, Apr. 22, 1920.
35. *SU*, Apr. 29, 1920.
36. Rhode, pp. 27-28.
37. Rhode, pp. 29 & 33.
38. Griffin, *Skyways*, No. 18, p. 42.
39. *AAW*, June 27, 1921, p. 364.
40. *SB*, Apr. 17, 1922.
41. *AAW*, Feb. 20, 1922, p. 560.
42. *AAW*, May 8, 1922, p. 207.
43. *AAW*, June 19, 1922, n.p.
44. *AAW*, May 15, 1922, p. 222.
45. *AAW*, Apr. 3, 1922, p.77.

Chapter 5

1. Abbott, Dan-San, *Lt. Colonel Harry W. Abbott*, Unpublished, p. 2-7.
2. Abbott, Dan-San, *Lt. Colonel Harry W. Abbott*, Unpublished, p. 2-7; Thad Kerns' contract on display at the Chico Air Museum in 2011.
3. Cleveland, pp. 39 &187.
4. Abbott, Dan-San, *Lt. Colonel Harry W. Abbott*, Unpublished, p. 3; Cleveland, p. 2.
5. Abbott, Dan-San, *Lt. Colonel Harry W. Abbott*, Unpublished, p. 5-11; Paul Chesebrough Album caption #21.
6. Abbott, Dan-San, *Lt. Colonel Harry W. Abbott*, Unpublished, pp. 12-13.
7. *AAW*, May 8, 1922, p. 207; *SU*, Dec. 17, 1922.
8. *SU*, Mar. 1, 1923.
9. *SU*, Mar. 11, 1923.
10. *SU*, Mar. 17, 1923.
11. *SU*, Mar. 25, 1922; Apr. 29, 1923; May 6, & 12-13, 1923.
12. *SB*, May 15, 1923; *SU*, May 15 & 18, 1923.
13. *SU*, May 21, 1923.
14. *SU*, May 21, 1923.
15. *AD*, July 1928, p. 108.
16. *SU*, June 5, 1923.
17. *SB*, June 6, 1923.
18. *NSJ* April/ May 1924.
19. *MD*, Mar. 28, 1925.
20. *NSJ*, Sept. 26, 1924; *SU*, Dec. 31, 1924.
21. *RDI*, May 9-11, 1925; *SB*, May 8-9 & 11, 1925, *The Ace*, June 1925, p. 8.
22. *SB*, Undated; Haller, pp. 53-55; *CG*, Jan. 1986
23. *SB*, July 1-4, 1925; *SU*, July 2-4, 1925.
24. *SU*, July 1, 1925.
25. *The Ace*, Aug. 1925, p. 12.
26. *SB*, July 1, 1925.
27. *SU*, Dec. 18, 1925.
28. *NSJ*, Apr. 16, 1926.
29. *WF*, Apr. 1926, p. 20.
30. *SB*, May 21, 1926.
31. *NSJ*, June 18, 1926.
32. *SB*, July 3, 1926.
33. *WF*, Mar. 1926, p. 20; *SU*, Sept. 8, 1970.
34. *SB*, July 3, 1926.
35. *NSJ*, Aug. 20, 1926.
36. *SU*, Aug. 29, 1926.
37. *WF*, Mar. 1926, p. 20; *WF*, Sept. 1926, p. 12.
38. *MA*, Sept. 29, 1926.
39. *WF*, Dec. 1926, p. 31.

Chapter 6

1. *WF*, June 1927, n. p.
2. *SB*, June 20, 1927.
3. *SB*, June 24, 1927.
4. *SB*, Oct. 25, 1927; *WF*, Sept. 1927, n. p.
5. *AD*, Nov. 1927, pp. 563-564.
6. *AD*, Nov. 1927, pp. 563-564; *PA*, Nov. 1927, p. 7.
7. *AD*, Nov. 1927, pp. 563-564.
8. *WF*, Dec. 1927, p. 51.
9. *AD*, Nov. 1927, pp. 563-564.
10. *AD*, Nov. 1927, p. 645
11. *SF Ch*, Dec. 19, 1927.
12. *SB*, Feb. 15, 1928.
13. *SB*, Feb. 22, 1928.
14. *SB*, Mar. 7, 1928.
15. *SB*, Mar. 21, 1928.
16. *WF*, Mar. 1928, p. 74.
17. *AD*, Apr. 1928, p. 634.
18. *SB*, Mar. 7, 1928.
19. *SB*, Apr. 11, 1928.
20. *SB*, Apr. 18, 1928.
21. *SB*, May 16, 1928.
22. *WF*, May 1928, p. 66.
23. *SB*, May 18, 1928.
24. *WF*, June 1928, p. 68.
25. *SB*, May 18, 1928.

Chapter 7

1. *MA*, Apr. 28, 1928.
2. *AD*, July 1928, p. 108.
3. *SU*, May 20-21, 1928.
4. *SU*, May 24, 1928.
5. *SU*, May 6 & 13, 1928.
6. *SB*, May 22, 1928.
7. *SB*, May 18, 1928.
8. *SU*, May 21, 1928.
9. *SB*, May 25, 1928.
10. *SB*, May 26, 1928.
11. *SB*, May 25, 1928.
12. *SB*, May 26, 1928.
13. *SB*, May 25-27, 1928; *SU*, May 25-27, 1928; *AD*, July 1928, p. 108.
14. *SU*, May 27, 1928; *WF*, May 1926, p. 8.
15. *SU*, May 27, 1928.
16. *SB*, May 26, 1928; *SB*, May 28, 1928.
17. *AD*, July 1928, p. 108.
18. Ibid.
19. *SB*, May 28, 1928; *SU*, May 28, 1928; *PF*, July 1928, p. 15.
20. *WF*, July 1928, p. 90.
21. *SU*, May 27, 1928.
22. Ibid.
23. *NSJ*, June 8, 1928.
24. *NSJ*, June 22, 1928.
25. *SB*, July 11, 1928.
26. *AD*, Aug. 1928, p. 276.
27. *WF*, Aug. 1928, p. 92.
28. *PF*, Aug. 1928, p. 19.
29. *SB*, Aug. 1, 1928; *WF*, Sept. 1928, p. 68.
30. *SB*, Aug. 8, 1928.
31. *NSJ*, Sept. 7, 1928.
32. *WF*, July 1928, p. 90.
33. *PF*, July 1928, pp. 17-20.
34. *WF*, Sept. 1928, p. 277.
35. *SB*, Aug. 2, 1928.
36. *SB*, Aug. 6, 1928.
37. *SU*, Aug. 10, 1928.
38. *SB*, Aug. 10, 1928.
39. *SB*, June 11, 1928.
40. *SB*, Aug. 13 & 16, 1928.
41. *SB*, Aug. 7, 1928.
42. *SB*, Aug. 24, 1928.
43. *SB*, Aug. 30, 1928.
44. *AD*, July 1928, p. 108.
45. *PR*, Nov. 9, 1979.
46. Ibid.
47. DeVries, p. 30.
48. *AD*, April 1928, p. 634.
49. *SB*, Mar. 14, 1928.
50. *SB*, Mar. 28, 1928.
51. *SB*, Apr. 11, 1928.
52. *SB*, Apr. 25, 1928.
53. *WF*, Aug. 1928.
54. *SB*, Aug. 14, 1928.
55. *SB*, Oct. 24, 1928.
56. *SB*, Dec. 12, 1928.
57. *CR*, June 25, 1928.
58. *AD*, Nov. 1928, p. 950.
59. *SB*, Jan. 30, 1928; *SB*, Feb. 13, 1928.
60. *SB*, Apr. 1, 1931.

Chapter 8

1. *SB*, Aug. 8, 1928.
2. *SB*, Aug. 22, 1928; *PF*, Oct. 1928.
3. *SB*, Aug. 20, 1928.
4. *SB*, Aug. 22, 1928.
5. *SB*, Sept. 26, 1928.
6. *SB*, Sept. 9, 1928.
7. *SB*, Sept. 26, 1928.
8. *MAD*, Sept. 29, 1928.
9. Cassagneres, pp. 176-179; Brown, pp. 166-167.
10. *SB*, Sept. 26, 1928.
11. *PF*, Oct. 1928, p. 25.
12. *SB*, Oct. 3, 1928.

Endnotes

13. *SB*, Oct. 10, 1928; *WF*, Sept. 1928, p. 78.
14. *SB*, Oct. 3, 1928.
15. *SB*, Oct. 10, 1928.
16. *SB*, Oct. 24, 1928.
17. *SB*, Oct. 24 & 31, 1928; *AD*, Dec. 1928, p. 1186.
18. *SB*, Oct. 31, 1928; *AD*, Dec. 1928, p. 1186.
19. *SB*, Oct. 10, 1928.
20. *SU*, Nov. 2, 1928.
21. *SU*, Nov. 5, 1928; *SB*, Nov. 5, 1928.
22. *SU*, Nov. 5 & 11, 1928; *WF*, Dec. 1928, p. 121.
23. *SU*, Nov. 11, 1928.
24. *WF*, Jan 1930, p. 118.
25. *SU*, Nov. 4, 1928.
26. *SB*, Nov. 7 & 11, 1928; *WF*, Dec. 1928, p. 106.
27. *GH*, Nov. 16, 1928.
28. *SU*, Nov. 12, 1928.
29. *SB*, Nov. 14, 1928.
30. *SB*, Nov. 21, 1928.
31. Ibid.
32. *SB*, Nov. 28, 1928.
33. *SB*, Dec. 19, 1928.
34. *SB*, Jan. 2, 1929.
35. *SB*, Jan. 16, 1929.
36. *SB*, Jan. 23, 1929.
37. *SB*, Jan. 30, 1929.
38. Ibid.
39. *SB*, Feb. 6, 1929.
40. *SB*, Jan. 23, 1929; *PA*, Feb. 1929, p. 75.
41. *WF*, Jan. 1930, p. 104.
42. *SB*, Feb. 6, 1929.
43. *SB*, Feb. 7, 1929.
44. *SB*, Feb. 27, 1929.
45. Ibid.
46. *SU*, May 2, 1929.
47. *SB*, Mar. 13, 1929.
48. *AD*, May 1929, p. 154.
49. *SB*, Mar. 1, 1929; *AD*, Apr. 1929, p. 154.
50. *SB*, Mar. 6, 1929.
51. *SB*, Mar. 20, 1929.
52. Ibid.
53. *SB*, Mar. 27, 1929.
54. Ibid.
55. Ibid.
56. *SB*, Apr. 3, 1929.
57. *SB*, Apr. 10 & 17, 1929.
58. *SB*, Apr. 24, 1929.
59. *WF*, May 1929, p. 92.
60. *SB*, May 1, 1929.
61. *SB*, Apr. 30, 1929.
62. *SB*, May 1, 1929.
63. *SU*, May 7-8, 1929.
64. *SB*, May 8, 1929.
65. *SU*, May 7, 1929; *SU*, May 8, 1929.
66. *SB*, May 8, 1929.
67. *SB*, May 22, 1929; *AD*, July 1929, p. 158.
68. *SB*, May 22, 1929.
69. *SB*, May 29, 1929.
70. *SB*, June 5 & 29, 1929.
71. *SB*, June 12, 1929.
72. *AD*, July 1929, p. 158.
73. *MAD*, July 1, 1929.
74. *AD*, July 1929, p. 160.
75. *SU*, June 2, 1929.
76. *PF*, July 1929, p. 19.
77. *SB*, June 12, 1929.
78. *SB*, June 19, 1929.
79. *SB*, Sept. 3, 1929.
80. *PF*, Sept. 1929, p. 21.
81. *SB*, Sept. 4, 1929.
82. *SB*, Sept. 11, 1929.
83. *SB*, Sept. 4, 1929.
84. *SB*, Sept. 25, 1929.
85. *SB*, Oct. 2, 1929.
86. *SB*, Oct. 6, 1929.
87. *SB*, Oct. 16, 1929.
88. *SB*, Oct. 23, 1929.
89. *SB*, Nov. 6 & 11, 1929.
90. *SB*, Nov. 20, 1929.
91. *SB*, Dec. 4, 1929.
92. *SB*, Dec. 11, 1929.
93. *SB*, Dec. 18, 1929; *SB*, Jan. 1, 1930

Chapter 9

1. *SB*, July 15, 1928.
2. *SB*, May 8, 1929.
3. *SB*, May 21, 1930.
4. *SB*, July 2, 1930.
5. *SB*, Oct. 1 & 8, 1930.
6. *PF*, Mar. 1931, p. 14.
7. *AD*, Oct. 1933, pp. 34-35; *SU*, July 26, 1919.
8. *SB*, Mar. 7, 1928.
9. *SB*, Mar. 14, 1928.
10. *SB*, May 16, 1928; *SB*, July 11, 1928.
11. *SB*, July 11, 1928.
12. *SU*, Aug. 26, 1928; *WF*, Aug. 1928, p. 92.
13. *SB*, Aug. 25, 1928.
14. *SB*, Sept. 26, 1928.
15. *AD*, Oct. 1933, pp. 34-35.
16. *WF*, Oct. 1938, p. 52.
17. *SB*, Apr. 17, 1977.
18. *SB*, May 16, 1928.
19. *SB*, July 16, 1928.
20. *PF*, Oct. 1928, p. 25.

21. *SB*, May 8, 1929.
22. *SB*, May 29, 1929; *SB*, Sept. 4, 1929.
23. *SB*, Jan. 15, 1930.
24. *SB*, Feb. 19, 1930.
25. *SB*, Aug. 13, 1930; *SB*, Jan. 28, 1931.
26. *SB*, Mar. 4, 1931; *SB*, Apr. 1, 1931.
27. *SB*, Apr. 8, 1931.
28. *SB*, Apr. 15, 1931.
29. *SB*, Apr. 22 & 29, 1931.
30. *SB*, May 6, 1931.
31. *SB*, May 13, 1931.
32. *SB*, Sept. 16, 1931.
33. *SB*, Nov. 11, 1931.
34. *SB*, Jan. 13, 1932; *SB*, Mar. 2, 1932.
35. *SB*, May 18, 1932.
36. *SB*, June 29, 1932.
37. *SB*, July 13 & 20, 1932.
38. *SB*, Aug. 10, 1932.
39. *SB*, Oct. 26, 1932; *SB*, Nov. 23, 1932.
40. *SB*, Dec. 14, 1932.
41. *SB*, July 4, 1928; *SB*, Aug. 1 & 22, 1928; *SU*, Aug. 25 & 26, 1928.
42. *SB*, Oct. 3, 1928.
43. *SU*, Nov. 4, 1928.
44. *WF*, Dec. 1928, p. 104.
45. *SB*, Nov. 14, 1928; *SB*, Dec. 26, 1928.
46. *SB*, Jan. 23, 1928.
47. *SB*, Jan. 23 & 30, 1929.
48. *SB*, Mar. 6, 1929.
49. *SB*, Mar. 27, 1929; *SB*, Apr. 3, 1929.
50. *SB*, May 8, 1929.
51. *SB*, May 15, 1929.
52. *SB*, June 5, 1929.
53. *SB*, June 19, 1929.
54. *WF*, Jan. 1930, p. 118.
55. *PF*, May 1930, p. 33.
56. *SB*, Feb. 19, 1930.
57. Photograph from the Sacramento Museum and Archive Collection Center with Catalog No. 77/X-17/168.
58. *SB*, Aug. 6, 1930.
59. *SB*, Nov. 23, 1932.
60. *SB*, Aug. 10, 1983.
61. *SB*, Aug. 10, 1983; Vanderford, Vince (II), Interview, Feb. 1998.
62. *SB*, Oct. 18, 1955.
63. *SB*, July 4, 1928.
64. *SB*, July 11, 1928.
65. *SB*, July 16, 1928.
66. *WF*, Aug. 1928, p. 92.
67. *SB*, Aug. 1, 1928.
68. *SB*, Aug. 22, 1928.
69. *SB*, Aug. 25, 1928.
70. *PF*, Oct. 1928, p. 25; *SB*, Sept. 26, 1928; *SB*, Oct. 3 & 10, 1928.
71. *SB*, Oct. 10, 1928; *WF*, Dec. 1928, p. 116.
72. *SB*, Oct. 31, 1928; *WF*, Dec. 1928, p. 116; *SU*, Nov. 4, 1928.
73. *SB*, Nov. 11, 1928; *SU*, Nov. 11, 1928; *SB*, Nov. 14, 1928.
74. *SB*, Nov. 21, 1928.
75. *SB*, Nov. 28, 1928.
76. *SB*, Dec. 5, 1928.
77. *SB*, Dec. 19, 1928.
78. *SB*, Mar. 6, 1929.
79. *SB*, Mar. 20, 1929.
80. *SB*, Mar. 27, 1929.
81. *WF*, May 1929, p. 94.
82. *SB*, July 24, 1929.
83. *SB*, Sept. 11, 1929; Grey, C. G., p. 63c
84. *SB*, Jan. 8, 1930.
85. *SB*, Jan. 15, 1930.
86. *WF*, Feb. 1930, p. 96.
87. *SB*, May 21, 1930.
88. *SB*, June 11, 1930.
89. *SB*, Aug. 13, 1930.
90. *SB*, Jan. 28, 1931.
91. *SB*, Jan. 6, 1932.
92. *SB*, Jan. 27, 1932.
93. *SB*, Feb. 10, 1932.
94. *SB*, July 27, 1932.
95. *SB*, Oct. 11, 1983.
96. *SB*, Dec. 2, 1966; *SB*, Sept. 26, 1928; Oct. 24, 1928.
97. *SB*, Oct. 24, 1928; *WF*, Dec. 1928, p. 116.
98. *NSJ*, Nov. 9, 1928; *SU*, Nov. 11, 1928.
99. *SB*, Nov. 12 & 14, 1928.
100. *SB*, Jan. 30, 1929; *SB*, Mar. 27, 1929.
101. *SB*, Aug. 8, 1930.
102. *SB*, Dec. 2, 1966.
103. *WF*, Aug. 1928, p. 92.
104. *SB*, July 11, 1928.
105. *SB*, Oct. 3, 1928; *SB*, Nov. 14, 1928.
106. *SB*, May 1, 1929.
107. *SB*, June 5, 1929; *SB*, June 12, 1929.
108. *SB*, June 26, 1929; *SB*, Sept. 25, 1929.
109. *SB*, Oct. 9, 1929; *SB*, Nov. 20, 1929; *AD*, Nov. 1929, p. 195.
110. *WF*, Jan. 1930, p. 120.
111. *SB*, June 4, 1930.
112. *SB*, June 11 & 18, 1930.
113. *SB*, Sept. 24, 1930; *PF*, Nov. 1930, p. 28.
114. *SB*, Feb. 25, 1931; Juptner, Vol. 3, pp. 9-10.
115. *SB*, Mar. 4, 1931; *SB*, Apr. 15, 1931.
116. *SB*, June 10, 1931.
117. *SB*, June 17, 1931.
118. Underwood, *Madcaps . . .*, p. 62; *SB*, June 17, 1931.

Endnotes

119. Underwood, *Grand Central* . . ., pp. 115 & 124; Beilby Obituary, *GNP*, Nov. 6, 1975.
120. *SB*, Aug. 8 & 22, 1928.
121. *WF*, Sept. 1928, p. 187.
122. *SB*, Sept. 19, 1928; *SB*, Oct. 17, 1928; *PF*, Oct. 1928, p. 18.
123. *SB*, Oct. 3, 1928.
124. *SB*, Oct. 17, 1928.
125. *SB*, Oct. 24, 1928; *WF*, Dec. 1928, p. 116.
126. *SU*, Nov. 5 & 11, 1928; *SB*, Nov. 7 & 14, 1928; *SB*, Jan. 9, 1929; *SB*, Feb. 27, 1929; *WF*, Dec. 1928, p. 116.
127. *SB*, Mar. 20, 1929.
128. *SB*, June 5, 1929.
129. *SB*, Feb. 12, 1930.
130. Betts, "Ken Blaney," *TWA Topics*, Undated, n. p.
131. *SB*, Aug. 25, 1928; *SU*, Nov. 4, 1928; *SB*, Jan. 30, 1929.
132. *SB*, Mar. 27, 1929.
133. Betts, "Ken Blaney," *TWA Topics*, Undated, n. p; *SB*, Sept. 21, 1989.
134. *SB*, Oct. 24, 1928; *WF*, Dec. 1928, p. 116.
135. *SU*, Nov. 4, 1928.
136. *SB*, Dec. 5, 1928.
137. *SB*, Dec. 19, 1928; *SB*, Feb. 27, 1929.
138. *SB*, Sept. 25, 1929.

Chapter 10

1. *PF*, Oct. 1928, p. 18.
2. *SB*, Feb. 6, 1929; *PF*, July 1929, p. 21.
3. *PF*, Aug. 1929, p. 22; *AD*, Sept. 1929, p.196.
4. *SB*, Oct. 29, 1929.
5. Oct. 16, 1929.
6. *SB*, Jan. 8, 1930.
7. *SB*, Feb. 12, 1930.
8. Ibid.
9. *WF*, Mar. 1930, p. 90.
10. *SB*, Apr. 17-18, 1930.
11. *SB*, Apr. 19-22, 1930.
12. *SB*, Apr. 24, 1930.
13. *AD*, May 1930, p. 154; *PF*, May 1930, p. 24; *SB*, Apr. 14, 1930.
14. *SB*, Apr. 30, 1930.
15. *WF*, May 1930, p. 103
16. *WF*, May 1930, p. 62.
17. *SB*, May 21, 1930.
18. *SB*, May 28, 1930.
19. *WF*, June 1930, n.p.
20. *SB*, June 2, 1930.
21. *SB*, June 4, 1930.
22. *SB*, June 11, 1930.
23. Ibid.
24. *SB*, June 18, 1930.
25. *SB*, June 25, 1930.
26. *SB*, July 2, 1930.
27. *WDD*, July 7, 1930.
28. *SB*, July 11, 1930.
29. *SB*, July 23, 1930.
30. *SB*, Aug. 12 & 19, 1930; *PF*, Sept. 1930, p. 22.
31. *SB*, Aug. 6, 1930.
32. *SB*, Aug. 13, 1930.
33. *PF*, Sept. 1930, p. 28.
34. *SB*, Sept. 24, 1930.
35. *SB*, Oct. 1, 1930.
36. *SB*, Oct. 22, 1930.
37. *PF*, Nov. 1930, p. 22.
38. *SB*, Nov. 5, 1930.
39. *SB*, Nov. 19, 1930.
40. *SB*, Dec. 1, 1930.
41. *SB*, Dec. 3, 1930.
42. *SB*, Dec. 10, 1930.
43. *SB*, Dec. 4, 1930.
44. *SB*, Dec. 10, 1930.
45. *PF*, Jan. 1931, p. 19.
46. *SB*, Jan. 7, 1931.
47. *SB*, Jan. 14, 1931.
48. *SB*, Jan. 21, 1931.
49. *SB*, Jan. 28, 1931.
50. *SB*, Feb. 4, 1931.
51. *SB*, Mar. 4, 1931.
52. *SB*, Feb. 11, 1931.
53. *SB*, Feb. 18, 1931.
54. *SB*, Feb. 25, 1931.
55. *SB*, Mar. 2-4, 1931.
56. *SB*, Mar. 18, 1931.
57. *PF*, Mar. 18, 1931, p. 10.
58. *PF*, Mar. 18, 1931, p. 13.
59. *SB*, Apr. 1, 1931.
60. Ibid.
61. *SB*, Apr. 8, 1931.
62. Ibid.
63. *SB*, Apr. 22, 1931.
64. *PF*, Apr. 22, 1931, p. 13.
65. *SB*, Apr. 29, 1931.
66. *SB*, May 6, 1931.
67. *SB*, May 13, 1931.
68. *SB*, May 20, 1931.
69. Ibid.
70. *SB*, June 3, 1931.
71. Ibid.
72. *SB*, June 6 & 10, 1931.
73. *SB*, June 6, 1931.
74. *SB*, June 12, 1931.
75. *SB*, Sept. 9, 1931.

76. *SB*, July 1, 1931.
77. *SB*, July 8, 1931.
78. Ibid.
79. *SB*, July 22, 1931.
80. *SB*, July 29, 1931.
81. *AD*, Aug. 1931, p. 92.
82. *SB*, Aug. 3, 1931.
83. *SB*, Aug. 12, 1931.
84. *SB*, Aug. 3, 1931.
85. *SB*, Aug. 26, 1931.
86. Ibid.
87. *SB*, Sept. 9, 1931.
88. *PF*, Jan. 1931.
89. *SB*, Oct. 7, 1931.
90. Ibid.
91. *SB*, Oct. 28, 1931.
92. *SB*, Oct. 31, 1931.
93. *SB*, Nov. 4, 1931.
94. *SB*, Nov. 18, 1931.
95. *SB*, Nov. 25, 1931.
96. *SB*, Nov. 18, 1931.
97. *SB*, Nov. 25, 1931.
98. *SB*, Dec. 2, 1931.
99. *SB*, Dec. 9, 1931.
100. Ibid.
101. SB, Dec. 16, 1931.
102. Ibid.
103. *SB*, Dec. 30, 1931.
104. Ibid.
105. *SB*, Jan. 6, 1932.
106. *SB*, Dec. 30, 1931.
107. *SB*, Jan. 6, 1932.
108. *SB*, Jan. 13, 1932.
109. *SB*, Jan. 20, 1932.
110. *SB*, Jan. 26, 1932.
111. SB, Feb. 3, 1932.
112. *SB*, Feb. 10, 1932; *SB*, Mar. 2, 1932.
113. *SB*, Mar. 2, 1932.
114. *SB*, Mar. 23, 1932.
115. *SB*, Mar. 30, 1932.
116. *SB*, Apr. 6, 1932
117. Ibid.
118. *SB*, Apr. 16, 1932.
119. *AD*, May 1932, p. 105.
120. *SB*, May 4, 1932.
121. *SB*, May 11, 1932.
122. *SB*, May 18, 1932.
123. *SB*, May 20, 1932.
124. *SB*, June 8, 1932.
125. *SB*, June 15, 1932.
126. *SB*, June 29, 1932.
127. *SB*, July 4, 1932; *SU*, July 4, 1932.
128. *SB*, July 6, 1932.
129. *SB*, July 20, 1932.
130. *AD*, Aug. 1932, p. 36.
131. *SB*, Aug. 10, 1932.
132. *SB*, Aug. 3, 1932.
133. *SU*, Aug. 22, 1932.
134. *SB*, Sept. 7, 1932.
135. *SB*, Sept. 21, 1932.
136. *SB*, Nov. 2, 1932.
137. *SB*, Nov. 9, 1932.
138. *SB*, Nov. 23, 1932.
139. *SB*, Dec. 14, 1932.
140. *SB*, Dec. 21, 1932.
141. *SB*, Dec. 28, 1932.
142. *SB*, Jan. 24, 1933.
143. *AD*, July 1933, p. 35.
144. *SB*, Oct 28, 1933.
145. Ibid.
146. *SU*, Oct. 29-30, 1933.

Chapter 11

1. *SB*, July 2 & 11, 1930.
2. *SB*, Feb. 18, 1931.
3. *SB*, Apr. 8, 1931.
4. *SB*, May 27, 1931.
5. *SB*, July 1, 1931.
6. *SB*, Nov. 25, 1931.
7. *SB*, May 30, 1932.
8. *SB*, Apr. 16, 1932.
9. *SB*, Apr. 27, 1932.
10. *SB*, June 22, 1932.
11. *SB*, Aug. 10, 1932.
12. SB, Sept. 4, 1929.
13. *SB*, Apr. 15, 1931.
14. *SB*, Apr. 22, 1931.
15. *SB*, May 30, 1931.
16. *SB*, Sept. 9, 1931.
17. *SB*, Dec. 2, 1931.
18. *SB*, Jan. 27, 1932.
19. *SB*, Mar. 9, 1932.
20. *SB*, Feb. 26, 1930.
21. *SB*, June 11, 1930.
22. *SB*, July 11, 1930.
23. *SB*, Aug. 13, 1930.
24. *SB*, Nov. 19, 1930; *PF*, Dec. 1930, p. 21.
25. *PF*, Jan. 1931, p. 22.
26. *PF*, Apr. 22, 1931, p. 17.
27. *SB*, May 27, 1931.
28. *SB*, Nov. 25, 1931.
29. *SB*, Dec. 2, 1931.
30. *SB*, Mar. 9, 1932.
31. *SB*, Apr. 16, 1932.
32. *SB*, Apr. 27, 1932.
33. *SB*, May 11, 1932.

Endnotes

34. *SB*, May 18, 1932.
35. *SB*, July 20, 1932; *SB*, Aug. 10, 1932.
36. *SB*, Oct. 19, 1932.
37. *SB*, Dec. 21, 1932.
38. *PF*, Oct. 1928, p. 25.
39. *SB*, Sept. 16, 1931.
40. *SB*, Oct. 14, 1931.
41. *SB*, Nov. 18, 1931.
42. *SB*, Nov. 25, 1931.
43. *SB*, Dec. 9, 1931.
44. *SB*, Jan. 6, 1932.
45. *SB*, Feb. 10, 1932.
46. *SB*, Mar. 2, 1932.
47. Ibid.
48. *SB*, Mar. 9, 1932
49. *SB*, Mar. 23, 1932.
50. *SB*, Apr. 16, 1932.
51. *SB*, Apr. 27, 1932.
52. *SB*, May 18, 1932.
53. *SB*, June 8, 1932.
54. *SB*, June 15, 1932.
55. *SB*, June 22, 1932.
56. *SB*, June 29, 1932.
57. *SB*, July 20, 1932.
58. *SB*, Aug. 3, 1932.
59. *SB*, Aug. 10, 1932.
60. *SB*, Nov. 9, 1932.
61. *SB*, Nov. 23, 1932.
62. *WDD*, Sept. 13. 1933.
63. *SB*, Jan 27, 1932.
64. Ibid.
65. *SB*, Feb. 10, 1932.
66. *SB*, Feb. 17, 1932.
67. *SB*, Feb. 24, 1932.
68. *SB*, Mar. 9, 1932.
69. *SB*, Apr. 27, 1932.
70. Ibid.
71. *SB*, May 4, 1932.
72. *SB*, May 11, 1932.
73. *SB*, June 8, 1932.
74. *SB*, June 29, 1932.
75. *SB*, July 13, 1932.
76. *SB*, July 20, 1932.
77. *SB*, July 27, 1932.
78. *SB*, Aug. 10, 1932.
79. *SB*, Sept. 21, 1932.
80. *SB*, Sept. 28, 1932.
81. *SB*, Oct. 19, 1932.
82. *SB*, Nov. 2, 1932.
83. *SB*, Nov. 23, 1932.
84. *SB*, Dec. 14, 1932.
85. *SB*, Dec. 28, 1932.
86. *SB*, July 11, 1928
87. *SB*, July 16, 1928.
88. *AD*, Aug. 1928, p. 286.
89. *SU*, Aug. 3, 1928.
90. *SB*, Aug. 8, 1928.
91. *SU*, Aug. 9, 1928.
92. *SB*, Aug. 18, 1928.
93. *SB*, Aug. 22, 1928.
94. *SB*, Oct. 31, 1928.
95. *SU*, Nov. 11, 1928.
96. Davies, *Airlines of the United States* . . ., pp. 60 & 70.
97. *SB*, Feb. 22, 1928.
98. *SB*, Feb. 15, 1928.
99. *WF*, Aug. 1928, P. 92.
100. *SB*, Sept. 26, 1928.
101. *WF*, Nov. 1928, p. 68.
102. *SB*, Dec. 19, 1928.
103. *SB*, Jan. 2, 1929.
104. *SB*, Apr. 3, 1929.
105. *SB*, May 29, 1929.
106. *SB*, Oct. 2, 1929.
107. *SB*, Nov. 6, 1929.
108. *SB*, Dec. 18, 1929; *SB*, Apr. 30, 1930.
109. *SB*, Mar. 5, 1930.
110. *SB*, May 21, 1930.
111. *SB*, Sept. 10, 1930.
112. *SB*, Sept. 10, 1930.
113. *MAD*, Mar. 18, 1931.
114. *SB*, May 27, 1931.
115. *SB*, June 10, 1931.
116. *SB*, June 17, 1931.
117. *SB*, July 22, 1931.
118. *SB*, Aug. 26, 1931.
119. *SB*, Sept. 16, 1931.
120. *SB*, Dec. 30, 1931; Davies, *Airlines of the United States* . . ., p. 180.
121. *SB*, Jan. 6, 1932.
122. *SB*, Feb. 3, 1932.
123. *SB*, Apr. 16, 1932.
124. *SB*, Apr. 27, 1932.
125. Ibid.
126. *SB*, May 11, 1931.
127. *SB*, June 8, 1932.
128. *SB*, June 15, 1932.
129. *SB*, July 27, 1932.
130. *SB*, Dec. 14, 1932.
131. *SB*, Dec. 19, 1932; *SB*, Dec. 21, 1932.
132. *AD*, Nov. 1934, p. 46.
133. *SB*, Sept. 11, 1931; Davies, *Airlines of the United States* . . ., p. 122.
134. *SB*, Oct. 7, 1931.
135. *SB*, Nov. 25, 1931; *SB*, Dec. 9, 1931.
136. *SB*, Dec. 30, 1931.

137. *SB*, Jan. 6, 1932.
138. *SB*, Jan. 13, 1932.
139. *SB*, Mar. 30, 1932.
140. *SB*, Apr. 16, 1932.
141. Davies, *Airlines of the United States* . . ., pp. 122-123.
142. *SB*, June 4, 1930.
143. *SB*, June 11, 1930.
144. *SB*, Sept. 27, 1930.
145. *SB*, Oct. 1, 1930.
146. *SB*, Oct. 8, 1930.
147. *PF*, Apr. 22, 1931, p. 17.
148. *SB*, Feb. 25, 1931.
149. *SB*, Apr. 8, 1931.
150. *SB*, Apr. 15, 1931.
151. *PF*, Apr. 22, 1931, p. 15.
152. *SB*, Apr. 29, 1931.
153. *SB*, May 6, 1931.
154. *SB*, July 22, 1931.
155. Ibid.
156. *SB*, July 29, 1931.
157. *SB*, Oct. 14, 1931.
158. *SB*, Oct. 21, 1931.
159. *SB*, Nov. 25, 1931.
160. *SB*, Jan. 13, 1932.
161. *SB*, Mar. 2, 1932.
162. *SB*, Mar. 9, 1932.
163. *SB*, Mar. 30, 1932.
164. *SB*, Apr. 27, 1932.
165. *SB*, May 11, 1932.
166. *SB*, June 15, 1932.
167. *SB*, June 29, 1932.
168. *SB*, July 13, 1932.
169. *SB*, Aug. 3, 1932.
170. *SB*, Aug. 10, 1932.

Chapter 12

1. Thaden, Bowen, Morgan, *WF*, Sept. 1932, pp. 28-29.
2. Ibid.
3. *WF*, Mar. 1930, n.p.
4. Thaden, Bowen, Morgan, *WF*, Sept. 1932, pp. 28-29; Schultz, p. 114; Jessen, p. 230; Whyte & Cooper, p. 110; *AD*, Feb. 1932, p. 77; Schultz, pp. 115-116; Veca, p. 230.
5. Avis Bielefeld Family Papers.
6. *SU*, Mar. 31, 1934.
7. Avis Bielefeld Family Papers.
8. Avis Bielefeld Flight Logbook.
9. *SU*, Oct. 5, 1936.
10. Avis Bielefeld Flight Logbook.
11. Ibid.
12. Avis Bielefeld Family Papers and Karen Ripley.
13. *WF*, Jan. 1939, p. 28.
14. *SB*, Oct. 3-5, 1936.
15. *SB*, Aug. 12-13, 1937.
16. Kozak, pp. 56-58.
17. *AAM*, June 10, 1938, p. 15.
18. *AAM*, Sept. 1, 1938, p. 28.
19. *WF*, Jan. 1930, p. 118.
20. *SB*, Jan. 8, 1930; *WF*, Mar. 1930.
21. *SB*, Jan. 15, 1930; *WF*, Mar. 1930, p. 90.
22. *SB*, Feb. 2, 1930.
23. *SB*, Feb. 19, 1930.
24. *SB*, Sept. 17, 1930.
25. *SB*, Sept. 24, 1930.
26. *SB*, Sept. 24, 1930; *PF*, Oct. 1930, p. 21.
27. *SB*, Oct. 8, 1930
28. *SB*, Nov. 19, 1930.
29. Ibid.
30. *SB*, Oct. 22, 1930.
31. *SB*, Nov. 12, 1930.
32. Saunders, Salle, Interview, Apr. 2000.
33. *SB*, Dec. 17, 1979.
34. *SB*, Nov. 19, 1930.
35. *SB*, Feb. 4, 1930.
36. *SB*, Feb. 18, 1931.
37. *SB*, Feb. 25, 1931.
38. *SB*, Mar. 4, 1931.
39. *SB*, Mar. 18, 1931.
40. *SB*, Apr. 15, 1931.
41. *SB*, May 29, 1931, NEG, Sept. 8, 1933.
42. *SB*, Aug. 12, 1931.
43. Miller, p. 20.
44. Miller, p. 41.

Chapter 13

1. WPA Writers Project, pp. 439-440.
2. *SU*, Sept. 28, 1919.
3. Baker, *AAHS Journal*, Vol. 14 No. 2, p. 115; Anderson, pp. 7-8.
4. Anderson, pp. 8-9.
5. Baker, *AAHS Journal*, Vol. 13 No. 1, p. 52.
6. *SU*, Sept. 17, 1916.
7. *SU*, Sept. 25, 1919.
8. *ODR*, Sept. 16, 1919.
9. *WM*, Apr. 2, 1918; *WM*, Jan. 3, 1918; *AAW*, Aug. 25, 1919.
10. *ODR*, Sept. 29, 1919.
11. *CR*, Sept. 14, 1919.
12. *CR*, Sept. 25, 1919.
13. *SU*, Sept. 24, 1919.
14. *WDD*, Oct. 13, 1919.
15. *WDD*, Oct. 17, 1919.
16. *ODR*, Oct. 14, 1919.

17. *CR*, Oct. 14, 1919; *ODR*, Oct. 15, 1919.
18. *WDD*, Oct. 21, 1919.
19. *WDJ*, May 3, 1920.
20. Grace, p. 141.
21. *CR*, Oct. 23, 1919.
22. *WDJ*, Apr. 1, 1920.
23. *PA*, Apr. 1938, p. 22.
24. Cleveland, p. 39.
25. Robert G. Fowler Collection Index No. 9, p. 101 (At the Hiller Aviation Museum, San Carlos, CA.
26. *WDJ*, May 24, 1920.
27. *ODR*, May 26, 1920.
28. *MA*, May 28, 1920.
29. Gwynn-Jones, p. 93.
30. *WDJ*, July 15, 1920.
31. *WDJ*, July 21, 1920.
32. *WDJ*, Sept. 7, 1920; *WDJ*, Sept. 14, 1920.
33. *WDJ*, Sept. 27, 1920.
34. *MD*, Sept. 3, 1925.
35. *WDJ*, Sept. 22, 1920.
36. *WDJ*, July 22, 1920.
37. *WDJ*, July 27, 1920.
38. *RCD*, Aug. 12, 1920.
39. *WDJ*, Sept. 1, 1920.
40. *WDJ*, Sept. 2, 1920.
41. *WDJ*, Sept. 29, 1920.
42. *WDJ*, Oct. 4, 1920.
43. *WDJ*, Oct. 9, 1920.
44. *GH*, Mar. 12, 1921.
45. *SDER*, Jan. 8-9, 1923; *SDER*, Jan. 10, 1923.
46. *WDJ*, July 26, 1974; *SU*, July 4, 1980.
47. *MSS*, Jan. 23, 1978.
48. *CDS*, May 31, 1930; *SB*, June 4, 1930.
49. *Sport Flying*, Apr. 1968, Vol. 2 No. 4, pp. 27-28.
50. *Sport Flying*, Apr. 1968, Vol. 2 No. 4, p. 24 & 28.
51. *SU*, July 4, 1932; *SB*, Dec. 28, 1932; *SB*, Oct. 3, 1936.
52. *TDJ*, Apr. 10, 1929.
53. Grambon, p. 25; Gordon, pp. 30-31; Ricklefs, p. 319.
54. *MAD*, July 27, 1929.
55. *MAD*, July 30-31, 1929.
56. *MAD*, Aug. 16, 1929.
57. *SCF*, Aug. 23, 1929; *AAHS Journal*, Fall 1968, p. 213.
58. *GH*, Mar. 7, 1930; *MAD*, Oct. 10, 1930.
59. *MAD*, Mar. 10, 1930.
60. *MAD*, Apr. 21, 1930; *WDJ*, Apr. 23, 1930.
61. *WDJ*, Apr. 23, 1930.
62. *MAD*, Apr. 24, 1930.
63. *SB*, Apr. 26, 1930.
64. *SB*, July 29, 1930.
65. *SB*, Sept. 3, 1930.
66. *PF*, July 1929, p. 16.
67. *PF*, July 1929, pp. 16-17; *CO*, July 9, 1929.
68. *MSS*, Jan. 23, 1978.
69. *TDJ*, Mar. 18-19, 1929; *TDJ*, Mar. 25, 1929.
70. *TDJ*, Mar. 23, 1929.
71. *TDJ*, Apr. 22, 1929.
72. *TDJ*, Apr. 12, 1929; *WF*, June 1929, p. 94.
73. *WF*, May 1930, p. 102.
74. *AD*, May 1930, p. 158.
75. *WF*, June 1930, p. 118.
76. *WF*, May 1930, p. 104.
77. *WF*, June 1930, p. 100.
78. *PF*, Sept. 1930, p. 22.
79. *PF*, Sept. 1930, p. 33.
80. *PF*, Nov. 1930, p. 12.
81. *Aero*, April 6, 1912, p. 15; Museum Society of Willows, p. 101; Anderson, p. 98; *WDJ*, Sept. 26, 1937; *WDJ* Obituary undated; Interview with Guy "Speed" Hughes, Aug. 2003.

Chapter 14

1. *PF*, Feb. 4, 1930, p. 6.
2. *PF*, Mar. 4, 1931, p. 9.
3. Beidleman, *AAHS Journal*, Vol. 38 No. 3, pp. 184-193.
4. *PF*, Mar. 4, 1931, p. 4.
5. *MAD*, Mar. 23, 1931.
6. *PF*, Apr. 22, 1931, p. 13.
7. *WDJ*, Aug. 22, 1931.
8. *PF*, Apr. 22, 1931, p. 10.
9. *PF*, Apr. 22, 1931, p. 13.
10. *MAD*, May 15, 1931.
11. *WDJ*, July 1, 1931; *SCF*, July 3, 1931.
12. *MAD*, Aug. 13, 1932.
13. Beidleman, *AAHS Journal*, Vol. 38 No. 3, pp. 190-191.
14. *SCF*, Feb. 23, 1933.
15. *OMR*, July 21, 1933.
16. *SCIF*, Sept. 14, 1934.
17. *SCIF*, Mar. 26, 1935.
18. *SCIF*, Apr. 30, 1935.
19. *SU*, June 16, 1935.
20. *SCIF*, June 28, 1935.
21. *MAD*, June 9, 1936.
22. *MAD*, Mar. 20, 1936.
23. *SCIF*, May 8, 1936.
24. *SCIF*, Aug. 28, 1936.
25. Anderson, pp. 81-83; Interview with Guy "Speed" Hughes, Aug. 2002.
26. Anderson, p. 83.

27. Interview with Guy "Speed" Hughes, Aug. 2002.
28. CDS, Apr. 8, 1911.
29. CDS, Apr. 18, 1911.
30. CDS, May 6, 1911.
31. CDS, May 25, 1911.
32. CDS, May 27, 1911.
33. CDS, May 30, 1911; CH, Sept. 29, 1916; CH, Oct. 8-10, 1916; CDS & CH, June 5-7, 1917; McConish & Lambert, p. 92.
34. PF, Oct. 3, 1928, p. 7.
35. PF, Nov. 1928, p. 13.
36. WF, Dec. 1928, p. 73.
37. SB, Nov. 7, 1928.
38. MAD, Jan. 23, 1929.
39. CDS, June 7, 1929.
40. SB, June 12, 1929.
41. Ibid.
42. MAD, June 12, 1929; SB, June 19, 1929; SB, July 3, 1929.
43. CDS, July 11, 1929.
44. CDS, Mar. 18, 1930.
45. CDS, Apr. 16, 1930.
46. CDS, Apr. 17, 1930.
47. MAD, May 23, 1930.
48. CDS, May 27, 1930.
49. CDS, May 28, 1930.
50. Ibid.
51. CDS, May 29, 1930.
52. CDS, May 28, 1930; SB, June 4, 1930.
53. CDS, May 29, 1930.
54. Ibid.
55. CDS, June 2, 1930.
56. MAD, June 2, 1930.
57. CDS, June 2, 1930.
58. SB, June 4, 1930.
59. CDS, June 2, 1930; WF, June 1930, p. 96.
60. MAD, June 2, 1930.
61. MAD, Nov. 30, 1930.
62. PF, Dec. 1930, p. 24; MAD, Mar. 18, 1931.
63. MAD, Mar. 31, 1931; dmairfield.com/people/brown-hf.
64. SB, Dec. 9, 1933.

Chapter 15

1. WDJ, June 23, 1926.
2. WDJ, Feb. 19, 1920.
3. WDJ, Feb. 26, 1920.
4. WDJ, Mar. 1, 1920.
5. WDJ, June 22, 1920.
6. WDJ, June 24, 1920.
7. WDJ, Sept. 4, 1920.
8. WDJ, Dec. 21, 1920.

9. WDJ, Mar. 19, 1920.
10. MD, Aug. 8, 1919.
11. SU, Sept. 18, 1919; SU, Sept. 28, 1919.
12. SU, Sept. 19, 1919.
13. SU, Sept. 20, 1919.
14. CR, Sept. 27, 1919.
15. WDJ, Mar. 24, 1920.
16. WDJ, Apr. 9-10, 1920.
17. WDJ, May 26, 1920.
18. WDJ, June 23, 1926.
19. IVP, July 3, 1926.
20. OU, July 6, 1926.
21. ODR, Aug. 14, 1926.
22. MD, Mar. 13, 1927.
23. WDD, Aug. 1, 1927.
24. AD, Sept. 1929, p. 487.
25. MAD, Jan. 12, 1928.
26. SU, May 21, 1928; AD, Sept. 1928, p. 532.
27. SU, May 25, 1928.
28. SB, July 10, 1928.
29. SB, Aug. 1, 1928.
30. SB, Aug. 15, 1928.
31. SB, Dec. 19, 1928.
32. SB, Feb. 13, 1929.
33. OU, Mar. 5, 1929.
34. OU, Mar. 8, 1929.
35. WF, May 1929, p. 118.
36. MAD, May 23, 1929.
37. SDI, Mar. 19, 1929.
38. WDJ, May 29, 1929.
39. WDJ, May 31, 1929.
40. WDJ, June 3, 1929.
41. WDJ, June 3, 1929; SB, June 3, 1929.
42. WDJ, June 22, 1929.
43. SB, July 3, 1929.
44. WF, Aug. 1929, p. 181.
45. PF, Aug. 1929, p. 22.
46. PF, Oct. 191, p. 21.
47. PF, July 1929, p. 26.
48. PF, Nov. 1929, p. 28; PF, Aug. 1929, p. 25.
49. PF, Nov. 1929, p. 21.
50. SB, Dec. 4, 1929.
51. WDJ, Jan. 4, 1930.
52. WF, Apr. 1930, p. 114.
53. WDJ, Apr. 16, 1930.

Chapter 16

1. WDJ, Apr. 17, 1930.
2. WDJ, May 26, 1930.
3. CDS, May 29, 1930.
4. PF, Sept. 1930, p. 28.
5. PF, Sept. 1930, p. 33.
6. WDJ, Sept. 15, 1930.

Endnotes

7. *WDJ*, Sept. 20, 1930.
8. *PF*, Nov. 1930, p. 23.
9. *PF*, Dec. 1930, p.20.
10. *PF*, Feb. 4, 1931, p. 7.
11. *WJ*, June 24, 1932.
12. *WJ*, Sept. 9, 1932.
13. *RBDN*, July 5, 1932.
14. *WJ*, Sept. 8, 1933.
15. *WJ*, Sept. 11, 1933.
16. *WJ*, Sept. 12, 1935.
17. Interview with Harry Middleton, Nov. 7, 2000.
18. *WJ*, Sept. 13, 1935.
19. *WJ*, Sept. 16, 1935.
20. *WJ*, Sept. 17, 1936.
21. *WJ*, Sept. 19, 1936.
22. *WJ*, Sept. 17, 1936.
23. *WJ*, Sept. 17, 1936; *WJ*, Sept. 21, 1936.
24. *WJ*, July 2, 1937.
25. *WJ*, Sept. 16, 1937.
26. *WJ*, Sept. 24, 1937.
27. *WJ*, Sept. 27, 1937.
28. *WJ*, Oct. 19, 1937.
29. *WJ*, Sept. 19, 1938.
30. *WJ*, Sept. 21, 1938; *WJ*, Sept. 23, 1938.
31. *WJ*, Sept. 22, 1938.
32. *WJ*, Sept. 23, 1938.
33. *WJ*, Sept. 24, 1938.
34. *WJ*, Sept. 26, 1938.
35. *WJ*, Oct. 11, 1938.
36. *WJ*, Sept. 21, 1938; Higham, p. 152.
37. *WJ*, Sept. 24, 1939.
38. *WJ*, Aug. 25, 1939.
39. *WJ*, Aug. 25, 1939.
40. Ibid.
41. *WJ*, Aug. 29, 1939.
42. *WJ*, Aug. 29, 1939.
43. *WJ*, Sept. 1, 1939.
44. *WJ*, Sept. 12, 1939.
45. *WJ*, Sept. 5, 1939.
46. *WJ*, Sept. 9, 1939.
47. Ibid.
48. *WJ*, Sept. 11, 1939.
49. *WJ*, Sept. 12, 1939.
50. *WJ*, Sept. 15, 1939.
51. *WJ*, Sept. 12, 1939.
52. *WJ*, Sept. 22, 1939.
53. *WJ*, Sept. 25, 1939.
54. Ibid.
55. *MAD*, Sept. 27, 1940.
56. Interview with H. T. Herr, Aug. 1999; Bohrer, p. 219.

Chapter 17

1. *CO*, July 23, 1936; *CO*, Sept. 15, 1975; *PA*, May 1939, p. 64.
2. *WF*, June 1926, n.p.
3. *CO*, May 6, 1922.
4. Russell, p. 119.
5. *CO*, May 6, 1922.
6. *AAHS Journal*, Fall 1974, p. 196.
7. *WF*, Nov. 1927, p. 38; *WF*, Dec. 1927, p. 60.
8. *CO*, July 21, 1938.
9. *AD*, Jan. 1928, p. 78.
10. *WF*, Jan. 1928, p. 64.
11. *SB*, Feb. 22, 1928.
12. *AD*, Apr. 1928, p. 636.
13. *SB*, Apr. 11, 1928.
14. *WF*, Aug. 1928, p.68.
15. *BWN*, June 30, 1928; Forden, p. 2.
16. *CO*, July 7, 1928; Forden, pp. 84-85.
17. *CO*, July 14, 1928.
18. *PF*, Aug. 1928, p. 21.
19. *BWN*, Aug. 4, 1928.
20. *WF*, Aug. 1928, p. 108.
21. *SB*, Aug. 11, 1928.
22. *CO*, Aug. 11, 1928.
23. *CO*, Aug. 11, 1928; Bohrer, p. 22.
24. *WF*, Sept. 1928, p. 297.
25. *SB*, Sept. 12, 1928.
26. *GH*, Nov. 6, 1928.
27. *AD*, Dec. 1928, p. 1186.
28. *CO*, Mar. 25, 1929.
29. The Cristero War in Mexico 1926-1929.
30. *CO*, Mar. 26, 1929.
31. *CO*, Apr. 10, 1929.
32. *PF*, Apr. 1929, p. 24.
33. *CO*, May 2, 1929.
34. *CO*, May 8, 1929.
35. *MNH*, July 2, 1929.
36. *CO*, June 20, 1929.
37. *CO*, July 26, 1929.
38. *CO*, July 29 1929.
39. *WF*, Aug. 1929, p. 122.
40. *CO*, Aug. 1, 1929.
41. *CO*, Nov. 6, 1929.
42. *CO*, Nov. 11, 1929; *CO*, Nov. 29-30, 1929; *CO*, Dec. 3-4, 1929.
43. *CO*, July 1, 1930.
44. *SB*, July 11, 1930.
45. *CO*, Oct. 6, 1930; *SB*, Oct. 8, 1930; *PF*, Oct. 1930, p. 21.
46. *PF*, Apr. 22, 1931, p. 13.
47. *CO*, May 28, 1931.
48. *SB*, June 10, 1931.
49. *CO*, June 10, 1931.

50. *AD*, Feb. 1932, p. 79.
51. *CO*, Aug. 30, 1932.
52. *CO*, July 1, 1932.
53. *CO*, July 6, 1932.
54. *CO*, July 26, 1932; *CO*, July 29, 1932.
55. Unnamed and undated newspaper clipping. (Probably the Corning Observer from the early 1930s.)
56. *CO*, Aug. 15, 1932.
57. *CO*, Aug. 31, 1932.
58. *CO*, Sept. 12, 1932; *RBDN*, Sept. 12, 1932.
59. *CO*, Sept. 26, 1932.
60. *CO*, Oct. 17, 1932.
61. *CO*, Nov. 10, 1932.
62. *CO*, Nov. 8, 1932.
63. *COR*, Jan. 28, 1933.
64. *CO*, Feb. 8, 1933.
65. *CO*, Feb. 20, 1933.
66. Ibid.
67. Ibid.
68. *CO*, Mar. 31, 1933; *COR*, Apr. 6, 1933.
69. *CO*, May 6, 1933.
70. *CO*, June 14, 1933.
71. *CO*, July 5, 1933.
72. *CO*, Aug. 11, 1933.
73. *CO*, Aug. 26, 1933.
74. *CO*, Sept. 7, 1933.
75. *CO*, Oct. 14, 1933.
76. *CO*, Apr. 5, 1934.
77. *CO*, June 8, 1934.
78. *COR*, Aug. 9, 1934.
79. *CO*, Aug. 24, 1934.
80. *CO*, Sept. 1, 1934.
81. *CO*, Nov. 1, 1934.
82. *COR*, Nov. 29, 1934.
83. *COR*, May 2, 1935.
84. *COR*, July 15, 1935.
85. *CO*, July 27, 1935.
86. *RBDN*, Oct. 21, 1935; *COR*, Oct. 24, 1935.
87. *COR*, Oct. 31, 1935.
88. *CO*, Dec. 12, 1935.
89. *CO*, Jan. 24, 1936.
90. *CO*, Feb. 6, 1936.
91. *CO*, Feb. 22, 1936.
92. *CO*, Mar. 9, 1936.
93. *CO*, Aug. 29, 1936.
94. *CO*, Sept. 17-18, 1936.
95. *CO*, Mar. 20, 1937.
96. Unknown and Undated Newspaper Article.
97. *CO*, July 29, 1937.
98. *CO*, Oct. 19, 1937; *CO*, Oct. 22, 1937.
99. *CO*, Oct. 21, 1937.
100. Unknown and Undated Newspaper Article.
101. *SB*, Mar. 20, 1938.
102. *CO*, July 21, 1938; *RBDN*, July 21-22, 1938.
103. Unknown and Undated Newspaper Article
104. *WJ*, Oct. 10, 1938.
105. *WJ*, Aug. 24, 1939.
106. *WJ*, Aug. 28, 1939.

Chapter 18

1. *SB*, Apr. 13, 1912.
2. *GH*, Aug. 3, 1918.
3. *ODR*, July 30, 1919.
4. *SU*, Sept. 18, 1919.
5. Haller, p. 44.
6. *SF Ex*, Apr. 11, 1920.
7. *CO*, May 6, 1922.
8. *CO*, May 6, 1922; Cleveland, p. 47; *MAD*, May 9, 1922.
9. *RBDN*, May 13, 1927.
10. *RBDN*, June 6, 1927.
11. *RBDN*, July 12, 1927.
12. *RBDN*, Aug. 25, 1927.
13. *RBDN*, Aug. 29, 1927.
14. *RBDN*, Aug. 31, 1927.
15. *RBDN*, Sept. 16, 1927.
16. Ibid.
17. *RBDN*, Sept. 17, 1927.
18. *RBDN*, Sept. 19-20, 1927.
19. *RBDN*, Sept. 20-21, 1927.
20. *RBDN*, Sept. 22, 1927.
21. Ibid.
22. *RBDN*, Sept. 22, 1927.
23. *RBDN*, Sept. 28, 1927.
24. *SB*, Feb. 8, 1928; *WF*, May 1928, p. 66.
25. *LMRR*, Apr. 12, 1928; *LMRR*, June 7, 1928; *WF*, Aug. 1928, p. 92.
26. *MAD*, June 14, 1928.
27. *PAN*, Aug. 1928, p. 14.
28. *RCFP*, Aug. 2, 1928.
29. *SU*, Aug. 3, 1928.
30. *SU*, Aug. 11, 1928; *SB*, Aug. 15, 1928.
31. *RBDN*, Sept. 11, 1928.
32. *RBDN*, Sept. 12, 1928; *SU*, Sept. 13, 1928.
33. *RBDN*, Sept. 14, 1928.
34. *RCFP*, Aug. 25, 1928.
35. *SB*, Aug. 28, 1928.
36. *SB*, Sept. 19, 1928.
37. *SB*, Oct. 17, 1928; *WF*, Dec. 1928, p. 68.
38. *SB*, Oct. 17, 1928.
39. *SB*, Jan. 9, 1929.
40. Ibid.
41. *AD*, Feb. 1929, p. 134.
42. *SB*, Apr. 24, 1929.
43. Bell, p. 138.

Endnotes

44. *SB*, Mar. 13, 1929.
45. *PF*, Apr. 1929, p. 24.
46. *SB*, July 3, 1929.
47. *CO*, July 29, 1929.
48. *CO*, Aug. 12, 1929.
49. *PF*, Sept. 1929, p. 21.
50. *PF*, Oct. 1929, p. 20.
51. *SB*, Nov. 27, 1929.
52. *SB*, Dec. 11, 1929.
53. *RBDN*, June 19, 1930.
54. Ibid.
55. *RBDN*, Dec. 1, 1930.
56. Interview with Gerald Beauchamp, Jan. 1978.
57. *PF*, Mar. 18, 1931, p. 14.
58. *PF*, Apr. 22, 1931, p. 13.
59. *SB*, July 15, 1931.
60. Ibid.
61. *SB*, Aug. 3, 1931.
62. *AD*, Oct. 1931, p. 104.
63. *RBDN*, Jan. 2, 1932.
64. *RBDN*, May 26, 1932.
65. *RBDN*, June 13, 1932.
66. *RBDN*, Aug. 10, 1932.
67. *CO*, Jan. 9, 1933.
68. *CO*, Aug. 24, 1934.
69. Red Bluff Airport Admin. Building Photo Display
70. *CO*, Mar. 5, 1936.
71. *CO*, Mar. 29, 1938.
72. *RBDN*, July 21, 1938.

Chapter 19

1. *RCFP*, July 2, 1909.
2. *RCFP*, July 6-7, 1909.
3. *CR*, Feb. 23, 1910; *ODR*, Feb. 23, 1909.
4. *RCFP*, Jan. 4, 1912; *RCFP*, Jan. 6, 1912.
5. *RCFP*, Jan. 11, 1912.
6. *Aero and Hydro*, Jan. 27, 1912, p. 341.
7. *RCFP*, Jan. 11, 1912.
8. *RCFP*, Jan 13, 1912.
9. *Aero and Hydro*, June 7, 1913, p. 190; *Aero and Hydro*, June 14, 1913, p. 221.
10. *RCFP*, July 22-23, 1919.
11. *RCFP*, July 23, 1919.
12. *RCFP*, July 28, 1919.
13. *RCFP*, Aug. 1, 1919.
14. *RCFP*, Aug. 2, 1919.
15. *RCFP*, Aug. 4, 1919.
16. *RCFP*, Aug. 9, 1919.
17. *RCFP*, Sept. 15, 1919; *SU*, Sept. 18, 1919.
18. Gardner, p. 21.
19. *RCFP*, Feb. 11, 1920.
20. *RCFP*, Feb. 12, 1920.
21. *RCFP*, Feb. 14, 1920.
22. *RCFP*, Feb. 17, 1920.
23. *RCFP*, Apr. 29, 1920.
24. Cassagneres, pp. 178-179.
25. *RCFP*, Aug. 19, 1920; *RCFP*, Aug. 21, 1920.
26. *RCFP*, Aug. 21, 1920.
27. *RCFP*, Aug. 26, 1920; *RCFP*, Aug. 28, 1920.
28. *RCFP*, June 29, 1923.
29. Gardner, p. 21.
30. *SB*, June 26, 1923.
31. *SU*, Dec. 30, 1924.
32. *SF Ch*, Sept. 6, 1926.
33. *MA*, Feb. 27, 1927; *AAHS Journal*, Vol. 38 No. 1, p. 92.
34. *RCFP*, July 2, 1929; *MAD*, Sept. 1, 1927; FAA 2012 San Francisco Sectional Map.
35. *RBDN*, Apr. 20, 1927.
36. *MAD*, June 8, 1927.
37. *MAD*, Sept. 1, 1927.
38. *AD*, Apr. 1928, p. 622.
39. *WF*, Apr. 1928, p. 46.
40. *MAD*, May 29, 1928.
41. *MAD*, June 4, 1928.
42. *AD*, July 1928, p. 114.
43. *BWN*, July 2, 1928.
44. *RCFP*, July 7, 1928.
45. Ibid.
46. *RCFP*, July 9, 1928.
47. *RCFP*, July 21, 1928.
48. *SB*, July 25, 1928.
49. *WF*, Aug. 1928, p. 66.
50. *AD*, Aug. 1928, p. 288.
51. *RCFP*, Aug. 10, 1928.
52. *SB*, Aug. 13, 1928.
53. *WF*, Sept. 1928, p.167; *WF*, Sept. 1928, p. 242.
54. *RCFP*, Sept. 3, 1928.
55. Ibid.
56. *RCFP*, Sept. 5, 1928.
57. *RCFP*, Sept. 7, 1928.
58. Ibid.
59. *RCFP*, Sept. 10-11, 1928.
60. *RCFP*, Sept. 15, 1928.
61. *SB*, Sept. 19, 1928.
62. *RCFP*, Sept. 21, 1928.
63. *RCFP*, Sept. 25, 1928; Interview with H. T. Herr, July 1998.
64. *SB*, Sept. 26, 1928.
65. *MAD*, Oct. 20, 1928; *WF*, Dec. 1928, p. 70.
66. *SB*, Mar. 20, 1929.
67. *SB*, Apr. 3, 1929.
68. *SB*, May 1, 1929.
69. *RCFP*, July 5, 1929.

70. *RCFP*, July 2, 1929.
71. Ibid.
72. *RCFP*, July 6, 1929.
73. *CR*, July 7, 1929.
74. *RCFP*, July 8, 1929; *SDI*, July 9, 1929.
75. *RCFP*, July 6, 1929.
76. *SB*, Dec. 11, 1929; *WF*, Jan. 1930, p. 1180.
77. *WF*, Jan. 1930, p. 172.
78. *PF*, Nov. 1930, p. 23.
79. *PF*, Mar. 18, 1931, p. 13.
80. *RBDN*, July 7, 1932; *RBDN*, July 9, 1932; *WJ*, July 8, 1932.
81. *AAM*, Nov. 15, 1939, p. 11.

Chapter 20

1. *SB*, Mar. 14, 1910.
2. *WDD*, July 29, 1970.
3. *ODR*, Feb. 26, 1910.
4. Crouch, p. 526.
5. *SB*, Aug. 6, 1910.
6. *SB*, Aug. 11, 1910; *WDR*, Aug. 13, 1910.
7. *CDS*, May 30, 1911; *CDS*, June 6, 1911.
8. *WDD*, Dec. 1-2, 1911.
9. *WDD*, Dec. 4, 1911.
10. *WDD*, June 27, 1918; *WM*, June 28, 1918; *WM*, July 2, 1918; *WM*, Aug. 4 & 14, 1918; *WM*, Sept. 13, 1918; *WDD*, Sept. 19 & 28, 1918; *WDD*, Dec. 2, 1918; *WDD*, July 12, 1919.
11. *WDD*, July 16, 1919.
12. *WDD*, July 18, 1919.
13. Ibid.
14. *WDD*, July 18, 1919; *WDD*, July 21, 1919.
15. *WDD*, Aug. 27, 1919.
16. *WDD*, Sept. 4, 1919.
17. *WDD*, Sept. 29, 1919.
18. *WDD*, Oct. 9, 1919.
19. *WDD*, Oct. 10, 1919.
20. *WDD*, Oct. 23, 1919.
21. *WDD*, Oct. 24, 1919.
22. *WDD*, Oct. 25, 1919.
23. *WDD*, Oct. 31, 1919.
24. *SU*, Apr. 9, 1920.
25. *WDD*, June 3, 1920.
26. *WDD*, June 16, 1920.
27. *WDD*, June 19, 1920.
28. *WDD*, Aug. 19, 1920.
29. *WDD*, June 26, 1920.
30. *WDD*, Aug. 23, 1920; *SF EX*, Aug. 23, 1920; *RCS*, Aug. 26, 1920; *AAW*, Sept. 13, 1920, p. 8; *The Ace*, Sept. 1920, p. 12; Dwiggins, p. 11.
31. Waterman, p. 150; *The Ace*, Oct. 1920, p. 12.
32. *AAW*, Feb. 14, 1921, n.p.
33. *WDD*, May 7, 1921.
34. *SU*, May 8, 1921; *WDD*, May 9, 1921.
35. Waterman, pp. 126-130; *AAW*, Sept. 13, 1920, p. 8.
36. *SU*, May 8, 1921; *WDD*, May 9, 1921.
37. Cleveland, pp. 37-40.
38. *SU*, May 24-25, 1923; Gudde, p. 426.
39. *WF*, June 1926, n.p.
40. *WDD*, May 25, 1927.
41. *WDD*, Apr. 16, 1927; *SU*, Apr. 17, 1927; Tillman, *AAHS Journal*, Fall 1971, p. 181.
42. *WDD*, June 27, 1927.
43. *WDD*, July 11, 1927.
44. *WDD*, July 20, 1927.
45. *WDD*, July 23, 1927.
46. *MAD*, July 31, 1927.
47. *WDD*, Aug. 6, 1927.
48. *WDD*, Aug. 10, 1927.
49. *WDD*, Aug. 11, 1927.
50. Ibid.
51. *WDD*, Sept. 28, 1927.
52. *MAD*, Sept. 21, 1928.
53. *SB*, Nov. 7, 1928.
54. *MAD*, Dec. 21, 1928; *WDD*, May 29, 2003.
55. *MAD*, Feb. 1, 1929.
56. *PF*, Apr. 1929, p. 24.
57. *SB*, May 1, 1929; *SB*, May 15, 1929.
58. *SB*, May 8, 1929.
59. *CR*, May 22, 1929; *WDD*, May 30, 1929; *PF*, June 1929, p. 19.
60. *WDD*, June 17, 1929; *SF Ch*, June 17, 1929.
61. *WDD*, June 17, 1929.
62. *PF*, July 1929, p. 22.
63. *PF*, May 1930, p. 23; *MAD*, May 6, 1930; *WF*, June 1930, p. 96.
64. *WDD*, July 1-3, 1930; Cleveland, pp. 148-153.
65. *SB*, June 25, 1930.
66. *WDD*, July 7, 1930.
67. *WDD*, July 2, 1930.
68. Ibid.
69. *SB*, Nov. 5, 1930.
70. *SB*, Nov. 12, 1930.
71. *PF*, Dec. 1930, p. 24.
72. *PF*, Apr. 8, 1931, p. 18.
73. *SB*, Nov. 4, 1931; Interview with Dan Best II.
74. *WDD*, Dec. 10, 1932.
75. *SB*, Dec. 14, 1932.
76. *SB*, Sept. 17, 1933.
77. *WDD*, Sept. 23, 1933.
78. *WDD*, Sept. 29, 1933.
79. *WDD*, Sept. 30, 1933.
80. *WDD*, Oct. 4, 1933.
81. *WDD*, Oct. 9, 1933.

82. *WDD*, Oct. 17, 1933.
83. *WDD*, Nov. 2, 1933.
84. *WDD*, Nov. 10, 1933; *WDD*, Nov. 15, 1933.
85. *WDD*, Nov. 14, 1933.
86. *WDD*, Nov. 29, 1933; *WDD*, Dec. 1-4, 1933.
87. *SB*, Dec. 7, 1933.
88. *WDD*, Dec. 27, 1933.
89. *AD*, July 1934, p. 45.
90. *PA*, June 1935, p. 359.
91. *AAM*, July 1, 1939, p. 8.
92. *WDD*, Mar. 22, 1941.
93. Davies, *Airlines of Latin* . . . , pp. 126-128.
94. *WDD*, May 9, 1941.
95. *WDD*, May 21, 1941.
96. *WDD*, May 9, 1941; *WDD*, May 21-23, 1941.

BIBLIOGRAPHY

Anderson, Mabry I. *Low and Slow*. San Francisco, CA: California Farmer Publishing Co., 1986.
Arbon, Lee. *They Also Flew*. Washington, D. C: Smithsonian Institute Press, 1992.
Bell, Dana. *Directory of Airplanes: Their Designers and Manufacturers*. London: Greenhill Books, 2002.
Bohrer, Walt. *Black Cats and Outside Loops*. Oregon City, OR: Plere Publishers, 1989.
Bowers, Peter M. *Curtiss Aircraft 1907–1947*. Annapolis, MD: Naval Institute Press, 1987.
Brown, Jim. *Hubbard: The Forgotten Boeing Aviator*. Seattle, WA: Peanut Butter Pub., 1996.
Cassagneres, Ev. *Ambassador of Air Travel*, Missoula, MA: Pictorial Histories Publishing, 2006.
Cleveland, Carl M. *Upside-Down Pangborn*. Glendale, CA: Aviation Book Co., 1978.P
Crouch, Tom D. *The Eagle Aloft*. Washington D.C: Smithsonian Institute Press, 1983.
Cummins, Julie. *Tomboy of the Air*. New York: Harper Collins Publishing, 2001.
Davies, R. E. G. *Airlines of Latin America Since 1919*. McLean,à VA: Paladwr Press, 1997.
—————————. *Airlines of the United States Since 1914*. Washington, D.C: Smithsonian Institute Press, 1998.
DeVries, Col. John A. *Alexander Eaglerock*. Colorado Springs, CO: Wolfgang Pub. 1994.
Dwiggins, Don. *Hollywood Pilot*. Garden City, NY: Doubleday & Co., 1967
Forden, Lesley. *The Ford Air Tours 1925–1931*. Alameda, CA: Nottingham Press, 1973.
Gardner, Lester D. *Who's Who in American Aeronautics 1925*. 2nd Ed., Los Angeles: F. Clymer Publishing, 1925.
Gordon, Dennis. *The Lafayette Flying Corps*. Atgen, PA: Schiffer Military History, 2000.
Grace, Dick. *I Am Still Alive*. New York: Rand McNally Co., 1931.
Grambon, Marion E., Editor. *Who's Who In World Aviation*. Washington, D. C: American Aviation Publishing, 1958.
Grey, C. G. (Editor). *Jane's All The World's Aircraft 1927*. London: Sampson, Low, Marston & Co., 1927.
Gudde, Erwin G. *California Place Names*. 4th Ed., Berkeley, CA: University of California Press, 1998.
Gwynn-Jones, Terry. *Wings Across the Pacific*. Atgen, PA: Schiffer Military/Aviation History, 1995.
Haller, Stephen A. *The Last Word in Airfields*. 1st Ed., San Francisco, CA: San Francisco National Park Service, 1994.
——————————. *The Last Word in Airfields*. 2nd ED., San Francisco, CA: Golden Gate National Parks Association, 2001.
Hallion, Richard P. *Legacy of Flight: The Guggenheim Contribution to American Aviation*. Seattle WA: University of Washington Press, 1977.
Hallion, Richard P. *Taking Flight:Inventing The Aerial Age From Antiquity Through The First World War*. New York: Oxford University Press, 2003.
Harwood, Craig S. and Gary B. Fogel. *Quest for Flight: John J. Montgomery and the Dawn of Aviation in the West*. Norman, OK: University of Oklahoma Press, 2012.

Hatfield, D. D. *Pioneers of Aviation*. Inglewood, CA: Northrop University Press, 1976.
Higham, Charles. *Errol Flynn*. New York: Dell Publishing Co., 1981.
Howard, Edwin T. *Travel Air Digest*. St. Louis, MO: Howard Pub., 1992.
Jessen, Gene Nora. *The Powder Puff Derby of 1929*. Naperville, IL: Sourcebooks Inc., 2002.
Juptner, Joseph P. *U. S. Civil Aircraft Series*. Blue Ridge Summit, PA: Tab Aero Division of McGraw-Hill, 1993.
Komons, Nick A. *Bonfires to Beacon*. Washington, D. C: Smithsonian Institute Press, 1989.
Kozak, Warren. *Lemay*. Washington, D. C: Regnery Publishing Inc., 2009.
Lewis, Thom. *West Sacramento*. San Francisco, CA: Arcadia, 2004.
Lincke, Jack R. *Jenny Was No Lady*. New York: W. W. Norton & Co., 1970.
Lipsner, Capt. Benjamin B. *The Airmail*. New York: Wilcox and Follett Co., 1951.
Lord, Myrtle Shaw. *A Sacramento Saga*. Sacramento, CA: Sacramento Chamber of Commerce, 1946.
Lyman, Robert H., Editor. *The World Almanac and Book of Facts for 1929*. Reprint, New York: The New York World Publishers, 1929.
Marrero, Frank. *Lincoln Beachey*. San Francisco: Scottwall Associates Publishing, 1997.
Maurer, Maurer. *Aviation in the U. S. Army 1919-1939*. Washington, D. C: Government Printing Office, 1987.
McConish, Chas. Davis, and Mrs. Rebecca T. Lambert. *The History of Colusa and Glenn Counties, California*. Los Angeles, CA : Historic Record Comp., 1918.
Miller, Maurice A., Editor. *McClellan Air Force Base 1936-1982*. Sacramento, CA: U. S. Air Force, Office of History, McClellan Air Force Base, December 1, 1982.
Murphy, Dan. *Sacramento's Curtiss Park*. San Francisco, CA: Arcadia, 2005
Museum Society of Willows, J. Wright, E. Whisman. *Willows*. San Francisco, CA: Arcadia, 2010.
Peek, Chet. *The Forgotten Barnstormer*. Norman, OK: Three Peaks Pub., 2110.
Rhode, Bill. *Bailing Wire, Chewing Gum, and Guts*. Port Washington, NY: Kennikat Press, 1970.
Richfield Oil Co. *Aviation Guide*. Publisher Not Indicated, August 1929.
Ricklefs, Jim. *Quiet Birdmen – San Francisco Hangar*, Privately Published, Date Unkwn.
Roseberry, C. R. *Glenn Curtiss: Pioneer of Flight*. Garden City, NY: Doubleday & Co., 1972.
Russell, Gene H. *The Land of Orland*. San Francisco, CA: Arcadia, 2008.
Scheppler, Robert H. *Pacific Air Race*. Washington, D. C: Smithsonian Institute Press, 1988.
Schonberger, William A. *California Wings*. Woodland Hills, CA: Windsor Pub., 1984.
Schultz, Barbara Hunter. *Pancho*. Lancaster, CA: Little Buttes Pub., 1998.
Shell Oil Co. *Airports 1936 Edition*. Hackensack, NJ: Airport Directory Co. 1936.
Smith, Herschel H. *Aircraft Piston Engines*. New York: McGraw-Hill Book Co., 1981.
Spearman, Arthur Dunning. *John Joseph Montgomery 1858-1911:Father of Basic Flying*. Santa Clara, CA: University of Santa Clara, 1967.
Underwood, James. *Grand Central Air Terminal*. San Francisco, CA: Arcadia, 2006.
---------------. *Madcaps, Millionaires and Mose*. Glendale, CA: Heritage Press, 1984.
Veca, Donna and Skip Mazzio. *Just Plane Crazy*. Santa Clara, CA: Osborne Pub., 1987.
Villard, Henry Serrano. *Blue Ribbon Of The Air*. Washington D.C.: Smithsonian Press, 1987.
Waterman, Waldo Dean and Jack Carpenter. *Waldo: Pioneer Aviator*. Carlisle, MA: Arsdalen, Bosch & Co. Publishers, 1988.
Whyte, Edna Gardner and Ann Cooper. *Rising Above It*. New York: Orion Books, 1991.
WPA Writers Project. *The WPA Guide to California*. Reprint, New York: Pantheon Books, 1984.

Articles From Journals And Quarterlies

Allen, Richard S. "Two Little Airlines (Consolidated)," *Skyways*, Jan. 2001, No. 57: 51-53.
Baker, Brian R., "Agricultural Flying." *AAHS Journal*, Spring 1968, Vol. 13, No. 1: 52-54, No. 3: 213
------------, "Early Dusting Experiments." *AAHS Journal*, Summer 1969, Vol. 14, No. 2: 115-118.
Beidleman, Lawrence E., "The Hawke Crop Duster." *AAHS Journal*, Fall 1993, Vol. 38, No. 3:184-193.
Betts, Tom, "Ken Blaney" *TWA Topics*, undated, n.p.
Billman, Owen S., "Jack Irwin – Lightplane Pioneer," *Sport Aviation*, Feb. 1977: 57- 65.
Glenshaw, Paul, "Ladies and Gentlemen: The Aeroplane," *Air and Space*, April/May 2008, 48-65.

Bibliography

Griffin, Larry and Helena. "Log of the Friesley Falcon," Part I, *Skyways*, Jan. 1991, No. 17: 33-39.

----------------------. "Log of the Friesley Falcon," Part II, *Skyways*, Apr. 1991, No. 18: 42-50.

Harp, Major Leland, "Biography of Joseph L. Cato," http:// www.rcooper.0catch.com.htm

Henley, James E., "1918 Sacramento Has An Aerocraft Factory And Mather Field," *Sacramento Historical Society Journal*, Vol. 3 Nos. 2 & 3: 37-42.

Raymond, A. E., "Early Non-Rigid Dirigibles 1898-1915." *AAHS Journal*, Spring 1985, Vol. 30 No. 1: 58-67.

Robinson, Douglas H. "Dr. August Greth and the First Dirigible Flight in the United States." *American Aviation Historical Society (AAHS) Journal*, Summer 1976, Vol. 21 No. 2: 84-91.

Snyder, J. J., "Dargue's Destiny." *AAHS Journal*, Summer 1993, Vol. 38, No. 2: 82-102.

Thaden, Louise, and Pansy Bowen with Mildred Morgan, "We Girls Must Stick Together," *Western Flying*, Sept. 1932: 28-29.

Tillman, Barrett, "Six Million Miles." *AAHS Journal*, Fall 1971, Vol. 16, No. 3: 175-183.

Wagner, William, "Ryan Mechanics Monoplane Co. and William J. Waterhouse." *AAHS Journal*, Fall 1974, Vol. 19 No. 3: 193-199.

Interviews

Gerald Beauchamp, Jan. 1978.
Dan Best II, Nov. 10, 2016
H. T. Ted Herr, Jan. 7, 1999.
Guy "Speed" Hughes, Aug. 14, 2002.
Harry Middleton, Nov. 7, 2000.
Salle Saunders, April 10, 2000.
Vince Vanderford (II) Feb. 1998
Rick Von Geldren, Mar. 7, 2000.

Unpublished Works

Lt. Colonel Harry W. Abbott by Dan-San Abbott in the care of Patricia L. Abbott

Avis Bielefeld Family Papers and Pilot's Logbook in the care of Karen Ripley

Index to Robert G. Fowler Collection at Hiller Aviation Museum in San Carlos, CA

Kemper, Lt. Seymour, "History of Mather Field 1918-1938," Unpublished article, 1944, in the Sacramento Archives and Museum Collection Center (SAMCC) Unknown author on Mather AFB, "Sacramento Saga" Unpublished article in SAMCC

PHOTOGRAPH CREDITS

The search for the photographs in this work began in 1999. A few are in public domain and the rest are from the following individuals and organizations kind enough to permit me to use photographs from their family albums or archives; their names are followed by the page numbers of their photographs.

Aerial Age Weekly, Pages 67, 147, 447.
Aeronautics, Pages 2, 10, 56.
Albert H. "Bert" Lane Collection held by Glen A. Lane, Pages 69, 71, 95, 96, 117, 260 (upper), 420, 421, 430.
Avis Sutfin Bielefeld Collection held by Karen Ripley, Pages 233, 260 (lower), 265, 267.
Beochanz Family Collection held by Wendelin Edward Beochanz, Pages 444, 445 (lower), 446, 468 (upper), 468 (lower).
Dan San Abbott Collection held by Patricia L. Abbott, Pages 99, 101, 102.
Center for Sacramento History, earlier known as the Sacramento Archives and Museum Collection Center, Pages 59, 60, 63, 66, 73, 74, 76, 82, 109, 113, 117 (lower), 118, 122, 170 (upper), 170 (lower) 174, 181, 197, 201, 204, 206, 211, 212, 234, 271, 276, 359, 360, 395, 429, 450, back cover.
Community Memorial Museum of Sutter County, Page xv.
Dan Best Collection held by Dan Best II, Pages 458, 460, 464.
Dan San Abbott Collection held by Phyllis Abbott, Pages 99, 101, 102.
Flying (Feb. 1914), Page 47.
Harry Middleton Collection held by Ben Middleton, Page 259.
Lenhoff Collection held by James Lenhoff, Pages 16 (upper), 16 (lower)
Marry Aaron Museum, Marysville, Calif., Page 430 (upper).
McClellan Aviation Museum, Page 339.
Orland Historical and Cultural Society Collection, care of Gene H. Russell, Page 429.
Pacific Flyer Magazine, Pages 131, 198.
Sacramento Public Library, Sacramento Room, Pages 111, 128.
The Ace, Page 445 (upper).
Wedderien Collection held by Bill Wedderien, Page 298.

All other photographs came from Allen Herr's collection. The front cover and the airports map were done by Allen Herr.

INDEX

A

"Aces Up" Flying Circus 397, 398
A'Sik, Cheung, 244
Abbott, Dan-San, 98
Abbott, Harry W., 97-99, 203, 318, 319, 337
Abbott, Wayne, 97, 319
Abreu, Alfred, 322, 323
Achaen Club inspect Willows Arpt., 342, 346
Ackerman, W. W., 391
Adams, Claude M., 243
Adams, Dr., 298, 346
Adams, E. W., 275
Adamson, Bob, 352
Adamson, J., 350
Aerial Crop Dusting Service, 348
Aerial League, 439
Aerial Navigation Co. of Sacto., 6
Aerial rice seeding 4/31, 308
Aerial weddings, 222
Aero Club of America (ACA), 7, 156, 439
Aero Club of the Northwest, 439
Aero Corp. of Calif., 205
Aero Corporation, 419
Aero Dusting Co., 308
Aeronautical Society of Calif., 439
Aerovias Centrales, 345
Agricultural Aviation Academy, 279
Agricultural Avtn. Activities, Inc., 295
Agricultural Park Racetrack, 10, 38, 39
Ahlf, Adolphus, 324
Ahlstrom, Harry E., 336
Air Commerce Act of 1926, 245
Air Ferries Ltd., 206, 207, 256, 258
Air Line Pilots Assn., 255
Air Mail Field (Diablo), 111
Air Mail Field renamed Blanch Field, 1924, 415
Air Mail Field, Reno, 91
Air Progress in Willows 9/11-24/39, 355
Air Service Field, 114, 125
Air Service fire patrols, 49
Air show has hog
Air Taxi Service Co., 236
Aircraft Board Wash. D. C., 60
Aircraft Industries, 310
Aircraft trade show at Willows '39, 355
Airmail night flights, 160
Airport Guide, 114
Airport sites being considered, 139
Airports at Corning and Mineral, 365
Airway beacons, 224, 427
Airway Development and Service Co.,
414, 442
AKA Redding-Boise Air Derby, 425
Alaman, Jim, 161
Alameda Airport, 232
Alderson, Bud, 178
Alexander Eaglerock aircraft, 105, 142, 419
Alexander, J. B., 208, 209
Alexander, J. Don, 142
Alexander, Mary C., 262
Alexandra, Lydia, 112
Alhambra Theater, 156
Allemanti, James, 144
Allen, Bob, 334
Allen, C. C., 122, 126
Allen, Clayton, 213, 257, 333, 426
Allen, E., 215,
Allen, John, 358
Allied shipping priority, 66
Almond Day Arbuckle, 55
Aloha, Dole Race plane, 136, 418
American Aircraft Corp., 420
American War Mothers, 287
Anderline, Frank W., 368
Anderson, Anneta, 166
Anderson, D. R., 358
Anderson, Ed, 178
Anderson, Gibert, 207, 460
Anderson, James, 255
Anderson, Judge O. W., 104
Anderson, M., 166
Andrews, Gerald "Jerry," 151, 158, 209, 334, 350, 366, 398
Andrews, H. G., hired by Maddux, 173
Andrews, H. P., 134
Andrews, H. to fly Glenn Co. fair, 328
Andrews, Henry G., 68, 81, 84, 85, 92, 107-130, 134, 139, 143, 157, 158, 171-179, 195, 209, 245, 246, 272, 328, 330, 401, 419, 449
Andrews, Maj. Frank M., 269
Andrews, Nicholson & Morris Co., 119, 123, 124, 127, 129, 136, 137, 140, 144, 172, 175, 184
Andrews, William K., DOC Inspector, 152, 166, 191, 197, 204-207
Andriotti, Mr., 296
Angel, Eddie, 106
Angel, James C. "Jimmie," 106, 107 166, 207
Angel, Parker, 106
Angeleno Buhl Airsedan, 208, 209
Antiaircraft Field, Sac., 114
Antweiler, Jack, 350
Arata, Winfield H., 439
Arbuckle Almond Fair, 84
Arbuckle Glider Club, 322
Arcade Creek, Del Paso Park, 138, 190
Arcade Farm Center, 140
Arcade School, 126
Armstrong, Lionel, 5
Armstrong, Louis, 6
Army Air Corps Air Maneuvers 1930, 318
Army plane at Webber Field, Woodland, 435
Army plane wrecked on Fliers Club Field, 453
Army planes from Hamilton Field, 346
Army versus Navy in Joint Maneuvers, 270
Arnold, Col. H. H. "Hap," 88, 390, 441, 443
Ashe, Harvey, 404
Ashfield, Nora, 414
Ashford, N. Dewey, 205, 346, 350
Associated Air Services, 404
Associated Oil Co. Boeing 40A, 162
Associated Oil Co., 223, 422
Attempt to light Mather, 154
Atterbury, Glenn, 457
Auburn Motor Co., 254
Aulthouse, Jack, dusting, 310
Aviation Act of June 1917, 58
Aviation Activities Inc., 294
Avro 504K, 442
Avro 504Ks, R. Fowler, 88
Axleson Motor, 154
Ayer, Denison, 167

B

B.B.T. Corp., lights, 134
Baby Ruth on Waco, 367
Bach Tri-motor, 154
Bachman, Bert, 226
Backman, Al, 240
Baily, Lt. Joe, 108
Baker, D. M., 111, 153
Baker, Floyd, 177, 219, 268
Baker, Merle, 388
Baker, Mrs. A. J., 357
Baker, R. R., 243
Balch, Ensign, 357
Balch, M., 358
Balch, Tom, 357
Baldwin crashes prior to Water Festival, 313
Baldwin, Capt. Ivy (William Ivy), 14-18, 313, 433, 434
Baldwin, Ivy, signs w/ Colusa, 313
Baldwin, Thomas S., 4, 5, 16, 17, 433
Ball, Gordon, 241

– 491 –

Ballough, E. E., 397
Bank of Sparks, Nev., 275
Bannister, "Bantie," 403
Bannister, M., 166
Barber, Bob,, 398
Barber, Frank, 297
Barden, Dorothy, parachutist, 349, 350, 388
Barker & Witney, Inc., 265
Barker, G. E. "Jerry," 264, 266, 269, 465
Barnes, Flor. L. "Pancho," 214, 263
Barnett, Robert, 227
Barrie, Allen, 164
Barrows, W. J. "Joe," 123, 152, 316, 425, 426
Baskins, Jack, 387, 405
Bass, Alfred M., 132
BAT (Boeing Air Transport), 217
BAT 1st flights out of Sac Muni, 217
BAT airmail, 200
BAT at Mather, 217
BAT becomes United Air Lines, 246
BAT bizarre incident, 210
BAT blind flying tests, 210
BAT forbids pilots to fly blind, 252
BAT starts at Sac Muni, 250
BAT Teletype reports, 251
Baugh, Gordon, chutist, 268
Baumgartner, Ray,457
Bay Farm Island, 365
Beach, Mrs. E. W., 264
Beachey, Lincoln, 1, 19, 38, 51-53, 392, 434
Beacon Airways, Inc.,145
Beale, Fern, 358
Beamer Park, Woodland, 437- 440
Bear, C. W., 216
Beardslee, John, 342
Beardsly, Archer, Indep. Flying Schl., 303
Bechtle, Chris, 424
Becket, Ralph, 216
Beckstrom, Bill, 180
Beckstrom, George, 180
Beedle, Hadley, 111
Beery, Wallace, 159,353, 376
Behan, Roscoe, Varney, 259
Beilby & Canning, 141
Beilby joins Varney, 192
Beilby, Jack, 143, 170, 176, 190-192,209, 216, 235, 236, 337
Bell, Bert, 398
Bellenger, E. N.,144
Belmont Park Air Meet 1910, 23, 29
Bendix, Howard, 244
Bennett & Bell Ranch Air Show, 364, 391, 392
Bennett and Bell Ranch
Bennett, C. E., 413
Bennett, Floyd, 117
Bennett, Forrest E., 191, 204, 215, 218, 226, 235, 236
Bennett, Frank, 174
Bennett, Pat, 178, 232
Bennett's Monocoach, 192, 216, 221, 236
Bent, Theodore, 393
Benton crashes at Reno, 91, 415
Benton Field Air Show, 418

Benton Field Ded., 424
Benton Field descript., 423
Benton Field gets a city block, 418
Benton Field named, 414
Benton Field on Johnson Hill, Redding, 417
Benton Field, 413, 418
Benton to S. Amer., 417
Benton, Lt. John W., 91, 108, 414,416, 424, 452
Benton, Mrs. Zelma, 424
Benton, Thomas Hart, 414
Bernthal races Overland, 24
Berry, J. M., 8, 9
Best Field Air Show,461, 462
Best Field, 458, 463
Best Field, new hangar ded. w/air show, 465
Best, Dan, 345, 461,462, 457
Best, Dan, flies under new Knight's Landing bridge, 463
Betsy Ross Corps, 261, 262
Bevan, A. D., 9
Biddlecome, Clementine, 331
Bidwell Airport taken over by city 1/29, 399
Bidwell Airport, Red Bluff, 399-405
Bidwell, C. H. S., Sacto Mayor
Bidwell, C. H., 256
Bidwell, Lt. Robinson E., died WWI, 390
Bielefeld, Al, 264, 267
Bielefeld, Avis Sutfin, 263-267
Biggs rice exp. station, 301
Billings, Cadet, 65
Bird, C. W., ad. prop., 461
Birnn, Lt. Roland, 202
Bishop, L., 200
Blache, Maurice, 327
Black Butte Reservoir, 332
Black, Josephine, 274
Blakely, H. W., 43, 45, 411
Blanch Field, Reno, 147, 183
Blanchfield, William F., 147
Blaney breaks back, 196
Blaney, Ken, 121, 124, 125, 134, 159, 174, 194-197
Blaney, Maddux copilot, 195
Blewett, Johanna, 254
Blohm, Henry F., 167
Blood, H. R., 127, 162
Bloodworth, H. B., 463
Bloodworth, W. A., 437
Blunt, H., 157, 167, 205
Bobuliski, Sergeant, 207
Bobzien, Lt. E. B., 222
Bodkin, Peter, 333
Boedefeld, L. R., 312, 313
Boeing 247 and B-9, 252
Boeing Air Transport, 122, 130, 134, 146-148, 153, 161, 199, 208, 210, 213, 217, 218, 229, 241, 247, 463
Boeing Model 40A, 134, 153, 247, 248
Boeing Model 80A, 153, 217, 247, 248, 250
Boeing School of Aeronaut., 205, 209, 215, 345-348
Boeing System, 230, 250-252

Boeken, Fred, 160
Boggs, S. S., 331, 422
Boland, F. E., 12
Boldt, L. J., 456
Boles, T. K., 342
Boller, Sterling, chief pilot CAL, 255, 256
Bond issue in Sacto., 206
Bond, E. J., 304
Boniface, Frank, 133
Bonnalie, Allen F., 156, 209
Booth, Fred, 148
Boquel, Joe, 54-56
Borello, Peter, 459
Borne before Judge, 290
Borth, Al, 143
Bottimore, Ebner, 230, 274
Bottimore, W. W., 274
Bottorff, A. V., 146
Bottoroff, H. C., 113, 127
Botts, F. W., 13
Botts, J. M., 12
Boucher, Jack, 125
Bounting, L. A., 88
Bourdeaux, Lt., 424
Bourne, Arthur A., 289, 396
Bovee, Courtney, 387
Bowen, Pansy, 233, 262
Bowen, Pansy, flies aerobatics, 268
Bowen, R. P., 229, 273, 351, 353
Bowerman, Jr., Mr., 136
Bowker, Earl, 154
Bowles, John, 358
Bowles, Tom, 358
Bowlus, Harvey, 319, 348
Bowman, Charlie, PAT, 249
Bowman, Les, 230, 345, 346, 383
Bowman, Martha, 230
Bowser, Charlie, 162
Boyd & Webdell sent to Chicago, 311
Boyd, Bob, 333
Boyd, Jr., Geo, w/Indep. Crop Dusters, 311, 325
Boyd, Mr. & Mrs., 159
Boyd, Robert E., 346, 353
Boyer, Mrs. A. H., 427
Boyle, Nev. Gov. E. D., 78
Bragdon, Ed, 399
Bragunier, Ace, 167
Brainard Bros. Foundary & Machine Shop, 38, 74
Brainard brothers, 38
Brainard, Ernest S., 32, 33, 36, 70, 74
Brainard, Omar L., 36, 70, 74, 76
Brand, L. C., 449, 451
Brandenburger, W. A., 383
Brander brothers, 148
Brander, Bill, 205, 311, 354, 357, 358
Brandt, Col. Gerald, 159, 424
Brandt, J., 462
Brandt, Mrs. G. C., 424
Branstetter, Charles, 354
Bray, C., 358
Brayfon, Lou, 199
Brazil, Tony, 177, 219
Breen, Capt. R. G., 367
Breese cabin planes, 129
Breese, Vance, 123, 209, 366, 401, 453,

INDEX

456,
Brett, Maj. George H., 415, 416
Brewer, W. R., 378
Brewster, Hugh, DOC, 381
Brien, Al, 343
Briggs, Dr. W. E., 81
Brisbin, Leslie, 304
British Airways, 246
British Columbia Airways Ltd., 213
Broadwick, "Tiny," 328
Broadwick, Charles, 440
Broadwick, Ethel, 328, 440
Broadwick's women parachutists, 440
Brock, William, 366
Bronte, Emory B., 162, 223,366, 422
Brooks, Frank, para., 164
Brookwalter, Vernon, 396, 397
Broughton, Don, 217, 250
Brown, Dick, 258
Brown, Earle, 31, 398
Brown, Harold F., 217, 223, 268, 307, 323, 324, 341, 347, 403
Brown, John Q., 81,
Brown, Kenneth C., 156
Brown, L., 358
Brown, Mr. & Mrs. J. H., 422
Brown, Norman, 308
Brown, Richard, 221
Brown, Warden A. J., 299
Browne, Carl, 38
Browne, Walter, cub act, 268
Browning, J. L., 296
Bruman, Frank, 358
Brush, Phil, 215
Brush, Shirley, 334, 462
Bryan, Al, 382
Bryant, Al, 354
Bryant, Dr. C. W.,414
Bryant, Frank, 44, 57, 58, 326, 327, 409, 411
Bryant, Harry, 58
Bryant, Henry, 58, 327
Buck, George, 259
Buckles, Rex, 220, 461
Bucklin, Buck, 398
Buckner, H. E., 88
Budwig, Gilbert "Bud," 451
Buffalo Park Exhibition, 31
Buffington, Lt. J. F., 61, 64
Bumblebee homebuilt ac, 132
Bundy, Lt. Harold, 203
Burging, Ernest, 144
Burhart, Charles, 358
Burk, Kathleen, 437
Burkhart, Dorothy, 240
Burleson, Evelyn, to fly air show, 354, 357
Burmeister, C., 286
Burnham, Lt. Sam. P., 62
Bush, Joan, 345
Bush, Joe, 383
Butte City Warehouse, 340
Byrd, Adm. Richard E., 133, 186, 462

C

CA airports lat.&long., 93
Caddo Co. filming *Hell's Angels*, 193
Caffery, Sgt. A. A., 105

CAL (Consolidated Air Lines), 256,
Cal Poly student ac, 166
Calahan Flying Ser., 193
Calif. Aero Manufact. and Supply Co., 312, 313, 434
Calif. Ag Society, 21
Calif. Air Tour, 1st, 163
Calif. Air Tour, 2nd, 209
Calif. Assn. for the Prom. of Aeronautics, 150, 151
Calif. Aviation Company, 32, 33, 42
Calif. Fish & Game, 280
Calif. Fruit Exch., 146, 247
Calif. Nat. Guard, 17, 55, 135, 205
Calif., first rice Butte, 279
California State Fairs, 20, 57, 61, 64, 84, 89-92, 105, 146, 165, 166, 219
California's first flight, 305
Cameron, A. E., 158
Camilli, Andy, 358
Camp 19 Bowman Lake, 224
Camp Sacramento, 34
Campbell camp snowed, 236
Campbell, Capt. H. D., 134,136
Campbell, Marston, 212
Campbell, Milo, 195, 316
Campbell, Ted, 368
Campbell, Will L., 224
Canning & Nicholson Flying Service, 226
Canning, Ralph, 125, 143, 165, 166, 176, 177, 190, 209, 221, 222, 225
Canwell, Robert, 367
Capay Valley emerg. fld.,455
Capital Air Lines ops. from Del Paso, 245
Capital Air Lines, 127, 129,134, 138, 149, 172-175, 192, 245, 246, 419, 422
Capital Airways, 163
Capital Flying Ser., 148, 149, 193, 246
Capital sold to Union, 245
Cardiff, Don, 145
Cardiff, Jack, 215
Carey, S. F., 215
Carey, Warren, 352
Carmichael, Cmdr. D. W., 83
Carnahan, Joseph, 21
Carroll, Lt., 205
Carter, Mrs. Charles H., 130
Casey, Jack, 148, 192, 246
Castalotti, Andy, 358
Castle, Don, 150, 151
Castle, O. W., 239-242
Catalpa sphinx larva, 278
Cates, W. K., 193
Cato, Joseph, 36
Cavalry Flat, Presidio, 43
Cecchetini, Joe, 176-178
Central Calif. Tractn Co., 7
Century pilots on strike, 255
Century-Pacific Lines, Ltd., 187, 219-222, 225, 254, 255
Century-Pacific start up, 254
Chadbourne, Jack, 161
Chadderton, Sydney, S., 319
Chadwick, Elmer, 399
Chadwick, Volney, 372, 380, 397-401, 405
Chamberlin & Levine, 371

Chamberlin, Clarence, 819
Chambers, Reed, 443-445
Chandler, A. E., 327
Chandler, B. C., 214
Chaney, S. M., 325
Chang, Henri, 358
Chanute glider, 40
Chapman, Allen, 158
Chapmenn, Ola, 322
Chappell & Brainard
Chappell & Brainard biplane, 32, 36
Chappell, Ernest, 32, 33
Chatterton, Ruth, 347
Checker Air Service, W. T. Varney, 106
Cheim Airport, Mrysvl., 184
Chen, Eugene, 99
Chew, Chancy, 97, 99
Chicago – NY Race, 29
Chico Contracting Co., 413
Chico Spring Festival, 42
Chinese-American Flying Circus, 100
Chow, William, 64
Choy, Bill, 244
Christal, Charles H., 439
Christensen & Burmeister Farms, 282
Christensen, L., 240
Christensen, rice farmer, 279, 282
Christiansen, Andy, 358
Christie engine, 23, 26-29
Christie, Walter, 16, 19, 21, 23, 26
Christie, Walter, race car, 53
Christofferson Aviation School, 54
Christofferson, Silas, 43, 46
Churchill, Rose, 134
Cirten, Milt, 86
City of Ottawa crash, 165
Civiln. Fligt. Trng. Pro., 359
Claiborne, Capt. Harry B., 166, 336
Clark, A. A., 457
Clark, Dustin, 242
Clark, Dwight "Suicide," parachutist, 346-348, 352, 382, 388
Clark, E., 358
Clark, Ernest, 354
Clark, Herbert L., 167
Clark, J., 296
Clark, Ken, 383
Clark, R. O., 308
Clark, Wilbur, 183
Clarke flies D.7 at YFC, 451
Clarke, Frank, L-6 J-1, 447
Clarke, James C.. 9
Clarke, Robert, 358
Clayton, Frank L., 336
Clevenger, Cloyd, 93, 330, 364, 366, 392
Cline, Virgil, 159, 164
Clohecy, Robert L., 93, 103, 105, 452
Clover Flying Serv., 207-210, 256, 322
Clyde, W. H., in Beech, 351
Coad, Dr. Bert, 279
Cody, Henry, 222,
Coenen, Virgil, 383
Coffee, Bud, 288
Coffing, Homer D., 131,194, 272
Coleman, Dorothy, 321
College of Pacific, 143, 205
Collier, Boyd, 233

COLUSA air marker, 318
Colusa Airport comm., 317
Colusa Airport, 316, 322, 322
Colusa Co. 1st Flight, 314
Colusa Flying Club, 323
Colusa Glider Club, 322
Colusa gun clubs, trip to, 316
Colusa opening air show, 255, 319, 320, 292
Colwell, Guy, 100
Condit, Robert, 126
Conley, R. E., 125, 138
Connolly, Howard, 221
Consolidated Air Lines (CAL), 213, 255, 268, 324, 347
Consolidated Arcrft Co., 143
Constable, Mrs. L., 143
Contact, the cat, 132
Continental Air Lines, 333
Conway Tract, Yolo Co., 282
Conway, B. F., 70
Conway, Sgt. Leo, 78
Cook, H. R., business on YFC Field, 457
Cook, John, 178
Cook, Leonard, 458
Cook, Weggers & Moe, 458
Cook, Weggers, Moe start dusting, 458
Cook's Woodland Flying Serv., 458
Cooley, Charles, 208
Cooper Co., Earl, Curtiss distrb., 80, 84, 85, 457
Cooper, Capt. H. J., 135
Cooper, Fred, 172
Cooper, Lt., 213
Cooper, Ned, 384
Cooper, Ray, 367
Cord Co., 230
Cord trades for Amer. Air. Stock, 255
Cord, E. L., 255, 254
Cordano, D. H., 110, 111
Cornelius Free-Wing, 220
Cornelius, G. Wilbur, 220
Cornell, Donald M., 93
Corning Air Shows, 352, 354, 382, 386, 388,
Corning Airport lighted, 377
Corning Airport, 365, 382
Corning Arpt. opening, 373
Corning winds, 382
Corning's new hangar, 385
Correa, Walter, 376
Cortopassi, W. H., 217, 237
Costello, J. L., 213
Cotrell, W. H., 334
Cotter, Claude, 322
Cotton fields dusted, 279
Cotton Palace 1918, 69
Coulter, M. E., 205
Courtland Chinese flying school, 98, 100
Covell, Genevieve, 84
Cowan Aviation Co., 138
Cramp, Charles, 370
Crandall, Harry, lands nr. Zamora, 455
Crandall, Harry, PAT, 249
Crane Co., 146, 247
Crane, Temple, 322
Crawford, Ray, 205, 215, 333, 334, 425

Creel, George, 462
Crissy, Maj. Dana H., 62
Cristiados War, 369, 423
Criten, B., 358
Crocker-Huffman exp., 301
Crocker-Huffman, 299
Crosby, Henry C., 33
Crosby, Roy W., 9-14, 18
Crosson, Marvel, 162
Crutchfield, Todd, 243
Cruze, James, 110
Cuddahy, Lt., 372
Culver City, Calif., 149
Culver Ranch, 284
Culver, Harry, 149
Culver, Mr. Holly, 288, 289
Cumberpatch, J. T., 87
Cunningham, Dudley, 311
Cunningham, Russ, PAT, 249
Curley, Eileen, 363
Curry, congressman, 110
Curtis Oaks, (South) Arpt, 85-88, 286
Curtis Park, Sacto. 86
Curtis, Lt. Tobin S., 78
Curtiss Aeroplane Co., 6-9, 61, 80, 85, 88, 286
Curtiss Eagle, 245
Curtiss Exhibit. Fliers, 29
Curtiss Falcon, USMC, 133
Curtiss Flying School, North Island, SD, 35, 40, 45
Curtiss Flying Ser. Sqn., 336
Curtiss Flying Service, 146, 166, 167
Curtiss Kingbird, 256
Curtiss N-9, 91
Curtiss OX-5 engine, 60
Curtiss sues Hamilton, 20
Curtiss-Wright Airport, 232
Curtiss-Wright dusting, 304
Curtiss-Wright Fly. Ser., 308
Curtiss-Wright, Buffalo, 244
Curtiss, Glenn H., 5-8, 15, 19-23, 29, 35, 41, 67
Cushman, Lt. T. J.,133
Cutter Jr., Curtis H., 85, 127, 172, 174
CWA money Yolo, 464

D

Danatti, Carl, 240
Danley, Glen, 345, 354, 358, 382, 388
Darbarn, G., 322
Dare, Prof. L. E., 7, 8, 33
Davie, W. L., 119
Davies, Leslie, 151
Davis Airport, Colusa, 402
Davis, Al, BAT 80A, 463
Davis, G. F., 393
Davis, John "Slim," 358, 401, 402, 404
Davis, L. F., 463
Davis, Manila, 262
Davison, Arch, 322
Davison, Dan E., 57, 58, 69, 98, 100, 442
Dawson, Joe, 98, 358, 361, 392
Day, Lt. E. M., 203
De La Mars, H. "Bud," 33
De Sabla Res. Crash, 369

Deaner's field, 437
Debois, George, 132
DeCetis, Joe, 216, 222, 225,237
Deckert, M, 442
Defolco, Robert, 53
DeFries, Donald, 384
DeHaven, Roy, 371, 372
Del Paso air shows, 167, 275
Del Paso Airport, 68, 87, 92, 106, 109-129, 135, 140, 146, 149-155, 162, 167, 172, 175, 176, 179, 182-186, 272, 275, 276, 280
Del Paso Park, 138
Del Paso, 8,000 at show, 272
Del Paso, Moore crash, 184
Del Paso's dimin. ops., 276
Del Pero, Adolph, 358
DeLarm, Ed, 398
Delarno, M., 93
Demo. of eagle shoot, 268
Denehie, Austin, 323
Dengler, Col. F. H., 222
DeRenzo, Sandy, 344
DeRosa, & Nicholson, 310
DeRosa, Elmer, 240, 241
DeRosa, Elmer, crash, 310
DeRosa, Irvin, 358
DeSaulles, Joseph, 443
Detroit Aircraft Co., 209
DeVaught, Edwin, 217
Develop. of Del Paso, 85
Devinna, Clyde, 354
DeVries, W. H., 203
DH-4 #372, 110
DH-4 patrol at Corning, 361
DH-4, Air Mail Service, 110
Diablo Field, Concord, 109
Dickerson, R. E., 273
Dickinson, R. H., 217
Dickson, G., 158
Dieudonne, James, 456
Diff, Jeff, 205
Diggs, Jackson, 309
Diggs, Marshall, 105, 452
Dillon, Tom, 49
Dinsmore, A. M., 256
Dirigible *America*, 407-409
Dirigible USS *Akron*, 227
Dirigible Zepplin type, 5, 227
Dirigible, *California Arrow*, 4, 5
Dirigible, *California Eagle*, 4
Dirigible, *Toledo III*,
Dirigible, US Zepplins, 227
Dittmar, F. C., 9
Dixon, Carl I., 167
Doane, Dick, 364, 392
Dobbins, Elliott F., 388
DOC (Department of Commerce), 224
DOC ac Mech. lic. #1, 293
DOC Aeronautics Branch, July '27, 190
DOC dislikes Cord, 255
DOC tells Willows to improve arpt., 341
Dolan, Walter, 224
Dole Race to Hawaii, 136, 294, 418
Dolzen, Lt., 228
Dome, David C., 113
Dominguez Hills air meets 1910-12, 7,

Index

12, 22, 38, 40
Don Carlos, F., 273
Don Lee Automobiles, 135
Donaldson, F. A., PAT, 249
Done, Richard, 290
Donnell, Robert, 354
Doolin, Mike "Mick," 344, 364, 392, 452
Doolittle, Capt., 334
Dormoy, Etienne, 279
Dorsett, Lt., 228
Dorst, Dorothy, 350
Doty, H. J., 316
Doty, Jeanette, 58, 314
Doty, L., flyd Grimes, 314
Doty, Lyman W., 314
Douglas & *Tioga Eagle*, 450
Douglas 0-2 USANG, 135
Douglas Aircraft Co., 58, 206
Douglas C-1, 124
Dowe, Noel, 396
Doyle, Lt. Harry, 324
Dozier, Dr. Ernest, 416
Drake, E. R., 9
Du Bose, Sydney, 93, 104
Dual instruction require., 64
Duck Air Service, 355
Duck patrol film made, 290
Duck patrol noted pilots, 285
Duck patrols, 172, 278, 285, 290
Dudley, A. H., 393
Dudley, Arthur S., 2, 17, 256, 269
Duke, R. H., 108
Duncan, James & Agnes, 358
Duncan, Joe, 233
Duncan, Wyatt G., Capay airport, 455
Dundas, Robert, 104
Dunham, Frank, 321
Dunn, Chauncey, 172
Duon, Chauncy, 127
Durand, Fern "Speed," 371
Durant Field, Oakland, 443
Durant, R. C. "Cliff," 87, 88, 441, 443
Durant's Ansaldo, 87, 444
Durant's aviators, 87
Durbrow, William, 224, 334
Duren, I., 48, 49
Dusting beans red spider, 296
Dusting Colusa & Sutter, 296
Dutton, Reeves, 80
Dye, Charles H., 243

E

Eagle Aviation Co. JN-4, 437
Eagle Club of Squaw Hollow, 382
Eagle Field at Dos Palos, 302
Eagle Rock Air Lines, 123-126, 135, 136, 142-144
Eagle Rock Airport, 105, 123-126, 135, 136, 141-144, 151, 162, 165, 176, 177, 221
Eaglerock dealers, 125
Eaglerock sales, 141, 142
Eaglerock *Yellow Canary*, 192
Eames Tricycle Co., 312
Earhart at Abilene, 218
Earhart at Lovelock, 217
Earhart, Amelia at Sac, 217

Earhart, Amelia, 160, 261,262
Earle, Evalen, 228
Early Aviation in Colusa & Glenn, 277
Early newspaper delivery, 79
Eaton, Sam, 93
Eddy, Selwyn, 216
Eden, F. G., 67
Edgar, J. O., 358
Edgar, Lt. James, 357
Edgar, Mark, 461
Edison Trust, 7
Edison, Eddie, 344
Edson, Frank, 455
Edwards, E. E., 137
Edwards, J. Paulding, 119, 125, 141, 452
Eighty-Sixes, 262
El Claro Oil Co., 377.
Elbridge FW engine, 9
Elder and Haldeman, 371
Elder, Ruth, 371
Eldridge hops the *Lark*, 328
Eldridge, J. A., 327
Elkus, Mayor, 110
Elliott & Duck Fly Ser., 207
Elliott, Chet, 463
Elliott, H. W., 358
Elliott, Jack, 207
Elliott, W. I., 245
Elm, Earl Cooper's pilot, 89
Elm, I. E., 444
Elmer, Mrs. Frank, 264
Elmhurst grassfire, 55
Elsen, Ted, 240
Ely, Eugene, 29, 30
Emenegger, Frank, 358
Emeryville Racetrack, 38
Emmett, Dan W., the flying legislator, 154, 156, 158, 216
Emmons, Maj. D. C., 62-65
Empire Air Circus, 457
English Channel crash, 165
Erickson, Chris, 62
Eureka Flying Club, 357
Evans, N. B., 369
Everett, Al, 254
Exhibition Years (1909-1914), 411, 434
Exhibition Years fliers, 56

F

F- 17 repaired at Galt, 173
FAA (Federal Aviation Admin.), 52, 302
Fabian-Grunauer Co., 291
Fagerskog air seeding, 183
Fagerskog Arpt. on Auburn Blvd., 121, 181, 221
Fagerskog, Fridtjof, 178
Fagerskog, Ingvald, 104, 112-115, 121-126, 131-137, 149, 151, 156, 158, 178-185, 203, 219, 227, 276, 292, 310, 334, 337
Fagerskog, Marie, 182, 183
Fagerskog's "Comet II," 181
Fagerskog's "Comet," 132
Fairbanks, Douglas, 369
Fairbanks, Gwendolyn, 369
Fairbanks, Mr.&Mrs. J, 369
Fairchild camera plane, 123

Fairchild, Dr., Wdlnd, 443
Fait,W. R., 437
Farman aircraft,12, 13, 32, 33
Farman biplane, Wiseman-Peters, 23
Farmers hire planes, 280
Farris aerial seed 1923, 291
Farris, Mr. Fauna W., 88, 291, 292, 444
Farris/Grunauer exper., 300
Farrow, Capt. K. W., 108
Faxson, R. S., 296
Fay, John D., 358
Federal beacon, Ksberg, 150
Federation Aeronautique Internationale (FAI), 8, 156
Federspiel, R. to muni, 200
Federspiel, Roland W., 126, 130, 137, 145, 158, 172, 191
Feds to imprv. Willows, 342
Feeny, William, 335
Feliz, Ruy, 215
Fender, Richard, 321
Fernsted, Mr., 358
Ferris, Dick, 1, 3, 19, 38-41
Fetters, Lt. Jay M., 79, 281, 285, 289, 290
Fiesta of Dawn of Gold, 433
Fillmore, Bill, 355
Finch, Charles H., 144
Finch, Milton, 370
Finnerty, Sam B., 112
Finson, James I.
Fire patrol Corning, 361, 391
Fire patrols at Redding, 411
Fire ptrls out of Redding, 414
Firefighting air exhibit., 351
Fires near Willows Arpt., 343
First air seedg. in Valley, 297
First civilians to Hawaii, 223
First crop dusting N.Cal., 294
First flight in Yolo Co. 431
First flight Woodland, 432
First National Airways, 213
First night flight Sierras, 289
First rice seed by air, 299
First rice seed Rathburn, 297
Fish & Game vs patrols, 290
Fish, Farnum, 32, 38, 41
Fishbeck, Del, 156
Fishbeck, Glen, 156
Fisher, Alva, 178
Fisher, Clay, 273
Fisher, Harry, 415
Fitzgerald, G. R. DOC, 331
Fitzgerald, Mrs. J. J., 80
Flanders, Lee, 104
Fleet trainer, 266
Fleet, Major Rueben, 62
Fleet, NC626M, 266
Flournoy, "Skeet," 384
Flournoy, Chet, 383
Flying Fleet, Best Field, 457
Flying Fleet, the, 285, 458
Fokker D. VII, 193
Fokker Super Universal, 256
Folk, J., 41
Fonda Flying Helmets, 134
Fong, Raymond, 355
Fontaine, aviator, 84

Foote, C. E., 438
Foote, Lou, 302
Foote, Lou, crashes Colonial Ford, 302, 303
Foote, Lou, disappears from Merced, 303
Ford Reliability Tours 1925-31, 163, 366, 367
Ford Tr. at Corning, 366, 367
Foriveno, Pete, 144
Fortney, John, 101
Fountain, Duane, 421-423, 427
Fourteen Counties Protective Assn., 326
Fowler sells Avro 504K, 286
Fowler, Robert G. "Bob," 19, 31, 46-50, 88, 281, 286, 414
Fowler, Tom, 231,422
Francis-Gage biplane, 410
Francis, Roy N., 43, 45, 409-411
Franciulli, J., 6, 8, 15, 20
Frank, Carl, 332
Franz, R., Waco dlr., 272
Freeman, Frank, 241
Freeman, George, 332-337
French, A. R., 334
French, Al, 425
French, F. M., 108
Fresno meet of dusters, 308
Friedman, Max, 43
Friesley Falcon airliner, 91, 239, 246, 284, at Yolo 451
Friesley, Harold M., 246
Frisbee, R.J., 295
Fry, Dale, 383, 405, 429
Frye, Capt., 423
Frye, Jack, 196, 205
Fuller Paint Family, 207, 318, 350, 401
Fuller, C. M., 422
Fuller, Dana, 350
Fuller, Frank, 350
Fuller, George P., 351
Fuller, Mrs. Bonnie, 351
Fuller, W. P., 401
Funke, E. G., 107, 113, 116, 124, 156

G

Gage biplane, 46
Gage tractor biplane, 46
Gage twin-tractor biplane, 43
Gage, Jay, 411
Gagen, W. E., 353
Galehouse, I. W.,167
Gallagher, Francis, 460
Galligan, Frank (not Gallison), 304
Galligan, Frank, C-W sales rep., 305
Gallison at Eagle Field, 302
Gallison flys in trout, 299
Gallison, Frank, 292, 294, 297, 300-303, 306, 308
Gallison, Frank, Merced-Wawona Airlines, 297
Galt High School aero. Classes, 134, 184, 188
Galt Junior Col. aeronautics program, 159, 194
Galt students fix *Miss Sacramento*, 184
Gannon, Atty. Chester, 89
Ganow, W. C., 176, 177, 225
Ganow, W., hauls wreck, 275

Gardiner, Ed, 44
Garey. W. E., 200
Garside, E., 358
Gastman, Henry, 224, 240
Gates Flying Circus, 91, 148, 285, 364, 391, 392, 457
Gates-Day Aircraft, 148, 272
Gates-Day New Stndrd., 167
Gates-Morris Co., 392
Gates-Morris Flyg Circus, 97
Gates, Ivan R., 12, 19, 43, 91, 98, 148, 272, 285, 363, 391
Gay, Carroll, 174
Gemignani, Adolph, 242
Gen. Aeronautics Serv. Co. (GAS), 157, 158, 163
General Electric Co., 134
Gerber, Ed, 173
Gerber, W. E., 366, 398, 399
German sympathizers, 60
Gerstner Field, LA, 278
Gianelli, Joseph L., 213
Gibralter Auto Club, 214
Gibson, Hoot, 135
Gibson, W. E., 389
Gifford, J. V., 316
Gilhausen, Al, PAT, 249
Gillette, Gov. J. N., 11, 12
Gilmore Oil Co., 236
Gilmore Oil mascot, 209
Gilmore, Beverly, 255, 256
Gilmore, Gen. W.E, 200, 202
Gilpin Airways, 214
Giminez, Louis, 458
Gish, Lilian, 369
Gleeson, Charles J., 305
Glenn Co. Fair, 328, 363
Glenn Co. farmers mad, 297
Glenn Grocery Store, 355
Glessier, Mrs. Bonnie, 288
Globe Iron Works, 58
Gnome rotary engine, 30
Godard, R., 180
Goddard Aircraft Co., 144
Goddard, Norman, 163, 164
Goebel, Art, 186
Goldborough, Lt. W. S., 415
Golden Bear monoplane, 337
Golden Gate, SF, 201
Golden State Aircraft Co., 136, 141, 143
Goldsmith, Capt. L. C., 369
Goodlow, Officer, 393
Goodrich, Mary, 262
Goodyear Blimp, 216
Goodyear No. 10 fabric, 42
Gordon & Stryker Co. 399
Gordon & Stryker *Miss Tehama*, 397, 400
Gordon A-3, 400
Gordon Bennett Cup, 23, 29
Gordon, Beston, 322
Gordon, Claude,398
Gordon, Frank, 397, 399, 401, 404
Gordon, Stan, 393
Gott, Paul, 290
Gov. Lic., July 1927, 163
Grace, Dick, 284
Grading Bidwell Arpt, 397

Graham-White, Claude, 29
Graham, Gene, 354
Graham, Ham, 322
Grand Central Air Term., 345
Grand International. Avtn. Meet, Sacto., 42
Granger, Jim, 371, 372
Grant dustg. Bolen Farm, 311
Grant, E., Kreutzer crash, 311
Gravel Day at Corning, 373
Gravell, Warham Singh, parachutist, 352
Graves, Lt. E. D., 203
Gray, Lloyd, 386
Great Diavalo chutists, 272
Great Western Power Co., 46, 48, 49, 51, 86
Greely, D. H., 124
Greely, Douglas, 130
Green, Manley, 241
Green, R. B., DOC, 167
Greene biplane, 10, 12, 33
Greene, Dr. William, 9, 13
Greer, Ed, 398
Gregg, Lt., 167
Gregory, John C., 134
Greth, Dr. August, 4
Gridley airport proposal, 304
Griffin, Raines, 400-404
Griffin, Raines, fired, 404
Griffith Park airfield, 135
Gronwoldt, Mr., 425
Gross, L. C., 88
Growney, George, 398
Grunauer/Farris seeding, 292
Grunaur, Abe, 291
Guernsy, H. N., 372
Guggenheim Fund, 114, 394
Guggenheim, Harry F., 394
Gugliametti, John, 159, 231
Guinther, Dolores, 349
Guinther, SF Bay Airdr., 349
Gundlach, Ray, 358
Gundrum, Dr., 181
Gunigani, Adolph, 358
Gunn, Tom Duck, 43, 45

H

Hackett, Lt. F., 78, 108, 203
Hadigan, John H., 167
Haekstra, Mildred Mae, 403
Haggin Land Grant, 115
Haggin Oaks Golf Cour.,182
Haig, Dr. Thomas R., 216
Halcomb, Mr.&Mrs. G., 428
Halcomb, Thomas, 428
Haldeman, George, 366
Hall-Scott Motor Car Co., 23, 27, 45, 364
Hall-Scott sent Deckert, 444
Hall, J. T. DOC Inspect., 399
Hall, Walter, parachutist, 143, 322, 334, 344, 398, 427
Hallanan, W., Sac police, 251
Halverson, Lt. H., 290, 452
Hamilton "Dip," 28
Hamilton "Glide," 28
Hamilton Field, 269
Hamilton, Charles K., 7, 10, 11, 15-30,

INDEX 497

34, 38-41, 433, 434
Hamilton, Craig, 398
Hamilton, Dillard, 144
Hamilton, Mrs. C. K., 45, 53
Hamilton's crash at fair, 26
Hamiltonian Aeroplane, 15-30, 41
Hampton, E. M., 321
Hancock, Bob, 229
Haney, George, 205
Hanna, R. W., VP of Standard Oil, 372, 398, 399
Hanna, W. J., 366, 418
Hansen, Anona, 263
Hansen, Carl, 456
Hansen, Lt., 424
Hansen, N. R., 399, 426
Hansen, W. G., 42
Hansen, W. R., 426
Hanson, Curtis, 458
Hanson, John, 458
Hanson, Ralph P., 57
Harbaugh, W. "Duke," 264
Harder, Karl, 232, 242, 274
Hargrove Air Service, 461
Hargrove, Joe, 214, 230, 461
Hargrove, Lt. & Mrs., 424
Harlow, Jean, 208
Harned, Tom, 358
Harper, O. G., 162
Harris, Al, 205, 206
Harris, Dr. Junius B., 27
Hart, Jess E., 364
Hart, Jess, Corn. Pioneer, 369
Hart's Cafeteria Co., 144
Hartz, Harry, 358
Harvard-Boston Air Meet, 20
Harvey, N. H., 358
Harvey, Walt, snowed in, 384
Hastings, Albt, 102, 105, 332
Hatch, Chester, 240
Hauser of Fish & Game, 290
Hawke Crop Dust., 307, 308
Hawke factory Modesto, 308
Hawke, E. R., 307
Hawks, Frank, 319, 366
Hawley, City Manager, 30
Hay, Del, 213, 311
Hay, Del, in Buzzards, 284
Haynes, Lt. C. V., 109
Hazeman, W. H., 161
Headless biplane, 32
Hearst, Mrs. Randolph, 215
Heath Parasol, 122
Heath, E. B., 121
Heaton, Vernon G., 269, 350, 358, 461
Heddinger, George, 398
Hegenberger, Capt. Al., 462
Hei, Nip, Kai, 98
Heidelburg, Henry, 160
Heilbron, Irving, 88
Hekerlie, N. R., 135
Hell's Angels ends shoot, 192
Hell's Angels Sikorsky, 303
Hell's Angels, 125, 208, 284, 293
Helm, Ed, 205
Helphenstine, Noel, 323
Hemsted, Don, 429

Henderson, James M., Liberty Iron Works Pres., 60
Henderson, James, 58, 358
Henley, Al, 366, 367
Hennessy, James R., 91, 415
Heringer, Bert, 193
Herndon, Jr., Hugh, 98, 457
Heron, F. C., 414
Herr, H. T. "Ted," 359
Herring-Curtiss Aeroplane Co., 431
Herring, Augustus, 7
Hershey, Ben, 382
Heryford, Milton, 413
Hester, Dorothy, 374, 375
Hewson, Jack, 254
Hicks, Joe, 374, 379
Hilderbrand, E., 177, 178
Hill, Marie Wilcox, 182
Hill, Prof. L. L., 18-21
Hippodrome Theater, 176
Hirth, Wolf, 348
Hispano-Suiza "Hisso" engine, 60
Hobday & Gold, 191
Hobson, Paul, 370
Hobson, Phil, 365
Hockin, W. H., 185
Hodge, Helen, 58
Hoffman, Ancil, 85
Hoffman, Ted, 358
Hoffman, V.W., 166
Hogan, Vic, 425
Hoganson, Vic, 259
Hogg, J. E., 290, 444
Hogland, Lt. Alander, 77
Holland, James, 388
Hollister, Charles, 49
Holman, C. W. "Speed," 397
Holmes Ranch, 348
Holt, H. F., 148
Holt, Wesley, 401
Homans, G. M. St. Frstr, 79
Hopkins, Lt., 202
Hosking, J., 159
Hoskins, W. A., 179-182
Hotchner, Mr., 14
Hotel Maywood, 371
Hotel Sacramento, 152
Hotzen, Lt., 229
Howard, Ben O., 366
Howard, W. M., 336
Hubbard Field replaces Blanch Field, 415
Hubbard Fld., Reno, 148, 153
Hubbard is today Reno-Tahoe Inter., 148, 415
Hubbard, Eddie, 148
Hudson, J. A., 243
Hudson, Tex, 233, 382
Hughes, David, 384
Hughes, E. C., DOC insp., 309, 358, 388
Hughes, Gene, 227, 243
Hughes, Guy "Speed," 306, 311
Hughes, Howard,, 125, 193, 208, 284, 292, 293
Huking, Harry, 210
Hulett, Edward, 358
Hull, Sheriff Floyd, 373, 404
Hulshizer, Martin, 380

Humbolt Air Service, 425
Humbug, Woodrow, 321
Hummingbird Aero, 162
Hunt and Asedo crash, 288
Hunt, Irwin, 285-287
Hunt, Irwin, arrested, 287
Hunt, Irwin, w/ Moffett, 288
Hunt, Mr. & Mrs. Alvis, 286
Hunter, Dale, 205, 236, 268
Hunter, J. E., Mr & Mrs., 354
Hurley, Henry T., 208
Hustan, Wallace, 458
Huston, A. C., 439
Huston, Bob, 437
Huston, Jr., Arthur, 437
Hutt, Louis, 290

I

Idahoe-Maryland Mine, 345
Ilano Seco, 283
Illing, Ernest, 437
Increase in crop dusting, 305
Independent Crop Dust., 325
Indian Arrow biplane, 10
Indianapolis 500 race, 105
Ingalls, David S., Asst. Sec. Navy, 372
Ingram, Dorothy, 167
Inland Aviation Club, 215
Inman, Walker, of Reno, 145
Interallied Air. Co, Can., 386
Interstate Airlines, Inc., 317
Inwood, Elizabeth, 363
IRS air passenger tax, 90
Irvin, Leslie "Sky High," 43
Irving at Meridian, 295, 299
Irving dusts at Grimes, 296
Irving dusts first, 297
Irving dusts w/ Eglrck, 295
Irving Eaglerock descrb., 295
Irving in Dole Race, '27, 455
Irving, L., Nav. Air Stn., 295
Irving, Livingston G., 123, 133, 152, 294, 296, 309, 453, 455
Irwin Aircraft Corp., 74, 169
Irwin Airport, Sacto., 73, 116, 117, 121, 169-171
Irwin Comet M-T, 74
Irwin In Mexico, 71
Irwin M-T-2 Meteorplane, 73, 148, 171, 397
Irwin, Aero School, 70
Irwin, John Fulton "Jack," 38, 69, 70, 74, 75, 121, 126, 148, 169-171,194, 227, 397
Irwin's Flying School, 171
Ishi's home territory, 392
Isleton Aviation Club, 131
Iverson, Fred, 357
Ives, Lt. N. H., 135
Ivy races train, 433
Ivy, Sgt. Span. War, 433
Ivy, William, 433

J

Jackson, Bottoms, YC, 286
Jackson, Paul C., 304
Jacobs, J. J., 247

Jacobson, H. O., 281
Jacuzzi brothers, 452
Jacuzzi J-7 at Yolo, 451
Jamison, Gus O., 18, 434
Jane's All The...'27, 169
Jansen, George, 348, 354
Jarvis, J. A., 272
Jaynes, J. B., DOC, 228
Jefferies, Temple, 321
Jeffers, Quentin, 358
Jellison, R. E., 319, 321
Jenkins, Capt., 424
Jenkins, N. "Jinx," 90, 398
Jenkins, W. B., 199
Jenny war cost $6,500, 61
Jensen jumps at air show, 293
Jensen proposed jump, 293
Jensen, "Red," mechanic, 232
Jensen, Charles "Red" parachutist, 293, 462
Jensen, Charles T. "Red," 73, 228, 232, 268, 292
Jensen, Harold, 150
Jensen, Martin, 136, 366, 418, 453
Jensen, Mrs. Martin, 136
Jerome, aerial laundry, 418
Jodoin, Ivy, 20
Johnson flies at Woodland, 434
Johnson Hill Fld, named Benton Fld., 417
Johnson Hill, W. Placer St., Redding, 414, 425
Johnson, Andy, 348, 351
Johnson, Berger, 281
Johnson, Byron, 354
Johnson, Dr. Julian P., 157
Johnson, E. E., 370
Johnson, E. L., 372
Johnson, Frank H. "Millionaire," 8-11, 14, 409, 431, 432
Johnson, G. R., 243
Johnson, G., 14
Johnson, George, farm, 100
Johnson, Gov. Hiram, 30, 55
Johnson, Gus, 1st flight *Miss Tehama*, 400
Johnson, Gus, 372, 380, 396, 405
Johnson, Gus, new airport mngr., 404
Johnson, Harry, 92
Johnson, P. G., BAT, 250
Johnson, Paul, 351
Johnson, R., Stin. rep., 230
Johnson, S. T., seeded, 297
Johnson, Wesley P., 443
Johnston, J. C., PAT, 249
Jones, A. S., 412
Jones, Dorothy, 264
Jones, E. M., 419
Jones, Ed, 240
Jones, F., Buck's Lake, 228
Jones, Frank, 176, 220, 240, 241, 276
Jones, W. H., 85
Jordan, J. A., 58, 59
Jordan, Jack, 208
Joseph, Ray, 215
Josephine Ford Fokker, 117
Junkans, Harold, 419
Junkers JL-6 at Yolo, 451

K

Kalinski, Lt., 151
Kaminski, J. C., 32
Karstan, Roy, 397
Kaseberg Field, Roseville, 150, 151, 155, 184
Keadle, Floyd of Tehama, 392, 397, 417-420, 423
Kearny, Horace, 38-41
Keeler, Herb, Yuba Coll. 348
Keener, Dorothy, 150
Kehoe, Donald E., 394
Keller, K., 322
Kelley, Alice Jane, 263
Kelley, John, 230
Kelley, Lawrence, 155
Kelly & Macready trans., 416
Kelly, Earl Lee, 215, 370, 398, 419-424
Kelly, Fred, 92
Kelly, Judge T. K., 368
Kelly, Lt. Oakley G., 416
Kelly, Sgt. Fred, 109
Kendall, Charles, 237, 465
Kennedy, Dr. G. M., 276
Kennedy, Mr., mechanic, 405
Kerns flies at Woodland, 434
Kerns, Thaddeus, 19, 31-33, 43, 392, 434, 435
Kerns' Curtiss copy, 435
Kerris, J., 167
Ketly, Betty May, 322
Kiel, Lt. E. C., 1st ptrl., 390
Kim, Mr., 325
Kim, Mr.& Mrs., 325
Kimball acquires Vega, 244
Kimball Flying Service, 224-227, 231, 242-243, 253
Kimball in hngr. No. 3, 242
Kimball trains Chinese, 242
Kimball, A. W. of Century-Pacific, 242, 254
Kimball, A. Weston, 221, 225, 230, 242-244, 254, 255
Kimball, Wilbur, 13
Kimball's Aeronca C-3, 243
King, Hermie, 176,
King, Jackson, 321
Kingham, Lt., bails out, 375
Kingsbury, Lt. W. C., 203
Kingsford-Smith, Charles, 87, 285, 286, 290
Kinograms, 327
Kitto, Ray S., 47, 49
Klamath Air Service, 364
Klamath Falls, Ore., 359
Kleaver, Ken K., 143, 144, 158, 162, 167, 207, 218, 225, 232, 273, 337, 426
Knabenshue, Roy, 1-6, 18, 19, 31, 42
Knight Park, Mrysvl., 93
Knight, Janet, 228, 239-242
Korean flying schl., 325, 327, 347
Korean flying students, 327
Koshall, George, 176, 215
Kotes, Eddie, 348
Kraft, Emil K., 439
Kraft, Herb, 324

Kraft, Herb, crashes at Willows, 335
Kraft, Herb, YFC, 455
Kranberg, Martin, 279
Krebeer, Norman, 403
Kreutzer Tri-motor, 166, 372
Kreutzer w/one engine, 311
Kreutzer, James, 166
Krines, Henry, 462
Kron, E. J., hired to dust, 305
Kron, w/Vndrfrd&Owen, 311
Krull, Lt. James S., 78,79
Kubota, S. J., 152
Kula, J., 358
Kunz, Opel Logan, 262

L

L & M Flying Service, 226
LA Inter. Air Meet, 3rd, 38
LA Inter. Air Meet, First, Jan. 1910, 5, 6, 389, 431
La Rene, Jean, 262
Lachner, Leo, 244
LaFollette, Super., 111
Lahm, Col. Frank P., 114
Laine, L., 152
Laird, Matty, at Yolo, 451
LaJotte, Charles, 351
Lake Charles, LA, 281
Lake dried up Mineral, 373
Lake, Byron, in jail, 151
Lam, Stephen, 99, 100
Lambari, J. D., 144
Lamkin sold Eaglebricks, 142
Lamkin, W. Lester, 141, 142
Lamphiere, Fay, 107
Landis, Cecil, 358
Lane, Albert "Bert," 122, 174, 325, 330-333, 337, 341, 359
Lane, Bert, at Stockton, 331
Lane, Bert, baseball, 331
Lane, Gladys, 423
Lane, Glen, 325, 343
Lane, L. E., 325
Lane, L. L., 330
Langille, Lloyd, 386
Langley's Aerodrome, 7
Larsen, Lloyd, 358
Lassen View Arwys, 418-420
Last, W., 358
Laurin, Bob, 192, 215, 216, 220, 221, 225, 226, 236, 237
Laurin, Eva Baily, 236
Laval, Bert, 166
Law, Col. Palin K., 326
Lawrence, E. J., 376
Lawrence, William W., 243
Lawson Airline, 81, 84
Lawson, Alfred, 81
Lawson, John S., 116, 124, 127, 149, 172, 179
Lazzarini, Paul, 176
Lear, Arthur, 276
Lechens, Henry, 373
Lederer, E. M., 341
Lee, C. C., 85
Lee, Charles, 327
Lee, Frances E., 181

Index

Lee, Harry, 398
Lee, Henrietta, 389
Lee, Lt., 228
Lee, Young S., 327
Leedy, J., 358
Lees, Jr., Richard, CAA, 354
Lefevre, Bert, 358
Legend creep, 305
Leland, Mathilde, 440
LeMay, Lt. Curtiss, 270
Lemcke, Harvey, 160, 161, 207, 401, 425-427
Leonard, J. E., 354, 358
LeRoy, R. S., 154
Levine, Charles, 419
Levy, Ellis J., 337
Lewis gun use, 65
Lewis, Dave, 358
Lewis, Jack, 241
Lewis, Joe, 352
Lewis, Joe, world class aerobat, 351, 352, 388
Lewis, Ned, 322
Liberty Iron Works WWI, 58-61, 80, 105, 106, 281
Limited Commercial requirements, 306
Lindbergh at Blanch Fld, 415
Lindbergh at Red Bluff, 394
Lindbergh Surge, 119
Lindbergh, Anne, 319
Lindbergh, Charles A., 119, 147, 183, 186, 319, 371, 394
Lindbergh's Cal. route, 394
Link, Jack, 456
Lipp & Sullivan Amb., 310
Lippiatt, N. C. won drby, 396
Lipps, Charles E., 108, 113, 124, 131, 155, 156, 176, 185,
Lite, B., 106
Little, D. E., DOC, 370, 400
Little, Mrs. L., 44
Little, Raymond J., 422
Lock, B. D., 205
Locke, Olive, 84
Lockheed Orion airliner, 258
Lockheed Vega air amb., 229
Lockheed Vega crash, 160
Lockhoof & "Sunfish," 190
Lockhoof & Cahill, 189
Lockhoof Arpt, 136, 137, 108
Lockhoof two crashes, 189
Lockhoof, Walter L.
Lockhoof, Walter L., the flying barber, 124, 125, 135-137, 150, 151, 188-190
Lockhoof's Eaglerock, 136
Lockwood, Harold, 135
Lockwood, W. P., 426
Loening Amphibians, 256
Long, Harvey, 358
Longshore, Mel, 106
Lorain, A. W., 45, 46
Lorenez, Joseph, 409
Lorenzo, Julio, 239
Louis, Elsie, 166
Love, Lt. George, 103
Lowe, Clem, 131, 453-456, 459, 464, 466
Lowe, Ted, 341

Ludlow, Israel, & kites, 19
Luilliwitz, H. M., 383
Lukens, J. P., 218
Lukov, M. H., Pac. Air., 256
Lum, Jim, 148, 173
Lundy, G. T., 189
Luppen and Hawley Co., 250
Lusk, Hilton F., 177, 205, 209, 217, 219, 226-230, 257,
Lusk's text, *Aero. Fund.*, 226
Lyon, Dorothy, 262
Lyons, Senator, 157

M

MacCalay, Lloyd, 420
MacDonald, Capt., 116
Macready tells Torrey, 378
Macready, 1st crop dust, 279
Macready, J., crashes, 378
Macready, John, 216
MacRobertson Race, 98
Maddux Air Lines, 145, 152, 159, 195, 246, 369
Maddux conct. at Fresno, 200
Maddux Ford mid-air, 303
Maddux Ford Tri., 369
Maddux merges w/ TAT, 173, 195, 256
Maddux ovr Lassen vol., 371
Maddux, J. L., 59, 61, 145
Maddux, TAT & Westrn, 195
Maitland, Capt. Lester, 462
Maj. Brett hits Dozier's auto on landing DH-4, 416
Maj. Brett wants lines moved at Redding, 416
Majors, W. J., 224
Makepeace, A. W., 108
Manning, Spud, 219, 230
Manwaring, Harry S., 103
Mar-Jones Mining Co., 372
March Field, Riverside, 201
Marchetti Motor Patents, 166, 337
Marely, Harold, 458
Marina Field, SF, 84, 364
Maritsas, Kath. H., 244, 264
Marley, Harold, 461
Mars, "Bud," (phony), 31-33
Mars, "Bud" (real), 5, 15, 33
Marsh, Bill, 166, 167, 337
Marsh, Bill, mech.&para. 175
Marsh, Dr. L. M., 240
Marsh, Maj., led Crissy, 373
Marshall, Ruth, 239
Martella, Louis, 274
Martin B-10, 269
Martin, Bill, 159
Martin, Charles, 322
Martin, Glenn, 5, 38, 40, 305
Martin, Jack, 45
Martin, Johnny, 347-349, 386
Martin, Johnny, UAL, 355
Martin, Larry, 351
Martin, Ross, 163, 205
Martin, Wallace, 419
Martland, R. W., 396
Marysville's Alicia Fld., 359
Masie, J. M., 92

Masli, Mr., 358
Masson, Dider, 1st flight in Tehama, 389
Mather – SF, 1st Flight, 63
Mather 1st over Sierras, 77
Mather Field air tour, 163
Mather Field dormant, 136
Mather runway complete, 63
Mather, 2nd Lt. Carl S., 62
Mathews, William, 213
Mathison, Herb, 366
Mattley Aircraft Co., 327
Mattley hits auto, 391
Mattley, O. H., 327, 391
Maurath, J. B., 439
Mautby, A. E., 191
Maxim Co. Flying Field, 38
Maxim Rotary Motor Co., 38
Maxwell, Lt. A. R., 203
May, Wesley, parachutist, 362, 392
Mayberry, James L., 136, 141-145, 392
Mayberry, Verbal, 321
Mayfield Aerial Surveys, 134
McAdoo, William Gibbs, 404
McAuliffe, D. C., 48
McAuliffe, J. C., 33
McBrier, C. S., 358
McCallum, Mr., 232
McCarthy, J. E., 167
McCauly, Lloyd, 423
McClaskey repl. Weaver, 276
McClaskey Sac Fly Ser., 276
McClasky, Les, 218, 220, 224, 276
McClellan AF Base, 135, 178
McCloud Aviation Club, 144
McColl, John B., 418
McCollum, Esther, 375
McCormac, Fred, 316, 317, 322, 324
McCracken, W. P., 116, 394
McCrillis, Capt., 200, 235
McCurley, L. H., 354, 358, 387, 388
McCurry, Harold J., 35, 109, 217
McCurry, Mr. theater, 179
McDaniels, A. B., 425
McDonnell, A. W., 62
McDonogh, S. J., 130
McGinnis, Hubert, 222
McGrew, Lester, 387
McGrew, Moses, 441
McGuire, Carlos, 241
McIntosh, R. U., 125
McKeehan Farm, 295
McKeehan, Al., 296
McKeen, Marion, 275
McKenly, Fred, 161
McKenzie, A. B., 365
McKinley Park, 107
McKinley, Fredrick, 255
McKinney, Ive, 93, 102, 103 148, 452
McKinnon, Don, 351, 354
McLaughlin, Don, 398
McManus Jenny repairs, 284
McManus, Frank W., 61, 80, 81, 84, 280-283
McMullan, E. A., 212
McMullen, Foster, 465
Mcmullen, Paul, 465
McNeal, Doc, 358

McNeil, H. S., 160
McRae, Eleanor, 262
McSwain, Tom, 299
McTadyer, J. C., 272
McTaranahan, J. T., 409
Meadows Airways, 144
Mealia, J., 108
Medico-Dental Fly Club, 219
Meinert, W. B., 296
Meisser, Roy, 157, 163, 175, 180, 191
Meister, A. & Son, 6, 31
Meister, George, 35
Mellard, Matthew, 42
Mello, Leo, 370
Memler, Archie G., 166, 174, 175, 176
Mendell, Loren W., 209
Menz, Ethel, 109
Menzel Field, 413
Menzel, Mayor William, 414, 420, 425
Merced Antique Fly-in, 302
Merced-Wawona Air Lines, 297-299, 302, 304, 308
Merced-Wawona, 1st rice seed, 297
Merced-Yosemite Glider Club, 304
Merchant, Harry, 148, 192
Meredith, Bud, 176
Merende, Vince, 388
Mererinck's Orchestra, 156
Merrill, Frank, 348
Merrill, Harold, 383
Merry, Fran, parachutist, 269
Merwin crashes in rice, 283
Merwin quits duck patrol 285
Merwin, Ogle C., 80, 81, 84, 280, 284, 290, 412, 413
Mess, R. W. 86
Meteor ac (not Irwin's), 226
Meteorplane, Irwin, 121, 126
Metro Air Service, 159, 179
Metzger, Sam, 179, 206
Meyer, Lt., 424
Meyerhoffer, Orvar, 286, 287
Meyerinck, Herbert, 156
Meyers, George, 348
Meyers, Ralph, 210, 253, 358
Meyling, Chris, 125, 126, 135, 142-144
Mickel flies for Hughes, 193
Mickel, Arthur F. "Pop," 125, 136, 140, 157, 174, 192-194
Mickel's Captl. Fly. Ser., 192
Mickle, E. J., 240
Middlecamp, L., 322
Middleton, Harry, 345
Miller bat-wing nixed, 357
Miller, Carter, DOC, 122
Miller, H. C., 416
Miller, Heber, PAT, 249
Miller, Lt. Walter, 108
Miller, Marion, 415
Miller, Royal, 129, 130, 245
Miller, Tony, 155
Miller, Tracy A., 9
Miller, Walter, bat-wing, 356
Mills Field, San Bruno, (SFO), 126, 131 132
Mills Orchard Co. plane, 328
Mills Station Fld, Mather, 61

Mills Station landowners, 62
Mills Station rail stop, 60, 61
Mills Stn. named Mather, 62
Milton, Tommy, 105
Mimic warfare Apr. '30, 201
Mineola Avtn. Fld. NY, 9, 13
Mineral Airport, 173, 366, 368, 373, 393, 398, 418
Miss Sacto-ornge&black, 184
Miss Tehama, 400, 401
Mitchell, Col. W., 116, 292
Mitchell, George N., para., 207, 208, 320, 322
Mitchell, Tom R., 157, 15
Mock, Albert, 221
Moe & Weggers – YFC, 460
Moe & Weggers leaflets, 459
Moe at Tegucigalpa, 466
Moe stricken on return, 467
Moe, Ernest P., 161, 178, 233, 244, 253, 456-458, 463, 465, 466
Moffett & Hunt's Avro, 286
Moffett Aero Patrol, 282
Moffett Aero Service, 282
Moffett airfield Willows, 286
Moffett and Hunt Co., 285, -287, 290
Moffett duck ptrl, 84, 93, 285
Moffett-Hunt ad, 286, 288
Moffett-Starkey Air Cir., 287
Moffett, Edmund J., 84, 88, 93, 280-286, 289, 329, 453
Moffett, W., (Moffitt), 285, 287
Moffitt-Hunt Vrny acft., 288
Moffitt, parachutist, 329
Molten, Lt. Comdr., 372
Molter, J. A., 137, 158, 199
Monday, Harry, 429
Mono Aircraft Inc., 191
Monocoupe Agency acquired by Willett, 197
Monocoupe distributor, 145
Monocoupe, 191
Monroe, J. W. 439
Monroe, Sheriff, 439
Montague land bought, 418
Montgomery, J., glider, 53
Montgomery, John J., 316
Moore drops food, 187
Moore ferries P-39s, 188
Moore flies food camp, 224
Moore surveys Reno, 186
Moore to new muni, 187
Moore, Bill, DOC, 216, 275
Moore, Capt. James aka J. L. Caulfield, 407, 409, 425
Moore, Courtney L., 295
Moore, Dr. Glen, 183, 184
Moore, Frank, 273, 350, 372
Moore, Gilbert, 358
Moore, J. M., Mr.&Mrs., 398
Moore, Leo, 131-136, 140, 145, 150-156, 167, 168, 183-188, 203, 223-226, 231, 233, 242-244, 253, 272, 292, 293, 310, 321
Moore, Les (not Leo), 177, 244
Moore, Ray, 164, 203, 256
Moore. L. A., 438

Mora, Tony, 358
Moran, Lee, 382
Moreau Flying Ser., 383
Moreau, Wes, finds Vance crash, 253
Moreing ballpark, 92
Moreing land levelers, 62
Moreing, Lou, 180
Morel, J., 358
Morely, C., 321
Morgan Aircraft Co., 401
Morgan Merced-Waw., 297
Morgan, Laura, 262
Morgan, Lt. John, 361
Morgan, M. bat-wing, 350
Morgan, Mildred, 263
Morris, C.E., lessee, 121, 157, 162, 166, 167, 273
Morris, Fred, police chief Sparks, 275
Morris, Leslie, 220, 461
Morris, W. L, 88, 93
Morris, Wm. "Bill," 364, 392
Morse Security, 21, 26
Moseley, Lt. Corlis C., 105
Motorcycle polo game, 167
Motordome of San Fran., 43
Moulton, Dr., 368
Mouton first mail to SF, 68
Mouton w/ Staggerwing, 345
Mouton, E. E., 1st DOC, 68, 122, 137
Mouton, Edison E. "Monty," 68, 88, 138, 149, 159, 202, 222, 223, 229, 273, 320, 322, 345-349, 355, 357, 452
Movie *Balaaika* Chico, 354
Movie *Robin Hood* " 353
Movie *Stand Up...* " 353
Mt. Shasta Arpt descr., 422
Mulhern, Tom, 409, 412
Municipal arpt, Del Paso, 144
Munkler-Irwin aircraft, 170
Munkler, Peter L., 135, 169
Munro, Fred, 181, 276
Murchie, E. S., 299-301
Murphy, Althea, 262
Murphy, G., 358
Murphy, John, 358
Murphy, Maurice "Loop-the-Loop," 93, 303, 451
Mutual Aircraft Co., 159
Myers, Capt., 424
Mygett, Milyon, 407

N

NAA glider club, 155, 268
NAA members, 202
NAA Sacto. Chapter, 156
NAA Yuba City Chapter, 318
Nakano, Shigeo, 358
Nall, J. G., DOC, 138, 149
Nall, W. F., 152
Napa Air Show 1930, 256
National Aeronautic Assn. (NAA), 124, 162-164
National Air Derby, 393, 395
National Women's Drby, 371
Natomas Dist. 171, 180
Navy bombers at show, 356
Neal, Viola, 263

INDEX

Nebeker, Genevieve, 178, 233, 264
Neighbors, Syd, 213
Neilson Steel Aircraft, 337
Nelson, Paul, 332
Neptune Gardens Park, 14
Nervino, Frank, 358
Nesbitt, Dr, Earl, 276
Ness, Jack, 398
Nevada Aviation Corp., 90
Nevada Highway Dept., 224
Nevada Irrigation Dist., 224
New muni work, 200
New Sac Muni runway, 200
New Sac Muni, Frprt Rd, 205, 247
New Standard biplanes, 148
New York Aero. Society, 13
Newberg, L., 390
Newbig, Lt. E. (Neubig), 411
Newman (Neuman), Harold L., UAL, 221, 229-231, 242, 250-253
Newton, Edsel, 168
Nicholson & Canning move to new muni, 176
Nicholson & Canning, 177
Nicholson and Meisser, 175
Nicholson barnstorms, 175
Nicholson seeds rice '33, 310
Nicholson, L., 358
Nicholson, Ray E. "Nick," 199-123, 127, 132, 156, 163, 166, 167, 175-178, 214, 218-226, 231, 253, 273-276, 310, 337
Nickels, Leslie J., 323
Nielsen, Mr.&Mrs. J. F., 419
Nightingale, J. M., 333
Ninety-Nines at Willows, 344
Ninety-Nines, 261, 263
Nolta, Dale to skywrite "airshow," 351
Nolta, Dale, 306, 345, 348-354, 357, 388
Nolta, Dale, flew Clark's jump plane, 353
Nolta, Dale, gas station, 354
Nolta, Dale, heroic try to save Lewis, 352
Nolta, Floyd, "Speed," 151, 292, 305, 325, 333-337, 341-348, 350-356, 359, 369, 374, 383, 386, 388, 462
Nolta, Floyd, 27 studnts, 336
Nolta, Floyd, 5th year seeding June '35, 310
Nolta, Floyd, air cop, 337
Nolta, Floyd, airport caretaker, 341
Nolta, Floyd, dusts for Harkey July '33, 310
Nolta, Floyd, eradicates eagles, 306
Nolta, Floyd, fire duty Mt. Shasta, 354
Nolta, Floyd, first to seed four counties, 306
Nolta, Floyd, to Chicago, 380
Nolta, Floyd&Dale fire fighters, 306
Nolta, Willows Flyg Ser. 346
Nomis, Leo, 203
Nor. Calif. Airports '26, 363
Nor. Calif. Soar. Meet, 274
Norboe & Slingsby, 224
Norboe, Paul, 224, 238, 241, 293
Norby, E. R., 157
Northern Bombing Group (France), 67
Novarro, Mike, 358
Noville, George, 133

Noyes, Blanche, 262

O

O'Connor, James, 337
O'Donnell, Gladys, 262
O'Donovan, Speed, 380
O'Hair, Mike, 321, 323
O'Hearn, Joe, 161
O'Rourke, Patsy, 41
Oakland – Del Paso, 132
Oakland Motordome (Emryvl.), 38
Oakland Muni air race, 132
Oakland Municipal Arpt. 127
Oakland, movie HQ, 193
Oakland's Durant Field, 88
Octoplane, 31
Odom, Culture, 41
Ogden, Harry, 215
Ohu, Peter, 327
Oldfield, Barney, 52, 53
Oldfield, Barney, Co., 438
Olds, Col. Robin, 269, 270
Olsen, L. W., 305
Omlie, Phoebe, 262, 366-7
Ong, Bill, 348
Oppose cutting trees, 140
Orange & Olive Expo, 185
Orange Bros. Arprt., 307
Oranges, Les, 203, 333, 426
Orht, Mr., 14
Orland air marker, 336
Orland Exchange Club, 332
Orland, poss. airport site, 332
Oroville Speedway Trck, 48
Orr, N. C., 215
Orr, Ted, 434
Orvis, William S., 237
Osler, E. B., 358
Otterson fliers, Willows, 353
Otterson, Bert, 353
Otterson, L. S. "Babe," 354
Outside Loops, 265
Overhouse, Charles, 232
Overland Airways, 166, 205, 212-215, 218, 229, 257, 333, 334, 425
Overland, Varney subsid, 257
Owen, Walter, 298, 305, 311
Owens, Charlotte, 85

P

Pabco Flyer, Dole race, 294
Pacer Aircraft Corp., 149
Pacer Racer, McKinney, 148
Pacific Aero Club, 58, 439
Pacific Aerodust in LA, 294
Pacific Air & Steamship, 213
Pacific Air Transport, 224, 249, 363, 364, 368, 428
Pacific Air Transport. a subsid. of BAT, 249
Pacific Airpln.&Supply, 444
Pacific Airway beacons, 399
Pacific Coast Air Derby, 396
Pacific Coast Air, 157, 316
Pacific Hawk airliner, 447
Pacific Rice Grow Assn., 281
Pacific Seaboard Air, 232

Packard, L. D., 124, 156
Padjan, Jack, 110
Page Teletype Sac Muni, 229
Pahlin, Henry, 335
Palace Hotel in SF, 288
Palmer, Burdette, GAS, 295
Pan-Amer. Good Will, 424
Pangborn "Flying Fleet," 457
Pangborn at Yolo meet, 451
Pangborn, Clyde "Upside Down," 91, 92, 97, 98, 148, 167, 272, 285, 363, 391, 451, 457, 458, 465
Pankost Boat Supply Co., 9
Parachuting dog, 135
Paraffine Co., 294
Pardee, Dick, 222
Parker, Kermit, 159, 194, 215
Parkinson, Frank, 307
Parle, E. of Parker Pen, 273
Parmalee, Phillip O., 38-41
Parmalee, S. N., 358
Parnham, Selden, 176, 177, 225, 233
Parrott Grant Ranch, 283-4
Part II, Tehama, Shasta & Yolo Counties, 361
Partelow, R., 358
Pastal, S., 215
PAT (Pacific Air Transport), 252-3
PAT pilot's salaries, 249
PAT pilots, 249
PAT's first six pilots, 249
Paterson Aeroplane Co., 312
Pathfinder flights, 77
Patrick, Garrison, 354
Patrols to Red Bluff, 391
Patterson, E. M., Torrey 378
Patterson, J., 84
Patterson, Pat, 164, 398, 456
Pattison, Mr., 296
Paulhan, Louis, 7, 12, 309
Peebles, Robert, 317
Peltior, George W., 7
Pendleton, E. H., 80-83, 280, 281, 390, 412, 413
Penfield, John, 203
Penfield, Tom, 164
Penney, Capt. Albert D., 62
Pennington, Bill, 48, 49
Peoples, Leland, 341
Perkins hires Mickel, 193
Perkins, Percival, 180, 193, 337
Perratt, Slim, 345
Perrine, Lyle, 358, 386, 387
Pershing, Gen. John "Black Jack," 71, 171, 439
Peters, Mark, 23
Peters, Spartan pilot, 153
Petersen, Jens, 199
Pettis, Lt., 424
Peyton, (or Payton) Jim, DOC, 217, 226, 232, 240, 245, 255, 428, 461
Phillipe, J. W., 354, 358
Phillips, aviator, 208
Piatt's Band, 28
Picket, Mr., 50
Pickford, Mary, 369

501

Pickup, Christopher V., 87, 88, 441, 443
Pickwick Airways, 149, 422
Pickwick Stage Lines, 245-6
Pierce Flying Ser., 357
Pierce, Lester, 348, 354, 357
Pierce, Lester, Mrs., 354
Pilgrim, Al, 200, 398, 419-422
Pilgrim, O. W., 308
Pimentel, Matt, property, 387
Pinnegar, Fred, 244
Pioneer Fliers Co., 93
Pirelli Cable Co., 317
Pitcairn Co., 217, 218
Pittenger, Ruth, 240
Placerville Airport, 193
Planes killing ducks, 283
Plant, Forrest A., 439
Plato, Abe, 329
Plughoff, A. B.
Poland's Stationary, 355
Polk crash Diggs Rnch, 309
Polk, C. A. "Al", 308, 309
Pollock, Mrs. G., 130
Polson, Thor, "Smokey," 228, 344, 347, 348
Pond, Charles McHenry, 246
Pond, Lt. C. F., 341
Pony Express rider, 110
Poor, R. C., 438
Pope, Francis, 222
Pope, George, 209
Pope, Herbert, 240
Population Colusa, 277
Porter, Lee, 350
Portland Air Show, 397, 418
Portland-Yakima Airline, 368
Post, Lt. Henry B., 45, 46
Post, Wiley, 160, 188
Postle, Dave, 215
Powell, Ira M., 419
Powell, Major R. F., 109
Power line patrol, 19, 47, 50
Power, R. Grover, Colusa Postmaster, 316, 323
Power, Sheriff Newt, 290
PPIE (Panama-Pacific Inter. Expo.), 46, 53
Pratt, O. W. H., 290, 437-440, 443
Pratt, O.H. W., told field unsafe, 454
Preble, Lucius E., 376, 379
Proberta's Jackson Field, 393
Prodger in Bristol YFC, 445
Prodger, Clifford B. 445
Prohibited flying WWII, 267
Pruett CAC-1 aircraft, 138
Pruett, Donald, 132
Pulington, Geo, 444
Punitive Expedition Mex 171
Purcell, Sam, 55-58, 134, 314
Purinton, Jimmie, 425, 426
Putrihaber, C. K., 358

Q

Quick, George C., duster, 311
Quimby, Harriet, 261
Quint District, Willows, 327
Quint District airfield, 327

Quint schoolhouse, 325

R

Radcliffe, Dan, 458
Radonich, John, 62
Ralls, Mrs., 42
Ram, Lt. Jack, 417
Randall, W. B., 346, 347
Rankin & Hester record outside loops, 374
Rankin Flying Service – Portland, 214, 368
Rankin flys Worlds Fair, 353
Rankin, Tex, 353, 355-357, 359, 374, 375, 419
Rasmussen, Richard, 405
Rea, Lt., 229
Reckless Rosie Cahill, parachutist, 185, 189, 193
Record, L. A., 414
Rector, Charles, 256
Red Bluff airfield, 393
Red Bluff airway beacon, 397
Red Bluff High School aero classes, 389, 403
Red Bluff Muni named, Bidwell Field, 390
Red Bluff passes bond, 397
Red Bluff Round-Up, 403
Red Devil Baldwin biplane, 5
Red Devils Sqdrn. tour, 349
Redding Air Show 1939, 429
Redding fire base, end W. Placer St., 390, 391
Redding Rec. Park, 407, 409
Redwood Aviation Sch., 326
Redwood Aviation, 327
Redwood City Airport, 92
Reed, C. Wesley, 240
Reed, Grafton, 239, 241
Reese, L. J., 67, 80, 81, 84-86
Reese, Mrs. J., 130
Reeves, J. R., 212
Reg. numbers, DOC, 402
Reid, Frank, 158
Reid's Ferry, 410
Reims Air Meet, France, 29
Reinhart, Norman, 177
Remey, Peggy, 262
Remlin, E. L., PAT pilot, 249
Reno-Tahoe Int. Arprt, 148
Renwick, Jack, 274
Republic Seabee amphib. 359
Resistal Goggles, 134
Resse, Al, 302
Retteruth, Freman, mngr. of airort, 272, 332
Rhinehart, James, 396
Rhodes, Allen, 296
Rhodes, H. W., 343
Ricard, Father, 92
Rice season 1931, 307
Rice seeding demo, 352
Rice, O. C., 438
Rice, Russell, 358
Rich Field, Waco, 69, 171
Richards, D., 458

Richardson Resort, 149
Richardson, A. L., 149, 179
Richardson's airfield, 150
Richel, William, 396
Richerson, O. C., 247
Richfield Oil Fokker Tri-motor, 152, 231, 422
Richfield Oil, 151, 159, 307
Richmond – Mather race, 107
Rickenbacker Auto, 105
Rickenbacker, Edward V. "Eddie," 105, 444, 451
Ridenour, Bill, 358
Rideout Hospital, 310
Rideout, R. L., 426
Riley Field, Oroville, 48, 330
Rinehart, R. B. "Pete," 207-209, 214, 215, 235
Ritchey, Harold F., 273, 332
Robbens, William, 199
Robertson, O. A., 60, 61, 309
Robinson, Dan, 367
Robinson, E. H., 166
Robinson, O. A., 115
Rockwell Field, N. Island, San Diego, 61, 171, 202, 294
Rodgers, Emory, 444, 452
Rodgers, Will, 188
Roland, Robert, 353
Rolph, Gov. James, 214
Rose, Frank, 87, 159, 164, 167, 179, 257-259, 273, 294, 322, 347, 350, 352, 355, 398, 425, 426
Rose, Frank, dusted '19, 279
Rose, J. A., UAL, 254
Rose, Mildred, 465
Rose, Ollie, 380, 428
Roseville air crashes, 152
Roseville Muni Airport, 150
Ross, Jack, 205
Rossen, Richard, 354
Round-The-World fliers, 108
Round-Up Ranch, 363, 364
Rowell, Maj. R. F., 108
Roxstall, J. N., 443
Royal Aero Corp., 297, 304
Roycroft, Mr., 422
Royle Air Lines, 159, 158, 316, 320, 333, 366, 398, 419, 423, 425
Royle, William H. "Bill," 320, 344
Rubens, Alma, 184
Ruggles, Lt. Francis W., 78
Russell Lobe parachutes, 176, 274
Russell, Mr., 93
Rutherford, aviator, 273
Ryan Brougham, 379
Rybitski, Otto (Arthur), 46
Ryker, Harrison C., 123

S

Sabihi, Gocen, 268
Sac (new) Muni Opening, 170, 177, 202, 226
Sac Aerial Nav. Syndic, 8, 9
Sac Aero Clb, 8-10, 25
Sac Air Depot opens '38, 276
Sac Air Markers, 152

INDEX 503

Sac Air Meet, 1st Annl., 107
Sac Air Show of Oct.'36, 268
Sac Aircraft Show, 126, 127, 130, 131, 134, 135
Sac Airport Comm., 141, 151, 153, 199, 202
Sac Aviation Club, 107, 113, 116, 124, 130, 132, 138, 140, 155, 156, 161, 164, 168, 179
Sac Aviation Co., 68, 84, 85, 87, 171, 328, 390
Sac Executive Aprt, 169, 271
Sac Flying Service (SFS), 166, 175, 218-220, 273-275
Sac High aero. Classes, 176
Sac High glider club, 274
Sac Inter. Airport, 171, 271
Sac Muni A1A rating, 225
Sac Muni activity, 220, 229
Sac Muni Air Show '33, 233
Sac Muni bond passed, 271
Sac Muni comml. pilots, 221
Sac Muni constrct. Details
Sac Muni fighter base, 271
Sac Muni hangar moved, 211
Sac Muni hangar No. 3, 219
Sac Muni landing siren, 219
Sac Muni runway, 211
Sac Muni, 18 poss. Sites, 199
Sac Muni, Summit HQ, 241
Sac Northern RR, 17, 282
Sac. Avtn. Co. Arbuckle, 328
Sac's five active airports, 137
Sacramento Airports, 219
Sacramento Aviation, 86
Sacramento Glider Club, 273
Sacramento Junior (City) College, 67, 205, 209, 215, 217, 220, 226, 230, 264
Saeltzer, R. M., 425
Sakamoto, Juichi, 44
Salisbury, H. S., 121, 418, 420, 423
Salisbury, Mrs. H. S., 419
Salisbury, S., 162
Sallee, Jimmie, 358
Salter Field, S. Willows, 331
Salter, Dr., of Williams, 328
Salzman, Joe, 132
San Francisco "bombed," 201
San Francisco Air Meet, 29
San Jose Air Show 1922, 98
San Martino, Paul, 167, 208,
Sanborn, Lt., 424
Sanborn, W. E., 452, 455
Sanders, Bill, 197
Sanders, W. A., 132, 365
Sandin, Edward, 176, 358
Sands, Charles, 241
Santa Clara College, 204
Santa Claus flies. 461
Sargeant, Mrs., 42
Saur, Chris, tire, 350, 386
Sayles, Don, Boeing, 381
Scarpino, Bill, 177
Scenic Airways Fokker, 346
Scenic Airways, 345
Schafer, Henry, 404
Schalif, Mr. & Mrs.,369

Schandhals, W. R., 225, 240
Sched. flights Sac to SF, 173
Schleuder, Mr., 159
Schloss, Lynn, 205
Schlosser, L., 322
Schmidt, Lt., 229
Schmitz, George, 348
Schoenbacker, E., 182, 337
Schoenhair, Lee, 331, 336, 366, 396
Schoening, O. M., 136
Schramm, Paul, 383, 405
Schreck, arpt. mngr., 272
Schreck, Paul S., 137, 167, 174, 192, 272, 276
Schunacho, J.,358
Schwartz, Lt. Charles W., 78
Scott, Blanche S., 38-41, 261
Scott, Randolph, 142
Scott, Roy, 313-314, 434
Scott, Tom Allen, 311
Scott, William K., 215
Scraggs, George, 12
Seagrave, Marshal, 403
Seal Beach flying school, 319
Seamans, G. H., 9
Seattle–LA airway lights, 149
Senator Hotel, 239
Senn, Martin, 244, 245
SERA airport grant, 324
Service clubs to fix Yolo, 457
SF Bay Airdrome, 205, 215 220, 221
SF Hngr Quiet Birdmen, 306
SF-Spok. Pac. Cst. Race, 396
Shadoan, Noel, 337
Shaffer, Fred, 437
Shaffer, Miss Reva, 437
Shalk, Jack, 103
Sham, Harry, 346, 348-352, 358, 462
Shanahan,Lt. P. E., 203
Shankle, Jean Fay, 262
Shannon, Super. Warren, 160
Sharpnack, J. W. crash, 224, 252
Shasta Aircraft Co., 420
Sheehan, Edgar M., 6-8, 15, 25, 27, 41
Sheep Camp Station, 18
Shell Oil Co., 216
Shellenbacker, Eddie, 151
Shelton, P. D., 167
Shelton, S. E., 74
Shepard, Wallace, 290
Sheridan Autos, 105
Sherman, Clay & Co., 88
Sherman, Fredrick, 88
Sherman, Peggy, 263
Shields, Peter J., 115
Shipley, W. W., 129
Short, A. M., 409
Short, Robert W., 337
Showboat, 1928, 184
Shrash, G. C., 358
Sieferman bros., 439
Sierra Aircraft Co., 102-105, 125, 141, 149, 332
Sierra Airport Air Show, 103
Sierra Airport, E. Sacto, 105, 114, 143, 153
Sierra Pacific Air Trans. Co., 371, 457

Sierra, an original "Pop" Wilde design, 307
Sierra/Eagle Rock Aprt., 177
Sik, Cheung, 244
Siler, Ray, 381
Simpson Arprt, Orland, 332
Simpson, Nora, 332
Sing, Wong, 244
Sisson, Hugh, 398
Sister's Hospital, 401
Sittman, Mr., 14
Siveris, Joe, 284
Siveris, Josephine, 284
Six, Robert, 333, 426
Slager, aviator, 210
Slaughterhouse Fld, 317, 318
Slaybaugh, Mr., 214
Slingsby to Echoe Lake, 238
Slingsby, Howard G. "Buzz," 192, 215, 216, 221, 224, 226, 228, 235-238, 241
Smith Estate Vinyards, 55
Smith of duck patrol, 289
Smith, A. W., 103
Smith, Al, 379
Smith, Alfred, DOC, 231
Smith, Art, 54, 370
Smith, B. B. 167
Smith, Babe, parachutist, 167
Smith, Bill, 161
Smith, Bill, chairman, 344
Smith, Bob, 344
Smith, Burrell E., 158
Smith, C. C., 460
Smith, Carl V., 113, 143, 144, 174, 178, 222, 232, 233
Smith, Dick, 272
Smith, Don, angry, 270
Smith, Donald B., new muni super., 177, 220-233, 241-244, 252, 266, 270, 347, 350, 358, 381, 398
Smith, Elinor, 261
Smith, Ernie L., 162, 223, 281, 397
Smith, Ernie, to Hawaii, 453
Smith, Howard R., 88
Smith, J. L., 126, 143, 155
Smith, Jack, 240
Smith, Lowell, given the *Tioga Eagle*, 450
Smith, Lt. Lowell, 107
Smith, M. M., 295
Smith, M., 358
Smith, Mervin, 214
Smith, Robert E., 411
Smith, S. B., 419
Smith, Sam, 354
Smith, Sergeant, 207
Smith, Sig, 106, 167
Smith, Warren B., 148
Soule, Cliff, 213
South China Air Serv., 97, 99
South Curtis Oaks, 85
Southern Cross, Fokker, 290
Southern Pacific RR, 9, 422
Spanhoff, Talbert, 274
Spartan factor Tulsa, 217
Spatz (later Spaatz), Maj. Carl, 88, 441, 442
Speed Johnson Sch., 372
Speichinger, Christine, 132

Spencer, Bond M., 284
Spherical balloon, *United States*, 1,
Spirit of St. Louis, 119, 394
Spitzer, J. J., 314
Sprague, Valentine, 263
Spreckels, Frank, 347
Spreckels, A. B., 346
Squadron 8, USMC, 136
St. Francis Dam Disaster, 143
St. John, Royal U., 124, 137, 140, 145, 150, 151, 155, 166, 189, 199, 205, 209, 220, 272, 381, 425, 426
St. Louis Centennial Fair, 4
Stadley, H. L., 223
Staff, Alberta, 183
Standard Airlines, 206
Standard Model Curtiss, 410
Standard Oil air marker, 330
Standard Oil Airport Dir. 393
Standard Oil at Sacto., 205
Standard Oil Beacon, 123
Standard Oil Ford Tri-motor 4-AT, 200, 209, 366
Standard Oil fuel pits, 200
Standard Oil of Calif., 134
Standard Oil, Willows, 343
Stanford – Cal football, 221
Starbuck, Art, PAT, 249, 363
Stark, Lowell, 334
Starkweather, Virginia, 321
State Ag Com., ag-flyng, 308
State's 1st lic, ag-plane, 294
Stead, W., 157
Stearman dusters, 311
Stearman-Hammond foolproof acft., 350, 351
Steele, Capt. Chas., 353, 357
Steele, Dudley, 334, 463
Steidlmayer, Francis, 322
Stephens, Bart, Sup., 161
Stephens, Gov. William, 58
Stephens, William, 62
Stephenson L-6 Stnd J-1, 447
Stevens, A. Leo, 4, 90, 322
Stewart, Harry, of GV, 243
Stewart, Thomas A., 138
Stillwell, Elgie, 370
Stinchfield, Sydney, 321
Stinson, Eddie, 366
Stockton Airport, 122
Stockton Arpt. air show, 333
Stockton Center Airport, 291
Stoddard, W. B., 439
Stoffer at Woodland 1919, 436, 437
Stoffer crash at Vallejo, 284
Stoffer in the Buzzards, 284
Stoffer to use Beamer, 436
Stoffer, at Ellington Fld, 437
Stoffer, Charles, 283, 284, 437, 438
Stokes, Bill, 322
Stoner, Earl, 358
Stribling, A. B., 243
Strief, Robert, 308, 374, 399, 423-425
Stryker bros. finish ac, 399
Stryker, Charles, 397
Stryker, Robert, 397
Stryker, Wally, 354, 358

Sturm, Edwin, 177, 178
Sugget land approved, 199
Sugget land, on Freeport, 199
Suggett, Dr. A. H., 208
Suisun City airport, 100
Sullivan, "Red" aka C. T. Jensen, 321
Sullivan, C. F., 158, 159, 425
Sullivan, William, 67, 107, 113, 264
Summers, H. S., 439
Summit Aircraft Co., 208
Summit begins at GV, 240
Summit Fleet in Reno, 223
Summit Flying Service, 220-223, 226- 229, 238-242, 264
Summit on Mills Field, 239
Summit reorgan. 9/31, 238
Summit Sacto. branch, 242
Sunnyvale dirig. Arprt., 372
Sunset Field, Alameda, 42
Sutro, Adolph G., 46
Sutter Hospital, 161
Swain, Bill, mngr. at Del Paso, 157-161, 204
Swalley, D. R., 226
Swallow Aircraft Co., 124
Swan Island - Silverton, 419
Swanson, Claude, 344
Swanson, Mary, 262
Sweely, LaVelle, 262
Sweeny, Carl, 121
Swingle - Webster's Stn., 433
Swingle in Yolo Co., 17-19
Switlik Parachute distr., 177
Sydney's Aviation Serv., 134
Sykes, Margaret, 357
Syracuse Flying Serv., 149

T

Tabor, Elliot, 124, 130, 139, 155, 158, 174, 193
TACA "flies anything," 466
Taff, Joe, 257
Talbot, Fred C., 347
Tallulah early dust. Exp., 279
Tanforan Park, San Bruno, 12, 29, 30
Tanner, Robert, 93
Target rail stop, 70, 71
Target, area's 1st arpt., 272
Tarter, Harold, 301
TAT merged West. Air, 173
TAT/Madx pilots report, 401
Tatham, Homer W., 165
Taws, Harold, 322
Taylor, Alice, 173
Taylor, Lt. Willis, 109
Taylor, N. R., 109
Taylor, Robert, 353
Teagarden, Les, 358
Tedrow, L. F., 299, 300, 304
Teed, Mrs. Elmo, 266
Tehama Co. Fair 9/28, 397
Tehama Petroleum, 377
Templeman, Don, 93, 162
Templeman, Sgt. F., 109
Teramoto, N., 180
Terrell, J. W., 214, 215
Terrell, Mr. & Mrs., 208, 209, 219

Terry, C. S., 274
Terry, Cadet Raleigh, 65
Thaden, Louise, 261, 262
Tharp, H. S., Hawke Dusters, 307, 308
The City of Roses plane, 396
The City of Vancouver, 396
Thomas Morse Scout, 103
Thomas, L. F., 458
Thomas, Margaret, 262
Thomas, W. P., Varney, 258
Thompson at Alameda, 315
Thompson crash, 315
Thompson fly to club, 315 Thompson, Arthur, 232
Thompson, Chadwick, 314
Thompson, Cyril C., 426
Thompson, Dana "Tommy," 213, 223, 228, 229, 239-242
Thompson, Lt., 454
Thompson, M., 459
Thompson, Melvin, 190
Thompson, W. J., 358
Tigar, Gene, 213
Tinker, Maj. Clarence, 220
Tioga Eagle, a LePere, 450
Todd, David, 90
Tong, George, 99
Torrey a UAL rep., 378
Torrey buys Ryan, 379
Torrey crash, 387
Torrey crashes on return, 376
Torrey for legal beer, 378
Torrey gets Pitcairn, 374
Torrey leaving Corning, 38
Torrey to Woodson Fld., 364
Torrey, Ben, 364, 365, 368-388, 402-405
Torrey, Ben, eagle hunter, 376, 382
Torrey, Ben, lic. his JN, 368
Torrey, Ben, starts grass fire
Torrey, Howell's Camp, 377
Torrey, Lillian, 381
Torrey, Ned, 364, 370, 377
Trans-Air Co., 232
Transcon. Reli.&Endur., 62
Transcon. route lighted, 154
Transient ac at Del Paso, 158
Transp. Pilot Lic. Req., 306
Trathem, Shf. Russell, 275
Travel Air *Comet* II, 181
Travel Air factory, 131
Travel Air *Miss Sacramento*, 151, 183-185, 188
Travel Air, Sac Fly Club, 209
Traxler, E. H., 139
Trayham, Harry, 220, 461
Tremain, Dr. I. R., 393
Tremaine, John 124, 138, 145
Tri-motor *Rising Sun*, 152
Tri-State Air Lines123, 125
Trit, Lt., Willows to hunt, 332
Trout, Bobbie, 155
Tryon, L. H., 133
Tucker, H. M., 113
Tucker, Milton, 121
Tung, Wong Ping, 98
Turkey Drop -'37 Corng, 386
Turkish Air Force, 268

INDEX 505

Turner, L. V., 387
Turner, Lewis, 388
Turner, Roscoe w/Leo, 209
Turner, Roscoe, 98, 236
Tuttle, Floyd, 439
Tyler, Grover, PAT, 148, 249
Tynan, J., 206

U

UAL drops fares, 252
UAL Radio technicians, 253
UCB Schl. of Mltry. Aero., WWI, 141, 294
Union Air Lines, 246, 422
Union Oil Co., 200
United Air Lines, 145, 218, 220, 251, 345, 349, 388
United Airport, Burbank, 223
United fare drop, 223
United flys PAT routes, 252
US Air Mail Service, 68, 109
US Army 1st Calif. Cav., 171
US Army 363rd Infantry, 79
US Army Air Corps, 276
US Army Air Service, (USAAS), 172
US Army Bal. School, 6
US Forest Service, 422
US Weather Bur., 153, 419
USAAC 14th Bomb Sq. 203
USAAC 1st Provis Wng. 200
USAAC 1st Pursuit Sqn., 203
USAAC 2nd Bomb Sqn., 203
USAAC 316th Obs. Sqn. 229
USAAC 91st Obs. Sqn., 159, 202
USAAC 95th Prst. Sqn., 203
USAAC 9th Aero Sqn., 364
USAAC Sac Air Depot, 276
USAAS 103rd Aero Sqn. 294
USAAS 3rd Av Instr. Cen 294
USAAS 91st Obs. Sqn., 109
USAAS 96th Day Bomb, 68
USAAS Crop dusting, 278
USAAS fire patrols '19, 390
USAAS fire patrols, 277, 422
USAAS First Aero Mex., 71
USAAS Ninth Aero Sqn. 361
USAAS Ninth Corps, 222
USAF 349th Fighter Wg, 294
USAF McClellan Field, 276
USS *Pennsylvania*, 30
Utah Exercise, the, 270

V

Valentine Gephart Trph, 418
Valley Air Lines, 238, 463
Valley Air Service, 125
Valley Dusting Ser., 307-8
Valley Flying Service, 200
Van Fleet, Lizzie, 67
Van Fleet, William C., 67
Van Gogh Starry Night, 181
Van Meter, Carl, 187, 243, 255
Van Tassall, Park, 14
Vance crashes Rio Vista, 253
Vance flew Oklnd-Reno, 248
Vance, 1700 trips over, 248
Vance, Clair Kinsey, 110, 247, 249, 253

Vandenberg, Lt. B. F., 62
Vandercook, E. V., 158, 199
Vanderford, Glen, 274
Vanderford, Mr&Mrs., 465
Vanderford, O. H., 297, 298, 305, 308, 311
Vanderford, Vince, 183, 296
Vardell, William, 162
Varney adds amphibs., 258
Varney Air Lines, 219, 243, 250, 255-258, 319, 322, 414
Varney Fld, Redwood, 414
Varney Lincoln-Stand., 286
Varney Mrysvl route, 192
Varney Orions, 259
Varney plane at Willows, 329
Varney run Sac–SF, 258
Varney Speed Lanes, 215, 218, 220, 257-259
Varney starts SF-Sac, 257
Varney stops Sac-Fres., 257
Varney to Yolo FC, 444
Varney, Ray, 348-357, 386, 388, 425, 429
Varney, Walter T., 92, 172, 257, 287, 414, 452
Vawter, George B., 138, 317, 460
VFW Air Show 8/32, 229
Vierra, Manuel, 177
Vieu, Charles, F., 454
Viking Kittyhawk bipe, 322
Villa, Pancho, 71, 171
Virden, Ernestine, 80
Virden, Ralph, PAT 249, 250
Voisin aircraft, 13
Vosmer (Volmer) Chas., 15
Voss, Lt., 79
Vowles, Reed, 418
Vremsak Ag. Air Ser., 311
Vremsak duster burns, 311
Vremsak flew rice '34, 310
Vremsak kidnapped, 310
Vremsak, Louis F., 226, 310

W

W. Placer St. Field, 413
Waage, John, 161, 324, 403
Wachorst, John, 113
Wachter, 296
Wagner, A. E., Royle Air Lines, 89, 316, 317, 322, 333, 335, 398
Wagner, E., 272, 273, 333
Wagner, Norman, 358
Wahl, Leo, 396, 405
Waite, Albert E., 177, 178, 232, 268, 465
Wakefield, Franklin W., 205
Wakefield, J. S., 180
Walker Jr., Fletcher, 425
Walker, C. C., 313
Walker, Charles, DOC, 264
Walker, Dave, 177, 178, 232, 233
Walker, Lt., 208
Wallace, Bill, 383
Wallace, H. A., 108
Wallace, Leo, 49
Wallace, N., 138
Wallace, Nathaniel, 177, 458
Wallen, Lt., 205

Walsh led DHs to YFC, 443
Walsh Station, JN mid-air, 64
Walsh, Jack, 144
Walter, E. H., 358
Walter, Lt. Ed, 357
Walthers, R., 412
Wanzer, Harry S., 61
War Mother's Air Show, 87
Ward, H., 321
Ward, Jimmie, 32
Ward, Ted, 243
Warner Bros Travel Air, 204
Warren hires Beilby, 191
Warren, Charles J., 320
Warren, D. C., 191, 203, 229, 320
Warren, D. C.,C-W distr, 191
Warren, D. Travel Air, 216
Warren, Jeff, 187, 207-210, 213, 256, 322
Wartime ban civil flight, 64
Wash.–Alaska Airways, 208
Washoe Co. Golf Cour,, 147
WASP, Womens Air Ser. 268
Water Festival deals fail, 313
Waterhouse Aircraft Inc., 364
Waterhouse Cruzair, 364
Waterhouse, Bill, 364
Waterman 3L-400, 450
Waterman, Waldo, 447, 449
Watkins, R. S., 129
Watson, A. L., 414
Watson, Col. H. L., 78, 88
Watsonville Airport, 171
Wawona lakes, 299
Wayne, Earl, 9
Weather Telegraph, 370
Weatherhead, L., 358
Weaver & Nicholson, 275
Weaver crashes, 275
Weaver leases Del Paso, 273
Weaver, "Buck," Laird, 452
Weaver, Earl, 358, 429
Weaver, H. L., 215
Weaver, Loretta, 275
Weaver, R., robs bank, 275
Weaver, Robert F., 166, 175, 191, 273-275
Webber property, 435
Webber, Bertha, 437
Webber, Mr., 190
Webdell, Tom, I. C.Dust, 311
Weber, Gordon, 240
Webster, A., 354
Webster's Stn. Yolo, 17, 18
Weems, pilot, 158
Weggers, Herbert, 292, 466
Weggers, Moe&Cook,457
Weinstock&Lubin store, 78
Weiss, Bill, 358
Welschke, Willis, 380, 381
Welsh, Martin I., 138, 139
Werle, Cliff, 333
Werlhoff, Victor, 387
West America Air Schools, Ltd., 200, 205, 206, 212, 272
West Coast Air sched., 266
West Coast Air Transport, 154, 250, 364, 369, 372, 378, 418, 421, 422
West Coast&Pickwick, 369

West, Bob, chutist, 207, 210
West, Charles, 415
West, Mrs., parachutist, 210
Western Aero Assn., 439
Western Aero Corp., 226
Western Air Express, 252
Western Aircraft Distrib, 187
Western Coast Air Lines, 200
Western College of Aeronautics, 207, 304
Western Dusters Co., 304
Western Front, WWI, 68
Western Inter. Glider, 274
Western Pacif. Petitn., 86
Western Pacific Air, 214, 256
Western Pacific RR Co., 43
Western Pacific shops, 86
Western Rice Co., 283
Western Sulphur Industries. Co., 295, 304
Wetzel, Harry H., 58
Wheeler, Andrew, 388
Whipple, D. A., 62
White Hospital, 86
White Thomas, 433
White, Bill, 358
White, Capt., 424
Whitehead, Lt. Ennis C., 417
Whiting, E. W., 206
Witney, W. W., 241
Whitsit, K., 358
Whittmore, Thomas, 240
Wicket, Byron, 414
Wieder, Will, 432
Wilcox, Arthur, 374
Wilcox, Marie, 126
Wilcoxon, Lewis, 95, 96
Wilde, Arthur "Pop," 100, 307
Wilhoite, J. A., 177
Wilkins, Charles E., 113, 116, 124, 130, 138, 156, 166, 199, 200, 235, 245, 256, 257
Wilkins, E. B., 166
Wilkinson, Ira, 163
Wilkinson, Stewart, 369
Willard, Charles F., 7, 29, 30
Williams at Willows, 329
Williams, "Red," 132, 241
Williams, Arthur, 456
Williams, E. J., 215
Williams, Ernie, 358
Williams, Jack, 274
Williams, W. A., 162
Willingham," Willie," 193
Willis, Patty, 263
Willits, S. L, 149
Willitt, (AKA Willett), Al, 132, 150, 151, 158, 164, 166
Willows "bombed" 1930, 340
Willows 800 see attack, 340
Willows air marker, 337
Willows Air Shows 1929-1939, 337, 343, 344, 346, 349, 350-356
Willows Airport beacon, 336
Willows Airport Dedication 6/29, 316, 333
Willows airport has no gas pump, 340
Willows Aviation Co., 286

Willows duck patrols, 284
Willows Flying Service, 348, 351, 352
Willows to take over, 332
Willows, duck ptrl. HQ, 285
Willows, west tract pick, 331
Wilson, Art, 179, 213, 216
Wilson, Cadet James E., 64
Wilson, Cadet William G., 64
Wilson, Charles, 163
Wilson, Claude R., 171
Wilson, Ira, 387
Wilson, J. Stitt, 64
Wilson, Pres. Woodrow, 49, 439
Wilson, Ralph, 241
Wilson, Stanley, 358
Wing Ranch, 348
Wing, E. V., 358
Wing, Jack, 352
Winslow, Burr H., 109, 111, 249
Winton, W. L., 304
Wiseman, Fred J., 23, 27, 31, 79
Wiseman, James, 354
Withrow, Bill, Benton, 429
Witney, Ivor, 220-223, 226, 239-242, 253, 264, 266, 269, 350, 461
Wolf, Frank, 358
Wolfskill's place, 439
Women's Air Reserve, 261-2
Wong, Ed, 178
Wong, Fred, 99, 274
Wood, Jimmie, 414
Woodbridge, Mrs. Cora, 151
Woodland duck patrols, 282
Woodland Fall Fiesta air show, 461
Woodland rvr "bombed," 340
Woodland-Watts Airpt, 465
Woodring, Lt., 202
Woodruff, Virg. & Bert, 358
Woodside, Mr., 14
Woodson Air Show, 351
Woodson Field 1928, 367
Woodson Field lights, 379,
Woodson Field Teletype, 379
Woodson Field, Corning, 363-365, 370, 405
Woodson loses hangar, 387
Woodson opened 1926, 363
Woodson, Warren N., Corning's "father," 156, 334, 362, 364-367, 373-376, 398
Woolsey, Capt. Clinton, 417
Wooster, Leonard, 437
Word, Norman, 258, 259
Worely, Phil, 462
Wrench, James, 333
Wright biplane, 410
Wright brothers, 5, 7, 13, 39
Wright Whirlwind J-5, 186
Wright, Charles E., 159, 161
Wright, E. J., 358
Wright, John, 332
Wright, Oroville, 5
Wright, W. D. "Denny," 132, 203, 215, 344, 398, 462 Wright, Wilber, 5
Wright, Wiley B., DOC, 176, 214, 215, 323
Wurgaft, Libby, 463
Wynn, W. E., 152, 371

Y

Yancy, Bud, 259
Yardley, H. E., 8
Yat-sen, Dr. Sun, 98, 99, 318
Yates, John, 422
YB-17 sqdn. Sac Muni, 269
YB-17 sqdrn. War Games 8/37, 269, 270
Yellowstone Air Derby, 424, 425
Yerex, Lowell, 91, 98, 285, 363, 391, 465, 466
YFC Air Meet, '21 races, 451
Yolo Co. resid. sell land, 465
Yolo Fliers Club expands, 447
Yolo Fliers Club Field 8/22/20, 443
Yolo Fliers Club Field, 87, 91, 105, 161, 451-453, 456, 458, 462, 465
Yolo Fliers Club membership 440, 463
Yolo Fliers Club, (YFC), 131, 290, 438-441, 443, 447, 448
Yolo Fliers Club, golf club, 453
Yolo Fliers plans hangars, shop, etc., 439
Yolo Internl. Airport, 465
Yost, Ken, 239
Young, Clarence, DOC director, 124
Young, E. I., 97
Young, Jimmy, Chinese parachutist, 418
Young, K. P, 97
Young, K. Y. (S. Y.), 98
Young, P. A., 15, 20, 24, 28
Young, R., 358
Young, S. Y., 97-99
Yuba-Sutter Flying Club, 205, 324
Yuen, Henry J., 178, 244
Yuravich, E. L., DOC, 228

Z

Zeman, Frank, parachutist, 341, 374
Zero, town of, 125
Zeulke, J., in prop accident, 438
Zumwalt, L. R., 323

ABOUT THE AUTHORS

Kathe and Allen Herr

Kathe Herr graduated with honors in liberal arts and sciences from the University of Illinois in Champaign/Urbana. Upon graduation from college, she began a 40-year teaching career. Nearly all of that time was spent teaching sixth grade students on Beale Air Force Base. In 1984 she discovered computers and shared her enthusiasm for technology with her students.

In 1969 Kathe took her first flight lesson on the day the astronauts landed on the moon. She then earned her private pilot's license and eventually her commercial license. She has raced a Mooney Mk. 21 in air races from California to Oregon. Kathe and the love of her life, Allen, have flown from coast to coast and had great adventures in their Bellanca Decathlon.

Kathe currently resides near Yuba City, California, with Allen and her beloved pups, Bella and Skyla.

Allen Herr was born in Marysville and raised in North Sacramento where he attended primary and Norte Del Rio High School while developing his talent playing the French horn. In 1963, at age 18, he was hired by the Sacramento Philharmonic Orchestra to play horn. A year later, the Sacramento Light Opera Co. (Music Circus) hired him for the pit orchestra of its summer stock productions. He joined the William Land Park Band, Forrey Long's Dance Orchestra, John Nelson's Big Band, and (his favorite) a Dixieland big band, Sugar Willy and the Ten Cubes. The income from these groups, plus other freelance work, enabled Allen to stay in Sacramento and attend college. He majored in music and minored in American history. While attending Sac State, Allen was hired to teach horn there and at the University of Pacific in Stockton. In the late '60s, Allen served with the 52nd Army Band at Fort Ord and later with the 59th National Guard Band at Sacramento. Retiring from music in 1982, he joined his father Ted in the well drilling business.

Allen began flying lessons at Sacramento's Branstetter Airport in 1964, and has over 1,800 private pilot hours. He has been an avid student of aviation history since he was given Douglas Rolfe's *Airplanes of the World* at age nine and has been a member of the American Aviation Historical Society (AAHS) and the Experimental Aviation Association over 45 years. He always wanted to contribute to aviation history literature, which has dominated his curiosity for so many years. Thus, he has authored articles for the AAHS journal, the British journal *Air Enthusiast*, and several regional historical society quarterlies. This is his third book in a series about early aviation in the Sacramento Valley and San Francisco Bay Area during the years 1910–1939. The other two are *Aviation in Northern California 1910–1939 Volume I: San Francisco Bay Area* and *Aviation in Northern California 1910–1939 Volume II: Yuba, Sutter, and Butte Counties,*

www.ingramcontent.com/pod-product-compliance
Lightning Source LLC
Chambersburg PA
CBHW070158240426
43671CB00007B/483